Bruce Ritchie has written a new, scholarly, ground-breaking biography of St Columba, weaving together historical narrative and theological exploration in a masterful way. We encounter the man, his times, his life, his teaching, and his legacy, set before us with depth, detail, and colour. This now surely has to be the starting point for all future studies of the Scottish saint. In my judgment, the book deserves the widest possible circulation among all serious students of Scottish church history.

NICK NEEDHAM
Church History Tutor, Highland Theological College
Minister of Inverness Reformed Baptist Church, Scotland

Living as he did in the twilight of antiquity, the memory of the remarkable Celtic Christian leader Columba has been both obscured by legend and claimed by various communities, which has only further obscured the real man. In this new study, Bruce Ritchie has put all who love the story of the Celtic Church in his debt as he untangles what we can truly know about Columba, his life in Ireland before coming to Iona, the Iona mission, and his thought. A solid historical monograph marked by scholarly heft, Ritchie's biography is also eminently readable—a rare combination and a delight to recommend.

MICHAEL A. G. HAYKIN
Chair and Professor of Church History
The Southern Baptist Theological Seminary, Louisville, Kentucky

In this scholarly and comprehensive account of Columba, Bruce Ritchie combines historical, theological and spiritual insights into his work. Deserving of a wide readership, his accomplished study will enrich our understanding of one of the great figures in Scottish church history.

DAVID FERGUSSON
Professor of Divinity, University of Edinburgh

Dr Bruce Ritchie's depiction of Columba as an 'Island Soldier', fighting the good fight of faith against the world, the flesh and the Devil, is both a pleasure to read and a thoroughly refreshing study of the saint's theology and beliefs as recorded in primary sources.

Dr Ritchie presents us with a robust figure who is something of contrast to the soft, sentimental and acquiescent 'Columba' of popular imagination.

Donald Meek
Professor Emeritus, Scottish, Celtic & Gaelic Studies

Columba

The Faith of an Island Soldier

Bruce Ritchie

MENTOR
Encouraging Christians to Think

ISBN 978-1-5271-0387-0
Ebook 978-1-5271-0429-7
Mobi 978-1-5271-0430-3

10 9 8 7 6 5 4 3 2 1

Published in 2019
in the Mentor Imprint
by
Christian Focus Publications,
Geanies House, Fearn, Tain,
Ross-shire, IV20 1TW, Great Britain.

www.christianfocus.com

Cover design by Peter Matthess
Printed by Bell & Bain, Glasgow

MIX
Paper from
responsible sources
FSC® C007785

CONTENTS

ABBREVIATIONS

ANF	Ante-Nicene Fathers
DSCHT	Dictionary of Scottish Church History and Theology
ICQ	Irish Church Quarterly
IQR	Irish Quarterly Review
ITQ	Irish Theological Quarterly
JCHAS	Journal of the Cork Historical and Archaeological Society
JCLAS	Journal of the County Louth Archaeological Society
JRSAI	Journal of the Royal Society of Antiquaries of Ireland
NEHS	New Edinburgh History of Scotland
NMS	National Museums of Scotland
NPNF	Nicene and Post-Nicene Fathers
NT	New Testament
PRIA	Proceedings of the Royal Irish Academy
PSAS	Proceedings of the Society of Antiquaries of Scotland
RCAHMS	Royal Commission on the Ancient and Historical Monuments of Scotland
SBET	Scottish Bulletin of Evangelical Theology
SCHS	Scottish Church History Society
SHR	Scottish Historical Review
UJA	Ulster Journal of Archaeology

REFERENCES

References in brackets in the main body of the text are to Adomnán's *Life of Columba.* Hence (II:2) refers to *Life of Columba*, Book II, Chapter 2, as in the Andersons' and Sharpe's editions. Reeves followed an earlier numeration. References to other frequently cited works, such as the *Amra Choluimb Chille* or the *Bangor Antiphonary*, are placed in the footnotes, or, if embedded in the main text, are source-indicated.

ACKNOWLEDGEMENTS

Thanks are due to my colleagues at Highland Theological College of the University of the Highlands and Islands, for their encouragement and interest. Thanks also to Dr Angus Morrison, Margaret Whyte Dravikula, Dr Ben van De Weil, and Professor Donald Meek, who assisted by reading and commenting on early drafts. I am likewise indebted to Christian Focus Publications, Stephen Greenhalgh and Alex Macaskill in particular, for the work involved in preparing the text for publication. Most of all, gratitude to my wife Grace, whose interest and support have accompanied the project throughout.

DEDICATION

In memory of my parents-in-law, Tom and Marion Dow, who had a lively interest in all matters connected with early Scottish history.

Introduction

Around the year A.D. 563 a middle-aged monk arrived in the west of Scotland. He was simply dressed. He was lean, sinewy, and weather-beaten. He was accompanied by a group of fellow pilgrims, and the boat from which he disembarked was a leather-hulled Irish curragh. Such curraghs, ranging from one-person coracles to double-masted vessels with ocean-going capabilities, were a familiar sight in the waters of the Irish Sea in the sixth century. In the 1970s the historian and explorer Tim Severin reconstructed a large curragh, following instructions found in early medieval texts, and proved that, with good seas and a fair wind, these vessels could reach the Faroe Islands, Iceland, and beyond.[1] The short voyage from the north of Ireland to the kingdom of Dál Riata in Argyll was no problem for the monk and his companions.

This was not just any holy man striking out for new pastures. This was Columba. In sixth-century Ireland, Columba already carried a formidable reputation as one of its movers and shakers. Yet, his home for the remaining thirty-four years of his life was to be Argyll. More specifically, it was to be Iona, lying off the larger island of Mull. Contrary to later legends, which claim that Columba never saw or set foot on his native soil again, he revisited Ireland many times, with the monastery at Derry particularly important to him. On one occasion he accompanied King Áedán of Argyll Dál Riata to a major political summit at the Convention of Druim Cett.[2] Manus O'Donnell's sixteenth-century compilation, *Life of Colum Chille*, tries to harmonise

1 Timothy Severin, *The Brendan Voyage* (London: Arrow, 1979).

2 Áedán ruled Argyll Dál Riata from 574 to 608, succeeding Conall, who was king when Columba arrived around A.D. 563. Áedán became a major power in the north. He had successful military campaigns in the Orkneys (580), Isle of Man (582), and in the lands of the southern Picts (590), plus exercising an overlordship in Ireland. He lost the battle of Degsastan in the south of Scotland in 603, which was a major setback.

the myth of Columba never visiting or even seeing Ireland again, with Columba attending Druim Cett. O'Donnell's solution is that Columba did return, but with a blindfold always over his eyes and a clod of Iona turf always under his feet. But early texts know nothing of this legal fiction. Despite such return visits, Iona was now Columba's home, and it was from that base that he left an indelible mark on the religious and political life of his new land.

Onlookers knew that the monks coming ashore were from the Irish Church. Their tonsure was a give-away sign. All monks, whatever tradition they belonged to, shaved the hair of their head, but did so in different patterns. Roman clergy shaved the crown of the head, leaving a circlet of hair above the temples. Irish monks shaved the front of the head, back to a line connecting ear to ear, allowing what remained to grow long at the back.[3] Both tonsures symbolised enslavement to Christ, but the differing styles became visible markers as to which group a monk belonged: and the tonsure, along with different ways of calculating the date of Easter, became a contentious issue wherever the Roman and Irish Church traditions collided. Not only did Columba's Irish Church have its own tonsure and its own date for Easter, but also its own way of organizing the Church; its own type of monastic organisation; its own system of bishops; and its own notion of autonomy vis-à-vis the Church in Rome.

Columba came to Argyll Dál Riata, a kingdom which already had a long-standing Christian heritage through its links with its sister kingdom in the north of Ireland (also named Dál Riata).[4] Columba did not introduce Christianity to the west of Scotland. He came in the wake of earlier missionary monks. Even during his own lifetime, Columba and his community were not the only group active in the region. Nevertheless, what was established on Iona through Columba's astonishing leadership, and through a succession of energetic and resourceful abbots, exerted a unique influence on the development of Christianity in Scotland and beyond. The quality of that work,

---

3 The Roman tonsure was attributed to St Peter. The Irish tonsure was attributed to Simon Magus. There is no historical basis for either claim. J. T. McNeill, *The Celtic Penitentials and their Influence on Continental Christianity* (Paris: Librairie Ancienne Honore Champion, 1923), 102, suggests the Irish style evolved from a pre-Christian druidical tonsure.

4 The long-standing assumption that Dál Riata in Argyll came into existence through conquest and colonisation from Dál Riata in the north of Ireland, has been questioned, and the issue now stands as unresolved; cf. Ewan Campbell, 'Were the Scots Irish?', *Antiquity*, vol. 75 (2001), 285-92.

allied to the publicity given to it by Columba's famous biographer Adomnán in his *Life of Columba*, has resulted in Columba's exploits becoming far better known than those of any of his peers such as Moluaig or Brendan, to name but two. Thus Columba's contribution dominates the narrative of early Scottish Christianity. And, as the centuries passed, it was Columba who acquired iconic status as *the* representative of Irish Christianity and its impact on Scotland's Western Islands and Highlands.

Columba is forever associated with Iona despite more than half his life being lived in Ireland. Thus, even though Adomnán's biography is mainly concerned with Columba as abbot of Iona, he also narrates numerous incidents which took place in Ireland itself. When Columba came to Argyll, it was after years of successful work in his homeland, exercising a free-ranging peripatetic ministry and founding numerous churches throughout the island. He had a following of monks. He conferred with kings. He had the reputation of being a strong and important figure. All of this was transferred into his Iona ministry where it was developed further. Columba was, and remained, monk, evangelist, pilgrim, abbot, scholar, statesman, advisor, diplomat, and disciplinarian.

This book explores Columba's faith. It probes his beliefs. It finds a man for whom a keynote motif of the Christian Gospel was: 'The triumph of Christ over Satan, and the setting free of God's people', a theme we examine in detail in chapters seventeen to twenty. This was the core axiom which informed, energised, and directed Columba's whole life. It was fixed deep within Columba's personal spirituality. It lay behind his daily labours. It informed his worship. It was a unifying principle of his theology. And it moulded his approach to evangelism, in which he viewed mission in terms of seeking out and destroying the rule of Satan wherever that still held sway. Our aim is to tease out this principle, and to examine its implications for Columba's approach to labour, scholarship, worship, theology, and mission. This book is not a history of Columba, though we touch upon many events in his life. Our focus is on Columba's thinking, his theology, his world-view, and the spirituality he brought to Iona.

COLUMBA'S LIFE

According to tradition, Columba was born on Thursday, 7 December 521, at Gartan, County Donegal, in the north-west corner of Ireland. The *Annals of Tigernach* suggest an earlier date of 518, but 521 is the preferred year for most historians. Adomnán states that Columba was born of noble lineage, echoing sentiments in Dallán Forgaill's early honour-poem in praise of Columba, the *Amra Choluimb Chille*.[5] The later *Old Irish Life* claims that Columba was eligible to the 'kingship of Eriu according to family'.[6] Admittedly, sixth-century Ireland abounded in families with claims to nobility; and, in a system of nomination to kingship rather than one of primogeniture, many young men could, in theory at least, become kings. What we can definitely conclude is that Columba had aristocratic credentials, though whether of a minor or a major status is less certain. His father was Fedelmid mac Ferguso who was descended from Niall of the Nine Hostages. His mother was Eithne whose grave, according to legend, is on Eileach-an-Naoimh of the Garvellach Islands, which lie between Mull and the Argyll mainland.

THE EARLY YEARS

Before Christianity came to Ireland it was traditional for sons of important families to be fostered by community leaders, with some parents giving their child to a High Druid, or a Chief Poet (*Ollam Fili*) for nurture and education. The offices of druid and poet were respected vocations, and the holders of such posts were trusted guardians. A son might also be placed in the household of another noble family, with the intention of strengthening the network of kinship relationships.[7] The higher a father's status, the greater was the fosterage-fee for his children.[8]

When Ireland was Christianised this long-standing custom of fosterage continued. Columba's parents would be no more than first or second generation Christians; and, in giving their son to a religious person for fostering, they respected both their traditional culture and their new Christian faith. But as Christian parents they gave their son

---

5 *Amra*, VII and VIII; cf. Adomnán, *Life of Columba*, Second Preface; Máire Herbert, *Iona, Kells and Derry: The History and Hagiography of the Monastic Familia of Columba* (Oxford: Clarendon, 1988), 26.

6 *Old Irish Life*, in W. F. Skene, *Celtic Scotland: A History of Ancient Alban* (first published 1877; American edition; New York: Books for Libraries, 1971), vol. II, 474.

7 Máire and Liam De Paor, *Early Christian Ireland* (3rd edition; London: Thames & Hudson, 1961), 108; Gilbert Markus, *Conceiving a Nation: Scotland to A.D. 900* (Edinburgh: EUP, 2017), 220f.

8 Kathleen Hughes, *Early Christian Ireland: Introduction to the Sources* (London: The Sources of History, 1972), 60.

to a Christian priest rather than to a druid; and within this system the priest became a full foster-parent, not just a teacher. Columba's foster-father was the priest Cruithnechan, described by Adomnán as a priest of 'admirable life' (III:2). It was Cruithnechan who was responsible for Columba's upbringing, and, apart from some basic first steps in literacy, which Columba may have received at home before fosterage began, he was Columba's first tutor. Any child who was placed in such an environment soon absorbed the ethos of ecclesiastical life.

As the years passed, Columba's education advanced at a succession of monasteries. Adomnán informs us that Columba studied 'divine wisdom' as a young deacon under Gemman of Leinster (II:25). The diaconate was the junior of the ordained offices of Deacon, Priest and Bishop, which were the three Church offices recognised across Christendom. Other callings, such as those of monk or abbot, were not ordained offices though they became immensely significant in the Church of the time. After Gemman of Leinster, Columba studied 'sacred Scripture' with a bishop known variously as Finnbarr, Finnio, Uinniau or Finnian (I:1, II:1, and III:4). It may have been during his time with Finnian that Columba was ordained a priest. Finnian's identity is a complex issue which we discuss in Chapter Three. According to the *Old Irish Life* Columba also studied with Mobii at Glaisnoide alongside other monks who went on to become famous leaders.[9]

IRELAND TO IONA

Until he was forty-two years old, Columba worked in Ireland, establishing monasteries and founding churches. Legends of that work fill up the pages of the *Old Irish Life*, and it seemed that the island of Ireland would be Columba's stage for the whole of his ministry. But all changed in his early forties. Adomnán tells us that Columba sailed to Britain two years after the battle of Cul Drebene to make his home there, choosing to become a 'pilgrim for Christ' (I:7). This is all that Adomnán writes about the 561 battle of Cul Drebene. Unlike later writers, such as Manus O'Donnell, Adomnán gives no hint of Columba having been a possible cause of the battle and its bloody carnage. And yet, Adomnán's silence raises suspicion. Was Adomnán supressing an inconvenient truth which was well known outside the official record?

---

9 *Old Irish Life*, in Skene, *Celtic Scotland*, vol. II, 480.

Did Adomnán edit out any involvement of Columba with the battle in order to protect the sanctity of his hero? Was it an indelicate topic avoided by Adomnán because of political sensitivities when he wrote his book at the close of the seventh century? Or was the legend of Columba doing penance for his part in the catastrophe a much later invention?[10] Certainly, other explanations of why Columba left Ireland have been put forward. Máire Herbert suggests that Columba left Ireland because that was the only way he could escape family ties and the privileges of aristocracy into which he had been born.[11] Ian Finlay proposes that Columba was sent to Argyll Dál Riata to help stabilise that kingdom in troubled times.[12] Others speculate it was all about a mid-life crisis! The reasons for his change of direction may never be identified. What we do know is that Adomnán only ever uses the battle of Cul Drebene as a way of dating other events. For Adomnán, Cul Drebene is simply a chronological reference point.

When Columba left Ireland, he did not go alone. An early appendix to Adomnán's *Life of Columba* states that the curragh brought not only Columba but twelve of his closest companions including his cousin Baithéne, who became the second abbot of Iona after Columba's death in 597.[13] It was common for early-medieval writers to assign twelve followers to holy men, in imitation of Jesus and His twelve disciples. Twelve would certainly be nearer the mark than the twenty bishops, forty priests, thirty deacons, and fifty students, which some later texts state as Columba's entourage![14] Whatever the number, this group, with Columba at its helm, made an impact over the next three decades which reverberates down the centuries. Adomnán contributed towards that by writing a blockbuster of a *Life*, ensuring lasting fame for Columba and his exploits.

---

10 Pre-dating Manus O'Donnell, the twelfth-century Latin *Life of Mo Laisse* asserts that exile was imposed on Columba as a penance. The relatively early *Annals of Ulster* record that the battle of Cul Drebene was won through the partisan prayers of Colum Cille. Neither the *Life of Mo Laisse* nor the *Annals of Ulster* accuse Columba explicitly of causing Cul Drebene.

11 Máire Herbert, 'An Tuairisc is Sinne', in John Randall (ed.), *In Search of Colmcille, The Legacy of St. Columba in Ireland and Scotland* (Laxay: Isle of Lewis, Islands Book Trust, 2015), 11; cf. Herbert, *Iona, Kells and Derry.*

12 Ian Finlay, *Columba* (London: Victor Gollancz, 1979), 105f.

13 Alan Orr Anderson and Marjorie Ogilvie Anderson, *Adomnán's Life of Columba*, (Thomas Nelson & Sons Ltd, 1961; revised edition; Oxford: Clarendon, 1991), 237ff., gives the full list.

14 *Old Irish Life*, in Skene, *Celtic Scotland*, vol. II, 491.

The early texts reveal a Columba who was comfortable in dealing with high-status individuals. All of his life he interacted with kings and power-figures. Though he may have had an uneasy relationship with Diarmait, the High-King in Ireland, his dealings with Conall of Dál Riata, Áedán of Dál Riata, Bridei of Pictland, and Rhydderch of the Britons of Strathclyde, appear to have been more productive. Columba first arrived in Argyll Dál Riata in 563, only a few years after that nation and Conall its king had suffered a heavy military setback at the hands of Bridei's Picts. In 563 Dál Riata's fledgling kingdom was in a precarious position. Bridei had not followed up his victory by driving the Scots of Dál Riata into the sea, but they were a cowed and weakened people, with Bridei in a dominant position. This is why Finlay suggests that Columba's arrival may have been a planned strategy, designed to prop up a bruised Dál Riata, and to help strengthen the political and spiritual foothold of a Christian kingdom in a pagan land.[15] Columba's arrival may not have been as calculated as Finlay suggests, but his presence would be welcomed by the beleaguered Conall. And when Adomnán recounts Columba's famous visits to Bridei of the Picts, which took place a few years later, then Adomnán may be chronicling Columba in the role of political ambassador on behalf of King Conall and the kingdom of Dál Riata, as much as in the role of religious evangelist on behalf of King Jesus and the kingdom of heaven.

THE MONASTIC COMMUNITY

Columba established a community on Iona which was under his direct personal control. As abbot he was 'father' to his monks. He had total authority over them. He carried responsibility for their spiritual well-being. He directed their devotional lives. He guided their search for salvation. He set their scholarly pursuits. He stipulated their penitential disciplines. He oversaw their missional activities. In turn, his monks trusted that Columba's captaincy of their lives on earth would give them the best possible chance of glory in heaven. The disciplines which he applied, the penance which he imposed, and the spiritual exercises which he demanded, were all welcomed despite their severity. These were embraced because the monks viewed Columba's rulings as commands from God Himself. Columba enabled them to know the

---

15 Finlay, *Columba*, 105ff.

mind of God in relation to their conduct, the shriving of their sins, and finding their path to eternal peace. Columba, as their abbot, was guardian of their souls. They had chosen to belong to his community because they believed that he could deliver them safely to the heavenly destination.

The monks' work included labour in the fields, study at the desk, worship in the church, and mission to the unconverted. Columba has been credited with taking Christian faith deep into neighbouring Pictland, and though he did have a number of incursions into Pictland, the title of 'Apostle to the Picts' claims too much for him. Other Irish and early Christian-Pictish monks worked full-time in Pictland much longer, and (arguably) more successfully, than Columba ever did. Adomnán does give us stories of individual Picts and their families being converted to Christ through Columba's preaching, but Columba's role as the first, or as the most important, evangelist to the Picts is dubious. Nevertheless, Columba and his Iona monastery were major drivers of the Christianisation of the west and north of Scotland.

THE LINDISFARNE MISSION

Columba died in 597, by which date Iona's influence was well established. Less than forty years after Columba's death, it was to Iona that King Oswald of Northumbria looked when he needed help to fully evangelise his own kingdom. The back-story to this starts in 616 when Oswald's father, King Aethelfrith of Northumbria, was killed in battle by Edwin of Deira.[16] Aethelfrith's widowed Queen Acha feared what might happen to her children at the hands of the victorious Edwin (despite Acha being Edwin's sister), and she fled with the royal family to the far west of Scotland for sanctuary. The boys, Eanfrith, Oswald, and Oswy, were aged twenty-six, twelve, and four at the time, with their sister Ebbe barely a year old. For the next sixteen years the family lived in Argyll Dál Riata where they were profoundly influenced by Iona. Each member of the family professed Christian faith and was baptised by Iona monks. In 632 their fortunes changed when Edwin was killed in battle by Penda of Mercia. The family returned to Northumbria, and Eanfrith (Aethelfrith's elder son possibly by a previous marriage) became king,

---

16 A very readable account is: Max Adams, *The King in the North: The Life and Times of Oswald of Northumbria* (London: Head of Zeus, 2013).

though he soon apostatised from his Christian faith. However, Eanfrith died within a year, and Oswald took over the kingship. Oswald, Oswy, and Ebbe, all remained loyal to the Christian profession, which they had made under Iona's tutelage. Oswy succeeded Oswald as king in 642, and Ebbe founded a female-led monastery at Coldingham, pioneering what was to become a strong Northumbrian tradition of female-led Columban communities.

It was when Oswald gained the kingship that he asked Iona to send a monk to help him evangelise his kingdom. The first monk was unsuitable, but he was replaced by Aidan, who became the bishop and abbot of a monastery built by Oswald on the tidal island of Lindisfarne, off the Northumbria coast. It was from Lindisfarne that monks of the Iona/Columban tradition took their faith all over Oswald's kingdom, with the full and active support of the monarch. Thus the flame of an Iona/Columban style of Christianity burned brightly, though briefly, in what now comprises the north of England and the central and eastern Borders of Scotland, though the present-day border between England and Scotland did not exist in the seventh century, nor indeed did England and Scotland as we know them.

By the time Oswald's brother Oswy became king, the Roman Church tradition was making an impact on Northumbria from the south. The clash between the two traditions resulted in Oswy calling a Synod at Whitby in 664, supposedly to deal with embarrassing inconsistences such as the date of Easter and the type of tonsure. But beneath the surface, deeper ecclesio-political factors acted as the real drivers. The result of Whitby was that Oswy decided that the Church within his realm should adopt Roman forms with respect to the tonsure and the date of Easter, and that there could be a closer relationship with Rome, though as yet with no suggestion that the Northumbria Church would be subject to Rome. After Whitby it was the Roman tradition, rather than the Irish tradition, which became increasingly dominant, not only in Northumbria but in Scotland. The churches of southern Ireland had already accepted the Roman dating for Easter by 632, though the churches of the north of Ireland, and Iona itself, held out for longer. Iona resisted change until the early eighth-century when Nechtan, the Christian King of the Picts, insisted on uniformity throughout his lands. Even after Roman norms in relation to Easter and other issues were adopted, the legacy of the early-medieval Irish Christianity which

Columba brought to Iona was substantial, influencing Christian faith throughout Scotland for centuries.

THE SOURCES

This part of the Introduction is more technical, and some readers may choose to refer to it only when early texts are mentioned in the main body of the work. Adomnán's *Life of Columba* is our main early text, but by no means the only one available to us. There are other extant documents, including some near-contemporary items written within a few years or even a few months of Columba's death. In this section we assess a selection of these important early works. Others, such as the *Bangor Antiphonary*, are discussed in the appropriate chapter.[17]

THE '*LIVES*'

There are several 'Lives' of Columba. These are available in editions which include both the original text and translation. There are also on-line versions of most works.

1. Adomnán's *Life of Columba.* Adomnán was the ninth abbot of Iona, of which Columba was the first. Adomnán's work was written a century after Columba's death and is a complex masterpiece. As such we devote the whole of Chapter Two to an extended discussion on how to read it. Is it a serious source? Is it fable rather than fact? Does it yield any hard data on Columba? Adomnán wrote in early-medieval Latin, and the early eighth-century Schaffhausen manuscript which was copied within twenty years of Adomnán's original, is the earliest still extant, but several English translations are available. William Reeves' nineteenth-century edition was the standard English text for many years, until superseded by Alan and Marjorie Anderson's highly-acclaimed 1961 work.[18] The Andersons re-evaluated the available manuscripts and produced a Latin and English version as part of the Oxford Medieval Texts series. A more recent translation, and the one most accessible for the general reader, is Richard Sharpe's work

---

17 The late seventh-century *Bangor Antiphonary* is discussed in Chapter Thirteen, 'The Worship-Driven Life'.

18 cf. footnote 13 above. Reeves first published his *Life of Columba* in 1856 in English for a limited readership through the Irish Archaeological Society and the Bannatyne Club. His work was then republished for a wider public eighteen years later: W. Reeves, *Life of Saint Columba, Founder of Hy* (Edinburgh: Edmonston & Douglas, 1874).

which was first published in the Penguin series in 1995.[19] All three have invaluable introductions plus detailed comments on the text.

2. *The Old Irish Life* (Anon), also known as *The Irish Life of Colum Cille* or the *Middle Irish Life*. Scholars have proposed a wide range of dates for when the *Old Irish Life* was first written, ranging from the ninth to the twelfth centuries, and it may also contain older material which previously circulated in the oral tradition.[20] In Máire Herbert's opinion this is the only known biography of Columba compiled after Adomnán's *Life of Columba*, which is not a derivative of that work, and she places its composition between 1000 and 1169.[21] In the nineteenth century William F. Skene made the *Old Irish Life* more widely known when he included a version of it as an appendix to the second volume of his series on Celtic Scotland.[22] The *Old Irish Life* has become a popular source for writers who want more biographical detail than provided by Adomnán. Yet, although it offers stories which occur nowhere else, it has less emphasis on Columba's political activities than Adomnán has in his biography. For example, the best texts of the *Old Irish Life* do not mention the Convention of Druim Cett which is a major event for Adomnán.[23] Nor does the *Old Irish Life* mention any controversy surrounding the battle of Cul Drebene. What it is interested in are the monasteries and churches which Columba founded throughout Ireland, especially the church at Derry. It also relocates to Ireland some episodes which Adomnán sets in Scotland.[24] It may be of course that Adomnán had himself transferred these from an Irish setting to a Scottish one! Despite its Irish interest, the *Old Irish Life* is aware of Columba as an Iona man. It states that on Iona Columba had thrice-fifty monks to pursue the contemplative life, with another sixty monks for active ministry. MacQuarrie suggests that a version of the *Old Irish*

19 Richard Sharpe, *Adomnán of Iona: Life of St. Columba* (London: Penguin, 1995).

20 cf. Herbert, *Iona. Kells and Derry*, 188f. Hughes, *Early Christian Ireland: Introduction to the Sources*, 236, suggests that the *Old Irish Life* may have been written in the ninth century. Reeves (*Life of Saint Columba, Founder of Hy*, xxvii) favours the tenth century.

21 Herbert, *Iona, Kells and Derry*, 181.

22 Skene, *Celtic Scotland*, vol. II, 467-507; cf. Paul Grosjean, *Scottish Gaelic Studies* II (University of Aberdeen, 1928), 111-71. Also, Herbert, *Iona, Kells and Derry*, 211-86. On-line versions are available.

23 *Old Irish Life*, Skene, *Celtic Scotland*, vol. II, 494ff., includes, albeit in parenthesis, a variant text which does feature Druim Cett, but this section is not regarded as being part of the original text of the *Old Irish Life*.

24 Herbert, *Iona, Kells and Derry*, 184.

Life may have been brought to Iona in the late twelfth century, and that it was used each year in the monastic liturgy as part of the Benedictine office for Columba's Festal Day on 9 June.[25]

3. Manus O'Donnell's, *Life of Colum Cille.* This is a sixteenth-century compilation which was completed in 1532. It is also known as the *Betha Colaim Chille.*[26] This work is regarded as notoriously unreliable, though there is a persistent suspicion that it may preserve traditions which circulated outside the official record for centuries before being collected by O'Donnell and put into print. O'Donnell claimed to have employed agents across Ireland to gather a bulk of folk material, both oral and written, but the provenance of stories which are unique to O'Donnell's work is unknown. If they did derive from ancient texts, available then but not now, this can no longer be checked-out. It is O'Donnell who gives us the extended story of Columba being at loggerheads with Bishop Finnian over a Psalter, which Finnian accused Columba of having copied illegally. This incident does not appear in Adomnán, though there is a hint of it in the twelfth-century Latin *Life of Mo Laisse.* According to O'Donnell's narrative, Diarmait, the Ui Neill Overlord of the north of Ireland, was asked to settle the dispute, but Diarmait adjudicated against Columba. Columba refused to accept Diarmait's verdict, and this inflamed tribal animosity, resulting in the battle of Cul Drebene. In O'Donnell's account, Columba left Ireland because he carried ultimate responsibility for having initiated a series of events which led to the battle and the slaughter of thousands of men. If the story is true (and we may never know if it is) then the Psalter which Columba copied illegally may be one and the same as an early Irish Psalter, rediscovered centuries later, and known as the Cathach or the 'Battle Book'. The Cathach is discussed in Chapter Eleven.

Columba stories also crop up in lives of several Irish saints. Such tales are usually unique to a particular life. They may be based on genuine memories of Columba within a monastic community. Or they may be legends which were invented with the aim of making Columba part of a local church's foundation story.

---

25 Alan MacQuarrie (ed.), *Legends of Scottish Saints: Readings, Hymns and Prayers for the commemorations of Scottish saints in the Aberdeen Breviary* (Dublin: Four Courts Press, 2008), 342. Skene, *Celtic Scotland*, vol. II, 468, on the basis of remarks made in the *Old Irish Life*'s preface, suggests it was read to congregations on Columba's Feast Day; cf. Reeves, *Life of Saint Columba, Founder of Hy*, xxvii.

26 Herbert, *Iona, Kells and Derry*, 129.

THE '*ANNALS*'

Iona kept its own record of significant historical events, the *Iona Chronicle*, and, in his role of abbot, Columba would be responsible for any entries during his lifetime. The sack of Iona by Viking raiders in the ninth century resulted in the loss of innumerable manuscripts, and though some were saved by being taken to Ireland or to Dunkeld in central Scotland, no *Iona Chronicle* now exists as a document under that name. But parts of it may have been copied into the so-called *Chronicle of Ireland*, which itself became a source for several ancient Irish *Annals* which are still available.[27]

1. *The Annals of Ulster.* These cover the years 431 to 1540 and are written in Irish with some in Latin. The entries are brief and succinct. The data may have come from both oral and written sources. It seems that when the compilers consulted written sources, they copied these word for word, without editing and without resolving contradictory features. Such literal transcriptions add to the usefulness of the *Annals* as a mine for original data, but also produce anomalies: for example, the *Annals of Ulster* has three entries for the battle of Cul Drebene, representing three different traditions, with three different dates. Moreover, dates given by the *Annals* do not always harmonise with modern dating systems, and sophisticated recalculation is required to determine when an event took place. Despite the possibility that the *Iona Chronicle* was a source for some of the earliest entries (either directly or through the *Chronicle of Ireland*), the *Annals of Ulster* has only a few references to Columba or Iona.

2. *The Annals of Tigernach.* These are named after Tigernach Ua Brain (d. 1088), who was the eleventh-century Abbot of Clonmacnoise, though he personally may not have written the *Annals* which now carry his name. The *Annals of Tigernach* cover the periods 489-766, 973-1003, and 1018-1178. The missing 766 to 973 section may now be part of another document, the *Chronicon Scottorum.* As with the *Annals of Ulster*, some early entries may have been sourced from the *Iona*

---

27 For the *Annals of Ulster* see *https://celt.ucc.ie//published/T100001A/index.html.* For the *Annals of Tigernach* see https://celt.ucc.ie/published/T100002A/index.html. Hughes, *Early Christian Ireland: Introduction to the Sources*, 99ff., has a helpful discussion of the various *Annals*; cf. Douglas Dales, *Light to the Isles: Missionary Theology in Celtic and Anglo-Saxon Britain* (Cambridge: Lutterworth, 1997), 59f. See also, Barbara Yorke, *The Conversion of Britain: 600–800* (Harlow: Pearson Longman, 2006), 6ff.; and Markus, *Conceiving a Nation*, 158.

Chronicle. Dates and data in the *Annals of Ulster* and the *Annals of Tigernach* do not always correspond. This gives historians plenty of scope for reconstruction and speculation.

THE '*ALTUS PROSATOR*'

In 1995 Thomas Clancy and Gilbert Markus published a landmark volume, *Iona: The Earliest Poetry of a Celtic Monastery.*[28] This is a vital source for Columba studies. Clancy and Markus give us the original text plus translation of several important early-medieval documents, with careful notes on authorship, background and interpretation. Their selection includes many of the main writings, contemporary or near-contemporary with Columba, which we cite throughout this book.

Subjecting themselves to strict conditions, Clancy and Markus allow two works, plus a fragment from another, to have come from Columba's own pen. The two works are *Altus Prosator* (The High Creator) and *Adiutor Laborantium* (O Helper of the Workers). The fragment is the first six lines of *Noli Pater Indulgere* (Father, do not allow).[29] Other compositions, which are sometimes included in modern hymn books or in modern prayer anthologies, and publicised as having been composed by Columba, do not pass Clancy and Markus's rigorous criteria. Since 1995, Gilbert Markus has revised his assessment of the *Adiutor Laborantium*, concluding that it was composed by Adomnán rather than Columba.[30] If so, this leaves the *Altus Prosator* as the only major document which we can ascribe to Columba himself with any confidence. Even this assertion is qualified because, whilst the language, poetic-style, and content of the *Altus Prosator* may date it to the sixth century, the earliest specific attribution to Columba occurs in an eleventh-century version of the Irish *Liber Hymnorum*. Nevertheless, the *Altus Prosator* is one hundred percent Columban in

---

28 Thomas Owen Clancy and Gilbert Markus, *Iona: The Earliest Poetry of a Celtic Monastery* (Edinburgh: EUP, 1995).

29 Clancy and Markus, *Iona: The Earliest Poetry of a Celtic Monastery*, 90. Thomas MacLauchlan was of the view that *Noli Pater Indulgere* was from Columba (*The Early Scottish Church: The Ecclesiastical History of Scotland from the First to the Twelfth Century*, Edinburgh: T&T Clark, 1865; reprint Forgotten Books, 2015, 198), as are Jean-Michel Picard and Notker Balbulus, 'Adomnán's Vita Columbae and the Cult of Colum Cille in Continental Europe', *PRIA* (1998), 1-23.

30 Gilbert Markus, '*Adiutor Laborantium*: A poem by Adomnán?' in Jonathan M. Wooding (ed.), *Adomnán of Iona: Theologian, Lawmaker, Peacemaker* (Dublin: Four Courts Press, 2010), 145-61.

content, and the general opinion is that it is from Columba's hand. This is our working hypothesis.

The *Altus Prosator* was written in a Latin influenced by Irish Gaelic. It has an alphabetic structure, with the first stanza beginning with A, the second with B, and so on. The alphabet is the early-medieval Latin alphabet which had twenty-three letters, corresponding to the modern English alphabet minus the letters J, U and W. Alphabetic structure was common at the time, and was based on biblical precedents such as Psalm 119.[31] The *Altus Prosator* draws on a wide variety of biblical texts, ranging from Genesis to Revelation. It opens with a strong declaration of trinitarian faith. It discusses the creation of the world. It elaborates on the fall of Satan and of disobedient angels. It considers the effect of sin. And it points to the final judgement.

THE '*AMRA CHOLUIMB CHILLE*'

Columba died on Iona in 597. Within a year the blind Irish monk Dallán Forgaill completed the *Amra Choluimb Chille* honour-poem, known more simply as the *Amra*. There is a tradition that Dallán drafted the *Amra* some years earlier in thanksgiving for Columba's support of the Bards of Ireland at the Convention of Druim Cett, but Columba forbade any publication until after his death.[32] Dallán may have met Columba at Druim Cett, or at a monastery on one of Columba's frequent visits back to his homeland. Dallán claims that his poem was commissioned by the royal figure Áed mac Ainmirech (d. 598), and we know that both Áed and his father Ainmere had close links with Columba.[33] Consistent with this, the *Amra* has a strong emphasis on Columba's noble ancestry, noted by Herbert who points out that the

31 cf. Psalms 25, 34, 37, 111, 112, 145. Jerome popularised the alphabetic model. The *Bangor Antiphonary* has several items with an alphabetic genre, as do other liturgical works.

32 Rory B. Egan, 'Stesichorus and Helen, Dallán and Columba', *The Classical World* (1993), 64-7, offers a radically different view of the *Amra*. Egan builds on a later Irish tradition that Dallán regained his sight, and he speculates that the *Amra* was composed in the ninth century to mimic the classical story of Stesichorus, who had been blinded by Helen of Troy, but later had his sight restored. Egan concedes that there is no evidence of Columba blinding Dallán as Helen blinded Stesichorus, and he also admits that other parts of his argument are weak.

33 Clancy and Markus, *Iona: The Earliest Poetry of a Celtic Monastery*, 118. Brian Lacey, 'The *Amrae Coluimb Cille* and the Ui Neill', *JRSAI*, vol. 134 (2004), 169-72, discusses date of composition and dedication in the light of the *Amra*'s internal evidence. Lacey is hesitant about dating the *Amra* as early as 600 but concludes that that was probably the case.

Amra celebrates Columba as a significant figure in the rapprochement between the secular aristocracy and Christian leadership.[34] The oldest extant copy of the *Amra* dates from the eleventh century, but Herbert is confident that linguistic evidence dates its composition to around the close of the sixth century.[35] Clancy and Markus include an English translation, and most of our quotations from the *Amra* come from this. P. L. Henry published a multi-lingual version of the *Amra* in 2006 under the title, *Amra Cholum Chille: Dallán's Elegy for Columba*.[36]

The *Amra* is not easy to interpret. For many years it was regarded as an arcane and difficult composition, shedding little light on Columba. But recently it has been viewed as providing more clues about Columba and his activities than previously supposed. It celebrates Columba founding numerous Christian communities. It speaks of him as the guardian of 'a hundred churches'. It highlights Columba's aristocratic connections. It stresses that Columba gave up great privileges when he followed the monastic life. In early-medieval Ireland, as in Christendom as a whole, the renunciation of wealth was viewed as a crucial indicator of a person's sanctity, and much was made of Jesus' teaching that a rich man could hardly enter the kingdom of heaven (Mark 10:25). On that basis the abandonment of this world's goods was regarded as an absolute pre-requisite for holiness and a heavenly hope. Accordingly, the *Amra* celebrates Columba living a wealth-denying lifestyle. It has Columba as a poet, going with 'two songs' to heaven. And it has a number of principal themes:

1. *Columba as Holy Man of God.* The *Amra*'s Columba is a visionary ascetic committed to fasting and vigils.[37] In this, the *Amra* differs from conventional secular honour-poetry in eulogising Columba's Christian ideals of renunciation rather than the attributes of the warrior hero.[38] The preface to the *Amra* ascribes saving powers to Columba, stating that whoever recites the *Amra* every day will receive from Columba 'the kingdom of God mightily', 'prosperity on earth', and 'save his soul

34 Herbert, *Iona, Kells and Derry*, 12.

35 Herbert, *Iona, Kells and Derry*, 9.

36 Clancy and Markus, *Iona: The Earliest Poetry of a Celtic Monastery*, give the Irish text and English translation of the *Amra Choluimb Cille*. P. L. Henry, *Amra Choluimb Cille: Dallán's Elegy for Columba* (Ultach Trust, 2006), has Old Irish, Modern Irish, Scots Gaelic, and English versions of the *Amra*; cf. Dales, *Light to the Isles*, 57.

37 Clancy and Markus, *Iona: The Earliest Poetry of a Celtic Monastery*, 119.

38 Herbert, *Iona, Kells and Derry*, 10.

past pain'.[39] However, the preface may be a later composition from the eleventh century and not from the hand of Dallán. Certainly, in the main body of the original early poem, Columba is not yet presented as a continuing patron in this life. Nevertheless, the *Amra* acknowledges miracles at Columba's grave, and expects help from Columba in the life to come.[40]

2. *Columba as Scholar and Interpreter.* The *Amra* majors on Columba's intellectual accomplishments, with Dallán showing a detailed awareness of Columba's scholarship. Given that the *Amra* is such an early work, this shows that Columba's scholarship was a major feature of his abbacy for those who knew him. The *Amra* describes Columba as 'learning's pillar'. It states that he was 'foremost at the book of complex law'. It claims that Columba studied Greek grammar. It celebrates his ability to 'explain the true word'. It emphasises that he 'made glosses clear' by his wisdom, and that he was a trusted exegete of the biblical text. Columba also 'read mysteries and distributed the Scriptures among the schools'. It is from clues in the *Amra*, allied to evidence in Adomnán's *Life of Columba*, that we learn more about the books which were available in the Iona Library even in its early years. This is discussed further in Chapter Eleven. Importantly, the *Amra* names two theologians whom Columba drew upon: Basil of Caesarea and John Cassian. They are major figures in our analysis of Columba's thinking. The *Amra* also tells us that Columba studied the moon and the stars and the 'course of the sea'. Columba's astronomical observations may have been for liturgical purposes.

3. *Columba as Missionary/Evangelist*? The *Amra* (I,VIII) has two references to Columba's ministry on the Scottish mainland but does not mention Columba's legendary visits to King Bridei of the Picts, which are prominent in Adomnán's *Life of Columba*. Instead, the *Amra* highlights interaction between Columba and the peoples of the Tay. This detail has spawned feverish speculation. James E. Fraser seizes on it to build a case for Columba never having operated in the Inverness area in any major way.[41] Alternatively, Máire Herbert suggests that the phrase 'peoples of the Tay' may simply be Dallán's

39 Clancy and Markus, *Iona: The Earliest Poetry of a Celtic Monastery*, 96.

40 Clancy and Markus, *Iona: The Earliest Poetry of a Celtic Monastery*, 99, 122.

41 James E. Fraser, *From Caledonia to Pictland: Scotland to 795* (Edinburgh: EUP, 2009), 105.

way of referring to North Britain as a whole.[42] Connected to this, Clancy and Markus point out that Columba lived for thirteen years after Bridei's death in 584, with these years seeing a shift of focus to Tayside, and it may be that later activity which the *Amra* features.[43] Dallán's immediate sources may have been monks more familiar with Columba's later years than with his earlier ones when he made expeditions further north.

4. *Columba and the King.* The *Amra* hints at a pact between Columba and the King of Dál Riata (VIII). Is this a reference to Iona being gifted to Columba as a monastic base? If so, then it bolsters the Iona version of the donation of Iona which insists that it was Conall of Dál Riata, and not Bridei of the Picts (as claimed by Bede), who gave the island.[44]

BECCÁN'S POEMS

Clancy and Markus also include poems by Beccán mac Luigdech, a close associate of Abbot Segene of Iona who ruled the monastery from 623 to 652. Beccán mac Luigdech may be the same as Beccán of Rum, whose death in 677 is recorded in the *Annals of Ulster*,[45] and what we find in Beccán's poems are evolving attitudes toward Columba even within fifty years of his death, and fifty years before Adomnán wrote his *Life of Columba*. In Beccán's first work, *Fo Reir Choluimb* (Bound to Columba), we find concepts echoing sentiments found elsewhere: asceticism, learning, industriousness, and wisdom:

He fought wise battles with the flesh,
Indeed, he read pure learning,
He stitched, he hoisted sail tops,
A sage across seas,
His prize a kingdom.[46]

The poem also celebrates Columba's regal status, and reflects a growing cult of Columba as a heavenly protector in the present life:

---

42 Herbert, *Iona, Kells and Derry*, 11.

43 Clancy and Markus, *Iona: The Earliest Poetry of a Celtic Monastery*, 207.

44 The Venerable Bede, *Ecclesiastical History of the English People (*trans. Leo Sherley-Price: London: Penguin revised edition, 1990), III:4.

45 *Annals of Ulster*, 677.6.

46 Beccán, *Fo Reir Choluimb*, XIII.

Royal kin of triumphant kings,
Lord full of grace, thus may he guard us,
I'll take off the devil's noose,
His bard's prayer perhaps may save us.[47]

Beccán's second work, *Tiugraind Beccain* (The Last Verses of Beccán), continues the theme of honouring Columba. It says of Columba: 'In scores of curraghs, with an army of wretches, he crossed the long-haired sea.'[48] 'Scores of curraghs' may refer to the many sea-journeys Columba made after settling on Iona, rather than to his initial arrival in Argyll. Or perhaps Beccán was employing poetic licence! The poem describes Columba as Wisdom's Champion, and that, 'all round Ireland, he was exalted'. Columba is 'shepherd of monks, judge of clerics'.[49] In Beccán's mind Columba is a spiritual giant, whose reputation increases rather than diminishes as year succeeds year.

LANGUAGE AND TERMINOLOGY

Our policy is to replace Latin by English wherever possible. Some documents, including Columba's *Altus Prosator*, Dallán's *Amra Choluimb Chille*, and liturgical pieces such as the *Nunc Dimittis* or *Sancti Venite*, are so well-known in their original Latin wording that Latin titles are retained, though English translations are used when quoting their main texts. Only once do we cite a longer Latin text. This is in Chapter Seventeen where we refer to the Latin text of the *Bangor Symbol*, in order to demonstrate that it derives from the *Apostles' Creed*, rather than from the *Nicene Creed*.

Concerning the spelling of the names of people and places, even Adomnán was aware that these could cause difficulties. In his First Preface he warns that the reader may encounter unusual terms:

> There are words here in the poor Irish language, strange names of men and peoples and places; names which I think are crude in comparison with the different tongues of foreign races. But let no one think this a reason to despise the proclamation of profitable deeds, which were not achieved without the help of God.

47 Beccán, *Fo Reir Choluimb*, XIV.
48 Beccán, *Tiugraind Beccain*, IV.
49 Beccán, *Tiugraind Beccain*, VI, *x*.

There was no need for Adomnán to apologise. But his discomfiture indicates he had a Latin readership in mind, beyond the circle of trainee Irish monks on Iona who were his immediate public, and Adomnán had no desire to be judged as an ill-educated monk from the edges of the world. Modern access to these 'crude' names is through copies of copies of copies of manuscripts, and repeated copying over the centuries has produced a plethora of variant spellings. For the sake of uniformity, we usually adopt Richard Sharpe's orthography in the Penguin edition of Adomnán's *Life of Columba.* Sharpe's version is the most-used text for English-speaking students of Columba, and it makes sense to follow him.

The term '**Celtic**' is not used by Adomnán, and today it is a word hedged around by scholarly and cultural hot potatoes! Consequently, we prefer the terms 'Irish' and 'Columban', though not totally shunning 'Celtic'. When we refer to the **Celtic Church**, we mean the non-Roman, Christian Church of a wide area of Atlantic Europe, including the Isle of Man, Wales, Ireland, western Scotland, parts of the north of France and parts of the north of Spain. This was the Christian Church occupying the so-called 'Celtic fringe' of Europe and is what Herren and Brown term the 'Common Celtic Church'.[50]

The phrase **Irish Church** refers to the early-medieval Christian Church in Ireland of Columba's era, and to churches planted by extension from Ireland, including those in Argyll, Pictland, Northumbria, and mainland Europe. Missionaries from this Church were known throughout Britain and Europe as 'Irish' missionaries. The **Columban Church** was an offshoot of the Irish Church. It was originally established on Iona by Columba. The Columban Church spread outwards from Iona but looked back to Columba as its inspirational founding figure. Hence, 'Columban' can apply to any monk, community, or mission, which saw itself as following in Columba's footsteps. In this sense, Lindisfarne was a Columban foundation, even though after Whitby in 664 it was increasingly Romanised. **Insular Christianity** refers to the Christianity of the islands of Ireland and Britain, including the Hebrides of Scotland, in contrast to the Christianity of mainland, continental Europe.

---

50 Michael W. Herren and Shirley Ann Brown, *Christ in Celtic Christianity: Britain and Ireland from the Fifth to the Tenth Century* (Woodbridge: Boydell, 2002), passim.

PROLOGUE

CHAPTER 1

Iona's Man

On a July Monday in 1869 the steamer, *S.S. Mountaineer* docked at Ardrishaig, Loch Fyne. Passengers came on board, some of whom had arrived earlier on a smaller boat from Tarbert, and all of whom were anticipating a relaxing voyage. They were scheduled to pass through the picturesque Crinan Canal before cruising the islands of the Inner Hebrides, setting down and picking up locals en route. The ship was a well-known sight in the west of Scotland, taking sightseers from Ardrishaig and Oban to Staffa, Iona, Fort William, and even Loch Coruisk in Skye. Built in 1852 by the Govan shipbuilders J. & G. Thomson, the *S.S. Mountaineer* was advertised as offering excellent accommodation for tourists. With her sleek lines, flush deck, comfortable deck-saloon, carved and gilded bow and stern, and capability of 15 knots, she was a classy vessel. Extended twice during her lifetime, the *S.S. Mountaineer* offered style and comfort to the Victorian traveller. Twenty years later, in September 1889, she ran aground whilst returning to Oban in bad weather. Fortunately, there was no loss of life, and initially the ship seemed to be only lightly damaged, but worsening seas broke her in two.[1] But in the summer of 1869 that undignified fate was far in the future. The *S.S. Mountaineer* was in her pomp, and coming aboard her that day were two passengers whose paths crossed for the first time, and who met at dinner that evening in an awkward encounter.

One was the Very Reverend Norman MacLeod, the 1869 Moderator of the General Assembly of the Church of Scotland. He was named after his father, Dr Norman MacLeod who was known as *Caraid nan Gaidheal* (Friend of the Gael) because of his passionate advocacy on behalf of the Gaelic-speaking folk of the Highlands and Islands. Though the younger Norman served in Glasgow as minister of the Barony Kirk

1 Ian McCrorie, *Steamers of the Highlands and Island* (Greenock: Orr, Pollock & Co., 1987), 16, 42.

rather than in the Highlands, he was admired like his father as having a heart for his ancestral people. Besides his parish work, he edited the popular *Good Words* Christian magazine, which was published twice a month with a circulation of 100,000 in Scotland alone. Recent editions of *Good Words* carried a series of articles on Iona written by George John Douglas Campbell, the eighth Duke of Argyll. The Duke had not limited himself to rhapsodising on the beauties of Iona but took the opportunity to criticise Roman Catholicism and condemn what he believed was its corrupting impact on the Columba story. The Duke lamented that Adomnán's classic work, his *Life of Columba*, was so riddled with superstitions (introduced in the Duke's opinion by Romanising influences) as to be almost unusable.[2] To the Duke's mind, Columba's true faith had been swamped by Roman Catholic accretions.

The other figure was Father John Stewart M'Corry, one-time priest of the Roman Catholic congregation in Perth. M'Corry was the author of several books in defence of the Roman Catholic faith and had read the Duke's contributions to the *Good Words* magazine with increasing annoyance. Not only had the Duke belittled Roman Catholicism in general, but he had rubbished Charles Forbes Montalembert's book, *The Monks of the West*.[3] M'Corry considered Montalembert his friend and was angered by the Duke's attack. M'Corry was not only offended by what the Duke had written but was annoyed that MacLeod, as editor, had allowed the articles to go into print. M'Corry was further irritated by MacLeod's recent keynote Moderatorial address to the General Assembly, which M'Corry interpreted as being anti-Catholic. Even as M'Corry boarded the *S.S. Mountaineer* en route to Iona, he had proof sheets in his pocket of a critical review he had written of MacLeod's General Assembly speech, almost ready for publication.[4]

---

2 In his later book the Duke wrote, 'To shut [Adomnán's] book and never to open it again might well be our first impulse ... What are we to make of [such] stories? ... Montalembert himself repeats all [Adomnán's] narratives without letting us clearly understand whether he accepts all, or only some, or whether he narrates them simply as part of the belief of the times, as such and as nothing more. Perhaps devout Roman Catholics do not choose to put any question to themselves upon the subject.' [Argyll, *Iona*, 43]. Norman MacLeod wrote similarly in *Good Words* (1860), 335: '[In Adomnán's *Life of Columba*] Columba is seen invested with such an atmosphere of legend and miracle that often, only with strained eye, in partial, broken glimpses, we can descry his human features. One moment we get a blink of his countenance as if by chance; the next it is lost in the mass of miracles, visions, and prophecies with which they have surrounded him.'

3 Charles F. Montalembert, *The Monks of the West from St. Benedict to St. Bernard* (1867).

4 John S. M'Corry, *The Monks of Iona: In Reply to 'Iona' by the Duke of Argyll* (1871), 42.

The exigencies of travel, and the dining arrangements on the *S.S. Mountaineer*, meant that the two men had to meet. Good manners would keep conversation within the polite constraints of Victorian civility, though M'Corry's account is ambivalent on this point. Two years later M'Corry published his views on MacLeod and the Duke of Argyll in book form, making reference to the ship-board encounter.

M'Corry's 1871 book, *The Monks of Iona*, starts with a courteous preface, congratulating the Duke of Argyll on the forthcoming marriage of his son John to Princess Louise, one of Queen Victoria's daughters. Pleasantries over, M'Corry attacks the Duke's anti-Catholic stance as set out in the *Good Words* articles. M'Corry stresses that any magazine with the title *Good Words* must also, at the very least, only allow *true* words. In M'Corry's view, what the Duke wrote and what MacLeod published, was simply untrue. M'Corry then devotes page after page in defence of Adomnán's portrayal of Columba from a Roman Catholic perspective, criticising the Duke's attempts to separate the faith of Columba from the faith of Rome. M'Corry knew that a nineteenth-century idealisation of a romantic 'Celtic' past had, in Protestant hands, promoted Columba as representing an earlier and purer form of Christianity than the Roman Catholicism which came later. M'Corry rejects this. He claims Columba for his own tradition. He argues that Columba's faith and Rome's faith were one and the same. At the same time, he is aware that the issue is not straightforward, prompting him to make this comment on Columba's faith as portrayed by Adomnán:

> As regards the theology of Columba's time, although it was not what we now understand as Roman, neither assuredly was it what we understand as Protestant. … in [Adomnán's book on] Columba's life we have proof of: the practice of auricular confession; of the invocation of saints; of confidence in their protection; of belief in transubstantiation; of the practice of fasting and of penance; of prayers for the dead; of the sign of the cross in familiar … use. Now, we submit that nothing could be more Roman and less Protestant than the very doctrines here enumerated and which were taught and practised so sedulously at Iona.[5]

5 M'Corry, *The Monks of Iona*, 79. M'Corry repeats concessions made by Montalembert, and noted by Argyll.

M'Corry concedes some differences between Columba's faith and his own nineteenth-century Catholic beliefs. He admits that Columba had no cultus of the Virgin Mary. He acknowledges that Columba's early-medieval Irish Church had little notion of the universal Bishopric of Rome. He recognises that there was not a one-to-one correspondence between the sixth-century Church on Iona and contemporary Roman Catholicism. Nevertheless, M'Corry is convinced that Columba's faith was infinitely closer to Roman Catholicism than to Presbyterianism.

M'Corry knew of Protestant attempts to represent Columba and other early Celtic monks as proto-Protestant or even proto-Presbyterian. He knew of a 'determined Protestant bid to portray the Celtic Columban order as a native, unadulterated and proto-Protestant Christianity, that had spread Gospel blessings throughout the isles and glens, [until] the Highlands [were] abandoned to the iniquities of Papists and Norsemen'.[6] Echoes of such claims of a 'Protestant' Columba and 'Protestant' early Irish missionaries would endure into the twentieth century. For example, G. N. M. Collins wrote in his 1944 biography of Professor Donald MacLean of the Free Church, that Christian light and culture had first arrived in Applecross via the Irish Church around 673, but that this early candle of 'true and pure Gospel faith' was later smothered by Rome.[7] In this reading of history, the first Irish monks to Scotland brought a faith which later Protestants could have owned as their own, but which Romanism snuffed out. This interpretation of Columba's era was adopted by Scots divines as early as the seventeenth century; and a nineteenth-century example was Thomas MacLauchlan, who, in his 1865 work, *The Early Scottish Church*, attempted to give the Columban Church a Presbyterian polity and doctrine, in which every reference to a bishop became a reference to an elder, and every article of faith anticipated the doctrines of Reformed Protestantism.[8] M'Corry was in direct opposition to this Protestant reading of spiritual history. In similar fashion, Father Allan MacDonald, the late nineteenth-century folklorist and champion of Gaelic Catholic spirituality, would claim Columba for Rome, believing

6 John MacLeod, *Banner in the West* (Edinburgh: Birlinn, 2009), 45ff.
7 G. N. M. Collins, *Donald MacLean* (Edinburgh: Lindsay, 1944), 1.
8 MacLauchlan, *The Early Scottish Church*, 165f.

that the only true unbroken link between Columba and the modern era was the 'indigenous' Catholic spirituality of the Western Isles.[9]

CLAIMING COLUMBA

Both traditions, Protestant and Catholic, have tried to claim Columba as their own. On the *S.S. Mountaineer*, these traditions collided in the persons of MacLeod and M'Corry. M'Corry claimed Columba for mainstream Roman Catholicism, though aware that Columba's faith did not perfectly harmonise with that of Rome. MacLeod, and the Duke of Argyll, after removing 'fantastical' and 'superstitious' stories which, in their opinion, had been foisted on Columba by a Roman-influenced Adomnán, claimed Columba for Protestantism, despite all early sources giving Columba a faith which no son of the Reformation could homologate in its entirety. So, to which was the 'real' Columba closer? Was he Roman Catholic? Was he Protestant? This is impossible to answer, because the issue goes beyond a simple binary option. Moreover, Columba has become such an iconic figure that suitors for his legacy are not confined within Catholicism or Protestantism.

Claiming Columba continues. Columba in particular, and Celtic Christianity in general, have been claimed by an ecologically focussed Green Spirituality, and we discuss this more fully in Chapter Seventeen in relation to God the Creator. Likewise, liberal Christianity sees itself as Columba's heir, though to what degree it can sustain that claim is less certain. For example, the core evangelistic concern of an Irish missionary monk was to help sinners avoid an everlasting hell, an issue which liberal Christianity tends to bypass, despite references to eternal judgement, and the need to be saved from a lost eternity, abounding in Adomnán's *Life of Columba* and Columba's *Altus Prosator*. This is where Ian Bradley, himself intuitively sympathetic to the values of modern liberal Christianity, is emphatically realistic. Bradley knows that any attempt to make Columba's Christianity reflect liberal agendas will fail,

> Whatever else he was; Columba was no liberal. The emphasis in [Columba's own] poem, *Altus Prosator* … is on the sovereignty of God, the reality of human sin, the depth of the fall of humanity, the power of divine judgement, the

---

9 Roger Hutchinson, *Father Allan: The Life and Legacy of a Hebridean Priest* (Edinburgh: Birlinn, 2010), 74f.

> terrible apocalyptic nature of Christ's second coming, and the reality of Hell.[10]

Herren and Brown, in their influential 2002 work, *Christ in Celtic Christianity*, write similarly. They note that the Irish Church was hell-orientated and obsessed with rescuing souls from the everlasting fire.[11] In this matter, though perhaps not in others, Columba and the early Irish Church were closer to conservative evangelicalism than to liberal Protestantism. Even that is a vast simplification, because vast swathes of Columba's beliefs would be anathema to traditional Presbyterians.

KNOWING COLUMBA

This ambiguity carries over into knowing what Columba was like. As far as his physical appearance is concerned, there are few clues. Like all monks he would be clean-shaven. And, because he followed an ascetic lifestyle, his physique would be wiry and spare. Beyond this we know little. When Adomnán wrote his *Life of Columba*, he was not interested in Columba's physical description. What mattered was Columba's holiness, faith, calling, and God-approved ministry. The *Amra*, written by the poet Dallán possibly within a year of Columba's death, does mention Columba's 'soft grey eye'. But Dallán was blind, so either others described Columba to him, or the soft, grey, eye, came from his poetic imagination. The novelist Nigel Tranter, drawing on hints scattered through the available literature, describes Columba as tall, handsome, fair-haired, well-built, a notable horseman, fond of sports, possessing a fine singing voice, and of hot temper![12]

The temper is significant. The Columba who helped his companions ashore in 563 was no shrinking violet. Though given the name Colum Cille (Dove of the Church), he was by no means the peaceable and innocent pilgrim which such a name might suggest. Moreover, 'dove' did not always imply 'peace'. In the Church Fathers the 'dove' was as much a symbol of the powerful and troubling presence of God the Holy Spirit than one of peace. And all through Columba's life there was a tension between being the humble servant of God, and being the

---

10 Ian Bradley, *Argyll: The Making of a Spiritual Landscape* (Edinburgh: St. Andrew Press, 2015), 58f.; cf. Clancy and Markus, *Iona: The Earliest Poetry of a Celtic Monastery*, 190ff.

11 Herren and Brown, *Christ in Celtic Christianity*, xiii, 152.

12 Nigel Tranter, *The Story of Scotland* (Glasgow: Wilson, 2000), 6.

dominant leader, power-broker, mover and shaker, fixer, and shrewd politician.[13] It is this dual quality of Columba's personality which makes Ron Ferguson compare Columba with George MacLeod, the founder of the modern Iona Community.[14] For Ferguson, both were firebrands. Both were passionate about justice. Both were energised by that disturbing dove, the Holy Spirit. Ian Finlay notes that Adomnán's *Life of Columba* reveals a man whose revered piety and devotion were capable of a rapid metamorphosis into surges of deep anger.[15] Columba could have a hair-trigger reaction to perceived wrongs, and readily called down judgement from heaven on erring individuals. For example, the custom of standing waist-deep or even chest-deep in the sea whilst praying to God was an expression of intense prayer; and on at least one occasion, Columba did exactly that. But he was not praying in this extreme manner to plead mercy from heaven on an erring soul, but asking that heaven's wrath might send a storm to drown an evil man (II:22).

Adomnán's portrayal of Columba reveals a complex, multifaceted, enigmatic personality. Two stories illustrate that complexity. One involves Erc moccu Druidi of the Island of Coll; the other features King Áedán of Dál Riata. In the first, we have a Columba full of compassion and sympathetic wisdom as shown by how he deals with the would-be thief, Erc moccu Druidi (I:41). Adomnán tells us that Erc hid on Mull, waiting for darkness, before sailing to a small island belonging to the monks which was a breeding-place for seals. Erc's intention was to kill seals, fill his boat with them, and strike for home. When Erc was apprehended and brought to Columba, Columba sought to deal with the causes lying behind Erc's actions rather than punishing him for his intended criminality. Columba knew that Erc had turned to crime because he was desperate, and said to Erc, 'If you are in need and come to us, you will receive the necessities you request.' Columba then slaughtered some sheep and gave them to Erc to take home. On a later occasion, knowing that Erc was dying, Columba sent him meat and grain. Here we see Columba ministering to the root cause of Erc's behaviour, which was desperation caused by poverty. Columba offered

---

13 Finlay, *Columba*, 173.

14 Ron Ferguson, *George MacLeod: Founder of the Iona Community* (London: Collins, 1990), 141ff.

15 Finlay, *Columba*, 141.

help and rehabilitation rather than retribution. Columba acted out a liberal and a progressive Christianity, treating the desperation and the root economic causes lying behind Erc's offending, rather than condemning him for what he planned to do.

If the Erc incident shows a compassionate Columba, the second episode (I:9) involving King Áedán of Dál Riata, raises the question: Was Columba really a man of peace? Gilbert Markus, in his 2017 book *Conceiving a Nation*, paints a picture of early-medieval Irish Christian piety, in which themes of peace, justice, and non-violence were core issues for Irish missions to Scotland, culminating in Adomnán's humanitarian activities, especially his 697 *Law of the Innocents* and its provisions for the protection of non-combatants in time of war.[16] There is little doubt that early-medieval monks would prefer peace to war, but was peace-making the key evangelical truth which drove their missionary zeal? Did that dominate their exposition of Christian faith? Was it central in their daily thoughts? Was it a non-negotiable axiom of faith? If promotion of peace is put forward as the central plank of Columba's ministry, then there is an inconvenient truth lying in the way. Adomnán's *Life of Columba* has no stories in which Columba urges peace instead of conflict. Columba never cries out, 'Stop the War!' This brings us to the King Áedán incident.

When Áedán of Dál Riata set off to battle the Miathi, Columba was filled with anxiety. But Columba's disquiet was not about the bloodiness of the coming campaign. Columba's worry was about the succession to the throne of Dál Riata if Áedán were to fall in battle. In this story, Adomnán does not present Columba as a 'dove of peace', tirelessly urging his warrior-monarch to desist from conflict and turn the other cheek whatever the cost. Columba's concern was not peace but the throne. Columba knew that the continued existence of Dál Riata as a nation was dependent on the stability of the kingship. Columba also knew that if Dál Riata were secure, his Church would be secure: if Dál Riata were strong, his Church would be safe. And when Columba intercepted his warrior-monarch, the issue at stake was not pacifism, nor was it the shedding of the blood of scores of

16 Markus, *Conceiving a Nation*; cf. Warren Bardsley, *Against the Tide: The Story of Adomnán of Iona* (Glasgow: Wild Goose, 2006); and Gilbert Markus (ed.), *The Radical Tradition: Saints in the Struggle for Justice and Peace* (London: Darton, Longman & Todd, 1992), 80-7.

men who would leave widowed wives and orphaned children. The vital issue was a smooth handover of power if Áedán were to fall.[17] Who would be king? Would there be a power struggle? Columba wanted this settled before Áedán left. In fact, in the culture of sixth-century Dál Riata, it would not be in Áedán's gift to determine his successor, and Adomnán may have constructed the story in order to argue for a system of primogeniture succession as part of the Christian Church's campaign for an alternative understanding of kingship. Nevertheless, whatever Adomnán's reasons for giving us the story, Columba is not presented in pacifist garb.

Is it surprising that Adomnán does not present Columba as pleading with Áedán to stay his hand for the sake of peace as a non-negotiable Christian virtue? Not really. As early as the first chapter of his *Life of Columba*, Adomnán tells of King Oswald of Northumbria triumphing in battle precisely because Columba aided him (I:1). In Adomnán's book Columba is never portrayed as a man for whom the cornerstone of his Gospel is an appeal to kings to live in a new way, the way of peace. This is not to say that Columba saw peace as unimportant. But Adomnán does not present *that* as the core message which was burning in Columba's soul. Gilbert Markus himself, whilst keen to stress the peace-credentials of the early Irish Church, concedes that churchmen accepted that some violence was necessary in order to govern and protect kingdoms.[18] Neither Columba nor Adomnán were absolutist pacifists.

On the other hand, the Columban Church did have an interest in peace and justice. Adomnán, through his epoch-making *Law of the Innocents*, passed at the Synod of Birr in 697, persuaded powerful chiefs in Ireland and Scotland to sign up to a policy of protecting women, children, and clerics during warfare. Pushing this through required vision, preparation, negotiation, courage, and tenacity on Adomnán's part. Thomas O'Loughlin notes with admiration that Adomnán stood his ground, challenging native law and culture, instead of compromising with the forces of power and wealth. Instead, Adomnán supplemented these quite radically from a Christian perspective.[19] And the Synod of Birr was not the only occasion when Adomnán's

17 cf. Markus, *Conceiving a Nation*, 172.
18 Markus, *Conceiving a Nation*, 131ff.
19 Thomas O'Loughlin, *Celtic Theology* (London: Continuum, 2000), 70.

radical and progressive Christian principles were put into practice. Earlier in Adomnán's abbacy he was involved in embassies to King Aldfrith of Northumbria (686, 688) arranging a release of hostages who had been carried off by Aldfrith's predecessor Ecgfrith some years earlier in a raid on the southern Ui Neill territory of Brega (II:46). Nevertheless, despite Adomnán originating and promoting one of the most significant humanitarian documents in Western political history, he never argues that warfare cannot be waged by Christian monarchs, and he never portrays Columba as an uncompromising pacifist. Adomnán's campaign was for civilised conduct. It was not a call to pacifism in every circumstance, whatever the cost in terms of self-suffering or self-sacrifice.

What we have in Adomnán's *Life of Columba* is a central figure who became, in modern parlance, 'a legend in his own lifetime'. This superstar celebrity status is wonderfully illustrated in Adomnán's account of Columba visiting the Clonmacnoise monastery in Ireland (I:2). Columba's arrival at Clonmacnoise caused a sensation. It was so tumultuous that, as Columba walked towards the monastery, four men kept pace with him, 'holding about him a square frame of branches tied together' to protect Columba from the pressing crowds. Modern images of yellow-jacketed, Big-Event, security-guards surrounding a celebrity come to mind. At Clonmacnoise huge numbers turned out for the man of the day. Adomnán's Columba was no ordinary person. He supped with kings. He dominated his monastery. He influenced religious life for centuries.

Columba's faith, spirituality and personality were those of an early-medieval Christian who lived on the 'fringes of the known world'. Protestants, Catholics, Greens, Conservatives, Liberals, all now claim him, each in their own way. But the debate concerning who he truly was and what he really represented continues. One place where we glimpse Columba's spirituality is within the pages of Adomnán's great book, his *Life of Columba.* How to read Adomnán's *magnum opus* is our focus in Chapter Two.

CHAPTER 2

Adomnán's Book

When the eighth Duke of Argyll researched his articles for the *Good Works* magazine, he read Adomnán's *Life of Columba*. The book frustrated him so much he was tempted to throw it across his study in Inverary Castle! The Duke expected clear data. Instead, he found implausible myths and legends; and he was not alone in being irritated by Adomnán's masterpiece. The Protestant historian Thomas MacLauchlan was similarly annoyed, concluding that, no 'greater congress of absurdity and pure fable' exists within the range of literature, civil or sacred, than in Adomnán's book.[1] MacLauchlan and the Duke opened Adomnán's pages with eager anticipation. They expected an informed biography. What they found was a seemingly disordered mish-mash of the bizarre and the incongruous. Few dates. Little chronological sequence. A narrative jumping from story to story, and majoring on prophecies, miracles, and visions. To their annoyance every incident recorded by Adomnán involved the fantastical and the bizarre. And every reader of Adomnán's book is faced with this. How do we use such a work?

ADOMNÁN'S MIRACLES

Adomnán's *Life of Columba*, simultaneously lauded and damned, dwarfs all other written sources for Columba. Can we find Columba through its pages? Or does the constant intrusion of the supernatural eliminate any possibility of seriously engaging with the real sixth-century saint? An Enlightenment principle, almost unquestioned in Western academia, is that academic investigation can only deal with natural events and natural causes: the proper study of man is of man

---

1 MacLauchlan, *The Early Scottish Church*, 148. In contrast, Hughes, *Early Christian Ireland: Introduction to the Sources*, 223ff., regards Adomnán as a valuable source of important information found nowhere else.

within a non-supernatural environment. This means that a historian can only permit natural causes and natural forces to influence actions. Within this methodology, the supernatural is deemed *ipso facto* not to be part of a scientific analysis; and though it may be valid for a historian to consider an author's *claim* of the supernatural, that is allowed only to understand how an author has subjectively interpreted an event. What is discounted is the possibility that the supernatural actually occurred.

This raises an immediate problem for Columba studies since supernatural events dominate Adomnán's narrative from start to finish. The miraculous is not an occasional visitor to the story, but a permanent resident. How do we handle a text in which the presence of the supernatural, through visions, prophecies, and miracles, is on every page and leaves its mark on almost every incident? Do we remove the fantastical and reconstruct the narrative with whatever remains? Do we look for a Columba behind the myths? Do we read the stories as figurative metaphors? Or do we give up searching for Columba, and assume that Adomnán's book only tells us about how Adomnán saw the world? Several lines of approach have been tried.[2]

1. One option is Christian Naturalism. This was the Duke of Argyll's position. Although the Duke had an issue with miracles in Adomnán's book, it was not because he disbelieved in miracles as such. He accepted the miracles of the New Testament, believing that there are arcane principles, hidden within nature, which enable uncommon things to happen. Such secret laws are themselves part of nature, but are embedded so deep that human beings have no normal access to them. The Duke held that these laws allowed unusual things to occur when a higher Mind activated them. The Duke saw himself as a modern scientific man of the nineteenth century. It was important to him that his defence of the biblical miracles would also preserve the scientific principle that laws of nature, established by God, cannot be broken.[3] God does not contradict, suspend, or oppose, the laws of nature

---

2 James Bruce, *Prophecy, Miracles and Heavenly Light?, The Eschatology, Pneumatology, and Missiology of Adomnán's* 'Life of Columba' (Milton Keynes: Paternoster, 2004), 7f., discusses Felim O'Briain's four classes of scholarly approach to miracle and wonder narratives: (a) credulous reverence; (b) *a priori* rejection; (c) naturalistic demythologised explanation; (d) historical objectivity, allowing the possibility that something unusual actually happened but not perhaps exactly as reported.

3 George Douglas Campbell, *The Reign of Law* (London: Strahan, 1867), 26f., 49f.

which He Himself has established. For the Duke, the unexpected events which are recorded in Scripture (commonly termed miracles) must be consistent with properties fixed by God within nature itself. When a 'miracle' occurs, no God-given natural law is broken. Instead, extraordinary principles are accessed by extraordinary persons.

Charles Babbage, the developer of early computers, had proposed this interpretation of miracle in his 1864 book, *Passages from the Life of a Philosopher*, and the Duke of Argyll adopted Babbage's thinking in his 1867 work, *The Reign of Law*.[4] As a Bible-believing rationalist, the Duke accepted that the signs and wonders recorded in the Gospels really took place, and were not to be explained away. And they occurred because Christ was able to access realities within nature, which were not available to other men and women.

Although the Duke defended biblical miracles, he rejected the signs and wonders recorded by Adomnán. In the Duke's opinion, Adomnán's stories were not true events, but products of an excited imagination affected by the exaggerations of early-medieval religion. The Duke was robustly anti-Roman Catholic. He viewed the medieval proliferation of stories about saints performing miracles as no more than Roman Catholic propaganda, and he regarded Adomnán as an early casualty of this tendency. Consequently, he dismissed the accounts of Columba as a miracle worker. In the Duke's opinion, miracles ceased with the Apostles, and in this he held to a cessationist position. This stance was common in some Protestant circles: accepting the biblical miracles

4 Campbell, *The Reign of Law*, 5ff., 14ff., 23f and 50: 'The laws of the spiritual world are in the highest sense laws of Nature, whose obligation, operation, and effect are all in the constitution and nature of things'; cf. Charles Babbage, *Passages from the Life of a Philosopher* (London: Longman, Roberts & Green, 1864), 488. This position was developed in response to objections posed by Hume, rejecting Hume's definition of miracle. Hume defined miracles as violations of the law of nature (487). This definition skewed debate on miracles by defining them at the outset as irrational. Babbage argued for the possibility of divine action within the natural world: '[We must] not forget that there is a Divine energy which overrides what we familiarly call the laws of nature.' Babbage defined a miracle as 'an effect which is not the consequence or effect of any *known* laws of nature' (489). Babbage's emphasis is on '*known*', reflecting on the limits of human experience: 'All that we see in a miracle is an effect which is new to our observation, and whose cause is concealed. The cause may be beyond the sphere of our observation, and would be thus beyond the familiar sphere of nature; but this does not make the event a violation of any law of nature.' (487f). For Babbage, nature is a complex mechanism, containing within itself the capacity to deviate from what we consider to be its 'laws'. Babbage's philosophy made miracle a natural event, preserving the miraculous phenomena, and also preserving the materialist thesis that natural effects have natural causes.

but believing that such wonders were only for the Apostolic age. This outlook helped to establish clear water between a Protestant faith exclusively focussed on Scripture, and a Roman Catholic tradition which continued to attribute miracles to saints down through the centuries. Protestants viewed these claims as superstition, and as a detraction from the pure truth of the Word of God. The Duke regarded miracles attributed to Columba in the same way as he regarded miracles attributed to any medieval saint. In his view, Adomnán's fabrications reduced, rather than enhanced, an account of a great Christian.

2. A second approach is Christian Supernaturalism. This is the position adopted by Ian Finlay in his book on Columba. Finlay held the post of Director of the National Museum of Scotland in Edinburgh from 1961 to 1971. He was also Professor of Antiquities of the Royal Scottish Academy, Vice-Chairman of the Scottish Arts Council, and Freeman of the City of London. His area of special interest was fine art, and, in his book on Columba, he blended his interest in art with his love of history. Finlay knew that Adomnán's *Life of Columba* raises the question of the miraculous from start to finish and was aware that any student of Columba has to come to grips with this. In his book, Finlay maintains that it is invalid to demythologise Adomnán's stories, remove the miraculous aspects, and re-present whatever is left as history. He argues that the miraculous should not be ruled out *a priori*. Instead, might it be that, in the frontier-missionary situation faced by Columba as in other frontier-missionary situations before and since, signs and wonders actually occurred? Truth may not lie in a narrative stripped of miracle. Truth may be in the miracle itself. In a remarkable passage, which is notable in being written by a scholar with an academic reputation to defend, Finlay writes:

> I have been told that when missionaries left some gospel-books behind in Ethiopia, and returned many years later, they found not only a flourishing church, but a community of believers among whom miracles like those mentioned in the New Testament happened every day, [and this was] because there had been no [modernist] missionaries to teach that such things were not to be taken literally. … We may yet have to weigh very carefully the doubts of the doubters.[5]

5 Finlay, *Columba*, 125f.

Finlay alludes to news of miraculous phenomena in contemporary situations and gives weight to these reports. They seem to indicate that unusual things occur on the interface between Christianity and paganism which may not occur to the same extent in settled Christianised societies. Are miracles the stuff of mission? Finlay is prepared to entertain the possibility that the miracles reported by Adomnán belonged to that category.

Unknowingly, Finlay replicates an idea suggested twelve and a half centuries earlier by the eighth-century historian the Venerable Bede. Bede is best known for his book *The Ecclesiastical History of the English People*, but he authored other treatises, one of which was a *Commentary on Mark's Gospel.* In his commentary on Mark, Bede wrote that miracles were to be expected especially and particularly in pioneer missionary contexts. Bede believed that new divine projects could expect signs and wonders, which became less frequent when Christianisation was more firmly established: 'When we plant bushes, we water them until they stand firm, but once they have taken root, the watering ceases.'[6] Bede's argument was that when the Gospel directly confronts the forces of paganism, or when it engages the powers of the demonic directly in frontier-evangelism, then signs and wonders are to be expected, but not when society has been more fully Christianised. For Bede, signs and wonders are extraordinary works of God, which are connected to full-on spiritual warfare in frontline situations. These became less frequent in the ordinary, settled, daily, Christian life. Bede and Finlay allow the same spiritual principle: in frontier-missions, signs and wonders may occur.

3. Source Characteristics. Professor Máire Herbert, in her book, *Iona, Kells and Derry*, offers another option. She discusses the various sources which Adomnán accessed, and how each affected his portrayal of the supernatural, concluding that the different sources had different approaches to the miraculous.[7] She begins by pointing out that Adomnán was not the first to compile a life of Columba. That honour fell to Segene, the fifth Abbot of Iona, who became abbot only twenty-six years

6 J. F. Webb and D. H. Farmer, 'Introduction', *The Age of Bede* (Penguin Classics edition: Harmondsworth: Penguin, 1965), 18. Bruce, *Prophecy, Miracles, Angels and Heavenly Light?*, 29f., notes that Pope Gregory I accepted miracles in missionary situations, but less inclined to accept them in established Christian cultures.

7 Herbert, 'An Tuairisc is Sinne' in Randall (ed.), *In Search of Colmcille*, 11.

after Columba's death, ruling the community from 623 to 652. Segene collected stories about Columba from Iona monks who had known Columba. He gathered them at a time when they were still fresh in the communal consciousness, and when their regular recitation, plus respect for Columba's memory, fostered inhibition against changes, fixing the form and content of the material.[8] Segene's collection was then used by his nephew Cumméne (Comyn the Fair, seventh Abbot of Iona from 657 to 669) who combined his uncle's material with additional data to produce a work entitled, *Book of the Powers of Saint Columba.*[9] No copy of Cumméne's book remains, but it is widely agreed that Cumméne's work is referred to by Adomnán when he claims to have drawn on written and oral sources, 'handed down by our elders, men both reliable and informed'.[10] Some of Book III, Chapter 5, of Adomnán's *Life of Columba*, may be word for word from Cumméne, and inserted by Adomnán himself or by a later scribe.[11]

Thus Cumméne provided Adomnán with a corpus of material from Iona. But Adomnán also used material from non-Iona (mainly Pictish) sources, and some analysists claim they can detect which of Adomnán's stories are from an Iona source and which are from a non-Iona (Pictish) source. For example, the presence of doublets (the same story repeated in two versions) is taken as indicating two sources. They each give their own account of an event, neither of which Adomnán wants to omit.[12] As a careful scholar, Herbert is well aware that source analysis is an inexact science. Nevertheless, she judges that the different sources are characterised by differing presentations of the miraculous. Her substantial point is that stories from the Iona monastic stratum of Adomnán's text are *muted* with respect to miracles; whereas in stories originating from places remote from Iona the instances of signs and wonders are *high-profile* and more frequent.[13]

---

8 Dales, *Light to the Isles: Missionary Theology in Celtic and Anglo-Saxon Britain*, 93.

9 Herbert, *Iona, Kells and Derry*, 25, notes that Cumméne may have given literary form to Segene's evidences.

10 Adomnán, *Life of Columba*, The Second Preface; cf. Máire Herbert 'The World of Adomnán' in Thomas O'Loughlin (ed.), *Adomnán at Birr A.D. 697: Essays in Commemoration of the Law of the Innocents* (Dublin: Four Courts Press, 2001), 38.

11 cf. Anderson and Anderson, *Adomnán's Life of Columba*, 189, note 214.

12 Herbert, *Iona, Kells and Derry*, 14.

13 Herbert, *Iona, Kells and Derry*, 16. Herren and Brown, *Christ in Celtic Christianity*, 167ff., 173, agree with Herbert but suggest that the high presence of the miraculous in Adomnán's *Life of Columba* is also linked to a Roman influenced emphasis on thaumaturgy and

If Herbert's analysis is correct, how is this to be explained? One explanation is that the contrast is perfectly consistent with Bede and Finlay's proposition: that in frontline mission situations, miracles occur more frequently.[14] But Herbert's own interpretation is that the Pictish corpus is characterised by more fantastical elements because that was how later Pictish Christians wanted to portray Columba. The argument is that, although in Columba's own lifetime Pictland had a low-key response to his evangelism, by the close of the seventh century there was a tendency for the Picts to glorify Columba and claim him as their apostle. As part of this process they exaggerated and enhanced accounts of mighty works which God had done through Columba in their land.

Whichever view a reader of Adomnán's *Life of Columba* adopts, he or she cannot avoid the centrality of miracle, sign, and wonder in Adomnán's book. The Duke of Argyll, Finlay, and Herbert, offer three perspectives. Others are possible. Whichever interpretation is chosen, any discussion of the spirituality of Columba and of the early-medieval Irish Church has to take into account this deep belief in the immanence of God's power on earth.

ADOMNÁN'S MOTIVES

Unlike other biographies which were read by the Iona monks, such as those of Anthony of Egypt and Martin of Tours, Adomnán's book only takes the form of conventional chronological narrative in two places. One is in its brief Second Preface. The other is in its long final chapter, which may have been read in later centuries on Columba's annual feast day of the 9 June.[15] Apart from the Second Preface and the final chapter, Adomnán's material is arranged thematically and not chronologically. This transforms the book from a normal biography into a theological commentary and extended meditation on the working of the Holy

---

special powers. They argue that Pelagian influences resisted the introduction of hagiography and miracles until the mid-seventh century.

14 Bruce, *Prophecy, Miracles, Angels and Heavenly Light?*, 22, observes in passing that 'the spiritual environment of Pictland was hostile because of its paganism, thus we should expect signs of spiritual warfare here'.

15 O'Loughlin, *Celtic Theology*, 78, suggests that much of Adomnán's *Life of Columba* was read in the liturgy on Columba's Feast Day. Hughes, *Early Christian Ireland: Introduction to the Sources*, 223, notes that Adomnán's two *Prefaces* and final chapter are reminiscent of Evagrius' translation of Athanasius' *Life of Anthony*, and Severus' *Life of Martin*.

Spirit in Columba's ministry.[16] Adomnán was aware of conventional biography, but he chose this way of presenting his material.

Adomnán puts his material into three Books, each of which is a themed collection of supernaturally empowered events. In his Second Preface he takes pains to describe what each Book is about.[17] Book One is on 'Prophetic Revelations'. Book Two deals with, 'Divine Miracles worked through Columba'. Book Three concerns, 'Angelic Apparitions and certain Phenomena of Heavenly Light seen above the man of God'. This is difficult material for historians to work with, but there is a logic to Adomnán's methodology. Adomnán is addressing the question: Was Columba a man approved by God? His answer is that any man who was given prophetic utterances, miraculous powers, and angelic visitations, was a man undoubtedly approved. Moreover, James Bruce suggests that, in arranging his material in this way, Adomnán is also proving that the signs of the outpouring of the Spirit on the Day of Pentecost are manifest in Columba:[18]

> 'In the last days,' God says, 'I will pour out my Spirit upon all people. Your sons and daughters will PROPHESY, your young men will see VISIONS, your old men will dream dreams … I will show WONDERS in the heaven above, and signs on the earth below, blood, and fire, and billows of smoke'. (Acts 2:17-19, NIV)

Adomnán is clear that Columba's abilities do not derive from some innate magical power, but are gifts from God by His Spirit (I:50). It is Adomnán's apologetic motivation on Columba's behalf which shapes the form and content of his work, and within this context Adomnán had a range of reasons for writing his book.

1. *Love of Writing.* Adomnán had a love of scholarship and literary activity *per se*, penning several works in addition to his *Life of Columba.* He composed hymns and prayers. He wrote a major book on *The Holy*

---

16 Dales, *Light to the Isles: Missionary Theology in Celtic and Anglo-Saxon Britain*, 61.

17 Adomnán, *Life of Columba*, Second Preface. Dales, *Light to the Isles*, 61, suggests that the tripartite structure of Adomnán's book deliberately echoed the threefold 'economy' of divine action in human history: Old Testament (prophecy and action); Gospels (miracles and the Word of God); and Apocalypse (visions and signs).

18 Bruce, *Prophecy, Miracles, Angels and Heavenly Light?*, 153, ref. to Acts 2:17-19 and Joel 2:28-30. Bruce (168) suggests that because Book One dealt with the prophetic aspect of Columba's ministry it was viewed by Adomnán as the most important.

Places, taking the reader to the sacred sites of the Middle East, having cribbed information from the wandering monk Arculf who arrived on Iona.[19] Adomnán presented a copy of *The Holy Places* to Aldfrith, King of Northumbria, which Bede uses in his *History*. Adomnán also authored the *Law of the Innocents*; and he may have written a commentary on the Roman poet Virgil.[20]

2. *Instruction of Monks.* Adomnán's given reason for writing the *Life of Columba*, is to teach new Iona monks about Columba, informing them about 'our blessed patron's life'.[21] In his book, new monks could read about their inspirational founder, and learn about Columba's continuing role as a heavenly intercessor.[22] Adomnán also wanted his book to unite Iona, not divide it, and so he avoided controversial issues.[23] Thus, he makes no reference to the date of Easter question, which was a disruptive issue on Iona during his abbacy. Admittedly, there may be a nod in that direction in the story of Columba's visit to the monks of Clonmacnoise when Adomnán makes Columba prophesy that strife will arise among the Irish churches concerning differing points of view vis-à-vis Easter (I:3). Adomnán differed from the rest of his community on Iona in this matter, having become persuaded that the Roman calculations were better than the Irish ones. However, he did not use his book to promote this. Harmony was more important. And in his final chapter he depicts Columba urging the monastic community to stay united in order to enjoy God's blessing (III:23).

3. *Hope of Heaven.* Adomnán also believed that if he honoured Columba by writing the *Life* then the saint would commend him to God, making Adomnán's eternal destiny more secure. This hope is

---

19 For a Latin/English edition see: Adamnan, *De Locis Sanctis*: Denis Meehan (ed.), *Scriptores Latini Hiberniae, Volume III* (Dublin: Dublin Institute for Advanced Studies, 1958). O'Loughlin, *Celtic Theology*, 79f., suggests that *The Holy Places* was written partly to resolve exegetical/geographical issues found in the Scriptures. Another speculation is that the monastic settlement on Iona was meant to replicate the holy city of Jerusalem, enabling 'pilgrimage to Jerusalem' by making a pilgrimage to Iona.

20 Hughes, *Early Christian Ireland: Introduction to the Sources*, 195.

21 Adomnán, *Life of Columba*, The First Preface.

22 O'Loughlin, 'Adomnán: A Man of many Parts' in O'Loughlin (ed.), *Adomnán at Birr*, 48; cf. Adomnán, *Life*, II:43-46.

23 Jennifer O'Reilly, 'Reading the Scriptures in the Life of Columba' in Cormac Bourke (ed.), *Studies in the Cult of Saint Columba* (Dublin: Four Courts Press, 1997), 103. O'Reilly sees an oblique reference to divisive issues on Iona in III:23, with Adomnán constructing his narrative so that Columba's final command to his people is for them to have mutual peace and charity among themselves.

also expressed in a prayer attributed to Adomnán, *Colum Cille Co Dia Domm Erail*, in which Adomnán writes: 'May Colum Cille commend me to God when I go (may I not go soon) to the place of the angel host: it is mine by right, my Christ, of my powerful sins.'[24] Through reverencing Columba, Adomnán will be aided by the saint when he dies. Clancy and Markus point out that Adomnán, like others, was intensely interested in Columba's powers after his death, and that these feature in many stories.

4. *Defence of a Hero.* But a major reason for Adomnán writing the *Life* was to defend Columba and Iona from critics in his own time. Adomnán had key power-figures in mind as he wrote, especially those in Northumbria. He wanted to remind them of their debt to Columba. A book's opening often reveals an author's overall aim, and in Book One, Chapter One, one of the stand-out stories, in prime, tone-setting position, is an incident which occurred years after Columba's death. It is the legend of King Oswald of Northumbria having a vision of Columba before battle. In Oswald's dream Columba assures him that God will give victory over powerful forces. Victory is achieved. And, in Adomnán's account, it is because Oswald's men believe that Columba had been aiding them that they adopt the Christian faith and receive baptism. Bede does not give this exact interpretation of events, but it was important for Adomnán.

When Adomnán cites this story, he goes out of his way to source it from the lips of Oswald himself, writing that at a later date Oswald returned to Iona and told Abbot Segene all that had happened.[25] But why was Adomnán anxious to give strong provenance to this particular story? And why did Adomnán place in his *first* chapter an event which supposedly occurred many years *after* Columba's death? Adomnán did not put it in his opening chapter by accident. He put it there because one of his major concerns was to remind Northumbrians that not only did their Christian faith first come from Iona, but that, even after his death, Columba was still being used by God in their cause. This was important to emphasise. Adomnán feared that the increasing presence of the Roman Church in Northumbria after the Synod of Whitby

24 Quoted by Clancy and Markus, *Iona: The Earliest Poetry of a Celtic Monastery*, 171ff.

25 Adomnán, *Life of Columba*, I:1: 'Abbot Failbe related all this to me, Adomnán, without question. He swore that he had heard the story of the vision from the lips of King Oswald himself as he was relating it to Abbot Segene.'

in 664 had made Northumbrians forget their historical and spiritual dependence on Iona.[26]

Jennifer O'Reilly, in her substantial article 'Reading the Scriptures in the Life of Columba', likewise argues that the story's presence in the opening chapter is significant, and is part of Adomnán's response to attacks on Columba from clerics in Northumbria.[27] She further suggests that Adomnán artfully constructs the narrative so that Columba appears to Oswald on the night before *his* battle, akin to how Christ appeared in a dream to the Emperor Constantine on the night before the battle of the Milvian Bridge. And, just as Constantine and his troops adopted Christianity after their victory, so Oswald's kingdom adopted Christianity after theirs. O'Reilly also points out that the words which Adomnán puts into Columba's mouth as he addresses Oswald are based on words which God spoke to Joshua after Moses' death, and that in early Christian tradition the Joshua story was interpreted as prefiguring Christ leading the new chosen people of God (the Church) into the heavenly promised land:

> Adomnán succinctly presents Oswald's victory as part of the *continuing* fulfilment of this Old Testament prefiguring of the Church by combining the Joshua story with a reminiscence of the dream of Constantine, whose divinely-ordained military victory had earlier led to the historical establishment of the Church throughout the peoples of the Roman Empire.[28]

In no uncertain terms, Adomnán was reminding those with ears to hear, of Northumbria's debt to Iona. It was through Iona that Northumbria

---

26 Jean-Michel Picard, 'The Purpose of Adomnán's *Vita Columbae*', *Peritia*, vol. 1 (1982), 166f., suggests that the principal aim of Adomnán's *Life of Columba* was to restore Iona's reputation after the Synod of Whitby. Bruce, *Prophecy, Miracles, Angels and Heavenly Light?*, 20, questions this, noting that Adomnán only refers to Northumbria twice, and makes little of Oswald's exile among 'the Irish'. However, Yorke, *The Conversion of Britain: 600–800*, 12f., 18, not only suggests that restoring Columba's reputation in Northumbria lay behind Adomnán's work, but his book was so effective that it stimulated the counter-production in Northumbria of various *Lives* of saints which argued the Whitby position.

27 O'Reilly, 'Reading the Scriptures in the Life of Columba' in Bourke (ed.), *Studies in the Cult of St Columba*, 80-106. O'Reilly refers to J.-M. Picard, 'The Purpose of Adomnán's *Vita Columbae*', *Peritia* (1982), 160-77.

28 O'Reilly, 'Reading the Scriptures in the Life of Columba' in Bourke (ed.), *Studies in the Cult of St Columba*, 85.

entered the promised land of Christian faith. Oswald had come to faith on Iona and was baptised there. And it was Iona to which Oswald had turned for help to Christianise his kingdom. Northumbria had been the jewel in the crown of Iona mission. And yet, despite this spiritual debt, Adomnán knew that the Iona heritage was being marginalised. At Whitby, part of the Roman argument involved undermining Columba's reputation and authority. Columba had never been a bishop. Nor had he been commissioned by a Pope. Against this, in Book One, Chapter One, Adomnán says to Northumbria: 'Do not forget who first brought Christ to you.'

On a personal level Adomnán was open to the merits of Roman Christianity, but he was also fiercely protective of Columba's reputation and viewed the post-Whitby sidelining of Columba as unacceptable. Hence, throughout his *Life of Columba*, Adomnán is anxious to persuade princes and churchmen in Britain and in Ireland that Columba was a man whom God had used mightily in the past, and a man who was still being used by God beyond his death. Adomnán's book was written to reinforce Columba's credentials. Adomnán was proving that Columba was a true prophet, through whom God did signs and wonders, and who was visited by angels and given revelatory visions. And Adomnán piles up example after example in support of Columba's God-approved saintliness. This is Adomnán's way of addressing the revisionism which gathered pace after Whitby, and which had profound implications for Iona.[29] Given this aim of exalting Columba's saintliness, it is unsurprising that Adomnán is coy about referring to any dark passages of Columba's life, including Columba's possible reasons for leaving Ireland.

At the close of his book Adomnán writes:

> Every conscientious reader who has finished reading this three-part book should mark well how great and special is the merit of our reverend Abbot; how great and special is his honour in God's sight; how great and special were his experiences of angelic visits and heavenly light; how great was the grace of prophecy in him; how great and how frequent was the brilliant light of heaven which shone on him as he dwelt in mortal flesh; and which, after his most gentle soul had left the tabernacle of the body, does not cease even today. (III:23).

---

29 Herbert, 'The World of Adomnán' in O'Loughlin (ed.), *Adomnán at Birr*, 39.

But if Adomnán wrote his *Life of Columba* with a Northumbrian audience in mind, would he not have given Northumbria a copy? And if he did, why does Bede, writing in 730 at the Wearmouth-Jarrow monastery, indicate he has not read it? Bede writes that Columba's life and sayings are *said* to have been recorded by his followers.[30] It is as if Bede has heard of such a book but has not seen it. If the book had been locally available, then Bede would have accessed it. But the explanation may be simple. The Northumbrian royal court only had a copy of Adomnán's work *The Holy Places* because one was delivered personally by Adomnán on a visit to King Aldfrith, who was his friend. Adomnán may simply have had no opportunity to visit Northumbria between writing the *Life* around 700 and his death in 704.[31]

ADOMNÁN'S IDEALS

Adomnán depicts Columba as a model Christian, a model monk, a model abbot, and a saint of God. The thematic structure which he adopts fits this goal. Moreover, because the book is designed to increase respect and devotion towards Columba, then many of its stories echo biblical patterns. The stories are also grouped to demonstrate that Columba's supernatural ministry proves that he was sent by God with divine authority, and that the Holy Spirit worked through him with power. Columba's standing had suffered at Whitby. Adomnán needed to rebuild Columba's reputation.[32]

---

30 Bede, *History*, III:4.

31 Adomnán visited Northumbria in 685/6 and 687/8. As far as we know, he did not travel there again. His *Life of Columba* was written after these visits. Whitaker, 'Regal Succession among the Dálriata' in *Ethnohistory*, vol. 23, no. 4 (1976), 347, argues it was written between 688 and 692: cf. Anderson and Anderson, *Adomnán's Life of Columba*, 5. Herbert, *Iona, Kells and Derry*, 142, judges it was compiled after Adomnán's Northumberland journeys and after Adomnán's personal adoption of Roman observances. She is of the view that I:3 presents a prophecy made by Columba about future diversity re the Easter Festival: this 'prophecy', plus Columba's death-bed plea for harmony (III:23) served Adomnán well. Fraser, *From Caledonia to Pictland*, prefers a post-697 date, with Adomnán using the *Life* to help commend his 697 *Law of the Innocents*. Dorbene, the scribe of the oldest surviving copy of the text, died in 713, within a decade of Adomnán's death in 704.

32 Herbert, *Iona, Kells and Derry*, 144, acknowledges that Adomnán feared that Northumbria no longer respected Columba, and refers to the significance of Columba appearing to Oswald in a dream. Herbert (Iona, Kells and Derry, 147f) claims that Adomnán's *Life of Columba* is an eloquent sermon addressed to his own community and to the Northumbrians, urging a new sense of perspective: Adomnán reminds the Northumbrians, with their pride in their neo-orthodoxy after 664, that 'sanctity is not the prerogative of those who uphold certain rules, but is a matter of divine affirmation', and that God affirmed Columba many times over.

1. *Columba as a Christ Figure.* In Irish monastic circles, Columba was portrayed as the ideal monk after the pattern of Christ Himself.[33] Hence, Adomnán presents events in Columba's life as paralleling incidents in the life of Christ. Like Christ, Columba experienced a glory similar to the glory of the Transfiguration, with a radiant 'ball of fire' shining from Columba's head as he stands in front of the altar (III:17).[34] Like Christ, Columba was able to heal at a distance, soothing the searing pain of a woman's broken hip even though not in her presence (II:5). Like Christ, Columba commanded the elements at sea: where Christ caused a storm to cease, Columba enabled a boat to sail into the wind (II:34).

Columba also imitated Christ in changing water into wine. In the opening chapter of Book One Adomnán relates how, when Columba was a young deacon, there was no wine for the mass but 'by virtue of prayer he changed pure water into true wine' (I:1). This event is so important to Adomnán that he cites it twice. On the second occasion (when he tells the story in greater detail) he notes suggestively: 'Christ the Lord made this the first proof of power in his disciple [Columba], performing the same miracle that he himself had worked as the first of his signs in Cana of Galilee' (II:1). Adomnán makes sure his readers realise that such a miracle indicates divine approval of Columba's ministry, and attributes huge significance to the incident. He views it as shining like a lantern at the start of his book, in the same way as Christ's miracle at Cana is a lantern at the start of John's Gospel.

Changing water into wine was incredibly important, placing Columba at the heart of the eucharistic event. But O'Reilly goes further. She interprets the whole of Adomnán's lengthy final chapter as a depiction of Columba as a Christ-figure. In a close analysis of the text she suggests that all of Columba's actions in that chapter, ranging from the specific blessings he bestows, to the manner of the death he dies, are crafted by Adomnán in order to prove a common spirituality between Columba and Christ.[35]

---

33 Herren and Brown, *Christ in Celtic Christianity*, 20.

34 Adomnán, *Life of Columba*, III:2, writes of the infant Columba having a fiery ball of light over his head as he slept, though that light did not emanate from within Columba as with Christ, but from a source close by.

35 O'Reilly, 'Reading the Scriptures in the Life of Columba' in Bourke (ed.), *Studies in the Cult of St Columba*, 94ff. O'Reilly also notes (106) a contrast between the early *Amra*

2. *Columba equal to Biblical Prophets and Apostles.* Columba could never be equal to Christ. Heavenly light could only shine *on* Columba, and not *from* him as with Christ (III:2). Nevertheless, for Adomnán, Columba was undoubtedly the equal of, if not greater than, many of the great men of Scripture.[36] Just as Moses struck a rock to release water, Columba did the same (II:10). When a child was brought for baptism there was no water. So Columba knelt, prayed, blessed the face of the rock, and immediately water bubbled from it. Columba also prophesied that the child would become a man of God, albeit after a dissolute youth. Hence the story not only proves Columba's miraculous powers, but validates him as a true prophet from God.

Just as Paul had visions, so had Columba (I:43). And like Paul, Columba was humble about these visions, only speaking of himself in the third person when describing them. Again, similar to other biblical figures, Columba was given divine insight, and was made aware of events and people far distant from where he lived (I:17). Columba was also given the rare power of raising the dead. When a Pictish layman and his family were converted, the joy of new faith was shattered when a child in the family died: but Columba went to the dead boy, knelt, wept over the corpse, prayed, and in the name of Christ commanded the dead boy to wake and stand on his feet: 'at the saint's glorious word the soul returned to the body, and the boy that was dead opened his eyes and lived again' (II:32; cf. I:1). Adomnán concludes: 'One must recognise that in this miracle of power our St. Columba is seen to share with the prophets Elijah and Elisha, and with the apostles Peter and Paul and John the rare distinction of raising the dead to

---

and the later *Life*, pointing out that in the early commemorative poem, *Amra Coluim Cille*, the emphasis is on Columba's great scholarship, whereas Adomnán's portrait of Columba in the *Life* exalts his similarity to Christ as wonder-worker and prophet, rather than his human knowledge and study.

36 T. M. Charles-Edwards, 'The Structure and Purpose of Adomnán's *Vita Columbae.*' in Wooding (ed.), *Adomnán of Iona*, 211, writes: 'What Adomnán was arguing was that Columba exemplified in his own lifetime the same combination of prophecy and power, to the same exceptional degree, that had been granted to the greatest Old Testament prophets and the three named apostles.' In this connection see the closing words of III:23 'joined with the apostles and the prophets'. Charles-Edwards argues that part of the function of Book III was to deal with the objection that at the final judgement Christ would disavow some who claim to have done great things in His name: thus the angelic visitations were confirmation that what Columba did he did for and by Christ. Bruce, *Prophecy, Miracles, Angels and Heavenly Light?*, 13f., sees Adomnán as building his description of Columba on the model of Jesus and, to a lesser extent, on Moses.

life.' Adomnán's use of *our* in referring to Columba is revealing. As an Iona man writing at the close of the seventh century, Adomnán is defending the saintliness of *our* founder against dismissive attitudes from elsewhere.

3. *Columba as a Great Figure in Christian History.* Adomnán ranks Columba with Patrick, who at the time was the greatest Irish saint yet known.[37] Just as Patrick made Ireland safe from snakes, Columba did the same for Iona, declaring, 'From this hour, from this instant, all poisons of snakes shall have no power to harm either men or cattle in the lands of this island for as long as the people who dwell here keep Christ's commandments' (II:28). Columba did not eliminate all snakes from Iona as Patrick had from Ireland. Instead, Columba neutralised their venom and removed the harm which a snake could inflict. In this way he introduced the vision of a redeemed creation in which not only lions and lambs, but snakes and humans, could live together without fear, making Iona a new Eden (Luke 10:19).[38] In that sense Columba achieved something greater than Patrick. He brought a foretaste of a restored Eden in which snakes exist but are now harmless. They were not excluded, as in a 'sticking-plaster' type of solution. Creation was healed, not bandaged.

Adomnán presents Columba as a spiritual giant, comparable with the greatest figures of Scripture and Church history. In this he follows Septimus Severus' portrayal of Martin of Tours in his *Life of Martin*, in which Martin's accomplishments echo those of the Old Testament saints and the New Testament apostles.[39] On this basis Adomnán argues that Columba was clearly a man used and approved by God, because no one could do such things unless God were with him. But this also means that Adomnán is not interested in recording Columba's failures in miracles or healings.[40] Adomnán has a mission. Writing in a post-Whitby environment, he has to prove that Columba was a true

---

37 In the Irish Church Patrick was comparable to the Angels and Apostles; cf. *Bangor Antiphonary*, Item 13:1.

38 Bruce, *Prophecy, Miracles, Angels and Heavenly Light?*, 119f. Bruce suggests that the snakes were metaphors for the heresies of Arianism and Pelagianism, or for dissenting and disruptive voices in Adomnán's day.

39 Dales, *Light to the Isles*, 25.

40 Finlay, *Columba*, 173. Adomnán, *Life of Columba*, III:5, has one story in which Columba is at fault. Columba initially refuses to accept that Áedán is God's choice as the next king of Dál Riata and has to be chastised before accepting God's will. This portrayal of Columba is unusual for Adomnán and may be a later insertion.

man of God. In his final chapter, addressing detractors as much as sympathisers, he writes:

> Even today, the place where his bones rest is still visited by the light of heaven and by numbers of angels, as is known from those of the elect who have themselves seen this. (III:23)

Adomnán's inference is clear. Only a man especially beloved by God would be granted spiritual manifestations continuing after his death. Such a man was Columba.[41]

ADOMNÁN'S HISTORICISING

James E. Fraser introduces another reason why Adomnán may have composed his *Life of Columba*. Fraser suggests it was written in order to justify Adomnán's own policies, in a method known as 'historicising the present'. For Fraser, Adomnán's *Life of Columba* is less about Columba and more about Adomnán's contemporary situation. Fraser's theory is that if a particular problem was being faced by Adomnán in the Iona of his own day, then he searched for a parallel incident in Columba's time (or even invented a scenario) and depicted Columba dealing with the issue in the way he wanted to deal with it with his own monks. Fraser sees the *Life* as written to homologate Adomnán's own policies, rather than soberly chronicling what Columba did or said. Adomnán was prepared to sacrifice historical accuracy as we know it, in order to make Columba's life a proxy for his own leadership and policies. Columba's story was hijacked to justify Adomnán's own actions.[42]

---

41 Picard and Balbulus, 'Adomnán's Vita Columbae and the Cult of Colum Cille in Continental Europe', *PRIA* (1998), 1-23, note that Adomnán concludes his *Life of Columba* with a theme already announced in his preface, namely the widespread fame of Columba not only in Ireland but also in England and on the Continent: 'God has conferred this great favour upon this man of blessed memory that, although he lived in this small and remote island in the Atlantic Ocean, his renown has merited to spread radiantly not only throughout the whole of our Ireland and throughout Britain … but to reach as far as triangular Spain and Gaul and Italy, situated beyond the Penine Alps, and even to the city of Rome, the head of all cities.' Picard and Balbulus examine the rapid growth of the Columba cult on the Continent which was aided by Adomnán's *Life of Columba*. An early copy of the *Life*, written on Iona by Dorbene (d. 713), was taken to the Continent during the eighth century and became the source of all the Continental versions. Dorbene's manuscript is kept in the Town library at Schaffhausen in Switzerland.

42 Fraser, *From Caledonia to Pictland: Scotland to 795*, 142; cf. Herbert, *Iona, Kells and Derry*, 13, and Yorke, *The Conversion of Britain: 600–800*, 18.

For Fraser, much of Adomnán's *Life of Columba* relates to the period of Adomnán's authorship rather than to Columba's era.[43] One story, which Fraser cites to illustrate this, concerns a man who pursued a girl in Leinster (II:25). In her flight she met Columba and his teacher and hid beneath their robes. However, her pursuer grabbed her and speared her to death. Fraser argues that when Adomnán wrote the *Life*, it was shortly after he had formulated the *Law of the Innocents*, which was designed to protect non-combatants, especially women and children, from outrages during war. Fraser sees the story of the ill-fated Leinster girl as a metaphor representing the distressed impotence of the Church prior to the introduction of the *Law of the Innocents*. In Adomnán's narrative, Columba and his teacher (representing the Church) are powerless to protect the girl: but the story concludes with Columba predicting that the killer will himself be struck down by God. Fraser interprets this as representing Adomnán's Church, newly armed with the *Law of the Innocents*, now able to protect the weak. For Fraser the story is a parable through which Adomnán creates support for his policies. Whereas previously a person seeking safety (even within the sanctuary of the church) might not have been guaranteed security, now they do. Clancy and Markus agree that when Adomnán includes this story in the *Life*, he may have been bolstering political support for his *Law of the Innocents*.[44] Gilbert Markus's interpretation is similar. He reckons that Adomnán placed the story within a group of incidents (II:22-25) which ostensibly illustrated Columba's mission to the poor and powerless, but which were more about Adomnán's own concern for justice than Columba's.[45]

How valid is Fraser's approach? Adomnán would certainly use precedent to add authority to his own policies, but Fraser tends to interpret almost the entire *Life of Columba* through this lens. More seriously, he implies that Adomnán not only tweaked existing Columba stories but invented some.[46] The Leinster girl story may be a 'tweaked incident', with Adomnán building on a known legend of Diarmait overriding the refuge which Columba had extended to a woman. An

43 Fraser, *From Caledonia to Pictland: Scotland to 795*, 6.

44 Clancy and Markus, *Iona: The Earliest Poetry of a Celtic Monastery*, 28.

45 Markus, *Conceiving a Nation*, 173f.

46 Bruce, *Prophecy, Miracles, Angels and Heavenly Light?*, 37, argues strongly that Adomnán was not writing seventh-century fiction in order to make his case.

example of an 'invented incident' may be Columba assisting an exiled Pictish nobleman called Taran (II:23). The Taran story is suspicious because Adomnán knew of a Pict in his own day with the name Taran, who had been exiled.[47] It seems too much of a coincidence that two noblemen with the same name were exiled, one in Columba's era, the other in Adomnán's! Might Columba's Taran have been invented by Adomnán, so that his dealings with the Taran of his time would be justified by Columba's policy towards the earlier one?

When a scholar develops a powerful analytic tool, there is a temptation to apply it universally, and Fraser may be guilty of this with his principle of 'historicising the present'. Fraser may be underestimating the controlling influence of a strong oral tradition within the Iona family. That tradition would question the emergence of new material. Existing narratives formed a canon. Stories were recited word for word on special occasions and would rarely be altered or added to. Even one hundred years after Columba's death, Adomnán would not have a free hand to create new material as he wished. The community would resist a cavalier approach. Nevertheless, Fraser is right to stress the contemporary agendas which historians are subject to. Adomnán had to deal with major issues on Iona during his abbacy. What better way to underpin his authority than by showing Columba had thought as he thought?

In Adomnán's book, there are at least three types of history. There is *history simpliciter*, with accounts of actual incidents handed down from Columba's time. There is *historicising*, in which Adomnán blends the present with the past so as to gain authority for his own policies through Columba's patronage. And there may be elements of *pseudo-history*, which have little or no basis in historical events.

Adomnán's *Life of Columba* occupies a dominating position as a written source. For some scholars this dominance is a problem. They know that the Christianisation of the Highlands and Islands involved monks other than Columba and involved missions from centres other than Iona. But the available texts nearly all come from the Columban/Iona tradition, and this has resulted in an almost exclusively Iona-centric reading of

47 cf. Fraser, *From Caledonia to Pictland: Scotland to 795*, 5.

the period. Frustration at this has resulted in the emergence of what can be termed an ABC methodology: Anyone-But-Columba! Sometimes this ABC tendency deliberately sidelines Adomnán's *magnum opus* in order to create room for a fresh perspective. It is undeniable that issues surround Adomnán's *Life of Columba*, and yet, when we tune in to Adomnán's way of thinking and when we understand his concerns, we are able to read his book not just as a propaganda document, which he penned during a difficult period for his own abbacy. It is more than that. It is a glimpse into the soul of the Columban Church.

All books about a person, whether autobiography, biography, or academic analysis, paint their own portrait. Nearly all that is written about Columba comes through the filter of Adomnán's great work. Modern historians, with varying degrees of success, have attempted to free themselves from bondage to Adomnán's book, and from an over-reliance on Iona's interpretation of events. Nevertheless, we are driven back repeatedly to Adomnán with all his strengths and weaknesses. But our focus is on Columba's spirituality, and our assumption is that contemporary and near-contemporary writers (Adomnán, Dallán, Beccán, and others) reflect the essence of Columba's faith precisely because they shared it with him. Even if we question the historical accuracy of some of Adomnán's stories, he would still be reflecting core components of Columba's spiritual beliefs. That being so, our portrait of Columba's spirituality may be one which he could recognise as his own.

CHAPTER 3

Columba's Influencers

The Irish Church was hard-wired into international Christendom, revering the Church Fathers of the Greek East and the Latin West. An older view which presumed that Ireland and its Church was cut off from wider European and Mediterranean civilisation following the Anglo-Saxon invasions of Britain has been replaced by an awareness that the Irish Church continued to have strong links with the rest of the Christian world.[1] It was that rich heritage which informed Columba's spirituality. And the theological instruction which was given in Irish monasteries was the same as that offered in institutions all over Christendom. From the deserts of Egypt to the western shores of Europe, a common teaching was imparted. Columba was taught the same faith. He recited the same Creeds. He studied the same Scriptures. He worshipped from a similar liturgy. There were local cultural variations (sometimes more, sometimes less) but that was true anywhere in Christendom, whether Palestine, North Africa, Cappadocia, Italy, Gaul, or Spain. Sixth-century Ireland was no theological backwater. A trainee monk in Ireland was exposed to the same theological curriculum as any of his peers across Christendom. Irish monks knew the thinking of the wider Church. They took inspiration from that universal Church, as well as from local traditions. Thus the piety of an early-medieval Irish Christian was fed by an array of influences, echoing the rich faith of international Christendom.

In this chapter we focus on five figures who influenced Columba: Anthony of Egypt, Martin of Tours, Basil of Caesarea, Cassian of Marseille, and Finnian of Clonard. The lives of Anthony and Martin

1 Leslie Alcock, *Arthur's Britain: History and Archaeology, 367-634* (London: Penguin, 1971), 206. O'Loughlin, *Celtic Theology*, 17, emphasises that early-medieval scholars believed that truth was, 'what was held always, everywhere, by everyone' and 'if they had suspected they were in any way idiosyncratic they would have been the first to adapt their ideas to that of the larger group.'

were considered to be idealised blueprints for monks.[2] Basil and Cassian were major thinkers, unique in being the only two theologians named in Dallán Forgaill's honour-poem to Columba, the *Amra Choluimb Chille*. And Finnian of Clonard was a pivotal figure from Ireland itself, and a principal developer of the Irish penitential system.

Adomnán gives sparse information concerning Columba's early monastic training, though he does highlight three of Columba's tutors. One was Columba's foster-father, the priest Cruithnechan. Another was Gemman of Leinster who taught Columba 'divine wisdom' (II:25). The third was Finnian of Clonard (also known as Finnbarr, Finnio, or Uinniau), under whom Columba studied scripture (II:1 and III:4).[3] Some sources assume that two Finnians tutored Columba at different times, namely Finnian of Movilla and Finnian of Clonard.[4] However, Padraig O'Riain has argued to wide acceptance, that the two are in fact one but described from two traditions.[5] Our choice is to designate him as Finnian of Clonard.[6] The *Old Irish Life* claims that Columba also studied under Mobii of Glaisnoide after his time with Finnian, but Adomnán does not mention this.[7]

ANTHONY OF EGYPT (d. 356)

Athanasius' fourth-century *Life of Anthony* was a core text for monks throughout the Christian world, with copies in all reasonably equipped monasteries. It was part of the Iona library during Adomnán's abbacy, with Adomnán quoting from Evagrius' Latin translation of Athanasius'

---

2 Dales, *Light to the Isles*, 10.

3 The Irish *Life of Finnian of Clonard* is probably tenth century; cf. Hughes, *Early Christian Ireland: Introduction to the Sources*, 237f.

4 cf. *Old Irish Life*, in Skene, *Celtic Scotland*, vol. II, 479.

5 Padraig O'Riain, 'St. Finbarr: a study in a cult', *JCHAS*, vol. 82 (1977), 63-82. O'Riain argues that Finnian's cult was set in Movilla and in Clonard, both giving him a local tradition. The *Annals* give the 'two' Finnians diverse dates.

6 In 2001, Clancy argued that Finnian's connections with Whithorn in south-west Scotland resulted in the story of Ninian of Whithorn being confused with Finnian's story due to an eighth-century scribal spelling error. Scholars are split on Clancy's hypothesis; cf. Thomas Owen Clancy, 'The real St. Ninian', *The Innes Review*, vol. 52 (2001), 1-28. Clancy prefers to designate him Finnian of Movilla. McNeill, *The Celtic Penitentials*, 54, notes that Columba was a pupil of 'both Finnians' and that the exercise of penance by Columba is a prominent feature in Adomnán's *Life*. Herren and Brown, *Christ in Celtic Theology*, 105, agree that the same Finnian (Uinniau) taught Columba as wrote the *Penitential of Finnian;* cf. O'Loughlin, *Celtic Theology*, 52.

7 *Old Irish Life*, in Skene, *Celtic Scotland*, vol. II, 480.

original Greek text.[8] And it is virtually certain that Iona had its own copy even during the early years of Columba's era, with Columba insisting his monks study such a seminal composition.[9]

Anthony's iconic status continued in Scotland well after Columba and Adomnán. Several of the large and highly-decorated stone cross-slabs, which were created by a later Christian-Pictish culture, feature the legend of Anthony and Paul of Thebes which was popularised through Jerome's *Life of St Paul the Hermit.* According to Jerome's story, Anthony travelled deep into the desert to meet Paul, a holy man who was fed bread daily by a raven sent by God. When Anthony arrived, the raven brought a double portion, and Anthony and Paul decided to break the bread together simultaneously so as not to outdo the other's sanctity. This meeting was regarded by some monks as constituting the first monastic community. The legend is graphically depicted on the Nigg cross-slab, now preserved in the old Nigg Church in Easter Ross,[10] with another representation on a Pictish cross-slab at St Vigean's.[11] These carvings emphasise Anthony's enduring appeal.

However, it was through Athanasius' biography that Anthony first became known to Irish monks, and they wanted to emulate his self-denying disciplined life. Like Anthony, they renounced the world. Like Anthony, they sought to triumph over the Evil One. Like Anthony, they tried to become so holy that their earthly pilgrimage would bring heavenly glory.

Athanasius portrays Anthony as a desert recluse, practising a form of monasticism known as *eremitic* monasticism, from the Greek *erēmos* meaning 'desert'. Ironically, Anthony's fame attracted so many visitors that he rarely experienced the solitariness which he sought. At other times he left the desert in order to assist the Church, but it was the desert which he craved. Anthony's theory was that through embracing desert isolation he could shed personal ambition, avoid sexual temptation, and

---

8 Thomas O'Loughlin, 'The Library of Iona in the Late Seventh Century: The Evidence from Adomnán's *De Locis Sanctis*', *Eriu*, vol. 45 (1994). Also, Clancy and Markus, *Iona: The Earliest Poetry of a Celtic Monastery*, 211ff.; cf. Sharpe, *Adomnán of Iona: Life of St. Columba*, 58, for discussion of Athanasius' *Life of Anthony* in Adomnán, *Life*, III:23.

9 Clancy and Markus, *Iona: The Earliest Poetry of a Celtic Monastery*, 213.

10 Several monks were named Paul. Paul the Anchorite was an early hermit, sometimes described as the 'first of the anchorites'; cf. Cassian, *Conferences* XVIII, 'Conference with Abbot Piamun', 6.

11 George and Isabel Henderson, *The Art of the Picts: Sculpture and Metalwork in Early Medieval Scotland* (London: Thames and Hudson Ltd, 2004), 139ff.

escape from the entrapments of wealth and luxury. This latter aspect was pivotal and would become a core principle of Irish monasticism. Wealth was seen as a crucial barrier to a person's salvation. Love of wealth (covetousness) was a form of idolatry. Thus, Athanasius begins his book with Anthony reflecting on key biblical passages on wealth such as, the disciples leaving everything to follow Jesus (Matt. 4:19; 9:9); Jesus saying to a rich man, 'If you would be perfect, go and sell what you have, give to the poor, and come, follow Me, and you will have treasure in heaven' (Matt. 19:21); and Jesus' teaching that it was easier for a camel to pass through the eye of a needle than for a rich man to enter the kingdom of heaven (Mark 10:25). These passages, plus the account of the first Christians selling their possessions and giving to the poor (Acts 4:32ff), were regarded as embodying key principles. It was believed that the early Christians gave away all possessions in order to become the first 'monks', and to gain greater certainty concerning eternal hope.[12] Anthony was convinced he had to act similarly if heavenly glory were ever to be attained.

Anthony embarked on a self-denying way of life, in which abandonment of possessions was but a first step.[13] However, though desert-living eliminated comfort, lures of the flesh were still strong. Athanasius writes that one night the devil took 'the shape of a woman and imitated all her acts simply to beguile Anthony'.[14] Other temptations came his way, but he overcame them through, 'filling his mind with Christ' and 'the nobility inspired by Him'. The wilderness was seen as the antithesis of God's Eden. It was Satan's home. And in going to the desert, a monk was reclaiming the world for Christ in a direct, frontline battle with the demonic.[15] The desert brought an intensified spiritual

12 Athanasius, *Life of Anthony*, 9.

13 Basil, *Shorter Rule*, Qu. 5, hints at disapproval of would-be monks giving their monies and possessions to relatives. Basil emphasises that the biblical command is to sell everything and give to the poor (Matt. 19:21).

14 Athanasius, *Life of Anthony*, 6.

15 Bruce, *Prophecy, Miracles, Angels and Heavenly Light?*, 32, disagrees with Clare Stancliffe's assertion in 'The Miracle Stories in Seventh-Century Irish Saints Lives', in J. Fontaine and J. N. Hillgarth (eds), *The Seventh Century: Change and Continuity*, (London: Warburg Inst., 1992), 102, that the devil and demons play no prominent role in the Judaeo-Christian revelation contained in the Bible and that their presence in early Christian literature was due to them being part of the shared thought world of (pagan) antiquity. Bruce argues that Satan and his demons feature large in the *Life of Anthony* and in the *Life of Martin* precisely because the authors were imbued with a biblical worldview. Our view is that Stancliffe was

struggle. It was in the wilderness that Christ came face to face with Satan; and the desert monks sought the same environment in order to participate in the same crucible of spiritual warfare.

Monasticism, as modelled by Anthony, was not about escapism. It was about engaging directly with the demonic. It was about overcoming Satan in the power of the Spirit. And Irish monasticism shared these assumptions. Irish monks saw themselves called to a lifetime of spiritual warfare as soldiers of Christ. The monk was a battle-zone warrior. He was involved in full-on engagement with the enemy of souls. Protected from Satan's clutches through lives of self-purification and prayer, monks interceded for a world still under Satan's thraldom. And they engaged the forces of Satan directly in evangelistic mission.

Divestment of wealth as an essential step towards salvation was a principle deeply embedded in Irish monastic piety. Beccán's honour-poem to Columba states: 'The one best thing of all things [about Columba, is that] he has freed his monks from wealth.'[16] Beccán praises Columba for *freeing* his monks from wealth. As abbot, Columba was able to ensure that his monks owned nothing, and they thanked him for doing so. His scrupulous pastoral supervision enabled them fulfil that essential precondition for heaven. There was an intense fear that wealth could cancel every spiritual advantage which was so laboriously gained elsewhere. Possessions could peremptorily disqualify a pilgrim from the kingdom.[17] Columba and his monks also learned from Anthony that endurance could bring a glorious outcome, for when Anthony died there was no uncertainty concerning his destiny. At his death Anthony was filled with a 'holy joy and gathered to the fathers'.[18] It was this which every monk longed to attain.

Athanasius' *Life of Anthony* taught the importance of crucifying personal ambition. It modelled a life of resisting temptation, engaging Satan, and overcoming him. Through purification, fasting, worshipping,

---

partly correct, since the Bible mentions the demonic rarely, apart from in the Gospels. The intensity of the demonic in the Gospels can be explained theologically as due to them featuring God in Christ interacting with His world making the demonic reveal itself. The presence of pure holiness draws out the demonic. If this was true for Christ, it could also be true for profoundly holy men such as Anthony, Martin and Columba.

16 Beccán, *Fo Reir Choluimb*, V. Clancy and Markus, *Iona: The Earliest Poetry of a Celtic Monastery*, 137f.

17 cf. Basil, *Homily 21*, 'On Detachment from Worldly Goods'.

18 Athanasius, *Life of Anthony*, 92.

praying, and evangelising, Anthony triumphed in the spiritual battle. His was the example par excellence to follow. And although an Irish monk had no access to a desert of sand and stones, he had deserts of the ocean in the form of the isolated islands of the Hebrides and rocky islets off Ireland. Monks who followed Anthony's strict regime gained reputations for great holiness and attracted crowds of the curious and the contemplative just as Anthony had done. This meant that Iona was constantly busy, though Columba seems to have revelled in its hustle and bustle. Cuthbert, the abbot-bishop of Iona's daughter monastery on Lindisfarne, was of a different temperament. He longed for true aloneness with God and with his soul.

MARTIN OF TOURS (d. 397)

Martin of Tours was mentioned in the regular Iona liturgy. We know this because Adomnán's *Life of Columba* records (III:12) that once, when the Iona monks were singing the Daily Office, they were halted by Columba on reaching the prayer which had Martin's name. On that occasion Columba wanted his monks to chant for Bishop Colman who had just died. Like Anthony, Martin was admired universally, both on the Continent and in Ireland.[19] The early Christian foundation at Whithorn in south-west Scotland was dedicated to Martin. Columbanus, Columba's younger contemporary, made a point of visiting Martin's tomb at Tours.[20] And Sharpe suggests that Adomnán may have borrowed the basic shape of Severus' *Life of Martin* for his own book on Columba.[21]

Whereas Anthony of Egypt preferred desert isolation, Severus portrays Martin as practising a communal form of monasticism. But what was common to both was a radical renunciation of possessions when they became monks, albeit with a difference. Anthony was anxiety-driven, fearing that wealth might bar him from everlasting glory. In contrast, Severus describes Martin's giving away of his wealth as motivated by altruism and wanting to assist his poor neighbours,

---

19 Dales, *Light to the Isles*, 25. Dales (61) points out that Adomnán, like Severus, divides his material into three books, though he treats his material somewhat differently.

20 Sharpe, *Adomnán of Iona: Life of St. Columba*, 366, note 379.

21 Sharpe, *Adomnán of Iona: Life of St. Columba*, 58. On the other hand, Bruce, *Prophecy, Miracles, Angels and Heavenly Light?*, 206, suggests that Adomnán's work is closer in flavour to the *Lives* of contemplatives such as Anthony and Benedict, than to missionaries Martin, Germanus and Patrick.

rather than by the needs of his own soul. Nonetheless, impoverishment was important, and freedom from the goods of this world was essential. For Martin, as much as for Anthony, wealth was an obstacle to salvation.

Severus stresses that Martin was humble even before he became a baptised Christian.[22] He had performed good works. He had supported those in trouble. He had brought help to the wretched. He had fed the poor. He had clothed the naked. He had kept nothing of his military salary apart from what was needed for food each day.[23] And it is Martin's readiness to give to others which becomes a central feature of his conversion narrative. Martin saw a naked beggar and wanted to give the beggar his own cloak, despite it being the only garment which he had left. So he cut the cloak in half, leaving himself only a ragged portion.[24] The next night he dreamt that Christ had clothed Himself in the part of the cloak given to the beggar, and he recalled the words of Jesus: 'As often as you do this to one of the least, you have done it to me' (Matt. 25:40). In Severus' narrative it was grace given to Martin, in and through his giving to others, which brought him to Christ.

The *Life of Martin* highlights poverty, exile from an easy path in life, and the spiritual power of virginity. It also features the relentless threatening presence of the demonic, with Martin being warned at the outset of his life as a soldier of Christ, 'Wherever you go, or whatever you attempt, the devil will resist you.'[25] Martin, like Anthony, was engaged in lifelong conflict with Satan. The reality of hordes of antagonistic demons was accepted without question.[26]

BASIL OF CAESAREA (330–379)

Basil of Caesarea is the only Church Father given the title 'Great' by the Greek-speaking Eastern Church. Moreover, along with Cassian, Basil is one of only two theologians mentioned in the *Amra* in connection with Columba. Basil and Cassian both made colossal contributions to monastic thinking, and their mention in the *Amra* indicates their importance, not only to Columba, but to the whole Irish Church. Importantly, although Basil influenced monasticism in Ireland, he was

---

22 Severus, *Life of Martin*, II:5.
23 Severus, *Life of Martin*, II:8.
24 Severus, *Life of Martin*, III:2.
25 Severus, *Life of Martin*, VI:2.
26 Dales, *Light to the Isles*, 25.

also required reading in monasteries on the Continent.[27] Like Anthony and Martin, Basil feared the corruption which wealth could have on holy Christian living, knowing this from bitter experience in his own diocese, in which some bishops accepted money for ordinations, despite being aware that the candidates were morally suspect.[28] Covetousness was a deadly sin because it fed idolatry. This was why a monk had to renounce everything. And Basil taught that true renunciation consisted of being free of all passions (not just wealth) whilst still in the body here on earth. Renouncing material possessions was but the start.[29]

Basil stoutly defended the Council of Nicaea of 325, with its unequivocal commitment to the full deity of God the Son; after Nicaea, he argued strenuously for an equally clear recognition of the Holy Spirit as the third person of the Trinity. Coincidentally, the reference to Basil in the *Amra* occurs soon after the *Amra* states that knowledge of the Godhead was granted to Columba. Clancy and Markus translate the lines as:

Knowledge of the Godhead was granted to [Columba].
Truly blessed when he died.
He was wise about apostles, about angels.
He applied the judgements of Basil,
Who forbids acts of boasting by great hosts.[30]

Henry renders the same section as:

Knowledge of the divinity was granted to [Columba].
His death was indeed holy.
He was familiar with apostles and angels.
He applied the judgements of Basil,
Who forbids the chanting of songs at large meetings.[31]

---

27 Benedict, *The Rule*, LXXIII. For a discussion on Basil's influence on Benedict see: Anna M. Silvas (tr.), *The Rule of St. Basil in Latin and English: A Revised Critical Edition* (Collegeville, Minnesota: Liturgical Press, 2013), 10f. Yet it should not be assumed that every monastery in the Latin world was either Benedictine or Irish. Jessie D. Billett, *The Divine Office in Anglo-Saxon England* (London: Henry Bradshaw Society, 2014), 5, stresses that few monasteries in Rome itself were strictly 'Benedictine' before the tenth century, in terms of fully embracing Benedict's *Rule*.

28 Basil, *Letters*, 53 and 54; cf. E. F. Morison, *St. Basil and his Rule: A Study in Early Monasticism* (London: OUP, 1912), 7.

29 Basil, *The Shorter Rule*, Qu. 4:1f., 9.

30 *Amra*, IV. Clancy and Markus, *Iona: the Earliest Poetry of a Celtic Monastery*, 107.

31 *Amra*, IV. Henry, *Amra Choluim Chille: Dallán's Elegy for Columba*, 37.

What were the 'judgements of Basil' which Columba applied? As with much of the *Amra*, interpretation is difficult. The *Amra* has brief allusions to issues, places, and people, and although these would be readily understood by its first readers, they are less obvious to us. Nevertheless, we can hazard a clarification. If the phrase, 'judgements of Basil' is meant to connect with the very next line of the poem, then the phrase may reference Basil's views on humility or indicate his views on the mode of singing in church.[32] But if the line stands on its own, without direct connection to what follows, then the phrase more likely refers to rules which Basil regarded as essential for a true Christian monk. One of Basil's lifelong objectives was to see the canons (decisions) of the Council of Nicaea enforced throughout the Church. Although Nicaea is best known for its famous Creed, it also laid down markers for Christian discipline, and subsequent theologians, such as Basil, sought to embed these decisions, concerning both theology and praxis, deep into the life of the Church. They endorsed Nicaea's theology by strengthening the Nicene doctrine of the deity of Christ; and they applied Nicaea's praxis by promoting its canons on Church order and Christian discipline. The canons dealt with practical questions. How are faults to be dealt with? How are lapsed Christians to be received? How are sinful clergy to be disciplined? Nicaea was not the first Council to consider these, nor would it be the last. Because Basil was an enthusiast for pure Christian living, especially in its monastic form, he embraced rules with gusto. His eagerness was shared by others, and his friend, Gregory of Nazianzus, wrote to him once about the joy of clear instructions: 'O for the contest and incitement to virtue which we secured by written rules and canons.'[33] In his Letters Basil reproduces and explains canonical rulings which he saw as important.[34] Hence, in the Amra, the 'judgements of Basil' may well be a reference to rules approved by the Greek Father.

A Basilean ethos permeated Irish monasticism. But the *Amra* indicates that Columba was influenced by more than a general ethos. One major

32 Forbidding 'boasting' may reflect Basil's oft-repeated insistence that human beings need to be humble in the face of the great mysteries, especially the mystery of the Godhead itself; cf. Basil, *On the Holy Spirit*, I-IV, and Basil, *Letters*, 7.

33 Gregory of Nazianzus, *Letters*, 6; cf. Morison, *St. Basil and his Rule: A Study in Early Monasticism*, 12.

34 McNeill, *The Celtic Penitentials*, 81, notes than in his *Letters* Basil includes traditional penalties alongside statements of his own opinions – not without inconsistencies.

direct link between Basil and Columba was the teaching of Finnian of Clonard since Finnian drew heavily on Basil in developing his own penitential theology.[35] Columba, as Finnian's student, was familiar with Basil. Also, on Iona, Columba may have had collections of Basil's rules or 'judgements' and may have used these to instruct and discipline the monks of his own community. Columba may also have had access to full works by Basil, such as Basil's *Shorter Rule, Longer Rule, On the Judgement of God, Concerning the Faith, Moralia*, or the widely-circulated *Letters* in which Basil outlined penitential penalties.[36] Columba may also have had copies of pseudo-Basil's *Ascetical Writings*, which, if not written by Basil himself, were in line with Basil's thinking. If Columba did read Basil directly, it would be through Rufinus' widely-circulated Latin version of Basil's *Shorter Rule*,[37] or through compendia of Basil's 'judgements' which were in circulation. Rufinus described Basil's *Institutes*, from which he took the *Shorter Rule*, as 'a kind of sacred case-law'.[38]

In later chapters, whenever we refer to Basil's thinking, or to a particular passage in Basil's writings, we do not assume that Columba had always read and studied the exact same section. But we do assume that Columba had read enough of Basil, and had absorbed Basilean principles to such an extent, that there was agreement of thought and practice between the great theologian and the abbot of Iona. Columba trusted the 'judgements of Basil'.

Three letters which Basil wrote to Amphilochius of Iconium are particularly important, as they were a fertile seed-bed for later Irish Penitentials.[39] In these letters Basil refers to graded stations of penance and

---

35 McNeill, *The Celtic Penitentials*, 35, also notes an association between the Welsh penitential writer Gildas, and Finnian of Clonard.

36 Morison, *St. Basil and his Rule: A Study in Early Monasticism*, 19. Morison questions if *Letters* 42-46, dealing with some monastic topics, are from Basil.

37 Basil's *Shorter Rule*, or *Small Asketikon*, was translated into Latin by Rufinus of Aquileia (c. 354-411), and it is Rufinus' Latin translation which is best known, since the Greek text of the *Shorter Rule* has not survived. An English translation of Rufinus' version is in Silvas, *The Rule of St. Basil in Latin and English*. Basil's *Longer Rule*, or *Great Asketikon*, is also in English, in Monica Wagner's, *Ascetical Works of St. Basil* (Washington: Catholic University of America, 1962).

38 Rufinus, *Preface to Basil's Shorter Rule*, 5.

39 Basil's three letters (as numbered in the *NPNF* series), are *Letters*, 188, 199, and 217. John T. McNeill and Helen M. Gamer, *Medieval Handbooks of Penance: A Translation of the principal* Libri Poenitentiales *and selections from related documents* (New York: Columbia University Press, 1938), 8, revises an opinion which McNeill gave in his earlier work, *The Celtic Penitentials*, 96, in which he stated: 'There is nothing to indicate that Gildas, David, Finnian,

indicates how long a penitent should spend in each. In Basil's system a typical period of penance had four stages, each of which might last for several years. The stages were: Weeping, Hearing, Kneeling, and Standing. All stages had to be completed before readmittance to the Eucharist was permitted. For example, concerning perjury, Basil stipulated,

> Perjurers shall be excommunicated for ten years; *weeping* for two, *hearing* for three, *kneeling* for four, and *standing* only during one year; then they shall be held worthy of communion.[40] [my italics]

Weepers were those at the first stage of penance: they were stationed away from the worshipping community (outside the door of the church) as a symbol of their current state of total exclusion from the kingdom of God. **Hearers** were allowed to be nearer the worshippers (inside the vestibule of the church) but dismissed after the Scripture lesson and sermon, and before the Eucharist was celebrated. **Kneelers** came to church clothed in sackcloth and with ashes on their head: they were stationed at the rear of the congregation, and, when others stood to pray, had to kneel. **Standers** could mingle with the congregation though not yet allowed to communicate. The three latter stages of Hearers, Kneelers, and Standers, were specified by the Council of Nicaea, with Basil himself introducing the Weepers' category.[41] If the *Amra*'s phrase, 'judgements of Basil', refers to penitential rules, then it may indicate that Columba applied a similar system on Iona, and indeed it is possible to trace faint allusions to these stages of penance in Adomnán's *Life of Columba*.[42] In our view, the likelihood is that the 'judgements of Basil' does refer to Basil's rules for monastic discipline and/or penance. Iona practices, following those of the Irish Church in general, reflected the ethos of Basil's monasticism and theology.

CASSIAN OF MARSEILLE (360-435)

John Cassian, like Basil, influenced not only Irish monasticism, but its Benedictine counterpart, with Benedict instructing his monks to

---

or Columbanus used Basil's or any other ancient penitential code as a basis for their penitential regulations. It is not till we reach Theodore of Tarsus that the influence of Basil appears.'

40 Basil, *Letters*, 217.

41 McNeil and Gamer, *Medieval Handbooks of Penance*, 7ff.

42 cf. Chapter Six, 'Enforcer and Protector'.

read Cassian daily.[43] Cassian's place of birth is unknown, but for part of his life he lived in the desert in order to familiarise himself with Egyptian monasticism. He later wrote down his thoughts on the desert monks in a collection of works known as *The Conferences*, in which he reconstructed conversations he had had with notable abbots of desert communities. Cassian was a prolific author. His writings were amongst the most copied of the age, with numerous Cassian manuscripts surviving into the late Middle Ages and the onset of printed books. This wide dissemination resulted in the principles of eastern Mediterranean monasticism, as interpreted by Cassian, influencing all monasticism in the West. His writings were widely circulated in Ireland, where they were valued by Columba. The *Amra* states:

The teacher [Columba] wove the word,
By his wisdom he made glosses clear.
He fixed the Psalms,
he made known the books of Law,
those books Cassian loved.[44]

Henry's rendering is:

The teacher [Columba] wove his words,
wisely explaining every gloss.
He made clear the text of the psalms,
And made known the books of the Law
as Cassian liked to do.[45]

What were 'those books Cassian loved'? Were they Cassian's own writings on monastic regulations? Probably not, since Cassian would hardly have been described as loving his own books! More likely the 'books Cassian loved' were the biblical books which he expounded.

---

43 cf. Benedict, *The Rule*, 42: '[After supper] someone should read from the *Conferences* or the *Lives* of the Fathers, or rate something else that will benefit the hearers … On fast days there is to be a short interval between Vespers and the reading of the *Conferences*, as we have indicated. Then let four or five pages be read, or as many as time permits.' cf. *The Rule*, 73. Cassian's semi-Pelagian combination of human effort and divine grace is reflected in the Preface to Benedict's Rule: 'We must, then, prepare our hearts and bodies for the battle of holy obedience to his instructions. *What is not possible to us by nature, let us ask the Lord to supply by the help of his grace.*'[my italics] Benedict's direct influence was limited in Britain and Ireland during Columba's lifetime; cf. Herren and Brown, *Christ in Celtic Christianity*, 21.

44 *Amra*, V. Clancy and Markus, *Iona: the Earliest Poetry of a Celtic Monastery*, 107.

45 *Amra*, V. Henry, *Amra Choluim Chille: Dallán's Elegy for Columba*, 41.

When he settled at Marseille, one of his aims was to prove that monastic principles were rooted in Scripture; and it was at Marseille that Cassian composed his three major treatises: *The Institutes*, *The Conferences*, and *On the Incarnation against Nestorius*.[46] In the *Institutes* Cassian set out rules for the conduct of a monk's life, including the Canonical Hours of prayer. In the *Conferences* he wrote at length on monasticism through his reconstructed conversations with desert abbots. And in his work *Against Nestorius*, he addressed some of the doctrinal issues of the day.

Central to the relevance of Cassian vis-à-vis Columba, is the fact that Cassian was dragged into debates involving Pelagius and Augustine of Hippo. The Pelagian debate is important in early-medieval Irish theology, with profound ramifications for Columba's theology, and a brief outline may be helpful at this juncture. Pelagius was a monk of British origin, living on the Continent, who reacted against aspects of Augustine's theology, especially Augustine's emphasis on God's sovereignty and the helplessness of men and women in relation to their salvation. Little of Pelagius' own work has survived, but he is understood to have taught – over against Augustine – that men and women could achieve perfection by an effort of free will even without divine help. He also denied any shared or inherited original sin and denied Augustine's strict doctrine of predestination.[47] Pelagius believed that men and women had within themselves a capacity to respond effectively to God's requirements. Consequently, he encouraged a strict, literal adherence to the law of Moses, revelling in any passage of Scripture which gave divine laws, because knowing all of God's laws was essential to living the perfect life.[48]

Augustine rejected Pelagius' entire position. Augustine held that no human action whatsoever, and no human merit of any type, could be instrumental in the soul's salvation. For Augustine 'grace alone' had to be taken literally. This debate pushed Augustine into teaching that grace was irresistible and indefectible. Hence, in 418, Augustine wrote to a priest named Sixtus, teaching a doctrine of absolute predestination based on the utter irresistibility of God's grace. Then, in 426, Augustine

46 Cassian linked Nestorianism with Pelagianism. He interpreted Nestorian Christology as teaching that the human nature of Christ, totally independent of any divinity, had strength of will to live without sin.

47 Herren and Brown, *Christ in Celtic Christianity*, 5.

48 Herren and Brown, *Christ in Celtic Christianity*, 190.

developed his thinking in two treatises, *Grace and the Freedom of the Will*, and *Concerning Corruption and Grace.* Pelagius' theology and Augustine's theology were mutually exclusive. For Pelagius, human effort on its own could make a person right with God. For Augustine, human effort had no part to play.

Cassian was aware of the debate, and his response was to promote a middle way involving a combination of divine grace and human effort. For many Christians, both lay persons and those in holy orders, Cassian's middle way made total common sense. It seemed reasonable that human beings should be obliged to 'do something' before receiving God's rewards. Augustine's radical doctrine of grace was especially unwelcomed in monastic circles. If human effort had no contribution to make, why strive to be holy? Why live a life of extreme hardship and self-denial? Augustine's theology discomfited those who admired the ascetic life with its strict disciplines and harsh austerity. And although Cassian did not involve himself directly in the dispute between Pelagius and Augustine, it was known that his Marseille community had reservations about the possible moral and theological consequences of Augustine's logic.

Cassian's middle-way theology has saddled him with the label 'semi-Pelagian'. But Cassian was no Pelagian and could just as easily be described as 'semi-Augustinian'.[49] He condemned Pelagius' position unequivocally. He affirmed that all humanity was affected by the Fall. He accepted that humanity always needed the grace of God for salvation.[50] However, Cassian also defended the role of the human will and human good works in salvation, albeit in conjunction with God's grace. For Cassian, good works were carried out not simply as responses of gratitude for salvation, but in order to gain salvation.[51] For Cassian,

---

49 cf. Cassian, *The Seven Books of John Cassian on the Incarnation of the Lord, against Nestorius*, I:3: '[The] heresy … which sprang from the error of Pelagius; viz., that in saying Jesus Christ had lived as a mere man without any stain of sin, they actually went as far as to declare than men could also be without sin if they liked.' (cf. *Seven Books*, V:1, 3).

50 Cassian, *Conferences*, XIII, 'Third Conference of Abbot Chaeremon', 9: 'Even of his own motion a man can be led to the quest of virtue, but always stands in need of the help of the Lord.' Cassian discusses grace and free-will in adjacent chapters, expounding Romans 7:18, 'For to will is present with me, but to perform what is good I find not.' Herren and Brown, *Christ in Celtic Theology*, 77, reckon that *Conferences*, XIII, was written with Augustine's doctrine of grace in mind.

51 cf. Cassian, *Conferences*, III, 'Conference of Abbot Paphnutius, on The Three Sorts of Renunciation', esp. 12:21, and *Conferences*, XIII, 'Third Conference of Abbot

it was important to have a theology which did not make monks feel that their stern asceticism was pointless. The effort which was put into crucifying carnal desires of mind and body had to be worthwhile. Therefore Cassian's middle-way theology, emphasising cooperation between divine grace and the human will, was readily embraced by the growing monastic movement and its admirers.[52] It gave meaning to all that they strove to achieve.

Augustine appeared to undermine the saving importance of good works. He seemed to diminish the need for purity, fasting, self-denial, isolation from the world, abandonment of luxury, and observance of penance, all of which were at the heart of monastic discipline. None of these contributed to gaining salvation if Augustine's interpretation of 'grace alone' were correct. It was feared that Augustine's theology would demotivate the monastic vocation, and that striving after holiness and purity would become a meaningless pursuit. It seemed that Augustine's notion of grace was a green light for moral laxity. Significantly, when Cassian debates free will, it is within the context of a discussion on chastity and holiness, indicating that Cassian engaged with the debate because of its possible impact on practical Christian living. Augustine could not accept this middle way. He could not yield on the principle of God's decree of election which, for him, was essential for 'grace alone'.

Because full-blown Pelagianism was regarded by the Western Church as an abominable heresy and because Augustine gave the strongest and most comprehensive rebuttal of Pelagianism, then within the Western Church Augustine's powerful writings became the official response to the heresy. This made Pope Celestine (d. 432), who was anxious to avoid being tarred with Pelagianism in any form, condemn not only Pelagius but also the Marseille teaching. Cassian himself was so respected that he was not subjected to direct attack. Nevertheless, he was never canonised as a saint by the Latin West, though neither was he declared a heretic.

Chaeremon, on The Protection of God'. Herren and Brown, *Christ in Celtic Theology*, 71f., reckon that for Pelagius grace was defined as (i) created nature itself (including the freedom of the will), (ii) the laws of Moses and of Christ, and (iii) instruction. Herren and Brown (79) also cite the British monk Faustus (d. 490) who, in his treatise *On Grace*, used arguments almost identical to Cassian, attacking Pelagius for arguing that man can be saved solely by his will and for opposing infant baptism; but also attacking Augustine's doctrine of predestination.

52 Dales, *Light to the Isles*, 29.

But did Augustine's position undermine Christian morals? Did it weaken incentive for the monastic life? That would be the case only if the motivation for living a holy life was fear of otherwise being unworthy for heaven. But *gratitude* for an assured salvation can be as powerful an incentive to live for God as *fear*. However, given that the Marseille school assumed that Augustine's theology subverted the monastic calling, this indicates that, for the Marseille school, it was a need to become worthy of salvation which drove the desire for purity. Monks wanted to become holy enough to be worthy of heaven. Cassian's semi-Pelagianism, with its complementary relationship between human merit and divine grace, gave a theological foundation for that understanding, and it was this spirituality which Irish monasticism adopted.

In Cassian's thinking, the human will did not become inert because of the Fall. The Fall severely weakened the human potential to respond, but, by God's grace, it still functioned. Hence, in Cassian's theology, divine grace did not displace human response. Instead, divine grace enabled human response.[53] And the gut-instinct of many Christians was that Cassian's position made more sense than Augustine's predestinarian doctrine. Hence, by the time of Pope Gregory the Great (d. 604), Cassian had become the silent victor.[54] Officially the doctrine of the Church remained Augustinian: but in terms of practical piety,

---

53 Herren and Brown, *Christ in Celtic Theology*, 75, stress that for Pelagius Christ's chief importance lay in being the giver of the New Law and in being the exemplar to imitate. Law and instruction were 'the truest forms of grace'. God was gracious in giving clear rules, laws and obligations. Semi-Pelagianism diluted this, but similar themes were still present. Pelagius interpreted the cross as the supreme example to be imitated by men, rather than as an act of atonement (88).

54 Philip L. Barclift, 'Predestination and Divine Foreknowledge in the Sermons of Pope Leo the Great', *Church History*, vol. 62, no. 1 (March 1993), 5-21, 5, argues that theologians, towards and after the end of Augustine's life, tried to moderate Augustine's more extreme positions concerning grace and predestination by realigning his ideas with accepted church tradition, defining 'accepted church tradition' as including Christian doctrines which were held by, and which were promoted most widely by, theologians regarded as orthodox up to, but not including, Augustine himself. This moderating process began in the monasteries in Gaul which Cassian had influenced. They reacted against Augustine's seeming deterministic thesis that human salvation flowed entirely from the divine initiative without involving human capacity for free choice. The monks in Gaul argued that human free-will was essential to the economy of human salvation. This became known as 'semi-Pelagianism.' It asserted the primacy of the will in the initial moment of the decision of faith. Yet this was not intended to be a rejection of all of Augustine's teachings. Herren and Brown, *Christ in Celtic Theology*, 80. O'Loughlin, *Celtic Theology*, 9, notes that the monastic community on Lerins not only read Augustine but 'quietly' corrected him.

it followed Cassian. As monasticism spread, and as the practice of penance began to dominate Christian spirituality, the place of human effort took centre-stage. Human effort *had* to have a place. If not, why the Law? Why striving for the holy life? Most of all, why penance? Cassian's notion of God's grace enabling human effort, and of God's grace perfecting nature, became the *de facto* day-to-day spirituality of the Church, even though Augustine's position was official dogma.[55] And so, in monasteries across Christendom Cassian's works were studied in depth, though sometimes tweaked and edited so as to appear officially orthodox.

All of this lies behind the *Amra*'s brief reference to Cassian. This is why the *Amra* mentions Cassian in conjunction with the books of the Law: '[Columba] made known the books of Law, those books Cassian loved.'[56] A *de facto* adoption of Cassian's theology pervaded the Irish Church's theology.[57] The spirituality of the early-medieval Irish Church emphasised a need for purity if heaven were to be reached, and it was observance of the Law of God which could achieve this.[58] Christ was the giver of the New Law: and Christ was the ultimate model for human imitation.[59] It was the holy life, allied to penitential exercises, which enabled a soul at death to be acceptable to God. And anxiety concerning the ultimate crisis of death was why monks submitted themselves to a trusted abbot. He could pilot them to a safe harbour in the eternal kingdom.

FINNIAN OF CLONARD (470–549)

Columba served as a deacon with Finnian of Clonard before being ordained a priest.[60] Finnian had earlier taught Comgall who went on to become the founding abbot of Bangor Monastery, and Columba and Comgall later developed a personal friendship. Finnian was a huge

55 Herren and Brown, *Christ in Celtic Christianity*, 7ff., emphasise the influence of both Pelagianism and semi-Pelagianism in the Celtic Churches, though in Gaul semi-Pelagianism was dominant.

56 *Amra*, v. Clancy and Markus, *Iona: the Earliest Poetry of a Celtic Monastery*, 107.

57 See below: Chapter 18, 'The Tendency of the Times'.

58 Herren and Brown, *Christ in Celtic Christianity*, passim.

59 Herren and Brown, *Christ in Celtic Christianity*, 15.

60 Following Adomnán, the 16th Century *Aberdeen Breviary* (25th September) notes: 'Columba soldiered for a long time under Finbarr's teaching in deacon's orders.' (MacQuarrie, *Aberdeen Breviary* 237).

figure for both men, not only as their teacher, but as a pioneer of a strict form of Irish monastic discipline. In his *Penitential of Finnian*, Finnian developed the penitential codes which had come to Ireland from the likes of Gildas in Wales, and from the Middle East via Gaul.[61] Finnian's book would influence all future Irish monasticism.[62] As young men under training, Comgall and Columba were exposed to Finnian's ideas and practices and they took these to their own monastic communities. The *Penitential of Finnian* is discussed in more depth in Chapter Six, but this section gives an opportunity to reflect on the growing practice of penance across Christendom.

From New Testament times onwards, the Church had disciplinary procedures which were designed to maintain the Church as 'a body of people of unpolluted holiness'.[63] As part of this process, there was the gradual development of formal penitential systems, with various factors feeding their evolution. One factor was the monastic movement itself. A monastery was a place for purification of the soul, with monks and nuns seeking ever greater purity. A major question was, 'How can I cleanse my soul after succumbing to sin?' There needed to be procedures for recovering lost ground, and penance seemed to fill that gap. Another factor was the very success of Christianity in becoming the favoured religion of the Roman Empire. When Christians lived as a persecuted minority, there was a relatively low level of moral laxity within their communities; but when Christianity became a preferred faith, the rush of nominal believers brought lower standards.[64] To counteract this, discipline was tightened.

But far and away the major factor accelerating the development of a formal penitential system, was the problem of the 'lapsed'. During persecution many believers heroically maintained their faith despite torture and death; but some Christians compromised under the intense pressure. What was to be done with them? Could they be re-integrated into the Church? If so, what conditions did they have to satisfy? It seemed unfair that the lapsed, who denied their faith to avoid suffering, should be restored immediately to full communion

---

61 McNeill and Gamer, *Medieval Handbooks of Penance*, offer a Latin/English version of the *Penitential of Finnian*.

62 Fraser, *From Caledonia to Pictland: Scotland to 795*, 74f.

63 McNeill, *The Celtic Penitentials*, 77.

64 cf. Dales, *Light to the Isles*, 26.

alongside those who remained faithful. This resulted in the emergence of a process in which the lapsed were only reinstated after a series of penitential steps were completed. Only after finishing these spiritual exercises were offenders readmitted to full fellowship. The thinking behind this process of reinstatement then widened to become a whole theology. And so, a system originally designed to deal with the spiritual condition of believers who lapsed during persecution, became a template applied to the spiritual condition of any who lapsed from grace through any serious sin. The penitential process became a way of solving the dilemma of how men and women, after committing serious post-baptismal sins, might be restored to God. If those who lapsed during persecution needed to complete a penance before being restored to fellowship here on earth, then those who lapsed through serious sin during their soul-journey needed a similar process before being worthy of heaven.

Penance originated in procedures designed to solve practical problems of church discipline. It then grew into a system which dominated medieval theology and piety; and, by the thirteenth century, it was referred to in Peter Lombard's *Sentences* as one of the Seven Sacraments. Penance appeared to solve some questions but created more. What if sufficient penance had not been completed before death? Could penance be continued after death? Could penance be undertaken by others on your behalf? Could holy saints give assistance to a penitent in this life or even beyond the grave? Might certain acts, such as taking the Eucharist, confer merit to remove the problem? Could penitential requirements be commuted into a financial payment to the Church?[65] These questions, and the thinking behind them, intensified as the centuries passed: but, from the start, the concept of penance contained the seeds of all of its future developments. In McNeill's view, it was the penitential scheme which lay at the root of the theological and moral issues which the sixteenth-century Protestant Reformers reacted against.[66] In order to break its suffocating stranglehold, the Reformers

---

65 Irish Penitentials frequently combined biblical sanctions with penalties in contemporary secular law. Irish Law allowed the giving of a monetary fine in lieu of other sanctions. This fostered the notion of giving a financial equivalent in place of spiritual penance. Monks could not take this option as they had no possessions.

66 McNeill, *The Celtic Penitentials*, 199f.; cf. Hughes, *Early Christian Ireland: Introduction to the Sources*, 89.

found themselves returning to Augustine's interpretation of God's sovereignty as the theological hammer with which to break the system. 'God alone', 'grace alone', and 'by faith alone', meant that God does it all, and human merit is not involved in any way.

The Irish penitential system was as severe as any in Christendom. It was applied more rigorously. Its penalties were more exacting. Those who followed in Finnian's footsteps, including Comgall and Columba, took it seriously. It was this penitential spirituality which Columba taught his monastic community. But whenever completion of penance becomes a pre-requisite for eternal salvation, it embodies semi-Pelagianism. And that was the position of the early-medieval Irish Church of Columba's era.

CHAPTER 4

Christ's Soldier

Adomnán uses a variety of phrases to describe Columba: 'the apostolic man', 'the blessed man', 'the holy man', 'a man prophetic and apostolic', etc. But Adomnán's most consistent descriptor, not only of Columba but of other serious monks, is 'soldier'. This title inhabits Adomnán's narrative from start to finish. Being a 'soldier of Christ' encompassed everything else: monk or non-monk; abbot or bishop; priest or layperson. Every Christian was commissioned to be a 'soldier of Christ' (*Miles Christi*).

'Soldier' had long been the term of choice to define serious believers. The Apostle Paul used military images to describe the Christian life (Eph. 6:10-17). Later in the first century, Clement of Rome reminded Christians in Corinth, 'Christ is our leader, and we are his soldiers'.[1] When Ignatius was martyred for his faith, the panegyric composed in his honour described him as a 'soldier for Christ' in one of the first documented usages of the phrase.[2] Subsequently, this became the standard way of referring to any Christian who was engaged in serious ministry. By the fourth century, Basil and Cassian use it regularly. Basil writes that he trained his monks to be, '[tried wrestlers], wounding and overthrowing the prince of the darkness of this world and the spiritual powers of iniquity, with whom, as the blessed Apostle says, is 'our conflict'.[3] And Cassian has 'soldier of Christ' as a synonym for those who embraced the monastic calling.[4] The concept was used by nearly all of the Church Fathers. It also appears frequently in early-medieval Irish Christian literature.[5]

Adomnán introduces the term and the concept of 'soldier' in the Second Preface of his *Life of Columba*. In this tone-setting introduction

1 Clement, *First Letter to the Corinthians*, 37.

2 *The Martyrdom of Ignatius*, 2.

3 Basil, *Letters*, 23.

4 Cassian, *Institutes*, II:1 etc.

5 cf. *Voyages of St. Brendan*, I, II, XXV, XXVI, etc.

Adomnán employs the notion twice: once in anticipation of Columba's ministry; and once when summarising that ministry at its close. The first reference comes within a prophecy concerning Columba's God-ordained calling, with Adomnán referring to a revelation given to a 'soldier of Christ' called Mochta, who stated that in Ireland there would be born a promised son (Columba) through whom God would do great things. The second reference occurs when Adomnán reviews Columba's life, and states that Columba lived on Iona for thirty-four years as an 'island soldier', not allowing even one hour to pass without applying himself to prayer, reading, writing, or some kind of work. What Adomnán gives us in the Second Preface is: first a 'soldier of Christ', foretelling Columba's birth; and then a summary of Columba's ministry on Iona as having been that of an *island soldier.* Significantly, Adomnán selects the term 'island soldier', rather than 'island monk' or 'island pilgrim', to sum up Columba's life. All of Columba's multi-functional activities as monk, missionary, brother, priest, abbot, and advisor of kings, are interpreted within this primary calling as a soldier of Christ.[6]

The term 'soldier of Christ', or its cognates, occurs over twenty times in Adomnán's book, and is applied not only to Columba but to other outstanding monks. Adomnán writes that certain information came to him through 'a religious old man, a priest and soldier of Christ, called Oissene mac Ernain' (I:2). Columba declares, 'Two strangers, consummating in a short space long years of service as soldiers of Christ, will depart in peace to Christ the Lord' (I:32). Adomnán describes Columba in Ireland when, 'fellow-soldiers of Christ stood on either side of the saint in Church' (I:40). Luigbe, 'himself a soldier of Christ, took Columba aside and began to question him' (I:43). Concerning a battle which Columba foretold, Adomnán states: 'A soldier of Christ called Finan was present at the battle' (I:49). Appealing to an eyewitness to prove the veracity of an incident, Adomnán says: 'We have the testimony of Silnan himself, a soldier of Christ' (II:4). Concerning a child brought for baptism, Columba foretells that this child 'will devote himself to service as a soldier of Christ to the end of his days' (II:10). When one of Columba's travelling companions, a young man named Fintan, became seriously ill, 'His fellow soldiers in Christ were

6 Herren and Brown, *Christ in Celtic Christianity*, 14.

saddened and begged St Columba to pray for him' (III:31). The monk Cormac is described as a 'soldier of Christ' (II:42). In a reference to Columba's exile from Ireland, Adomnán writes that Columba crossed to Britain with twelve disciples as his 'fellow soldiers' (III:3). Elsewhere, an Irish pilgrim says, 'I know a soldier of Christ who built a little monastery for himself in the district where he and I used to live' (III:7). Another monk, Fergnae, dies 'as a victorious soldier of Christ' (III:23). Other instances abound.

The term 'soldier' is significant because it identifies a central characteristic of the monastic life. Everything which was done within the monastery was part of soldiering. Monks were not military soldiers of Christ (as they disastrously became during the Crusades) but spiritual warriors. Spiritual-military duty was the task of all monks everywhere, with Benedict's *Rule* stressing this dimension when reflecting on the life of a solitary monk:

> [They] have built up their strength and go from the battle-line in the ranks of their brothers, to the single-combat of the desert. Self-reliant now, without the support of another, they are ready with God's help to grapple single-handed with the vices of body and mind.[7]

Columba had many skills. He had a powerful intellect. He had political expertise. He had leadership qualities, and the ability to inspire. But informing and moulding each persona, was his work as a spiritual warrior. At the heart of any soldier's calling is warfare, and in Columba's case it was spiritual warfare. This is why the depiction of Columba and his fellow-monks as 'soldiers' is a key description. It summarises their self-understanding of what they were and did. As monks they were many things, but they were supremely soldiers of Christ on active service every hour of every day. Each day was to be lived out as a soldier of Christ. Each day they battled on Christ's behalf against Satanic hordes of hell. Spiritual conflict dominated their faith horizon; and every phase of life, and every circumstance, was interpreted in relation to that warfare. Being a soldier of Christ encompassed all other aspects of Columba's Christian life: his calling to be a monk, his role as an abbot, his responsibility as the guardian

7 Benedict, *The Rule*, I.

of the monastic community; all were subsumed within the grand reality that the task at hand involved hard fighting and the life of a spiritual warrior.[8]

THE FOE OF SOULS

The controlling paradigm of faith for Columba was that of being a participant in the spiritual battle between Christ and Satan.[9] Pseudo-Basil writes:

> Be assured, then, that you will not escape doing battle with the Renegade nor will you gain the victory over him without much striving to observe the evangelical doctrines. How will you, stationed in the very thick of the battle, be able to win the contest against the Enemy? That he wanders over all the earth under heaven and ranges about like a mad dog seeking whom he may devour, we learn from the history of Job. If then, you refuse battle with your Antagonist, betake yourself to another world where he is not; avoidance of conflict with him will then be possible for you, as well as relaxation without peril to evangelical doctrines. But, if this cannot be, make haste to learn how to fight with him, taking instruction from the Scriptures in the art of conflict, that you may not be defeated through your ignorance, and consigned to everlasting fire.[10]

Because Columba's calling, work, worship, theology, and evangelism, were set within this overarching context of spiritual warfare, then understanding what spiritual warfare meant to him is key to unlocking his spirituality and practice of Christian faith. On the principle that the start of a book highlights its principal themes, it is striking that the first chapter of Adomnán's *Life of Columba*, has a direct reference to spiritual battle:

8 cf. Bruce, *Prophecy, Miracles, Angels and Heavenly Light?*, 136ff.

9 Benedict, *The Rule*, I, emphasised that anchorites, were: 'Trained to fight against the devil; they have built up their strength and go from the battle-line in the ranks of their brothers to the single-combat of the desert. Self-reliant now, without the support of one another, they are ready with God's help to grapple single-handed with the vices of body and mind.'

10 Pseudo-Basil, *An Ascetical Discourse and Exhortation on the Renunciation of the World and Spiritual Perfection.*

> When countless hosts of horrible devils were making war against [Columba], visible to his bodily eyes, and beginning to inflict deadly diseases on his monastic community, he, one man alone, with God's help repelled them and drove them out of this our principal island. With Christ's help, he curbed the raging fury of wild beasts sometimes by killing them and sometimes by driving them away. (I:1)

Other incidents, such as Columba's fierce battle against demons at an isolated spot on Iona (III:8), have him contending against Satan's forces, echoing Christ's battle against Satan in the wilderness. Adomnán's focus is typical of the literature of the early Irish Church in which the theme of spiritual warfare is ever-present. Comgall's monastery at Bangor viewed the life of faith in similar terms, and Michael Curran reads the *Bangor Antiphonary* as teaching that, 'the victory of the apostles and of the other martyrs was achieved through a struggle comparable to that of Christ, through spiritual armour, through strength and fidelity.'[11] Curran points out that the concept of combat with Satan appealed in a marked degree to the Irish monastic spirit. And James Bruce, in his book, *Prophecy, Miracles, Angels and Heavenly Light?* is also sharply aware of this being a major dimension of Irish and Columban spirituality.

Curran and Bruce apart, this theme is rarely examined in studies of the early-medieval Irish Church. Other questions take centre stage. To what extent were pre-Christian beliefs preserved in the theology of the Irish Church? Did indigenous Irish culture inform and mould the prayers, hymns, and philosophy of Columba and his contemporaries? Was there continuity with pre-Christian culture or a break with it?[12] All these questions are important, and all require research. But the many descriptions of battle with the demonic, which pervade the literature, are often read only as metaphors for crisis events experienced by the monastic community, or are regarded as products of excited imaginations with

11 Michael Curran, *The Antiphonary of Bangor and the Early Irish Monastic Liturgy*, (Dublin: Irish Academic Press, 1984), 79.

12 Bruce, *Prophecy, Miracles, Angels and Heavenly Light?* 39-94 and 201, discusses this and related issues in detail. He concludes that the early Irish Church was far more influenced by biblical concepts than by those of the surrounding culture. Whilst not denying the importance and influence of indigenous culture, Bruce's comments are a reminder that biblical categories informed the core thinking of early Irish Christianity.

monks wanting their personal narrative to replicate Christ's conflict with Satan. It can be tempting to dismiss these stories as entertaining embroideries to the text created by the over-anxious. But spiritual battle was at the heart of a monk's faith: it saturated all he thought; it pervaded all he believed; and it affected all he did. His calling, worship, theology, and evangelism, in both form and content, were determined by a spirituality moulded by notions of spiritual warfare.

THE SOLDIER'S BATTLEFIELD

Columba's poem, the *Altus Prosator*, describes how the physical human environment of space and time is infested by Satan's demons:

Driven out from the midst [Lucifer] was thrust down by the Lord;
the space of air is choked by a wild mass of his treacherous attendants,
invisible, lest, tainted by their wicked examples and their crimes,
(no fences or walls ever concealing them)
folk should sin openly, before the eyes of all.[13]

In this extract, Columba states that the 'space of air' is full of the demonic. Viewing the air as a physical location of the demonic was mainstream thinking among the Church Fathers. Scripture describes Satan as 'prince of the powers of the air' (Eph. 2:2), and the Church Fathers took the phrase literally. It was a belief held by major figures such as Tertullian,[14] Laurentius,[15] Origen,[16] Athanasius, Augustine,[17] and John Chrysostom.[18] For them, the concept of Satan as 'prince of

13 *Altus Prosator*, Stanza H.

14 Tertullian, *Against Marcion*, V:17: 'Who then is he? Undoubtedly he who has raised up "children of disobedience" against the Creator Himself ever since he took possession of that "*air*" of his.'

15 Laurentius, *Commentary on the Apostles' Creed*, XIV.

16 Origen, *Against Celsus*, VIII:58.

17 Augustine, *City of God*, X:21, 22: 'We call our martyrs heroes … not because they lived along with the demons *in the air*, but because they conquered these demons or powers *of the air*, and among them Juno herself…It is by true piety that men of God cast out the hostile power *of the air* which opposes godliness; it is by exorcising it, not by propitiating it; and they overcome all the temptations of the adversary by praying, not to him, but to their own God against him. For the devil cannot conquer or subdue any but those who are in league with sin; and therefore he is conquered in the name of Him who assumed humanity, and that without sin, that Himself being both Priest and Sacrifice, He might bring about the remission of sins.'

18 Chrysostom, *Homilies*, IV: Satan occupies the space under heaven, and incorporeal powers are spirits *of the air* under his operation.

the powers of the air', was not to be interpreted metaphorically. They believed that the physical atmosphere was inhabited by the demonic, and it was into this demon-infested air that Christ entered when He was lifted up on the cross. Athanasius expresses this worldview perfectly in his influential work *On the Incarnation*:

> [Jesus said], when he indicated by what manner of death he would ransom men, 'When I shall be raised up I shall draw all men to myself'… The enemy of our race, the devil, having fallen from heaven moves around *in this lower atmosphere*, and lording it here over his fellow demons in disobedience… to cheat men, and tries to prevent them from rising upwards. The Apostle speaks of this also, 'According to the ruler of the power *of the air*, who now works in the sons of disobedience'.
>
> But the Lord came to overthrow the devil, *purify the air*, and open for us the way up to heaven, as the Apostle said, 'Through the veil, that is, his flesh'. This had to be effected by death, and by what other death would these things have been accomplished save by that which takes place *in the air*? I mean the cross. For only he who expires on the cross dies *in the air*. So it was right for the Lord to endure it. For being raised up in this way he *purified the air* from the wiles of the devil and all the demons, saying, 'I saw Satan falling as lightning'. And he reopened the way *up to heaven*, saying again, 'Lift up your gates, princes, and be raised, everlasting gates'.[19] [my italics]

Athanasius asks fundamental questions. Why did Christ come? What did He do on the cross? Athanasius' answer, reflecting the theological emphasis of the time, is that Christ came to overthrow the devil, purify the air, and open up a way to heaven through that air. And it was as Christ passed through the air in His ascension, that He created a safe way past Satanic dangers for those who followed, an idea which is

19 Athanasius, *On the Incarnation*, XXV. In his Festal Letter for the year 350 Athanasius returned to the same themes: 'Where our Lord Jesus Christ, who took upon Him to die for all, stretched forth His hands, not somewhere on the earth beneath, but in the air itself, in order that the Salvation effected by the Cross might be shown to be for all men everywhere: destroying the devil who was working in the air: and that He might consecrate our road up to Heaven, and make it free.'

directly alluded to by Adomnán in *The Holy Places.*[20] It was believed that when a believer died, he or she had to complete a perilous journey through the air in order to reach glory. This was Cassian's worldview:

> The *atmosphere* which extends between heaven and earth is ever filled with a thick crowd of spirits, which do not fly about in it quietly or idly, so that most fortunately the divine providence has withdrawn them from human sight.[21] [my italics]

The physical space of air was infested with Satan and his treacherous attendants. Clancy and Markus comment that, for Irish monks, the very air which they breathed was filled with demons, and was a place of danger, both physical and spiritual, brought by the fall of Satan and the sin of Adam.[22] Hence Columba and his monks saw themselves living in a space which was surrounded by demonic forces. This influenced how they interpreted Christ's victory on the cross. And this was an outlook woven into the fabric of daily life in the early Irish Church, though not unique to that tradition. In this matter, as in others, early Irish spirituality shared the worldview of Christendom.

The view that the air was the natural habitation of demons explains why, in several episodes of Adomnán's *Life of Columba*, the air is where spiritual conflict is at its most intense. Angels fight with demons 'in the air' (III:6). Souls of dead men and women have to pass through the hostile medium of the 'air' in order to reach heaven (III:13). When such souls are passing through the air they need saintly or angelic guardians (III:10, 11, 12, 14). When Columba confronts the water-beast of the River Ness (II:27), he makes the sign of the cross in the 'empty air' (with 'empty' indicating that demons are unusually absent, possibly because of the sheer holiness which Columba brings).[23]

---

20 Adomnán, *The Holy Places*, I:23.

21 Cassian, *The Second Conference of Abbot Serenus*, 'On Principalities', 31 and 12; cf. Cassian, *Institutes*, V:18.

22 Clancy and Markus, *Iona: The Earliest Poetry of a Celtic Monastery*, 58. On Satan inhabiting the air, and its implications for the atoning work of Christ, see especially: Chapter 19, 'The Triumph of the King'.

23 Reeves and Sharpe, render this simply as 'in the air' in their translations of II:27, whereas the Andersons give the full force of the Latin: 'in the empty (*vacuo*) air'. Adomnán's inclusion of 'empty' would be deliberate. Columba traditions, outside of Adomnán's *Life*, portray Columba having contact with a range of supernatural beings; cf. Cary, 'Varieties of supernatural contact in the *Life* of Adomnán' in John Carey, Máire Herbert and Pádraig

When describing Columba blessing a milk-pail, Adomnán emphasises that Columba makes the sign of the cross 'in the air' (II:16); and in the narrative the words 'in the air' are superfluous unless Adomnán intends to alert the reader to something significant. And the something significant happens: as Columba makes the sign of the cross 'in the air', the milk-pail is violently disturbed because a demon has been concealed in it.

THE SOLDIER'S VOW

Columba was a soldier of Christ. Any soldier, enlisting in any army, took a vow or an oath. So also did monks. All male members of the community referred to one another as 'brothers' (*fratres*), but the term 'monk' (*monachus*) denoted a brother who had committed himself to the abbot and the community through a vow or a promise (*votum*),[24] and one of the earliest evidences of men or women taking a vow when entering the monastic life is found in one of Basil's letters.[25] We have no record of the actual form of words which comprised a monastic vow within the early Irish Church, nor can we assume that all vows referred explicitly to celibacy, poverty and total obedience. Nevertheless, any new recruit would be well aware that he was entering a life of spiritual, military service in which unquestioned obedience toward his superior

Ó Riain (eds), *Saints and Scholars: Studies in Irish Hagiography* (Dublin: Four Courts Press, 2001), 49-62.

24 Anderson and Anderson, *Adomnán's Life of Columba*, li. All monks were termed brothers. An 'oath' taken to another person was '*iuramento*'; cf. II:39. The vow taken by the two men in I:32 (x2) was *votum*. *Votum* is also used of Libran's monastic vow in II:29. This corresponds to the vocabulary of the Vulgate. In the Vulgate the New Testament references most closely approximating to a 'holy vow' occur in Acts 18:18 and 21:23, where *votum* is used. Similarly, *votum* is the consistently preferred term in the Vulgate Old Testament (cf. Genesis 28:20; 31:13; Leviticus 7:16, 22:18; Numbers 6:21, etc.)

25 Basil, *Letters*, 199, 'Concerning fallen virgins, who, after professing a chaste life before the Lord, *make their vows vain*, ... I do not recognise the profession of men, except in the case of those who have enrolled themselves in the order of monks, and seem to have secretly adopted the celibate life. Yet in their case I think it becoming that there should be a previous examination, and that *a distinct profession should be received from them*, so that whenever they revert to the life of the pleasures of the flesh, they may be subjected to the punishment of fornicators.' cf. Basil, *The Shorter Rule*, Qu. 7:14, and also, Silvas, *The Rule of St. Basil in Latin and English: A Revised Critical Edition*, 89, fn. 41, who argues that Basil was the first to institute a formal monastic profession, and was deliberately introducing the idea of an irrevocable public vow for both men and women as something of a new principle. Morison, *St. Basil and his Rule: A Study in Early Monasticism*, 92f., agrees with Silvas. Basil, *The Longer Rule*, 10, advises great care in admitting a new brother: a would-be monk should be given every opportunity to understand what monastic life meant.

was expected. When he made his vow, he went to the church, knelt, and offered himself to God as a 'living-sacrifice'. There was a simple form of words signalling his acceptance of the abbot's authority and his own commitment to the holy life. If poverty, chastity, and obedience were not avowed explicitly, they were part of the reality of monasticism. Renunciation of wealth was a *sine qua non.* Sexual self-control was demanded. And, undergirding all else, the assumption of obedience to the abbot was undisputed.[26]

Adomnán cites two instances of monastic vows being taken. The first is when two men arrive on Iona wanting to be pilgrims at Columba's monastery for a year (I:32). Columba explains that they cannot stay for such a long period without first taking the monastic vow. They accept Columba's conditions. They enter the church with Columba. They kneel. They make that commitment, and in doing so they place themselves under the abbot's authority. The story is unusual in that they take the monastic vows without a period of probation. The monastic life was exacting, and the vow was irrevocable; therefore, it was standard practice to make eager recruits wait before making a final decision. After becoming monks, there could be no going back.[27] Good abbots warned new arrivals that the monastic life was hard, not easy. That was also Benedict's approach. He emphasised that newcomers were not to be admitted too easily. They were given every opportunity, over a length of time, to see how demanding it could be.

The second instance of vow-taking is when a man named Libran comes to Columba wanting to do penance for sin and also wanting to join the community (II:39). In this instance, Columba makes Libran aware of the heavy discipline of monastic life. Libran's story is complicated by the fact that he arrives on Iona in the aftermath of having committed grave sins. This means that Columba immediately obligates him to complete seven years of penance. These seven years double up as preparation for taking his monastic vows. After seven

---

26 Benedict's monks had to obey the abbot unreservedly; cf. Benedict, *Rule*, IV.

27 Benedict, *The Rule*, LVIII, implies that any desire to leave the monastery would be a suggestion from the devil; cf. Basil, *The Shorter Rule*, Qu. 7:14-15: 'Once they have been received, if perchance they transgress their resolve, then they ought to be regarded as those who have acted perversely against God, before whom as witness they professed the covenant of their confession.'

years, Libran was well aware of what being a monk involved as he 'devoutly vowed the monastic vow'.

Having made the vow, a monk was tied to the will of his abbot, and all abbots expected total obedience.[28] A monk could not come and go as he wished.[29] Even if a monk wanted to go on a spiritual retreat, permission had to be sought and granted. On one occasion, Columba prophesied that a voyage made by the monk Cormac to find a place of spiritual contemplation would come to nothing (I:6). This was not due to any fault of Cormac's, but because in his group there was a brother who had sailed without seeking his abbot's consent.[30] Every community was under the firm control of the abbot, who had the awesome responsibility of piloting them to a heavenly haven. That was a huge task, and there could only be a successful outcome if monks complied unquestioningly with their abbot's rule and direction. As soldiers of Christ they regarded their abbot as commanding officer standing in Christ's place, and they gave to their abbot the same obedience as any soldier gave to his Field Marshall in time of war.

THE IONA ARMY

The cohort of monks on Iona comprised several groups.[31] There were **Pupils** (*alumni*), not yet full monks, having not yet taken the vow. These were usually older youths of at least seventeen years of age. One promising youth, named Virgno, is described by Adomnán as being of 'good ability' (III:19), and is referred to as a brother. He eventually became Iona's abbot (605–623). There were **Working-Brothers** who did physically demanding work: some in agriculture and fishing, and some busying themselves in the monastic workshops, specialising in wood and metal. When Columba visited Clonmacnoise in Ireland, the monks at work in the fields flocked to meet him, 'assembling with

28 cf. Benedict, *The Rule*, V.

29 Basil, *The Shorter Rule*, Qu. 80:1f., 'Ought one to go anywhere without a mention from the one who presides? Since the Lord says, "I have not come that I might do anything of myself, but it was he who sent me" (John 7:28), how much less ought each of us to give himself permission!'

30 Herren and Brown, *Christ in Celtic Christianity*, 34, argue that Iona monks had to stay within the monastic enclosure. However, they may be giving too strict an interpretation. If the island was wholly populated by the monastic community (III:23), such limitations would be unnecessary in order to maintain separateness from the world.

31 Finlay, *Columba*, 113. Anderson and Anderson, *Adomnán's Life of Columba*, li.

those who were inside' (I:3). Yet these young, fit, and active brothers were not restricted to labour, and took their turn at literary activities and tutoring. The **Seniors** were older monks, regarded as wiser and more experienced. Seniors who were no longer physically strong occupied themselves in the more sedentary aspects of monastic life, such as reading, writing, and teaching, though some still took part in light manual labour (I:37). It is important to note that terms such as 'Working Brother' or 'Senior' are functional descriptions used for practical purposes, and do not signify different orders of monks. There was no ceremony marking the transition from a Working Brother to a Senior. Another group were the **Lay-brothers**, and these were monks who were not ordained to the holy offices of deacon or priest, and perhaps never would be. Some Lay-brothers lived in the villages nearby, and some were married.

Early Irish monasteries aligned themselves closely to their local tribe (*tuath*), and the presence of the local lay population was a natural part of monastic life. Few monastic communities could survive without support from that wider community.[32] But was there a resident lay population on Iona? It appears not. It seems that the island community consisted only of brothers and monks, with Iona becoming a spiritual citadel par excellence. Evidence indicating the lack of a resident lay-population on Iona comes in Adomnán's account of Columba's death.[33] In Adomnán's text, Columba prophesies that, 'The men and women of the lay-population will not be able to come to my funeral at all. Only the monks of my own community will carry out my burial and perform the funeral duties' (III:23). Adomnán then describes how a week-long violent storm meant that no one was able to land on the island during the week of Columba's funeral, fulfilling Columba's prediction. This story has been interpreted to mean that no one lived on the island outside the monastic community, with the phrase, 'monks of my own community' referring to all members of the monastic household, even to those who had not taken vows.[34] Iona was taken over by monks.

32 David Clarke, Alice Blackwell and Martin Goldberg, *Early Medieval Scotland: Individuals, Communities and Ideas (*Edinburgh: National Museums of Scotland 2012), 84.

33 cf. Aidan MacDonald, 'Adomnán's Monastery of Iona' in Bourke (ed.), *Studies in the Cult of Saint Columba*, 32.

34 Anderson and Anderson, *Adomnán's Life of Columba*, lii.

There is no clear evidence of nuns on Iona during Columba's abbacy, or during the abbacies immediately following. The early-medieval Irish Church did have some female communities, and Adomnán alludes to a 'monastery of maidens' (II:41), though not on Iona but on Rathlin Island off the northern coast of Ireland. We know that fifty years before Adomnán penned his *Life of Columba*, communities of nuns were established in Iona-inspired Northumbria, one of which was founded at Coldingham by Ebbe, the sister of King Oswald. The Northumbrian Church went on to have a proliferation of female monastic communities, often led by an unmarried or widowed member of the royal family. The Iona Nunnery whose ruins can be seen today, is from a later period.

Whichever identifying label was applied to an individual, all were soldiers of Christ. A brother was a soldier of Christ. A monk was a soldier of Christ. An abbot was a soldier of Christ. A bishop was a soldier of Christ. Nuns and abbesses were female soldiers of Christ. The calling to be *miles Christi* was at the heart of every appointment and every activity. That description indicates the true nature of the work which monks were involved in. Daily they donned their spiritual armour. Daily they engaged in battle with Satan and his legions. Daily they fought for the good of their own souls. Daily they battled for the extension of God's kingdom in the world around them. And in this military campaign their leader was the abbot.

PART ONE
ABBOT

CHAPTER 5

Status, Reputation, Office

Columba was the unquestioned leader on Iona, with his status described as *abbas*, *pater*, *sanctus pater*, *patronus*, and *senior*. The term 'abbot' recognised Columba as Father of the Community and invested him with a level of authority equal to that enjoyed by a father in any sixth-century household. Benedict went as far as to state that an abbot held the place of Christ in a monastic community, and had the titles 'lord' and 'abbot' out of honour for Christ Himself.[1] Benedict stressed also that high honour brought with it high responsibility, and abbots should be aware that, 'at the fearful judgement of God, not only the abbot's teaching but his disciples' obedience will come under scrutiny'. The Irish Church viewed its abbots likewise.

Columba was also his community's patron (*patronus*), since he was considered to have been the founder of Iona's monastery, discounting any Christian presence on the island before his arrival. In due course his protective patronage was viewed as continuing beyond his death, and all subsequent abbots of Iona were regarded as heirs of Columba (*comharba Choluim Chille*).[2]

In the Irish system, each major monastery had its own *paruchia*, consisting of groups of geographically scattered religious houses, each acknowledging the abbot of the main monastery as the common head.[3] The abbot was autonomous within his *paruchia* and, if he had the ability to lead his communities with inspirational zeal and energy, then the *paruchia* could expand almost limitlessly. No higher ecclesiastical authority dictated the limits of its bounds. Subsidiary monastic settlements were managed by a senior monk, often carrying the title of

1 Benedict, *The Rule*, II, LXIII.

2 Markus, *Conceiving a nation*, 157. Markus suggests that subsequent abbots 'inherited' something of Columba's authority. When Adomnán wrote about Columba, he was underlining his own authority as Columba's successor.

3 Hughes, *Early Christian Ireland: Introduction to the Sources*, 71.

'prior', who was appointed by the abbot and subject to him.[4] Iona, plus its subordinate institutions in Scotland and Ireland, formed Columba's *paruchia*, with Columba selecting monks from his own community to govern the daughter-institutions under his authority.[5] In these appointments, kinship was as important as in secular society,[6] and few without kinship ties to the abbot were ever appointed to authority roles. This was accepted as normal within the prevailing culture. Columba made his cousin Baithéne prior of the daughter-monastery on Tiree, and he appointed his uncle Ernan as prior on Hinba.[7]

CREDIBILITY

Despite the growing importance of monasteries, monasticism was not a recognised part of Church order in the same way as the diocesan system was. However influential the monastic movement became, it was essentially a para-organisation. Likewise, taking a monk's vow was not the same as being ordained to one of the three recognised offices of deacon, priest, or bishop. Similarly, abbacy was merely about being the leader, guardian and mentor of a group of monks, with each abbot elected by the monks themselves and not appointed by the wider Church. Nor was an abbot's appointment an ordination. Abbacy was a function, not an office. Throughout Christendom there were only three universally recognised clerical offices, and abbacy was not one of them. At the Columban daughter-monastery on Lindisfarne the post of abbot was combined with that of bishop (at the insistence of the Northumbrian kings), but the ordination which accompanied that appointment related to the abbot's episcopal role and not to his abbacy. Deacons, priests, and bishops were regarded as having been established by divine command, with their terminology mentioned in the New Testament, but monks were not. Nor were abbots. Such roles, however commendable, were humanly instituted. For some, this created a problem with Columba.

---

4 cf. Benedict, *The Rule*, LXV: 'The prior for his part is to carry out respectfully what his abbot assigns to him and do nothing contrary to the abbot's wishes or arrangements.'

5 Herbert, *Iona, Kells and Derry*, 33.

6 In an early-medieval context 'secular' meant 'non-monastic' in contrast to the modern meaning of 'non-religious'. Thus, there could be 'secular priests' and 'secular monks'.

7 Adomnán refers to the post of prior four times. Twice Baithéne is termed prior of Iona's daughter-monastery on Tiree (I:30; I:41). Ernan is referred to as prior on Hinba (I:45). Luigne is referred to as prior on the 'island of Elen' (II:18).

In the early 700s Bede was scholar-in-residence at the Wearmouth-Jarrow monastery in northern England. His day job was as 'principal private secretary' to the abbot, alongside which he busied himself with bookish activities, writing his *Ecclesiastical History of the English People*, his *Lives of the Abbots*, plus an array of biblical and religious treatises. Bede belonged to the Roman Church tradition, which had advanced steadily northwards ever since Augustine of Canterbury arrived in Kent in 597. In his *History*, Bede wanted to celebrate the achievements of his own Church tradition, but was also aware that an Iona mission, based on Lindisfarne, had evangelised parts of Northumbria several decades before the Roman Church arrived. That Lindisfarne mission achieved brilliant results despite its heyday of supremacy being surprisingly brief – from the early 630s when King Oswald first invited missionaries from Iona, until 664 when it was eclipsed by the Roman tradition after the Synod of Whitby.

Bede was intellectually and spiritually convinced of the superiority of his Roman tradition. Nevertheless, he had no intention of editing out the contribution made by others. Bede was fair-minded. He was aware of the saintliness of men and women such as Aidan, Cuthbert and Ebbe. And although Bede disagreed profoundly with many of their practices, he accepted that their reputations transcended ecclesiastical divisions. Bede also knew that these spiritual giants had a faith moulded by Iona spirituality, even if some of them had never visited the island.[8] He was also aware that it was Columba who had made Iona what it was, and so Bede included Columba in his *History.* This brought two problems.

THE PROBLEM OF STATUS

Bede's first difficulty concerned Columba's reputation as it was now viewed in Northumbria. At Whitby, Wilfrid had been the main protagonist for the Roman Church over against the Columban tradition, and he insinuated doubt about the validity of Columba's ministry. Wilfrid was a brilliant if an unscrupulous debater. He lambasted what he saw as the arrogance of the Irish Church in thinking it was correct and the rest of the Christian world was wrong: 'The only people who stupidly contend against the whole world are those Irish men, and

8 Bede, *Life of Cuthbert*, XVI, lauded Aidan. Herren and Brown, *Christ in Celtic Christianity*, 40, suggest that Bede saw Aidan's model of the abbot-bishop as consistent with Pope Gregory's recommendations to Augustine of Canterbury.

their partners in obstinacy the Picts and Britons.'[9] Wilfrid knew that if he could undermine Columba's personal spiritual legitimacy, then his opponents would be seriously weakened. He therefore hinted heavily that Columba was well-meaning but misguided. Crucially, Columba was suspect in that he had only been an abbot and never a bishop. In the Roman Church, bishops were the leaders, strategists, authority figures, and the men whose advice and direction could be followed with confidence. Abbots were not mentioned in Scripture, but bishops were. Abbots were not part of an apostolic succession in an unbroken line from the first apostles, but bishops were. Throughout Christendom, it was bishops, not abbots, who were bestowed with authority through ordination. Columba had never been ordained to the office of bishop. Therefore, to what extent had his role ever been valid? Had he been self-appointed? Had he usurped a leadership position which should belong to a bishop whose abilities, gifts, and orthodoxy were recognised by the wider Church? Wilfrid pushed his arguments home, damaging Columba's standing in Northumbria; and when Bede wrote about Columba, he knew this was a problematic issue for many of his readers.

Bede was never as abusive in his comments as Wilfrid could be, but he was equally uncomfortable with the Irish set-up, and particularly with what he understood to be its relationship between bishop and abbot. It was not that the Irish Church had no bishops: it had scores of them. But the available literature does not portray bishops of the Irish Church as the power-players, which bishops of the Roman tradition were. In the Roman Church it was the bishop who had power, whereas in the Irish Church that belonged to the abbot. An Irish bishop was a spiritual person rather than a leader. Meek notes that an abbot such as Columba, who was the central figure throughout the Iona *paruchia*, was in effect the 'chief executive officer' of a group of businesses, 'closer to our own management-driven form of secular life than we might dare to think: and abbots of monasteries, like Chief Executives of our day, were powerful people'.[10]

Lying behind this were the different ways in which the Roman and Irish Churches were organised. In the Roman Church the base unit was

---

9 Bede, *History*, III:25.

10 D. Meek, 'St. Columba and Celtic Christianity' in Randall (ed.), *In Search of Colmcille*, 35.

the geographical diocese, of which the diocesan bishop was head. But in the Irish Church the base unit was the monastery, where the abbot held sway.[11] The diocesan structure of the Roman Church evolved from the political structures of the later Roman Empire, with the Church on the Continent copying the Empire's form of secular governance. But Ireland had never been colonised by Rome, and Irish society had never been organised on the Roman model. Instead, the Irish Church modelled itself on the core structures of indigenous Irish society, which were the various tribes or *tuaths*. Thus, whereas the Roman Church was geographically organised, the Irish Church was, by and large, tribally organised with an emphasis on kinship ties.[12] Each monastery had an association with a particular *tuath*, making the Irish Church a decentralised organisation.[13]

Diocesan bishoprics were not unknown in early Irish Christianity; and Curran, Hughes, and Markus all suggest that later monastic writers may have exaggerated the role of the abbot and may have downplayed the role of diocesan bishops during Ireland's earliest Christian period.[14] Similarly, Máire and Liam de Paor are aware of a view that Patrick's Church was not primarily monastic, with Patrick described as placing bishops and priests in charge of churches, and with only one instance in his era of a church being handed over to an abbot.[15] Be that as it may, it was centuries after Columba before a truly diocesan system was re-introduced to Ireland. During the 'golden

11 MacLauchlan, *The Early Scottish Church*, 165, argues that when Patrick planted 300 bishops in Ireland the term 'bishop' equated to that of 'presbyter', 'priest', or 'pastor', rather to that of diocesan bishop. This interpretation is contested.

12 De Paor, *Early Christian Ireland*, 50f.

13 Herren and Brown, *Christ in Celtic Christianity*, 4.

14 Curran, *The Antiphonary of Bangor and the Early Irish Monastic Liturgy*, 159ff., points out that the earliest missionaries to Ireland may have tried to introduce a diocesan system. Hughes, *Early Christian Ireland: Introduction to the Sources*, 71ff., argues that ancient Irish Law Tracts may be more reliable indicators than monastic texts for what really happened during the sixth and seventh centuries. She notes that these indicate a continuing power tension between bishops (who regarded themselves as having diocesan powers) and abbots of monasteries, but that the later writers of history, the monastic scribes, gloss over this. Monastic scribes give the impression that bishop's powers were non-existent. When the Irish Church exported itself to Argyll etc., it did so through the monasteries, which partly explains why Bede thought that abbots were all-powerful. Hughes holds that the Law Tracts, from the earliest days of the Church in Ireland, may more truly represent what was happening on the ground, since they deal with real life legal situations, and not 'edited' history; cf. Markus, *Conceiving a Nation*, 138f.

15 De Paor, *Early Christian Ireland*, 33.

years', the monastery was the fundamental unit, not the diocese, and abbots carried more power than bishops. Bede was aware of this. He did not approve:

> Iona is always ruled by an abbot in priest's orders, to whose authority the whole province, including the bishops, is subject, *contrary to the usual custom.* This practice was established by its first abbot Columba, who was not a bishop himself, but a priest and a monk.[16] [my italics]

In writing that Irish bishops were subject to abbots, Bede may have misunderstood their relationship. Nevertheless, Columba not being a bishop was a major stumbling-block, and Rome struggled with the legitimacy of any Church which was not *de facto* governed by bishops. How could a Church not governed by bishops be approved by God? Ninian, Patrick, and Augustine of Canterbury had all been bishops, but not Columba. Bede's ideal was Cuthbert of Lindisfarne who was both abbot and bishop.[17] But in Ireland there was no extensive ecclesiastical hierarchy as was rapidly developing in the Roman Church.[18] In Ireland the abbot was king. Moreover, in Ireland, although the Pope was deeply respected, neither he nor any part of the Roman Church was deemed to have authority over what happened there. All of this was a problem. Had Columba ever been a legitimate leader, appointed and approved by God? From the viewpoint of the Roman tradition the answer was 'No'.

---

16 Bede, *History*, III:4. Markus, *Conceiving a Nation*, 140, argues that Bede may be citing Iona as an *exception* to what was found everywhere else (even in Ireland); that bishops exercised day-to-day authority in the Church; and that the phrase 'contrary to the usual custom' implies contrary to the usual custom in Ireland, not just contrary to the custom of the Roman Church. However, Markus's argument is heavily dependent on his interpretation of Bede and on Irish documents from two centuries later than Columba.

17 Clare Stancliffe, 'Cuthbert and the polarity between Pastor and Solitary' in Bonner, G., Rollason, D. and Stancliffe, C. (eds), *St. Cuthbert, His Cult and Community to A.D. 1200* (Rochester: Boydell Press, 1987), 40; cf. Herren and Brown, *Christ in Celtic Christianity*, 171, '[Cuthbert] was a model figure for Bede in that he governed Lindisfarne as a monastic bishop after the fashion of Augustine at Canterbury.' Given that there was no resident bishop on Iona, presumably monks were ordained priests by bishops in Ireland or brought from Ireland for the purpose. Who ordained Aidan as a bishop before he went to Northumbria? Was he given the title in retrospect? cf. Barbara Yorke, *The Conversion of Britain: 600–800*, 153.

18 Similarly, in the indigenous Irish political system the primary allegiance was to the local 'lord' or 'king', with no 'central government'; cf. Hughes, *Early Christian Ireland: Introduction to the Sources*, 53.

THE PROBLEM OF SOURCES

Bede's second difficulty concerned sources. Bede was not a twenty-first-century historian, but he had the instincts of a first-class scholar. For example, his commitment to high standards made him secure primary documents from the papal archives in Rome in order to flesh out his account of the mission sent by Gregory in 597.[19] Wherever possible, Bede built on good evidence, but sometimes all he could do was to retell another's tale and use material saturated with a strong flavour of legend. But Bede tried to assess his sources critically, and when he turns his attention to Columba, he indicates that some of his information is from sources which cause him concern:

> [Columba's] life and sayings are *said to have been* recorded in writing by his disciples; but, whatever type of man he *may have been*,[20] we know for certain that he left successors distinguished for their purity of life, their love of God, and their loyalty to the monastic rule.[21] [my italics]

This extract introduces several issues. First, Bede indicates he is aware that accounts of Columba's life had already been written but has not been able to consult them.[22] This means that the extensive Wearmouth-Jarrow monastic library did not have copies of Cumméne's *Book of the Powers of Saint Columba*, or of Adomnán's *Life of Columba.* Aldfrith, who was King of Northumberland from 686 to 705, had a library at his royal palace, and the Wearmouth-Jarrow monastic library was also well-stocked. A substantial collection of manuscripts was brought to it by Benedict Biscop from his five trips to the Continent; and Abbot Ceolfrith virtually doubled its capacity. It also had books borrowed from Lindisfarne and Canterbury.[23] However, there is no indication

---

19 Bede, *History*, 'Preface'. Bede's 'Preface' is an impressive example of a scholar explaining his methodology; cf. Bede, *Lives of the Abbots*, Chapter 11, in which he describes the library set up by Benedict Biscop at Monkwearmouth-Jarrow.

20 Does Bede's phrase, 'whatever type of man he may have been', hint at Columba's reputation having been questioned? Does it contrast Columba with his successors? Was Columba so much belittled in Northumbria that his very character was in doubt? Or is Bede simply indicating that his own knowledge of Columba is limited?

21 Bede, *History*, III:4.

22 cf. Dales, *Light to the Isles*, 60.

23 See: Bede, *Lives of the Abbots*, and the anonymous, *Life of Ceolfrith*. The Biscop/Ceolfrith collections would be too early to include Adomnán's *Life of Columba;* cf. M. L. W. Latimer, 'The Library of the Venerable Bede' in Hamilton Thomson (ed.), *Bede: His Life, Times, and Writings* (Oxford: Clarendon, 1935), 238-47.

that a copy of Adomnán's *Life of Columba* was available for consultation by Bede, either in the royal library at Bamburgh or in the monastery. Second, the phrase 'said to have been', which Bede uses in reference to Columba, resembles phrases employed by him elsewhere in his *History* where he indicates reservations about the available data. An instance of this is in connection with a legend about Gregory the Great.[24] Another is in connection with Bede's sources for Ninian of Whithorn and the impact which Ninian was 'said to have had' on the 'southern Picts'.[25] In each case Bede is asking the reader to note that, in this particular section of his work, he is merely echoing what others have told him.

All of this impinges on Bede's account of Christianity north of Hadrian's Wall. Much of Bede's information for the spread of the Christian faith in the west and north came from two sources. One source was his friend Pecthelm, the seventh-century abbot of Whithorn, who relayed to Bede some Whithorn traditions about the Church in south-west Scotland and its reputation further afield. The other source was envoys sent by the Christian King Nechtan of the Picts to Abbot Ceolfrith of Wearmouth-Jarrow in the 710s, when Nechtan sought advice from Ceolfrith about changing the Church polity of his own Pictish kingdom. Bede was in his thirties when Nechtan's emissaries arrived and may have quizzed the envoys himself about how Christian faith came to Pictland. If so, these envoys would relate the Columba story as understood by them more than a century after the events. By that date the northern Picts were Christianised, and they may have revised their history to give the impression that their Pictish forebears responded with enthusiasm to Columba's preaching, in contrast to the Iona tradition which indicates a flatter response.[26] The same Pictish spin may account for Bede believing that Iona had been gifted to Columba by the Picts, whereas the Irish/Iona tradition was that the island had been granted by King Conall of Dál Riata.[27] Bede may have been unaware of contradictory data;

---

24 Bede, *History*, II:1. P. H. Blair, *The World of Bede* (London: Secker & Warburg, 1970), 75ff., discusses Bede's careful use of language when using such sources.

25 Bede, *History*, III:4.

26 Markus, *Conceiving a Nation*, 178, argues that by 697, when the *Law of the Innocents* was adopted in Ireland and much of Pictland, Columba was held in high honour in Pictland.

27 *Annals of Ulster*, 574.2: 'Conall son of Comgall, who granted the island of I to Colum Cille.'

but he was conscious of relying on a thin line of evidence. Hence his cautious wording.

DEACON, PRIEST, AND ABBOT

In post-Whitby Northumbria, Columba's legitimacy came under hostile scrutiny; but in the Irish Church tradition his status was unquestioned. Of the three recognised ordained offices within the Christian Church, Columba occupied two of them during his lifetime. He was first a deacon and then a priest. The diaconate was the junior office, and Columba served as a deacon during his training in Ireland, first under Gemman of Leinster and then under Finnian of Clonard (I:1, II:1, 25). In this role Columba gave practical assistance to the priests and was responsible for making some of the arrangements for the Eucharist. The *Penitential of Finnian* informs us that, in early-medieval Ireland, deacons were also permitted to baptise, which may have been a functional necessity given a scarcity of priests and given the desire of parents to have their infants baptised as soon after birth as possible.[28] This elevated deacons above ordinary monks who could not baptise or receive alms.[29]

Though deacons could baptise, only an ordained priest could celebrate the Eucharist or pronounce absolution. It appears that Columba was ordained a priest before he left Finnian's tutelage. On Iona, at least three, and possibly four, of the monks were priests. These were Columba, Baithéne, and Ernan, with Mael Odrain mocu-Curin the other possibility (II:15, I:20, 44, 45). In his *Life of Columba* Adomnán employs *presbyter* as his preferred and almost exclusive term to refer to priests.[30] This contrasts with Bede whose preferred term for a priest is *sacerdos*, a word which Adomnán rarely uses.[31] Why this difference in vocabulary? Was one used by the Irish tradition, and the other by the Roman tradition? Not necessarily, since *sacerdos* is used in the Irish liturgical document, the *Bangor Antiphonary*.[32] Adomnán may have preferred *presbyter* for the ordained office since that was the most

---

28 *Penitential of Finnian*, Canon 49.

29 *Penitential of Finnian*, Canon 50.

30 Adomnán, *Life of Columba*, I:2, I:20 (in conjunction with *sacerdos*); I:36 (4x); I:40 (2x); I:44 (Andersons: 'presbyters', Sharpe: 'priest'); I:45 (2x); II:9 (2x); II:15 (2x); III:2; III:9. Reeves, Andersons, Sharpe, nearly always render 'presbyter' as 'priest'.

31 Adomnán, *Life of Columba*, I:20 (in conjunction with *presbyter*).

32 e.g., *Bangor Antiphonary*, Items, 6, 8, 41, etc.

common term used in the Latin translations of the New Testament which he was familiar with.

Was there a bishop on Iona? There may have a resident bishop on the island during Adomnán's abbacy, since a Bishop of Iona is one of the guarantors of *The Law of the Innocents* at the Synod of Birr in 697.[33] But there is no indication in the *Life of Columba* that there was a permanent bishop there during Columba's abbacy. From time to time bishops came to Iona to visit Columba, sometimes anonymously (I:44), but there is no suggestion that Columba ever regarded himself as being under the authority of a bishop, nor would we expect this within the Irish system. Instead, fellow abbots had a system of mutual recognition of authority across monastic *paruchiae*. This meant, for example, that if an individual was disciplined by any abbot in any of the *paruchiae*, then that discipline was respected and enforced by all the others.

Columba was tough. As abbot, he exercised total control over his monks, and complete obedience was given, because each monk trusted that his abbot could bring him safely to the heavenly kingdom. That was the abbot's fundamental duty. It was belief in an abbot's ability in that vital role, which created his reputation. Men did not come to Iona as dilettantes, who were vaguely seeking spiritual insights. Men became monks in order to be saved, and to have union with God through purification of the soul.[34] They put themselves under Columba's rule for a purpose. And the one thing that mattered about any abbot was his ability to deliver those in his care to eternal glory. That was what counted. All else was embellishment.

Columba's status was enhanced by being a nobleman of the powerful Ui Neill. This gave him natural links with secular leaders, and his monastic federation profited from these.[35] Reeves, in his introductory

33 cf. MacDonald, 'Adomnán's Monastery of Iona' in Bourke (ed.), *Studies in the Cult of Saint Columba*, 28.

34 Morison, *St. Basil and his Rule: A Study in Early Monasticism*, 22; cf. Pseudo-Basil, *Ascetical Discourse (II)*: 'The ascetical life has one aim: the soul's salvation, and all that can contribute to this end must be observed with as much fear as a divine command. The commandments of God themselves, indeed, have no other end in view than the salvation of him who obeys them. It therefore behoves those undertaking the ascetical life to enter upon the way of philosophy, stripped of all worldly and material things in the same manner as they who enter the bath take off all their clothing.'

35 Herbert, *Iona, Kells and Derry*, 124.

notes to Adomnán's *Life of Columba*, points out that whatever type of exile from Ireland Columba embraced when he moved to Iona, it did not cut him off from the connections which he had there.[36] Similarly, Herbert emphasises that Columba maintained contact with movers and shakers on both sides of the Irish Sea, receiving regular news of Irish political events.[37] Columba sent emissaries to his homeland. He welcomed a stream of pilgrims, penitents, and aspiring monks. He returned to Ireland many times. And he was visited on Iona by highly respected fellow abbots.

Columba did not go to seed on Iona. The opposite was the case. He had vibrant links with his peers; he fostered contacts with the power-figures of society; he dealt with kings such as Conall and Áedán of Dál Riata, Bridei of Pictland, and Rhydderch of Strathclyde. The abbot of Iona may not have had the name or office of a bishop, but he carried all the influence of one. Although abbacy was not a formal, ordained holy office such as that of deacon, priest or bishop, the *de facto* reality was that it operated as such, especially in the Irish Church. Columba's outstanding abilities and energy exploited this role to the full. And if the power of an abbot of the Irish church life confused and disturbed Bede, it did not trouble Iona's monks. They accepted that their abbot was their commander-in-chief. Monks revered their abbot. He was their inspirer, spiritual director, and interpreter of the Word of God. He safeguarded orthodoxy of belief and practice. He saw to it that his community adhered to the liturgy, creeds, and culture of Christendom. Above all else, he piloted his monks through the hazards and dangers of this life to glory in the next.

---

36 Reeves, *Life of Saint Columba, Founder of Hy*, xxxiv-xxxvii.

37 Herbert, *Iona, Kells and Derry*, 30.

CHAPTER 6

Captain, Guardian, Enforcer

A monastery and its community were like a ship and a ship's company, with the abbot exercising the same autocratic power as the captain of a great vessel.[1] Like masters of sea-going ships, abbots had total control, and for good reason. A sea captain has personal responsibility for ensuring that his vessel and all carried within it reach journey's end safely. To achieve this, he is given comprehensive authority. In similar fashion, abbots had personal responsibility for ensuring that those in their monastic vessel completed their pilgrimage and reached the heavenly harbour.[2] This was why monks submitted to their abbot's dictatorial leadership. His captaincy would determine the outcome of their pilgrimage. Any penance which the abbot imposed, and any discipline which he enforced, were accepted for that reason. The journey was a perilous one. Souls could flounder on the way. The abbot was the captain of the barque they had chosen to sail in, and it was he who had the responsibility of navigating a turbulent, spiritual ocean. For the good of all, his word was law, and submission was a price worth paying, because a skilled abbot could pilot to the safe haven. This was why men came to Iona. They committed themselves to Columba's captaincy. They trusted that under his abbacy they had a surer hope of reaching glory.

---

1 *Bangor Antiphonary*, Item 95 (cf. Item 41), likens a monastic community to a Ship or Ark: 'Ship never turbulent, though skimmed by waves, also prepared for wedding festivities, as spouse for the Lord King' [Tr. D. R. Howlett, *The Celtic Latin Tradition of Biblical Style* (Dublin: Four Courts Press, 1995) 191]. O'Reilly reflects on this in her article, 'Reading the Scriptures in the Life of Columba' in Bourke (ed.), *Studies in the Cult of St Columba*, 91f., where she discusses (II:42) in the light of the 'ark' metaphor. She points out that the Bangor community saw itself as the living embodiment of the Ark of the Covenant as did other monasteries. The monastic community saw itself as a special location of the divine presence in the midst of the new chosen people (the Church) on its pilgrimage through this life to the heavenly paradise of the new Jerusalem. The monastic community was the new 'Ark'. Belonging to it could take a person safely to the end of the journey.

2 cf. Basil, *The Longer Rule*, 25.

This aspect of an abbot's responsibility is explicit in Adomnán's narrative. When he writes about Columba's birth, he records that Eithne, Columba's expectant mother, heard a voice declaring that her son was predestined to be a 'leader of innumerable souls to the heavenly country' (III:1). Elsewhere, he writes that the monk Finten is destined to be an abbot in order to become, 'leader of souls to the heavenly kingdom' (I:2). Adomnán repeats this sentiment a few sentences later, noting that Finten is to build a monastery and 'lead unnumbered souls to the heavenly country'. For Adomnán, Columba, Finten, and all abbots, a central feature of their calling was leading those under their charge to glory. Benedict saw abbacy in the same way, reminding colleagues that on judgement day each abbot 'will surely have to submit a reckoning to the Lord for all their souls, and indeed for his own as well'.[3]

The abbot was accountable for ensuring that his flock pilgrimaged successfully. To achieve this, he was given unquestioned power; and though Columba may never have compiled a formal written *Rule* for Iona monks as Benedict did for his, he directed his community as a powerful enforcer.[4] He enforced poverty. He enforced piety. He enforced purity. He enforced penance. These enforcements were welcomed by his monks, because these kept them safe from spiritual shipwreck. In being their enforcer Columba also became their guardian, with the *Amra* describing him as, 'the leader of nations, who guarded the living'.[5] Columba disciplined his community with uncompromising high standards because he had the serious duty of enabling them to reach heaven itself.

'HE HAS FREED HIS MONKS FROM WEALTH'

Wealth was a major obstacle on the pilgrimage to heaven. The *Life of Anthony* and the *Life of Martin* both taught that abandonment of riches was a prerequisite for salvation. Wealth hindered a soul from gaining the kingdom of God, and the issue was so serious that love of possessions could result in automatic exclusion from heaven, no matter what else a pilgrim might do for God. The Scriptures taught that the

3 Benedict, *The Rule*, II.

4 The so-called *Rule of St. Columba* was not written by Columba. Skene includes it in his *Celtic Scotland*, vol. II, 508, Appendix II.

5 *Amra* I; cf. *Amra*, VI, 'He was an ample fort for the stranger' which also stresses the notion of guardianship and refuge.

love of money was the root of all sin, with Jesus' parable about camels and needles warning of the difficulties faced by the wealthy in entering the Kingdom of Heaven (Mark 10:25). This was a big issue.

Some came to Iona to pray. Some to escape their enemies. Some to do penance. Some to live out the remainder of their days. A significant number came because they needed to divest themselves of possessions, goods, and wealth, before they could even begin to think of being saved. Taking the monk's habit placed riches out of reach, since the monastic life involved the immediate shedding of worldly assets. Hence, becoming a monk was a positive step towards safety. Beccán's honour-poem to Columba, *Fo Reir Choluimb*, declares:

The one best thing of all things:
He has freed his monks from wealth. [6]

In these lines Beccán expresses gratitude that Columba's abbacy and discipline meant that his monks lived lives divested of possessions. Columba imposed a lifestyle which freed them from that clawing evil, and his enforcements resulted in them running the spiritual race unencumbered. Beccán's poem may also hint that Columba himself had feared that wealth and privilege might disqualify him from salvation. Though Columba had been a monk from his youth, he came from a reasonably high-ranking family, and could still access comforts of life if he wanted to. It may have been in order to embrace a truly austere life and to fully separate himself from ease, that Columba exiled himself.

Basil and Cassian both connect acquisition of wealth with distance from God's kingdom. Basil taught that gold is the soul's foe and is 'the father of sin and the agent of the devil'.[7] Elsewhere, Basil makes a theological connection between greed and original sin, writing that covetousness is the root of all evil because it involves idolatry of possessions, making it the 'approach to hell'.[8] Over against the evils of

6 Clancy and Markus, *Iona: The Earliest Poetry of a Celtic Monastery*, 137f.; cf. Columbanus, *Monk's Rules*, VI: 'Nakedness and disdain for riches are the first perfection of monks. The second is the purging of vices. The third the most perfect and perpetual love of God and unceasing affection for things divine, which follows the forgetfulness of earthly things.'

7 Basil, *Letters*, 52.

8 Basil, *Letters*, 53. Commenting on the sin of accepting money from candidates for ordination Basil writes: 'They think that there is no sin because they take the money not before but after the ordination … I exhort you, abandon this gain, or, I would rather say, *this approach to Hell*, … Covetousness is the root of all evil and is called idolatry (Eph. 5:5).'

wealth, Basil portrays poverty as a positive force, personifying it as a Friend who is the nurse of true philosophy, and as a Mate who should not be driven from the home.[9] Basil commends poverty as something to be nurtured, protected, and cherished. For Basil, poverty is not a negative entity, crudely defined by a lack of material goods. This is Basil's positive theology of 'Poverty as the Good Companion'.[10] Cassian was similarly uncompromising about riches.[11] And Finnian of Clonard followed both Church Fathers in equating covetousness with idolatry.[12]

The problem of wealth occurs in several of Adomnán's stories. In one incident Columba was approached by a man named Columb mac Áedo who was in obvious distress (I:50). Columb mac Áedo had been listening to Columba preaching on what constitutes acceptable offerings to God, with Columba saying that he could not bring himself to even 'taste' the gift of a greedy man 'unless he first truly does penance for his sin of avarice'. This so troubled Columb mac Áedo that he 'recognised his guilt and came forward to kneel before the saint and do penance'. Columba was deeply impressed by Columb's sincere resolve to 'renounce avarice, mend his way of life, and practise generosity', and declared that from that very hour 'his sin was healed'. Columb was a wealthy man, but Columba's preaching convinced him that outward displays of generosity counted as nothing if greed and avarice still lay within. Accordingly, he did penance to shrive his sins. Columb mac Áedo needed to deal with his attachment to worldly goods. Some became monks for similar reasons; from fear as much as from piety.

But true divestment of wealth involved more than giving things away. The action of giving away was relatively easy. Much more demanding was losing a *desire* for riches. It was the longings of the heart which were the real challenge, and the monk's ultimate aim was to be free from covetous desires, of which the destructive love of wealth was but one.[13] The monk wanted to become unmoved by what used to excite

9 Basil, *Letters*, 4.

10 cf. *Bangor Antiphonary*, Item 15:3 which describes Caomlach as rejoicing in poverty.

11 Cassian, *Institutes*, II:3. Herren and Brown, *Christ in Celtic Christianity*, 24, point out that Pelagius stressed poverty more than virginity, and that for both Cassian and Columbanus 'poverty' was 'the first perfection'.

12 *Penitential of Finnian*, XXVIII.

13 Benedict, *The Rule*, XXX, disapproved of private ownership and wealth: 'Above all, this evil practice must be uprooted and removed from the monastery. Without an order from

him. This fostered the pursuit of *apatheia*, which is achieved when worldly desires are no longer felt with any strength, whether these are longings of the flesh, appetite, personal ambition, or individual ego. To gain *apatheia* unmoved by good or ill, by comfort or discomfort, is a sign of true consecration.[14]

Although early monasticism prioritised the radical abandonment of possessions, one of the ironies of history is that wealth became the curse of the medieval monastery because of the very respect in which monks were held. Kings and nobles gave rich lands and generous endowments to monasteries, paying them vast sums to pray for their souls. With wealth came corruption and a loss of moral ideals. But, in the early centuries, monasteries such as Columba's on Iona, were unaffected by the problems of mammon.

DOCTOR TO THE SOUL

As abbot of Iona and as guardian of the souls of his community, Columba's power was robustly enforced through his role as the arbiter of penance. Within the community, sins needed to be shriven, and breaches of authority had to be dealt with. Columba supervised both of these aspects of monastic life. He was responsible for the spiritual health of his community. He was also responsible for monastic discipline. Spiritual health was damaged by sins against the divine law. Monastic discipline was compromised by breaches of the monastic code. In theory these were distinct. In practice, spiritual health and monastic discipline were regarded as one. God's dignity and the abbot's God-given authority were so closely aligned that if a monk flouted the abbot's rules, he was regarded as also flouting God's will. Therefore, penance was imposed for breaches of the monastic code as well as for moral sins.

Although penance originated as a mechanism to deal with really serious sins, it was eventually applied to a wide range of misdemeanours. In the monastery it was the abbot who determined the nature and level of penance, and this was not unwelcome. The community accepted what he imposed because they trusted that their abbot knew which

---

the Abbot, no one may presume to give, receive, or retain anything as his own, nothing at all – not a book, writing tablets, or stylus – in short, not a single item.'

14 cf. Basil, *The Shorter Rule*, Qu. 128.

penance would be acceptable to God Himself, and salvation depended on God being satisfied with that penance. An incorrect penance would be penance served in vain. Each monk believed that his abbot had the gift of discernment and trusted that what his abbot demanded was what God Himself required. Penance was welcomed as purgative medicine for the soul,[15] and abbots were seen as soul-doctors with spiritual skills.[16] They were able to diagnose sin and able to apply a remedy. In this area, Irish penitential thinking owed a heavy debt to Cassian.[17]

1. *The Diagnosis of Sin.* Cassian was the first to list the eight principal vices which might affect a person's spiritual health: gluttony, fornication, avarice, anger, dejection (bitterness of heart), languor (idleness), vainglory, and pride.[18] 'Pride' was the most serious, because it lay at the root of the others. Cassian devoted Books V-XII of his *Institutes* to describing these sins and how they could be treated. Following Cassian, it was standard practice for penitential writings to be structured around his list of eight vices.

2. *The Medicine for Sin.* Cassian also promoted the 'Principle of Contraries' as the means of dealing with the eight vices, drawing on a theory in classical medicine that 'contraries are cured by their contraries'. Themison of Laodicea, Soranus of Ephesus, and Alexander of Thales were among the best known practitioners of this principle, with Alexander of Thales stating: 'The duty of a physician is to cool what is hot, to warm what is cold, to dry what is moist, and to moisten what is dry.'[19] Several Church Fathers approved of the principle, but it was Cassian who linked it with the appropriate soul-medicine for erring sinners:

15 McNeill and Gamer, *Medieval Handbooks of Penance*, 19ff. and 44ff.

16 The *Bangor Antiphonary*, Item 129, refers to Abbot Segan as a 'great physician of Scripture'. The phrase probably refers to Segan's ability in applying Scripture as pastoral soul-medicine, rather than to his exegetical skills. O'Loughlin, *Celtic Theology*, 61, points out (in relation to *The Penitential of Cummean*) that the administrators of a *Penitential* were neither gurus nor wonder-workers, but spiritual General Practitioners dealing with sick-souls, prescribing courses of therapy.

17 Basil, *The Longer Rule*, 51, has elements of this. Finnian, Columba, and Columbanus, owed much to Cassian's penitential thinking. See McNeill, *The Celtic Penitentials*, 52. O'Loughlin, *Celtic Theology*, 49, bemoans the fact that in most popular books on 'Celtic Christianity', the *Penitentials* get little mention, possibly because their severe penalties do not conform to the popular romantic picture of early Irish Celtic faith. In reality, the *Penitentials* were the 'most distinctive feature of the insular churches'.

18 Cassian, *Institutes*, V:1. Pride included blaspheming, and treasuring any novel idea outside of Scripture.

19 Cited in McNeill and Gamer, *Medieval Handbooks of Penance*, 19.

> When anyone discovers by those signs which we described above, that he is attacked by outbreaks of impatience or anger, he should always practise himself in the *opposite and contrary things*...The cure for ailments (anger, vexation, impatience, etc.) has been shown to consist in opposing to them their contraries.[20]

Cassian's treatment for sin followed the principle of contraries.[21] It then transferred into Irish penitential thinking, with Finnian of Clonard making explicit usage of the principle in his *Penitential*, teaching that a person's penance for an offence is that he 'cures and corrects contraries by contraries'.[22] Expanding on the idea Finnian writes:

> By contraries, let us make haste to cure contraries, and to cleanse away the faults from our hearts and introduce virtues in their places. Patience must arise for wrathfulness. Kindliness, or the love of God and of one's neighbour, for envy. For detraction, restraint of heart and tongue. For dejection, spiritual joy. For greed, liberality.[23]

Finnian never claims originality and portrays himself as simply codifying and applying a system of penance which came from others.[24] Finnian's actual list of tariffs for offences owes more to Basil than to Cassian (since Cassian never listed tariffs as Basil did), but he absorbed much of Cassian's philosophy.[25] Cummean, who flourished a century after Finnian, was likewise indebted to Cassian's ideas. At the start of Cummean's own penitential treatise he describes penance as the 'health-giving medicine of souls' and takes Cassian's two core concepts of the 'eight vices' and the 'principle of contraries' into the heart of his system, stating that the 'eight principal vices contrary to human

---

20 Cassian, *Conferences*, XIX, 'Conference with Abbot John', 14, 15 [my italics]

21 McNeill, *The Celtic Penitentials*, 91.

22 *Penitential of Finnian*, XXVIII.

23 *Penitential of Finnian*, XXIX.

24 McNeill, *The Celtic Penitentials*, 39.

25 McNeill and Gamer, *Medieval Handbooks of Penance*, 86-97. McNeil and Gamer note that the *Penitential of Finnian* is fuller than any sixth-century Welsh document. It not only has a methodical treatment of sins and their appropriate penalties for clergy (Canons 1-34) and laity (Canons 35-53), but offers theoretic explanation. Oscar D. Watkins, *A History of Penance, vol. II: The Western Church from 450 to 1215* (London: Longmans, Green & Co., 1920), 756, emphasises the dependence of Finnian on Welsh teachers such as David and Gildas.

salvation shall be healed by … eight contrary remedies. For it is an old proverb: contraries are cured by contraries'.[26] All Irish penitential thinking was governed by these principles.

ARBITER OF PENANCE

Minor faults could be dealt with by expressing genuine remorse in face of the community. Serious sin required something more.[27] Even in New Testament congregations, grave offences resulted in exclusion from the fellowship (1 Cor. 5:3-5). In later centuries, exclusion became a standard feature of penance, sometimes amounting to years at a stretch. This automatically involved exclusion from the Eucharist, which was a drastic penalty given the growing belief that participation in the Eucharist was essential to being in a state of grace. Serious sins included blasphemy, adultery, and murder.[28] In the Old Testament there were sins for which no sacrifices could atone, and a few Church Fathers, including Tertullian, regarded idolatry, fornication, and murder as absolutely irremissible. A less rigorous position eventually prevailed, but in all cases, penance was the way to deal with sin.[29]

All of Iona's monastic community were subject to Columba's spiritual guardianship, as were local believers. So too were the penitents who flocked to Iona to have their sins shriven. Many had committed detestable sins against God. Some had sinned 'with a high hand', committing murder, blasphemy, incest, or adultery.[30] Some had offended their tribe, such as the former king Áed Dubh who was obliged to live a penitential life as a cleric because he had slain his Ui Neill overlord (I:36). In all cases the burning question was: After committing serious sin, how can I reclaim hope of heaven? Re-baptism was not an option, so another mechanism had to apply. That mechanism was penance. Baptism might

26 McNeill and Gamer, *Medieval Handbooks of Penance*, 98, reckon that *The Penitential of Cummean* was written c. 650. Cummean's identity is uncertain. He was not the seventh-century abbot of Iona with a similar name. Nor was he the Irish bishop who wrote to Iona in the mid-seventh century trying to persuade them to adopt Roman forms.

27 O'Loughlin, *Celtic Theology*, 50.

28 McNeill and Gamer, *Medieval Handbooks of Penance*, 6, stress that not all offenses were subject to penalty. Lighter or 'everyday' sins were dismissed by open acknowledgement to the congregation, usually before the Eucharist on a Sunday. See the second-century *Teaching of the Twelve Apostles.*

29 McNeill and Gamer, *Medieval Handbooks of Penance*, 5f.; cf. Watkins, *A History of Penance, vol. II*, 751f.

30 cf. O'Loughlin, *Celtic Theology*, 50.

wash away original sin and any actual sins committed before baptism, but it was penance which dealt with post-baptismal transgressions. As arbiters of penance, abbots were sought out by the soul-anxious. Those who came to Columba did so because his reputation for knowing the mind of God meant they could trust his judgement concerning the correct penance for absolving guilt. The eternal destiny of the soul was at stake, and penitents had to be confident that any decision made, and any penance imposed, reflected God's own will.

In practice, penitential penalties in the Irish Church frequently dovetailed with the legal penalties of secular law. Sanctions from pre-Christian Irish society were often the starting-points for religious penance, and sometimes Old Testament rules were subtly modified so as to allow, for example, the eating of pork which was a traditional delicacy![31] But there was one route, becoming increasingly prominent in secular law, which was not open to a monk. This was the option of commuting a penalty into a financial payment. Monks had no money to make payments. Hence, any penance assigned to a monk, including years of penitential exile, was served in full.

Basil, Cassian, and Finnian of Clonard, all influenced Columba's decision-making. Compendia of Basil's penitential decisions were available. Cassian was widely read.[32] And Finnian's *Penitential* would be a familiar document, since Columba had been Finnian's student. Columba belonged to a wave of new abbots who were putting Finnian's ideas into practice, and, if anything, Columba applied rules more

---

31 McNeill and Gamer, *Medieval Handbooks of Penance*, 36, comment that the principle of restitution (Exod. 22:12) dovetailed with native law. They also note (25) that, 'apart from the question of pagan survival as a whole, the penitentials themselves proclaim their accommodation to native custom in countless details'. The penalty of exile was a native element, as was redemption of penance by financial payment. This accommodation to pre-Christian customs aided the acceptance of Church discipline. McNeill, *The Celtic Penitentials*, 55, 99ff., discusses the off/on relationship between Church canons, penitential exercises, and native law within the Celtic tradition; cf. Hughes, *Early Christian Ireland: Introduction to the Sources*, 43ff. and 76f: 'The main aim [of the Irish canonists] was not to bring the Church into line with continental practice, but to adjust it to native law.' cf. O'Loughlin, *Celtic Theology*, 55f. and Yorke, *The Conversion of Britain: 600–800*, 221. Markus, *Conceiving a Nation*, 129f., cites the eighth-century prologue to the Gaelic law-text *Senchus Mor*, which represents pre-Christian laws and traditions as fully acceptable except where they clashed with the Word of God in the Old and New Testaments. Such 'ancient judgements of nature' had been given by the Holy Spirit 'through the mouths of righteous judges and poets' before the coming of the faith.

32 McNeil and Gamer, *Medieval Handbooks of Penance*, 92, note 25, also identify specific instances of dependence by Finnian on Cassian, e.g., Canons 25 and 26.

strictly than his teacher.[33] For example, Finnian assigned seven years penance for fratricide and incest, whereas Columba set it at twelve (I:22). Admittedly, Adomnán's text may be reflecting the tariffs of Adomnán's time, but nothing in Columba's character makes such strictness unlikely.[34] Columbanus, Columba's younger contemporary, was even harsher.[35] Watson thinks that Columba and Columbanus set the bar too high, and suggests that the Irish Church's oppressive discipline (masquerading as high Christian standards) eventually became an unbearable burden.[36] Watson argues that this led to an intolerable severity, and may be a key to both the rise and fall of the Irish Church. Initially, seriously minded people were attracted by the strictness of the Irish Church, since strictness seemed to indicate authenticity. But when the system became over-strict, then the milder Benedictine Rule became more attractive.

Strict or otherwise, there was no doubt concerning an abbot's power as Arbiter of Penance. He judged with the authority of God. And it was disastrous for a person to die without completing penance. One day Columba heard loud shouting from Mull and commented to his companions that the man shouting was to be pitied since, 'He has come to us to ask for medicines to heal the body, but it would be better today

---

33 Fraser, *From Caledonia to Pictland: Scotland to 795*, 78. McNeill, *The Celtic Penitentials*, 39, notes that Finnian increased penalties when there was public scandal. One year of penance was prescribed for fornication which was kept secret; but six years if the same crime was publicly known (Canons 10 and 21).

34 The pseudographical text, *The Canons of Adomnán*, comprises twenty canons dealing with the question of clean and unclean meats and remarriages. O'Loughlin, *Celtic Theology*, 74f., allows *The Canons of Adomnán* as authentic to Adomnán. Yorke, *The Conversion of Britain: 600–800*, 229, suggests that students or monks collected Adomnán's teaching as a compilation under his name.

35 F. E. Warren, *The Liturgy and Ritual of the Celtic Church* (Oxford: Clarendon, 1881), 17: '[Columbanus' Rule] was very severe, far more so than the Rule of St. Benedict. It is difficult to read it today without thinking that it represents a disturbed mind. Its principles were absolute and unreserved obedience, constant and severe labour, daily self-denial and fasting; and the least deviation from the Rule was visited with corporal punishment or a severe form of fast, the precise number of blows and of days or hours of fasting being minutely prescribed.' Columbanus advocated flogging as part of penance: 200 strokes for a monk conversing alone with a woman; cf. McNeill, *The Celtic Penitentials*, 45ff. for a detailed analysis of Columbanus' sanctions in comparison to Finnian's. Yet Columbanus' severe *Rule* was venerated to such a degree that some (Benedictine) Continental monasteries adopted it conjointly with Benedict's *Rule;* cf. Louis Gougaud, *Gaelic Pioneers of Christianity: The Work and Influence of Irish Monks and Saints in Continental Europe* (tr. Collins) (Dublin: Gill (1923), 8f.

36 Warren, *The Liturgy and Ritual of the Celtic Church*, 13, 17, 55.

for him to do penance for his sins because at the end of this week he will die' (I:27). It was fearful to die before penance was completed. The same dread is expressed by Beccán in his elegy to Columba:

May mercy come to me before death.
May it be penance that I seek.
May I be in my mind and my sense,
bound to Colum while I speak.[37]

A severe penance was imposed on the monk Berchan who spied on Columba to see the 'heavenly brightness' which shone around him (III:21). Berchan's sin would have damned his soul for ever had not God determined that, since Berchan had been Columba's pupil, he might obtain mercy before his death if he did a 'tearful penance'. But if penance were not completed, then Berchan was doomed. Another penance involved standing waist or chest-deep in sea water for lengthy periods whilst engaged in prayer.[38] This discipline was also thought to expel erotic thoughts from the mind. It had been practised in pre-Christian druidical religion, and it had a future-history, featuring in the thirteenth-century *Orkneyinga Saga*.

Years of penance might be required, but occasionally forgiveness was granted immediately. Once a 'learned man' named Fiachnae came to Iona to perform a 'fearful penance', but even as Fiachnae disembarked, Columba discerned that Christ had already accepted Fiachnae's repentance, and declared, 'Stand up, my son, and be comforted; your sins have been forgiven, because, as it is written: "A broken and a contrite heart God will not despise." ' (I:30). In this case Fiachnae's penitential exercises were completed out of gratitude for a forgiveness already received. Immediate forgiveness also came to Columb mac Áedo who was conscience-stricken about his greed and wealth (I:50). Columb's resolve to 'renounce avarice, mend his way of life, and practise generosity', meant that 'from that very hour' Columb's sin was healed.

Adomnán refers frequently to Columba imposing penance, yet only twice does he set out the fault and the accompanying penalty. The form of penance echoes those given by Basil and Finnian, though the tariffs may reflect Adomnán's era rather than Columba's.

37 Beccán, *Fo Reir Choluimb*, 25.
38 cf. Bede, *History*, V:12.

Fault	Penance
A man slays his brother (fratricide) and sleeps with his mother (incest), (I:22).	He has to do penance among the Britons, weeping and wailing for twelve years, and is not to return to Ireland till his death (perpetual exile).
Libran commits many sins, including killing a man, and breaking a binding oath he gave to a relative who had obtained his freedom and release from a death sentence, (II:39).	Libran has to spend seven years in penance at the monastery on Tiree. After this, during Lent, he is to return to Columba in order to receive the Eucharist at the Easter Festival. After this, he is to return to Ireland and put things right with those he has wronged.[39]

At first glance, the Libran incident appears to indicate that Columba applied a less stringent penance than set out by Finnian, since Finnian states in his *Penitential*:

> If any cleric commits murder and kills his neighbour … he must become an exile for ten years and do penance seven years in another region. He shall do penance for three years of this time on an allowance of bread and water, and he shall fast three forty-day periods on an allowance of bread and water; and for four years abstain from wine and meats. And having thus completed the ten years, if he has done well and is approved by testimonial of the abbot or priest to whom he was committed, he shall be received into his own country and make satisfaction to the friends of him whom he slew, and he shall render to his father or mother, if they are still alive, compensation for the filial piety and obedience [of the murdered man] and say, 'Lo, I will do for you whatever you ask, in the place of your son'. But if he has not done enough he shall not be received back forever.[40]

39 Markus, *Conceiving a Nation*, 195, in discussing the *Penitential of Finnian*, points out that penalties related to both 'spiritual' and 'secular' law systems. Homicide was both a sin and a crime: therefore, two things had to be done: (1) penance for the sin and (2) redress to the victim's kin in accordance with native law for the crime.

40 *Penitential of Finnian*, Canon 23.

Libran was a cleric who committed murder: therefore why was seven years of exile applied by Columba, and not the ten years required by Finnian? The answer is that the penance assigned by Columba was not for the murder, but for Libran breaking his oath to the kinsman who paid the murder-fine on his behalf.[41] In gratitude, Libran had bound himself to his kinsman for 'all the days of my life' but then broke that bond and fled the country to become a monk. Thus the penalty which Columba imposed was for Libran breaking his oath, and not for the murder which was already dealt with by the fine.

Finnian and Adomnán both exhibit traces of Basil's stages of separation from the community during the period of penance. Basil constructed a system in which penitents were successively: weepers, hearers, kneelers, and standers. These are not replicated explicitly by Finnian, though in the above example the period of penitential exile is made up of blocks of three, three, and four years. Yet, although Finnian does not replicate Basil's full terminology, he does allude to a 'weeping' stage,[42] as does Adomnán (I:22). It may be that because any extended penance for Iona monks involved exile to an adjacent island such as Tiree, then Adomnán simply refers to the whole period of exile from Iona, rather than to the discreet stages of the penitential process which would be observed on the island of exile.

THE SOUL-FRIEND

The path of lifelong pilgrimage had risk and danger, but each brother, including the abbot, had a 'soul-friend' or *Anmcara*, who was a mixture of counsellor and confessor, and who provided pastoral care and support. Confidentiality was of prime importance in this system, with the later *Martyrology of Óengus (Felire Óengus)* stating that if an Anmcara divulged information given to him by a penitent then he committed a sin for which there was no penance.[43] Columba's Anmcara was his fellow monk Diarmait, and Columba may have been Anmcara to King Áedán of Dál Riata. The *Martyrology of Óengus* suggests that the monk Donnán of Eigg (d. 617) asked Columba to be his Anmcara. If Donnán asked, so would others.

41 McNeill, *The Celtic Penitentials*, 136.

42 *Penitential of Finnian*, Canons 8, 12, 29,

43 McNeill, *The Celtic Penitentials*, 96.

An Anmcara did not determine the penance his soul-friend might serve, unless the Anmcara happened also to be the abbot. No one could usurp the abbot's role in this area. What the Anmcara could do was to advise his friend on how to deal with issues and temptations assailing him. He could also advise his friend when to approach the abbot for counsel, especially if there was sin needing penance. The duties of a soul-friend are well described in Carthach of Druim Fertain's seventh-century *Rule*, and include: leading by example, encouraging an honest and contrite confession, listening with silence, and teaching the penitent the way of truth from the Scriptures.[44] A good Anmcara had a genuine concern about the spiritual health of his friend, and the role of the Anmcara reinforced Basil's principle that true Christian life could only be lived in community. It was in community, not in isolation, that faithful friends were present who could identify areas of life needing correction.[45] Comgall of Bangor is credited with saying: 'A person without a soul-friend is a body without a head.'[46]

An Anmcara of the Irish Church encouraged his friend to confess his sins regularly. Through time, this contributed toward a change of thinking across Christendom in which confession and penance became regarded, not as one-time exercises just before death, but as spiritual disciplines to be repeated through life.[47] Tertullian had argued that only one repentance was possible after baptism.[48] But the Irish Church did not restrict confession of sin to a once-only event, as close to death as possible. It regarded confession as a repeatable spiritual discipline.

The concept of soul-friend went hand in hand with trying to deal with sin in a private and confidential manner. In the early Church,

44 The *Rule of St. Carthach*, and the ninth-century *Rule of Cormac*; both describe duties of an Anmcara. He is to lead by example; encourage a true confession of sin; listen with silence; teach a penitent the way of truth; encourage reading of the Scriptures; and encourage living a holy life. Not every Anmcara could bestow absolution, but all were spiritual doctors directing the penitent back to God.

45 Basil, *The Longer Rule*, 7, and Basil. *The Shorter Rule*, Qu. 3:1-37.

46 McNeill and Gamer, *Medieval Handbooks of Penance*, 29.

47 The Council of Toledo (589) attempted to forbid the iteration of penance.

48 Tertullian, *On Repentance*,VII: 'Although the gate of forgiveness has been shut and fastened up with the bar of baptism, [God] has permitted it still to stand somewhat open. In the vestibule He has stationed the second repentance for opening to such as knock: but now once for all, because now for the second time, *but never more*, because the last time it had been in vain.' [my italics]

confession of sin and its absolution was public.[49] Cassian wanted to retain this public accountability, arguing that minor faults could be quickly expiated by public confession rather than through a drawn-out process.[50] Inexorably, public confession to the community morphed into private confession to an individual, possibly to avoid the penitent losing face. Basil taught that sins should be confessed to those entrusted with the 'stewardship of the mysteries of God', and within a monastic context, this meant the abbot.[51] In theory, the required penance was also private. In reality, sanctions such as exile and exclusion from the Eucharist, made penance a known state. The *Irish Penitentials* assume the theoretical position that penance was determined in private conference, and Finnian's intention was that it should all be kept secret.[52] But that was unrealistic. Some penalties could never be kept secret, and a degree of public humiliation was inevitable.[53]

SANCTIONS AND PENALTIES

Penalties and punishments included: extended fasts, extended devotional exercises, and degrees of exile. In Celtic spirituality, fasting, singing the psalms, and exile, were therefore major aspects of both penance and of the regular devotional life.[54] What was given voluntarily in the normal life of a monk (fasting, praise, exile), was transformed into a punitive exercise in the penitential state.

1. *Extended Fasts.* Penitents observed extended fasts, receiving less food during their penitential period. Sometimes the provision amounted to little more than bread and water. This severe fasting was sometimes relaxed, as on one occasion when Columba arrived on Hinba and ordered that more food should be allowed that day, 'even to the penitents' (I:21).

---

49 McNeill, *The Celtic Penitentials*, 78.

50 Cassian, *Institutes*, II:15, 16. In the early centuries it was assumed that even serious faults committed by a Church member would be dealt with publicly, believing this was the New Testament pattern. When 'righting of wrongs' evolved into 'penance' the public arena remained the norm for a while. This morphed into private discipline in which a penitent confessed to a trusted Confessor who advised on the appropriate steps to take. See: Curran, *The Antiphonary of Bangor and the Early Irish Monastic Liturgy*, 159.

51 Basil, *The Shorter Rule*, Qu. 21:4.

52 McNeill and Gamer, *Medieval Handbooks of Penance*, 9; cf. *Penitential of Finnian*, Canon 10: 'Sins are to be absolved in secret by penance and by very diligent devotion of heart and body.'

53 McNeill, *The Celtic Penitentials*, 80.

54 McNeill, *The Celtic Penitentials*, 130f., 134f., 137f.

2. *Extended Devotions.* Increased recitation of the psalms was also imposed as a penitential duty.[55] McNeill and Gamer see parallels with the penitential singing of sacred hymns in ancient India as prescribed in the Brahman codes, and they suggest that so many penitents may have been reciting the Psalter that some monasteries could achieve their goal of perpetual praise![56]

3. *Exile and Exclusion.* Penance could also involve exile until sin had been purged. Although Basil's four stages of penitential exile (*weeping*, *hearing*, *kneeling*, and *standing*) may not have been replicated exactly in the Irish penitential system, there was certainly a strong concept of exile from God's grace and from God's people. Celtic secular culture regarded 'exile' and 'outcast' as synonymous. And the seriousness of this is highlighted in ancient Welsh law, in which an outcast/exile was known as a 'kin-wrecked' man.[57] As an exile, a person was deemed to lose the essential bonds which tied him or her to kinfolk. He or she no longer belonged. He or she became a non-person. When this concept was translated into the spiritual realm, penitential exile became an actual exclusion from God's presence, church, fellowship, and the Eucharist. In a very real sense he or she lost their identity. He or she was kin-wrecked, especially their kinship in the family of Christ. During penance a penitent became Israel in exile in Egypt, a non-people who needed to be freed from the bonds of Satanic captivity and darkness in order to even exist.

In Irish spirituality, *voluntary exile* (white-martyrdom) had no penitential overtones. It was an act of self-consecration in which an exiled Christian believer abandoned natural kinship ties for a life lived exclusively for Christ. This voluntary exile involved giving up the comforts of home and living somewhere which was difficult or dangerous or both, with some commentators interpreting Columba's exile from Ireland to Iona in these terms. *Penitential exile* was somewhat different. It required a penitent to live in geographic exile for years at a

55 McNeill and Gamer, *Medieval Handbooks of Penance*, 30f.; cf. McNeill, *The Celtic Penitentials*, 31, who notes that in the *Preface of Gildas Concerning Penance*, penalties include the nocturnal singing of psalms and deprivation of the evening meal. McNeill (49) also notes that penitential singing of the psalms was insisted on by Columbanus 'for all manner of trivial monastic failings'.

56 McNeill, *The Celtic Penitentials*, 105ff.

57 McNeill, *The Celtic Penitentials*, 111, 134ff.

stretch, and an Iona penitent would be sent to satellite islands such as Tiree or Hinba. These islands were dual purpose. They were places for voluntary spiritual retreat. They were also 'penal colonies'.

But far more important than geographic exile was the spiritual exile. We have already noted in chapter three that the Council of Nicaea defined three degrees of separation within penitential discipline, which Basil extended to four. Each stage not only involved a degree of separation from other believers, but also from the Eucharist. However, if a penitent was at risk of death, then he or she was permitted access to the sacrament:

> If any man or woman is nigh unto death, although he (or she) has been a sinner, and pleads for the communion of Christ, we say that it is not to be denied to him if he promises to take the vow, and let him do well and he shall be received by Him. ... We are not to cease to snatch prey from the mouth of the lion, or the dragon, that is of the devil, who ceases not to snatch at the prey of our souls; we may follow up and strive [for his soul] at the very end of a man's life.[58]

On completion of penance, a penitent not only returned to the Eucharist but 'to the world' (I:21). During the penitential period they had had a shadow, non-person, existence. Having returned, they were once more on the way of salvation, and reaching the heavenly kingdom was again a possibility. Sin had been shrived, and the abbot's role in setting the correct penance had been crucial. Although penance was not yet a sacrament within the early Irish Church, it was the given means of restoring a sinner after he or she had lapsed from grace.[59]

The Irish penitential system addressed a major problem. There was a real fear that post-baptismal sins could not be forgiven. What it did was to create a process of absolution through a continuing programme, rather than through the gamble of one great repentance which might

---

58 *Penitential of Finnian*, XXXIV. The New Testament concept of being delivered to Satan for a season (cf. 1 Corinthians 5:5; 1 Timothy 1:20), was interpreted by some Church Fathers as exclusion from sacramental grace.

59 Herren and Brown, *Christ in Celtic Christianity*, 125.

or might not take place in time before death occurred.[60] However, it also fuelled a piety which increasingly relied on the merits of human penitential actions rather than on God's grace. Moreover, there were always some sins not expiated before death. In time this would feed the notion of purgatory as a state in which purification could continue post-death. Nevertheless, the intention of the *Penitentials* was to provide a humane ministry and offer hope and rehabilitation.[61] The *Penitentials* gave guidance on how to restore relationships with God, society, and the Church. And the *Penitentials* tried to reform a person's character by offering medicine for the soul. O'Loughlin points out that while many Church Fathers simply lamented how a 'perfection once given in baptism had been lost', Finnian started by accepting the reality of flawed discipleship, and asked how it could be 'repaired, improved, and hastened towards its purpose [of reigning with Christ]'.[62] The penitential writers tried to offer a way out of a spiritual cul-de-sac, and attempted to shift the emphasis from the crime to the cure.[63] And Yorke argues that, in their methodology and aims, penitential rulings and their spiritual tariffs were ideally suited to early-medieval societies in Britain and Ireland, whose native law systems already included the concept of making reparations for a crime.[64]

The system was intended to give hope. It was to be a way to be put right with God. Yet, despite these laudable objectives, the *Penitentials* contained the seeds of later difficulties. The option of paying money instead of doing penance eventually led to the Church becoming immensely wealthy and corrupted. The system also introduced the notion of a holy person (usually a saint) being able to do more than what was required for his or her own purification. This created the idea that their acts of supererogation (accumulation of surplus virtue) could become a 'treasury of transferable merits'. In turn, this led to

60 On the fears raised by a 'one-chance' penance, see Watkins, *A History of Penance*, 752: 'When men were about to die they clamoured eagerly for the one accorded Penance of the life-time; and trusted in its efficacy to find a remedy for all the lapses of a careless life.' Herren and Brown, *Christ in Celtic Christianity*, 123, note that sixth-century Britain was probably where a ritual of repeatable penance was created, and where manuals were written to assist its implementation, with Gildas and Finnian major figures.

61 McNeill and Gamer, *Medieval Handbooks of Penance*, 46. The *Life of Columbanus*, 11, calls penance 'a saving grace'.

62 O'Loughlin, *Celtic Theology*, 59.

63 O'Loughlin, *Celtic Theology*, 62, 66.

64 Yorke, *The Conversion of Britain: 600–800*, 229.

the later medieval practice of purchasing Indulgences, with all of their attendant abuses.[65] Even a relatively early document such as the *Bangor Antiphonary* has embryonic traces of a treasury of merits.[66]

Penance fostered a piety in which good works were deemed essential for salvation.[67] Basil taught that the rewards of heaven were strictly conditional on a moral life, and this assumption carried over into the early-medieval Irish Church.[68] This reinforced its semi-Pelagianism. Salvation came as a combination of God's grace and human effort.[69] And within that milieu, penance was more than simply a spiritual discipline. It was a conditional requirement for salvation, as vividly illustrated in Adomnán's story about Berchan (III:21), in which divine mercy was totally conditional on Berchan completing his penance.

---

65 McNeill, *The Celtic Penitentials*, 118, argues that commutation of penance into money payments is traceable to the Celtic penitential books; cf. O'Loughlin, *Celtic Theology*, 65f.

66 *Bangor Antiphonary*, Item 129:6: 'We invoke the loftiest most faithful merits of these holy abbots ... so that we can wipe out all our sins, through Jesus Christ.' [Tr. Howlett, *The Celtic Latin Tradition of Biblical Style*, 129].

67 McNeill and Gamer, *Medieval Handbooks of Penance*, 15: '[Penance] was thought of not merely as a discipline for the restoration of sinners to the privileges of membership in the Church, but as a means of supernatural grace annulling the consequences of sin and recovering the favour of God.' cf. McNeill, *The Celtic Penitentials*, 58; D. Meek, 'Columba's Other Island? Columba and Early Christianity in Tiree' (lecture given at the Tiree Feis, July 1997, transcript), suggests that penance may have been a means of testing monastic devotion.

68 Morison, *St. Basil and his Rule: A Study in Early Monasticism*, 26.

69 Herren and Brown, *Christ in Celtic Christianity*, 9, 243.

CHAPTER 7

Simplicity, Austerity, Severity

Continental monasticism and Irish monasticism each evolved from the spirituality of the Desert Fathers. As such, hard contrasts should not be drawn between them.[1] There were differences. But they believed the same doctrines. They confessed the same Creeds. They practised similar spiritual disciplines. They observed similar Canonical Hours of prayer. They read the same Church Fathers. And both ran the risk of spiritual elitism, with key theological writings in each tradition encouraging the idea that monasticism was the most perfect expression of the Christian way. Other forms of Christian living were inferior since they involved unavoidable compromises with the world and the flesh. In theory, the ascetic life of a monk and the married life of a layman were both divine callings. In reality, the monk's life was spiritually superior.[2]

The monks of the Egyptian deserts were not the Friar Tuck figures of later centuries. For them, self-denial was central. And, in one of his letters, Basil describes the life which an erstwhile brother had once committed himself to:

> You pricked your body with rough sackcloth. You tightened a hard belt around your loins. You bravely put wearing pressure on your bones. You made your sides hang loose from back to front, and all hollow with fasting. You would wear no soft bandage and, drawing in your stomach, like a gourd, made it adhere to the parts around your kidneys. You emptied out all fat from your flesh. All the channels below your belly you dried up. Your belly itself you folded up for

1 Hughes, *Early Christian Ireland: Introduction to the Sources*, 90.

2 cf. Pseudo-Basil, *An Ascetical Discourse and Exhortation on the Renunciation of the World and Spiritual Perfection*: 'The benevolent God, solicitous for our salvation, ordained two states of life for men (marriage and virginity): that he who is not able to endure the hardships of virginity might have recourse to the married state'; cf. Basil, *The Larger Rule*, 78.

> want of food. Your ribs, like the eaves of a house, you made to overshadow all the parts about your middle, and, with your body contracted, you spent the long hours of the night in pouring out confession to God, and made your beard wet with channels of tears.[3]

Only a monk could live such a life, and this view was reinforced whenever monks studied exemplars such as Anthony and Martin. Simplicity had to pervade every area of life, because simplicity and godliness went together theologically. Simplicity was a prominent ideal in the Middle Eastern Christian tradition, which regarded pure simplicity as a key perfection of the divine nature. Hence, in order to be godly and to live in the image of God, a believer had to live out that divine principle of simplicity. In practical terms, the easiest way to do this was by adopting austerity. Austerity was seen as the practical equivalent of simplicity.

CLOTHING AND FOOD

Columba strove to express divine simplicity in his clothing. He gave up expensive garments and wore clothes of only basic material. On this matter Basil gave ready advice:

> The tunic should be fastened to the body by a girdle, the belt not going above the flank, like a woman's, nor left slack so that the tunic flows loose like an idler's. The gait ought not to be sluggish, which shows a character without energy; nor on the other hand, pushing and pompous, as though our impulses were rash and wild. The one purpose of dress is that it should be a sufficient covering alike in winter and summer. As to colour, avoid brightness. In material, [avoid] the soft and delicate. To aim at bright colours in dress is like women's beautifying when they colour cheeks and hairs with hues other than their own. The tunic ought to be thick enough not to want other help to keep the wearer warm. The shoes should be cheap but serviceable. In a word, what one has to regard in a dress is the necessary.[4]

---

3 Basil, *Letters*, 45.

4 Basil, *Letters*, 2; cf. Basil, *The Shorter Rule*, Qu. 11:1ff.

One body garment – plus hood, plus sandals – was enough.[5] Monks publicised the embracing of simplicity and rejection of luxury by wearing a simple white costume and a hood of natural wool, with the wool coming from sheep kept by the monastery.[6] Shoes and sandals were essential, but these were also kept simple. The type of footwear is illustrated in the *Book of Kells*, which has drawings of Jesus' disciples wearing sandals, with similar images in other early Celtic manuscripts. In 1979, archaeological excavations of a ditch on Iona found leather shoes which were radiocarbon-dated to the late sixth or seventh century, close to Columba's later years.[7] Adomnán refers to footwear in passing, writing that Columba's friend Cainnech was once so anxious to get to church that he went with one shoe on his foot and the other shoe left behind (II:13). Adomnán also writes of the monks strapping on footwear, ready to start their daily work, when Columba halted proceedings and called for a special Eucharist (III:12).

Monks had only one main meal each day. This was taken after the ninth-hour service (None) at 3 p.m. in the afternoon (apart from Sundays and special Feast Days when the monks ate soon after the mid-day service). They may also have had a small breakfast, consisting of bread and water. This spartan regime was deliberate, with Irish monks imitating the Desert Fathers. Bede notes that on Lindisfarne, which originated as an Iona daughter-monastery, there was a custom of fasting each day until three-o'clock, except at Easter.[8] Benedict's system was similar, but less austere.[9] MacDonald argues that on the official fasting

---

5 Basil, *The Shorter Rule*, Qu. 11:39, 40, 129.

6 Benedict, *The Rule*, LV: 'We believe that for each monk a cowl and tunic will suffice in temperate regions. In winter a woollen cowl is necessary; in summer a thinner or worn one; also a scapular for work, and footwear (both sandals and shoes)'. 'For bedding the monks will need a mat, a woollen blanket and a light covering as well as a pillow.' 'In order that this vice of private ownership may be completely uprooted, the Abbot is to provide all things necessary; that is, cowl, tunic, sandals, shoes, belt, knife, stylus, needle, handkerchief, and writing tablets.'

7 Sharpe, *Adomnán of Iona: Life of St. Columba*, 365, note 376; cf. Warren, *The Liturgy and Ritual of the Celtic Church* (1881), 122.

8 Bede, *History*, III:5.

9 Benedict, *The Rule*, XLI: 'From Holy Easter to Pentecost the brothers eat at noon and take supper in the evening. Beginning with Pentecost and continuing throughout the summer, the monks fast until mid-afternoon on Wednesday and Friday, unless they are working in the fields or the summer heat is oppressive. On the other days they eat dinner at noon. Indeed, the Abbot may decide that they should continue to eat dinner at noon every day if they have work in the fields or if the summer heat remains extreme. Similarly, he should so

days of Wednesdays and Fridays, the community enforced an actual total fast until three in the afternoon, and cites as evidence a story in which Columba relaxed the Wednesday fast because a guest was scheduled to arrive on the Wednesday morning (I:26).[10] The presence of a total fast on Wednesdays and Fridays supports the assumption that on other days the monks were allowed a simple breakfast. Bede may have disregarded this modest breakfast when recording that Lindisfarne monks fasted until after None. There was also an additional small meal on Sundays and solemn Feast Days (III:12).[11] MacDonald interprets Adomnán as implying that working monks were given extra food and rest if they had to cope with heavy labour or bad weather (I:29).

Eating was never to be a pleasure-seeking, gourmet indulgence. That was sinful. Food was for survival, nothing more.[12] Cassian writes that some desert monks, guarding themselves against any link between eating and self-indulgent pleasure, survived on two small, hard, biscuits (*paxamatium*) per day.[13] True anchorites were excruciatingly severe in denying themselves food in order to 'crucify the flesh'. The meals of an Irish monastery were not so grim, but they still tended towards the very least a monk needed to survive. This followed Basil's advice:

> One ought not to eat with any exhibition of savage gluttony. But in everything that concerns our pleasures to maintain moderation, quiet, and self-control. And, all through, not to let the mind forget to think of God, but to make even the nature of our food and the constitution of the body that takes it, a ground and means for offering him the glory. We think on how the various kinds of food, suitable to the needs

---

regulate and arrange all matters that souls may be saved and the brothers go about their activities without justifiable grumbling. From the 13th of September to the beginning of Lent, they always take their meal in mid-afternoon. Finally, from the beginning of Lent to Easter, they eat towards evening. Let Vespers be celebrated early enough so that there is no need for a lamp while eating, and that everything can be finished by daylight. Indeed, at all times let supper or the hour of the fast-day meal be so scheduled that everything can be done by daylight.'

10 MacDonald, 'Adomnán's Monastery of Iona' in Bourke (ed.), *Studies in the Cult of Saint Columba*, 35.

11 Sharpe, *Adomnán of Iona: Life of St. Columba*, 324, note 239.

12 Basil, *The Shorter Rule*, Qu. 48:1: 'How is one not to be conquered by the delight and pleasure of food? If one makes it a rule not to seek what pleases, but rather what is helpful and what is sufficient for use and not for delight'; cf. McNeill and Gamer, *Medieval Handbooks of Penance*, 102.

13 Cassian, *Institutes*, IV:14.

> of our bodies, are due to the provision of the great Steward of the Universe. Before meat let grace be said, in recognition alike of the gifts which God gives now and which he keeps in store for time to come. [Also] say grace after meat in gratitude for gifts given and petition for gifts promised. Let there be one fixed hour for taking food, always the same in regular course. That of all the four and twenty of the day and night, barely this one may be spent upon the body. The rest, the ascetic ought to spend in mental exercise.[14]

Basil refers to saying grace before and after 'meat'. In the Greek text, the word translated 'meat' is '*trophe*', which can simply mean 'food' or 'sustenance'. Given that elsewhere Basil disapproves of flesh-eating, 'food' may be the better rendering.[15] Jerome also disliked meat-eating, writing that meat-eating was only for those on a lower spiritual level who needed to raise families.[16] In the light of this, was Columba's Church non-meat eating? Opinion is split.

Aidan MacDonald points out that Adomnán only ever mentions bread, fish, fruit, and milk as food for the monks, and argues from this evidence that the community did not eat meat.[17] Certainly, the later Irish work, *The Voyages of Saint Brendan*, states that Brendan never ate meat after his ordination, though that statement may reflect a later culture.[18] On the other hand, recent archaeological evidence suggests that meat was eaten, with Finbar McCormick referring to a filled-in ditch on Iona containing objects from the early Christian period, including bone fragments with butchering marks. The bones were from cattle,[19] red deer, roe-deer, sheep, pigs, horses, otters, grey seal, and possibly a whale.[20] Given that Iona was populated almost

---

14 Basil, *Letters* 2.

15 Basil, *Letters*, 51, indicates that no cooking and no eating of meat took place under Basil's roof, though the provenance of this letter is questioned.

16 Jerome, *Letters*, 79: 'Let those feed on flesh who serve the flesh, whose bodies boil with desire, who are tied to husbands, and who set their hearts on having offspring.'

17 MacDonald, 'Adomnán's Monastery of Iona' in Bourke (ed.), *Studies in the Cult of Saint Columba*, 35f. But see also Sharpe, *Adomnán of Iona: Life of St. Columba*, 331f., note 280.

18 *The Voyages of St. Brendan*, XVI.

19 De Paor, *Early Christian Ireland*, 90, notes that in early-medieval Ireland it was common for cattle to be killed off in the autumn since winter fodder was scarce.

20 Finbar McCormick, 'Iona: The Archaeology of the Early Monastery' in Bourke (ed.), *Studies in the Cult of Saint Columba*, 56; cf. Bruce, *Prophecy, Miracles, Angels and Heavenly Light?*, 125, who suggests that slaughter was common on Iona as evidenced by I:41;

exclusively by monks, these remains appear to indicate that the monastic diet did include meat. McCormick also cites the ninth-century Céilí Dé document, *The Monastery of Tallaght*, in which the eating of venison is associated with monastic holiness.[21] Moreover, despite being aware of apparent monkish revulsion to eating horsemeat, McCormick is unperturbed by the butchered horse bones found in the Iona ditch, arguing that horsemeat was occasionally on the table.[22] He further notes that in the secular legal text *Bretha Crolige*, concerning care of the sick, the eating of horsemeat was not completely forbidden: it was simply deemed unsuitable for invalids, as it 'tended to stir up sickness in the stomach'.

McCormick's views on a meat-eating, monastic diet are supported by archaeological evidence from the Pictish Christian monastery at Portmahomack.[23] Martin Carver, the lead archaeologist at Portmahomack, has deduced that the diet of its monastic community consisted predominately of beef, pork, milk, butter, cheese, plus traces of barley, nuts, a little fruit and veg, and limited amounts of fish and

---

II:19, 20, 21, 26, 27. Yorke, *The Conversion of Britain: 600–800*, 157, 182, draws attention to Gildas' criticism of non-meat-eating monks: Gildas allowed meat-eating, whereas David of Wales embraced an extreme asceticism, with monks, rather than oxen, pulling the ploughs themselves. The *Old Irish Life* (Skene, *Celtic Scotland*, vol. II, 494) states that on one occasion, 'Baithene left Colum Cille cooking a beef for the labourers', and the entire incident is a celebration of beef-eating. Yet, towards the close of Skene's translation of the *Old Irish Life* (505), though in a section incorporated from an alternative text, there is the statement that Columba 'used not drink ale, and used not eat meat, and used not eat savoury things'.

21 *Monastery of Tallaght*, 6: 'Not a morsel of meat was eaten in Tallaght in Maelruain's lifetime, [unless] it was a deer or a wild swine. What meat there was [at Tallaght used to be consumed by] the guests.'

22 McCormick, 'Iona: The Archaeology of the Early Monastery' in Bourke (ed.), *Studies in the Cult of Saint Columba*, 57.

23 Martin Carver, Justin Garner-Lahire and Cecily Spall, *Portmahomack on Tarbat Ness: Changing Ideologies in North-East Scotland, Sixth to Sixteenth Century AD* (Edinburgh: Society of Antiquaries of Scotland, 2016), 59, note that examination of human remains (almost all male) at Portmahomack from the monastic period shows they ate meat. The Period 2/3 populations, which include Portmahomack's monastic era of 680-810, consumed meat but no fish. Later medieval populations had a broad diet including deep-sea marine fish. Carver (60) deduces that the Period 2 monastic community hunted red deer and roe deer, trapped wild geese and capercaillie, and acquired plenty of seals, plus cattle, etc. Carver provides full archaeological evidence in tabular form on pages 63-5. He also notes (12): '[The skeletons of periods 1, 2, 3] were found to depend largely on terrestrial plants and animal protein, with no marine component.' On 222f. he points out that Period 2 at Portmahomack had cattle as 75 per cent of the meat species; that the cattle were slaughtered at 3+ years; and that there was secondary product exploitation e.g., milk etc. There is evidence of sharp butchery knives, especially on marine mammals (223f.).

dolphin. The Christian monks at Portmahomack were not averse to meat. Carver also notes that, in the Lindisfarne tradition, Cuthbert was once provided with a miraculous meal of roast dolphin.[24] Both Lindisfarne and Portmahomack had Columban roots. All of this calls in question the long-held presumption that monks never ate meat.

Clancy and Markus suggest that eating horsemeat may have happened during the early Christian period despite Adomnán despising the practice (I:21).[25] Adomnán's attitude comes in his story about Neman mac Cathir who was undergoing penance. Columba allowed Neman a temporary reprieve of the meagre diet normally allowed to penitents, but Neman petulantly refused the offer. His rejection infuriated Columba, who was never a man to contradict! Columba prophesied, 'I have allowed a relaxation in the rules of diet, and you refuse it: but the time will come when, in the company of thieves in the forest, you will eat the flesh of a stolen mare.' Refusal of the abbot's generosity was more than disrespect. It was a sin. Consequently, later in Neman's life extreme hunger compelled him to eat what he found repugnant. Eating horsemeat was eventually forbidden within the Irish Church, despite not being prohibited by Old Testament codes.[26]

COMMUNALITY AND SOLITARINESS

Athanasius' *Life of Anthony* was inspiring, but it also contained the seeds of future tensions: communality versus solitariness; contemplation versus labour; and celibacy versus marriage. Most Irish monks lived in a communal, or coenobitic lifestyle, and the tension between the communal and the solitary in Columban monasticism is discussed by Clare Stancliffe in relation to Cuthbert, the abbot-bishop of the Iona-originated community on Lindisfarne.[27] Stancliffe notes that Augustine of Hippo emphasised communality, teaching that the core Christian template to be taken from Scripture is the

---

24 cf. *Prose Life of Cuthbert*, II:4. Carver et al., *Portmahomack on Tarbat Ness*, 224, note that whilst marine animals were eaten, the oil they could supply was just as important. Oil could be burned to give light and may be why dolphins were depicted on Roman lamps. Christian communities had rituals which required oil, including the maintenance of the altar light and chrisms to anoint the new-born and dying.

25 Clancy and Markus, *Iona: The Earliest Poetry of a Celtic Monastery*, 21.

26 Sharpe, *Adomnán of Iona: Life of St. Columba*, 282, note 118.

27 Clare Stancliffe, 'Cuthbert and the polarity between Pastor and Solitary' in Bonner et al., *St. Cuthbert, His Cult and Community to A.D. 1200*.

communal life of the Apostles, rather than the solitariness of an Elijah or an Elisha.[28] Gregory the Great agreed with Augustine, with both echoing Basil's view that the communal life was the more perfect. This was Basil's conviction despite his huge admiration of lone ascetics.[29] For Basil, the Christian ideal was social rather than solitary, and he listed a formidable array of arguments in favour of the communal life.[30] He argued:

- men require assistance from others even in bodily requirements;
- the law of love concerns the needs of a neighbour, and neighbours only exist in a community;
- a person who lives alone becomes unaware of his own faults with no one to reprove him in a kindly fashion;
- some divine commands can only be fulfilled within communality, such as the command to share;
- only the community can be the biblical model of the Church in which believers are members one of another through union in one body by the Holy Spirit;
- the gifts of the Spirit are not all given to one individual, but are distributed across the family of believers;
- the solitary life fosters self-complacency with little opportunity to practice true humility;
- in solitariness there is no opportunity to 'wash one another's feet' or to imitate the first believers who had all things in common;

28 Augustine, *Confessions*, IX:10; cf. Stancliffe, 'Cuthbert and the polarity between Pastor and Solitary' in Bonner (ed.), *St. Cuthbert, his Cult and Community to A.D. 1200*, 37.

29 Basil, *Letters*, 42.

30 Basil, *The Shorter Rule*, Qu. 3:22, 25. Gregory of Nazianzus, *Orations*, XLIII, 62, writes at length in admiration of how Basil brought hermits together, 'in order that the contemplative spirit might not be cut off from society, nor the active life be uninfluenced by the contemplative, but that, like sea and land, by an interchange of their several gifts, they might unite in promoting the one object, the glory of God'; cf. Basil, *The Longer Rule*, 7, and Basil, *The Shorter Rule*, Qu. 3:1-37. Silvas, *The Rule of St. Basil in Latin and English: A Revised Critical Edition*, 7, points out that Basil's idea of Christian community went hand in glove with his theology of communion and order in the Trinity, and with the image of God in men and women reflecting God as a social being.

- prayer is stronger when prayed by the many with one mind and heart;
- finally, and of crucial importance for spiritual warfare, the communal life is more effective in warding off the Evil One.

In contrast to Basil, and despite being the founder of a community at Marseilles, Cassian saw the solitary, or at least the semi-solitary, life as the more perfect. Cassian viewed the contented life of the hermit as spiritual perfection and believed that pure worship could not be achieved in the communal experience.[31] For Cassian the coenobitic life was for beginners. It was a stage on the way to the ideal. This was one area in which Cassian's admirer, Benedict, disagreed with him. Benedict held that membership of the community until death was the most perfect form of monasticism. For Benedict the communal life was not a staging post on the way to perfection. It was itself the highest form of Christian living. Every pilgrim was always a beginner. Every pilgrim needed the *Rule*. Every pilgrim lived by the support of the common life.

Irish monks embraced Cassian's emphasis on solitariness more than their Benedictine counterparts did. Many sought the 'deserts of the ocean', on Hebridean islets or on hard-to-get-to islands such as Skellig Michael off south-western Ireland. Yet Jill Harden suggests that the *eremitic* experience may only have been sought on a temporary basis, and that few Irish monks were permanent recluses, even those on Skellig Michael.[32] Isolation may have been for a specified length of time, possibly the holy period of forty days.

One notable recluse was Cuthbert of Lindisfarne. Though Cuthbert's spirituality came from the Iona coenobitic tradition, he longed for the solitary life as he grew older.[33] He relinquished his post as abbot-bishop on Lindisfarne. He moved to a hut outside the main monastic compound. He then transferred to a cell on an islet adjacent to Lindisfarne. Finally, he relocated to one of the uninhabited Farne

31 Cassian, *Institutes*, III:2.

32 Jill Harden, 'Following in St. Brendan's Wake: Distant Early-Christian Islands between Ireland and the Faroes', Groam House Lecture, 31st August 2017.

33 Stancliffe, 'Cuthbert and the Polarity between Pastor and Solitary' in Bonner (ed.) *St. Cuthbert, his Cult and Community to A.D. 1200*, 36, indicates several, possibly deliberate, similarities between the *Life of Cuthbert* and Athanasius' *Life of Anthony*, including an increasing tendency to isolation.

Islands. There he spent his time in intense spiritual combat against the demonic as a soldier of Christ.[34] Cuthbert went to extremes, enclosing himself within a building and cutting himself off from everything apart from a view of the sky. He never wanted to be an abbot. Nor had he ever wanted to be a bishop. He was by nature a loner. Although some of Cuthbert's actions may be attributed to a derangement of the mind as he grew older, he illustrates that, for some, there was an overpowering desire for solitariness. In this respect the hermits of the Irish Church replicated the desert anchorites in a way in which others rarely did. Only in isolation, away from all people and away from all distractions, could the soul be purified, could life be truly simple, and could God be found.

In his *Life of Columba* Adomnán refers to monks seeking isolation. There was 'a soldier of Christ' called Finan who lived for many years as an anchorite beside the monastery of Durrow (I:49). There was the monk Baetan who sought Columba's blessing before setting out with others to seek a place of retreat (I:20). Nevertheless, the majority of Irish monks lived in a communal existence. Only occasionally did they pursue solitariness.

What of Columba himself? In the *Altus Prosator*, Columba makes it clear that this world is not a Christian's true home, and only those who despise this present world and hold it in contempt can please God in the last time.[35] Does this make Columba a loner like Anthony and Cuthbert? Not really. Adomnán portrays Columba seeking solitariness from time to time (especially during night hours), but nowhere does he describe Columba as restlessly seeking that experience. At heart Columba was a different personality-type from Cuthbert. Columba relished being at the centre of events. He enjoyed the buzz of action. He revelled in the company of the powerful and influential. He was a man born to be a leader. He needed people around him whom to lead. The ethos of Iona reflected the personality of its founder, and in Iona spirituality it was the communal outlook which dominated. MacDonald notes that Adomnán's Columba is only conventionally an ascetic and in no sense a solitary.[36] Significantly, Iona's foundation

---

34 Bede, *Life of Cuthbert*, XVII.

35 *Altus Prosator*, Stanza Z.

36 MacDonald, 'Adomnán's Monastery of Iona' in Bourke (ed.), *Studies in the Cult of Saint Columba*, 26.

story symbolises communality, with Columba arriving in Britain accompanied by twelve companions (III:3). It is the community which is apart from the world, not the individual. This is reflected in Adomnán's account of Columba's funeral, when it is the community alone who are in attendance, separated by wind and storm from the rest of the world.

CONTEMPLATION AND LABOUR

A second tension, with roots in early desert monasticism, was between the contemplative and the practical. Though Cassian saw both the contemplative life and the practical life as acceptable to God, he viewed the contemplative as preferable.[37] Cassian also warned that women (sexual desires) and bishops (church politics) had to be avoided if a monk were to have any hope of pursuing the contemplative life![38] Gregory the Great had a different view.[39] Just as Gregory favoured the communal rather than the solitary, so he advocated a mixed contemplative and active life. In Gregory's model, Jesus was the perfect pattern. Jesus was a man of prayer. He was also a carpenter practising His trade. In doing so, Jesus hallowed all labour, and united the practical and the contemplative. Jesus made toil, as well as prayer, part of the ideal Christian experience. But not everyone agreed with this theology. There was a view that labour and toil were part of human experience only because of the Fall of humanity. Labour and toil might be *necessary* for human existence, but they were not an original part of the *essential* life of men or women. Moreover, in heaven there will be no toil or labour, but only holy contemplation of God. Labour and toil belong to a fallen world. They are not part of the true life of a child of God.

Stancliffe suggests that Martin of Tours was never at ease with the notion that holy perfection combines the contemplative and the practical. Hence, instead of accommodating himself to the daily practical necessities of physical labour and administration, Martin tried to delegate these to others in order to focus on prayer. For

37 cf. Herren and Brown, *Christ in Celtic Christianity*, 240.

38 Cassian, *Institutes*, XI:18.

39 Stancliffe, 'Cuthbert and the polarity between Pastor and Solitary' in Bonner (ed.) *St. Cuthbert, his Cult and Community to A.D. 1200*, 40.

Martin, physical work was not an extension of the spiritual. Toil was an obstruction to prayer. Within this milieu, workaday activities were not regarded as complementary features of the balanced spiritual life, but as barriers and obstacles.

Where did Columba stand on this? Did his Iona regard the whole of monastic life, from its liturgy in church to its labour in the fields, as an offering of worship? Did the monks live out a harmony of prayer and toil? If Cuthbert of Lindisfarne were typical of the Columban tradition, the answer would be in the negative. Cuthbert was not work-shy. When he expended himself actively, he gave one hundred percent commitment, making long pastoral and evangelistic journeys all over the Borders. But the mixed life never truly worked for him. He tried to slough off responsibilities, even his Episcopal duties, in order to be free for prayer and meditation. For Cuthbert, even a bishop's role was unsuited to the truly contemplative life.

But Cuthbert was not Columba. Therefore, were workaday activities part of a holistic spirituality for Columba? This is certainly a feature of 'Celtic' spirituality in Alexander Carmichael's *Carmina Gaedelica*, his nineteenth-century compilation of Gaelic prayers and blessings. In recording prayers associated with everyday tasks such as house cleaning, milking cows, and working in the fields, Carmichael gives the impression that in Celtic spirituality the whole of life was seen as spiritual. But does Carmichael represent the spirituality of sixth-century Iona? The notion that Celtic spirituality viewed the whole of life as spiritual was certainly attractive to nineteenth-century readers, living in an era when the bleak spectre of industrialisation cast a dehumanising shadow on the soul. But Carmichael took his material from the nineteenth-century Catholic Gaelic culture of the Western Isles, and not from Columba. Did that nineteenth-century culture echo Columba's of thirteen centuries earlier? Or did it read nineteenth-century romanticism back into the sixth century? Cuthbert, even as an extreme case, shows that within early Columban Christianity, there was not always a harmony between the meditative life and that of labour and toil.

We cannot assume too readily that sixth and seventh-century Iona monks embraced a harmony of contemplation and toil. And yet, there do seem to be elements of this in the spirituality of the period. Was Columba's blessing of a milk-pail a hallowing of labour (II:16)? The story is complicated by including the expulsion of demonic forces lurking within the milk-pail, introducing spiritual warfare alongside the simple blessing of a milking. Nevertheless, an appeal to bless the milk-pail was the original request; and detection of the demonic lurking within it was an unexpected development. Elsewhere in Adomnán's *Life of Columba* there are examples in which the ordinary toils of life appear to be viewed as part of a spiritual calling. Unlike Cuthbert, Columba incorporated all of the messy and awkward duties of his abbacy (leadership, discipline, labour, advising kings) into his spiritual calling – with enthusiasm!

CELIBACY AND MARRIAGE

Adomnán writes that Columba was 'one of the company that follows the Lamb, a virgin without stain, pure and whole without fault, through the grace of our Lord Jesus Christ' (III:23). In similar vein, the *Amra* states that Columba 'lit up the east with chaste clerics'.[40] There is no evidence that any abbot of Iona married. There are no references to children of abbots. There was no hereditary succession. Was celibacy a requirement for the monastic life on Iona?

At this point we need to distinguish between monks and priests, since it was not uncommon in the early centuries of the Christian era for priests to be married. The Fourth Canon of the Synod of Gangra (340) indicates that married priests existed and defends them against their critics. Then, in the fifth century, Patrick writes in his *Confessions* that he was the son of a deacon and the grandson of a priest.[41] Patrick himself was unmarried, and the *Bangor Antiphonary* celebrates Patrick keeping his flesh chaste on account of his love for God.[42] However, other early Irish canons allude to the wives of priests.[43] There is also prodigious evidence for married clergy in the Celtic Church in Wales, with frequent notices of married bishops, priests, and deacons. Records of strong opposition to attempts at enforced clerical celibacy in tenth-century Wales also show that the Welsh branch of the Celtic Church

40 *Amra*, II.

41 Patrick, *Confessions*, I.

42 *Bangor Antiphonary*, Item 13:10.

43 Warren, *The Liturgy and Ritual of the Celtic Church*, 14; cf. Herren and Brown, *Christ in Celtic Christianity*, 32.

had married clergy until at least then.[44] Papal decrees were issued from Rome from the fourth century onwards with the aim of imposing celibacy, but these were regularly ignored, especially in Britain and Ireland. The fact that decrees were issued shows that clerical celibacy was not universally observed.[45] In the eastern Church, there were married deacons, priests, and bishops until the Trullo Synod of 691–692, after which bishops and patriarchs (but not priests) had to be unmarried, as is the case today.[46]

The situation was different for monks. Although marriage existed among the *manaig* who lived outside a monastery, celibacy was the norm within it; and indeed, whether the *manaig* should be termed 'monks' at all is an undecided issue.[47] Concerning 'real' monks,

---

44 Warren, *The Liturgy and Ritual of the Celtic Church*, 14. Warren cites married priests in the Celtic Church in Brittany.

45 MacLauchlan, *The Early Scottish Church*, 192, consistent with his 'Protestantising of the Columban Church', argues that in Scotland the marriage of clergy was practised for centuries after Columba's era. James Morton, *The Monastic Annals of Teviotdale: The History and Antiquities of the Abbeys of Jedburgh, Kelso, Melrose, and Dryburgh* (Edinburgh: Lizars, 1832, Forgotten Books edition), 190, cites three eighth-century Scottish clergymen including John of Melrose (from the Melrose/Lindisfarne/Iona tradition) disputing against Boniface of Mainz who held that celibacy should be compulsory for all clergy. Boniface called a Council in 742 and decreed that anyone marrying after becoming a priest, or not sexually abstinent if already married, or living with a concubine if unmarried, should be severely whipped and imprisoned for two years. Boniface's reaction shows that some were marrying after becoming priests, and some already married men were being admitted to the priesthood. The First Lateran Council (1123) forbade those in orders to marry and ordered those already married to renounce their wives and do penance.

46 Demetrios J. Constantelos, *Understanding the Greek Orthodox Church* (4th edition; Massachusetts: Hellenic Press, 2005), 99, suggests that the requirement for a celibate episcopate was due to the increasing influence of monastic ideals.

47 Hunwicke, 'Kerry and Stowe Revisited' in *PRIA: Section C: Archaeology, Celtic Studies, History, Linguistics, Literature*, vol. 102C, no. 1 (2002), 1-19, notes the 'almost monks' living on the fringes of monastic communities who were married. Hughes, *Early Christian Ireland: Introduction to the Sources*, 79, notes that in the later Irish canons: 'Every first-born son of the *manaig* (i.e. the lay-monks who farmed the monastic lands and were married) was to be offered to the Church and educated by the Church: later he inherited his share of the family land and farmed it as a free-client of the Church.' In Irish, *manaig* is the plural of *manach* meaning 'monk'. *Manaig* were counted as being *within* the monastic family even though located outside the monastery; whereas the tenants of a Benedictine monastery were not part of the monastic family. Herren and Brown, *Christ in Celtic Christianity*, 14, discuss these lay-monks, or 'faithful laity', who had to practise sexual abstinence for three forty-day periods each year (the three 'Lents') and had to submit to the guidance of a confessor. Herren and Brown (33) state that *manaig* were married folk with families, providing services for the church in return for pastoral care (the sacraments, burial, prayers for the dead); they lived under the rule of the community. O'Loughlin, *Celtic Theology*, 132, notes that a monastery was not just the band of monks who kept the monastic Rule but

Canon 16 of the Council of Chalcedon (451) stated that monks and nuns should not contract marriage, and if they did, they were to be excommunicated. Hence, monks based in monasteries were celibate. Their lives were wholly dedicated to their calling, and celibacy was strictly enforced.

But celibacy did not remove erotic longings. Sexual temptation had to be overcome, despite later writers sometimes over-idealising early Irish monks as giants of holiness who had eliminated carnal desires. Warren quotes an eighth-century text which describes the early Irish Church in glowing terms:

> They had one head, Christ; and one chief, Patrick. They observed one mass, one celebration, one tonsure from ear to ear. They celebrated one Easter, on the fourteenth moon after the vernal equinox. And what was excommunicated by one church all excommunicated. They rejected not the services and society of women; because, founded on the rock of Christ, they feared not the blast of temptation.[48]

This excerpt promotes the myth that monks of the early Irish Church were so pure that they were untouched by sexual temptation and were able to live near women because they had attained lack of passion in *apatheia*. But this is a later age looking back. In their own day Columba, Comgall, Cormac, and Cuthbert were only too aware of the temptations of the flesh. Cassian was equally realistic: perhaps obsessively so. One of Cassian's arguments for minimal sleep, and for observing compulsory vigils until dawn, was that deep sleep might bring dreams which, ungoverned by the conscious will, would flood the soul with sinful thoughts and images. Monks were to watch and pray during the night hours for three main reasons: to glorify God; to avoid laziness; and that Satan might not, 'by some illusion in a dream pollute the purity which has been gained by the Psalms and prayers of the night'.[49] Prayer during the long hours of the night was not just an

---

included many who were socially and legally identified with the monastery, who farmed its land, who carried on their trades in the service of the community, and who had their religious needs met by the monks.

48 Warren, *The Liturgy and Ritual of the Celtic Church*, 80.

49 Cassian, *Institutes*, II:13 and II:14. Basil, *Letters*, 2, expresses similar sentiments: 'To be overcome by heavy torpor, with limbs unstrung, so that a way is readily opened to

act of devotion. It was an alternative to slumber, since slumber could expose the soul to sinful thoughts.

Adomnán's Columba engages with every aspect of life. He thrives in the company of others, but also seeks times of retreat. He is at home in the devotions of the prayer-house, but also in the work of the field. Adomnán's Columba personifies Gregory's vision of the mixed life as the ideal. Columba's Iona was a place where liturgy and labour, worship and work, were each a positive part of the spiritual life.

wild fancies, is to be plunged in daily death. What dawn is to some, this midnight is to athletes of piety.'

CHAPTER 8

Prayer, Fasting, Seclusion

Each monk wanted his life to be an unbroken offering of praise and prayer, and the set daily Canonical Hours of worship were stepping-stones toward this ideal. Between the Canonical Hours each monk was expected to continue in prayer through repeating the psalms, even as he worked. Slumber was an unwanted evil, interrupting a life of constant prayer. One reason why Columba was seen as a perfect exemplar of the spiritual life was because he stayed awake in prayer during winter nights when (so it was rumoured) angels came to him. At such times Columba was in a 'thin place', close to God. Beccán wrote of him:

He served with a blessed band,
He often spent nights withdrawn.
Silence, too, thinness of side.
Britain's beacon, his mouth's wisdom.[1]

But what was prayer for Columba? Was it reflective meditation? Was it discerning God's will? Could prayer move God's hand and change history? On the latter point, Adomnán certainly presents a Columba who believed that prayer did affect God's actions. On one occasion, Columba learned that his life had been extended by four years, simply because so many churches prayed that he might stay longer on earth to aid them (III:22).

Three physical postures could be adopted during prayer: standing, kneeling, and prostration. The first pose was to stand erect, with arms spread out towards heaven, and with eyes gazing upwards. When Columba was at sea, and his boat in danger of sinking, he stood in the prow, extended his hands to heaven, and prayed to the Almighty (II:12). Another time, he was secretly followed by monks who saw,

1 Beccán, *Fo Reir Choluimb*, 19.

'Columba standing on a knoll among the fields and praying with his arms spread out towards heaven and his eyes gazing upwards' (III:16). Another time, his monks raised 'their hands to heaven in great joy, and worshipped Christ in the holy and blessed man' (I:37). The second pose involved the supplicant kneeling. Columba knelt in church before he died (III:23). Similarly, when he prayed for Cormac whose ship was in peril, 'he bent his knees before the altar and in a tearful voice prayed to the omnipotence of God which controls the winds and all things' (II:42). However, when intense prayer was needed, the third pose was adopted, with the supplicant prostrating himself on the ground, as Columba did when urging his monks to pray for the soul of a man drowned in Belfast Lough, whose eternal destiny was at stake (III:13).

Prayer was a serious matter. Basil makes the point that if it is a solemn thing for a private individual to speak to an Emperor, how much more for a mere man to speak to God![2] Such seriousness brought severe penalties for reciting prayers incorrectly. For example, the *Penitential of Cummean* prescribed fifty lashes for any monk who stammered over the *periculosa* which is recited when the chalice is raised during the Eucharist. This increased to one hundred lashes for two offences, and to a severe fast for three.[3] Adomnán accepted that God might use fear to increase the intensity of prayer. Thus, when Bishop Colman mac Beognai encountered rough seas on his way to Iona, and tried to lessen the danger by sitting in the prow of the boat and blessing the turbulent waters, Columba commented:

> The Lord terrifies him in this way, not so that the ship in which he sits should be overwhelmed and wrecked by the waves, but rather to rouse him to pray more fervently that he may sail through the peril and reach us here (I:5).

More important than posture is the question: To whom was prayer directed? Adomnán's Columba worshipped and prayed to the triune God of Father, Son, and Holy Spirit, and not to an anonymous Supreme Being. This focus on the triune God is powerfully conveyed in early texts such as the *Amra Choluimb Chille* and the *Altus Prosator*. At the same time, Adomnán portrays an Iona spirituality familiar with

2 Basil, *Letters*, 41:2.

3 *Penitential of Cummean*, XI:29.

prayer involving departed saints. In early-medieval times this had three aspects: prayer *to* the departed saints; prayer *for* the dead; and prayer involving Mary.

1. *Prayer to Departed Saints.* Adomnán has several stories indicating that this was common practice on his Iona. For example, after Columba's death, some relics, including Columba's white tunic and his books, became part of a prayer vigil at a time of drought (II:44). In that narrative Columba was referred to in the prayers, though it is unclear whether the prayer was directed to Columba or directed to God with a plea to remember Columba's people.[4] On that occasion it may be that relics were brought forward as symbols in order to 'remind' God to honour Columba's memory. But other incidents leave no doubt that Columba was appealed to in prayer. Thus, when Adomnán and his companions are delayed by inclement weather as they tow oak trees from the River Shiel to Iona, Adomnán appeals directly to Columba for help:

> Is this troublesome delay in our efforts what you wanted St. Columba? To this point I had hoped that by God's favour you would bring help and comfort in our labours, since I thought you stood in high honour with God. (II:45)

In the same chapter Adomnán records a prayer made when returning from an Irish Synod, and again delayed by weather:

> Is it your wish, O saint, that I should stay here among the lay people till tomorrow, and not spend the day of your feast in your own church [on Iona]? It is such an easy thing for you on a day like this to change an adverse wind into a favourable one, so that I might partake of the solemn masses of your feast day in your own church. (II:45)

These are clear examples of praying to the departed Columba, and regarding Columba in heaven as being involved in answering the prayer. In these instances, it is not God who is addressed, directly. Nor is Columba mentioned only in a context of God being appealed

4 Yorke, *The Conversion of Britain: 600–800*, 191, suggests that Adomnán cast the incident in a form reminiscent of an account of a procession involving Italian saints written by Gregory the Great in his *Dialogues*.

to for the sake of Columba's honour, or for the good of Columba's people. Columba himself is supplicated. There is no reason to doubt that such practices existed in Columba's time as well as in Adomnán's. Columba would pray to figures who had been great saints of God. This theme comes to a climax in Adomnán's final chapter, where he portrays Columba promising to intercede for Iona after his death:

> These my last words: Love one another unfeignedly. Peace. If you keep this course according to the example of the holy fathers, God, who strengthens the good, will help you, and I, dwelling with him, shall intercede for you. (III:23)

All of this is at odds with Warren's generalisation that liturgies of the ancient Celtic Church contain no instances of prayer to departed saints.[5] Warren acknowledges that there may have been a belief in the efficacy of the prayers of the glorified saints on behalf of those still on earth but insists that departed saints were not expected to answer prayer in their own right. However, the foregoing examples question that argument. Warren holds to his position despite being aware that Item 124 of the *Bangor Antiphonary* has direct address to departed saints, arguing that Item 124 is more an appeal for the holy martyrs to *remember* the church on earth than a direct prayer for their *aid*.[6] But this relies on a subtle distinction between 'remembering' and 'aiding'. Is that permissible? In context, 'remember' meant being asked to 'help'.[7] What Warren may be doing is attempting to separate the piety of the early-medieval Irish Church, from the Catholicism of his own era in the nineteenth century, in which direct supplication of the saints was a massive feature of popular

5 Warren, *The Liturgy and Ritual of the Celtic Church*, 102.

6 Warren, *The Antiphonary of Bangor: Part II (Antiphonarium Benchorense): An Early Irish Manuscript in the Ambrosian Library at Milan, Part II* (London: Harrison, 1895), 81. Paul C. Stratman, *The Antiphonary of Bangor and the Divine Offices of Bangor* (Beaver Dam: Stratman, 2018), translates Item 124 as: 'Remember us always in the presence of the Lord, so that from the Lord we may receive help.' Item 13:24 is even more obvious: 'Bishop Patrick, pray for us all, that the crimes we have committed may be erased immediately.' [Stratman translation]

7 Adomnán, *Life of Columba*, I:1, claims that Columba's name was so powerful that its invocation, even by evil men could bring protection: 'Certain men, wicked and blood-stained from a life as brigands, were protected by songs that they sang in Irish in praise of St. Columba and by the commemoration of his name. For on the night they sang these songs, they were delivered from the hands of their enemies, who had surrounded the house of the singers, and escaped unhurt through flames and swords and spears. But a few of them made little of the holy man's commemoration and would not sing these songs. Miraculously, these alone perished in the enemies' attack.'

piety. But even if early-medieval practice was less extreme than that of Warren's day, it still existed. In the early-medieval era, prayer was not only directed to God. It was also addressed to departed saints.

2. *Prayer for the Dead.* Several early-medieval writers close their works with requests for the continued prayers of their readers, though in some cases these requests may have applied only during the beneficiaries' earthly lifetime. Adomnán closes his book on *The Holy Places* with such a plea.[8] Dorbene, the scribe of an early eighth-century copy of Adomnán's *Life of Columba*, adds a similar petition at the close of his manuscript. Warren, still wary of confusing early-medieval Irish piety with later practices of prayers for the dead *en masse*, points out that Item 61 of the *Bangor Antiphonary* stops short at a passage which, in the later *Stowe Missal*, led into intercession for the departed.[9] Despite these caveats the pleas appear to be for prayer for the authors from the living, even after the authors have died.

3. *Prayer involving Mary.* In the century following Columba's death there was an increase of attention to the Virgin Mary. This may have sprouted from a devotional concentration on Christ's nativity, sparked by the Theotokos controversy and Mary's role as the God-bearer.[10] Yet, throughout Christendom, Mariology was a slow-burner.[11] In sixth-century Irish texts, such as the *Amra* and Columba's *Altus Prosator*, Mary is conspicuous by her absence. Equally, the short prayer *Adiutor Laborantium* (perhaps partially composed by Columba), has

8 Adomnán, *The Holy Places*, III:6.

9 Warren, *The Antiphonary of Bangor: Part II*, 66.

10 R. E. Messenger, *The Medieval Latin Hymn* (Washington DC: Capital, 1953), 8.

11 The scholarly blogger Anglandicus (www.anglandicus.blogspot.co.uk) notes that Marian piety and veneration developed relatively late in Christianity. Ignatius mentions Mary for Christological purposes, in order to defend the virgin birth etc. Tertullian in the third century affirms the virgin birth but denies that Mary remained ever-virgin or sinless. Mary remaining sinless was open for discussion, and several Church Fathers, such as Origen, Basil, Cyril of Alexandria, Athanasius and John Chrysostom write of Mary's personal sins of doubt and ambition. By the fourth century prayer and invocation of the saints, including Mary, is common practice. Jerome and Augustine teach that Mary lived a sinless life though she had original sin. Jerome and Augustine were hugely influential in early Ireland. The sixteenth-century Council of Trent declared dogmatically that Mary was free from actual sin, and in 1854 Pope Pius IX declared the dogma of the Immaculate Conception, that Mary had no original sin. Augustine does not teach a doctrine of Immaculate Conception, and it is not found in Latin writings until the twelfth century, when it is opposed by Bernard of Clairvaux among others. In 1950 Pope Pius XII defined the doctrine of the Assumption of the Virgin Mary into heaven, stating that Mary reigns in heaven with her Son.

no reference to Mary or any request for her aid. Mary's absence from the *Adiutor Laborantium* is striking. Its petitions seem a ready-made opportunity to invoke Mary's aid, but it is Christ who is appealed to, not her. Similarly, the *Bangor Antiphonary*, echoing older forms of worship (though composed in the early eighth century), has no focus on Mary.

Nevertheless, we know that by the time Adomnán wrote his *Life of Columba* in the last decade of the seventh century, the cult of Mary was gathering strength. Why then does Adomnán have no references to prayers to the Virgin in his book? The answer may be that Adomnán's concern is to present Columba as such a great man of God that his prayers are second to none in their power and efficacy. If Columba needed additional help (through Mary, for example) that would indicate something lacking in him. Hence, when Columba is faced with a girl agonising in a difficult childbirth (II:40), he prays to 'Christ the Son of Man' and not to Mary, even though childbirth would be a perfect setting for such an appeal.[12] Adomnán wants all of the focus to be on Columba. His aim is to prove Columba's intercessory powers, not Mary's.

Adomnán does refer to Mary in his *Law of the Innocents*, where he argues that the reason women should be treated as non-combatants in time of war is because the God-given destiny of any woman is as a giver of life, not its destroyer. For Adomnán, Mary is the ultimate example of this calling. Adomnán opens his work by claiming that an angel spoke to Adomnán, saying:

> Go forth into Ireland and make a law in that women be not killed in any manner by man … You shall establish a law in Ireland and Britain for the sake of the mother of each one, because a mother has borne each one, and for the sake of Mary, the mother of Jesus Christ through whom the whole [human race] is.[13]

Mary's importance is in being the giver of life to Jesus Christ. Through him, she is life-giver to the whole human race. In his other major work, *The Holy Places*, Adomnán refers to Mary as ever-virgin, but with no hint of the later dogma that Mary was taken up to heaven before

12 Adomnán, *Life of Columba*, II:40, 'Now the Lord Jesus, born of woman, shows favour, and giving timely help to the sufferer has released her from her distress.' (tr. Anderson and Anderson)

13 Adomnán, *The Law of the Innocents*, 33, in O'Loughlin (ed.), *Adomnán at Birr*, 57-68.

death.[14] Yet, Adomnán is not uninterested in Mary. Several times in *The Holy Places* he notes the quadrangular church in Jerusalem which was dedicated to Mary.[15] He also tells us that his source, Arculf, claimed to have seen a cloth which Mary wove.[16] But despite this interest, he nowhere translates this into an emphasis on Mary as a heavenly intercessor. At the close of his book it is Christ, and not Mary, to whom he urges his readers to pray on his behalf.[17]

Nevertheless, even as Adomnán ruled as abbot of Iona, the cult of the Virgin was growing. Pope Sergius I (d. 701) established her four great feasts in the Church calendar. And Irish stone-crosses, hitherto devoid of references to Mary, began to depict the Virgin and child.[18] On Iona itself the monk Cu Chuimne wrote the hymn *Cantemus in Omni Die* (Let Us Sing Every Day), revealing a spirituality never referenced by Adomnán:

Let us sing every day, harmonising in turns,
Together proclaiming to God, a hymn worthy of Mary.
In two-fold chorus, from side to side, let us praise Mary,
So that the voice strikes every ear with alternating praise.[19]

Cu Chuimne's early eighth-century hymn reveals how Mariology was starting to influence the devotional life of Iona. In the hymn, Mary has a strong role in salvation. She is born of the tribe of Judah. She is mother of the most-high Lord. She is the venerable Virgin. She is unique of all human mothers. Critically, as a woman, she reverses the fault of the first woman:

---

14 Adomnán, *The Holy Places*, I:12. Adomnán does not know where Mary's body is as it 'awaits resurrection'.

15 Adomnán, *The Holy Places*, I:4.

16 Adomnán, *The Holy Places*, I:10.

17 Adomnán, *The Holy Places*, III:6: 'I admonish the reader of these experiences that he neglects not to pray to Christ the judge of generations on behalf of me, the writer, a wretched sinner.'

18 Sharpe, *Adomnán of Iona: Life of St. Columba*, 80. Jane Hawkes, 'Columban Virgins: Iconic Images of the Virgin and Child in Insular Sculpture' in Bourke (ed.), *Studies in the Cult of Saint Columba*, 107-35, gives a comprehensive account of images of the Virgin and Child in insular art. The earliest extant insular image of Virgin and Child may be incised on the Cuthbert coffin produced at Lindisfarne. However, Christopher De Hamel, *Meetings with Remarkable Manuscripts* (London: Penguin, 2017), 113, believes that the earliest representation of the Virgin and Child in western European art may be on folio 7v in the Book of Kells, created towards the close of the eighth century.

19 Cu Chuimne, *Cantemus in Omni Die*, I; cf. Clancy and Markus, *Iona: The Earliest Poetry of a Celtic Monastery*, 177.

By a woman and a tree, the world first perished,
By the power of a woman, it has returned to salvation.[20]

The word 'power' is the Latin '*virtutem*', signalling that Mary's virtue contributes materially to the salvation of the world. Cu Chuimne also speaks of believers being 'perfected by God' and 'taken up by Mary'. Overall, he has a strong notion of Mary aiding salvation:

Truly, truly, we implore, by the merits of the child-bearer,
That the flame of the dread fire be not able to ensnare us.[21]

Clancy and Markus note that in Cu Chuimne's poem Mary's place in the story of salvation is at the incarnation rather than at the cross.[22] This is because she is the *Theotokos*, the God-bearer, the mother of the one in whom divine nature and human nature are conjoined in one person.[23] It is her consent which allows the incarnation to take place, and which initiates the consequent drama of redemption. Hence, in the Iona monastery of the eighth century, there is a regard for Mary which is more than polite reverence. She has a mediating and a saving role.[24] But little of this can be projected backwards on to Columba. The transition from reverencing Mary as the mother of Jesus, to making Mary a focus for prayer and devotion, had not yet taken place in Columba's lifetime, at least in the Irish Church.

FASTING

Ritual fasting existed even in pre-Christian Ireland. Sometimes it was a religious discipline, and sometimes it was a means for subjects to bring issues to the attention of their rulers.[25] The indigenous practice then dovetailed with Christian disciplines, with fasting indicating the seriousness of a supplicant's prayers. Fasting, with its rejection of bodily comforts, encouraged concentration on things of the spirit. It aided weaning from the world. It helped to slough off bodily desires for

---

20 Cu Chuimne, *Cantemus in Omni Die*, VII.

21 Cu Chuimne, *Cantemus in Omni Die*, XII.

22 Clancy and Markus, *Iona: The Earliest Poetry of a Celtic Monastery*, 187.

23 Clancy and Markus, *Iona: The Earliest Poetry of a Celtic Monastery*, 188f.

24 Clancy and Markus, *Iona: The Earliest Poetry of a Celtic Monastery*, 190, point out that the Christology of *Cantemus in Omni Die* reflects phrases used at the 675 Council of Toledo. Toledo spoke of Christ being both Father and Son of the blessed Virgin. Similarly, Cu Chuimne wrote: 'Mary, amazing mother, gave birth to her Father.'

25 Yorke, *The Conversion of Britain: 600–800*, 220.

comfort and food. And, in putting these aside, the pilgrim became more like a heavenly being, finding fulfilment in God alone. The *Amra* (VII) portrays Columba as a champion of battles won over the flesh and is proud that he destroyed 'his body's desire'.[26] He 'won battles with gluttony' (V). He 'avoided the fill of his mouth' (VI).

This self-denial was seen as a power-driver of Columba's inner spiritual life.[27] Fasting did much more than hone the body. It perfected soul and intellect. It gave Columba increased virtue. It provided him with greater understanding of the Scriptures. It shaped his unsurpassed skill in scholarship. And it bestowed on him an incomparable gift of teaching. Fasting was credited with enhancing every dimension of Columba's spirituality. It opened channels through which God, by his Spirit, could work powerfully in his life.[28] Notably, fasting is one area in which the *Amra* and the *Life of Columba* are in full agreement, despite at other times having divergent images of Columba. The *Amra* is less focussed on miracles which are so high-profile in the *Life*; but both the *Amra* and the *Life* celebrate the importance of fasting.[29]

1. *Fasting as an Exercise in Spiritual Self-Denial*: The Amra (VI) notes that Columba 'avoided the fill of his mouth', and argues that this discipline enabled him to subdue ungodly desires.[30] It was repeated fasting and repeated prayer which made him a saintly figure. Fasting deepened piety and created a virtuous cycle, reinforcing a resolve to pursue ever-more intense self-denial.

2. *Fasting as a Weapon in Spiritual Warfare*: In the core ministry of fighting demonic forces, the discipline of fasting was a mighty weapon. Adomnán describes how once, when Columba went off to pray alone, he 'saw a line of foul, black devils, armed with iron spikes and drawn up ready for battle' (III:8). When Columba was aided by angels, the

---

26 cf. Basil, *The Shorter Rule*, Qu. 8:16, 17.

27 Herbert, *Iona, Kells and Derry*, 10f.

28 McNeill, *The Celtic Penitentials*, 133, suggests that Celtic Christian fasting also drew on pre-Christian notions that fasting could help obtain boons from supernatural beings.

29 Clancy and Markus, *Iona: The Earliest Poetry of a Celtic Monastery*, 124, note similarities between Columba and Cassian in relation to fasting. Herren and Brown, *Christ in Celtic Christianity*, 119f., argue that semi-Pelagian Irish Christianity was averse to miracles (explaining why the *Amra* has few), preferring to concentrate on Columba's moral and spiritual virtues.

30 *Amra*, VI: 'A sound, austere sage of Christ/ No fog of drink nor fog of delights/ He avoided the fill of his mouth/ He was holy, he was chaste, he was charitable/ A famous stone in victory'.

demons fled to Tiree. But the demons also failed on Tiree, because the monks triumphed through 'prayer and fasting', though one of Baithéne's monks, and some monks belonging to other Tiree monasteries, perished in the demonic attack. Adomnán may be suggesting that non-Columban Tiree monasteries suffered more because they were less spiritual and less protected from demonic onslaught.[31]

3. *Fasting as a Means to Increase the Intensity of Prayer*: Decades after Columba's death, Adomnán and other monks were bringing timber from the mainland to Iona, when contrary winds impeded their journey (II:45). To increase the intensity of prayer, Adomnán not only laid Columba's vestments and books on the altar but, 'by fasting and singing psalms', entreated Columba to obtain favours from the Lord.

4. *Fasting as a Preparation for God's Guidance*: Columba once advised fasting to help solve a couple's marital problems. He was staying on Rathlin Island when he was approached by a man complaining that his wife would not sleep with him (II:41). Columba sent for the wife. Berating her, he pointed out that the marriage vows meant becoming one flesh. However, the lady stood her ground, adamant that she would no longer share the marital bed. Columba then suggested fasting and prayer, and Adomnán reports that, after all three fasted and prayed, the woman's aversion disappeared: 'The husband whom I hated yesterday I love today.' The story may actually be about a disempowered woman submitting after being browbeaten by a power-figure. But for Adomnán it was an example of a miracle made possible through fasting.

Wednesday and Friday on Iona were fast days, and the Scots-Gaelic names for the days of the week came to reflect this. *Diciadain* (Wednesday) is the day of the first fast. *Dihaoine* (Friday) is the day of the fast. *Diadaoin* (Thursday) is the day between the fasts. Eastern Christians fasted on Wednesdays and Fridays, as did the Roman Church of the Middle-Ages, with each fast having theological significance. In the East the Wednesday fast was in commemoration of Christ's betrayal by Judas Iscariot, and the Friday fast in commemoration of Christ's crucifixion. There were also seasonal fasts, such as the great fast through Lent leading up to Easter, plus other fasts commanded by the abbot. However, East and West did not agree as to which days of the week apart from Wednesdays and Fridays should be regular fast days. Cassian notes

31 Bruce, *Prophecy, Miracles, Angels and Heavenly Light?*, 137, note 99.

that in the Latin West it was common to fast on the Sabbath (Saturday), a practice alien to Middle Eastern Christianity. Thus the Greek tradition allowed feasting on Saturdays after the rigours of the vigil from Friday through to Saturday morning.[32] In the East, Saturdays were regarded as Festal Days, and both dinner and supper were supplied on Saturdays, Sundays, and all Holy Days.[33] The question of whether to fast or not to fast on Saturdays became a point of dispute between the Latin and Greek traditions, with each thundering condemnations on the other. It was the Greek practice of not fasting on Saturdays which was absorbed into the early-medieval Irish Church and taken to Scotland by Columba and others. This may be what the *Amra* (VII) refers to when it states that Columba, 'would do no fast which was not the Lord's law'.

Because the Columban tradition did not fast on Saturdays, even during Lent, this became an issue in the eleventh century when Queen Margaret attempted to bring the Scottish Church into line with continental practices. In Margaret's opinion the Scottish Church did not observe the forty-day Lenten fast properly. The Scottish fast started on the wrong day. It was broken when it should be continuous. It abstained on only thirty-six days, not forty.[34] Margaret got her way, but the controversy shows how deeply Columban practices were embedded in the Scottish Church.

Fast-day strictures could be eased by an abbot if a visitor arrived. Once, Columba informed the brothers, 'Tomorrow is a Wednesday when we usually keep a fast: however, we shall be disturbed by a visitor and our normal fast will be relaxed' (I:26). Adomnán indicates that the whole community broke its fast to welcome the visitor. This differed

32 Cassian, *Institutes*, III:9, 10. Warren, *The Antiphonary of Bangor: Part II*, xxiv, notes Augustine's explanation that the East preferred to relax the fast in order to symbolise Christ's rest in the tomb on Saturday, whereas churches in the West fasted on Saturdays on account of Christ's humiliation and death.

33 *Apostolic Constitutions*, II:59, 1; VIII:33, 1. *Council of Laodicea*, Canons XVI, XLIX, LI. Cassian, *Institutes*, III:12.

34 Cassian knew his system gave only 36 days of fasting (*Conferences*, XXI: 35). Turgot, *The Life of Margaret*, 18, refers to a Council involving representatives of the old Celtic Church, Margaret, her husband Malcom III, and three Benedictine advisors. The Roman date for Easter was adopted in Scotland in the century after Whitby in 664, but the date for the *start* of Lent was disputed. The old Celtic Church did not fast on Sabbaths. Hence, though it observed six weeks for Lent (nominally amounting to forty-two days), lack of fasting on six Sabbaths reduced the number to thirty-six. Margaret argued that, for Scotland to harmonise with the rest of Christendom, uniformity concerning Lent was essential.

from the practice in Benedictine communities where only the abbot broke his fast if a visitor arrived.[35]

SECLUSION

This section could be titled, 'Times of Retreat', but that may conjure up thoughts of twenty-first century church members on an away-weekend, with spiritual reflection combined with a recreational-holiday. For Columba, times of seclusion were of a different stamp. The key notion was exile. And exile was embraced as a pilgrim discipline in which whatever comforts existed at the main monastery were exchanged for a season of even stricter asceticism. Voluntary exile for spiritual reasons was part of an intensification of humility before God; and the exile of a pilgrim-monk echoed the exile embraced by the Son of God when He left the glory of heaven and dwelt on earth.[36] True exile involved a crucifixion of the self.

Voluntary exile could be shared with others. Or a brother might choose to become truly isolated up a distant glen, on an out-of-the-way islet, or in a remote cave. Because exile was part of a monk's calling, some interpret Columba's decision to leave Ireland wholly in terms of him embracing this spiritual discipline.[37] But there was also an enforced exile, when a penitent was ordered to live in an isolated location; and in secular Irish culture the imposition of exile on an individual was a severe form of punishment and disgrace. Exile put a penitent in a state of 'non-being' in relation to the world, society, and the things of God.

Columba's monks spent most of their time in community. They lived together. They worked together. They ate together. It was a coenobitic lifestyle. The Iona monastery was never an enclosed community. It had no fortress-like boundary, and the archaeological evidence indicates that

---

35 Benedict, *The Rule*, LIII.

36 Yorke, *The Conversion of Britain: 600–800*, 123. The *Old Irish Life* saw pilgrimage as a counsel given by God to Abraham and something that 'might abide always with the church'. True 'sons of Abraham' are those who imitate Abraham's perfect faith. (*Old Irish Life*, in Skene, *Celtic Scotland*, vol. II, 469f.). The *Old Irish Life* portrays Columba requesting three gifts from God: chastity, wisdom, and pilgrimage. Pilgrimage is represented as a positive spiritual gift.

37 Sharpe, *Adomnán of Iona: Life of St. Columba*, 335, note 293, observes that the normal Irish Latin meaning of *peregrinus* refers to separation from one's homeland, rather than shrine-visiting in the continental/medieval sense. Hence, when Adomnán describes Columba's life as *peregrinatio*, he is describing Columba's whole thirty-four-year sojourn following his leaving of Ireland in 563; cf. Bruce, *Prophecy, Miracles, Angels and Heavenly Light?*, 210.

the encircling *vallum* was incomplete during Columba's era.[38] Irish monasteries were open-walled and connected to the local *tuath*, or tribe, with the typical monastery a busy, bustling centre. Iona retained that cultural context despite its island location. This meant that the main monastery was not the best place for isolation and quietness. Consequently, if a monk wanted privacy, his first recourse might be a hut beside the monastery, where he could live in parallel with the community but with private space (I:49). That might be enough, but some craved more.[39] And when Irish monks sought true seclusion, they looked to the remote islets of the Hebrides, the 'deserts' of the ocean. These islands were their Arabia. For example, the monk Fergnae spent twelve years in isolation at Muirbolc Mar, 'the place of the anchorites' (III:23), though in his case Muirbolc Mar was not an island by itself but an isolated spot on Hinba.[40]

Watson notes that although Adomnán sometimes uses the Greek *erēmos* to describe a retreat location, his most common descriptor is the Latin *desertum* meaning 'desert'. Several places in Ireland begin with *disert*, usually followed by the name of a saint.[41] Scotland also has examples, though fewer than in Ireland; and in Scotland the saint's name is not always preserved. Scottish instances include Dysart in Fife, and Kirkton of Dysart at the foot of Glen Orchy. The scarcity of occurrences in Scotland may be because Scottish monks sought islands, and, with islands, the convention was to prefix the saint's name with the word for 'island' and not the word 'desert'. This may explain why in Scotland the term 'desert' is restricted to mainland sites. Paradoxically, there were so many monks looking for secluded isolation that finding an uninhabited island became well-nigh impossible. Cormac tried in vain to find a place of retreat in the ocean (II:42). This made Columba appeal on Cormac's behalf to Bridei of the Picts, asking Bridei to grant Cormac and his companions safe conduct if their wanderings brought them to Orkney. The Orkneys were under Bridei's authority,

38 McCormick, 'Iona: The Archaeology of the Early Monastery' in Bourke, *Studies in the Cult of Saint Columba*, 68. There was a vallum, pre-existing Columba's arrival, which did not totally enclose the settlement. Thus Columba had an 'open' monastic site. The monastic vallum may have been symbolic more than functional.

39 Clancy and Markus, *Iona: The Earliest Poetry of a Celtic Monastery*, 132.

40 W. J. Watson, *The History of the Celtic Place-Names of Scotland* (1926), 256.

41 cf. Adomnán, *Life*, I:20. Columbanus' *Precamur Patrem* (We pray to the Father), which is Item 3 of the *Bangor Antiphonary*, speaks of learning from the Exodus experience so as to 'spurn the acts of the world, and to dwell together in the desert of virtues'.

and Columba's request on Cormac's behalf may have been part of sophisticated political machinations. Even so, the story illustrates how every island was sought after.

Between the bustling community on Iona, and the lonely islets to which a monk might go for seclusion, there were satellite communities on nearby islands, with Adomnán viewing the Iona monastery as being spread over several islands, referring to them as 'our islands' (I:2, 13).[42] Each satellite community was presided over by Columba's appointee. His cousin Baithéne (abbot of Iona after Columba) served terms as prior on Hinba and at Mag Luinge on Tiree, each time under Columba's authority. Other trusted senior men, invariably kinsmen, were appointed elsewhere. These islands were places for spiritual solitude, and were also places to which penitents could be sent for years of penance. Exile under supervision enabled them to complete their penance successfully. Tiree and Hinba were used for both penance and seclusion.

TIREE

Tiree is the most westerly of the Inner Hebrides.[43] It is also the flattest, sometimes appearing as a thin line on the horizon, giving it the romantic sobriquet, 'the land below the waves'. Though Tiree is exposed to the fury of Atlantic storms, it has high levels of sunshine, and frost is rare. Thirty square miles of rich and fertile land make it a land of abundance, able to support crops and cattle.[44] This is why the monastery on Tiree was able to send a 'fat beast' and 'six measures of grain' to Erc of Coll, whom Columba rehabilitated from a life of crime (I:41). Adomnán's *Life of Columba* is peppered with references to monks spending time at the Tiree monastery of Mag Luinge (e.g. I:30, II:39), though no traces of its buildings survive.[45] Curiously, Adomnán never

42 cf. O'Loughlin, *Adomnán and the Holy Places: The Perceptions of an Insular Monk on the Locations of the Biblical Drama* (London: T&T Clark, 2007), 20.

43 For Tiree, see: Kennedy, *The Land below the Waves: The Island of Tiree, Past and Present* (Tiree: Tiree Publishing Company, 1994); Aidan MacDonald, 'Adomnán's *Vita Columbae* and the Early Churches of Tiree' in Wooding (ed.), *Adomnán of Iona*, 219-36. Also, various references in Watson's *The History of the Celtic Place-Names of Scotland*; and Donald Meek, 'Columba's other Island? Columba and Early Christianity in Tiree'.

44 Meek, 'Columba's other Island?', disputes the assumption that Tiree was a main supplier of grain to Iona. However, the Erc story (I:41) does seem to indicate Tiree as an island of abundance.

45 Cumméne and/or Adomnán may have drawn on a corpus of Mag Luinge stories, possibly compiled by Baithéne, which they incorporated into their works on Columba.

records Columba visiting Tiree, but it is inconceivable he did not. Meek relates a story from Tiree tradition involving a petulant Columba cursing a rock (*Mallachdaig*/cursed-one) because seaweed on the rock, to which Columba unwisely moored his coracle, broke, resulting in the coracle drifting off-shore.

Sixth-century Tiree had a vibrant community, albeit on a lesser scale than Iona, and was not a place of complete isolation. When a monk went there, he did not become a true anchorite, but at least he was away from busy Iona with its stream of Columba-admiring visitors. Meek, rather darkly, interprets the Columban settlement on Tiree as a 'spiritual-concentration-camp', because of its use as a penitential colony, which downplays its positive function as a place for spiritual seclusion. It is likely that Tiree fulfilled both roles.

Adomnán records that a whale once threatened monks sailing to Tiree: the moral of the story being monastic obedience (I:19). Adomnán also has the story of demons attacking Tiree after being driven from Iona, with the Tiree monasteries suffering from their onslaught (III:8). Adomnán's use of the plural 'monasteries' indicates that Tiree had more than one monastic settlement. In addition to Columba's Mag Luinge there was a monastery at Artchain (Fair Cape/Fair Height) though its exact location is unknown. The Artchain monastery was founded by Columba's contemporary Findchan, and Adomnán has a decidedly negative view of Findchan's community.[46] Findchan brought a man named Áed Dub from Ireland (I:36) whom Adomnán disapproved of, claiming that he had been a 'very bloody man and had killed many people'. Adomnán also criticises Findchan's irregular ordination of Áed Dub as a priest and implies there was a same-sex attraction between the two men. He portrays Columba as being deeply disturbed about the situation, with Columba pronouncing a fearful judgement on them, which is followed by Findchan's right hand becoming withered and dead. Findchan lived for many more years, but eventually 'rotted' and was buried on the unidentified island of Ommon. Áed Dub, being 'a priest in name only', returned to his wicked ways before perishing in a threefold death of stabbing, falling, and drowning. As far as the Columbans were concerned, Findchan's group was improperly

46 Watson, *The History of the Celtic Place-Names of Scotland*, 304. Kilfinnichen in Mull commemorates Findchan.

constituted, badly led, morally corrupt, and unwisely governed. There was clear ill-feeling between the Columban community at Mag Luinge and Findchan's group.[47]

Were there other monasteries on Tiree? In the story of demons attacking other 'monasteries', the plural does not include Mag Luinge itself, implying there must have been at least one other monastic group besides the one at Artchain. We know of a chapel of Kilbride at Cornaig Mor, a quarter of a mile south-east of a corn-mill near Loch Bhasapol, but whether that was the site of an ancient monastery is less certain.[48] There is also a tradition that Comgall founded a monastery on Tiree before Columba ever came on the scene.[49] If so, then Comgall's monastery may have been pillaged by Pictish raiders in the mid-sixth century, and Columba's Mag Luinge may be Comgall's monastery reborn.[50] The mention of sixth-century Pictish raiders is a reminder that the seas of the Hebrides were infested with marauding desperadoes long before Viking incursions. Another of Columba's friends, Cainnech, may also have had a foothold on Tiree, and Aidan MacDonald cites clues in the *Life of Cainnech* indicating that Cainnech lived there.[51] The evidence is inconclusive, but, if true, it may have been at the site known today as Church of Kilkenneth.

HINBA

Columba stayed on Hinba for times of prayer and reflection. Whereas Tiree is mentioned six times in Adomnán's *Life*, Hinba has seven references. Moreover, whereas Adomnán has no stories of Columba on Tiree, he has four featuring him on Hinba. Adomnán implies that Columba was the original founder of the monastic community on Hinba (I:45), but that may be exaggeration. The claim may reflect Columba spending time on Hinba before settling on Iona. Or Adomnán may be alluding to Columba initiating a monastery on Hinba additional to a pre-existent one. At some point Columba appointed his elderly uncle Ernan as prior on Hinba (I:45), just as he appointed Baithéne to Mag Luinge on Tiree.

---

47 Meek, 'Columba's other Island?'.

48 Erskine Beveridge, *Coll and Tiree, Their Historic Forts and Ecclesiastical Antiquities,* (Edinburgh: 1903), 146.

49 MacDonald, 'Adomnán's *Vita Columbae* and the early churches of Tiree' in Wooding (ed.), *Adomnán of Iona*, 228f.

50 Watson, *The History of the Celtic Place-Names of Scotland*, 62.

51 MacDonald, 'Adomnán's *Vita Columbae* and the early churches of Tiree' in Wooding (ed.), *Adomnán of Iona*, 225f.

But where was Hinba? Skene espouses Eileach-an-Naoimh of the Garvellachs,[52] and for many years this was taken as fact, with translations of Adomnán's *Life of Columba* placing Eileach-an-Naoimh in brackets after each mention of Hinba in the text. The truth is we do not know. At one time or another, most of the inner-Hebridean islands have been suggested as its location, with strong arguments made for Jura, Colonsay, Oronsay, Tiree, Canna, and many more.

One theory is that when Columba first left Ireland he sailed intentionally to a known monkish community on Hinba, from which he could make easy contact with King Conall on the Argyll mainland at Dunadd. Eileach-an-Naoimh in the Garvellachs would certainly place Columba only a dozen miles from Dunadd by sea and land. Eileach-an-Naoimh also has remains of an early stone-built monastery, bee-hive cells, chapel, and a graveyard, all of which indicate ancient usage of the island by Irish monks. Admittedly, other Hebridean islands have the same features, though Eileach-an-Naoimh also has the long-standing legend that Columba's mother, Eithne, was buried there. Despite this evidence, it is not at all certain that Eileach-an-Naoimh is Hinba, and Watson argues extensively against it, preferring Jura.[53] Meek and Sharpe prefer Oronsay, off Colonsay.[54] John Lorne Campbell champions Canna.[55] A tour of all possible Hinba sites would make a wonderful summer voyage around the Hebrides! Wherever Hinba was, it was important to Columba, and it may have been his temporary home before he ever saw Iona. Significantly, in Adomnán's *Life of Columba*, it is on Hinba, perhaps more than on Iona, that Columba has some of his most intense spiritual experiences:

1. *Danger of Death*: Though associated with piety and prayer, Hinba was not totally safe, and Adomnán tells of an assassination attempt on Columba whilst he was on retreat there (II:24).[56] Columba had excommunicated the pirate sons of Conall mac Domnaill who had been raiding churches. In revenge, one of them, named Lam Dess,

52 Skene, *Celtic Scotland vol. II: Church and Culture*, 128f.

53 Watson, *The History of the Celtic Place-Names of Scotland*, 81ff.

54 Meek, 'Columba's other Island?'. Sharpe, *Adomnán of Iona: Life of St. Columba*, 308, note 194.

55 John Lorne Campbell: *Canna, The Story of a Hebridean Island* (London: OUP, 1984), 5f.

56 Sharpe, *Adomnán of Iona: Life of St. Columba*, 306, note 194, has a detailed discussion on Hinba, favouring Colonsay.

attacked Columba on Hinba with a spear; but the monk Findlugan stepped in, ready to die instead of his abbot. According to Adomnán, Findlugan was wearing Columba's cowl and this acted miraculously like a breastplate that could not be pierced. Lam Dess fled the scene, but poetic and divine justice triumphed. Exactly a year later he was killed by a thrown spear.

2. *Revelation of Kingship*: Adomnán writes that Columba was on Hinba when he received instructions through an angel to ordain Áedán as King of Dál Riata after the death of Conall in 574 (III:5). Adomnán portrays Columba as resisting this divine prompting. The vision needed to be repeated over three nights, accompanied by physical discipline, before Columba complied. But why does Adomnán portray Columba as slow and reluctant to obey? One reason might be that Adomnán wants to present Columba as a second Samuel, and Samuel also needed several promptings before accepting that the voice he heard was God's voice. Or it may be that Adomnán (ever sensitive to the politics of his own day) is anxious to show to his own contemporaries that Columba had thought that Áedán's brother Eóganan was worthy of the kingship. Whatever the reason, the outcome was that Columba ordained Áedán as king in obedience to divine revelation, and forged a successful relationship with him.

3. *Meeting with Leaders:* On another occasion, four of Columba's friends, Comgall, Kenneth, Brendan, and Cormac, all of whom were regarded as spiritual giants in their own right, came from Ireland to meet with Columba on Hinba. These A-list Christian leaders elected Columba to lead them in the Eucharist (III:17). This was interpreted as a strong indication of Columba's status even in a stellar gathering of remarkable holy men.

4. *Experience of the Spirit*: Another time, Columba had a deep experience of the Holy Spirit on Hinba (III:18). Adomnán writes that the grace of the Holy Spirit was poured on Columba and remained over him for three days. During this period, he stayed locked in his room, which was 'filled with heavenly light'. Columba sang spiritual chants 'of a kind never heard before'; and was given knowledge of deep secrets which 'had been hidden since the world began'. Afterwards, Columba regretted that Baithéne had not been present to record these wonderful things. This may imply that Baithéne normally kept notes as he accompanied Columba.

Hinba continued in importance after Columba's era. In the last chapter of his *Life of Columba*, Adomnán writes that knowledge of Columba's death was supernaturally conveyed far and wide, including to the monastery of Cluain Finchoil in Ireland where an old man, Lugaid mac Tailchain, became aware of the saint's departure (III:23). Lugaid shared the news with a 'fellow soldier of Christ' named Fergnae, who then sailed to Hinba (rather than to Iona), and spent the 'rest of his days' amongst the brothers there 'living faultlessly'. For the final twelve years of his life Fergnae withdrew from the other monks on Hinba, and it was he who lived in continuous isolation 'at the place of the anchorites in Muirbolc Mar', before dying as a 'victorious soldier of Christ'. Though Muirbolc Mar was on Hinba itself, this does not mean that Hinba had to be a large island, since a relatively small distance between Fergnae and the main community could be enough for isolation.

OTHER CENTRES

Adomnán notes that Columba stayed a few days on Skye (II:26). Whilst there Columba went alone into a dense forest to pray, encountering a huge boar which was being pursued by hunting dogs, and was in a highly agitated and aggressive state. With remarkable composure Columba stood his ground, raised his hand, prayed to God, and commanded the boar to stop and perish at that very spot. By 'the power of Columba's word' the boar fell dead before his face.

Other daughter-churches, doubling up as destinations for monks spending time away from Iona, include one on an unidentified island called Elen. Adomnán also mentions the church of Diun by the River Awe, whose prior was a monk named Cailtan (I:31). This is almost certainly the church known as Cella Diuni, which Clancy, Markus, Lane, and Campbell conclude was on the mainland at Annat, west of where the River Awe enters Loch Awe.[57] Adomnán implies that Cailtan was under Columba's authority, making Cella Diuni a daughter-church of Iona. Cailtan is described as its prior, and priors were under the authority of the abbot of the home monastery.

57 Clancy and Markus, *Iona: The Earliest Poetry of a Celtic Monastery*, 10, 224. Alan Lane and Ewan Campbell: *Dunadd: An Early Dalriadic Capital* (Oxford: Oxbow, 2000): 25. Watson, *The History of the Celtic Place-Names of Scotland*, 93, suggests Cella Diuni was named after Cailtan's brother, which may explain why it does not carry Cailtan's name.

PART TWO
WORKER

CHAPTER 9

Labour and Skills

At the Eighth International Insular Art Conference, held at the University of Glasgow in 2017, Ewan Campbell and Adrián Maldonado presented a paper whose conclusions became a global sensation.[1] They had re-examined artefacts, first collected on Iona by Charles Thomas between 1956 and 1963, and had come to a remarkable conclusion. Thomas excavated several locations, including the rocky outcrop Torr an Aba (Hill of the Abbot), thought to have been the site of Columba's personal cell or hut, and had unearthed remnants of ancient wood in the form of hazel charcoal. The age of the wood was indeterminate because 1960s radiocarbon-dating techniques lacked modern precision. Thomas also noticed that the charcoal remains had been covered by beach pebbles, and that there were signs of a post-hole. All this generated speculation. Had the wood been part of a wattle hut? Had the post-hole held a cross? Had Columba's hut been dismantled after his death? Was the site strewn with pebbles from the beach after its demolition? These were imaginative conjectures, but hard evidence was lacking.

Thomas went on to teach in Edinburgh and Leicester before becoming the first Professor of Cornish Studies at Exeter University. Each time he moved he took the hazel charcoal fragments with him, and in retirement stored them in his garage at Truro. There they stayed until 2012 when Campbell and Maldonado asked if they could test the fragments using modern radiocarbon methods. The results were astonishing. The wood came from between 540 and 650, dates which perfectly straddle Columba's years on Iona from 563 to 597. A speculative surmise became a strong probability. The wood may well have come

1 Ewan Campbell and Adrián Maldonado, 'New Discoveries from Iona', paper presented to the 8th International Insular Art Conference, University of Glasgow, 10th-14th July 2017; BBC News Report 11th July 2017.

from Columba's own hut. This was what Campbell and Maldonado published to the world.

THE HUT

On Iona, as at other Irish monasteries, the monks had two types of accommodation. One was the Great House. The other was the individual hut made of wood, wattle, and daub. The hut style followed the example of Martin of Tours who lived in a small cell made of wood, rather than in a stone-built beehive cell.[2] There were two types of hut. There were sleeping-huts (*hospitiolum*), and there were work-huts (*tegorium*). The hut on Torr an Aba appears to have been Columba's work hut where he studied, wrote, and copied sacred texts.[3] From this vantage point he could survey his community, and Aidan MacDonald interprets its commanding position as a visible expression of Columba's authority. From this hut Columba not only watched over the monastery, but the sea-straits between Iona and Mull, making him aware of who was coming and going.[4] He could also hear; and Adomnán records an occasion when a man shouted from the other side of the Sound, and Columba, in his raised wooden hut, heard everything (I:25). In the same story Adomnán indicates that the work hut had a wooden floor resting on wooden beams. The beams probably helped to level the uneven ground of the rocky tor.[5] This was all relatively luxurious compared to what was normally available for monks. A wooden floor was far more comfortable than the clay or rush strewn floors of other cells.[6] The doorway would face east, away from the prevailing wind.

Columba also had a sleeping-hut which, counter-intuitively, was less comfortable than his work hut.[7] Instead of straw or a wooden floor,

2 Severus, *Life of Martin*, X:4.

3 Clancy and Markus, *Iona: The Earliest Poetry of a Celtic Monastery*, 20. Anna Ritchie and Ian Fisher, *Iona Abbey and Nunnery* (Edinburgh: Historic Scotland, 2004), 7.

4 MacDonald, 'Adomnán's Monastery of Iona' in Bourke (ed.), *Studies in the Cult of Saint Columba*, 41f.

5 Sharpe, *Adomnán of Iona: Life of St. Columba*, 285, note 127. Yet, McCormick, 'Iona: The Archaeology of the Early Monastery' in Bourke (ed.), *Studies in the Cult of Saint Columba*, 54, argues that evidence for use of joints in other contemporary buildings is scarce.

6 Timothy O'Neill, 'Columba the Scribe' in Bourke (ed.), *Studies in the Cult of Saint Columba*, 75.

7 McCormick, 'Iona: The Archaeology of the Early Monastery' in Bourke (ed.), *Studies in the Cult of Saint Columba*, 52.

he had bare rock. Instead of a soft pillow, he had a stone (III:21, 23). These ascetic conditions are referred to in two of Beccán's poems. In *Tiugraind Beccain*, Beccán writes of Columba:

He crucified his body, left behind sleek slides.
He chose learning, embraced stone slabs, gave up bedding.[8]

In *Fo Reir Choluimb*, Beccán further describes the austerity of Columba's accommodation:

It was not on cushioned beds,
He bent to his complex prayers;
He crucified – not for crimes –
His body on the grey waves.[9]

Beccán's emphasis is on Columba embracing a severe lifestyle. But Beccán is careful to state that Columba accepted this personal crucifixion of discomfort and exile 'not for crimes'. Was Beccán aware of suspicions that Columba had been forced into exile as penance for sin? Was he trying to quash such rumours? Beccán presents Columba's exile as a self-imposed martyrdom; and implies that Columba's rejection of worldly comforts was voluntary. For Beccán, if not for everyone, neither of these were sparked by guilt for past faults.

Acceptance of discomfort was a sign of holiness. This is why a monk's sleeping hut was so bare. The stone slab referred to by Beccán, is also mentioned by Adomnán in his account of Columba's last day (III:23):

> When the saint had finished his verse at the bottom of the page, he went to the church for Vespers on the night before Sunday. As soon as it was over, he returned to his lodgings and rested on his bed, where at night instead of straw he had bare rock and a stone for his pillow.

The Museum of the Isles at Lews Castle in Stornoway has an example of an early Christian pillow-stone. The one on display (labelled as a grave marker) is flattened and almost circular, with an equal-armed cross carved in relief on one of its surfaces. It was discovered in 2000 during excavations of a Blackhouse on Eilean an Tighe, one of the

8 Beccán, *Tiugraind Beccain*, 16.

9 Beccán, *Fo Reir Choluimb*, 2.

Shiant Islands off the east coast of Harris and Lewis.[10] The geological characteristics of the pillow-stone indicate that it was brought to the Shiants from elsewhere, and the closest geological match is an outcrop of red sandstone at Torridon on the mainland, just north of Applecross. Applecross was a monastic centre from the seventh century onwards, founded by Maelrubha from Bangor, and the Shiants may have been an outpost of the Applecross Monastery, functioning either as a place of retreat and/or penance, or as a base from which to evangelise the Outer Hebrides. The Shiant stone has been dated to between the seventh and tenth centuries and is of the same type used by monks as pillows during life and as markers after death. Columba's pillow-stone on Iona would be similar.

In his sleeping-hut a monk could enjoy a degree of solitariness, and the eighth-century Irish text *The Hermit* describes the experience of one hermit:[11]

Alone in my little hut without a human being in my company,
Dear has been the pilgrimage before going to meet death.
A remote hidden little cabin: for forgiveness of my sins,
A conscience upright and spotless: before holy heaven.

A bare floor, a stone pillow, difficulty, and discomfort, prepared the soul for God:

Making holy the body with good habits, treading it boldly down,
Weak tearful eyes for forgiveness of my desires …
A cold anxious bed, like the lying-down of the doomed,
A brief apprehensive sleep, invocations frequent and early …

The yearning for 'aloneness' is expressed with increasing strength as the poem continues:

Treading the paths of the Gospel, singing psalms every Hour,
An end of talking and long stories, constant bending of the knees …
Alone in my little hut, all alone so,
Alone I came into the world: alone I shall go from it.
If being alone I have done wrong at all, through the pride of the world,
Hear my wail as I lament all alone, O God!

10 http://www.shiantisles.net/archaeology/index.htm (31/7/2017).

11 *The Hermit* in K. H. Jackson (ed.), *A Celtic Miscellany* (London: Penguin, 1971), 281.

PHYSICAL TOIL

Though monks of the Irish tradition are praised for their literary accomplishments, all able-bodied monks had also to engage in manual labour. The community needed food, shelter, and clothing. Commitment of body and muscle, as well as of soul and spirit, was required. This made a monk's life as physically demanding as that of any of the lay-population. In some respects, it was more severe, because compulsory participation in midnight prayers and compulsory long night-vigils were added to the physical labours of the day.

Sleep was disapproved of. Basil and Cassian both held that deep sleep was unnecessary and to be avoided if possible. Deep sleep and heavy torpor interrupted what should be a life of continual praise (*laus perennis*) and put a monk at risk of experiencing dreams with sinful and ungodly content.[12] Consequently, monastic discipline denied monks the unbroken hours of slumber enjoyed by others. Snatched sleep, demanding prayer schedules, strict discipline, and hard labour made some monks abandon their vows. These lapsed brothers were not looked on sympathetically, and a considerable number of monastic canons were directed at failed brethren. Lapsed monks were viewed as men who had put their hand to the monastic plough, physically as well as spiritually, but had looked back. Basil, in a letter sent to a former monk, warns him to abandon his apostasy:

> Resume once more the toils of your youth, and, by a fresh course of good deeds, destroy the indulgence that creeps foully along the ground. ... Never let that most awful sentence apply to you, 'Depart from me, I never knew you.'[13]

For those who stuck it out there was much to be done. Muscle-work and soul-work were related spheres of activity, not least because it was believed that hard work helped to repel the devil's insistent suggestion that the rigours of monastic life might simply be a huge waste of time. Concerning this thought, which must have come to many monks, Basil advises:

12 Cassian, *Institutes*, II:13; II:14; cf. Basil, *Letters*, 2: 'Let sleep be light and easily interrupted, as naturally happens after a light diet; it should be purposely broken by thoughts about great themes. To be overcome by heavy torpor, with limbs unstrung, so that a way is readily opened to wild fancies, is to be plunged in daily death.'

13 Basil, *Letters*, 45; cf. 44.

> Train your body to hard work, … when the evil thought starts up and says, 'What is the good of you passing your life in this place? What do you gain by withdrawing yourself from the society of men?' … When the evil thought rises against you, with all these ingenuous pretexts and wishes to destroy you, – oppose it by pious reflection.[14]

Hard work could distract a monk from demoralising thoughts, and hard work was easy to find. Cassian stresses that monks should follow the Apostle Paul's example and supply their own needs.[15] This brought a raft of practical duties. The first requirement was to produce food, not only for the resident community, but for the many guests who arrived. This meant that a monk's life had a rhythm which was hard-wired to daily and annual cycles. There was a daily cycle of working in the fields, looking after stock, fishing, and workshops. And there was an annual cycle of ploughing, sowing, harvesting, and threshing.[16] There were animals to be cared for. There were fish to be caught. There was hay to be mown. There was ploughing to be done. There were crops to be ingathered. There were goods to be made. All of this in addition to prayer, teaching, and scholarly reflection.

AGRICULTURE

The machair of Iona is fertile ground. Iona's beaches had shell-sand to lime the soil, and its coastline yielded masses of seaweed to be processed as fertiliser. Excess dried seaweed was burnt as fuel.[17] With these resources the island produced good crops, and yet it was unable to feed everyone because so many people came. As Columba's fame increased the community grew, the number of visitors multiplied, and Iona's food-supply had to be augmented from elsewhere. Inchkenneth in the mouth of Mull's Loch na Keil, and Tiree, several sea-miles to the west, were Iona's granaries, with one derivation of Tiree being 'the land of corn'. Though Inchkenneth and Tiree had to provide for their

---

14 Basil, *Letters*, 42; cf. Benedict, *Rule*, XLVIII: 'Idleness is the enemy of the soul. Therefore, the brothers should have specified periods of manual labour as well as for prayerful reading.'

15 Cassian, *Institutes*, II:3; cf. 1 Thessalonians 4:11.

16 Adomnán, *Life of Columba*, I:37 and I:28. In II, 20 Adomnán refers to the 'trench of a threshing floor'.

17 Ritchie and Fisher, *Iona Abbey and Nunnery*, 31. Finlay, *Columba*, 109.

own resident populations, they were able to export a surplus to help the community on Iona.

Not every year was one of abundance. As abbot, one of Columba's tasks was to challenge his farming monks to live as men of faith and not to worry about the vagaries of climate. On one occasion, when the weather delayed sowing until late in the season, Columba said to his monks, 'Let the man trust in God's omnipotence: though his crop be sown when half the month of June has gone, it shall still be harvested at the beginning of August' (II:3). As well as fields there was a monastery garden, and Adomnán makes an indirect reference to the community growing medicinal herbs. This comes in the story of the man who shouted across the Sound from Mull, asking for medicines to heal his body (I:27).

LIVESTOCK

The monks tended cattle, sheep, goats, and pigs. Sheep grazed on Iona and also on a small islet off its southern tip. Seal meat was eaten, with Adomnán hinting that the monks had rights to hunt seals off Mull. This comes in the story of Columba sending two of his monks to search for the thief Erc moccu Druidi. They were to look for him on 'the little island that is the breeding-place of the seals we reckon as our own' (I:41). Sealskin and seal-oil were as important as the meat itself, with oil needed for light and for liturgical purposes. Seal bones found in the monastic midden on Iona reveal that some seals were young or newborn. The remains of an older seal has a hunting wound in its pelvis.[18]

The most important of the domesticated animals were the cattle. In early-medieval culture cattle were the gold-standard indicator of status and wealth, with the land itself measured in 'hides'.[19] The economic and social value attached to cattle in Adomnán's *Life of Columba* is reflected not just by the number of times Adomnán mentions them, but in his portrayal of Columba as a man able to make people richer by healing their cattle or by making their herds increase (II:4, 17, 20, 21). Nesan of Lochaber had only five cows and was reckoned to be very poor, but Columba increased his herds (II:20). On another

18 McCormick, 'Iona: The Archaeology of the Early Monastery' in Bourke (ed.), *Studies in the Cult of Saint Columba*, 57. McCormick suggests seal food may have been a special food in the monastery He cites Martin Martin who, in 1703, wrote that Catholics in the Hebrides ate seal flesh on fast days as they believed it was the equivalent of fish.

19 Sally Foster, *Picts, Gaels and Scots* (London: Batsford, 1996), 53.

occasion, Columba was unwilling to bless a knife which had been used in killing bulls, because bulls were meant for ploughing and not for meat (II:29). Aidan MacDonald interprets this story as evidence that Columba and his monks were vegetarian.[20] However, the point of the story may be that, because cattle were immensely valuable, they were not to be slaughtered needlessly for human consumption, especially a bull. On the same theme, when Columba helped a very poor family in Lochaber and gave the husband a special sharp stake for hunting, Columba stressed that the stake was only for killing wild animals or fish and was not to be used to harm men or cattle (II:37). Columba's warning was taken so seriously that the man's wife feared that if any cattle were killed by the stake then the whole family might be killed or sold into slavery: the law being that if someone was wronged, and the perpetrator could not pay the honour-price, then the guilty party could be put to death or enslaved.[21]

Cattle were kept on Iona itself. Adomnán writes of a young man, Colman Ua Briun, returning from milking the cows and asking Columba to bless the milk-pail (II:16).[22] The story presupposes that Colman Ua Briun milked the cows nearby before passing Columba's hut. Another story, indicating that cattle in general, and not just milking-cows, were kept on Iona, is one in which an aged and frail Columba travels by cart to visit monks building a stone wall on the west side of Iona (II:28). He blesses them and declares that from now on no snake poison would harm either men 'or cattle' in the lands of 'this island' so long as its inhabitants continued to follow Christ's commandments. Other evidence of cattle on Iona includes the monk Molua illicitly trying to kill a bullock 'outside the boundary bank of the monastery' (II:29). Cattle were amongst the community's most valuable assets and were guarded as closely as possible. It would be virtually impossible for rustlers to lift cattle from Iona, but a herd on Mull, or on an adjacent island, would be at far greater risk.

Modern archaeology reinforces Adomnán's references to the Iona monks tending a range of livestock and reveals which animals were

---

20 MacDonald, 'Adomnán's Monastery of Iona' in Bourke (ed.), *Studies in the Cult of Saint Columba*, 35f.

21 Markus, *Conceiving a Nation*, 207.

22 Adomnán, *Life of Columba*, III:23 refers to the 'booley' or 'milking-pen'. This would be in fields near the monastery.

butchered for their meat as part of the monastic diet. As noted previously, one of the filled-in ditches on Iona has objects dating from the early Christian period, including bone fragments with butchering marks, from cattle, red deer, roe-deer, sheep, pigs, horses, otters, grey seal, and a whale.[23]

FISHING

Though sea-fishing is not referred to explicitly by Adomnán, the sea was a massive food-larder, and we know that the community had its own harbour and constructed its own boats (II:45).[24] McCormick, whilst noting that Adomnán's few references to fishing are to freshwater fishing, adds that these seldom relate to Iona itself. This is logical, since Iona has only small streams.[25] For McCormick, archaeological data prove that the early-medieval community were heavily involved in sea fishing, since excavations in the areas of the Guest House and ditches show evidences of gurnard, cod, hake, saithe, and red sea bream. Some cod were in excess of ten kilograms in weight, and fish of that size are not found in shallow inshore waters. Similarly, saithe, hake and grey gurnard are generally deeper water fish.

Adomnán features river-fishing on several occasions, with frequent references to monks netting catches. Adomnán's primary purpose in relating incidents of miraculous catches is to accumulate even more evidence of Columba's credentials as a true man of God; but the stories also reveal that fishing was a popular social activity. On one occasion, Columba was with a 'company of hardy fishermen' on the 'fishful' River Shiel, when five fish were caught in the net (II:19). Columba told the fishermen to cast again, and they drew in a salmon 'of wonderful size'. On another occasion, Columba's companions want to fish on Lough Key, but he tells them, 'Today and tomorrow there will not be a single fish caught in the river: but I will send you fishing on the third day and you will find two great salmon caught in the net' (II:19). For Adomnán, these stories are gold-standard evidence of God's approval of Columba's ministry. And in case the reader misses the significance

---

23 McCormick, 'Iona: The Archaeology of the Early Monastery' in Bourke (ed.), *Studies in the Cult of Saint Columba*, 56.

24 Bardsley, *Against the Tide: The Story of Adomnán of Iona*, 55.

25 McCormick, 'Iona: The Archaeology of the Early Monastery' in Bourke (ed.), *Studies in the Cult of Saint Columba*, 59.

of the latter incident, Adomnán states up front that such episodes show the power of miracle, and the gift of prophetic foreknowledge, which Columba was given by God.

Fishing enters the final chapter of Columba's life. When Columba dies, a monk named Ernene moccu Fir Roide, who was fishing in Ireland, saw supernatural signs and reported, 'On the night of Columba's blessed and blissful passing from the world to the heavens, I and the men with me were hard at work fishing in the fishful River Finn, when all at once we saw the whole sky light up: later we learnt that many other fishermen, fishing in various places along the same river, saw a similar apparition, and they were seized with a great fear' (III:23). 'Fishful' was a favourite descriptor for good fishing rivers.

INDUSTRY

Self-sufficiency requires skills beyond farming and fishing. In this respect the profile of the average monk was similar to that of missionaries recruited by organisations such as the London Missionary Society in the late eighteenth and early nineteenth centuries. The LMS looked for artisans of practical ability as much as for men and women with intellectual gifts. It was thought that would-be missionaries who were only used to soft and refined living would not survive in frontier situations. In like manner, Columba's monks needed not only to be educated, but to have invaluable, artisan, hands-on, skills.

1. *Metal-working.* Almost every excavated site of early-medieval Irish culture has evidence of metal-working and Iona is no exception.[26] Iona discoveries include slag, plus fragments of three triangular crucibles from the early Christian period which were used for collecting smelting products or for melting metals prior to casting.[27] Fragments of moulds used for casting bronze have also been discovered.[28] Martin Carver has identified signs of metal-

26 De Paor, *Early Christian Ireland*, 96.

27 Finbar McCormick, A. MacSween, J. N. Dore, A. O'Berg and Wilthew, P, 'Early Christian metalworking on Iona: excavations under the 'infirmary' in 1990' in *PSAS*, vol. 122 (1992), 208f. See also, Hughes, *Early Christian Ireland: Introduction to the Sources*, 25, who points out that furnaces used charcoal fuel, and that traces of slag and iron smelting exist on many small Irish ring-forts.

28 McCormick, 'Iona: The Archaeology of the Early Monastery' in Bourke (ed.), *Studies in the Cult of Saint Columba*, 60.

working within the precincts of the Pictish-Christian monastery at Portmahomack.[29] Given that the Portmahomack monastery may have originated through the agency of monks from the Irish or Columban tradition, these similarities are unsurprising, and support a story told by Adomnán in which monks 'who knew the blacksmith's craft' melted down the iron of a knife and coated the liquid metal on the other tools in the monastery (II:29).[30]

2. *Wood/Leather-working.* McCormick is of the view that Iona had a wood-working workshop, with evidence of bowls made of alder, dating from at least the seventh and eighth centuries. Considerable leather remains have also been discovered, and these are dated to the same period, indicating that Iona had a leather-workshop, producing footwear and book-satchels. [31]

3. *Water-mill:* To the north of the main enclosure on Iona is a small stream running towards the eastern shore of the island. This is called Sruth a'Mhuilinn (Mill-Stream), suggesting a water-mill in ancient times, though no signs remain today.[32] Adomnán refers to the monastery using barley (II:3), and milling of some kind would be required. Excavations in 1994 uncovered a large, sub-rectangular pool to the side of the stream, which might have been the undercroft of a horizontal watermill, but this is undated.[33] As a monk not shy of work, Columba would be no stranger to the mill.

4. *Corn-drying Barn*: Adomnán may also refer to a corn-drying building on Iona, though this has yet to be located. The allusion is in a story concerning Columba's aged uncle, Ernan (I:45). Columba appointed Ernan as prior of the monastery on Hinba, but Ernan took ill after only a few days, and asked to return. Immediately he reached

29 Martin Carver, *Portmahomack: A Monastery in* Pictland (Tarbat: Highlands & Islands Enterprise, 2007), 20ff.

30 Sharpe, *Adomnán of Iona: Life of St. Columba*, 332, note 282, discusses problems raised by Adomnán's claim that the monks 'melted' the iron. Iron only melts at a very high temperature, perhaps higher than the monks on Iona could raise. Sharpe suggests that the monks used the term 'melt' to describe a process in which iron was simply softened.

31 McCormick, 'Iona: The Archaeology of the Early Monastery' in Bourke (ed.), *Studies in the Cult of Saint Columba*, 61f.

32 Michael Herity, 'Early Irish Hermitages in the Light of the *Lives* of Cuthbert' in Bonner (ed.), *St. Cuthbert, his Cult and Community to A.D. 1200*, 52. See also, RCAHM vol. IV, Iona (1982), 32.

33 McCormick, 'Iona: The Archaeology of the Early Monastery' in Bourke (ed.), Studies *in the Cult of Saint Columba*, 55.

Iona he collapsed and died. In Sharpe's translation Ernan died 'in front of the door of the corn-kiln [*canaba*]'. However, translating the Latin *canaba* as 'corn-kiln' is disputed, with the Andersons rendering *canaba* simply as 'shed'. Sharpe's view is that *canaba*, though capable of various translations, was used in Hiberno-Latin in a specialised sense, referring specifically to a building which housed the equipment for drying corn before threshing.[34] It is difficult to give a definitive verdict on this. We do know that Iona had several barns and at least one shed. These were situated away from the monastery, with tracks radiating from them to fields in various parts of the island. One may have been a corn-drying barn.

TRADE

Trade routes existed between Ireland and continental Europe long before Columba; and as early as the late first century the Roman historian Tacitus mulled over the possibilities of increased commerce with Ireland.[35] Such trade was by the Atlantic seaways, with the Western Isles of Scotland regarded as northerly extensions of the main trade destinations.[36] Merchants came to these remote islands from Gaul, Spain, and the Mediterranean, and Adomnán recounts that Columba and Luigbe once talked with sailors from Gaul about a recent tragedy which had taken place in Italy (I:28). On that occasion Columba and Luigbe had travelled from Iona to the *caput regionis* (head of the region) of Dál Riata where they conversed with the sailors. The precise whereabouts of the *caput regionis* is debated. Was it a main harbour on the Kintyre peninsular, near Dunadd, the capital of Dál Riata? Was it at Dunaverty on the southern tip of Kintyre? Was it elsewhere? The question of location aside, what the meeting with the Gaulish sailors illustrates is that there was a ready contact with the wider world. David Clarke, in his essay on 'Communities' in the National Museums of Scotland publication, *Early Medieval Scotland*, suggests that Adomnán's casual and matter-of-fact description of Gallic sailors and traders in Argyll indicates that the presence of ships from Gaul was unexceptional. It was part of life.[37]

---

34 Sharpe, *Adomnán of Iona: Life of St. Columba*, 309, note 195.

35 Tacitus, *The Life of Gnaeus Julius Agricola*, XXIV.

36 cf. Yorke, *The Conversion of Britain: 600–800*, 77.

37 Clarke (ed.), *Early Medieval Scotland*, 116.

It was through such trade that exotic goods from Mediterranean lands made their way to the 'edge of the world', as Ireland and the Western Isles of Scotland were known. Amongst other articles, a fragment of an African red slipware bowl has been discovered on Iona.[38] Red slipware is a type of pottery, made in North Africa near Carthage between the second century and the seventh century, but believed to have been imported into Atlantic Britain only during the second quarter of the sixth century, with Clarke of the view that its importation ceased before Columba arrived in Argyll in 563.[39] Similar fragments of African red slipware pottery have been found at Whithorn in south-west Scotland, and in England and Wales. It is unlikely that major trading vessels docked in Iona's small harbour, and the presence of exotic pottery on Iona point to such goods coming from centres elsewhere in Dál Riata or brought by pilgrims.

Trade involves a two-way process. What could the monks give in return? In wider society the normal trade goods were slaves, leathers, furs, sealskin, eiderdown, and freshwater pearls.[40] Apart from slaves, the Iona monks could supply all of these. It is probable that major trading arrangements in Dál Riata would be authorised by the king, and the sixth-century monastery on Iona would not establish major trading contracts in its own right. Thus, any involvement of the monks of Iona in commercial enterprises may have been within the context of a larger agreement between the royal court and the traders; although, with an abbot as influential as Columba, what Iona wanted Iona would get. Ships which arrived in Dál Riata from far afield would stay in a port for several weeks. This gave ample opportunity for news of the ship's arrival to spread; for goods to be brought to the harbour from the surrounding region; and for the ship's own cargo to be traded. That may have been why Columba and Luigbe were at the *caput regionis* when they met the sailors.

---

38 Clarke (ed.), *Early Medieval Scotland*, 114.

39 Hughes, *Early Christian Ireland: Introduction to the Sources*, 28, holds that although some pottery importation took place in Ireland in the late-fifth, sixth, and early-seventh centuries, it was not until the Viking settlements that trade on any considerable scale was maintained. The same may have been true in Argyll.

40 Clarke (ed.), *Early Medieval Scotland*, 117.

CHAPTER 10

Literacy and Speech

Loch Glashan lies two miles from Dunadd, and in 1960 leather remains were found on a crannog in the loch. Crannogs were small artificial islands, often connected to the shore by a causeway just below the surface of the water. The causeways were rarely straight, but had bends and kinks which helped to defend the crannog's inhabitants from a surprise attack. The leather strips found at Loch Glashan puzzled researchers until it was realised they were the remnants of a book-satchel, probably dating from around the ninth century. Five such book-satchels, from various sites, have survived the centuries, with the Loch Glashan specimen the earliest. Book-satchels were essential accessories for monks as they visited scattered communities; and images of clerics with book-satchels are carved on two stone cross-slabs in the Shetlands, one on Bressay and the other on Papil. Like a modern laptop computer bag, the satchels had straps for slinging round the shoulder; some were ornamented by stamping the leather, though the Loch Glashan example is simple, plain, and undecorated.[1] A seventh-century Irish text, *Hisperica Famina*, gives instructions on making book-satchels, and when the National Museum of Scotland commissioned the artist Ian Dunlop to make two reproductions, he based his work on the Irish text and on the images on the Shetland cross-slabs.[2]

THE SATCHELS

Satchels carried books. And holy books with holy words were a feature of Christian faith in early-medieval Ireland. Christianity had a book-based culture. In this respect it differed sharply from pre-Christian druidical religion. The Bible was the book of books, and it was the

---

1 Ewan Campbell, 'The archaeology of writing in the time of Adomnán' in Wooding (ed.), *Adomnán of Iona*, 141.

2 http://www.bbc.co.uk/news/10407225 and Clarke (ed.), *Early Medieval Scotland*, 110.

foundational text for all matters of belief, piety, and worship.[3] Faith and worship were based on written words.[4] This contrasted with the orally-based druidical religion and its colleges. It was not that druidical training had low intellectual standards. On the contrary, it was a demanding programme, with Julius Caesar recording that training was only completed after twenty years of intense study.[5] Nevertheless, though druids were exceptionally learned, they were not literate in any advanced way. Ogham script, which was used prior to and during the era of Christian influence, could record a modicum of information, but it lacked the flexibility and comprehensiveness of the written culture brought by the Church.[6] Eventually, this lack of advanced literacy placed druidical religious leaders at a disadvantage in comparison with Christian monks. It affected their status in the eyes of the community. And it undermined their political value to local chiefs.

Adomnán features book-satchels in his *Life of Columba.* He writes of a young man, with a satchel of books, travelling on horseback in the north of Ireland (II:8). As the youth crossed the Boyne, he fell into the river and was drowned. Body and books were retrieved twenty days later, with the books ruined, having been under water for three weeks. They were totally spoiled, apart from one page which Columba had written with his own hand! Elsewhere, Adomnán refers to other miraculous book preservations, such as a book of the week's hymns also written by Columba, and also lying under water, though in its case not just for three weeks but all winter from Christmas to Easter (II:9).[7] When it was retrieved in its now heavily-rotted satchel, it also was found to be unharmed, clean, and dry. Adomnán's point is that anything written by Columba was miraculously preserved by supernatural agency. Aware that some readers might doubt these stories, Adomnán adds that the men who gave him the information were of exemplary honesty and good

3 cf. O'Reilly, 'Reading the Scriptures in the Life of Columba' in Bourke (ed.), *Studies in the Cult of Saint Columba*, 80-106.

4 Markus, *Conceiving a Nation*, 111.

5 Caesar, *The Gallic Wars*, VI:13, 14.

6 Yorke, *The Conversion of Britain: 600–800*, 22f.

7 If the plagiarised Psalter story is true (see later in this chapter), then Adomnán would know of the accusation that Columba had illegally copied Finnian's book. It may have been to offset this that Adomnán takes every opportunity to stress that copies made by Columba's own hand had miraculous qualities, indicating divine approval of Columba's work as a copyist.

faith. For Adomnán, these incidents prove that God's blessing attended Columba's ministry, since God would only protect text written by a holy hand.[8] The stories also indicate that anything thought to have been written by Columba's own hand would be conserved with great care.

THE BOOKS

Máire and Liam de Paor suggest that Irish monks valued letters and learning even more than their Middle Eastern progenitors had.[9] Certainly, monks who were skilled in copying sacred texts were so valued in an Irish monastery that the penalty for killing a scribe was as great as that for murdering a bishop or an abbot.[10] Monks who were able to write words, record truth, copy documents, read texts, and interpret what had been written, were accorded deep respect. If an abbot were also a renowned scribe, then that added to his already substantial dignity. Adomnán has numerous references to Columba transcribing manuscripts, demonstrating that copying the sacred text was viewed as a high calling and was not something to be palmed off to underlings as an unwanted burden. It was an important ministry in its own right, and Columba had a reputation both as an academic and a copyist.[11] Significantly, when Adomnán records the last day of Columba's life, he portrays Columba spending these precious hours in copying the psalms (III:23). Columba's last task on earth was one of the most important duties of any monk: making copies of God's Word. Baithéne, who became Columba's immediate successor, was also a scribe, and it was Baithéne who was charged with completing the Psalter which Columba had been working on. This made Baithéne

8 *Old Irish Life* emphasises the incorruptibility attaching to Columba's writings (Skene, *Celtic Scotland*, vol. II, 487).

9 De Paor, *Early Christian Ireland*, 52.

10 Warren, *The Liturgy and Ritual of the Celtic Church*, 18.

11 cf. M. Joynt, 'The Cathach of St. Columba', *ICQ*, vol. 10, no. 39, 193: 'In the sixth century books were a rare and greatly valued possession, and it is not surprising to find even saints, who had renounced all the other vanities of life, setting their hearts on this one earthly treasure. St. Columcille, we know from abundant testimony, was an ardent student and an indefatigable copier of manuscripts, and there is a story told in the notes to the old Irish Martyrology known as the *Felire Oengusa*, of his paying a visit to St. Longarad of Ossory, who had a library, and requesting permission to examine his books. But Longarad refused or (as the original puts it), "hid his books on him", whereat St. Columcille "left a word", to wit, a malediction on the books, that they might be of no use to anyone after their owner's death. And that was fulfilled, for on Longarad's death "his books were read by none".'

a worthy successor to Columba, not only because of his holiness, experience, judgement, and leadership qualities, but because he was able to continue Columba's own task of furthering God's work through copying God's Word.

All copies were made by hand. Monks produced books rather than scrolls, with a book (*codex*) consisting of leaves stitched together, making it compact enough to be carried in a book-satchel. Protected in this way, books could be taken by monks as they navigated seas, sailed rivers, traversed mountains, and penetrated remote glens on pastoral and missionary journeys. These portaged books were not complete Bibles, which would be far too heavy and bulky. Instead, the monks took abbreviated versions containing the Gospels, the Psalms, and some liturgical material. Full copies of the Scriptures were kept on Iona itself.

During the dark months of the year, the only indoor light was from candles or from small lamps fuelled by seal oil. Yet, when we read Adomnán's *Life of Columba*, we are given the impression that painstaking accuracy was everything. Sloppiness was a sin because careless copying could change divine truth into the devil's falsehood. Accordingly, Adomnán depicts Columba as demanding high standards, insisting on meticulous precision. On one occasion, Baithéne completed a copy of the Psalter and asked Columba to appoint another monk to proof-read it (I:23). Through spiritual insight Columba knew immediately that the copy was perfect apart from one detail, and informed Baithéne that there were no mistakes, neither one letter too many nor one too few, except that in one place the letter 'I' was missing. This still obliged Baithéne to proof-read every line, searching for the missing 'I'! And Adomnán implies that Baithéne had to trawl his entire work. Columba did not use his miraculous abilities to identify where the error was![12] What the story really illustrates is that Adomnán wants his readers to see perfection as Columba's only standard. This accuracy was to apply to all texts, not just to the Scriptures, and when Adomnán completes his *Life of Columba* he insists that his book should be treated with similar scrupulousness, giving the following instruction to future copiers:

> After carefully copying they compare them with the exemplar from which they have been written, and amend

12 Adomnán, *Life of Columba*, I:23: '*Having gone through the whole Psalter*, it was found … as the saint predicted.' [my italics]

> them with the utmost care, and also that they append this adjuration in this place. (III:23)[13]

Copiers had to copy this instruction about copying to future copiers! In reality, copies made by monasteries were not perfect. Bernard Meehan, Curator of early Irish manuscripts at Trinity College Dublin for many years, points out that even the celebrated *Book of Kells* has numerous inaccuracies and instances of miscopying.[14]

THE CATHACH

Total accuracy was the ideal, but the frequent variant readings which occur in early Irish texts show this was not always achieved. This introduces the question of the Cathach which some think may have been penned by Columba himself. If so, then, alongside the radiocarbon-dated remains of Columba's hut on Torr an Aba, it is one of a small group of objects which we can connect to him. The name 'Cathach' means 'Battler' or 'Champion', which may be either a reference to the battle of Cul Drebene, or to the alleged practice of Irish chiefs parading the casket containing the Cathach thrice around their army before going into battle. Prior to its opening, it was thought that the sealed casket contained bodily relics of Columba himself.

The Cathach is an ancient copy of the Psalter which was discovered when a medieval silver-lined casket was opened in 1813 by Sir William Betham, Deputy Ulster King of Arms. It is one of the earliest surviving Irish illustrated manuscripts, and consists of fifty-eight partially mutilated parchment leaves on which are written Psalms 30:10 to 105:13 in Jerome's Latin Gallican version, with a small mixture of pre-Jerome readings.[15] Internal evidence dates it as early as the sixth century.[16] Its discovery renewed speculation on the legend that one of the causes of the bloody battle of Cul Drebene (561) was Columba illegally copying a Psalter owned by his mentor Finnian of Clonard.

---

13 The Andersons, *Adomnán's Life of Columba*, 235, note 263, are of the view that these words were part of Adomnán's original text, rather than an addition by Dorbene the scribe. Either way, they emphasise concern for accurate copying.

14 Bernard Meehan, *The Book of Kells* (London: Thames & Hudson, 1994), 86.

15 cf. Michael Herity and Aidan Breen, *The Cathach of Colum Cill: An Introduction* (Dublin: Royal Irish Academy, 2002), 1ff.

16 Herity and Breen, *The Cathach of Colum Cille: An Introduction*, 60, conclude that, over a range of criteria, there is nothing which argues against a date of origin before 600.

The gist of the legend is that Finnian lent Columba the Psalter to read but was furious when he discovered that Columba had made a copy without his permission. Finnian then claimed that the copy, as well as the original Psalter (returned by Columba), belonged to him. The case was taken to the High King Diarmait mac Cerbaill, who found in Finnian's favour, declaring, 'To every cow her calf; to every book its copy'. Columba ignored Diarmait's judgment. This created a standoff, which fed into tribal tensions, which in turn resulted in the battle of Cul Drebene. The story does not appear in Adomnán's *Life of Columba*, and although the *Annals of Ulster* (561.1) record that the battle was won through the partisan prayers of Colum Cille, they are silent concerning cause or possible blame. The earliest hint of the legend is in the twelfth-century, Latin *Life of Mo Laisse* which states that, because of the great numbers killed at Cul Drebene, the penance imposed on Columba was exile. The story then crops up in an extended version in Manus O'Donnell's sixteenth-century *Life of Colum Cille.*

Despite the copyright incident not being recorded in Adomnán's *Life of Columba*, there is a persistent suspicion that it might be true. Did oral tradition preserve the legend outside official church records which only recognised sanitised and hagiographical accounts of Columba's life?[17] O'Donnell claimed to have consulted very old manuscripts, but if he did, then these are no longer extant. But even if true, why would Columba be so keen to make a copy of Finnian's Psalter? Would Columba not already have a Psalter? Was there something unique about Finnian's book? Was it a new(ish) version, perhaps one of Jerome's Latin translations? Had Finnian visited Rome and obtained Jerome's work? Had Columba snapped up the chance to make his own copy? When did Jerome's Psalter first came to Ireland? Had it been in Ireland for over a century, as some argue? Or did it only become commonly available

17 Joynt, 'The Cathach of St. Columba', 191, notes that the tract *De Causa Peregrinationis S. Columbae*, cited in a *Life* found in two Bodleian manuscripts, attributes the battle to Columba's wrath at the unjust judgement passed by Diarmaid in the matter of 'a certain book'. What the 'certain book' was, or who the other party in the dispute was, we are not told. There is also the testimony of an ancient stanza preserved by O'Donnell and attributed to Diarmaid, in which he is made to say that one of the things which deprived him of the kingship of Tara was 'the judgement concerning the book of Columcille and of Finden, "When with deceptive intent I said the saying: To every book its booklet (*re gach lebar a lebhrdn*)".'

around the time Columba is said to have borrowed from Finnian?[18] Was this why Columba succumbed to temptation?

In support of the legend is the fact that the Cathach is full of errors, more than 250 of them.[19] This is far beyond what would be expected of a document which was copied with normal care under normal conditions. Was the copying carried out in extreme haste and under high pressure? Does the high error count point to Columba making a quick illegal copy before returning the original to Finnian? The very high number of mistakes in the Cathach text may well be an indication of authenticity. Moreover, unless it were a very special book, why would an error-ridden copy be preserved so carefully in a special casket believed to contain relics of Columba? We may never know the answer to these questions, but the large proportion of errors does suggest a desperate hurriedness on the part of the scribe.

THE MANUSCRIPTS

The manuscripts of Columba's era, were not the dazzling illuminated versions of a later era, but working copies intended for everyday use. Nevertheless, the production techniques behind later manuscripts throw light on the scriptorial methods carried out on Iona during Columba's era. One of the most famous of the later illustrated manuscripts is the aforementioned *Book of Kells* which may have originated on Iona before being taken to Ireland.[20] If the *Book of Kells* did start life on Iona, it would be the ninth-century Viking raids which prompted its removal, first to Kells in County Meath before finding its present home in Trinity College Library, Dublin. The *Book of Kells* is an illustrated rather than an illuminated manuscript since it now has no gold leaf, but

18 Martin McNamara and Maurice Sheehy, 'Psalter Text and Psalter Study in the Early Irish Church (A.D. 600–1200)', *PRIA, Section C: Archaeology, Celtic Studies, History, Linguistics, Literature*, vol. 73 (1973), 262, are of the view that Patrick primarily used a pre-Jerome Gallic Old Latin text, arguing that Jerome's revision could hardly have established itself as early as Patrick's time. Yet, when Newport White analyses nineteen direct quotations by Patrick from the Psalter, he concludes that Patrick's preferred Old Testament text was an Old Latin version, but with intrusions from several Jerome translations. (Newport: J. D. White, *Saint Patrick: His Writings and Life* (London: SPCK, 1920), 3f.

19 For a discussion on the errors in the Cathach see Herity and Breen, *The Cathach of Colum Cille: An Introduction*, 6ff.

20 The *Book of Kells* was first sighted in 1007. From the start it was attributed in Kells to Columba. Before the 1620s it was known as the *Book of Columba*. De Hamel, *Meetings with Remarkable Manuscripts*, 138f., is of the view that it was made partly at least on Iona.

it does have intricate decorations, each of which took days to produce, though the main text could be copied relatively quickly.[21] Traditionally, the *Book of Kells* has been seen as the work of four scribes plus an illustrator, though Donncha MacGabhann, in his 2016 doctoral thesis, argues that such books were the work of only two hands.[22] One was the Master Artist responsible for the illustrations, the other was the Master Scribe who transcribed the main text. If MacGabhann is correct, then during Columba's era, and before texts were enhanced by elaborate illustrations, one scribe might copy a whole volume from start to finish.

Viking raids destroyed vast quantities of Iona scholarship, including Liturgies, Psalters, and Chronicles, not to mention a corpus of original compositions by Iona monks. One tradition, born more from optimism than from evidence, is that some of Iona's books were saved by being wrapped in hides and buried on the rocky islet of Cairn a'burgh. If so, this treasure has yet to be rediscovered.[23]

Modern interest in manuscripts often centres on their artistic qualities, but the books were originally produced as works to be used. Finlay emphasises Coptic influence in the artwork of Irish manuscripts of Columba's era and later.[24] He specifically refers to the *Codex Usserianus Primus* (also held in Trinity College Library, Dublin) which he judges as more Coptic than Celtic, and which dates from around the time of Columba's death in 597.[25] Finlay is convinced that the interlace patterns of 'Celtic art' were not derived from pre-

21 cf. De Hamel, *Meetings with Remarkable Manuscripts*, 96-139.

22 Donncha MacGabhann, 'Magnificent Obsession: An Artist's response to George Bain and The Book of Kells', *Inaugural George Bain Memorial Lecture*, 24th September 2015, in the Groam House Lecture series. See http://www.groamhouse.org.uk/index.asp?pageid=617918. De Hamel, *Meetings with Remarkable Manuscripts*, 129, alludes to the older theory that the Book of Kells was the work of four different scribes, and mentions Abbot Connachtach of Iona (d. 802), a known Master Scribe, as possibly one of those responsible (139). This view of four main scribes is also held by Meehan, *The Book of Kells*, 78ff. MacGabhann reckons that a proficient scribe could write 180 to 200 words per hour, working perhaps six hours per day; cf. Hughes, *Early Christian Ireland: Introduction to the Sources*, 256f. Meehan makes similar calculations.

23 Marian Pallister, *Argyll Curiosities* (Edinburgh: Birlinn, 2007), 99.

24 Finlay, *Columba*, 214, 217 and 223; cf. De Hamel, *Meetings with Remarkable Manuscripts*, 118, who writes that some of the illustrations in the *Book of Kells* seem to replicate Coptic textiles which 'are extraordinarily' similar.

25 cf. Dales, *Light to the Isles*, 42. De Hamel, *Meetings with Remarkable Manuscripts*, 127, notes that the *Codex Usserianus Primus* has an Old Latin text. De Hamel (118) also alludes to a school of scholarship which sees the origins of Irish Christianity in 'Coptic North Africa'.

Christian Irish culture, but from the Middle East,[26] and that the art forms of the Irish Church owed more to these influences than to indigenous inspiration. This whole field is a can of worms, in which conclusions are invariably affected by a scholar's presuppositions. One scholar emphasises continuity with indigenous culture. Another scholar emphasises a displacement of the previous culture. Finlay does concede that elements of pre-Christian Irish art, such as its bird-lore tradition, were carried over into the Church of Columba's time. However, the proportion to which the Irish Church, in its art and faith, drew from indigenous Irish culture over against Middle Eastern culture, is an area of intense debate.

THE TOOLS

Monks could either use black carbon ink derived from lamp soot, or iron gall ink made from crushed oak galls and iron sulphate.[27] The Andersons suggest that the intensely black ink of Dorbene's early eighth-century Schaffhausen copy of Adomnán's *Life of Columba* may have used Iona holly as an ingredient.[28] Columba held his ink in a shaped animal horn, and ink-horns from Irish monasteries usually had long spikes anchoring them into a hole in a desk or suitably prepared chair, or even into the ground.[29] Such precautions were not infallible. On one occasion, a man arrived on Iona in a highly excited state (I:25). Variously described as the 'clumsy guest' or the 'troublesome visitor', he upset the ink-horn with the edge of his clothing as he rushed forward to kiss Columba, spilling the ink. The presence of ink indicates that Columba was in the process of making a permanent copy on vellum,

---

26 Warren, *The Liturgy and Ritual of the Celtic Church*, 50ff., has an extended section arguing on artistic and stylistic grounds for a profound eastern influence on 'Celtic' art and script.' Herity and Breen, *The Cathach of Colum Cille: An Introduction*, 17, 23, 27f., 35, 39, see traces of pre-Christian La Tene central European culture on the script of the Cathach, as well as Coptic influences (28). Herity and Breen (30) conclude that the Cathach combines pagan Celtic and early Christian features in its art, and was produced in an artistic milieu that was predominantly Irish La Tene in character (39).

27 O'Neill, 'Columba the Scribe' in Bourke (ed.), *Studies in the Cult of Saint Columba*, 74. The ink used for the early *Cathach* was brown or black and identified as Gall (Herity and Breen, *The Cathach of Colum Cille: An Introduction*, 6).

28 Anderson and Anderson, *Adomnán's Life of Columba*, li.

29 The Bodleian Library, Oxford, has a late eleventh-century manuscript attributed to Hugo Pictor, which includes an illustration of an ink-horn attached to a chair. (De Hamel, *Meetings with Remarkable Manuscripts*, 243).

and if the spillage was over the writing surface rather than over the desk or floor, that would have been calamitous.

Quills were usually made from the wing feathers of geese or swans and tempered by heat to fuse and harden the barrel, enabling a high quality nib to be cut. The scribe of the Cathach, whoever he was, used an edged rather than a pointed quill, holding it at a flat angle to the horizontal, producing thick downstrokes and thin horizontals.[30] Similar processes and techniques were common throughout Christendom, and had been standard for generations. Like the perishable wooden styli which were used to make impressions on wax tablets, quill-feathers rarely survive as archaeological artefacts.[31]

Three surfaces were available for writing on: slate, wax tablets, and vellum. Slate and wax tablets were used for non-permanent inscriptions because their surfaces were easily erased by rubbing, scraping, or placing the wax tablet briefly in an oven.[32] Vellum was for a permanent record.

1. *Slate.* Slate was readily available. Not far from Iona is Easdale which later became the site of extensive slate quarries. However, there is a dearth of slate in Iona's archaeological record. This is surprising given slate's durability, but there may be slate panels lying buried beneath the present abbey. We know that other early monasteries used slate as a writing surface, and a cache of inscribed slates was discovered at Inchmarnock monastery off the Isle of Bute. The Inchmarnock slates are still decipherable, with the inscriptions revealing they were used for teaching pupils to write and memorise texts.[33]

2. *Wax Tablets.* In 1914 a quantity of wax tablets was recovered from Springmount Bog, seven miles north of Ballymena in the north of Ireland.[34] The Springmount Bog wax tablets are dated to the year 600, and comprise a book of six wooden leaves. Each leaf is approximately eight inches by three inches, inlaid with wax on both sides, apart from the two outer leaves which act as covers and have no wax on the external surfaces. The six leaves are bound together by a leather thong, which

30 Herity and Breen, *The Cathach of Colum Cille: An Introduction*, 7.

31 O'Neill, 'Columba the Scribe' in Bourke (ed.), *Studies in the Cult of Saint Columba*, 73; cf. (II:29) for reed usage.

32 Sharpe, *Adomnán of Iona: Life of St. Columba*, 296, note 155.

33 Clarke (ed.), *Early Medieval Scotland*, 6.

34 McNamara and Sheehy, 'Psalter Text and Psalter Study in the Early Irish Church', *PRIA* (1973), 201-98.

is stitched through holes perforating one edge of the tablets forming a spine.[35] In a few places the script is still legible, and the Springmount Bog tablets have quotations from Psalms 30, 31, and 32 in the Latin Vulgate. These were exemplar inscriptions, with pupils' attempts scrawled below.[36] The Springmount Bog tablets yield rich information about wax tablets and their usage in the Church of Columba's era.

The reusable characteristic of wax made it ideal for taking notes, and Adomnán records the monk Colgu mac Cellaig working in this way (I:35). Colgu and Columba were studying together in Columba's hut, when Columba became supernaturally aware of a crisis occurring in Colgu's own village: 'Hearing what the saint said, Colgu wrote down the date and the hour on his tablet.' Wax tablets also feature in Adomnán's book, *The Holy Places*, in which Adomnán describes taking notes of what the monk Arculf told him: 'I first wrote it down on the tablets: it will now be written succinctly on parchment.'[37] Adomnán records that he also questioned Arculf carefully on details about the Church of the Holy Sepulchre in Jerusalem, again writing the information on a wax tablet.[38]

Wax tablets took impressions from a stylus, and several Romano-British and Anglo-Saxon archaeological sites on mainland Britain have yielded examples of styli, though fewer have been recovered in Ireland or Scotland. Two styli have been identified at the Pictish Christian monastery at Portmahomack, but none on Iona itself. Campbell suggests that their scarcity in Ireland and Scotland may be due to the abundance of slate which uses chalk.[39] Alternatively, the Iona monks may have used perishable styli. Styli could be made from metal, wood, or bone, and, whereas the Portmahomack examples were bone styli, Iona may have preferred wooden versions. Wood breaks, and broken wooden styli would be used as kindling for a fire.[40]

---

35 McNamara and Sheehy, 'Psalter Text and Psalter Study in the Early Irish Church', *PRIA* (1973), 277f.

36 Ewan Campbell, 'The Archaeology of Writing in the time of Adomnán' in Wooding (ed.), *Adomnán of Iona*, 139.

37 Adomnán, *The Holy Places*, Introduction; cf. *Voyage of St. Brendan*, XII: 'The Abbot at once would take up his stylus and write down on a tablet whatever God had revealed.'

38 Adomnán, *The Holy Places*, I:2.

39 Campbell, 'The Archaeology of Writing in the time of Adomnán' in Wooding (ed.), *Adomnán of Iona*, 139, 143.

40 Hughes, *Early Christian Ireland: Introduction to Sources*, 33, notes with regret that an 'Irish farmer's wooden tools would have rotted away under normal temperate conditions,

3. *Vellum.* The deluxe writing surface was vellum (parchment), which was prepared from the treated and stretched hide of calves. All permanent records were made by ink on vellum, and the eighth-century *Lucca Manuscript* describes how vellum/parchment was prepared. The skin was placed in lime water and left for three days; it was then extended on a frame and scraped on both sides with a sharp knife; it was then left to dry.[41] One hide produced a single pair of leaves, and Christopher De Hamel estimates that the 1,030 leaves of the *Codex Amiatinus* Vulgate Bible would require 515 skins.[42] If necessary, sheepskin or goatskin could be used. Glue came from animal by-products; and animal sinews were used for binding. Excavations at Portmahomack have uncovered a vellum-making workshop within the monastic complex itself, along with shaped stones which were used to work and stretch the hides. Evidence for a similar workshop on Iona has still to be found. That also may lie beneath later buildings.

THE PUPILS

The monastery was a place of education, and Adomnán refers to one of Columba's pupils, Berchan Mes Loen, who was studying 'wisdom' (III:21). In a monastic context 'wisdom' meant sacred learning rather than philosophy.[43] Sharpe suggests that Berchan was foster-son to Columba, as Columba had been foster-son to the priest Cruithnechan, and also argues that this was why Columba educated Berchan even though Berchan was not set for the religious life. However, Sharpe may be going beyond the evidence of the text. He translates '*alumnus*' as 'foster-son', whereas the Andersons translate it more literally as 'pupil'. Berchan may have been fostered by Columba as Sharpe suggests, but the term *alumnus* is insufficient evidence for that conclusion. In any case, the unfortunate Berchan disobeyed Columba, spying on him when Columba was experiencing heavenly visions and heavenly light. Columba prophesied that, because of his disobedience, Berchan would live lecherously all his days; but, since he had been Columba's pupil, the penance he did before death could

---

whilst his iron ones would have been handed on. Therefore, finds today are not representative of the amount of equipment then current.' As with wooden tools, so also with styli.

41 Carver, *Portmahomack on Tarbat Ness*, 210.

42 De Hamel, *Meetings with Remarkable Manuscripts*, 82.

43 cf. Sharpe, *Adomnán of Iona: Life of St. Columba*, 371, note 393.

bring mercy from God. Mercy was not automatic. It was strictly conditional on Berchan's penance.

Fostered children were exposed to a standard method of instruction.[44] The alphabet was memorised. Letters were copied. Words and sentences were reproduced. The main text was the Latin Psalter, meaning that learning to read and write went hand in hand with learning the psalms. This made a child both literate and liturgically competent, preparing him for participation in the ministry of the Church. It was a purpose-driven education, and a core aim was to learn by heart the one hundred and fifty psalms of David, colloquially known as the 'three fifties'. Because of this, psalms were rarely written out in full in liturgical books, but were briefly indicated by their opening words. That was enough. Each monk knew what followed.

Discoveries at Inchmarnock monastery are strongly suggestive of a monastic schooling for the wider populace, including adults as well as children.[45] But was this only for the elite? And did this also happen on Iona? We cannot be certain. However, the Inchmarnock inscribed slates, which were used for tuition in literacy and for the memorisation of Christian texts, reveal that the pupils practised two types of scripts, Ogham and Latin.[46] The scholars were taught in two cultures: the older, pre-Christian culture, as well as that which was introduced by the Church. This contrasts with Watson's view that Ogham was so much associated with paganism that the Church banned it totally.[47] On Inchmarnock, if not elsewhere, pupils were familiar with the ancient script of their ancestors. Alphabet stones were also used as teaching aids, and their possession was a statement which advertised not only a person's literacy but their access to the Word of God.

---

44 McNamara and Sheehy, 'Psalter Text and Psalter Study in the Early Irish Church', *PRIA* (1973), 206.

45 David Clarke, 'Communities', in *Early Medieval Scotland*, 90f.

46 Jill Harden, *The Picts* (Edinburgh: Historic Scotland, 2010) 20. Ogham writing originated in Ireland and was later adopted by the Picts. Twenty different 'letters' were formed from straight lines. Ogham was read from bottom to top, with between one and five horizontal or diagonal lines attached to a single vertical line.

47 Watson, *The History of the Celtic Place-Names of Scotland*, 222. Watson cites MacNeill who 'gives good reasons' for believing that the Ogham cult was seen as distinctively pagan, banned by the Church, and its development arrested by the growing power of Christianity; cf. Warren, *The Liturgy and Ritual of the Celtic Church*, 19. Patrick may have been among the first to introduce the Latin-Irish alphabet which supplanted the earlier Ogham characters, though definite conclusions cannot be reached.

Since no lay community lived on Iona, a regular education for the wider populace may not have taken place there, though we do know of high-status tutelage.[48] In the early seventh century, the exiled Northumbrian royal family was schooled by Iona, with the children also instructed in Christian beliefs, professing faith, and being baptised. Their circumstances were exceptional but demonstrate that some monks became teachers to the young. A generation later, the future King Aldfrith of Northumbria was similarly educated by Irish monks, and when he became king after the death of Ecgfrith in 685, his relationship with Adomnán, forged on Iona, continued.

LITERACY AND POWER

Christianity introduced a sophisticated literacy to both Ireland and Scotland. Monks were able to read and write, not only in Church Latin but in the newly scripted Gaelic. This advanced literacy was almost exclusively owned by the Christian community. It was a tool for communication. It brought status and importance. And it was an avenue to power, especially when kings asked clerics to act as recorders or as ambassadors. Literate churchmen become important envoys, and Columba's visits to Bridei of the Picts may have been as much ambassadorial as missionary, with Columba acting as an envoy from Dál Riata. Literate churchmen were trusted. It was assumed they had high ethical standards. And because they were able to put their monarch's thoughts in writing, that gave added confidence that the king's policies would be accurately represented. Foster points out that the power of literacy should not be underestimated.[49] It was a major avenue to influence. It had an ability to radically affect how society operated. And it was the church which held the key. Kings were aware of this, not least because many of them had been educated though the Church.

The facility to record data and preserve knowledge in written form changed everything. Literacy brought an ability to accumulate knowledge. It enabled records to be transmitted from one leader to

48 Campbell, 'The archaeology of writing in the time of Adomnán' in Wooding (ed.), *Adomnán of Iona*, 144, suggests that lay literacy was more widespread than used to be thought, with the likes of King Aldfrith of Northumbria and many lay people spending time in monasteries as pilgrims or as penitents sometimes for years at a stretch. They would acquire basic literacy at the very least.

49 Foster: *Picts, Gaels and Scots*, 71.

another, and from one generation to another. Documents, and those who wrote the documents, became the custodians of truth, rather than the traditional bardic poets. Literacy facilitated the sharing of ideas. It enabled genealogical lists to be preserved (so vital in validating kingly legitimacy), and it was the Church which became the curator of such lists. Literacy also aided the publishing of laws and edicts over a kingdom. In turn this enabled land titles to be recorded, meaning that land ownership began to be defined by legal decision rather than by custom. Literacy also impacted on evangelism. It meant that the Christian scriptures, especially selections from the Gospels and the Psalter, became the highpoint of spiritual wisdom. The power of literacy brought a focus on the Word of God, and monks took that Word to remote corners of the land.

These connections between literacy and evangelism raise questions. Did Christianity succeed because missionaries hijacked the language of the people? A Columba in the sixth century, or a David Livingstone in the nineteenth century, would believe that Christianity's success lay in its inherent truth; but was its triumph really due to missionaries taking control of a people's language through their ability to reproduce it in writing?[50] This argument is proposed by Paul Landau, and by Jean and John Comaroff, in relation to the nineteenth-century South African context. They argue that when missionaries put a people's language into written form, then the missionaries effectively took custodianship of that language, gaining control and dominance in relation to the culture, ideas, and beliefs of the people.[51] Hunter advocates a similar dynamic operating with Columba's missionaries, and that a major factor in the success of the Iona missionaries was the power of the written word.[52] Pagan priests were *learned* and enormously intelligent, but they were largely illiterate. Hunter argues that this placed them

---

50 cf. David Livingstone, 'Letter to William Thompson, 27th September 1855' in Schapera (ed.), *Livingstone's Missionary Correspondence: 1841-1856* (London: Chatto and Windus, 1961), 286: 'The Word of the living God has been brought in contact with their hearts and minds. This word has life and power. Few human souls can withstand its force, and no hatred, however deep, can quench its power.'

51 Paul Stuart Landau, *The Realm of the Word: Language, Gender and Christianity in a Southern African Kingdom* (Cape Town: David Philip, 1995), Jean and John Comaroff, *Of Revelation and Revolution: Christianity, Colonialism, and Consciousness in South Africa, vol. 1* (Chicago: Chicago University Press, 1991).

52 James Hunter, *Last of the Free* (Edinburgh: Mainstream, 1999), 61.

at a disadvantage in their dealings with Columban clerics, whose religion was so closely bound up with an ability to read and write.[53] He maintains that enormous prestige attached itself to those who could access the wisdom of past ages and who could make a permanent record of what was being said and done around them. In his view that was what brought success for missionary monks.

Columba would argue that success came because of spirituality, the prayers of God's people, the witness of God's servants, and the power of God's Holy Spirit. Here, as elsewhere, the secular historian looks for non-supernatural mechanisms, and works with a methodological naturalism. For an academic scholar, the success of a movement has to be explicable by material causes and effects. But, for Columba himself, the ultimate factor was spiritual and supernatural. In both analyses, literacy is key.

David Bogue was the theological tutor for the London Missionary Society in the early nineteenth century, and in his *Missionary Lectures* he emphasised that language is key to mission. He taught that the first duty of a missionary is to learn the language of the indigenous people, and that this should occupy the first year in the mission field.[54] Centuries earlier, did Columba do this in Pictland, or was his native Irish Gaelic enough? Adomnán twice, though only twice, mentions Columba using an interpreter when conversing with Picts. The first occasion was when Columba was staying for a few days on Skye (I:33): an old man heard the word of God from Columba 'through an interpreter', believed, and was baptised. The second occasion was when

53 Pre-Christian Celtic culture had its own form of literacy. Harden, *The Picts*, 9, points out: 'The use of symbols [on stones] is now generally seen as the Pictish response to literacy, at a time when the written word was emerging as an important apparatus of power. … one strong possibility is that the combinations of symbols represent the names of specific individuals in a form of writing. The suggestion that they recorded tribal lineages or marital agreements is no longer generally accepted.' Bury in J. B. Bury and Jon M. Sweeney, *Ireland's Saint: The Essential Biography of St. Patrick* (Massachusetts:Paraclete, 2008), 171, notes that writing was in use among the Celtic Iberians of Spain and among the Celts of Gaul before the Roman conquest of Britain (A.D. 43). The Iberians had their own script, and some of the Spanish peoples had a considerable literature. Caesar notes that in Gaul the lore of the Druids was not written down, but that Greek text was used for public and private purposes. Bury concludes: 'These facts show, at least, that the art of writing might have reached Ireland at an early period. But there is no proof that it did.'

54 David Bogue, *Missionary Lectures*, Lecture 2: 'The Employment of a Missionary' in Archives of the School of Oriental and African Studies, University of London.

Columba was in the province of the Picts, preaching the word of life 'through an interpreter' (II:32): a Pictish layman heard him and, along with his entire household, believed, and was baptised. What do these interpreter-stories tell us? Do they imply that Columba's language was not understood by some groups?[55]

At the very least the interpreter-stories indicate a gap in Columba's range of abilities. This makes it unlikely that Adomnán fabricated such cameos out of his imagination. One of Adomnán's aims is to heighten Columba's reputation as a great man. Accordingly, we expect Adomnán to *enhance* a story in order to *raise* Columba's status and add to his prestige. We do not expect him to invent a detail which might *lower* Columba's standing or reveal limits to his skill-set. Given the implausibility of Adomnán inventing the interpreter-stories, these incidents were probably long-established anecdotes, with the Iona oral tradition recalling that Columba sometimes needed help when communicating with Picts. At the same time, interpreters are not mentioned every time Picts are conversed with. For example, there is no mention of interpreters when Columba meets with King Bridei of the Picts. The most we can conclude is that sometimes interpreters were required, and sometimes they were not. This leads to the question of Columba's own tongue.

MOTHER SPEECH

Columba's mother tongue was early Irish Gaelic, which belonged to the Q-Celtic branch of a family of Celtic languages spoken across the British Isles at the time. The Picts spoke a P-Celtic form. In this designation of language-types, the 'P' refers to 'proto' (rather than to 'Pictish') indicating that linguistic scholars once thought that P-Celtic was the prototype root from which the other forms derived.[56] Opinion is now less certain, and there is currently a reluctance to go further than to state that P-Celtic and Q-Celtic were kindred tongues with a common root, but not necessarily mother and daughter.[57] One theory is

55 Anderson and Anderson, *Adomnán's Life of Columba*, 139, note 168, on II:32.

56 O'Loughlin, *Celtic Theology*, 13ff., suggests that 'P' and 'Q' refer to predominant sounds within the Welsh and Irish language families respectively.

57 Watson, *The Celtic Place-Names of Scotland*, 126, gives the prevailing opinion in 1926: 'The evidence at our disposal goes to show that at the time of the Roman occupation the language current all over Britain was Celtic of the P-group, that is to say, Old British,

that Q-Celtic (Goidelic) may have been in the British Isles for centuries before Brythonic or P-Celtic arrived.[58]

Whatever the origins of Q-Celtic and P-Celtic, the variances between them may explain why Columba needed an interpreter when communicating with some Picts though not with all. Foster notes that late nineteenth-century scholars speculated that the Picts had a distinctly separate non-Indo-European, pre-Celtic, component to their vocabulary and that Pictish was fundamentally different from Columba's Irish: however, recent work has moved away from that supposition, concluding that the Picts simply spoke another form of a common Celtic language.[59] Yet, there may be an element of truth in the nineteenth-century speculation. What may have been the case is that, in remote areas, some pre-Celtic components had been retained and were mixed into the local P-Celtic, creating a hybrid version, explaining why, in these areas, Columba had difficulties in communicating. Columba may have gained proficiency in 'standard' P-Celtic, but not in local variations. Although this is a speculative hypothesis, it is possible, and it allows a scenario in which Columba was able to converse with most Picts in their P-Celtic tongue but needed help where local people had an idiosyncratic version.

Columba lived in Dál Riata where Q-Celtic was dominant, following ethnic immigration from the north of Ireland. However, P-Celtic groups still existed in areas under Dál Riatan control, and Dál Riata's powerful neighbours, the Britons of Strathclyde, had a P-Celtic Brythonic-based language. Hence, Columba could have absorbed the rudiments of P-Celtic on his doorstep. This, plus any inherent similarities between Q-Celtic and P-Celtic, may have been enough in most situations. However, as a high-status individual and ever conscious of his dignity, Columba would be unwilling to look

---

represented now by Welsh.' Modern analysis offers a different view, and though Watson may not have been wide of the mark, the separation of languages probably started sooner.

58 Martin Dougherty, *The Celts: The History and Legacy of One of the Oldest Cultures in Europe* (London: Amber, 2015), 41, suggests that, 'although there were differences between the Celtic languages, common roots made it likely that any given group of Celts could communicate reasonably well with any other.' This is also the view of Colin Scott Mackenzie, 'St. Columba's Church' in Randall, *In Search of Colmcille*, 125, who writes that Brythonic Celts displaced the original Goidels in many areas, or at least supplanted their language and possibly culture. He comments, 'just how far they were mutually intelligible is hard to figure out'.

59 Foster: *Picts, Gaels, and Scots*, 24.

foolish by stumbling in his speech or vocabulary. This may be why, in places with strong local dialects, he used an interpreter. In sophisticated Pictish society, which had a more standard P-Celtic, Columba may have been relatively fluent, explaining why there is no mention of an interpreter when he meets Bridei. Nonetheless, an interpreter may have been used in conversations with Bridei but is not mentioned because Adomnán has more important issues to record. Another possibility is that Bridei was fluent in Columba's language rather than vice-versa.[60] A high-status individual such as Bridei would be well educated and may have known the language of Ireland, whose people had been settling on his west coast for several generations.

Over the centuries Columba's Q-Celtic, brought to Scotland by the Irish Church, evolved into Scottish Gaelic, with Scottish Gaelic often labelled as 'Erse' or the 'Irish tongue'. It was described as such not only by Dr Johnson and other travellers in the Highlands, but in official Parliamentary and Church Reports. Pictish P-Celtic disappeared as a distinct spoken tongue by the tenth century, though residual traces survive to modern times.[61]

LITURGICAL SPEECH

Columba and his monks communicated with the local people in the vernacular, but liturgical language was different. Though no Iona Liturgy is extant for us to refer to, it is unlikely it would have been in the language of the people. Warren argues that there is no trace of a vernacular Liturgy in any portion of the Celtic Church, though his conclusion is based on a very small number of surviving truly early liturgical manuscripts.[62] Supporting Warren's thesis, the near-contemporary *Bangor Antiphonary* is totally in Latin, indicating that monastic worship services were conducted in Latin, including prayers, hymns, psalms, scripture readings, and celebration of the Eucharist. The sermon would be in the vernacular, but little else. Hence, although Columba gained the reputation of being a protector of the Irish bardic

60 Donald Mackenzie, *Scotland: The Ancient Kingdom* (London, 1930), 146.

61 cf. Harden, *The Picts*, 19, points out that Pictish has not survived as a spoken tongue, and gradually died out during the tenth and eleventh centuries when Gaelic became the everyday language of former Pictish regions. In the Western Isles, Skye and the north-west mainland, Pictish was swamped by Norse and then by Gaelic.

62 Warren, *The Liturgy and Ritual of the Celtic Church*, 155.

tradition, and although he is sometimes represented as the promoter of all things vernacular, there is little indication that liturgical items were in the mother tongue.

On the other hand, many poems and praise-songs were in the vernacular, and Adomnán alludes to these. One of his stories features bandits who were having a riotous evening singing songs, some of which featured Columba (I:1). Absorbed in their wild revels, they were attacked: but the only ones who perished were those who had not sung in praise of Columba! In another story, some of Columba's monks ask Columba why he did not request the poet Cronan to 'sing a tuneful piece of his own composition, as custom allows' (I:42). Columba replies that it would be inappropriate to ask Cronan for a merry song, since he was an unhappy fellow and soon to die. Over time, the Psalms were translated into Irish Gaelic, but full vernacular liturgical usage came much later.[63]

Modern worshippers might react against having to attend religious services conducted in an alien tongue, but in the sixth century the ordinary worshipper may not have found this situation at all strange or off-putting. Mystery, and a sense of the holy, may have been more important than understanding every word. The actual meaning of the liturgical actions would be explained to converts. And when they gathered for worship and received the sacrament, they would take in their stride the fact that eucharistic mystery and linguistic mystery went together. For them it made sense that holy sacramental actions required a holy sacramental language.

WRITTEN SPEECH

Ancient Irish culture was predominantly an oral culture, with its Ogham script able to record only basic data. The dominant medium was the spoken word. In Finlay's opinion, even when Christian monasteries displaced the older druidic schools, the culture of the spoken word retained immense importance.[64] Finlay maintains that, despite their renowned book-culture, Irish monks were instinctively more comfortable with the spoken word than with written text. He argues that our modern preoccupation with the wonderful art of the Irish Church in its texts and illustrated manuscripts, makes us

63 The *Book of Deer* was much later.

64 Finlay, *Columba*, 212ff.

assume that writing rather than speaking was the preferred medium. Finlay's substantial point is that our focus on monks busily copying out superb manuscripts makes us assume that the written word was what enthused them, came naturally to them, and was their favoured mode of communication.

Finlay questions these assumptions. He proposes that one of the monks' aims was to overcome frustrations created by the limitations of the written word. They wanted, somehow, to transmit the nuances of live oral expression into frustratingly static written texts. He suggests that they tried to inhabit what they wrote with what they normally expressed much better through rhetoric and oral communication. Finlay's theory is that this desire to communicate something of the quality of speech through written words may lie behind embellishments to the text in Irish manuscripts. Irishisms, such as dots and symbols, may be an attempt to voice rhetorical nuances in a manner impossible in plain script on its own. In Finlay's opinion, it was the treasure chest of Celtic symbolisms which enabled them to imbue written text with virtual speech. They used the art of their pagan past to give fuller expression to the Christian words which they copied. Finlay's thesis is not proven, but it is a reminder that communication through speech was as important as communication through script, if not more so.

CHAPTER II

Learning and Scholarship

The Irish Church expected high standards of scholarship. When the *Amra Choluimb Chille* celebrates Columba's erudition, it is his study of the Scriptures which takes centre-stage. The *Amra* (I) claims that Columba, 'could explain the true Word', a boast which is made in its opening stanza, indicating the importance of that skill.[1] The *Amra* is effusively generous, since the Iona *familia* was proud of the scholarly reputation of its founding abbot, as monks of other communities were of theirs. The *Bangor Antiphonary* praises Comgall in similar fashion, styling him as a man who was learned in the Scriptures and careful in the administration of the sacraments, 'a scholar among his peers in the Old and New Testament'.[2] If the *Amra* goes over the top, praising Columba's scholarship wherever possible, then that was because its depiction of Columba's academic interests reflected Columba's reputation in his own lifetime. A century later, in his Second Preface to his *Life of Columba*, Adomnán claims that Columba never let an hour go past in which he was not either praying, or reading, or writing.

Columba was a fine scholar. But it was his ability to handle the 'book of books' which was regarded as his most important quality. Consequently, the *Amra* focuses on two areas of Columba's scholarship. One is Columba's ability to interpret Scripture. The other is his wider knowledge of theological literature.

---

1 On early Irish Church learning see: Hughes, *Early Christian Ireland: Introduction to the Sources*, 193ff. Herren and Brown, *Christ in Celtic Theology*, 114, argue that literacy and learning was a by-product of Pelagianism, since only by being literate could one read the Scriptures where God's will and the rules which should be followed were made known. They argue (117) that the preferred Gospel was Matthew, with its extensive sections on law, commandments, and instruction.

2 *Bangor Antiphonary*, Item 14:9 (Stratman's translation); cf. Ian Adamson, *Bangor: Light of the World* (Newtonards: Colourpoint, 2015), 246.

THE BIBLICAL TEXT

Which Bible did Columba use? A definitive answer is elusive, but there are clues. Most of the evidence comes from psalm-texts since the Psalter was the most read, and most frequently cited, part of Scripture. The Psalter was also the basis for all acts of worship and devotion, both corporate and personal. Hence it is the examination of quotations from early Irish Psalter-texts which enables scholars to deduce which Scripture versions were in use at any one time or place.

The Bible was written in Hebrew for the Old Testament, and in Greek for the New Testament. Small portions were in other Near Eastern languages, but Hebrew and Greek were the principal tongues. Around 200 B.C. the Hebrew Bible was translated into Greek in a version known as the Septuagint (LXX), named after the seventy scholars to whom tradition gives the honour of having completed the translation. In the early Christian era the whole Bible was translated into Old Latin (*Vetus Latina*) versions. In this context 'Old Latin' is not a different type of Latin, but indicates that these versions predated Jerome's translations. There were a range of Old Latin versions, of varying quality and accuracy. One was named the Gallic Old Latin version due to its popularity in Gaul, and it was also popular in Ireland. There was no standard Latin text until several centuries after Columba's era. Hence, it is common to find quotations from a variety of Latin versions within one manuscript.

In 382 the variable quality of the Old Latin translations prompted Pope Damasus I to commission Jerome to make a scholarly Latin revision of the Bible. Centuries later, the fruit of Jerome's labours became known as the Vulgate (*Versio Vulgata*); and, at the Council of Trent in 1546, the Vulgate was adopted by the Roman Catholic Church as its official Latin text. However, this official status, granted to a particular Jerome text, was far in the future in the fifth and sixth centuries. Moreover, that official Vulgate was not a single work by Jerome, but an aggregate of his translations. The version known today as the Vulgate took shape over a period of time during which several of Jerome's new Latin translations circulated alongside older Latin versions. Columba's era, the latter half of the sixth century, was within this period of flux, with a variety of options. Pope Damasus I died in 384, and by that date Jerome had already completed a new Latin translation of the four Gospels from the best available Greek texts. However, given the centrality of the Psalter in the Church's theology and liturgy, it is Jerome's several subsequent translations of the Psalms which are crucial.[3]

1. *The Roman Psalter.* Jerome started with a quick revision of the Old Latin text of the Psalter, basing his revision on the Greek Septuagint. This is known as the Roman (R) Psalter, and Jerome may have completed this as early as 383.

2. *The Gallican Psalter.* Jerome then made a second, more careful, revision of the Old Latin text of the Psalter. This second revision, known as the Gallican (G) Psalter, was to have a long life. This was also based on the Greek Septuagint text, albeit a revised and improved edition, and was completed around 387. It was an immediate success, becoming widely popular during the fifth century. It was introduced by Gregory of Tours into the Church in France, giving it its name, the Gallican (G) Psalter.

3. *The 'H' Psalter.* Jerome's third rendering of the Psalter into Latin was a completely new translation, referred to as the (H) version because this time Jerome translated the Psalms from the original Hebrew rather than from the Greek Septuagint. Jerome worked on this version between 390 and 405 as part of a larger project in which he translated all thirty-nine books of the Hebrew Bible into Latin. However, by the ninth century his much-loved Gallican Psalter (G) ousted his (H) Psalter, and so today the 'Vulgate Psalter' is essentially the Gallican (G) Psalter.[4] Thus, the current Vulgate Old Testament is principally Jerome's (H) apart from the Psalms which are Jerome's (G). The oldest complete extant text of the Vulgate anywhere in the world is the *Codex Amiatinus*, which was produced in Northumbria at Abbot Ceolfrid's request around the year 700, when Bede was a young man.[5]

---

3 cf. White, *Saint Patrick: His Writings and Life*, 3f.

4 Vulgate numbering of the Psalms differs from standard Hebrew psalm numbering. The Vulgate numbering is based on that of the Septuagint, whereas the standard Hebrew numbering is based on the Masoretic text which is widely accepted as the standard Hebrew text. The numbers are the same for Psalm 1 to 8. Psalms 9 and 10 (Hebrew) are combined as Psalm 9 in the Vulgate. This different numbering continues until Psalm 113 in the Hebrew which is Psalm 112 in the Vulgate. Psalms 114 and 115 in the Hebrew are combined to become Psalm 113 in the Vulgate. But Psalm 116 (Hebrew) is split into Psalms 114 and 115 in the Vulgate. The Vulgate then continues, one number behind the Hebrew numbering until Psalm 147 (Hebrew) which is split into Psalms 146 and 147 in the Vulgate. Psalms 148, 149, and 150 are the same in both.

5 Howlett, *The Celtic Latin Tradition of Biblical Style*, 55; cf. De Hamel, *Meetings with Remarkable Manuscripts*, 54ff.

Despite Jerome's scholarly work, the pre-Jerome Old Latin versions were replaced only slowly across Europe. Not only did new work need time to spread geographically, but the familiar phrases of the Old Latin versions were deeply embedded in local liturgies and in the minds of worshippers. For example, the *Book of Kells* is standard Vulgate but with Old Latin intrusions, and De Hamel speculates that variant readings may have been inserted unconsciously by monks who knew the Old Latin text by heart.[6] Even in Rome, and as late as the closing years of the sixth century, Pope Gregory the Great notes that both the Vulgate and the Old Latin were in use in the Apostolic Palace. Gregory used the Vulgate, except where the earlier version seemed better.[7] This is similar to what occurred centuries later when the much-loved phrases of the King James' Authorised Version persisted long after other translations became available. Moreover, at no point in the early centuries did a Church Synod declare that such-and-such a translation was the official version and was to be used exclusively. Hence, Jerome's fresh new translations were soon corrupted by Old Latin readings where these were preferred, as they often were for centuries to come.[8]

Consistent with all of this, analysis of early Irish Church texts reveals that writers frequently quote from several versions even within one document. They may quote from personal memory, in which case several versions compete for attention. Or, if they consult a written text, then that text may itself include a variety of renderings. In order to identify which biblical texts were used by Columba, the first step is to review manuscripts straddling Columba's era.

1. Patrick (5th C.) cites Scripture in his *Confessions* and in his *Letter to the Soldiers of Coroticus*. McNamara and Sheehy point out that Patrick primarily uses a pre-Jerome Gallic Old Latin text.[9] They also think that Jerome's revision may not have established itself as early as Patrick's era, though White concludes differently. In an analysis of nineteen direct quotations by Patrick from the Psalter, White points out: seven times Patrick uses identical (R/G) texts from Jerome; ten times Patrick has a

6 De Hamel, *Meetings with Remarkable Manuscripts*, 127.

7 De Hamel, *Meetings with Remarkable Manuscripts*, 33.

8 Herity and Breen, *The Cathach of Colum Cille: An Introduction*, 42.

9 McNamara and Sheehy, 'Psalter Text and Psalter Study in the Early Irish Church', *PRIA* (1973), 262. No complete Irish copy of an Old Latin Psalter survives. They were superseded by the Gallican so completely that they ceased to be copied.

rendering in which (R) coincides with some Old-Latin versions; in one case Patrick agrees with Jerome's (H); and in one case he agrees with Jerome's (G).[10] White's conclusion is that Patrick was aware of Jerome's translations alongside Old Latin versions. Despite this, Jerome may not have been widespread in Ireland during Patrick's era.

2. In the Springmount Bog wax tablets (*c.* 600) it is Jerome's Gallican (G) translation which dominates, with occasional readings from Old Latin versions.[11] Thus, by the year 600, Springmount pupils were learning literacy primarily through Jerome's Gallican (G) Psalter.

3. Columbanus (d. 615) was educated at the Bangor monastery. He normally uses Jerome's Gallican (G) Psalter, but cites from a variety of versions, including Old Latin renderings.[12]

4. Cummain (d. 661) was a seventh-century Irish Bishop who wrote a *Paschal Letter* in 632 trying to persuade Iona to adopt the practices of the Roman Church. Cummain cites the Psalter four times, three of which entirely replicate the Jerome Gallican (G) text.[13]

5. The *Bangor Antiphonary* (*c.* 690) predominantly uses the Jerome Gallican (G) text, but with variations which reveal an enduring fondness for Old Latin texts. Warren notes that thirty of the forty-one psalm quotations in the *Bangor Antiphonary* are identical with Jerome's Gallican (G) version, and Warren devotes several pages to a detailed tabulated comparison of the Bangor text with the Vulgate.[14] Outside the Psalms, two major portions of Scripture cited by the *Bangor Antiphonary* are the Song of Moses (Exod. 15:1-19) and the Speech of Moses (Deut. 32:1-43). Both these Canticles were chanted regularly in the liturgy: hence we would expect them to conserve

---

10 White, *Saint Patrick: His Writings and Life*, 3f.

11 McNamara and Sheehy, 'Psalter Text and Psalter Study in the Early Irish Church', *PRIA* (1973), 207.

12 McNamara and Sheehy, 'Psalter Text and Psalter Study in the Early Irish Church', *PRIA* (1973), 260, demonstrate that Columbanus' Psalter text is Gallican in fifteen out of a total of twenty-six readings. Three citations are Old Latin; four are uncertain; and four more are peculiar to Columbanus.

13 McNamara and Sheehy, 'Psalter Text and Psalter Study in the Early Irish Church', *PRIA* (1973), 260.

14 Warren, *The Bangor Antiphonary: Part II*, xxxiiff.; cf. D. S. Nerney, 'The Bangor Symbol, I', *ITQ* (1952), 371, who agrees that the *Bangor Antiphonary* Scripture text is 'Old Irish mixed' (partly Vulgate and partly Old Latin). When Warren uses the term 'Vulgate' to refer to the main Latin biblical texts in the *Bangor Antiphonary*, it is Jerome's Gallican (G) text which he has in mind for the Psalter.

older forms of expression. Thus, although the *Bangor Antiphonary*'s Song of Moses is mainly Jerome's (H) text, it also has strong traces of Old Latin renderings. An Old Latin version also dominates the *Antiphonary*'s citation of Daniel 3. New Testament references in the *Bangor Antiphonary* also preserve some Old Latin readings.

These examples confirm three things. First, during the period in question, there was no official Latin biblical text. Second, Jerome's Gallican (G) text was the preferred choice for the Psalter. Third, whenever quoting Scripture 'worn smooth' by liturgical repetition, the familiar Old Latin texts still shone through. The Springmount wax tablets, Columbanus, Cummain, and the *Bangor Antiphonary* all indicate that, from 600 onwards, Jerome's Gallican (G) text dominated the Psalter.[15] This makes it highly probable that Columba, during the late sixth century, also used Jerome's increasingly popular Gallican (G) Psalter, whilst occasionally retaining Old Latin wordings. This supposition is supported by Columba's *Altus Prosator*, with biblical quotations within the *Altus* including both Old Latin and Jerome versions.[16]

An intriguing detail, relevant to this discussion, comes in Adomnán's account of Columba's last day (III:23), in which Columba busied himself transcribing part of the Psalter. According to Adomnán, Columba reached Psalm 34 (Vulgate 33).[17] If Adomnán's quotation corresponds to what Columba actually wrote, then Columba was transcribing an Old Latin version rather than Jerome's. If so, then Columba sometimes used a very early form of the Psalter when elsewhere it was being superseded by Jerome's Gallican (G). Columba may have been mixing versions: and a 'pick and mix' approach would be entirely consistent with what we find in Patrick, Columbanus, and Bangor. But all of this depends on Adomnán accurately reproducing Columba's last transcriptions, and

---

15 McNamara and Sheehy, 'Psalter Text and Psalter Study in the Early Irish Church', *PRIA* (1973), 263.

16 Clancy and Markus, *Iona: The Earliest Poetry of a Celtic Monastery*, 42. M. Esposito, 'The Cathach of St. Columba', *Journal of the County Louth Archaeological Society*, vol. 4, no. 1 (Dec., 1916), 83, also notes that the *Altus Prosator* cites Old Latin versions.

17 O'Reilly, 'Reading the Scriptures in the Life of Columba' in Bourke (ed.), *Studies in the Cult of Saint Columba*, 103, comments on Columba's last task, his transcription of part of Psalm 34. She notes that in the *Epistle of Clement of Rome* and other late first-century documents, Psalm 34:12 was interpreted as an invitation to eternal life issued by Christ; the same verse opens Ambrose's *De Officiis Ministrorum* and was used in baptismal catechesis, as well as forming part of a chain of texts on the spiritual life used by monastic writers. As such it was significant for a man on the brink of eternity.

can that be assumed?[18] Remarkably, perhaps it can. What Columba wrote that afternoon was his final handwritten work before his death. As such, the Iona monks may have safeguarded the last book Columba copied, the last page he touched, and the last words he wrote. Awe for Columba's writings, added to the probability that whichever text Columba preferred would be the community's choice for generations, may mean that Adomnán cites the actual words which Columba wrote.[19] If so, then Columba's own Bible included not only psalms from Jerome's Gallican (G) Psalter but favourites from Old Latin texts. Interestingly, this mixture is preserved in the Cathach. Is this additional evidence that the Cathach came from Columba's hand? Was the Cathach the basis of all his future copies? [20] Against this, Reeves notes that Psalm 34, verse 11, in the Cathach, differs from what is cited by Adomnán.[21] Being a textual detective is not straightforward!

Old Latin biblical texts were eventually replaced by Jerome's (G) for the entire Psalter, and by Jerome's (H) elsewhere. But that wholesale substitution was still in the future in Columba's day. Even Bede, in early eighth-century Northumberland, records Abbot Ceolfrid quoting Genesis both in an Old Latin version and in Jerome's new translation.[22] The old wording was lodged deep in the communal memory. The beauty of language, the richness of expression, and the connections with the past, all created an affection for a particular rendering within a worshipping community. The early Irish monasteries had a love of the

18 McNamara and Sheehy, 'Psalter Text and Psalter Study in the Early Irish Church', *PRIA* (1973), 260.

19 On the biblical text which Adomnán uses in *The Holy Places*, see: O'Loughlin: *Adomnán and the Holy Places*, 14, who identifies overwhelming use of the Vulgate.

20 Esposito, 'The Cathach of St. Columba', *Journal of the County Louth Archaeological Society* (1916), and M. Joynt, 'The Cathach of St. Columba', *ICQ* (1917), 186-204. Esposito is of the view that though Jerome's version may have come to Ireland a century before Columba, Columba may not have possessed a copy. Columba would know the Psalms in the Old Latin versions by heart, but Finnian's book may have been his first opportunity to make a copy of this version. Joynt (197), states that the text of the Cathach, 'appears to be based on Jerome's Gallican Psalter. A comparison of psalms 90-93 with a passage of corresponding length in the *Book of Kells* shows that the variation of the *Book of Kells* from the Vulgate is twice as great as that of the Cathach from the Gallican text, and that the *Book of Kells* Old Latin mixture exceeds that of the Cathach in the proportion of more than two to one.' Joynt (199f) also points out that the rubrics of the Cathach are squeezed in later but consistent with texts known to be to the fore in Bede's time, indicating the Cathach itself predated Bede's era.

21 Reeves, *Life of Saint Columba, Founder of Hy*, lxxxv.

22 Bede, *History*, V:21.

ancient texts, especially any version which their founders were known to have used.[23]

One more speculation. Joynt suggests that although Columba had a fondness for the Old Latin versions, he may have played a part in popularising Jerome in Ireland. Joynt points to a line in the *Amra* which states that Columba 'secured the psalms'.[24] An early copy of the *Amra* comments on this phrase, explaining that it means Columba 'separated the psalms under *obelus* and *asterisk*, or, under titles and arguments'. Elsewhere, a fragment from an Irish treatise on the Psalter notes that, in translating from the Hebrew and the Greek, Jerome corrected the biblical text 'under *obelus* and *asterisk*', meaning that Jerome provided his version of the Psalter with *obeli* and *asterisks* to indicate the relation of his text to the Septuagint and the original Hebrew. For Jerome, an *obelus* indicated a passage which was in the Septuagint but not in the Hebrew; an *asterisk* indicated words which were in the Hebrew but not in the Septuagint.[25] Jerome instructed all future copyists to reproduce these critical signs along with his translated text. Might the *Amra*'s comments on Columba 'securing the psalms', indicate that Columba knew of Jerome's request and complied accordingly? This argument is not watertight, but worthy of consideration. Significantly, the Cathach has *obeli* and *asterisks*.[26]

COLUMBA AS BIBLICAL SCHOLAR

Columba was well versed in Latin. Was he also proficient in Hebrew and Greek? The *Amra* (VIII) claims that Columba studied Greek grammar. If so, then Greek texts on Iona would include Scripture, plus writings from Greek Fathers such as Basil or Cassian (though Latin versions of both were more common). The last folio of Dorbene's early eighth-century Schaffhausen manuscript of Adomnán's *Life of Columba* has the Lord's Prayer in Greek which may confirm interest in Greek on Iona.[27]

---

23 O'Loughlin, 'The Library of Iona in the Late Seventh Century: The Evidence from Adomnán's *De Locis Sanctis*', *Eriu (*1994), 37.

24 Joynt, 'The Cathach of St. Columba', *ICQ* (1917), 199.

25 Warren, *The Antiphonary of Bangor: Part II*, 3f. Origen of Alexandria (d. 254) borrowed the *obelus* and *asterisk* from Alexandrian philology for his work on the biblical text (Herity and Breen, *The Cathach of Colum Cille: An Introduction*, 41).

26 Herity and Breen, *The Cathach of Colum Cille: An Introduction*, 42ff.

27 Clancy and Markus, *Iona: The Earliest Poetry of a Celtic Monastery*, 26. Clancy and Markus note instances of Greek in the *Altus Prosator*. For an older discussion on the knowledge of Greek and Hebrew on Iona and in Bangor, see Gougaud, *Gaelic Pioneers of Christianity*, 57ff. Gougaud may underestimate knowledge of Greek in such centres.

Did Columba also have Hebrew? This is an unresolved issue. Clancy and Markus point to stanza M of Columba's *Altus Prosator* which uses an unusual noun '*iduma*' which may be a Latinised form of a Hebrew word.[28] But the term may have come to Ireland from elsewhere, without any awareness of a possible Hebraic origin. Apart from this doubtful detail, evidence for Columba as a Hebrew scholar is weak. All we can be certain of is that Columba was at home with the Latin text.

'HE MADE GLOSSES CLEAR'

The *Amra* (V) comments that Columba 'made glosses clear'. Glosses were a commentator's annotations on the text, which were written in the headings, the margins, or even between the lines. In manuscripts from the early Irish Church, such marginal notes and glosses often provide the earliest written examples of Old Irish.[29] McNamara and Sheehy suggest that Psalters were heavily glossed in order to make the text more understandable for both students and worshippers. They also propose that because the psalms were recited at such a slow pace during the Divine Office, the monks had time to read these comments even as they worshipped, enabling them to reflect on the meaning of what they sang.[30]

The *Amra*'s statement that Columba 'made glosses clear' means one of two things. It can point to Columba giving a definitive explanation where there were competing interpretations of a portion of Scripture. Or, because glosses sometimes dealt with textual variances, it can mean that Columba defined the text of Scripture for his monks.[31] Given the absence of a single authorised version of Scripture during Columba's lifetime, the latter possibility has some credibility. However, most glosses went further than simply establishing what the text should be. They involved the interpretation of the Scripture in question.

Title-headings given to the psalms were themselves glosses and a commentary, because they interpreted the spiritual context within

28 Clancy and Markus, *Iona: The Earliest Poetry of a Celtic Monastery*, 42. Elsewhere in Irish literature the word is used of Christ Himself as the hand of God; and of Christ and the Spirit as the hands of God especially in creation.

29 O'Neill, 'Columba the Scribe' in Bourke (ed.), *Studies in the Cult of Saint Columba*, 72.

30 McNamara and Sheehy, 'Psalter Text and Psalter Study in the Early Irish Church', *PRIA* (1973), 271.

31 McNamara and Sheehy, 'Psalter Text and Psalter Study in the Early Irish Church', *PRIA* (1973), 212.

which a psalm was to be read. In Irish Psalters the practice was to supplant Hebrew headings with Christian captions.[32] The Psalter was assumed to be a book about Christ, and each psalm was to be read as the voice of Christ, or as the voice of the Church to Christ.[33] For example, some Irish Psalters titled Psalms 3 and 6 as, 'The Voice of Christ to the Father'. Thus the Irish Church read the psalms allegorically through a Christological lens rather than historically within the original Old Testament context. McNamara and Sheehy point out that title-headings occasionally reveal which commentaries were used by the scribes who penned the glosses, with frequent quarrying from Augustine's notes on the Psalms. These glosses, whether as title-headings or as comments adjacent to the text, enabled the reader to read Old Testament Jewish psalms as Christian prayer and Christian instruction.[34]

'HE KNEW THE LAWS FROM OLD TO NEW'

The Psalter was central to worship. It was read. It was sung. It was memorised. But Columba studied more of Scripture than simply the Psalter, and the *Amra* commends him on his ability to handle the various types of literature found in the Bible. He 'separated the elements according to figures among the books of the Law' (*Amra*, V), which is a reference to Columba's skill in distinguishing between the allegorical and the literal. The *Amra* (V) also singles out Columba's talent in teaching and in applying the Wisdom Literature sections of Scripture: 'The books of Solomon, he followed them.'[35] The Wisdom Books (Proverbs, Ecclesiastes, Wisdom of Solomon, Ecclesiasticus) were key documents for Pelagians and semi-Pelagians because of their high incidence of rules and instructions; and the *Amra*'s highlighting

32 McNamara and Sheehy, 'Psalter Text and Psalter Study in the Early Irish Church', *PRIA* (1973), 215.

33 Herity and Breen, *The Cathach of Colum Cille: An Introduction*, 47.

34 The headings of the psalms in the Cathach refer to the original historical context, but with some Christianised reinterpretations (e.g., Psalm 45, 65 and 69 / Vulgate 44, 64 and 68). See the facsimile and translations supplied by Herity and Breen, *The Cathach of Colum Cille: An Introduction*, in the digital CD-ROM format bundled with their publication. For a detailed discussion of the Cathach's rubrics and headings see Herity and Breen, *The Cathach of Colum Cille: An Introduction*, 45-51.

35 Basil, *Letters*, 42:3, warns that careful interpretation of Scripture is necessary: 'Never neglect reading, especially of the New Testament, because very frequently mischief comes of reading the Old, not because of what is written is harmful, but because the minds of the injured are weak. All bread is nutritious, but it may be injurious to the sick.'

of their importance to Columba may indicate sympathy with semi-Pelagian spirituality.[36] Strictly speaking, an interest in the biblical Wisdom Literature is not itself proof of semi-Pelagianism, though it is entirely consistent with that position. Semi-Pelagian or otherwise, rules and regulations were important in the monastic understanding of the spiritual life, and Columba was seen as a scholar with an ability to explain the Law of God in relation to holy Christian living. Monastic life gave the soul-anxious an opportunity to live in conformity to God's requirements: but that commitment would be in vain if God's Law was followed incorrectly. For God's Law to be followed properly, Scripture had to be read aright. Thankfully, Columba's interpretations could be relied on. That was an important abbatical task. This is why the *Amra* repeatedly celebrates Columba's ability in this area: 'He knew the laws from Old to New, he who knew no falsehood' (VI); 'He was foremost at the book of complex law' (II); 'By his mighty skill he kept the law firm' (IV).

In praising Columba as expounder of God's Law, the *Amra* touches on an important aspect of an abbot's duties vis-à-vis his community. Keeping the Law enabled a monk to live a purer life. Living a purer life gave him more hope for the salvation of his soul. But to live the pure life, a monk needed to understand the requirements set out in the Old and New Testaments. In this context, 'Law' included all the rules and regulations which Scripture contained, and a monk trusted that his abbot could identify all precepts of Scripture which needed to be observed. Consistent with this, the *Amra* (IV,V) recognises Columba's respect for Basil and Cassian. Cassian's semi-Pelagianism meant that observance of the laws and rules of Scripture was seen as a vital component of a soul's salvation. This lay behind the stringent and severe lifestyle of monasticism. And this asceticism, rooted in the Law of God, was something which Columba not only taught but practised. The *Amra* (VII) notes with approval that he 'prepared under the holy Law', 'averted his side's softness', and destroyed 'his body's desire'.

All of this meant that, on Iona, there was a close study of the biblical text. Understanding Scripture brought understanding of God's Law. This enabled a monk's life to be lived according to the proper rules. Keen study of Scripture was vital. This may be why, when Bede

36 Herren and Brown, *Christ in Celtic Theology*, 117.

compares the Roman and Irish Christian tradition, he judges the Irish monks to be even more deeply biblicist than those of his own church.[37]

'SECRETS ... CLEARER THAN LIGHT'

Adomnán also claims that Columba was given supernatural aid to interpret Scripture. He records that, when Columba was on Hinba, the Holy Spirit gave him exceptional insight into the mysteries of faith and the meaning of Scripture. Adomnán credits Columba with an experience similar to that of Paul who was 'transported into the third heaven' (2 Cor 12:2f), and to that of John who was 'in the Spirit on the Lord's day' (Rev 1:10).[38] Admittedly, Adomnán's aim is to accumulate yet more evidence that Columba was a man approved of by God, and a man to be respected as a second Paul or as a second John. But Adomnán is also conveying the idea that Columba, whilst in this spiritual state, was given unique and profound understanding of the things of God:

> He was also heard singing spiritual chants of a kind never heard before. And, as he afterwards admitted to a few people, he was able to see, openly revealed, many secrets that had been hidden since the world began, whilst all that was most dark and difficult in the sacred Scriptures lay open, plain, and clearer than light in the sight of his pure heart. ... If [Baithéne] had been present for those three days, he could have recorded from the saint's lips a great number of mysteries, both of ages past and future, unknown to other men, together with some interpretations of the sacred books. (III:18)

It was divine aid which enabled Columba to understand what was 'most dark and difficult' in the Scriptures. God Himself gave Columba an understanding which was 'open, plain, and clearer than light'. Columba was given insight 'unknown to other men'. This was how Iona viewed Columba: holy man, wise scholar, true interpreter, and reliable guide.

COLUMBA AS ACADEMIC READER

Columba was familiar with writings outside of the Bible, with the *Amra* (II) declaring that he was 'learning's pillar in every stronghold'.

---

37 Bede, *History*, III:4.

38 *Bangor Antiphonary*, Item 14, claims similar direct divine revelation for Comgall.

The 'stronghold' was the monastic community itself, reflecting Basil and Cassian's expectation that monasteries would become bulwarks of orthodoxy. After referencing Columba's knowledge of the Divine Law in Scripture, the *Amra* adds: 'Rome was known, order was known, knowledge of the Godhead was granted to him.' Here the *Amra* stresses that Columba was not from the backwoods. He was not an inadequately educated Irish monk. He was not a man with limited horizons. On the contrary, Columba knew the thinking of the wider Church; and the *Amra*'s specific references to Columba's knowledge of Basil and Cassian reinforce this. And Basil and Cassian would not be the only authors available for study on Iona during Columba's abbacy. Though the sixth-century Iona library would not be as extensive as it became during the next two hundred years until the time of the Viking raids, it would have works from a variety of authors. Columba did not paddle from Ireland in a tiny coracle. He arrived on a large curragh, which was capable of transporting goods as well as men. And when Columba and his companions set out from Ireland, they took with them essential texts for study and devotion.

Clancy, Markus, and O'Loughlin reconstruct lists of the contents of the later Iona library from clues given by Adomnán and others.[39] Though these lists are too extensive to quote in full, they show that the later Iona had a rich selection of books, including works by: Athanasius, Basil, Jerome, Philip the Presbyter, Cassian, Cassiodorus and Constantius. Also available were Apocryphal texts, Augustine's *City of God*, Sulpicius Severus' *Life of Saint Martin*, and Gregory the Great's *Dialogues*. Liturgical books, histories, and works of canon law added to the mix.[40] O'Loughlin is of the view that Jerome's Commentaries on Matthew, Ezekiel, Nahum, and the Letters of Paul, were particularly well used.[41] Clancy and Markus point to the possible

39 Clancy and Markus, *Iona: The Earliest Poetry of a Celtic Monastery*, 211ff.; cf. O'Loughlin, 'The Library of Iona in the Late Seventh Century: The Evidence from Adomnán's *De Locis Sanctis*', *Eriu* (1994), 33-52.

40 Bardsley, *Against the Tide: The Story of Adomnán of Iona*, 56.

41 O'Loughlin, 'The Library of Iona in the Late Seventh Century: The Evidence from Adomnán's *De Locis Sanctis*', *Eriu* (1994), 39. Herity and Breen, *The Cathach of Colum Cille: An Introduction*, 51ff., argue that the Cathach exhibits signs of familiarity with the commentaries of Eusebius, Athanasius and Gregory of Nyssa. If the legend of Columba being its copyist is true, then the copy (with possibly the interpretative headings added by Columba himself) would be made before he left Ireland. The De Paors, *Early Christian Ireland*, 65, note that Columbanus (as a typical product of Irish schools of the sixth century) was familiar

presence of a Greek glossary which may have aided Columba and his fellow monks. Although these lists relate to Adomnán's period rather than to Columba's, standard theological texts would have been brought by Columba at the very start of his time in Dál Riata.

---

with 'Virgil, Ovid, Horace, Prudentius, Juvenal, Eusebius, Jerome, Sedulius, Dracontius, Ausonius, Gildas, Fortunatus, Gregory the Great, and perhaps of Statius, Persius, Jevencus and Lucan as well as with the Scriptures.'

CHAPTER 12

Lord's Day and Sabbath

A week before he died, Columba went with his servant Diarmait to bless a barn, and took the opportunity to share some thoughts with him:

> Scripture calls this day the Sabbath, which means 'rest'. Today is truly my Sabbath, for it is my last day in this wearisome life, when I shall keep the Sabbath after my troublesome labours. At midnight this Sunday, as Scripture saith, 'I go the way of my fathers'. For now, my Lord Jesus Christ deigns to invite me. (III:23)

For Columba, Saturday was the Sabbath, and Sunday was the Lord's Day. This was the case across the early Irish Church, and Seventh-Day Adventist scholars, such as David Marshall and Leslie Hardinge, draw heavily on the Celtic distinction between Sabbath and Lord's Day in support of their own Church tradition.[1] They argue that the earliest Christians in Britain observed Saturday as the Sabbath, with the change to Sunday a later development enforced by the Roman Church. A Saturday Sabbath followed the Jewish practice, and, despite increasing Romanisation from 664 onwards, a form of Saturday Sabbath continued in Scotland until the time of Queen Margaret in the eleventh century, when she attempted to harmonise Scottish Church practice with continental Christian culture.

This assumption that the early-medieval Irish Church had a Saturday Sabbath has not gone unchallenged, despite there being a clear distinction between Saturday as Sabbath and Sunday as the Lord's Day in Adomnán's *Life of Columba* (III:23). Adomnán starts his account of the last week of Columba's life by commenting on Columba's calm

1 David Marshall, *The Celtic Connection* (Grantham: Stanborough, 1994); Leslie Hardinge, *The Celtic Church in Britain* (London: SPCK, 1972).

cheerfulness during mass 'on Sunday'. It is six days later (Saturday) when Columba explains to Diarmait that 'Scripture calls this day the Sabbath which means "rest".' During the remainder of that day (Saturday), Columba sat in his hut copying the psalms. He then went to church for Vespers, after which he rested. He then returned to church for the Midnight Service: and in church, whilst kneeling in prayer, he died.[2] Columba died as Saturday moved into Sunday, and as Sabbath moved into the Lord's Day. The community would see God's timing in this. Gilbert Markus points out that Columba's death occurring on the transition from Sabbath to Lord's Day meant that on the Saturday Columba ceased from his labours and enjoyed God's original Sabbath; then, by dying at midnight at the beginning of the Lord's Day, Columba entered not only God's rest but the risen life of Christ and the new creation.[3]

What Adomnán's narrative establishes that his Sabbath was not Sunday. All through his account of Columba's last days, Adomnán distinguishes between events which occur on the Saturday (Sabbath) and those which take place on the Sunday (the Lord's Day). But what did Adomnán's Saturday Sabbath involve? Was 'Sabbath' merely a title for Saturday? Was Saturday Sabbath observed as a day of rest from work? Was Saturday Sabbath a main day for public worship? How did it relate to Sunday, the Lord's Day? Some of these issues are addressed later in our discussion of the *Cain Domnaig*, but a number of comments can be made at this stage.

Iona observed the Saturday Sabbath as a day of rest. Adomnán makes Columba say to Diarmait that Sabbath means 'rest', and, by putting this explanation in Columba's mouth, Adomnán is teaching his readers that Sabbath and 'rest' go together. But what kind of 'rest' was observed on Columba's Iona? Was it the all-embracing 'rest' of later Presbyterian Scotland? If Adomnán's narrative is our guide, then blessing a barn was not viewed as a breach of Sabbath protocol. More

2 O'Reilly, 'Reading the Scriptures in the Life of Columba' in Bourke (ed.), *Studies in the Cult of Saint Columba*, 100f., points out that earlier in III:23, Adomnán notes Columba's frailty, needing to travel in a wagon, and Diarmait lifting Columba's right hand for him to give a blessing. Yet, at midnight he *ran* into the church. O'Reilly interprets this as Adomnán showing that Columba was hastening (at the close of the physical Sabbath) to enter the eternal Sabbath. This fits with Hebrews 4:11, 'Let us hasten to enter into that rest.'

3 Markus, *Conceiving a Nation*, 144.

controversially, Adomnán records that for the remainder of the Saturday Sabbath Columba sat in his hut copying out Scripture. Transcribing Scripture was certainly laborious. It required keen concentration. It induced tiredness. But it must not have been viewed on Iona as 'labour' in the same sense as tilling the fields or working at a forge. If Adomnán's narrative reflects the Iona norm – there is little reason to doubt otherwise – then the copying of Scripture was classified as a spiritual exercise and hence an appropriate Sabbath activity. These examples indicate that Iona interpreted 'Sabbath rest' as cessation from workaday physical labour.[4] Spiritual activities such as blessing a barn, or copying Scripture, were not work in the same sense. Hence, Saturday Sabbath on Iona was a special day of rest.

But was Saturday Sabbath a special day of worship? Or was that reserved for Sunday, the Lord's Day? This is a more complex issue.

THE *CAIN DOMNAIG*

Donald MacLean (1869–1943) came from the Gaelic speaking township of Lochcarron, Wester Ross, in the north-west Highlands of Scotland.[5] As an able pupil at the village school, MacLean earned a bursary to the Old Aberdeen Grammar School, before proceeding to the University of Aberdeen for his Arts degree. He then studied theology at New College, Edinburgh, also attending classes in Celtic Studies at Edinburgh University. After serving as Free Church minister at Moy near Inverness, and at St Columba's Free Church in Edinburgh, MacLean took the Chair of Church History and Free Church Principles at the Free Church College. He had also been nominated for the Chair of Celtic Studies at Edinburgh, a post which went to W. J. Watson, the renowned Celtic Scholar. The two men, once rivals for the same post, maintained scholarly contact and a warm friendship for many years.

In 1926 MacLean published a book, *The Law of the Lord's Day in the Celtic Church.* He produced this work, not just because of his interest in his Gaelic heritage, but because of his teaching role at the College. MacLean wanted to demonstrate that the principles and practices of the Free Church (such as Sabbath observance) were not

4 Constantine decreed a 'Day of Rest' in 321. Other decrees, dealing with activities on the Sabbath, were promulgated in ensuing centuries. Charlemagne's decree in 791 forbade all ordinary work on Sunday.

5 G. N. M.Collins, *Donald MacLean D.D.* (1944).

only biblically based but were in continuity with early Christianity in Scotland before it was Romanised. MacLean argues in his book that strict sabbatarianism was a feature of Columba's Iona as much as it was of the Scottish Highlands and Islands in the early twentieth century.[6] And, in his view, Columba's sabbatarianism was observed on Sundays.

Maclean bases his argument on a detailed analysis of a Gaelic manuscript, the *Cain Domnaig* (Law of the Lord's Day).[7] MacLean was aware that the copy which he had access to in the National Library of Scotland was a ninth-century text, but was convinced that it derived from a much earlier original. We now know that the National Library's copy of the *Cain Domnaig* is inferior to others held elsewhere, and Vernon Hull, in a detailed 1966 article, points out that MacLean was hampered in only being able to consult that version.[8] Hull regards the National Library's manuscript as ten percent indecipherable, and that MacLean's interpretation of its contents was seriously affected by this. Hull was able to access other early *Cain Domnaig* manuscripts, and uses them to correct MacLean's translation and interpretation. Nevertheless, MacLean's arguments, based on his reading of the *Cain Domnaig*, are what occupy our attention. Maclean does not dispute that Adomnán and the early-medieval Irish Church gave the title 'Sabbath' to Saturday. What he argues is that although Adomnán's Saturday had the *title* 'Sabbath', all of the Sabbath's religious aspects, including rest and worship, had been transferred to Sunday. Hence, Saturday was Sabbath in name only. Sunday was the day on which sabbatarian observance of rest and worship took place.

MacLean's translation of the National Library's manuscript sets out in detailed fashion what the *Cain Domnaig* permits and prohibits in sabbatarian observance.[9] The list is formidable, and in Hull's revised translation (based on several manuscript copies) the rules are no less

6 Donald Maclean, *The Law of the Lord's Day in the Celtic Church* (Edinburgh: T&T Clark, 1926).

7 *Cain Domnaig*, NLS, MS. XL 72-5; cf. Donald Mackinnon, *A Descriptive Catalogue of Gaelic Manuscripts in the Advocates' Library, Edinburgh, and elsewhere in Scotland,* (Edinburgh: Brown, 1912), 91.

8 Vernam Hull, 'Cain Domnaig', *Eriu, The Royal Irish Academy* (1966), 151-77. Comparing the various *Cain Domnaig* manuscripts, Hull argues (155) that they are not all from a common progenitor or have a similar line of descent.

9 MacLean, *The Law of the Lord's Day in the Celtic Church*, 4ff.

extensive.[10] In MacLean's version, *permitted* actions include: going to communion; going to baptism; going to a place for water; going to a milking place; providing food for guests; clerics and nuns travelling to a (distant) church; and journeying to a person in the toils of death. The *prohibited* actions involve: no riding; no beginning a journey (apart from special circumstances); no suing; no giving a judgment (i.e. no legal processes); no cropping of hair; no shaving; no washing; no bathing; no churning; no wood-splitting; no grinding of corn; no house-cleaning; etc.[11]

In addition to prohibitions and permissions, the *Cain Domnaig* also details penalties for transgression of the rules. Some sanctions are bitingly severe, such as a fine of four three-year-old heifers together with forfeiture of equipment. Moreover, any person who sees the day being transgressed, but does not claim and exact the penalty from the transgressor, is liable to the same fine as the culprit. Everyone is expected to be his brother's keeper and his neighbour's policeman. The importance of this Law is summed by the *Cain Domnaig* itself:

> Worse than demons are they who would destroy the Law of the Lord's Day, and they would shut fast the kingdom of heaven if they were to reach it, so that there would be no rest therein for ever.[12]

MacLean builds his argument on the fact that the *Cain Domnaig* applies the list of permitted and forbidden actions to Sunday (Lord's Day) rather than to Saturday. Hull agrees that the list applies to Sunday, with its provisions running from Vespers on Saturday to Morning Prayer on Monday.[13] In the *Cain Domnaig*, it is Sunday which is to be kept in a sabbatical manner. The crucial point for MacLean, based on his conviction that the *Cain Domnaig* originated in the early Irish Church, is that Columba's Iona must also have treated Sunday as the true Day

---

10 Hull, 'Cain Domnaig', *Eriu*, 163f., has alternative translation of the *Cain Domnaig*, Section One, featuring permitted and forbidden actions. Hull also suggests a list of fines which he believes are more accurate than in MacLean's version.

11 Herren and Brown, *Christ in Celtic Christianity*, 6, point out that although Pelagians did not recommend Sabbath observance, their numerous injunctions to obey all of God's commands created an appetite for it. Sabbath observance would be eagerly adopted by monks who wanted to 'obey all the rules' since by doing so they were more fit for heaven.

12 MacLean, *The Law of the Lord's Day in the Celtic Church*, 14.

13 cf. Hughes, *Early Christian Ireland: Introduction to the Sources*, 80.

of Rest even if Saturday retained the name of Sabbath. But all hinges on when the *Cain Domnaig* was first written.

MacLean knows that the National Library's *Cain Domnaig* manuscript is a ninth-century and not a sixth-century document. He also knows that if the original *Cain Domnaig* went back no further than the ninth century then his argument could fall, because by the ninth century the Roman Church, with its preference for a Sunday Sabbath, was highly influential in Scotland. A ninth-century document might reflect the practice of the Roman Church rather than that of the early-medieval Irish Church. Aware of this, MacLean offers several arguments in support of an early date of composition. First, he argues that although the National Library's Gaelic manuscript is ninth-century, it has signs that the original from which it was copied was much earlier. Second, he believes that because the *Cain Domnaig* started life as a Gaelic rather than as a Latin text, then that indicates early composition. Third, he notes that the *Cain Domnaig* refers to the Apostolate as a whole rather than to the Primacy of Peter in particular, concluding that, because the *Cain Domnaig* does not give Peter a high profile, and because it respects Patrick as God's vice-regent rather than Peter, then it must have originated before the triumph of the Roman Church at Whitby in 664, after which a focus on Peter was the norm. Fourth, MacLean judges that the penalties of the *Cain Domnaig* reflect ancient Irish Law rather than Roman Law. Fifth, he argues that because the *Cain Domnaig* is itself referenced in the eighth-century document, the *Martyrology of Óengus*, then it must have existed before the ninth century.

Strong as these arguments appear, they have weaknesses. For example, the possible reference to the *Cain Domnaig* in the *Martyrology of Óengus* is less convincing than at first sight. When F. N. Robinson reviewed MacLean's book a few months after its publication, he pointed out that although the *Martyrology of Óengus* itself is eighth-century, its alleged reference to the *Cain Domnaig* only occurs in a much later commentary attached to it.[14] Another argument, based on the *Cain Domnaig* not giving Peter a high-profile, is also weaker than first appears, because, even when the Irish Church became increasingly Romanised, it continued to celebrate an array of saints and not Peter

14 F. N. Robinson, 'Review of MacLean, *The Law of the Lord's Day in the Celtic Church*', *Speculum* (1927), 491f.

alone. It was centuries before a mono-Petrine culture became the norm. Similarly, the fact that the penalties of the *Cain Domnaig* reflect ancient Irish law is not conclusive of early origin, since ancient law was so deeply embedded in Irish culture that traditional penalties applied for many centuries.

MacLean's argument that because the *Cain Domnaig* originated as a Gaelic document then it must be very early, is also speculative. MacLean builds on the legend that at the Convention of Druim Cett (*c.* 574) Columba's defence of the bardic tradition in Irish society resulted in a flowering of songs and prose-writings in the indigenous languages. MacLean concludes that the *Cain Domnaig* was part of this blossoming, and because the *Cain Domnaig* shows no signs of having been translated from a Latin original, then it could never have been composed in a Romanised Church. But it is a huge supposition to assume that any document originally written in Gaelic must have been composed in a pre-Roman Irish Church. Christopher De Hamel, when discussing other medieval manuscripts, makes the observation that literacy (in England at least) only *returned* to Latin following the Norman Conquest of 1066, implying that previous to the Conquest the Anglo-Saxon vernacular was used in places of learning and scholarship.[15] A similar situation could have been the case in Scotland. It may well be that, until Queen Margaret's reforms in the eleventh century, the vernacular was widely used, with many eighth and ninth-century texts composed in the vernacular, though now only existing as Latin copies, with the original manuscripts, from which the Latin copies were made, all being disposed of, apart from a few such as the *Cain Domnaig.*

McLean weakens his position with a misreading of Adomnán. When Columba ordered the Iona monks to rest and worship on the day Colman mocu Loigse died, Columba said, 'as on the Lord's Day' (III:12). MacLean argues from this that if Saturday had been the 'rest day' then surely 'Sabbath' rather than 'Lord's Day' would be the phrase used. But the passage does not support this interpretation. When Columba says, 'as on the Lord's Day', he is not referring to the monks 'resting', but to them having an additional 'small meal'. It

15 De Hamel, *Meetings with Remarkable Manuscripts*, 257.

is the additional 'small meal' which is linked to the Lord's Day, not cessation of work.

MacLean's work on the *Cain Domnaig* was good in its time but has been eclipsed. Hull's detailed analysis undermines MacLean's case for a very early date, with Hull concluding that the *Cain Domnaig* originally appeared in the early eighth century, and not in the sixth century.[16] Admittedly, Hull's lower limit of the early eighth century still involves a major change from a Saturday Sabbath in the sixth century to a Sunday Sabbath in the eighth century. How can that be explained? One possibility is that both days (Saturday and Sunday) had sabbatarian features during the early-medieval era.

DOUBLE-OBSERVANCE

MacLean interprets Iona's practices as matching the Presbyterian Lord's Day Sabbath of his own culture. Conversely, Marshall and Hardinge, as Seventh-Day Adventist scholars, want to reinforce their tradition, and are convinced that the main diet of worship in the Celtic Church took place on the Saturday Sabbath, with Marshall citing an impressive array of scholars who appear to support his position, including the Andersons.[17] He argues that Roman scribes amended the records so as to convey the impression that the very earliest Irish saints held Sunday sacred, whereas they observed a seventh-day Sabbath.[18] But is it valid to argue that an Adventist type Saturday Sabbath applied in Columba's era?

Marshall notes that Adomnán regularly uses *sabbatum* for Saturday, the seventh day of the week. That is not contested. Marshall further argues that Adomnán's text implies that Iona observed Saturday as a day of rest from manual labour. That also is not contested. But what Marshall does not prove so decisively is that Saturday was Iona's main day for Christian worship. Any conclusion on this is made more difficult by the fact that the Irish Church often operated outside Christian practices elsewhere in Europe. Various Church Councils on the Continent issued diktats concerning Saturday, Sunday, and

16 Hull, 'Cain Domnaig', *Eriu*, 156f. Hull conceded that the *Cain Domnaig* may no later than c. 750.

17 Marshall, *The Celtic Connection*, 29. Marshall refers to Hardinge's Ph.D. thesis, *The Celtic Church in Britain* (1972).

18 Marshall, *The Celtic Connection*, 26ff.

Sabbath, with the aim of moving everything to Sunday (the Lord's Day), but the Irish Church did not concern itself too much about such edicts. All of this means that there are three issues to consider. Did the Irish Church advocate cessation of work on a Saturday? That is agreed. Did the Irish Church view Saturday as a day of special worship? That is probable. Did the Irish Church regard Saturday as the principal day of worship? That is debateable. The conundrum may be solved by considering 'Double-Observance'.

Warren suggests that the *Bangor Antiphonary* points to both Saturday and Sunday as special liturgical days in the Irish Church, and although the Lord's Day may have been the more important, Saturday had a liturgical standing in its own right. If Warren is correct, this would be in line with the practice of double-observance. Double-observance was an ancient Christian tradition, which is referenced in early Christian works such as the fourth-century Syriac treatises known as the *Apostolic Constitutions.*[19] The *Apostolic Constitutions* leave no doubt that though Sunday was special, and though Sunday was probably the main worship day of the week, Saturday had liturgical importance. The *Apostolic Constitutions* exhort Christians to,

> Assemble yourselves together every day, morning and evening, singing psalms and praying in the Lord's house: in the morning saying the sixty-second Psalm, and in the evening the hundred and fortieth, but principally on the Sabbath-day. And on the day of our Lord's resurrection, which is the Lord's day, meet more diligently, sending praise to God that made the universe by Jesus, and sent Him to us, and condescended to let Him suffer, and raised Him from the dead.[20]

Theological reasons are given for observing both days. The Saturday-Sabbath is a memorial of creation, remembering the Lord who 'made the universe by Jesus'. And the Sunday-Lord's Day is a memorial of the resurrection, celebrating the Lord who 'sent Him to us and condescended to let Him suffer and raised Him from the dead'.[21]

---

19 The Eighth Treatise, sometimes named the *Apostolic Canons*, may have been a later insert.

20 *Apostolic Constitutions*, II:59; cf. Paul F. Bradshaw, *Daily Prayer in the Early Church, A Study of the Origin and Early Development of the Divine Office* (Eugene: Wipf & Stock, 1981), 68, 88f.

21 *Apostolic Constitutions*, VII:23.

Crucially, the *Apostolic Constitutions* give practical advice on how the sanctity of both days should be preserved. And there is sabbatarianism on both days. Servants are to work on five days but must be allowed to rest on the Sabbath and on the Lord's Day in order to go to church for the teaching of piety.[22] Additionally, the eighth treatise of the *Apostolic Constitutions* contains the *Apostolic Canons* which stress that both Saturday and Sunday are to be joyful Festal Days and not solemn Fast Days. The *Apostolic Canons* insist that observing the Saturday Sabbath as a Festal Day is important, with both Saturday and Sunday as Festal Days. As such, both differ from other days of the week, and if any cleric fasts on the Lord's Day, *or* on the Saturday-Sabbath (except the Sabbath of Easter Eve), then that cleric should be deposed. Any lay man who commits the same fault should be excommunicated.[23] This severe attitude to fasting on the Sabbath was an overreaction to practices in the Western Church where Saturdays were becoming Fast Days. Nevertheless, the message is clear. Both Saturday and Sunday, Sabbath and Lord's Day, are days of festal celebration and worship. Both are days of rest. Both differ from the rest of the week.[24]

The *Bangor Antiphonary* indicates that the Divine Office which was observed on Saturday and Sunday contrasted with that of the other five days. Warren sees this as pointing to a pattern of double-observance, re-emphasising parallels with early Middle Eastern Christianity in which Saturday and Sunday, Sabbath and Lord's Day, were both marked for festal celebration.[25] Given the early Irish Church's debt to influences

---

22 *Apostolic Constitutions*, VIII:33.

23 *Apostolic Canons*, 64; cf. Warren, *The Antiphonary of Bangor: Part II*, xxiv, who notes that canons 49 and 51 of the Council of Laodicea (364), marked out the Sabbath and the Lord's Day as days to be observed *festally* in Lent. Canon 39 stated that clerics were to be 'outlawed' for keeping the Jewish Sabbath!'

24 Cassian also views both Saturday and Sunday as holy days (*Institutes*, III:8-12). Palladius, an early chronicler of monastic traditions, notes that the monks of Nitria assembled at the church only on Saturdays and Sundays (Morison, *St. Basil and his Rule: A Study in Early Monasticism*, 39).

25 Warren, *Bangor Antiphonary*, xxiii; cf. Herren and Brown, *Christ in Celtic Theology*, 109, who argue that the Church in the first five centuries had a clear distinction between Sabbath and the Lord's Day, with many Christians observing both, worshipping on the Lord's Day, and observing prohibitions against work and travel on the Sabbath. Herren and Brown (285) also point out that a series of Councils held in Gaul at Arles, Orleans, and Macon, through the sixth century and especially after 585, had the effect of sabbatising the Lord's Day. Prohibition of labour on a Sunday became secular law in England in the late seventh century. It is this sabbatising of the Lord's Day which the *Cain Domnaig* represents.

from the East, it appears that double-observance was absorbed into the spirituality of early Christianity in Ireland.

If we seek parallels to the early-medieval Irish Church's observance of Saturday and Sunday, then it is the culture of the *Apostolic Constitutions* and the *Apostolic Canons* which come closest. The early Irish Church had double-observance.[26] Both Sabbath and Lord's Day had sabbatarian features. Both Saturday and Sunday had liturgical elements. Various Councils tried to enforce total abandonment of Saturday observance (as the Church cut its ties with its Jewish roots) but Saturday still had a special place in the Irish Church.[27] Saturday did not have the full glory of Sunday since Sunday was the Lord's Day, the Day of Resurrection. But Saturday was different from the other days of the week. It was a Festal Day in its own right. And in the early Irish Church, no manual labour took place during it.

26 Herren and Brown, *Christ in Celtic Christianity*, 62.

27 Herren and Brown, *Christ in Celtic Theology*, 109f., argue that Pelagian and semi-Pelagian influences in the British and Irish Churches meant they preserved a deep regard for Jewish aspects of Christianity, contrasting anti-Jewishness elsewhere.

PART THREE

WORSHIPPER

CHAPTER 13

The Worship-Driven Life

On Iona there could be many reasons for the pealing of a bell.[1] It might be that the king was going into battle. Or someone may have died, and their now-vulnerable soul was requiring help. Or travellers might be in danger on the seas. Numerous circumstances warranted urgent intercession. But what a bell sounded for most often were the Canonical Hours of the Daily Office, which were non-sacramental services recited by the community. The brothers were summoned to the church, and the abbot led them through the appropriate liturgy for the Hour.[2] Psalms were chanted. Collects were recited. Scripture was read. Hymns were sung. Everyone had to attend. Even monks at work in fields distant from the monastery, or monks on a journey, were expected to observe each Hour as best they could.[3] Benedict taught that absent monks should kneel and pray where they were. Similar procedures would apply on Iona.

Iona had its own liturgical books specifying the precise form of prayers and readings to be followed by the community. None of these survive.[4] All have disappeared, destroyed by time and Viking raids. Parts of an Iona liturgy may have been integrated into other works, but if so, then any reference to Iona as the place of origin has been lost. Hence, there is no Iona equivalent of the *Bangor Antiphonary* to

---

1 George Petrie, *The Round Towers of Ireland* (2nd edition; Dublin: Hodges & Smith, 1845), 389, suggests Iona had a belfry. Sharpe and the Andersons both render '*Clocam pulsa*' (I:8), when Columba orders Diarmait to summon the community to prayer, as, 'strike the bell', suggesting a fixed bell. Others maintain that Columba was referring to a hand-bell.

2 cf. Benedict, *The Rule*, L and XLVIII.

3 Basil, *The Shorter Rule*, Qu. 107, recognises that some tasks made attendance at prayers impossible; but cautioned against work being an excuse not to be there.

4 Warren, *The Liturgy and Ritual of the Celtic Church*, 81, holds that the ancient Scottish (Columban) Church had its own liturgy. He points to an idiosyncratic fragment in the *Book of Deer*, III:5, and notes the claim of the *Aberdeen Breviary* (June 1st), that St. Serf lived 'under the form and ritual of the primitive Scottish church'.

enrich our knowledge. Despite this, we can reconstruct elements of the Iona Daily Office from clues in Adomnán and other near-contemporary writings. This is important because prayer and worship were central to each monk's life and spirituality, including Columba's.

'PRAY WITHOUT CEASING'

Monks attempted to replicate on earth the pure worship of God offered by the angels in heaven. Night and day, the angels around the throne of God give glory to the Most-High, never pausing or resting in their praise. In its worship, the community saw itself as being one with this heavenly host, which offers unceasing praise and adoration to God. Indeed, true worship is only ideal, pure and perfect, if it is also continuous and unbroken. Perpetual praise (*laus perennis*) was what humanity had been created to give to God, and one of the aims of monasticism was to live out that original human destiny. Monasticism was a setting in which constant prayer and worship could take place, and in which God's will could be realised on earth as it was in heaven. Basil writes:

> What state can be more blessed than to imitate on earth the choruses of angels? To begin the day with prayer, and to honour our Maker with hymns and songs? As the day brightens, to betake ourselves, with prayer attending on it throughout, to our labours, and to sweeten our work with hymns, as if with salt?[5]

However, the human needs of work, meals, rest, and sleep, disrupt the perfect spiritual life of continuous praise and prayer. Nevertheless, the biblical command to pray without ceasing (1 Thess. 5:17) should be taken literally.[6] Paul's words were not to be interpreted simply as an encouragement to be ready to pray at any time or in any circumstance. His words were understood to imply that prayer, often in the form of

5 Basil, *Letters*, II:2; cf. Morison, *St. Basil and his Rule: A Study in early Monasticism*, 13.

6 cf. Colossians 4:2; Ephesians 6:18; Luke 18:1. Some Old Testament Scriptures could be cited in support of this principle. I Chronicles 9:33 states that singers and priests were employed in worship 'day and night'. Isaiah 30:29 refers to perpetual praise in the Temple. Robert Taft, *The Liturgy of the Hours in East and West* (Collegeville, Minnesota: Liturgical Press, 1986), 5, stresses the importance of the command to 'pray without ceasing' in the development of the Divine Office.

recitation of the psalms, should be on the lips of every monk, during every moment of every day, whether working in the fields, writing in a cell, or walking along the way. And one reason why sleep was looked upon askance, was because it automatically interrupted the ideal of unbroken worship.[7]

Cassian taught that a soldier of Christ trained himself to pray without ceasing, through 'learning the psalms and observing the Canonical Hours'.[8] But he also viewed the system of Canonical Hours as only for beginners. In his view, coenobitic monks were on a lower spiritual level because they needed the set structure of Canonical Hours to help them approximate semi-continual prayer, whereas true anchorites had gone beyond this. Cassian claimed to know desert monks who needed no Canonical Hours because, as they worked and prayed in their cells, they spent the whole day, non-stop, in offices which other monks only celebrated at fixed times. Reflecting on this, Cassian writes:

> That which is *continually* offered is more than that which is rendered at *intervals* of time. And it is more acceptable as a free gift than duties which are performed by the compulsion of a rule.[9]

Cassian's ideal monks had no communal prayer during the daylight hours, though they did gather for Vespers and Nocturns, and they did meet on Saturdays and Sundays for Holy Communion. Even then, they allowed only limited conversation with one another, returning to solitary meditation as soon as possible.[10] Cassian approved of this single-mindedness. He lauded their habit of continually repeating psalms and other passages of scripture by heart and, by doing so, giving no opening for 'idle talk, dangerous schemes, or evil designs'. Minds and hearts were fully occupied with spiritual meditations. And yet,

---

7 Ian Adamson, *Bangor: Light of the World* (2015), 66, speculates that the 3,000 students and monks at Bangor had a continuous chorus of Divine Praise sung by relays of large choirs. The *Old Irish Life* (Skene, *Celtic Scotland*, vol. II, 492) states that there were 'thrice-fifty' persons on Iona in 'monastic rule'. This may refer to three groups of monks, each fifty strong, who took turns in prayer, ensuring unbroken prayer 24/7. The *Old Irish Life* also states there were sixty persons to do the work of manual labour and portrays an idealised monastic settlement.

8 Cassian, *Institutes*, II:1.

9 Cassian, *Institutes*, III:2.

10 Cassian, *Institutes*, II:15.

although Cassian's thinking permeated the Irish monastic system, it was the system of Canonical Hours which provided structure for prayer and devotion for the average monk of the Columban tradition.

THE DAILY OFFICE

From the first century onwards, Christians observed a rhythm of daily prayer. Sometimes they built on practices rooted in Jewish worship – though the relationship of early Christian worship to Jewish worship is a complex issue, with varying views held by scholars.[11] In the New Testament, the Book of Acts records Peter and John attending daytime (3 p.m.) Temple services (Acts 3:1ff). But away from Jerusalem, the earliest Christian pattern may only have involved morning and evening prayer.

By the late second century, Christian prayer-patterns were more formalised, though not uniform.[12] Clement of Alexandria (d. 215) knew of Christians who had prayers at the third, sixth, and ninth hours. He also knew of believers who prayed when rising, before retiring, at night, and before, during, and after meals.[13] Tertullian (d. 240) was of the view that prayers at the third, sixth, and ninth hours, plus prayers in the morning and evening, were something which no Christian was at liberty to neglect.[14] Tertullian also introduced a theological underpinning for these observances. He saw the requirement to pray three times during daytime as a living symbol of the Trinity in the Christian's life. In similar vein, Cyprian (d. 258) clothed the prayers of the third, sixth, and ninth hours with spiritual meaning, describing

---

11 Taft, *The Liturgy of the Hours in East and West*, differs from Bradshaw, *Daily Prayer in the Early Church: A Study of the Origin and Early Development of the Divine Office* (1981). See also: Gregory W. Woolfenden, *Daily Liturgical Prayer: Origins and Theology* (Aldershot: Ashgate, 2004); Dom Gregory Dix, *The Shape of the Liturgy* (2nd edition; London: A & C Black, 1993); Messenger, *The Medieval Latin Hymn*; and Arnold Blaes, *The Canonical Hours: Their Origin, Symbolism and Purpose* (Conception: Conception Abbey Press, 1956). Taft (3ff), warns against building too much on links between Jewish hours of prayer and early Christian practices. Nevertheless, he agrees that the NT Apostles observed the regular daily prayer times in the Temple, and that Christians adopted the Jewish custom of praying at fixed times. Taft questions whether the later Canonical Hours of Terce, Sext, and None were taken from Jewish practice, despite their mention in biblical books, and offers his own account of the development of the Canonical Hours.

12 Taft, *The Liturgy of the Hours in East and West*, 21, argues that for Cyprian himself the opposite was true. Frequent references to morning and evening prayers in the Psalms influenced Jewish and early Christian prayer.

13 Clement of Alexandria, *Stromata*, VII:7.

14 Tertullian, *On Prayer*, XXV.

their triple-threeness as a sacrament of the Trinity itself. For Cyprian, the three times of prayer, and the three hours between them, all had spiritual significance, because the 'perfect Trinity' was numbered every three hours. Cyprian believed that Old Testament heroes who observed these hours, such as Daniel and his companions (Dan. 6:10), honoured the Trinity unknowingly, and benefited from an inherently trinitarian sacramental blessing.[15] At the same time, Cyprian stressed that no hour of the day should be exempt from praising God.

Within its first three centuries, the Christian Church developed patterns of daily prayer.[16] It strove to root these patterns in Old and New Testament precursors; and its theologians brought spiritual and theological significance to each observed Hour. Monasticism accelerated this developing system.[17] When Christianity became the favoured State religion, it attracted tens of thousands of supposed converts and the Church was flooded with nominal believers. Some Christians regretted this overnight popularity. In their view acceptance by the State introduced a populist superficiality, and they longed for a more earnest spirituality. This yearning for authenticity drove some to ascetic monasticism, and, as monasticism grew, the monks' use of regular Prayer Hours influenced the practice of worship throughout the Church, leaving a mark on Cathedral worship as much as on the

15 Cyprian, *On the Lord's Prayer*, XXXIV: 'We find that the three children with Daniel, being strong in faith and victorious in captivity, observed the third, sixth, and ninth hour, as it were, for a sacrament of the Trinity, which in the last times had to be manifested. For both the first hour in its progress to the third shows forth the consummated number of the Trinity; and also the fourth proceeding to the sixth declares another Trinity; and when from the seventh the ninth is completed, the perfect Trinity is numbered every three hours, which spaces of hours the worshippers of God in time past having spiritually decided on, made use of for determined and lawful times for prayer. And subsequently the thing was manifested, that these things were of old Sacraments, in that anciently righteous men prayed in this manner.' Tertullian, *On Prayer*, XXV: 'We pray at least not less than thrice in the day, debtors as we are to Three, Father, Son, and Holy Spirit: of course, in addition to our regular prayers which are due, without any admonition, on the entrance of light and of night.' cf. Cassian, *Institutes*, III:3.

16 Messenger, *The Medieval Latin Hymn*, 9, suggests that before Christianity was the Empire's favoured religion, Christians held a vigil on Saturday night in preparation for Sunday. As part of that vigil, there were services of prayer at candlelight, night-time, and dawn. In the fourth and fifth centuries, following Christianity's elevation, this simple arrangement was added to by a range of services, in which the day-time series (*diurnal cursus*) was complemented by a night-time series (*nocturnal cursus*).

17 Curran, *The Antiphonary of Bangor and the Early Irish Monastic Liturgy*, 160. Blaes, *The Canonical Hours: Their Origin Symbolism and Purpose*, 5ff.

monasteries themselves. Though details varied across Christendom, Canonical Hours became part of church life everywhere. If the aim of prayer was unbroken communion with God, then the adoption of specific Prayer Hours was to aid that end.[18]

Some desert monks attempted to pray constantly in a quite literal fashion; but most recognised that that was impossible in this life. The next best approximation was to follow the words of the Psalmist: 'Seven times a day I praise you for your righteous laws' (Ps. 119:164).[19] This text was interpreted as a God-given direct instruction for distinct times of prayer during every twenty-four hours. But what did seven mean? Was it code for 'all the time', since seven symbolises the ideal? Did it mean 'exactly seven'? Did it mean 'at least seven'? Eight was a popular number in some medieval monasteries, and Warren refers to an early Irish gloss which claims that Columba celebrated ten Canonical Hours, but the gloss has a weak evidential basis.[20] Nevertheless, whether the number of observed Canonical Hours was seven, eight, nine or more, the psalmist's instruction, 'Seven times a day I praise you' drove the move towards specific hours being set aside as times for prayer.[21]

THE ISLAND HOURS

For early-medieval Irish monastic communities, such as Columba's Iona and Comgall's Bangor, six Canonical Hours are readily identifiable, with the seventh more elusive. The six straightforward Canonical Hours are: Third Hour (Terce), Sixth Hour (Sext), Ninth Hour (None), Vespers, Midnight and Morning. The twelve day hours were counted from 6 a.m. Hence the Third Hour (Terce) was 9 a.m. Sixth Hour (Sext) was noon. Ninth Hour (None) was 3 p.m. The twelve night

---

18 Bradshaw, *Daily Prayer in the Early Church*, 151.

19 cf. Benedict, *The Rule*, VI: 'We will fulfil this sacred number of seven if we satisfy our obligations of services at Lauds, Prime, Terce, Sext, None, Vespers and Compline, for it was of these times during the day that he said, "seven times a day have I praised you. … and let us arise at night to give him praise".'

20 Warren, *The Antiphonary of Bangor: Part II*, xxvi. The eleventh-century 'Vision of Adhamhnan' in Jackson (ed.), *A Celtic Miscellany*, 290, 295, refers to, 'eight Canonical Hours', assuming this was commonplace. Morison, *St. Basil and his Rule: A Study in Early Monasticism*, 66, suggests that Basil observed eight services (Prime, Terce, Sext, None, Vespers, Compline, Nocturns, and Lauds), though this is questioned.

21 Bradshaw, *Daily Prayer in the Early Church*, 127, notes that Aurelian of Arles (d. 553) mentions nine daily offices.

hours started at 6 p.m., meaning that the 'eighth hour of the night' was 2 a.m. Moreover, terms such as 'First Hour' were sometimes applied to the whole period of three hours before the next Canonical Hour. Under this interpretation, First Hour could refer to any time between 6 a.m. and 9 a.m.[22] Not all Canonical Hours were observed outside the monasteries; and Cathedral Canonical Hours could differ slightly from monastic ones.

There were two principal groupings of Hours: the day-time series (*Diurnal Cursus*) and the night-time series (*Nocturnal Cursus*). The services themselves could be described as prayer-meetings, and were not sacramental occasions. When the Eucharist was celebrated in a monastery (on a Sunday for example), it displaced the normal prayer and praise liturgy. And when monasteries observed the Eucharist, they followed the general eucharistic rites of the Church.

On Iona, Columba could mark the passage of time with some accuracy by noting the position of the sun in the sky. Noon is when the sun is due south and at its highest. At six in the morning (zero hour in monastic reckoning) the sun is due east. At six in the evening, the sun is due west. Vespers is linked to the appearance of the Evening Star (Venus) before sunset. Other important hours such as Third Hour and Ninth Hour can be interpolated. The Midnight hour can be approximated. On cloudy days (not unknown on Iona) an educated sense of time, possibly aided by a sand-clock, could be brought to bear. Gauging time by the position of the sun in the sky can become an intuitive skill. We recall that once, in the remote rural Malawian village of Mbalachanda, a villager, of whom we asked the time, instinctively looked at the position of the sun before confirming his judgement with his wrist-watch! In modern monasteries, such as Pluscarden in north-east Scotland, Terce is not rigidly fixed to 9 a.m., or Sext to noon, or None to 3 p.m.[23] Likewise, in later medieval institutions such as Dryburgh Abbey in the Scottish Borders, Nocturns was at 2 a.m. rather than at midnight. Similar elasticity may have operated on Iona, though our suspicion is that the earliest Columban monks were fastidious about doing things at the 'proper' time.

---

22 Blaes, *The Canonical Hours: Their Origin, Symbolism, and Purpose*, 31.

23 cf. Dom Augustine Holmes, *Pluscarden Abbey* (Derby: Heritage House Group, 2004), 30. Pluscarden observes Sext at 12.35, and None at 2.15.

Iona's northern latitude brought challenges, with its hours of sunset and sunrise varying enormously in the course of a year, affecting services which are linked to sunset or sunrise. Even in the Middle East, with its more moderate fluctuations of daylight, Cassian acknowledged that the changing times of sunset and sunrise forced adaptations.[24] If sunset and sunrise were always twelve hours apart, then services linked with day and night, light and darkness, could follow one another at constant intervals. But on Iona in the month of June, sunset is at 10 p.m. and sunrise at 2 a.m., with ample light in the sky for at least half-an-hour after sunset and half-an-hour before sunrise. If no allowances were made, then this superabundance of daylight could result in services overlapping one another. Similarly, in autumn, winter, and spring, Vespers falls comfortably into an afternoon slot: but what should be the rule in high summer when sunset is not until late evening and daylight lingers even longer? Should Vespers be held over to that late hour? Or should it stay as an afternoon service? The shortness of the summer night certainly affected the sequence of events when Columba died in June 597 (III:23). Columba died as the Midnight Office began, but the monks did not cancel the night vigil which followed the Midnight Office, probably because the period of actual darkness was extremely short. Adomnán tells us that, after the morning hymns were ended (perhaps only an hour after midnight itself) they took Columba's body from the church.

Like monks everywhere, the Iona monks not only marked the Canonical Hours, but had extended vigils of prayer and reflection. A vigil might be observed by a monk alone in his quarters; or it might be observed with the community in the church. In the Irish Church a vigil was not itself a Canonical Hour, though a vigil might be book-ended by Canonical Hours. For example, the night vigil would normally start with the Midnight Office and close with Morning Prayer. Thus, the Midnight Office could morph seamlessly into the night vigil, though the two were distinct liturgically. In some modern

24 cf. Cassian, *Institutes*, III:4 and 8: 'In the winter time when the nights are longer, the vigils which are celebrated every week on the evening at the commencing of the Sabbath, are arranged by the elders in the monasteries to last until the fourth cock-crowing for this reason: that after the watch during the whole night they may, by resting their bodies for the remaining time of nearly two hours, avoid flagging through drowsiness the whole day long, and be content with repose for this short time instead of resting the whole night.'

monasteries, such as Pluscarden, the term 'vigil' applies to pre-dawn prayers starting at around 4.30 a.m. Elsewhere the pre-dawn prayers might go under the terms 'Morning Prayers' or 'Matins', though 'Matins' has various meanings, depending on the Church tradition in question. In the early Irish Church of Columba's era, 'vigil' nearly always refers to the time of prayer and reflection between the Midnight Office and pre-dawn Morning Prayers.

Importantly, each Canonical Hour was assigned a spiritual and theological meaning, which was linked to events recorded in Scripture as having taken place at that hour of the day. The monks read Scripture as divinely inspired in every detail. They assumed no part of Scripture was superfluous, and no recorded fact was incidental. Each detail had spiritual import. Hence, all events in Scripture, which were recorded as having taken place at a precise hour of the day (e.g. at the third hour), must have a spiritual connection with the liturgy of the corresponding Canonical Hour (e.g. the Third Hour liturgy). Basil, one of Columba's major theological influencers, wrote that each period contained a reminder 'peculiar to itself' of blessings received from God.[25] All incidents in Scripture connected with that hour of the day were relevant. The narrative of Christ's Passion gave profound meaning to certain Canonical Hours: and closely allied to Christ's death and resurrection was Israel's deliverance from Egypt in the Exodus story. That historical Exodus foreshadowed the mighty act of God in Christ in delivering His people from the captivity of Satan and the bondage of death. Each Canonical Hour found its meaning in events. It focussed on narrative; and dramatic action-images dominated the spiritual imagination.[26]

THE RECONSTRUCTION

Several documents aid our reconstruction of Iona's Daily Office. Adomnán's *Life of Columba* has incidental evidence, and though Adomnán may be sometimes describing his own time rather than Columba's, his liturgy would echo the earlier period. Resistance to change was embedded in Irish monasticism. There was so much respect

25 Basil, *The Longer Rule*, Qu. 37.

26 In some later texts, such as *The Spinola Hours*, the spirituality of the Canonical Hours was related to Mary, and to various events in her life. (De Hamel, *Meetings with Remarkable Manuscripts*, 530).

for a monastery's founder that each generation of monks conserved what they believed had been their founder's way of doing things. There was also a belief that received liturgical practices had divine sanction and must be handed on unaltered. Orthopraxis in worship was as important as orthodoxy in theology. The original liturgy had come from a saintly figure, who was thought to have discerned God's exact will for his community through careful study, deep piety, and angelic revelations. Cassian expresses this when commenting on the number of psalms for each service,

> This arrangement, fixed ever so long ago, has continued unbroken to the present day throughout so many ages in all the monasteries of those districts, because it is said that it was no appointment of man's direction, *but was brought down from heaven to the fathers by the ministry of an angel.*[27]

For Cassian, liturgical practice was not a product of human creativity. It had been brought down from heaven to the Church Fathers. It had been revealed by the ministry of angels. Basil was of the same mind, seeing what had gone before as a sacred model.[28] Clement of Rome thought similarly, writing that devotional exercises should be observed at times and hours appointed by God's own supreme will, 'in order that all things, being piously done according to His good pleasure, may be acceptable to Him'.[29] It was assumed that there was a divinely approved way of doing things, which was fixed by God's will. Novelty was to be avoided. Consistent with this, Iona's own literature claims that Columba was divinely instructed, reinforcing the notion that great

---

27 Cassian, *Institutes*, II:4 [my italics]. Billett, *The Divine Office in Anglo-Saxon England:597-1000*, 26, makes the same point: 'All liturgy tends towards conservatism, and monasticism's strong adherence to tradition meant that deviation from established norms was especially frowned upon, above all when it came to the Divine Office, the central activity of any monastery.'

28 Basil, *Letters*, 28, commends a recently departed brother whom he praises as, 'guardian of the principles of his fathers', 'enemy of innovations', 'making the state of the Church put under him conform to the ancient constitution, *as to a sacred model*', and who 'put forth nothing of his own, no novel invention'.

29 Clement of Rome, *First Letter to the Corinthians*, XL. Warren, *The Antiphonary of Bangor: Part II*, xviii, points out that Cassian spoke at length and deprecatingly in *Institutes* II:2 of too much variety in the structure and arrangement of the Church's services. Cassian wanted uniformity, fixity, and homogeneity. Warren concedes that the Celtic Church was guilty of some variations from the standard models found elsewhere.

leaders received direct revelation to shape the life of their communities for ever.[30] Thus the *Amra* (VIII) states that what Columba conceived by keeping vigil, he ascertained by action. We can assume with some confidence that the Iona liturgy of Adomnán's day would be essentially the same as that of Columba's era, in its structure and spirituality.

Early poems from the Iona family also have hints on liturgical practice.[31] Likewise, there are clues in documents from daughter-monasteries, such as Lindisfarne, which stood full-square in the Iona tradition, at least until the Synod of Whitby of 664.[32] And Columbanus (d. 615) also sheds light, having published a *Rule* for his monks (*Regula Monachorum*), which includes a brief description of an Irish monastic cursus. Columbanus was near-contemporary to Columba, and though he was a product of Bangor in Ireland, he may have spent time on Iona. Columbanus was a hard taskmaster, and his extreme approach is reflected in his liturgy, with its gruelling routine of unremitting all-night psalmody in contrast to a less intense approach in the Roman tradition.[33] We suspect that Columba inclined towards the rigorous end of the spectrum.

Beyond these texts, our understanding of early-medieval Irish liturgical worship is aided immensely by the *Bangor Antiphonary*, which is a late seventh-century liturgy originating from the monastery of Bangor. The next earliest Irish Church liturgy is the *Stowe Missal*, but

---

30 *Amra*, VIII, claims that Columba 'spoke with an angel'. The *Amra* may be citing a strand of tradition also referred to by Adomnán (III:18) when he wrote of Columba receiving direct divine instruction whilst on Hinba. All of Columba's teaching was regarded as having an angelic/divine imprimatur.

31 cf. Columba, *Altus Prosator*; Dallan, *Amra Choluimb Chille*; Beccán, *Tiugraind Beccain* (which speaks of adoring God nightly and daily); and the anonymous *Cantemus in Omni Die* which has a reference to antiphonal singing. All these are early writings from Iona or its close family.

32 Billett, *The Divine Office in Anglo-Saxon England: 597-1000*, 132, strikes a cautious note: 'We have no idea … how the Office was sung at the Irish foundation of Lindisfarne during Wilfrid's boyhood.' The *Voyages of St. Brendan* has frequent references to liturgical observance. However, though Brendan was contemporary to Columba, the *Voyages* was probably composed centuries later. Despite this, Padraig O'Neill, 'Welsh *Anterth*, Old Irish *Anteirt*', *Eriu*, vol. 41, 1-11 (5f.), suggests that though the Brendan text may have received its present form in the early tenth century, it is essentially backward-looking, presenting a picture of the ideal monastic life of the Old Irish Church and of the Divine Office as it was then. Against this, its frequent mention of Compline indicates later Benedictine influences, since the term Compline was not used in the early Irish Church. The term is totally absent from Adomnán's *Life of Columba*, and from the *Bangor Antiphonary*.

33 Taft, *The Liturgy of the Hours in East and West*, 114.

that is dated to the late eighth century.[34] If the *Bangor Antiphonary* is used with care it becomes an open window through which to view the worship and theology of the early-medieval Irish Church. The key is to use it 'with care'. The *Bangor Antiphonary* is not the Iona liturgy in disguise. We cannot assume a one-to-one relationship between it and the Iona liturgy. Nevertheless, if used judiciously, it illuminates our understanding and is a gold-mine of supportive evidence. No other ancient liturgy brings us so close to Iona. Nevertheless, there are issues to be discussed before using it to help understand worship on Columba's island.

USING THE BANGOR ANTIPHONARY

The *Bangor Antiphonary* was written at the Bangor Monastery between 680 and 691. This precise time-span is based on evidence within the *Bangor Antiphonary* itself, with its list of Bangor abbots implying that Abbot Cronan (Bangor's abbot between 680 and 691) was alive when it was written.[35] At some point a copy was taken to mainland Europe where several Irish-originated monastic houses had been established. It was kept at Bobbio until 1606, when it was taken for safe keeping to the Ambrosian Library in Milan during a period of political turbulence. Shelved in obscurity, the *Antiphonary* next saw the light of day in 1713, when an edition was printed by the scholar Ludovico Muratori, better known for his discovery of the *Muratorian Fragment*, which has one of the earliest lists of New Testament books.[36] The *Bangor Antiphonary* then reappears in the nineteenth century when F. E. Warren made a close examination of its text on behalf of the Henry Bradshaw Society, publishing his findings in two volumes, including a detailed introduction and commentary.[37] Warren's work is still a benchmark

34 O'Loughlin, *Celtic Theology*, 130, dates the *Stowe Missal* to between 792 and 812. It was named after Stowe House in Buckinghamshire, England, where it was once kept, but originates from a monastic setting, probably Tallaght. O'Loughlin points out that Tallaght was the driving force in a new 'reform' movement at that time the *Stowe Missal* was composed and that its basic text was the Roman rite.

35 *Bangor Antiphonary*, Item 129.

36 Ludovico Antonio Muratori (1672-1750) was uncertain whether the Milan manuscript was an original or a copy. Warren, *The Antiphonary of Bangor: Part II*, x, saw no reason to dispute it as an original.

37 Warren's work on the *Bangor Antiphonary* was published as two volumes, in the Henry Bradshaw Ancient Liturgical Texts series. Volume One, a facsimile edition, was published in 1893. Volume Two, published in 1895, has most of Warren's scholarship on

study. His sober and meticulous analysis established solid foundations for future researchers, with the likes of Michael Curran emphasising the enduring worth of Warren's scholarship.[38]

At Bangor, the *Antiphonary*, along with Psalter and Bible, was used by the abbot as he led worship. It is a short document and does not provide a full liturgy for every service of the year. Warren sees it as a companion volume to Psalter and Lectionary, and designed for Easter Eve and Easter Day, *or* for Saturdays and Sundays in Eastertide, *or* for all Saturdays and Sundays plus perhaps feasts of martyrs.[39] Other interpretations have been suggested. However, even if its usage was restricted to the Easter season, its structure and content echo the normal Daily Office. And even as a partial and seasonal liturgy, the *Bangor Antiphonary* has rich content for each Canonical Hour. As well as collects and psalms it includes hymns, several of which come from wider Christendom. All of these enrich our awareness of the worship of the early-medieval Irish Church.

Nonetheless, there are issues to address. The hundred-year gap between Columba's death and the *Bangor Antiphonary*'s creation is one. The thousand-year gap between it first arriving on the Continent and a copy being discovered in Milan is another. Does the fact that Bangor was founded by Comgall and not by Columba make a difference? Did the Roman Church, with its increasing influence in Ireland during the seventh century, alter Bangor's liturgy from what Comgall instituted? Was the *Antiphonary* re-edited *after* it arrived on the Continent? Might differences be so great that its relevance to Iona in the late sixth century is minimal at most?

---

the *Bangor Antiphonary*. The Henry Bradshaw Society was founded in 1890 to promote the study of medieval and early modern liturgies through the publication of scholarly editions and studies. A growing corpus of scholarly articles on the *Bangor Antiphonary* is also aiding academics and lay-readers. Paul C. Stratman published his new translation of the *Antiphonary* in 2018.

38 Curran, *The Antiphonary of Bangor and the Early Irish Monastic Liturgy*, 1. Daibhi O Croinin, reviewing Curran's book in *Irish Historical Studies*, vol. 24, no. 96, 530-1, notes that 'Bangor's book' has been fortunate in its modern students, and that Warren's two-volume edition for the Henry Bradshaw Society was one of the finest works of nineteenth-century scholarship. Croinin adds that Curran's complementary study, with its detailed and valuable liturgical commentary, was a welcome addition by an Irishman in a field of research hitherto dominated by continental scholars.

39 Warren, *The Antiphonary of Bangor: Part II*, x. O'Neill, 'Welsh Anterth, Old Irish Anteirt', 4, holds that, despite the *Bangor Antiphonary*'s limitations as an Office Book, it can be used to help reconstruct the Daily Office.

1. Time-difference is a minor factor. We have already noted the inherent conservatism of the Irish Church, and that a founder's pattern was regarded as semi-sacred. Modernity places high-value on innovation, but in the early-medieval Irish Church it was antiquity which was important. Communities clung to the one 'God-given' and 'correct' way of doing things. Irish monks were particularly conscious of traditions inherited from sixth-century patriarchal figures, and Bangor monks would conserve what they thought Comgall had instituted.[40] Practices would be kept constant. Novelty would be avoided. Divinely revealed order would be obeyed. Cassian's view that right-practice had been revealed from heaven by the ministry of angels was axiomatic.[41] This was the mindset of Christendom as a whole. In worship, and in other issues such as the date of Easter and the tonsure, it was believed that there was only one divinely sanctioned way of doing things, and to act contrary to God's will was sin. Changes might occur, and did occur, but only slowly. Monastic culture meant that worship at Bangor at the close of the seventh century would not differ radically from what Comgall laid down a century previous.

2. Comgall was not Columba. Nevertheless, the likelihood is that Comgall's practices were the same as Columba's. They were contemporaries. Comgall founded Bangor around 555; and Columba instituted his community on Iona around 563. Moreover, Adomnán's *Life of Columba* depicts Comgall and Columba as colleagues, mentioning Comgall three times, each time portraying Comgall and Columba as close in spirit.[42] Both studied under Finnian of Clonard, though not simultaneously. Just as future Bangor and Iona monks kept the traditions they inherited, so Comgall and Columba would

40 Curran, *The Antiphonary of Bangor and the Early Irish Monastic Liturgy*, 160.

41 Cassian, *Institutes*, II:4 (my italics); cf. Cassian, *Institutes*, II:6 for another apposite quotation.

42 Adomnán depicts: Columba and Comgall fellowshipping together (I:49); Columba being concerned about Comgall's monks drowning (III: 13); and Comgall sharing the Eucharist with Columba (III:17). Sharpe, *Adomnán of Iona: Life of St. Columba*, 314 note 205, refers to the late ninth-century *Martyrology of Notker* which describes Comgall as sole heir of Columba's virtues and merits, a passage which may come from an earlier source. Over against this, Adamson, *Bangor: Light of the World*, 69, refers to a tradition that, around 579, there was a dispute between Columba and Comgall regarding the Church of Ros-Torathair, a Bangor foundation, which resulted in a battle at Coleraine between the Cruithin and the Ui Neill. This later tradition has been used by some writers to develop a narrative in which Columba and Comgall were at loggerheads.

respect what they were taught by their master.[43] They had a common training. They had a common theological outlook. They inherited a common liturgical tradition. They would institute similar, if not identical, practices in their monasteries. Details might vary, but with no huge differences. The few sea miles between Ireland and Scotland meant little. Geographic distance was less a factor than cultural and ecclesial continuity. Both belonged to the Irish Church. Both were shaped by its culture. Both followed liturgies common to the beliefs, practices, and rituals of the Church to which they belonged.

3. Did Romanising influences change things at Bangor? Even if Bangor monks would prefer to keep things unaltered, did other factors kick in? Was the late seventh-century *Bangor Antiphonary* a Romanised text? Herren and Brown fear this may have been the case,[44] but Warren and Curran are satisfied that the copy discovered in Milan's Ambrosian Library does not exhibit signs of Romanisation. Although the middle decades of the seventh century saw some Irish monasteries abandoning their traditional Easter dating in favour of the Roman calculations, the Irish Church was not yet Romanised culturally. Full absorption into Rome did not occur for several centuries, during which time Irish liturgy and Irish theology remained vitally alive, and it was an Irish churchmanship which produced the *Bangor Antiphonary*. In support of this, Warren highlights Item 13 of the *Antiphonary*, which states that Patrick of Ireland received his apostleship directly from God, independent of Papal authority.[45] Warren argues that if Roman influence had changed the *Bangor Antiphonary* significantly, then Item 13 would have expressed Patrick's reliance on Rome more clearly. Instead, the *Bangor Antiphonary* refers to Patrick in a manner totally consistent with the early-medieval Irish Church's position in relation to Rome. In the *Antiphonary* it is Patrick, not Peter, who is appointed Pontiff by Christ for Ireland.[46] The Irish Church had long respected Rome, and it recognised Rome's importance within Christendom, but it never acknowledged Rome's claim to universal authority. When

43 The *Old Irish Life* claims that Columba and Comgall also studied under Mobhi at Glasnevin.

44 Herren and Brown, *Christ in Celtic Christianity*, 279.

45 *Bangor Antiphonary*, Item 13:3, 15, 16, 21. Patrick was 'chosen by God's own self … appointed from heaven'; cf. Warren, *The Antiphonary of Bangor: Part II*, 50.

46 *Bangor Antiphonary*, Item 13:16.

Columbanus wrote to Pope Boniface IV in the early seventh century, defending the Irish Church on a range of issues, he acknowledged the *de facto* primary role which Rome occupied, but he never accepted that Rome had a *de jure* primacy over Christendom.[47] Rome was respected. Rome was a vital centre. Rome was where Peter and Paul had been martyred. Rome was a pilgrimage destination for Irish Christians. The Irish Church never isolated itself deliberately from the Roman Church. It accessed the same books. It respected the same Church Fathers. It affirmed the same fundamental orthodoxies. But it did not view itself as subject to Rome. Warren reasons that Item 13 of the *Antiphonary* is from an early stratum of Irish liturgical material, perhaps fifth century, and that it illustrates the relationship between Ireland and Rome perfectly. It affirms the Irish Church's independent status, as having been established by God directly through Patrick.

4. Is the extant manuscript of the *Bangor Antiphonary* a true copy of the original? Warren, Nerney, and Curran are all confident that the Milan manuscript is so. It has Irish script. It has Irish orthography. It has Irish-style idiosyncratic dotted ornamentation. It has Irish idioms reproduced in Latin. Moreover, the style of the prayers within the *Antiphonary* suggest that the manuscript is a direct copy of an Irish text and not an adaptation.[48] Nothing, of course, was 'purely Irish'. Irish monks happily absorbed material from a variety of sources; and detailed analysis by Warren and Curran shows that the *Bangor Antiphonary* includes liturgical items from Gaul, Spain, north Italy, and the eastern Mediterranean, reflecting long-standing trade and cultural links between the regions.[49] An outstanding example of this eclecticism

---

47 Columbanus, *Letter V to Boniface IV*; cf. Dales, *Light to the Isles*, 70.

48 Warren, *The Antiphonary of Bangor: Part II*, xxvi-xxviii., 98; Nerney, 'The Bangor Symbol: Part I', *ITQ* (1952), 369f.; Curran, *The Antiphonary of Bangor and the Early Irish Monastic Liturgy*, 160. Curran suggests that the Old Latin text of the canticles, *Cantemus, Benedicite,* and *Benedictus*, in the *Antiphonary* implies they were used in Ireland in the pre-monastic period.

49 Curran, *The Antiphonary of Bangor and the Early Irish Monastic Liturgy*, 151. John Ryan, 'The Mass in the Early Irish Church', *IQR* (1961), 374, suggests that any liturgy introduced by Patrick into Ireland would be Gallican at its core. Yet, at the same time, the early Irish churchmen 'were frankly eclectic; they were looking for a liturgy that was devotional and were not slow to accept it from any recognized Catholic source. If the bunting was of many colours, they rejoiced rather than repined'; cf. Woolfenden, *Daily Liturgical Prayer: Origins and Theology*, 288, who stresses close similarities between the *Bangor Antiphonary* and the Ambrosian Office.

are two collects in the *Antiphonary* which Curran has established as verbatim transcriptions of sermons by Zeno of Verona (d. 371).[50] Previous to Curran's findings, the earliest known Zeno citations were in works by Ratherius (d. 974). And yet, despite this diversity, Warren stresses that the *Antiphonary* has original Irish elements, some of which we highlight later.[51] Any Iona liturgy would exhibit similar variety.

The *Bangor Antiphonary* was birthed from the spirituality of the early-medieval Irish Church. It provides insights into the common worship of early Irish monasticism. And yet, precisely because it originates from a specific monastery, and because it was used only on specific occasions, insights need to be applied with care. But what it can do is to give collaborative evidence concerning Iona's Daily Office. Hence, the method which we follow in reconstructing the Iona Daily Office involves gathering available direct evidence for that Daily Office and comparing that with evidence from Bangor and the wider Church.[52] These comparisons and contrasts will inform our discussion of Columba and Iona's liturgical practices and their accompanying spirituality.

To uncover the theology behind each of Iona's Canonical Hours, we draw on the teaching of Basil, Cassian, Benedict, and Bangor, along with insights from other Church Fathers. Basil and Cassian are important because of their direct influence on Irish monasticism. Benedict often arrived at similar solutions to similar problems. And Bangor is significant because the *Bangor Antiphonary* sheds a bright light on liturgical practices in the early-medieval Irish Church.

---

50 Curran, *The Antiphonary of Bangor and the Early Irish Monastic Liturgy*, 145.

51 Curran, *The Antiphonary of Bangor and the Early Irish Monastic Liturgy*, 32ff., 38, argues for a primary Irish origin of some hymns. Many Irish-originated hymns adopted the alphabetic structure and started 'Audite'.

52 cf. Woolfenden, *Daily Liturgical Prayer: Origins and Theology*, 272ff.

CHAPTER 14

The Canonical Hours

In the *Bangor Antiphonary* the lists of Canonical Hours are headed by *Ad Secundam.* This was an early, post-dawn, service which took place before the Third Hour (Terce) observance. Warren and Curran both suggest that the liturgical day in Irish monasteries commenced with this service, with *Ad Secundam* at Bangor being the equivalent of Prime elsewhere.[1] (The relationship between *Ad Secundam* and Prime requires some explanation which we adjourn until later in this chapter.) In contrast, Sharpe has the Irish liturgical day starting with Vespers, making it harmonise with the Jewish day which ran from sunset to sunset.[2] Others suggest Terce was the beginning.[3] We begin our discussion with Terce, but not because we have decided that it initiated the liturgical day. It is simply that this enables us to start with the fairly straightforward *diurnal cursus,* before examining the more ambiguous *nocturnal cursus.*

We also note that Adomnán sometimes cites the daily hours as liturgical events (e.g. worship at the Third Hour or at the Sixth Hour), but he can also refer to them as time-of-day indicators (e.g. a person arriving before the third hour, or an event occurring after the ninth hour). Both forms of reference were in common usage in the Church of the period.

THE THIRD HOUR (TERCE)

The Daytime Hours of Terce (9 a.m.), Sext (Noon), None (3 p.m.) and Vespers (pre-sunset), are common to Basil, Cassian, Benedict, Iona, and Bangor.[4] From Monday to Friday, the Terce, Sext, and None services

1 Warren, *The Antiphonary of Bangor: Part II,* xvi; Curran, *The Antiphonary of Bangor and the Early Irish Monastic Liturgy,* 162.

2 Sharpe, *Adomnán: Life of St Columba,* 323, note 238.

3 Bradshaw, *Daily Prayer in the Early Church,* 128.

4 Basil's system is detailed in *The Longer Rule,* Qu. 37. Cassian's model is in his *Institutes,* III:3. Benedict set out his system in *The Rule,* VI, XVI, listing: 'Lauds, Prime, Terce, Sext,

were short, though longer on Saturdays and Sundays. Initially, the Church Fathers may have regarded the third, sixth, and ninth hours as periods of private prayer, at least before they became part of a recognised liturgy of the Hours.[5] The noontide Sext office could be extremely brief, coming as it did in the middle of a working day.[6]

1. *Scripture and the Third Hour.* The New Testament has two major third-hour references. The Holy Spirit came in power on the Church at the third hour at Pentecost (Acts 2:15); and, according to Mark, Jesus was crucified at the third hour (Mark 15:25). However, nearly all early Third Hour liturgies only refer to the Pentecost event. This is because most Church Fathers associate Jesus' crucifixion with the onset of darkness over the land from the sixth to the ninth hours.[7] For example, Ignatius and Augustine both interpret Mark's mention of the 'third hour' as being the hour Jesus was condemned by Pilate, and not the hour he was nailed to the cross. They argue that because Pilate's verdict sealed Jesus' fate, then Mark could legitimately call it 'the hour of crucifixion', even though the nailing to the cross took place later.[8] This leaves the coming of the Holy Spirit at Pentecost as the major biblical event associated with the third hour. This was centre stage in early liturgies.[9]

2. *Adomnán and the Third Hour.* Adomnán twice refers to the third hour. In the first instance (II:15), Columba assured Baithéne that he would have a following wind for his journey from Iona to Tiree.

None, Vespers, and Compline.' Bangor's Hours are taken from the *Bangor Antiphonary* (e.g., Items 17-24, 27-39). O'Neill, 'Welsh *Anterth*, Old Irish *Anteirt*', *Eriu*, vol. 41, compares the Bangor Hours with those listed in an eighth-century Old Irish gloss on the Psalms, preserved in a Latin commentary in the Vatican Library: Antert (Prime); Tert (9 a.m.); Sest; (Midday), Noon (None); Fescer (Vespers); Midnoct (Media Noctis/Nocturna); Mate (Matutina/Matins). O'Neill comments on the omission of *Initium Noctis* (First Nocturns) in the Vatican list, concluding that its absence from the Vatican list may be a deliberate omission by the Old Irish glossator, who wanted only seven Hours, agreeing with Psalm 119. O'Neill sees the Vatican list as reinforcing Bangor, and as defining the Hours for the Irish Church. The omission of the term 'Compline' in the Vatican document, despite its Northumbrian eighth-century origin, suggests early Irish terminology took precedence over Benedictine terminology which used the word 'Compline' from an early date.

5 Woolfenden, *Daily Liturgical Prayer: Origins and Theology*, 292.

6 Hughes, *Early Christian Ireland: Introduction to the Sources*, 92f.

7 cf. Cassian, *Institutes*, III:3. Hippolytus (d. 235) was one of the few who linked the third hour with Jesus' death.

8 Ignatius, *Epistle to the Trallians*, IX. Augustine was inconsistent: in *On the Trinity*, IV:6, Christ is 'suspended on the cross at the third hour'; in *Harmony of the Gospels*, III:13, 50, it is the sixth hour; cf. *Apostolic Constitutions*, V:3.

9 Tertullian, *On Prayer*, XXIV and Cyprian, *The Lord's Prayer*, XXXIV.

Baithéne set off and, at 'the third hour', Columba was able to tell the priest Colman that Baithéne had safely arrived at his destination. In this story Adomnán uses 'third hour' as a time-of-day marker. In the second instance (II:45), Adomnán illustrates the efficacy of a prayer made to Columba many years after Columba's death. Adomnán had been in Ireland and was anxious to reach Iona for Columba's feast day, but contrary winds hampered his return. By the eve of the feast day, he was only part-way. Prayer was made to Columba. A south wind blew. And Iona was reached 'after the third hour of the day'.[10] Adomnán had time to wash hands and feet before celebrating 'the solemn Mass at the hour of Sext for the feast of St. Columba and St. Baithéne.' In this story the third hour again indicates the time-of-day when Iona was reached, and does not necessarily indicate a service at Terce, though that was standard monastic practice.

3. *Spirituality and the Third Hour.* Basil and Cassian connect the Third Hour liturgy with the coming of the Holy Spirit on the Apostles,[11] as does Item 28 of the *Bangor Antiphonary*:

> With our dependent prayers, we beseech you, Christ the Lord, who in the Third Hour of the day sent the Holy Spirit on the disciples as they prayed, to give to us who come after them participation in the same grace.

This prayer illustrates that Canonical Hour spirituality was not just about remembering God's actions in biblical history, but had daily-life application. The climax of the prayer is its request for the Spirit to enable the monks to share the same grace as bestowed on the original disciples. This reflects Basil's theology of the Third Hour, in which he teaches that the Spirit was given to the Church for two reasons: first, to aid believers in their striving to be worthy to receive the gift of sanctity; second, to give instruction in what is good and useful.[12] Basil bases this

10 Sharpe's translation is, 'after the hour of Terce'. The Andersons are more literal: 'after the third hour of the day'.

11 Basil, *The Larger Rule*, Qu. 37 and Cassian, *Institutes*, III:3.

12 cf. Basil, *The Longer Rule*, Qu. 37: 'At the third hour the brethren must assemble and betake themselves to prayer, even if they may have dispersed to their various employments. Recalling to mind the gift of the Spirit bestowed upon the Apostles at this third hour, all should worship together, so that they also may become worthy to receive the gift of sanctity, and they should implore the guidance of the Holy Spirit and His instruction in what is good and useful.' Morison, *St. Basil and his Rule: A Study in Early Monasticism*, 66, argues that

theology on several psalms in which God is asked, 'to create a clean spirit in me', 'to strengthen me with a guiding spirit', and, by His Spirit, 'to lead me into the right land'. Item 28 of the *Bangor Antiphonary*, with its plea for 'participation in the same grace', is consistent with Basil's plea for the Holy Spirit to come on the Church, purify the hearts of God's people, and guide them.[13] Item 18 is a similar Third Hour collect, requesting gifts of grace from Christ: 'Through the Third Hour we pray for the mercy of Christ, that he may bestow on us his perpetual grace'. Iona's Third Hour liturgy would have the same focus, celebrating the giving of the Holy Spirit at Pentecost. Near the start of each working day, it sought the bestowal of the Holy Spirit, and the Spirit's guidance and instruction.

THE SIXTH HOUR (SEXT)

The Sixth Hour Office was at midday, and its observance on working weekdays was brief. This brevity enabled monks to mark it where they were before continuing their tasks.

1. *Scripture and the Sixth Hour.* Pilate handed Jesus over to be crucified at the sixth hour (John 19:14). There was darkness from the sixth hour to the ninth hour as Jesus hung on the cross (Matthew 27:45; Luke 23:44).[14] The sixth hour was when Peter had a vision instructing him to treat the Gentile soldier Cornelius as an equal (Acts 10:9ff). The Samaritan woman came to the well at the sixth hour (John 4:6), a detail noted by Adomnán in *The Holy Places*,[15] though little significance was made of the woman at the well incident in early liturgies.

2. *Adomnán and the Sixth Hour.* Adomnán has two references to the sixth hour. On the same day as Baithéne travelled to Tiree, the priest Colman left for Ireland from Iona *after* mid-day (II:15, *post meridiem*).

---

because Basil was a strong apologist for the godhead of the Holy Spirit, it was important to him that Terce gave special honour to the third person.

13 Morison, *St. Basil and his Rule: A Study in Early Monasticism*, 66, suggests that Basil's emphasis on brothers worshipping together with one accord was that they may be found worthy of the Spirit's sanctification.

14 Taft, *The Liturgy of the Hours in East and West*, 22f., offers a reconstructed text of the *Apostolic Tradition*: 'Pray likewise at the sixth hour. For when Christ was nailed to the wood of the cross, the day was divided, and darkness fell. And so at that hour let them pray a powerful prayer, imitating the voice of him who prayed and made all creation dark for the unbelieving Jews.' The concept of the day 'divided' resulted in some institutions splitting Sext into two services.

15 Adomnán, *The Holy Places*, II:21.

It may be that Colman waited until midday prayers at Sext were over before commencing his journey, though the phrase 'after mid-day' is a time-of-day marker in the narrative rather than a liturgical statement. In a second story, Adomnán records that when he hurried back to Iona to mark Columba's feast day, he arrived in time to celebrate solemn mass at Sext (II:45).

3. *Spirituality and the Sixth Hour.* It is the drama on Calvary, and the vision to Peter, which dominate the Sixth Hour liturgies of the Patristic era.[16] As noted, the Church Fathers identified the sixth hour rather than the third hour as the hour of crucifixion. For them, the darkness which covered the land at the sixth hour made it the decisive moment. It was a spiritual darkness as well as a physical darkness. And because Jesus' ascent of the cross and the onset of darkness came together, this made the sixth hour the crisis-moment when Jesus' battle with Satan came to its climax. This is totally consistent with the Church Fathers' literal reading of Ephesians 2:2, and their interpretation of Satan's status as 'Prince of the powers of the air'. The physical air-space between earth and heaven was Satan's habitat. When Jesus was lifted up into the air on the cross, He entered that demonic realm and fought face to face with the Evil One.[17] This engagement between Jesus and the 'Prince of the powers of the air' is integral to Sixth Hour spirituality.

Basil stresses the importance of noon prayers, citing Psalm 55:17: 'Evening, morning, and at noon I cry out in distress and he hears my voice.'[18] For Basil, prayer is important at the sixth hour in order 'to be saved from invasion and the noonday Devil'. Basil emphasises the risk of being invaded by darkness and Satanic forces; and believers should chant Psalm 91 (Vulgate 90) to protect themselves from such perils. The same psalm should be appealed to whenever Satan might be near, such as before sleep and the onset of night. Both noon and evening were vulnerable times of the day with respect to the demonic. The evening was obviously so with its coming darkness. But noontide was also a

---

16 Tertullian, *On Prayer*, XXIV, linked the Sixth Hour to Peter's vision. Cyprian, *The Lord's Prayer*, XXXIV, explained that Peter was being taught to include all peoples in the grace of salvation, despite previously being doubtful of baptising Gentiles. Cyprian had an atonement reference: 'From the sixth hour to the ninth, the Lord, being crucified, washed away our sins by his blood; and, that he might redeem and quicken us, he then accomplished his victory by his passion.'

17 cf. Athanasius, *On the Incarnation*, XXV.

18 Basil, *The Longer Rule*, Qu. 37.

danger-point because of what happened on Calvary. For the monks, this noonday crisis was prophesied by Psalm 91: 'You will not fear the terror of night, nor the arrow that flies by day, nor the pestilence that stalks in the darkness, nor the plague (destruction) that destroys at midday.' But Psalm 91 also reaffirmed God's shelter, God's protection, and God's shielding from harm. In recalling these realities, monks were strengthened to withstand both the noonday devil and the terrors of the night. For Basil, the liturgy of the Sixth Hour is profoundly connected with Christ being raised up on the cross into Satan's realm, and with the furious onset of a demonic darkness on that first Good Friday. Though Basil does not refer directly to the crucifixion, his focus is Christ's sixth-hour encounter with Evil.[19]

Cassian goes further. In his account of the Sixth Hour liturgy he links Christ's ascent of the cross with Peter's vision. Each is important in itself, but they are also interrelated. For Cassian, the cross was where Jesus despoiled principalities and powers, and where Jesus set sinners free from Satanic captivity.[20] But Peter's vision was also of such importance that Cassian refers to it as 'nothing else than the Gospel'. Cassian gives Peter's vision this high status because, for Cassian, the fact that God's grace is not restricted to the Jews is at the heart of the Gospel message. This makes Cassian connect two massive realities in his interpretation of the Sixth Hour liturgy: Christ on the cross, and a Gospel for the whole World. And he makes the connection through words which Jesus spoke on the night before his crucifixion: 'If I be *lifted up*, I will *draw all men* to myself' (John 12:32). For Cassian, these words of Jesus unite the major themes of the Sixth Hour.[21] 'Being lifted

19 Ambrose, *Commentary on Psalm 118* (PG XV, 1315) writes that at the middle of the day 'our adversary is most especially powerful' but yet also 'that at the middle of the day the power of divine light is most operative'; cf. Blaes *The Canonical Hours: Their Origin, Symbolism and Purpose*, 38.

20 Cassian, *Institutes*, III:3: '[At the Sixth Hour] the spotless sacrifice, our Lord and Saviour, was offered up to the Father, and, ascending the cross for the salvation of the whole world, made atonement for the sins of mankind, and, despoiling principalities and powers, led them away openly; and all of us who were liable to death and bound by the debt of the handwriting that could not be paid, he freed, by taking it away out of the midst and affixing it to his cross for a trophy.'

21 Cassian, *Institutes*, III:3: '[He offered himself up] to the Father by the lifting up of his hands for the salvation of the whole world; which spreading forth of his hands on the cross is quite correctly called a "lifting up". For when we were all lying in Hades he raised us to heaven, according to the word of his own promise when he says, "When I am lifted up from the earth I will draw all men unto me".'

up' refers to Christ on the cross. 'All men' refers to a Gospel for the whole world. It was in being lifted up on the cross that Christ not only overcame Satan, but also embraced the world, including the Gentiles. These two concepts were linked together, not only by Cassian, but by Ignatius, Origen, Chrysostom, and Athanasius.[22]

The *Bangor Antiphonary* has similar thinking in its Sixth Hour prayers. Item 19 not only refers to Christ being nailed to the cross and crucified for our salvation but asks Christ to pardon supplicants who kneel before Him at the sixth hour, because that was the hour He died 'for all of us'. The collect not only rejoices in salvation but celebrates the fact that that salvation is for all peoples. In this way it combines the two themes of 'Christ on the cross' and 'a Gospel for the whole World'. Item 29 goes deeper into Sixth Hour spirituality, stating that in the very act of humbling Himself and ascending the cross at that hour, Christ illuminated the darkness of the world and the darkness of our hearts. In other words, it was in the very act of being lifted up on the cross into the darkness of the demonic, that Christ brought light to the world: and in early Christian thinking 'light to the world' referred to inclusion of the Gentiles. Iona's liturgy for the Sixth Hour would have the same emphases as those of Basil, Cassian, and Bangor.[23]

THE NINTH HOUR (NONE)

The Ninth Hour (None) was at three in the afternoon. Though its observance was brief on weekdays, it was one of the most solemn of all the Hours because of its association with the moment of Christ's physical death.

1. *Scripture and the Ninth Hour.* The ninth hour was when Jesus gave up his life and breathed his last (Mark 15:34; Matt. 27:45f; Luke 23:44).[24] It was when Cornelius had his vision (Acts 10:3), a day before Peter had

---

22 Ignatius, *To the Smyrnaeans*, II; Origen, *Commentary on the Gospel of Matthew*, XVIII; Chrysostom, *Homilies*, LXVII; Athanasius, *On the Incarnation*, XXV.

23 MacLean, *The Law of the Lord's Day in the Celtic Church*, 3, refers to an early Irish text which speculated that, as it was midday when Christ was placed on the cross, so it had been the sixth hour when Adam sinned. Early Christian thinking frequently used analogy and symmetry, viewing Christ's actions as reverse-engineering human sin: e.g., undoing Adam's actions at the same place and at a similar hour. Cassian, *Institutes*, XII:8, listed several ways in which God healed humanity by reversing Satan's actions. This linked with the idea of healing 'contraries by contraries'.

24 Cassian, *Institutes*, III:3, sees the ninth hour as the hour when Jesus descended into hell.

his. It was when Peter and John visited the Temple and a paralysed man was restored to health (Acts 3:1). For non-Jewish Christians, the vision given to Cornelius ranked with that given to Peter, since it underscored that salvation was for the Gentiles without any need to be circumcised or to observe Jewish ceremonies and food-laws. Cornelius' vision meant that the Gospel was for all peoples, justifying the very existence of Gentile Churches.

2. *Adomnán and the Ninth Hour.* Adomnán mentions the ninth hour three times. On the first occasion (I:48), Columba said to his monks:

> After the ninth hour, a guest will arrive from the north of Ireland, a heron, buffeted by the wind on its long flight, tired and weary. Its strength will be almost gone and it will fall on the shore in front of you. Take care how you lift it up, having pity for it, and carry it to the nearby house. Look after it and feed it there as a guest for three days and three nights. Afterwards, at the end of three days, when the heron is revived, it will no longer want to stay as a pilgrim with us, but when its strength is recovered it will return to the sweet district of Ireland from which it came.

Is this ninth hour only a time-of-day reference? Or is Adomnán embedding a theological metaphor? The heron, with life almost gone from its body, arrives after the ninth hour (the hour when Christ on the cross was at His weakest and about to give up His spirit); the heron rests for three days on Iona (just as Christ rested three days in the tomb); then, on the third day (as if with resurrection strength), the heron, full of new life, sets off for its true home 'in a straight line of flight'. If the story is a faith metaphor (though we cannot be certain that it is), then the ninth-hour reference is more than a time-of-day marker. It has liturgical significance.[25]

In Adomnán's second mention of the ninth hour, he records Cainnech praying for Columba and his companions who were at sea and being pounded by a storm (II:13). Cainnech was in his Aghaboe monastery in Ireland. The ninth hour had passed, and Cainnech was

25 Herren and Brown, *Christ in Celtic Christianity*, 273, note that in early Irish stories it was common for the souls of the dead to adopt the shape of birds. Though they do not apply that to Adomnán's 'heron story', it is a suggestive interpretation.

starting to 'break the bread of blessing in the refectory'.[26] As he did so he felt an overwhelming urge to pray for Columba 'even now in peril on the sea'. He immediately stopped what he was doing, left the table, and ran to the church.

Adomnán's third mention of the ninth hour is when he describes Columba speaking to fellow monks after None (II:38). In this story, Adomnán uses the term 'None' rather than the phrase 'ninth hour', indicating a liturgical event.

3. *Spirituality and the Ninth Hour.* Basil majors on Peter and John going to the Temple at the ninth hour, viewing this as Scripture setting a pattern for statutory ninth-hour prayer for all Christians.[27] Basil is anxious to have biblical validation for the emerging system of Canonical Hours, and Peter and John's actions serve that aim. In contrast, Cassian focusses on a deeper spirituality. He reflects on Christ's death and His descent into the Abyss as the Harrower of Hell. Death enabled Christ to penetrate Hades, reach the saints held captive there, and set them free:

> By the brightness of his splendour he extinguished the indescribable darkness of hell. Bursting its brazen gates and breaking the iron bars, he brought away with him to the skies the captive band of saints which was there shut up and detained in the darkness of inexorable hell. By taking away the fiery sword, restored to paradise its original inhabitants by his pious confession.[28]

This is how Cassian understands the mechanism of salvation. He sees it as Christ setting saints free from the darkness and doom of Satan's captivity. This interpretation was common across Christendom and was embraced by the Irish Church. The theme of Christ setting captives free was revisited in prayers offered during the night Canonical Hours, with the darkness of night likewise associated with Christ in hell. That intense drama coloured the spirituality of the Ninth Hour, and also the spirituality of the night-time prayers and vigils.

---

26 This breaking of bread was not the Eucharist, but a common meal which the monks shared.

27 Basil, *The Longer Rule*, Qu. 37; cf. Tertullian, *On Prayer*, XXIV.

28 Cassian, *Institutes*, III:3.

What the *Bangor Antiphonary* emphasises in its Ninth Hour liturgy is the visit of the angel to Cornelius (Item 20). The *Antiphonary* also presents the ninth hour as the moment when the penitent thief on the cross was offered mercy by Christ (Item 121). Surprisingly, its Ninth Hour collects do not focus on the actual moment of Christ's death. This took Warren by surprise, making him speculate that the 'divine wonders' (*divina miracula*) referred to in Item 30 (a Ninth Hour collect), may be prompted by thoughts of the extraordinary phenomena which occurred when Christ died: the veil of the Temple being rent in two; earthquakes; and the opening of tombs of the dead.[29] But this speculation is more indicative of Warren's bewilderment than of his academic convictions.[30]

Did Iona's Ninth Hour liturgy have an explicit reference to Christ's death and the harrowing of hell? We do not know. The likelihood is that Iona would reflect Bangor, and at Bangor the notion of release of captives from Satanic darkness belonged to the Midnight Office rather than to that of the Ninth Hour. We suspect this was the case across the early-medieval Irish Church. Iona's Ninth Hour liturgy would concentrate on Cornelius' vision. And it would be Iona's Midnight Office which deliberated on the harrowing of hell.

VESPERS

Benedict specified that Vespers was to be celebrated whilst there was still light in the sky.[31] Iona and Bangor would almost certainly do likewise. They assumed that Old Testament evening prayers took place before dark, hence Christian Vespers should take place before the evening candles were lit.[32] This made Vespers a late afternoon service, to be celebrated before daylight turned to darkness. However, because summer sunset in northern lands could be extremely late, the custom was for Vespers to remain a late-afternoon/early-evening service. This was the sequence of events in June 597 when Columba celebrated Vespers, and then had rest time before going to the church at midnight (III:23).

---

29 Warren, *The Antiphonary of Bangor: Part II*, 60.

30 cf. Warren, *The Antiphonary of Bangor: Part II*, 59.

31 Benedict, *The Rule*, XLI. In Benedictine monasteries Vespers was followed by a meal, followed by Compline, followed by sleep. Lamps were required for Compline. The monks then rose for night prayers at 2 a.m.

32 Warren, *The Antiphonary of Bangor: Part II*, xvif., admits uncertainty as to whether Vespers in Bangor was the last of the Day Hours or the first of the Night Hours. He notes that although the hour for Vespers was 6 p.m., it varied with daylight.

1. *Scripture and Vespers.* References to evening prayers include Psalm 141:2: 'May my prayer be set before you like incense; may the lifting up of my hands be like the evening sacrifice', which is still sung daily in Greek and Armenian Churches. Other Old Testament texts, read as precursors for Vespers, included 2 Chronicles 13:11: 'And they burn unto the Lord every morning and every evening burnt sacrifices and sweet incense.'[33] Cassian argues that these scriptures made evening prayer a perpetual obligation, not just an Old Testament practice.[34]

2. *Adomnán and Vespers.* Adomnán has three references to Vespers. The first concerns Cainnech coming to Iona on a day of crashing storms and high waves (I:4). Columba told the monks to prepare the Guest House and draw water to wash the feet of important visitors. His monks refused to believe that anyone could cross the Sound of Iona in such conditions. But Columba insisted, saying: 'There is one, a chosen saint, to whom the Almighty has granted calm in the midst of storm, so that he may reach us in time for Vespers.' As Columba prophesied, so it happened.

Adomnán's second Vespers reference concerns Columba outside the fort of King Bridei (I:37). Columba's prayers at Vespers were interrupted by hostile druids. Undaunted Columba continued the service, with his voice overwhelming the opposition:

> The saint was saying Vespers, as usual, with a few brethren, outside the king's fort, and some wizards came quite close to them, trying as best they could to make them stop: for they were afraid that the heathen people would hear the sound of God's praise from the brethren's mouths. Knowing this, St. Columba began to chant the forty-fourth psalm,[35] and at that moment his voice was miraculously lifted up in the air like some terrible thunder, so that the king and his people were filled with unbearable fear.

---

33 Exodus 30:1-8, 29:38f.; 2 Kings 16:15-16; I Chronicles 16:39-40; 2 Chronicles 2:4, 13:11. Etc.

34 Cassian, *Institutes*, III:3. Though the sacrifices themselves were temporary figurative offerings, Cassian held that Psalm 141:2 signified something permanent. Cassian argued that evening worship was practised by Christ at the Last Supper when He instituted the holy mysteries of the Church, and that evening worship was given its ultimate validation when Christ gave Himself on the cross at the time of the evening sacrifice. Christ's sacrifice was the true evening sacrifice, the sacrifice offered 'at the end of the ages'; cf. Woolfenden, *Daily Liturgical Prayer: Origins and Theology*, 52.

35 Psalm 45 (Vulgate 44).

The third Vespers reference is in Adomnán's account of Columba's final hours (III:23). During the day Columba busied himself copying the Scriptures, and by late afternoon he was working on Psalm 34 (Vulgate 33):

> When the saint had finished his verse at the bottom of the page, he went to the church for Vespers on the night before Sunday. As soon as it was over, he returned to his lodgings and rested on his bed, where at night instead of straw he had bare rock and a stone for his pillow.

3. *Spirituality and Vespers.* Basil and Cassian offer little on the spirituality of Vespers, apart from an emphasis on thanksgiving. In typical fashion, Cassian adds that, though the day's labour is finished, there should be no sleep as there is much prayer needing to be made.[36] Some Vesper liturgies focussed on Jesus' body being removed from the cross before sunset and before the start of the Jewish Sabbath. Consequently, Vespers could introduce reflection on Christ in the darkness of death. But Vespers' main emphasis was on asking for forgiveness of sins as the monks reflected on a day now ending.[37]

The *Bangor Antiphonary* is rich in Vesper material. It has two full cycles of Vesper prayers, though with little reference to Jesus' body being taken from the cross. Its concern is with sunset worship, and with celebrating God as Lord of Creation and Redemption. Item 31 is a typical Vesper collect, possibly alluding to the evening Psalm 141:2:

> Let our evening prayer ascend
> into the hearing of your divine majesty.
> And may your blessing descend, Lord, upon us,
> as we have placed our hope in you.[38]

Item 21 is another Vesper collect,

> At the time of evening we invoke you O Lord.
> Our prayer is always that you pardon our sins.[39]

---

36 Basil, *The Longer Rule*, Qu. 37. Cassian, *Institutes*, V:35.

37 Woolfenden, *Daily Liturgical Prayer: Origins and Theology*, 174.

38 *Bangor Antiphonary*, Item 31 (tr. Woolfenden, 273).

39 *Bangor Antiphonary*, Item 21 (tr. Woolfenden, 273).

The plea in Item 21 is for God to pardon sins as the day draws near its end. This parallels Basil's thoughts concerning close of day prayers, though Basil does not use the term Vespers:

> When the day's work is ended, thanksgiving should be offered for what has been granted us or for what we have done rightly therein and confession made of our omissions whether voluntary or involuntary, or of a secret fault, if we chance to have committed any in words or deeds, or in the heart itself; for by prayer we propitiate God for all our misdemeanours. The examination of our past actions is a great help toward not falling into like faults again; wherefore the Psalmist says: 'The things you say in your hearts, be sorry for them upon your beds.'[40]

There was a fear that if death came in the darkness of night, when demonic powers were intensely active, then any soul carrying unconfessed sins would be at enormous risk. The Iona liturgy would replicate this thinking. Whether it had a more explicit reference to Christ being laid in the tomb, is unknown.

After Terce, Sext, None, and Vespers, came the *nocturnal cursus*. At this point analysis of the Canonical Hours becomes more complex. Different terminology is used by different monasteries. Sometimes the same terminology refers to different realities. And within the confines of this chapter we cannot debate, far less solve, long-standing liturgical points of contention. But what we can do is to indicate the most probable situation for Iona.

Blaes suggests that the evening ritual of the primitive Church had three elements: the lighting of the lamps (*lucernarium*); the banquet of love (*convivium caritativum*); and the chanting of hymns and psalms (*euchologium*).[41] A Christian lighting of lamps ceremony is certainly referred to by third-century authors such as Tertullian and Cyprian; but by the sixth century the lamps ceremony may have lapsed in the West, along with the 'banquet of love', leaving only the *euchologium*,

40 Basil, *The Longer Rule*, Qu. 37.

41 Blaes, *The Canonical Hours: Their Origin, Symbolism and Purpose*, 17ff.

with its chanting of hymns and psalms.[42] Cassian alludes to an 'hour of the lamps' which he links with the Eleventh Hour.[43] This occurs in Cassian's discussion of Jesus' parable about hiring labourers for work in the vineyard (Matt. 20:1-6). The eleventh hour (5 p.m.) is almost at the close of the day, and Cassian's point is that labourers may be hired for kingdom work at any hour, no matter how late that may be. Several Church Fathers note that Jesus' parable of the labourers in the vineyard mentions specific hours for hiring: early morning, the sixth hour, the ninth hour, and even the eleventh hour when the evening lamps were being lit. For Cassian, each of these has liturgical significance.

Because the lighting of the lamps was associated with the coming of the Light of the World, some Western traditions sang the Magnificat at Vespers since the Magnificat was Mary's song of thanksgiving for the Light of the World dwelling in her womb. In contrast, in the East the Magnificat is the 'morning canticle *par excellence*'.[44] Adomnán has no clear reference to 'lighting the lamps', though Warren claims to detect it in Item 9 of the *Bangor Antiphonary*.[45]

All of the above raises the question: 'In early Irish monasteries, were there evening prayers after sunset, distinct from Vespers before sunset?' This is possible, though not certain. Some early Irish monasteries may have had some form of evening prayers after darkness fell, at least in the winter months when there were many hours before the Midnight Office. This possibility is strengthened by the *Bangor Antiphonary*'s mention of a First Nocturns service (*Ad Initium Noctis*).[46] However, though it may be tempting to equate Bangor's First Nocturn with Benedict's Compline,

---

42 Cyprian, *The Lord's Prayer*, XXXV. Tertullian, *Apology*, XXXIX:18: 'After the washing of hands and the lights, someone who is able is prompted to stand in the centre and sing to God a hymn from Sacred Scripture or one of his own composition.' Tertullian's *Apology* (c.197), is the earliest evidence for the 'agape' supper with its evening lamp ritual. Messenger, *The Medieval Latin Hymn*, 6, notes that Prudentius (d. 413) wrote hymns for the evening *lucernare.*

43 Cassian, *Institutes*, III:3; cf. Cyprian, *The Lord's Prayer*; Basil, *The Greater Monastic Rules*, Qu. 37, and *Apostolic Constitutions*, VIII:34.

44 Woolfenden, *Daily Liturgical Prayer: Origins and Theology*, 285.

45 Warren, *The Antiphonary of Bangor: Part II*, 45.

46 The *Bangor Antiphonary* lists the Hours in sequence from Item 17 to Item 24: Second Hour (*Ad Secundam*); Third Hour (*Ad Tertiam*); Sixth Hour (*Ad Sextam*); Ninth Hour (*Ad Nonam*); Vespers (*Ad Vespertinam*); First Nocturn (*Ad Initium Noctis*); Nocturns/Midnight (*Ad Nocturnam*); Towards-Morning (*Ad Matutinam*). This list is repeated in Items 27 to 39. All were distinct Canonical Hours rather than vigils. Stratman simplifies the terminology by naming *Ad Secundam* as Prime.

that may be too simple. That aside, the period before the Midnight Office was one of the few opportunities for real rest.

The term 'Compline' derives from the Latin *completorium*. Compline is connected with completing the working day, and was usually observed just before the monks lay down to sleep. Benedict's *Rule* mentions Compline by name, as do later monastic liturgies.[47] However, early-medieval Irish monasteries such as Bangor and Iona do not use the term Compline at all, even though later Irish texts such as the *Voyages of Saint Brendan* do. Here we note that although some scholars identify Bangor's First Nocturn with Compline, lying as it does between Vespers and the Midnight Office, it was not named as such. Moreover, as we discuss later in this chapter, we suspect that for Bangor and for Iona, First Nocturn may have been observed only at certain times of year.

THE MIDNIGHT OFFICE

Monastic night prayers (Nocturns) had an eschatological focus. Just as the virgins of Jesus' parable looked for the coming bridegroom (Matt. 25:1-13), so the Church looked for the coming Christ. There was a long-held belief that Christ's Second Coming would be during the watches of the night.[48] Middle-of-the-night prayers also fulfilled the scripture, 'At midnight I rise to give You thanks' (Ps. 119:62). Benedict recommended that monks should rise at the eighth hour of the night (2 a.m.) rather than at midnight itself, arguing that, by sleeping until a little past midnight, the brothers would rise with their food fully digested.[49] That was his practice from the first of November until Easter, months in which there were many hours of darkness after 2 a.m. in which to complete the night vigil. Rising at 2 a.m. also gave the monks more rest after Compline before the nocturnal disciplines were upon them. Here, as elsewhere, Benedict was aware

---

47 Benedict, *Rule*, VI. Morison, *St. Basil and his Rule: A Study in Early Monasticism*, 66f., interprets Basil, *The Longer Rule*, Qu. 37, as providing evidence for Compline, along with: Prime, Terce, Sext, None, Vespers (Compline), Nocturns and Lauds. Morison admits there is little evidence for the term 'Compline' before Benedict, even though Basil may have originated the office. Blaes, *The Canonical Hours: Their Origin, Symbolism and Purpose*, 48, suggests that Compline existed 100 years before Benedict, and that it was an accepted Canonical Hour in the East before recognition in the West.

48 Herren and Brown, *Christ in Celtic Christianity*, 264, point out that sculptured Irish crosses, albeit slightly later than Columba, display the final judgement on their east sides facing the rising sun, from which direction Christ was to reappear.

49 Benedict, *The Rule*, VIII.

of human limitations and applied common sense. Iona and Bangor may not have been so flexible, given Irish monasticism's reputation for uncompromising strictness.

Nocturns is a standard Canonical Hour in the *Bangor Antiphonary*'s list of recognised Hours in Items 17 to 24.[50] Its collects use the phrase *media nocte*, which may mean that Bangor's Nocturns were observed as near to actual midnight as possible. If so, this would make Bangor's Nocturns equivalent to Iona's Midnight Office, which is mentioned by Adomnán in his account of Columba's death (III:23). A night-vigil until dawn followed the Midnight Office.

Midnight brought the darkest hour. And darkness was a threatening reality. It spoke of Christ dead in the tomb. It symbolised the hopelessness of sinners bound in captivity by Satan. It signified uncertainty about the future. This made midnight prayers and the following night-vigil, a conscious stand against Satanic oppression. The menacing darkness, and the terrors of the night, prompted Cyprian to urge his people to deliberately pray at that hour in order to make a defiant statement, both to themselves and to Satan, that in Christ they were in fact always in the light. Darkness did not exist for them.[51] And yet, despite Cyprian's bold theology, the night brought real fear. It was vital to obey Christ's command to 'watch and pray', first given to the sleepy disciples in Gethsemane. It was important to do so, not only to succeed where they had failed, but to keep the believer alert and ready if Jesus returned in glory.

1. *Scripture and Midnight Prayer.* Midnight was when God passed over His people in Egypt, smiting the first-born male Egyptians, initiating the Exodus, and bringing liberation from bondage (Exod. 12:29). Midnight prayer was powerfully commanded in Psalm 119:62. Midnight was when the bridegroom arrived unexpectedly at the bridal chamber in Jesus' parable (Matt. 25:6). Midnight was also when Paul and Silas, whilst singing praise to God in prison in Philippi, were supernaturally set free (Acts 16:25). What link these biblical passages are: salvation, darkness, unexpected release by the mighty hand of

50 cf. Warren, *The Antiphonary of Bangor: Part II*, 47. Hughes, *Early Christian Ireland: Introduction to the Sources*, 93, suggests that the later practice at Tallaght was for two monks to stay in the church saying the psalms until joined by the others for the night office. This ensured perpetual praise during the night.

51 Cyprian, *The Lord's Prayer*, XXXIV.

God, and the sudden coming of the King. These were all part of the spirituality of the Midnight Office.

2. *Adomnán and the Midnight Office.* Adomnán's clearest reference to the Midnight Office is in his account of Columba's death (III:23). When the bell sounded at midnight, Columba hurried to the church ahead of the brothers in order to pray alone. In Adomnán's chronicle of that June evening he mentions no service between Vespers and the Midnight Office (such as First Nocturns, listed in the *Bangor Antiphonary*). Did Iona's Canonical Hours differ from Bangor's? Not necessarily. It may be that First Nocturns (in both monasteries) was only observed during the winter months with their many hours of darkness between Vespers and Midnight. In summer, First Nocturns may not have happened.

3. *Spirituality and Midnight Prayer.* Basil validates the Midnight Office as a God-appointed, Canonical Hour by citing Psalm 119:62, and by referring to the example of Paul and Silas.[52] He also writes to Gregory: 'What dawn is to some, midnight is to athletes of piety.'[53] These words are a reminder that sleepiness had no place in a monk's life. In another letter, Basil infers that night prayers morph into a vigil, which itself morphs into dawn prayers:

> Among us the people go at night to the house of prayer, and, in distress, affliction, and continual tears, making confession to God, at last rise from their prayers and begin to sing psalms. And now, divided into two parts, they sing antiphonally with one another, thus at once confirming their study of the Gospels, and at the same time producing for themselves a heedful temper and a heart free from distraction. Afterwards they again commit the prelude of the strain to one, and the rest take it up; and so after passing the night in various psalmody, praying at intervals as the day begins to dawn, all together, as with one voice and one heart, raise the psalm of confession [Ps. 51] to the Lord, each forming for himself his own expressions of penitence.[54]

52 Basil, *The Longer Rule*, Qu. 37.

53 Basil, *Letters*, 2: 'Let sleep be light and easily interrupted, as naturally happens after a light diet; it should be purposely broken by thoughts about great themes. To be overcome by heavy torpor, with limbs unstrung, so that a way is readily opened to wild fancies, is to be plunged in daily death. What dawn is to some, this midnight is to athletes of piety.'

54 Basil, *Letters*, 207.

The early-medieval Irish Church embraced these universal themes for the Midnight Office. It imitated Christ and the Apostles by praying at midnight. It made itself alert for the return of Christ at midnight. And it was well aware that midnight was when temptation was strongest.

But the dominant spiritual emphasis at midnight was liberation by the mighty hand of God. Hence, Item 10 of the *Bangor Antiphonary*, as a long middle-of-the-night hymn which is borrowed from the wider Church, begins by affirming God as the triune God of Father, Son and Holy Spirit who brings freedom to Israel by smiting all the first-born in Egypt. The hymn continues, 'We are the true Israel, rejoicing in you, O Lord', 'We laugh to scorn our malicious enemy'.[55] Just as God liberated historical Israel from Pharaoh and from the stygian darkness of captivity, so God liberates the 'true Israel' (the Church) from Satan.[56] Because of this, Satan can be scorned and mocked (not feared) because, like Pharaoh, he has lost his captives. This primary theme of liberation is reinforced later in the hymn when it celebrates Paul and Silas being set free at midnight from their prison cell in Philippi. Curran points out that these historical liberations spoke of a deeper spiritual liberation from darkness and the demonic which was available to the monks themselves. The *Bangor Antiphonary*'s Midnight Office also reminds monks that Paul and Silas experienced deliverance precisely because they prayed at that hour, even whilst bound in prison.[57] Hence, though God's people may feel bound, they too must pray at midnight in order to be delivered from spiritual captivity, and in order to praise Christ their God for ever.

Another Bangor collect for midnight, Item 57, states: 'At the middle of the night there is a cry; grant that we may prepare to meet the bridegroom.'[58] This references Jesus' parable about the coming bridegroom at the midnight hour, and reminds God's people to be

55 *Bangor Antiphonary*, Item 10; cf. Arthur Walpole, *Early Latin Hymns: With Introduction and Notes* (Cambridge: CUP, 1922), 209.

56 *Bangor Antiphonary*, Item 13:21, skilfully connects political liberation from physical slavery and the Christian's spiritual liberation in Patrick's mission: 'Setting prisoners free from the hold of two tyrants: ransoming slaves from the chains of men who held them in bondage; freeing from Satan's rule numberless souls that were his.' This dovetails with awareness of links between Israel's political liberation and the need to be freed from spiritual captivity to Satan, as very fully articulated in Items 76, 88.

57 Curran, *The Antiphonary of Bangor and the Early Irish Monastic Liturgy*, 182.

58 cf. *Bangor Antiphonary*, Items 23, 37, 57.

wakeful, since Christ may return suddenly.[59] But Jesus' return should bring joy, not fear. If midnight brings a surprise visitation, then, for the wise at least, it will be accompanied by deliverance, joy, and peace.[60] The *Bangor Antiphonary* also makes midnight the hour of Christ's birth and the hour of Peter's deliverance from prison, though in doing so it goes beyond the text of Scripture.[61] Nevertheless, these events of Christ's birth and Peter's deliverance coincide with core emphases of the Midnight Office. The midnight liturgy had strong spiritual meaning. Midnight was dark and fearful. But it was also the hour of liberation. Because of that reality Satan could be mocked, not feared. And the coming Christ could be welcomed with joy, not terror.

Midnight is viewed as the hour of many Exoduses. It was when Israel was released from bondage in Egypt. It was when Paul and Silas were delivered from prison. It will be the hour when Christ, the heavenly bridegroom, returns in glory.[62] This gave midnight a specific piety; and the core spiritual truth at its heart is redemption of God's people by God's mighty power.[63] The misery of bondage is replaced by the joy of deliverance. This meant that the monks awaited the dawn with hope. Its light would signal, not simply a new day, but the emancipation of God's people in the resurrection of Christ. The community was not to sleep. It was to keep vigil. It was to watch and pray. It was to remember that Christ lay dead in the tomb during the terrifying hours of darkness. It was to remember that Satan's triumph had seemed assured, and that his power had seemed unstoppable. Most of all, it was to remember that it had always been during the times of deepest darkness that God stretched His mighty hand to set His people free. This piety was wedded to Columba and Iona's core theology of liberation from the power of Satan.

THE NIGHT-VIGIL

The night-vigil was not a Canonical Hour. Nevertheless, it was an important spiritual exercise. Jerome writes that because men and

59 Blaes, *The Canonical Hours: Their Origin, Symbolism and Purpose*, 11.

60 Curran, *The Antiphonary of Bangor and the Early Irish Monastic Liturgy*, 180.

61 *Bangor Antiphonary*, Items 37, 23.

62 cf. the long hymn of the *Bangor Antiphonary*, Item 10.

63 Maclean, *The Law of the Lord's Day in the Celtic Church*, 3, notes that the *Cain Domnaig* states it was midnight when God created the elements. This resonated with the themes of liberation and resurrection, since, like creation, liberation and resurrection were only possible by God acting in sovereign power.

women of prayer were appointed as guardians and keepers of God's people, they should be able to say with the Psalmist: 'He who watches over Israel will neither slumber nor sleep' (Ps. 121:4).[64] Darkness and sleep were connected with sin and the power of Satan. As such, slumber was to be resisted and there should be continuous vigil from the close of the Midnight Office until the start of the pre-dawn Office. On very sacred occasions, such as during the transition from Saturday to Sunday, or on the eve of a Festal Day, the vigil was in church. At other times monks prayed in their own hut or chamber, imitating Jesus' solitary vigil in Gethsemane. There was a strong biblical and theological basis for night-vigils. It not only followed Jesus' example (Luke 6:12), but it imitated the angels who need no sleep and who praise God night and day.[65]

The hours after midnight were not for slumber, but for active watchfulness. Cassian, tireless in his disapproval of sleep, advises monks who feel drowsy to mix meditation with work during times of private vigil.[66] Desire for sleep was a real problem, and although Cassian believed that enough sleep had already been allowed for, he permitted abbots to make allowances for human weakness.[67] The night-vigil was especially long and demanding in winter, and even Cassian conceded that monks needed more rest after its completion. Benedict's *Rule* was more accommodating.

Whenever the formal night-vigil was held in church, the Midnight Office led into it. The night-vigil itself led into the pre-dawn Office of *Ad Matutinam*, though some *Rules* had a brief pause between the two.[68] Were there vigils every night on Iona? Were there night-vigils

---

64 Jerome, *Letter to Riparius*, CIX:3. Columbanus, *Regula Monachorum*, VII, insists on an all-night rendering of psalmody, 'sniffing' at Catholics who only had a *pensum* of twelve night psalms.

65 Basil, *The Shorter Rule*, Qu. 75, praises whoever wakened the brothers for prayer; cf. Woolfenden, *Daily Liturgical Prayer: Origins and Theology*, 286: 'The whole night part of the ancient office seems to have been a vigil before dawn for which the recitation of the Psalter in course was particularly appropriate.'

66 Cassian, *Institutes*, II:13f., gives reasons why monks should not sleep after the night service. The danger of sinful dreams. The risk of cultivating laziness. A duty to glorify God at all times. The risk of losing a sanctification previously gained.

67 Cassian, *Institutes*, III:4.

68 Basil, *The Longer Rule*, Qu. 37: 'We must anticipate the dawn by prayer, so that the day may not find us in slumber and in bed.' This may imply that the monks retired for bed after the midnight office. The general trend was less and less sleep.

only on special occasions? Were individual monks expected to observe a private vigil in their own quarters every night? Some monks may not have had the physical stamina to observe every requirement without flagging: but Columba was regarded as the ideal monk, and one of the reasons he is praised in Beccán's poem *Fo Reir Choluimb*, is because, like Christ Himself, he had the reputation of being able to maintain spiritual devotions all through the hours of darkness.[69]

TOWARDS-MORNING

In the *Bangor Antiphonary* the pre-dawn Office has the Latin title, *Ad Matutinam*, which we render as 'Towards-Morning'. This is a cumbersome translation, and designating it Matins would be much simpler, but the term 'Matins' has a range of meanings which vary across Church traditions. Some communities use 'Matins' as a catch-all for all prayers after midnight, including: midnight prayers, the night-vigil, pre-dawn prayers, and sunrise prayers.[70] The *Old Irish Life* terms the midnight prayers when Columba died as 'Matins',[71] whereas other communities use 'Matins' only to describe prayers immediately before dawn. Benedict did not use the term at all and named Lauds as the first Canonical Hour of a new day. This confusion of terminology is why we prefer to translate *Ad Matutinam* as 'Towards Morning', since, at Bangor (and probably on Iona), *Ad Matutinam* led to first light. The word *Ad* is capable of a range of translations including: 'to', 'near to', 'at', and 'towards'. Our choice is the latter.

Bradshaw suggests that in the Celtic Churches, *Ad Matutinam* was not a genuine morning office but a vigil.[72] Conversely, our conviction is that the night-vigil was distinct from the office of Towards-Morning, with Towards-Morning the last and the longest of the night hours at Bangor, ending with the three psalms: 148, 149 and 150. These three psalms became the basis of Lauds, which was to develop as a distinct

69 Beccán, *Fo Reir Choluimb*, 19.

70 Blaes, *The Canonical Hours: Their Origin, Symbolism and Purpose*, 11ff., defines Matins as prayers from midnight onwards, arguing that originally the night-vigil was predominant, and Matins was only a part of the vigil, with the latter part of the vigil said at dawn becoming the office of Lauds, when the dawn brought back light, hope, and joy to the world. Taft, *The Liturgy of the Hours in East and West*, 191ff., has an extensive and helpful discussion on Nocturns, Matins, and Prime.

71 *Old Irish Life* (Skene, *Celtic Scotland*, vol. II, 507).

72 Bradshaw, *Daily Prayer in the Early Church*, 134.

sunrise service.[73] However, there is fierce debate among liturgists concerning the development of Lauds. It is agreed that Psalms 148, 149 and 150 were originally part of Matins, and because these psalms emphasise 'praising God' or 'lauding God' they were known as the 'lauds section' of Matins. Hence, when the same three psalms were made the basis of an additional and distinct act of worship, it was given the title 'Lauds'. But, Towards-Morning and Lauds were not always distinct, and the *Bangor Antiphonary* reflects the older practice of no distinct Lauds, and with the three critical psalms – 148, 149 and 150 – still part of *Ad Matutinam*. We assume that Columba's Iona followed Bangor in this.

1. *Scripture and Morning Prayer.* Pre-dawn prayers were rooted in biblical references: 'I rise before dawn and cry for help' (Ps. 119:147); 'Very early in the morning, while it was still dark, Jesus got up, left the house and went off to a solitary place, where he prayed' (Mark 1:35). Approaching dawn meant more than the coming light of a new day. Just as release from captivity by the mighty hand of God was at the heart of the Midnight Office, so Towards-Morning moved towards the ultimate outcome of that deliverance, with its liturgy featuring the triumph of the risen Christ and the loosening of the bonds of death and hell. This made Towards-Morning an appropriate time at which to chant Moses' Song of Triumph, in celebration of the Exodus.[74]

2. *Adomnán and Morning Prayer.* Adomnán does not use the term Matins, but he does mention 'morning hymns' in his account of Columba's death:

> After the departure of the saint's soul, the morning hymns (*hymnis matutinalibus*) were sung, and his sacred body was carried from the church to his lodging (III:23).[75]

The Iona monks stayed beside Columba's body from midnight until morning. Sunrise on Iona was around 2 a.m. that night, with

---

73 Warren, *The Antiphonary of Bangor: Part II*, vii.

74 cf. Warren, *The Antiphonary of Bangor: Part II*, 35. Dawn also had a dark side, brought out in the later Irish document *Cain Domnaig*, associating dawn with Peter's denial of Christ, and Christ being beaten in the house of Caiaphas (cf. Maclean, *The Law of the Lord's Day in the Celtic Church*, 3).

75 Anderson and Anderson, *Adomnán's Life of Columba*, 230, footnote 257, link this with Bangor's *Ad Matutinum*, the longest of the nocturnal offices.

daylight earlier. Columba's body, having lain in church through the brief darkness, was carried by the monks into a new dawn. Curran suggests this may prove that Iona only observed one Canonical Hour after midnight (*Ad Matutinam*) with no intermediate Office at 3 a.m. as suggested by others, including Warren.[76] Curran's conclusion may be correct, but an argument based on the conditions in June, with its brief darkness, is weak. Warren concedes that at Bangor the Towards-Morning service was moveable and always timed to approach daybreak, though he is reluctant to abandon his theory of a fixed service at 3 a.m.[77]

3. *Spirituality and Morning Prayer.* Basil writes that a believer should already be at prayer when dawn broke, so that 'the day may not find us in slumber and in bed'.[78] Wakefulness would ensure that the first fruit of a believer's daily life was prayer to God. Cassian teaches similarly, quoting Abbot Tomas on the importance of morning prayer for all believers, and stressing that the first fruits of each day should be praise and prayer, rendered through the High Priest Jesus Christ.[79]

Towards-Morning was important at Bangor. Its prayers anticipated dawn and the coming of light.[80] Its collects mention: cockcrow, the expelling of darkness, and waiting for the morning light which 'liberates' the soul from sleep.[81] These themes confirm that *Ad Matutinam* started before sunrise and led up to dawn. *Ad Matutinam* was no cursory affair. In the *Bangor Antiphonary* it takes up more space than any other Office, and Curran sees it as consisting of two parts: extensive psalmody followed by extensive prayer.[82] The psalmody of Towards-Morning at Bangor included recitation of the final three psalms of the Psalter every day without fail, plus any other psalms

---

76 Curran, *The Antiphonary of Bangor and the Early Irish Monastic Liturgy*, 162.

77 Warren, *The Antiphonary of Bangor: Part II*, xxi, 60. Warren (63), commenting on Item 38 which is a Collect, *Ad Matutinam*, reckons that '*illuminator caliginum*' pointed to the dawn of day or about 3 a.m. He argued similarly concerning Item 58. But in midwinter 3 a.m. was nowhere near daybreak. In modern Pluscarden, Vigils (Matins) always begin at 4.45 a.m. whatever the month (Holmes, *Pluscarden Abbey*, 30).

78 Basil, *The Longer Rule*, Qu. 37.

79 Cassian, *Conferences*, XXI:26.

80 *Bangor Antiphonary*, Items 25, 26, 58.

81 Woolfenden, *Daily Liturgical Prayer: Origins and Theology*, 274; cf. *Bangor Antiphonary*, Item 58. Note that the soul is 'liberated' from sleep.

82 Curran, *The Antiphonary of Bangor and the Early Irish Monastic Liturgy*, 183ff. *Bangor Antiphonary* collects assigned to Towards-Morning include Items 38, 39, 58, 59, 60, 120, drawing on Psalms 4, 5, 45, 50, 62, 100, 112, 134, 143.

which the liturgy required. But the nearness of a new day also called for thoughtful reflection on serious issues. Obvious themes included creation and resurrection; equally important was preparing for the day ahead. Cassian makes much of Jesus' parable on hiring labourers for the vineyard, pointing out that early morning is when an employer hires his main body of workers.[83] For the monks, this associated dawn with being recommissioned by God daily. The start of each new day was a time of serious prayer. Accordingly, the liturgy included extensive guidance for whom and for what to pray, with each item headlined by a *versicle*, or rhyming stanza, introducing a series of collects covering a range of important topics.[84]

Because morning was when each monk was 'rehired', then prayer for the day ahead was essential. There was: prayer for our sins; prayer for the baptised (all Christian people); prayer for priests and for those consecrated to God in various ministries; prayer for the abbot; prayer for the brothers; prayer for fraternity; prayer for the peace of the people and for the peace of kings; prayer to the martyrs; and prayer for the penitents. All were important. Prayers for a monarch and people not only fulfilled a biblical command to intercede for nations and their rulers (cf. 1 Tim. 2:2), but, by daily naming a particular king, such prayers strengthened the legitimacy of his rule. If Columba prayed for Áedán, then Áedán was seen as the one approved by God. In this subtle way kingship was legitimised by the Church.

PRIME/AD SECUNDAM

It is likely that Iona observed at least seven Canonical Hours, and not just six. Our hypothesis is that Iona observed Prime (a daylight Office between Towards-Morning and Terce) with the term 'Prime' deriving either from it being celebrated at the First Hour, or from it being the first service occurring after dawn. At Bangor it was known as *Ad Secundam*.

Cassian gives his own explanation of how Prime became a Canonical Hour.[85] He describes how, although not originally part of the Divine

83 Cassian, *Institutes*, III:3.

84 *Bangor Antiphonary*, Items 40 to 56. Curran, *The Antiphonary of Bangor and the Early Irish Monastic Liturgy*, 89f. Versicles may have been a uniquely Irish contribution to Christian liturgy, reflecting indigenous bardic culture.

85 Cassian, *Institutes*, III:4.

Office, it was introduced at Bethlehem at the end of the fourth century, to fill a gap between Matins and Terce. According to Cassian, some Bethlehem monks were scandalised by other brothers who were so exhausted by the long night-vigil that they went to bed after Matins and missed Terce completely! To thwart this, the new service of Prime was introduced. Cassian approves of this. It made the number of Canonical Hours a perfect seven. And it halted the nonsense of too much sleep! Though Cassian's account is debated by liturgical scholars it is, at the very least, a good story.[86]

1. *Bangor and Prime/Ad Secundam.* The *Bangor Antiphonary* has many references to *Ad Secundam*, and O'Neill argues persuasively that clues within the *Antiphonary*, combined with evidence from elsewhere, prove that *Ad Secundam* took place when daylight broke and at the same hour as occupied by Prime in other liturgies.[87] Warren and Curran concur: *Ad Secundam* is Prime.[88] Stratman, throughout his translation of the *Bangor Antiphonary*, simply replaces the title *Ad Secundam* with Prime.

2. *Adomnán and Prime/Ad Secundam.* Given Bangor's practice, it is reasonable to assume that Iona's was the same.[89] Nevertheless, direct evidence for the observation of Prime on Iona is thin, and any conviction that it was part of Columba's liturgy needs to be inferred from elsewhere. Adomnán gives one hint:

---

86 cf. Bradshaw, *Daily Prayer in the Early Church*, 106f.

87 O'Neill, 'Welsh *Anterth*, Old Irish *Anteirt*', *Eriu*, vol. 41, 5ff. O'Neill bases the identification of Prime with *Ad Secundam* on two arguments: (a) In the *Bangor Antiphonary*, the wording of the *Ad Secundam* liturgy, the choice of *Ad Secundam* Psalms, and the choice of *Ad Secundam* Anthems all fit in with daybreak worship, placing *Ad Secundam* after Towards-Morning and before Terce; (b) Though the *Voyages of Saint Brendan* received its present form in the early tenth century, its numerous references to the Divine Office (admittedly influenced by Benedictine practices) retain clues to earlier Irish monasticism, and, in the *Voyages* Brendan celebrates the first Hour of daytime by singing repeatedly, '*Et sit splendor Domini Dei nostri super nos*', an antiphon reserved in the *Bangor Antiphonary* for the observance of *Ad Secundam*, and to be sung at daybreak. This tallies with the Hour when the anthem was sung in *The Voyages*, i.e., after Matins and preceding Terce.

88 cf. Curran, *The Antiphonary of Bangor and the Early Irish Monastic Liturgy*, 58, and Warren, *The Antiphonary of Bangor: Part II*, 58. *Bangor Antiphonary*, Item 27 uses the phrase, '*hac hora prima diei*' in connection with *Ad Secundam*. Curran, *The Antiphonary of Bangor and the Early Irish Monastic Liturgy*, 162, suggests Prime was when night turned to day.

89 Curran, *The Antiphonary of Bangor and the Early Irish Monastic Liturgy*, 162, concludes that Iona's Hours were: Prime, Terce, Sext, None, Vespers, Midnight, and Matins (*Ad Matutinam*), the latter consisting, 'at least in summer', simply of the morning psalms without any vigil.

> Once, while St. Columba was living in Iona, he called to him in the first hour of the day (*prima diei hora*) one of the brethren, Lugaid, named in Irish 'the strong', and said to him: 'Make ready at once for a speedy voyage to Ireland' (II:5).

In this extract, Adomnán may be using 'first hour' as a time-of-day marker (cf. 'tenth hour' in II:42). Yet, given that a Canonical Hour was observed in Bangor at that hour of the day, there seems to be a liturgical allusion.[90] Adomnán may be implying that Columba's conversation with Lugaid took place after Prime/*Ad Secundam* had been completed. Alternatively, the first hour of the day, between 6 a.m. and 7 a.m., may have been the first opportunity to talk to Lugaid after the night-vigil and after *Ad Matutinam* prayers.

Was Prime/*Ad Secundam* observed all year? Did it only take place in summer when there were several hours between sunrise and Terce at 9 a.m.? Did it lapse in winter when dawn broke close to Terce? And, if seasonality affected which Hours were observed at the start of the day, did seasonality also affect the Hours at its close? Was First Nocturns observed in winter but omitted in summer? Was Prime/*Ad Secundam* observed in summer, and First Nocturns in winter? Were there dates on which the community switched from an extra service in the morning to one in the evening, and vice versa? That arrangement would ensure that exactly seven Canonical Hours were observed each day all year. Hence, did Bangor have eight daily Canonical Hours as the *Bangor Antiphonary* indicates on first reading, or did it have only seven, with the seventh moveable? More research is required on this.

3. *Spirituality and Prime/Ad Secundam.* The spiritual themes of Prime/*Ad Secundam* prayers follow on from those of Towards-Morning, with God asked to protect the thoughts, words, and deeds of the monks through the coming day. Item 16 of the *Bangor Antiphonary* states:

---

90 O'Neill, 'Welsh Anterth, Old Irish Anteirt', *Eriu*, vol. 41, 4, suggests that 'antert' may mean 'ante-tert', i.e., an Hour before Terce. He notes that later Irish lists usually had six or eight Canonical Hours but acknowledged that evidence for Ireland during the early period is fragmentary. By the high Middle Ages, the norm was for eight Canonical Hours (Matins, Lauds, Prime, Terce, Sext, None, Vespers, Compline). But eight was not the original number of Canonical Hours.

> Protect us this day, O Lord, holy Father, almighty and eternal God, and in your compassion and mercy, help and guide us. Enlighten our hearts and keep our thoughts, words and works pleasing in your sight, that we may do your will and walk in the path of righteousness our whole life long.[91]

In later monastic traditions, Prime evolved into a service in which the community reflected on its traditions, founders, famous figures, and history. Also, whereas Cassian and Benedict expected the monks to go to work immediately after Prime, a custom developed in which the Superior took the monks aside to reflect on their Rule, read the Martyrology and Necrology of their monastery, and assigned duties for the day. Having meditated on the example of the saints who went before them, the monks set out on their daily tasks.

91 *Bangor Antiphonary*, Item 16 (Stratman).

CHAPTER 15

The Regular Liturgy

Adomnán has no reason to describe Iona's liturgy in detail. Similarly, the *Bangor Antiphonary* was written for liturgically informed monks. The absence of clear liturgical information in such documents make Warren and Curran wary about reconstructing early-medieval Irish monastic worship, and cautious about extrapolating from any hints which are provided.[1] But we do have some facts. We know that worship at the Canonical Hours always involved chant, prayer, and Scripture, though with no regular preaching on weekdays. We know that the Saturday and Sunday liturgies were more substantial.[2] We know that martyrologies were recited at appropriate festivals. Furthermore, Cassian and Benedict provide insights concerning their own systems, and, although Columba's pattern would not have replicated either *in toto*, these are starting-points.[3]

The psalms were chanted, with Cassian insisting that each verse should be evenly enunciated, and with no rushing or mumbling.[4] Each psalm was separated from the next psalm by a prayer. And the longer psalms were split into several sections with prayers between each unit. For Cassian, it was important that the mind was properly engaged, since 'the intelligence of the mind' was more important than the number of verses able to be squeezed into a service. Benedict had a similar approach.[5]

---

1 Warren, *The Antiphonary of Bangor: Part II*, xix. Curran, *The Antiphonary of Bangor and the Early Irish Monastic Liturgy*, 184. Woolfenden, *Daily Liturgical Prayer: Origins and Theology*, 275, notes similarities between the Bangor and Milanese forms of worship. Stratman, *The Antiphonary of Bangor and the Divine Offices of Bangor*, 79-133, presents a reconstruction of all of Bangor's daily services, based on evidence from within the *Antiphonary* allied to known common practice.

2 The East taught Scripture on Saturdays and Sundays; cf. Taft, *The Liturgy of the Hours in East and West*, 39.

3 Cassian, *Institutes*, II:4, and Benedict, *The Rule*, IX, XI, XVII, etc.

4 Cassian, *Institutes*, II:1.

5 Cassian, *Institutes*, II:11; cf. Benedict, *The Rule*, XVIII.

Vespers and Nocturns (Cassian)	
(The service starts with a Greeting and Versicle, which, though not mentioned by Cassian, were standard practice. The main body of the service is as follows)	
12 Psalms with Prayers	The final psalm concludes with all responding '*Alleluia!*' (*Institutes*, II:5). No other psalm has the response '*Alleluia*' unless so marked in the title (*Institutes*, II:11).
'Glory to the Father, to the Son, and to the Holy Spirit.'	Sung by the entire community at the conclusion of the psalmody section (*Institutes*, II:8).
Old Testament Reading New Testament Reading	On Sundays both readings are from the New Testament: one is from the Epistles or the Acts of the Apostles and the other is from the Gospels (*Institutes*, II:6).
(Followed by more prayers, a blessing, and the dismissal, which, though not mentioned by Cassian, were standard practice)	

Cassian also ruled that if the cantor went beyond what was scheduled to be sung, he should be stopped by the Senior clapping his hands and making all rise for prayer! Devotion was good. Going on too long was bad! Cassian favoured frequent short prayers, rather than long and wordy supplications.[6] Cassian's Terce, Sext, and None services were brief, with only three psalms rather than twelve. Cassian was convinced that the form of observance had been divinely appointed, twice emphasising that the pattern was a divine providence given by angels. It was not a human construction decided by men.[7] As such, it was to be an unalterable formula.

6 Cassian, *Institutes*, II:10; cf. Benedict, *The Rule*, XX: 'God regards our purity of heart and tears of compunction, not our many words. Prayer should therefore be short and pure, unless it is prolonged under the inspiration of divine grace. In community, however, prayer should always be brief.' Both Cassian and Benedict made provision for late-comers, with penalties only applied to those who arrived after the 'gathering-praise'; cf. Bradshaw, *Daily Prayer in the Early Church*, 143.

7 Cassian, *Institutes*, II:4, 6.

Terce, Sext, and None (Benedict)	
Greeting and Versicle	Benedict's *Rule*, XVIII, stipulates that each of the Day Hours should begin with 'God, come to my assistance'.
The Hymn for the Hour	(Psalm 69:2), followed by 'Glory to the Father', followed by the appropriate hymn.
3 Psalms with Prayers	Each psalm ends with everyone singing, 'Glory to the Father'. Prayer separates each psalm from the next one.
Scripture Reading	
(Followed by: 'Glory to the Father'; a Versicle; 'Lord have mercy'; and the Dismissal)	

Benedict knew that small gatherings of worshippers might struggle to sing everything. In light of this, he advised that the refrains after each psalm should only be sung if many were present. In general, Benedict's system reflected the practices of southern Gaul, rather than those of the East. These differences were noticed by Cassian when he moved to Marseille. For example, in southern Gaul everyone stood up after each psalm and everyone sang 'Glory to the Father', whereas in the East the congregation kept silent, with the leader alone offering prayers at that point. Moreover, in the East, 'Glory to the Father' was recited only once, at the close of the psalmody section.[8] Overall, Benedict's Vespers service was more elaborate than Cassian's, with an Ambrosian hymn, a Gospel Canticle, an extended Litany, and the Lord's Prayer.[9]

Because patterns of worship were broadly similar across Christendom, it comes as no surprise that Curran's reconstruction of the Bangor Day and Nightfall Services has an order similar to those of Cassian and Benedict.[10] There is high probability that the proceedings on Iona were the same as those at Bangor. The universal pattern was:

8 Cassian, *Institutes*, II:8.

9 Benedict, *The Rule*, XVII.

10 Curran, *The Antiphonary of Bangor and the Early Irish Monastic Liturgy*, 169ff. The Eucharist was more elaborate.

Bangor's Secunda, Terce, Sext, None *(Omitting opening and concluding sections)*
3 Psalms with Prayers
Collect
Prayers of Intercession

Bangor's Nightfall Service *(Omitting opening and concluding sections)*
12 Psalms with Prayers
Collect
Intercessions for Peace
Apostles' Creed
The Lord's Prayer

Bangor's Midnight Office *(Omitting opening and concluding sections)*
12 Psalms with Prayers
Hymn
Collect

Opening Verses

Psalms and Prayers

Scripture Readings

Prayers

Blessing

Dismissal

Specific liturgical elements, such as the Lord's Prayer and the Creed were recited at set Canonical Hours: sometimes at Vespers before darkness enveloped the monastery; sometimes at Nocturns; sometimes before a new day began.

Nearly all readings were taken from Scripture, but reconstructing the monastic lectionary for each Canonical Hour is a specialist study beyond the scope of our discussion. We also know that, for vigils, Benedict encouraged his monks to read commentaries on Scripture which had been written by reputable Church Fathers as well as reading Scripture itself.[11] The same may have taken place at Bangor and on Iona.

THE HYMNS

Hymns were sung, and in the story of the book-satchel which fell into a Leinster river, Adomnán writes that it contained a 'Book of the Week's Hymns' which had been copied by Columba's own hand (II:9). This was probably a collection of sacred songs designed to cover the weekly cycle of worship. In his narrative, Adomnán uses the Latin term *hymnus*, but what did he mean by that? Was *hymnus* a synonym for psalms?[12] Did

11 Benedict, *The Rule*, IX.

12 cf. Sharpe, *Adomnán of Iona: Life of Columba*, 322, note 231. Messenger, *The Medieval Latin Hymn*, 10, notes: 'The word *hymn* came to mean specifically a hymn of the Divine

hymnus include canticles, i.e. songs found within Scripture but outside the Psalter? Did *hymnus* include non-scriptural compositions, perhaps some composed by Columba himself?

There was a long-standing debate across Christendom as to whether sung items in Christian worship should be exclusively from the Psalter, or at least from Scripture. Tertullian, writing around 200, refers to believers singing hymns 'of their own composition' at evening worship.[13] Conversely, the Council of Laodicea (364) forbade 'private hymns', though Bishop Ambrose of Milan (d. 397) ignored that ruling and was not alone in doing so. Ambrose saw how the Arian heresy had been popularised by songs conveying Arian doctrine.[14] He was convinced that the orthodox faith should respond in kind and encouraged his congregations to sing hymns expressing orthodox doctrine. Like Hilary of Poitiers (d. 366) before him, Ambrose knew that hymns could be powerful propaganda tools, and his congregations in Milan were soon chanting the praises of the Trinity antiphonally. Ambrose also created a new type of hymn. Whereas previous compositions retained the Hebrew poetic style of rhythm and parallelism, Ambrose preferred rhyming stanzas. This may make him the true 'originator of the medieval Latin hymn with its uniform series of metrical stanzas adapted to congregational use'.[15]

The psalms debate rumbled on. Around the time Columba arrived on Iona, the Council of Braga (563) forbade the secular clergy from using hymns. The Braga ruling was ambiguous as it permitted non-scriptural hymns in a monastic setting, whilst forbidding them elsewhere! A few years later, the Council of Tours (576) permitted the secular clergy to use hymns, and this was encouraged by Pope Gregory I, who was enthusiastic about hymn-writing and hymn-singing. In 633 the Spanish Fourth Council of Toledo upheld the validity of hymns by Christian authors over against the argument that Church singing should be restricted to the psalms of the Old Testament.[16] One of the Toledo

---

Office, later associated with the Breviary. The word *hymnal* was applied to a cycle or collection of Office hymns.'

13 Tertullian, *Apology*, XXXIX:18.

14 Eusebius, *Church History*, VII:30, also noted this problem.

15 Messenger, *The Medieval Latin Hymn*, 2.

16 Messenger, *The Medieval Latin Hymn*, 13, cites the Fourth Council of Toledo, Canon 13: 'As with prayers, so also with hymns written for the praise of God, let no one of you disapprove of them but publish them abroad both in Gaul and Spain. Let those be punished with excommunication who have ventured to repudiate hymns.'

arguments was that if prose prayers can be 'new compositions' so can hymns, since all hymns are prayers.

In reality, such rulings had little impact on the Irish Church, and there is evidence that Gaulish and Irish monastic communities sang non-scriptural compositions in formal worship long before Councils gave official approval.[17] These hymns were commonly linked to annual festivals and the liturgical year. The authors were often anonymous, though names of famous hymn writers such as Prudentius, Hilary, or Ambrose were frequently attached to them. Thus Item 2 in the *Bangor Antiphonary* is described as a hymn by Hilary of Poitiers. Columba was also a hymn writer, and the *Amra* (VII) claims that Columba went 'with two songs' to heaven. Columba's compositions would have been used on Iona alongside time-honoured items.

Though the divinely inspired Psalter was central to worship, the *Bangor Antiphonary* included other items of sung praise. It is also the earliest manuscript from the Celtic Church which contains hymns, and, as such, is a key source for understanding early Irish liturgies. Apart from psalms, the *Bangor Antiphonary* has three main types of sung praise: non-Psalter scriptural songs (canticles); non-scriptural hymns; and songs commemorating Christian leaders. The liturgy on Iona would incorporate similar items.

CANTICLES

The *Bangor Antiphonary* includes three ancient Canticles. Columba would be familiar with all three of these, and all three would be sung on Iona.

Bangor Antiphonary *(Non-Psalter Scripture-Songs [Canticles])*		
Song of Moses	Deuteronomy 32:1-43 Exodus 15:1-19	*BA* 1 *BA* 5
Benediction of Zacharias	Luke 1:67-80	*BA* 4
Song of the Three Young Men	Daniel 3	*BA* 6

17 Benedictine foundations used hymns. Benedict may have adopted the *Old Hymnal* of the Gallican Rite; cf. Messenger, *The Medieval Latin Hymn*, 11.

1. *The Song of Moses.* The liberation of Israel from Egyptian captivity is a central feature of the hymns and prayers of the *Bangor Antiphonary.* The Exodus narrative, and its emphasis on deliverance from the powers of darkness, was a core paradigm in the theology of the early-medieval Irish Church. Significantly, the 'Song of Moses', celebrating this mighty act of God in redemption, is the very first Item of the *Bangor Antiphonary*, and colours all that follows. Warren reckons that it was sung at *Ad Matutinam*, especially on Saturdays and Sundays.[18]

2. *The Benediction of Zacharias.*[19] The *Benedictus* is Zacharias' song after the birth of his son, John the Baptist (Luke 1:67-80). This is Item 4 of the *Bangor Antiphonary*, but is also alluded to elsewhere in the document.

3. *The Song of the Three Young Men.* The *Benedicite* is taken from a lengthy section of Daniel chapter 3 which is found in the Greek Septuagint (LXX) text of the Old Testament but not in the Hebrew text. It was sung in Eastern and Benedictine liturgies, and also sung in the Irish Church as the *Bangor Antiphonary* indicates. The *Benedicite* is an extended paean of pure praise to God for the wonders of His works, and has remained popular through the centuries, even in traditions which reject the canonicity of the section of Daniel text from which it comes. As Shadrach, Meshach, and Abednego stand in the flames of Nebuchadnezzar's fiery furnace, they sing the *Benedicite*: 'Bless the Lord! All you works of the Lord; sing praise to him and exalt him forever.' For monks, this story of the three young men reaffirmed faith in a God who saves His people from the clutches of evil even when all seems lost. Just as remembrance of the Exodus event brought the theme of liberation into the heart of the *Antiphonary*, so also the setting free of the three young men from the fiery furnace highlighted God's mighty acts of deliverance. Because of this, it is frequently alluded to in the *Antiphonary*. The enduring popularity of the *Benedicite* within Irish spirituality is confirmed by the many references to it in the *Voyages of St. Brendan*.

---

18 Warren, *The Antiphonary of Bangor: Part II*, 35.

19 Warren, *The Antiphonary of Bangor: Part II*, 110, notes that this song, in various forms, occupies a prominent position in the *Bangor Antiphonary*, inferring that it formed a constituent part of the Celtic liturgy as it did of the Gallican and Mozarabic Liturgies where it was sung before the Gospel (Gallican) or before the Epistle (Mozarabic) on all Sundays and Saints' days.

NON-SCRIPTURAL HYMNS

As with the Canticles, Columba would know most of the *Bangor Antiphonary's* Non-Scriptural Hymns.

Bangor Antiphonary (*Non-Scriptural Hymns*)		
Hymn concerning Christ	Hilary of Poitiers	*BA* 2
Hymn of the Apostles	Irish (Columbanus?)	*BA* 3
Te Deum	Nicetas?	*BA* 7
Hymn when Priests take Communion	Anon. (Irish?)	*BA* 8
Hymn of Fire and Creator of Fire	Anon. (Irish?)	*BA* 9
Hymn for Midnight	Nicetas?	*BA* 10
Hymn in honour of Martyrs	Anon.	*BA* 11
Hymn for Matins on the Lord's Day	Anon. (Irish?)	*BA* 12

1. *Hilary's Hymn*. Item 2 is attributed to Hilary of Poitiers (d. 366). Like Ambrose, Hilary knew that the Arians used hymns to spread their teaching, and he responded by writing hymns on the deity of Christ. Item 2 is an early version of a Hilary hymn, combining a strong declaration of Christ's deity with an account of Jesus' life.[20] By the sixth century it was widely sung. We can be certain that Columba used it on Iona.

2. *Hymn of the Apostles* (*Precamur Patrem*) was probably post-Columba in date. Stancliffe suggests it was composed by Columbanus.[21] At the heart of the hymn is a celebration that because the Word was made flesh then eternal light floods the world and 'the old enemy [Satan] had to release the world from the bonds of death'.

---

20 Walpole, *Early Latin Hymns: With Introduction and Notes*, 1-15. Herren and Brown, *Christ in Celtic Christianity*, 138, argue oddly that because stanza 27 refers to Christ being 'raised by his Father's right hand' rather than by 'raising himself', this reflects Pelagian exegesis of the resurrection downplaying Christ's miraculous abilities. But Hilary was simply repeating standard NT phrases which speak of Christ being raised by the Father (Eph. 1:20 and Col. 2:12).

21 cf. Stancliffe, 'Venantius Fortunatus, Ireland, Jerome: the evidence of *Precamur Patrem*', *Peritia*, vol. 10, 91-7. The title *Precamur Patrem* was to suggest that the Apostles would have sung the same truths; cf. Howlett, *The Celtic Latin Tradition of Biblical Style*, 169ff. Herren and Brown, *Christ in Celtic Christianity*, 284ff., have extensive notes on the *Precamur Patrem*, and note the three stanzas (33-35) devoted to the harrowing of Hell and the rescue of the saints.

3. *Te Deum*. The author of the *Te Deum* (*We praise you, O God*) is unknown. It was once thought to be an Ambrosian hymn (based on Psalm 113), but the current favoured author is Nicetas (d. 414), Bishop of Remesiana in Dacia. The *Te Deum* was, and is, a standard liturgical item. It would be sung on Columba's Iona.

4. *Communion Hymn*. Item 8 is the ancient communion hymn, *Sancti Venite Christi Corpus Sumite* (Come holy ones, and take the body of Christ). This is found only in two manuscripts: the *Bangor Antiphonary* and the seventh or eighth-century *Leabhar Breac*. Walpole suggests that its absence of rhyme indicates a very early date, making it a well-established liturgical item in Irish monasteries.[22] It is highly probable that Columba used it on Iona.

5. *Hymn of Fire and Creator of Fire* (*Ignis Creator Igneus*) only appears in the *Bangor Antiphonary* and in one other manuscript. In Walpole's view this is a hymn of Irish origin, perhaps as early as the fifth or sixth century.[23] If it is early Irish, then Columba's liturgy on Iona would include it. It may have been sung at the lighting of the Paschal Candle, and Walpole favours that context rather than at a daily lighting of the lamps. The hymn includes a strong Exodus motif, with references to: the escape from Egypt, the pillar of fire by night, and the pillar of cloud by day. These familiar themes of Light and Exodus are complemented by the intriguing metaphor of the 'bee', in which the candle is fashioned from purified beeswax, and the bees represent the pure newly-baptised who have tasted the baptismal honey.

6. *Hymn for Midnight*. Warren attributes Item 10 to Ambrose. However, Nicetas may have been its author, as well as being the author of the *Te Deum*.[24] Item 10 is full of theological significance, not the least of which is the familiar link between the Exodus liberation of Israel, and Christ's liberation of His people through sacrifice. An emphasis on release from Satan's captivity is a consistent feature of Bangor spirituality, and is typical of Irish piety in general. Given this hymn's early date, it would be known to Columba and used on Iona.

7. *Hymn in honour of the Martyrs*. Few early Irish Christians were killed because of their faith. Nevertheless, the Irish Church followed

22 Walpole, *Early Latin Hymns: With Introduction and Notes*, 344ff.

23 Walpole, *Early Latin Hymns: With Introduction and Notes*, 346ff.

24 Warren, *The Antiphonary of Bangor: Part II*, 43, 47. Walpole, *Early Latin Hymns: With Introduction and Notes*, 205ff.

the practice of commemorating well-known Christian martyrs, and Item 11 is in this tradition. It is not well known, with Warren unaware of it outside the *Bangor Antiphonary*.[25] It may have originated in Gaul or Spain.

8. *Hymn for Matins on the Lord's Day*. Warren notes that Item 12, *Spirit of the Divine light of Glory*, is another hymn which is only found in the *Bangor Antiphonary*. In his view the irregularity of its metre points to Ireland as the place of composition.[26] Theologically, it draws heavily on the Nicene Creed. Because it is unique to the *Bangor Antiphonary*, dating is difficult, and we do not know if Columba knew of it. It may have been composed after his death.

SONGS COMMEMORATING CHRISTIAN LEADERS

Another group of songs are hymns in praise of heroes of the faith.[27] In the *Bangor Antiphonary* these include hymns dedicated to Patrick (Item 13), Comgall (Item 14), and Camulacus (Item 15). Patrick and Comgall are well known. Camulacus is less so, and he may have been a bishop ordained by Patrick. Whereas Items 13, 14 and 15 feature specific individuals, Item 129 commemorates many figures, especially the abbots of Bangor. Hymns or prayers recalling past soldiers of Christ and outstanding champions of the faith were a standard feature of monastic liturgies. It was a practice adopted by Columba himself, with Adomnán noting the mention of Martin of Tours in Iona's liturgy (III:12). Citing human leaders in the liturgy was regarded as a legitimate part of worship. Just as God is praised because He blesses His people with bountiful gifts, so God should be praised because He blesses His Church with special people. The *Old Irish Life* mentions Columba composing hymns which were eulogies of God's people.[28] In such songs the worship and thanksgiving are normally directed to God, though the saintly figure himself was sometimes the one addressed.

Iona and Bangor drew on common resources, and there would be broad overlap between the songs and hymns sung in Bangor and those sung on Iona. Scriptural songs, non-scriptural hymns, and songs commemorating Christian leaders, were all part of Columba's Iona liturgy.

---

25 Warren, *The Antiphonary of Bangor: Part II*, 48.

26 Warren, *The Antiphonary of Bangor: Part II*, 48.

27 *Bangor Antiphonary*, Items 13, 14, 15, 129.

28 *Old Irish Life* (Skene, *Celtic Scotland*, vol. II, 490).

THE PSALMS

The northerly monasteries of Iona and Bangor experienced huge fluctuations in the times of sunrise and sunset over the course of a year. This affected not only when certain services could begin or finish, but how long services could last. In high summer, with few hours between sunset and sunrise, no night service could be too lengthy. In deep midwinter, the night services could be prolonged. All of this affected the number of psalms to be recited. Warren tabulates this for Bangor:[29]

Canonical Hour		**Number of Psalms**
Ad Secundam	First Hour (Prime)	3
Ad Tertiam	Third Hour (Terce)	3
Ad Sextam	Sixth Hour (Sext)	3
Ad Nonam	Ninth Hour (None)	3
Ad Vespertinam	Vespers	12
Ad Initium Noctis	First Nocturn	12
Ad Medium Noctis	Midnight	12
Ad Matutinam	Towards-Morning	24 to 36 (Mon-Fri) 36 to 75 (Sat/Sun)

This Bangor list tallies with what Cassian specifies for eastern monasteries. Cassian wrote that Terce, Sext, and None all close with three psalms and prayers.[30] Cassian also fixed the number of psalms for Vespers and Nocturns at twelve.[31] The Bangor list also tallies with Columbanus' brief description of his liturgical practices, which is to be expected since Columbanus was a product of Bangor, albeit a century before the *Antiphonary* was written. For Columbanus, the psalms of the

29 Warren, *The Antiphonary of Bangor: Part II*, xvi.

30 Cassian, *Institutes*, III:3; cf. Columbanus, *Regula Monachorum*, VII.

31 Cassian, *Institutes*, II:4: 'The number of Psalms is fixed at twelve both at Vespers and at the office of Nocturns, in such a way that at the close two lessons follow, one from the Old and the other from the New Testament.' Cassian argued this arrangement was given by angelic revelation and unalterable. In *Institutes*, II:5, he indicates that prayers separate each Psalm from the next one. In *Institutes*, II:6, he writes that on Saturday and Sunday both lessons are from the New Testament, one from the Epistles or Acts, and one from the Gospel. Benedict had similar practices: cf. Benedict, *The Rule*, VIII, IX.

night hours were grouped in units (*chora*), with the first two psalms of each unit recited without any antiphon (such as 'Glory to the Father'), but with the third psalm followed by an antiphon.[32] Taft points out that Columbanus, in his *Regula Coenobialis*, indicates that after each psalm the monks knelt and prayed. At Eastertide Columbanus' monks also bowed, and said privately three times, 'O God, come to my assistance; O Lord, make haste to help me' (Ps. 69:2).[33]

Only three psalms were sung at daylight services such as Terce, Sext, and None, ensuring these were easy to observe if a monk were in the field or on a journey. However, from Vespers through to Midnight Prayer the services had twelve psalms, and Warren sees this (including the prolonged night-vigil merging into *Ad Matutinam*) as deriving from an Eastern influence. The *Ad Matutinam* service had a hugely variable number of psalms, and many of these – though nominally assigned to the *Ad Matutinam* Canonical Hour – were probably recited as part of the solemn night-vigil held from the Midnight Office to dawn. The next table has more detail.[34]

Ad Matutinam *(Saturday and Sunday)*	
Nov 1st – March 25th	25 anthems and 75 psalms each night
March 25th – June 24th	Weekly reduction of 1 anthem and 3 psalms as nights shorten
Midsummer Night	12 anthems and 36 psalms
June 24th – Nov 1st	Weekly increase by 1 anthem and 3 psalms as nights lengthen

The long dark nights were from the first of November to the twenty-fifth of March, one hundred and forty-five in all. The midpoint was the twelfth of January, traditionally associated with the Celtic New Year. During this period the entire Psalter of one hundred and fifty psalms was sung as a combined Saturday and Sunday liturgy each week. Seventy-five psalms were sung before dawn on Saturday. The other seventy-five psalms were sung before dawn on Sunday. One

32 Taft, *The Liturgy of the Hours in East and West*, 114. In this context antiphons, or anthems, can be any sung refrain.

33 Taft, *The Liturgy of the Hours in East and West*, 114.

34 cf. Columbanus, *Regula Monachorum*, VII.

anthem was sung after every three psalms. Singing the entire Psalter was regarded as an important spiritual exercise.

How long would Columba and his monks take to sing seventy-five psalms and twenty-five anthems, plus prayers? Columba would not rush worship, and McNamara and Sheehy suggest that the psalms were recited so slowly that monks had time to reflect on the marginal glosses whilst doing so.[35] The length of time needed to sing half the Psalter, including pauses, repetitions, and responses, could easily extend up to seven hours or more. This would fit in with Saturdays and Sundays having a continuous vigil from the close of Midnight Prayers through to sunrise. It also explains why, in some traditions, the term 'Matins' became a catch-all title for the entire night-vigil of prayers and psalms from midnight through to dawn. All of the hours of darkness following the Midnight Office were needed.

Similar principles governed the Monday to Friday services, although we have less evidence for there being a graduated increase or decrease in the number of items. All we definitely know is the number of anthems and psalms allotted to the longest and shortest weekday nights.

Ad Matutinam *(Monday to Friday)*	
Longest nights	12 anthems and 36 psalms
Shortest nights	8 anthems and 24 psalms

Columba would follow the same system. Iona and Bangor had similar liturgical problems to solve. They would arrive at similar solutions. However, identifying the specific psalms sung at each Canonical Hour is more difficult.[36] Psalm 141 was always associated with Vespers. Psalms 148, 149, and 150 were always recited around dawn. Basil wanted Psalm 91 (Vulgate 90) to be recited at Sext and at night. Any further analysis is too detailed for our purposes.

---

35 McNamara and Sheehy, 'Psalter Text and Psalter Study in the Early Irish Church', *PRIA* (1973), 271.

36 Curran, *The Antiphonary of Bangor and the Early Irish Monastic Liturgy*, 169ff., offers structure and content for services at Bangor. Benedict gave clear instructions for his monasteries; cf. *The Rule*, IX. Though the *Voyages of St. Brendan*, XVII, give detailed information concerning which psalms were sung at the Canonical Hours, we cannot assume these applied in Columba's era. Woolfenden, *Daily Liturgical Prayer: Origins and Theology*, 204ff., has analysis of the content of the Roman and Benedictine Offices, and other traditions.

THE SINGING

Columba sang Vespers outside Bridei's fort. Adomnán sang psalms when he prayed for a favourable wind for ships bringing pine and oak to Iona. The monks sang as they carried Columba's body from the church. And the style of song was a chant, though not a Roman chant in either a Gregorian or an earlier form.[37] We know from Bede that the Roman style of singing came to England in 678, through the agencies of Abbot John from Rome, and Abbot Benedict Biscop of Wearmouth.[38] Use of the Roman style then spread, with Wilfrid, the hammer of the Irish Church, zealous in introducing it to the previously Columban monasteries of the north. But all of this was in the future when Columba was abbot of Iona. In his day, both Iona and Bangor had a song-form distinct from the church-style of subsequent centuries.

Just as Columba insisted on precise scholarship, he would insist on high standards in worship. He would never allow the psalms to be rushed even during the long, cold, dark winter nights.[39] As abbot he led the praise, and Adomnán claims that Columba's voice was so powerful that it not only drowned out druids who tried to disrupt Vesper worship, but could carry over the strait between Iona and Mull. It was clear and distinct 'more than a mile' away without Columba straining, a phenomenon which Adomnán attributes to the grace of the Holy Spirit and further proof of God anointing Columba's ministry (I:37). According to the *Old Irish Life* Columba's voice was not only strong but 'sweet and tuneful'. These attributes aided Columba as the leader of worship, especially since the entire service was sung, including the prayers.[40]

Adomnán refers to choir singing (I:37, III:12). In the sixth and seventh centuries, the sung-praise on Iona and at Bangor was responsorial rather than truly antiphonal. This was despite Bangor's liturgy

---

37 Warren, *The Liturgy and Ritual of the Celtic Church*, 125, 127. Warren argues that the Irish/Celtic form of singing was Eastern, introduced into Gaul by Cassian, and then to Ireland and Scotland.

38 Bede, *History*, IV:18.

39 Warren, *The Liturgy and Ritual of the Celtic Church*, 98, notes that the Lord's Prayer was an essential part of the Celtic Liturgy, with heavy penalties at Iona in the case of any mistake in its recitation; cf. Benedict, *Rule*, XLV: 'Should anyone make a mistake in a psalm, responsory, refrain or reading, he must make satisfaction there before all.'

40 Warren, *The Liturgy and Ritual of the Celtic Church*, 125; cf. *Old Irish Life* (Skene, *Celtic Scotland*, vol. II, 478).

being called an *Antiphonary*.[41] With typical brashness, Wilfrid claims credit for bringing the antiphonal style of singing to Britain.[42] Though Wilfrid's claim is egotistical, it does indicate that something new was introduced in the seventh century. In the early-medieval period there were four main ways in which to render praise: (a) *Individual*: one person sings the words and the community listen 'in the Egyptian manner'.[43] (b) *Communal*: the community recite the psalm together. (c) *Responsorial*: one person, or a small group, sing the bulk of the words and the community give a set response at given junctures, which might simply be 'Alleluia', or a verse, or part of a verse from the psalm itself.[44] (d) *Antiphonal*: the community splits into parts and the praise is sung antiphonally, with each part taking up the singing in a continuous relay. Responsorial and antiphonal singing are both categorised as 'call and response' anthemic styles, though the terminology can be elastic.[45]

Within a hundred years of Columba's death, antiphonal singing became the norm on Iona, with the hymn *Cantemus in Omni Die* (Let us sing every day), composed around 700, describing true antiphonal singing. The poem also signals increased devotion to the Virgin Mary a century after Columba; but its form of worship is what interests us here. *Cantemus in Omni Die* pictures monks chanting alternately from either side of the choir,

Let us sing every day, harmonising in turns,
Together proclaiming to God, a hymn worthy of holy Mary ...
... In two-fold chorus, from side to side, let us praise Mary
So that the voice strikes every ear, with alternating praise.[46]

---

41 Clancy and Markus, *Iona: The Earliest Poetry of a Celtic Monastery*, 177ff.

42 Eddius, *Life of Wilfrid*, 47: 'Did I not teach you to chant according to the practice of the early church, with two choirs singing alternately, but simultaneously for responsories and antiphons and doing the responses and chants together antiphonally? Did I not bring the monastic life into line with the Rule of St. Benedict never before introduced into these parts?'

43 Curran, *The Antiphonary of Bangor and the Early Irish Monastic Liturgy*, 167.

44 Bradshaw, *Daily Prayer in the Early Church*, 83.

45 Bradshaw, *Daily Prayer in the Early Church*, 90, agrees that 'antiphonal psalmody' did not always refer to the later Western practice of two choirs singing alternate verses of a psalm, but sometimes to an earlier responsorial form in which soloists still sang the verses while the refrain was repeated by two choirs in turn; cf. Woolfenden, *Daily Liturgical Prayer; Origins and Theology*, 280; Taft, *The Liturgy of the Hours in East and West*, 139; Basil, *Letters*, 207.

46 *Cantemus in Omni Die*, I and II.

The community harmonises in turns. There is a twofold chorus. It echoes from side to side. The sung worship strikes every ear with alternating praise. This is true antiphonal singing. First one side of the church, and then the other, takes up the song. However, although monastic chants became predominantly antiphonal, the earlier form was responsorial, and it was that responsorial form which Columba's monastery was familiar with. The same was true at Bangor. This is why the *Bangor Antiphonary*, despite its name and despite being written in the late seventh century, is regarded as reflecting an older form of worship rather than the newer antiphonal style. Many of the *Bangor Antiphonary*'s collects are set out for responsive chant, which is added evidence that the *Bangor Antiphonary* preserves an ancient form of worship, and one known to Comgall and Columba.

Warren is of the view that, by the close of the seventh century, the responsorial had given way almost everywhere to the antiphonal.[47] And yet there was opposition to such changes. And resistance was not confined to Irish monasteries. Even the more Romanised English Church only slowly adopted the form of chanting sung at St Peter's in Rome. However, even in Ireland the traditional style of worship became eclipsed by the Roman, and the antiphonal replaced the responsorial.

THE PRAYERS

Irish monastic liturgies had many short prayers which we term 'collects', and these were normally recited by the abbot.[48] During worship, each psalm, either on its own or as part of a group of psalms, had an assigned collect.[49] The phrase 'Saviour of the World who reigns' – which is often abbreviated in the *Bangor Antiphonary* to simply 'Who reigns' – closes many of the collects, and Warren and Curran see this as a feature peculiar to Irish and Gallican texts. Collects are important sources for monastic spirituality, and when collects appeal to Christ as 'Saviour of the World who reigns', this is not a casual nod to Christ's rule, but a real-life, existential appeal to Christ to protect His people. The Church needed protection from Satan the Old Enemy (*vetus inimicus*),[50] and

47 Warren, *The Antiphonary of Bangor: Part II*, 35.

48 Warren, *The Liturgy and Ritual of the Celtic Church*, 96. Curran, *The Antiphonary of Bangor and the Early Irish Monastic Liturgy*, 110.

49 Warren, *The Antiphonary of Bangor: Part II*, xix.

50 *Bangor Antiphonary*, Item 91.

it needed protection from a multitude of dangers in the same way as God's people needed defending from Pharaoh and his pursuing hosts at the Red Sea. Another repeated phrase in the collects is 'the blood which redeems'. This phrase is occasionally placed alongside references to baptism, making a spiritual connection between the waters of the Red Sea, the waters of Baptism, and salvation.[51]

What shines through the collects is the full-on orthodoxy of the Irish monastic tradition vis-à-vis the Trinity and the deity of Christ. In the *Bangor Antiphonary* six out of the eight collects which are available for use after singing the 'Song of Moses' are addressed to Christ; one is addressed to God the Father and one is indeterminate.[52] Curran sees this as indisputable proof that the *Bangor Antiphonary*, and the monastic tradition which produced it, had a high-Christology. It emphasised Christ as divine. It worshipped Him as Creator. It celebrated Him as the Word incarnate. It viewed Him as the Light sent by the Father into the world, as the King enthroned at the right hand of God, as the Judge who is to come, and as the Saviour.[53] This high-Christology is also evident in the seven collects for use after Item 6 (Song of the Three Young Men), all of which are addressed to Christ.[54] Warren argues that, even when a collect begins with the word God (*Deus*), that does not mean it is directed to God the Father. He gives three examples of collects which address God (*Deus*) but which are clearly directed to Christ.[55]

On Iona, as in Bangor, the prayers of the community honoured Christ as God. And if departed heroes of the faith were occasionally prayed to, they were never honoured as God in the way Christ was. Evidence from documents from Iona's own monastic family, such as the *Altus Prosator* and the *Amra Choluimb Chille*, reveal a robust Nicene understanding of the Trinity and of the person of Christ, which we discuss further in Chapter Seventeen. At the same time, Nicaea taught that Christ is 'truly man' as well as 'truly God'. This meant that the humanity of Christ was also important in prayer on Iona. It was the Christ of human flesh and

51 *Bangor Antiphonary*, Items 68, 76, 88, 94.

52 *Bangor Antiphonary*, Items 62, 68, 71, 76, 81, 88, 91, 94; cf. Warren, *The Antiphonary of Bangor: Part II*, xxi.

53 Curran, *The Antiphonary of Bangor and the Early Irish Monastic Liturgy*, 105. In Item 39, Christ is spoken of as He who IS salvation, hope, life in Himself. Curran notes this as characteristic of Spanish prayers.

54 *Bangor Antiphonary*, Items 63, 69, 72, 77, 82, 89, 92.

55 *Bangor Antiphonary*, Items 71, 72, 73; cf. Warren, *The Antiphonary of Bangor, Part II*, xxi.

blood to whom Columba appealed when he prayed for a young woman in a difficult childbirth. Adomnán records that Columba knelt down and prayed to Christ the 'Son of Man', saying, 'Now has our Lord Jesus, who was born of woman, shown favour on the poor girl, and brought timely help to deliver her from her difficulties' (II:40).

Any liturgy can become stale through repetition, and Basil notes this danger:

> Variety and diversity in the prayers and psalms recited at appointed hours are desirable for the reason that routine and boredom, somehow, often cause distraction in the soul; while by change and variety in the psalmody and prayers said at the stated hours it is refreshed in devotion and renewed in sobriety.[56]

Columba would work hard at keeping his monks focused intelligently on the words they chanted, and he may have insisted on silence before and after services to achieve this concentration. Cassian advised monks not to speak to one another before or after prayers, observing silence as they gathered and silence as they left.[57] Benedict thought similarly, writing that, after worship, 'all should leave in complete silence and with reverence for God, so that a brother who may wish to pray alone will not be disturbed by the insensitivity of another'.[58] We can assume that, apart from Clonmacnoise when Columba's arrival was greeted with noisy exuberance (I:3), quietness and decorum characterised the start and finish of each service of worship.

The cumulative effect of years of worship in which the Psalter was chanted and meditated upon, meant that the spirituality of the Psalms moulded the faith of the community. The Psalter's phrases, imagery, teaching, and portrayal of humanity before God, were driven deep into the souls of Columba and his fellow monks.

56 Basil, *The Longer Rule*, Qu. 37.

57 Cassian, *Institutes*, II:10, 15.

58 Benedict, *The Rule*, LII.

CHAPTER 16

The Eucharistic Mystery

Adomnán employs several phrases to describe the Eucharist: 'Most Holy mystery' (I:1); 'Sacred Ministry of the Eucharist' (I:40; II:1; III:11, 12.); 'Sacred Mysteries of the Eucharist' (III:12, 17); 'the Mass' (I:40; II:45; III:11, 17, 23.); 'Sacrificial Mystery' (II:1); 'Sacred Oblation' (III:12, 17). As has become common, Adomnán uses the term 'mystery' even though nowhere in the New Testament is it associated with the Lord's Supper as such. In the New Testament the great 'mystery' is God's grace itself: a grace which redeems sinners, breaks down the dividing-wall between Jew and Gentile, and incorporates believers into Christ as His holy bride (Rom. 16:25-27; 1 Cor. 2:1; 4:1; Eph. 1:8ff.; 3:1ff.; Col. 1:25-27; 2:2-15; 1 Tim. 3:9-16). Nevertheless, the term 'mystery' was attached at an early stage to the Eucharist.

Each monastery celebrated the Eucharist according to what it understood to be the common practice of Christendom. By the sixth century the relatively simple eucharistic celebrations of the early Church had become more elaborate, though the rudiments were the same. Dom Gregory Dix, in his epic work *The Shape of the Liturgy*, concludes that, for the first 800 years of the Christian Church, every tradition (Eastern, Western, Roman or Gallican) had the same basic structure.[1] Local variations existed. But the main elements were constant.[2]

Columba brought to Iona what he learned in Ireland. And the early-medieval Irish Church drew on Gallican influences and further afield. All developed from a very early liturgical model, the fullest description of which is given by Justin Martyr (d. 165). Around the year 150 Justin set out a defence of Christian faith in a work now known as *The First Apology of Justin Martyr*. In his *Apology* Justin explains to critics what Christians actually believed, and how Christians actually worshipped,

1 Dom Gregory Dix, *The Shape of the Liturgy*, 434-72.

2 Warren, *The Liturgy and Ritual of the Celtic Church*, 63ff.

aiming to demonstrate that Christians were harmless, sensible, rational people, and a danger to no one. As part of his defence, he outlines a Christian act of worship, describing a form of liturgy which was to characterise Christian worship for centuries to come.[3] Constancy of practice through succeeding generations means that Justin's liturgy has key elements which were discernible centuries later, both in the *Bangor Antiphonary* and in Adomnán's *Life of Columba*.

THE EUCHARISTIC LITURGY (JUSTIN MARTYR)	
	THE GATHERING
The Faithful assemble on Sunday	On Sunday all believers, from city and country, meet in one place. Local gatherings take place on other days.
	THE TEACHING
Readings from the Memoirs of the Apostles, and from the Prophets	'Memoirs' include NT *Epistles*, *Acts of the Apostles*, and *Gospels*. Readings continue 'as long as time permits', indicating that a large section of the service is devoted to them.
The President preaches	Justin uses the term 'President', not 'Bishop'. He emphasises that the Homily exhorts believers to imitate the moral lifestyle highlighted in the readings.
	THE PRAYERS
All stand and recite prayers together	Prayers are offered by the Congregation immediately after the Homily. This is common in subsequent liturgies.
The Kiss is exchanged	Catechumens and non-believers are dismissed immediately after the Homily. Only full believers can share a 'kiss of fellowship'.[4]

3 Justin Martyr, *First Apology of Justin Martyr*, 65-7.

4 cf. Tertullian, *On Prayer*, XVIII: 'Such as are fasting withhold the kiss of peace which is the seal of prayer ... [but] what prayer is complete if divorced from the "holy kiss"?' Tertullian connects the Kiss with affirming unity in Christ after corporate prayer. Taft, *The Liturgy of the Hours in East and West*, 333f., argues (against Dix), that dismissal was not restricted in the early centuries to eucharistic occasions but occurred at every service.

THE EUCHARISTIC LITURGY (JUSTIN MARTYR)	
THE RITE	
The Offertory: Bread, wine and water are laid before the President	These are prepared beforehand. Mixing wine with water was a well-established custom, and the practice of the early Irish Church (Adomnán, II:1). One interpretation was that the water represents humanity and the wine represents divinity; just as water mixed with wine can never be separated, so also, in Jesus, humanity can never again be separated from God.
The President prays and thanks God	This prayer would later be regarded as a 'blessing' of the bread and wine/water.
Consecration of the elements	The 'blessing' is followed by formal consecration. Justin notes that at the consecration the 'Prayer used by Christ himself' is employed. In the early Irish Church it was only a portion of 'blessed' bread which was selected for consecration.
Holy Communion distributed by the deacons	The whole congregation receives the consecrated elements. After the service the Deacons take the elements to those who are absent.
THE GIFTS	
The Gift Offering	The President is to use the gift offerings to help widows, orphans, the sick, the needy, the imprisoned, and strangers.

Justin aims are apologetic. He is anxious to describe a form of religious observance which will appear reasonable to any fair-minded person. He omits description of how the service opens and closes. He also omits references to hymn-singing (mentioned in other early sources), not because he thinks that hymn-singing might be offensive to a critic, but because he wants to focus on the misunderstood Eucharistic Rite which needed a clear explanation.

If Justin's outline is supplemented with standard opening and closing features, then it becomes almost indistinguishable from later liturgies. On the basis of Justin's model, we can outline a basic Eucharistic Rite which was common across traditions in East and West, and in Celtic

BASIC EUCHARISTIC RITE
Greeting & Response
Readings interspersed with Psalmody
Sermon
Exclusion of the Catechumens
The Intercessory Prayers of the Faithful
Kiss of Peace
Offertory
Eucharistic Prayer
The Fraction
Communion
Dismissal

as well as continental Churches. The accompanying table, setting out this basic Eucharistic Rite is a direct development from Justin Martyr's model. There is high probability that it represents the shape of a liturgy familiar to Columba on Iona.[5]

Tantalisingly, there is extant an early Gallican liturgy known as *The Eucharistic Rite of Germanus of Paris*, attributed to Germanus (d. 576) who laboured in northern Gaul in the sixth century.[6] Given the close ties between Ireland and Gaul, it is tempting to draw on Germanus' rite when discussing the Eucharist in the early-medieval Irish Church. The temptation is especially strong because *The Eucharistic Rite of Germanus of Paris* gives rich and detailed information concerning exactly which responses and canticles were sung at specific points of the service. Moreover, there are indications in the *Bangor Antiphonary* that the Bangor liturgy includes some of the responses and canticles listed in Germanus' Rite. This increases the temptation to fill gaps in our knowledge of early Irish liturgies with data from Paris.

If only it were so simple! If only we were sure of a one-to-one correspondence between Paris, Iona, and Bangor! But we need to be careful. We resist the temptation to extrapolate. Key to our caution is the uncertain provenance of Germanus' Rite. Hence, when searching for a model for a typical sixth-century Irish liturgy, our wisest course is to keep within the broad parameters indicated by Dom Gregory Dix as common across Christendom at the time. The basic Eucharistic Rite is our template for Columba's Iona, and Adomnán provides us

5 Dom Gregory Dix, *The Shape of the Liturgy*, 434f.

6 Germanus, *Expositio Antiquae Liturgiae Gallicanae*, in E. C. Ratcliff (ed.), *Expositio Antiquae Liturgiae Gallicanae* (London: Henry Bradshaw Society, vol. XCVIII, 1971).

with just enough clues to connect eucharistic observance on Iona with that broad outline.

THE PREPARATION

The first section of the liturgy concerns the Preparation. Was there fasting prior to the Eucharist? Was pre-Eucharist Confession mandatory? Could priests be disqualified by contamination? Was incense used?

1. *Fasting.* Warren finds no clear evidence of a formal pre-Eucharist fast in the Irish Church.[7] Nevertheless, if the Eucharist was normally taken at an early hour then that would occur before the night's fast was broken anyway. Complicating this, is the story of Columba stopping the monks from starting daily work and ordering them to celebrate the Eucharist to venerate Colman who had just died (III:12). Had the monks already taken a light breakfast, unaware of Columba's plans? If so, it did not bar them from the Eucharist. Adomnán notes that Columba was uncomfortable with having to act as celebrant on that occasion. Why the discomfort? Had Columba compromised himself by taking food before discovering that God intended him to celebrate the sacrament? Or was Columba out of sorts because of Colman's death?

2. *Confession.* There is no evidence of statutory Confession immediately prior to the sacrament. Nonetheless, it was forbidden to come to the Eucharist, either as priest or lay person, with serious unconfessed sin.[8] Any priest who concealed sin and administered the Eucharist was guilty of a grave evil. This happened when Columba was in Ireland visiting the small monastery of Trevet (I:40). The Trevet monks chose a priest to be the celebrant because he seemed to be deeply religious. During the Eucharist, Columba became aware that the priest was tainted, and Columba interrupted proceedings, declaring, 'Clean and unclean are now seen to be mixed up together: the clean ministry of the sacred offering is administered by the unclean man who at the same time hides in his heart the guilt of a great sin.' The priest had to confess his sin in front of everyone.

---

7 Warren, *The Liturgy and Ritual of the Celtic Church*, 146.

8 Warren, *The Liturgy and Ritual of the Celtic Church*, 147. In the *Stowe Missal* the Eucharistic Rite begins with a litany in which confession of sin is central, and in which the community calls on departed saints to intercede for them as the community approaches the sacred mystery.

3. *Non-contamination.* The Andersons suggest that in the early-medieval Irish Church the presence of a priest at a death could make him ritually unclean, preventing him from celebrating the Eucharist. In support of this they refer to the ninth-century *Tallaght Discourse.*[9] If this rule applied on Iona, then Columba would take great care to avoid contamination since the same rule required a bishop to reconsecrate parties after contamination, and Iona had no resident bishop. This raises questions about Columba dying in church when the whole community was present. His dead body was carried out of the church by the brothers (III:23). Was everyone contaminated by being there? Were only those who touched the body contaminated? Did lay-brothers carry the body? Did Columba's saintliness cancel any pollution? Or was the rule not observed on Iona?

4. *Incense.* Censing of church and altar probably took place. Was it reserved for the Eucharistic Rite? Was it part of every service? Morning and evening prayer in biblical times always involved incense, and monastic communities copied several Old Testament liturgical practices. The *Bangor Antiphonary* has no clear mention of incense, but omission in such a fragmentary text is not decisive. There was no need to state what everyone knew. Hunwicke observes that despite 'remotest Hibernia' being far from the sources of the myrrh and olibanum which were used as incense, many exotic substances did make their way to Britain and Ireland.[10] He cites evidence of olive oil from Tunisia and Cilicia being used at Tintagel, Cornwall, in the fifth and sixth centuries, and Ireland is only a few sea-miles more. Any available market stimulates supply. Hence, although textual evidence is thin, and although early Irish censers are lacking in the archaeological record, censing probably occurred on Iona.

THE EXCLUSIONS

Only believers could be present for the Eucharist. This meant that a dismissal took place before the full Eucharistic Rite commenced.

9 Anderson and Anderson, *Adomnán's Life of Columba*, 190, note 215, suggest that III:6 may reflect taboo surrounding a corpse; cf. E. J. Gwyn and W. J. Purton (eds), *The Monastery of Tallaght*, *PRIA*, vol. XXIX, Section C, no. 5 (Dublin: Hodges, Figgis & Co. 1911), 153: Canon 65: 'If he be present in the house at the death, it would not be allowable for him to perform the sacrifice until a bishop should consecrate him.'

10 Hunwicke, 'Kerry and Stowe Revisited', *PRIA* (2002), 1-19.

Non-believers, catechumens, and those at certain stages of penance, had to leave. This was fully consistent with early Church practice as described by Justin Martyr. Catechumens and non-believers were dismissed after the homily because only full believers could exchange the kiss of fellowship which preceded sharing the bread and wine.

Cassian and Finnian both stipulate exclusion from the Eucharist as a standard feature of penance. This was not just an exclusion from receiving the bread and wine. It was being barred from where the Eucharist took place. On Iona such proscriptions could last for many years, as in the case of a man from Connachta who made a long pilgrimage to Iona in an attempt to wipe out his sins (II:39). After confessing his faults to Columba he was sent to live for seven years in penance at Mag Luinge on Tiree before returning to Iona during Lent. Only then, at the Easter Festival, was he allowed to approach the altar and receive the sacrament. On the other hand, a penitent could receive the sacrament before penance was completed if he or she was at risk of death.

Did children take the sacrament? Warren thinks the Eucharist may have been administered symbolically to children immediately after their baptism, but admits that the evidence is ambiguous.[11] On this issue Adomnán offers little help. His few references to Columba baptising infants contain no hints that they were also given the Eucharist. Eastern Orthodox Christianity has always administered the sacrament to newly-baptised infants, but we cannot assume that the early-medieval Irish Church did things in exactly the same way, despite its roots in the Eastern tradition.

THE KISS

Monastic culture included giving and receiving a kiss as a sign of welcome, brotherliness, and belonging. It sealed the deep bonds of community, and in one letter Basil writes in bewilderment and

---

11 Warren, *The Liturgy and Ritual of the Celtic Church*, 136: 'There are traces of the once universal custom of administering the Eucharist to children after baptism in the Stowe Missal, where a formula of communion and several collects of thanksgiving after eucharistic reception are placed at the close of a Baptismal Office, the language of which implies that it was intended to be used in the case of infants as well as of adults.' Warren also refers to a twelfth-century Irish Order for Baptism which directs that newly-baptised infants shall be confirmed if a Bishop be present. Warren also cites the possible significance of Matthew 19:14, 'Let the little ones come to me', as a Communion Antiphon in the Stowe Missal, 6.

frustration to a lapsed monk: 'Remember how many mouths of saints you saluted with a kiss; how many holy bodies you embraced; how many held your hands as undefiled; how many servants of God, as though in worship, ran and clasped you by the knees'.[12] Basil cannot understand how someone who had belonged to such a close community could walk away from it. Within the community the kiss was important. It expressed peace. It expressed fellowship. It expressed union in Christ. And it occurred in liturgical and non-liturgical contexts.

1. *The Welcome Kiss.* Adomnán has several examples of the kiss at times of welcome and departure.[13] Fintan kissed Columb Crag before sailing to Iona (I:2). The monks of Clonmacnoise welcomed Columba with a kiss (I:3). The clumsy visitor who spilled Columba's ink-horn was rushing forward to kiss him (I:25). When pilgrims arrived unexpectedly one Lord's Day they were kissed in welcome (I:32). When Columba arrived at the Synod of Teltown under a disciplinary cloud, his friend Brendan welcomed him with a kiss (III:3), though Brendan was reprimanded by Synod officials for doing so. They reminded him that no excommunicated person should be welcomed with a kiss. But Columba's excommunication was soon revoked.

2. *The Liturgical Kiss.* All the foregoing are examples of the kiss outside a service of worship, although it might be argued that the kiss of welcome given to Columba at Clonmacnoise had a liturgical association since it was followed by hymn-singing and procession to church. Apart from that speculation, Adomnán has no instances where the kiss is connected with initiating a service of worship. Nor does Adomnán give instances of the kiss being given during worship. Nevertheless, there is little doubt that the kiss was exchanged on Iona during worship. In his *Life of Columba*, Adomnán focusses on portraying Columba's godliness, and is not discoursing on the Iona liturgy. What actually took place on Iona during worship can be inferred from the wider Celtic Church. For example, Gildas, the sixth-century historian and compiler of penitential codes, stipulates exclusion from communion *and* from the kiss of peace as the punishment for some offences in

---

12 Basil, *Letters*, 45.

13 cf. *Voyages of St. Brendan*, XII: 'The Abbot came forward and kissed Brendan and the brethren in turn, then each of the monks in procession did the same. Everyone gave everyone else the kiss of peace, the guests were led inside, and prayers were recited as they went, as is customary in monasteries in the East.'

the Welsh Church.[14] This dovetails with Adomnán's account of the Brendan incident at Teltown, when Brendan was reminded, in no uncertain terms, that excommunicants should not be welcomed with a kiss. The kiss of peace was a quasi-sacramental action. It was not to be extended to the excluded.

Warren argues that the *Bangor Antiphonary* assumes the kiss of peace during worship and interprets Item 34 accordingly. He further argues that examination of ancient Celtic formulae of benediction indicates that those with the word '*pax*' were connected with a physical bestowal of the kiss of peace. Warren sees the kiss of peace as rooted in the liturgies of the Eastern churches, echoing the 'universal custom of the first Christians, never to meet together for purposes of worship without the salutation of the kiss of peace'.[15] Warren reckons that in the eucharistic liturgy of the Celtic Church the kiss of peace was given *after* the prayer of consecration of the bread and wine, but *before* the communion of the people, though acknowledging problems with this sequence.[16] This would certainly differ from Justin Martyr's description in which the kiss occurs *before* and not *during* the eucharistic actions.[17] Gildas' comments, plus Warren's observations, make it likely that the kiss was part of the eucharistic liturgy on Iona. As a sign of fellowship, it may also have taken place at each of the Canonical Hours.[18]

THE OFFERTORY

The Offertory was not a donation of gifts or money, but an offering of bread and of wine to the priests in readiness for the Eucharist. The bread and wine were prepared earlier, then brought in procession to the altar following the prayers, readings, and dismissal of the catechumens. Germanus' *Rite* indicates that in Gaul the Offertory and Consecration took place just after the reading from the Gospel, and this matches

14 Warren, *The Liturgy and Ritual of the Celtic Church*, 102.

15 Warren, *The Antiphonary of Bangor, Part II*, 61.

16 Warren, *The Antiphonary of Bangor, Part II*, 61.

17 Justin Martyr, *First Apology*, 65; cf. Benedict, *The Rule*, LXIII. Justin's sequence was probably and primarily based on Matthew 5:23-24.

18 Benedict, *The Rule*, LIII: 'Once a guest has been announced, the superior and his brothers are to meet him with all the courtesy of love. First of all, they are to pray together and thus be united in peace, but prayer must always precede the kiss of peace because of the delusions of the devil.' Prayer helped discern if the guest was a true believer, and ensured the kiss was not carnal.

evidence from Adomnán's *Life of Columba*. In Adomnán's account of Columba celebrating the Eucharist on Hinba (III:17), the sacrament was preceded by a reading from the Gospels: 'Columba entered the church as usual on the Lord's Day after the Gospel had been read.' The normal practice was for the Gospel reading to take place outside the church or oratory if laity were present. It was listened to by everyone and might be followed by a homily. After these, the priestly party moved inside the church for the Consecration. This was the equivalent of later clergy moving behind the rood-screen for the Consecration. Sharpe speculates that, on the occasion in question, there was no sermon between the Gospel and the start of the Eucharistic Rite, with Columba moving into the privacy of the church for the Consecration immediately following the Gospel reading.[19]

1. *Water and Wine.* Mixing water and wine at the Eucharist was a long-established practice of the early Church and continued in the Irish Church.[20] Adomnán alludes to this in a story about the young Columba fetching water for the sacrament as part of his regular duties as a deacon (II:1). On that occasion the water was miraculously changed into wine because no wine was available through a bizarre oversight. But the water had not been fetched with the aim of it being changed miraculously into wine. That was unexpected. The water was required for the Eucharist anyway. In a regular Eucharist, the mixing of water and wine took place at the consecration of the elements. Around 1849 a small bronze spoon was found beneath St Martin's Cross on Iona.[21] Warren saw similarities between it and two bronze spoons from the early-Christian period found at Llanfair in Wales.[22] These spoons may have been used by the clergy to convey water to the chalice when it was mixed with wine for the eucharistic celebration. Alternatively, if the

---

19 Sharpe, *Adomnán of Iona*, 368, note 387; cf. Warren, *The Liturgy and Ritual of the Celtic Church*, 99.

20 Justin Martyr, *First Apology*, 65; cf. Clement of Alexandria, *The Instructor*, II:2: 'As wine is blended with water, so is the Spirit with man. And the one, the mixture of wine and water, nourishes to faith; while the other, the Spirit, conducts to immortality. And the mixture of both, of the water and of the Word, is called Eucharist, renowned and glorious grace; and they who by faith partake of it are sanctified both in body and soul.' It is more than likely that Justin and Clement had John 19:34 in mind.

21 J. Huband Smith, 'Iona', *UJA* (1853), 79-91.

22 Warren, *The Liturgy and Ritual of the Celtic Church*, 133, referring to: *Archaeologia Cambrensis*, Third Series, vol. XXXI, July 1862, 208-19; cf. Herren and Brown, *Christ in Celtic Christianity*, 187f.

laity did not drink directly from the chalice, they may have received the wine on a spoon.

2. *The Bread.* The bread was prepared with some ceremony long before the service began. This started with the grinding of the flour for the eucharistic bread, with the grinder using a special stone marked with a cross, an example of which has been found at Dunadd.[23] These stones were reserved for sacred purposes and were not used for grinding flour for normal bread. Ordinary bread used flour which was ground by ordinary stones. This newly baked bread was brought to the officiating priests during the Offertory section of the service. The whole of the offered bread was blessed by prayer, but only a portion of it – not all of it – was selected for the Eucharist.[24] The unselected portion of the blessed bread was called the *eulogium*, which was now viewed as 'blessed bread' and reserved for special usage after the service. The portion which was chosen for the Eucharist itself was taken from the sight of the laity and consecrated. As in the story of Columba and his fellow-abbots on Hinba, whenever a service took place away from the monastery, the officiating clergy moved into a chapel for the consecration, with the people remaining outside. These local chapels were small. Away from prying eyes, there was no need for a screen separating priests and laity.[25] And when going into an oratory for the sacred consecration, shoes or sandals were removed.[26]

THE RITE

For the Eucharist, the altar was covered with a purple cloth, and the monks wore white garments (III:12).[27] Columba's ceremonial robes are alluded to by Adomnán when he writes of placing Columba's books and vestments on the altar during a time of prayer (II:45). These may have been Columba's regular vestments which he wore during Canonical

23 Clarke (ed.), *Early Medieval Scotland*, 148.

24 Sharpe, *Adomnán of Iona: The Life of St. Columba*, 319, note 219. Ryan, 'The Mass in the Early Irish Church', *IQR* (1961), 372.

25 Hunwicke, 'Kerry and Stowe Revisited', *PRIA* (2002), 1: 'The Stowe Missal provides evidence for a liturgical culture in which the liturgical building was intended to house only the celebrant bishops and priests during the *Missa Fidelium*; the congregation, and probably the deacon, remaining outside except when (and if) they entered to receive the Lord's body and blood.'

26 cf. *Old Irish Life* (Skene, *Celtic Scotland*, vol. II, 500).

27 Warren, *The Liturgy and Ritual of the Celtic Church*, 124.

Hours, or they may have been his robes for the Eucharist. Altars were usually hard against the east wall of the church, with the priest facing the altar, his back to the congregation. In standing as the congregation stood, the priest signified that he stood with them.[28]

1. *The Diptychs.* Germanus' *Rite* refers to Diptychs between the Offertory and the Eucharistic Prayer. Physically, diptychs were two folding-boards which were hinged together, and which were decorated with icons or lists of names. There were two groups of names. Names of the living were on one board: names of the dead were on the other. Those named were commemorated in a section of the liturgy which also had the title Diptychs. Adomnán mentions Martin of Tours' name being chanted during a service (III:12), and Martin's name would be in the list of departed saints. The *Bangor Antiphonary* lists deceased *prominenti*, who would also be celebrated at this point of the service.

2. *The Fraction.* The 'Fraction' was the breaking of the bread. The late eighth-century *Stowe Missal* describes the bread being broken into a specific number of pieces, each with its own symbolic meaning, but whether that degree of symbolism was functioning in Columba's era is unknown. In some liturgies the Fraction was accompanied by singing the *Agnus Dei*.

3. *The Priests.* The officiating clergy took communion first, and the *Bangor Antiphonary* has important detail as to what happened at this sacred point of the Eucharist.[29] As the priests took bread and wine, they sang the hymn *Sancti Venite*, which is Item 8 of the *Bangor Antiphonary* and described as 'A Hymn when the Priests are Communicating'. The *Sancti Venite* was almost certainly part of eucharistic practice throughout the whole of the Irish Church and not just in Bangor. Significantly, the *Bangor Antiphonary*'s reference to the *Sancti Venite* homologates a tradition previously known only in a single source, the seventh or eighth-century *Leabhar Breac*. In its preface the *Leabhar Breac* has a legend about angels being heard chanting the *Sancti Venite* in the church of St Sechnall, and a note inserted by the author of the *Leabhar Breac* claims that singing the *Sancti Venite* was long-established in the liturgy. Nevertheless, prior to the discovery

28 Warren, *The Liturgy and Ritual of the Celtic Church*, 111.

29 O'Loughlin, *Celtic Theology*, 137. O'Loughlin notes Columbanus imposed a penalty of six slaps for those who damaged the chalice with their teeth, indicating that priests drank straight from the chalice.

of the *Bangor Antiphonary*, there was no corroborating evidence for this. The *Leabhar Breac* also hints that the *Sancti Venite* was sung whilst the people were communicating, and not just the priests. This contrasts with Warren's opinion that it was sung immediately *after* the prayer of consecration, during the communion of the clergy but *before* the communion of the people.[30] Of spiritual significance is the *Leabhar Breac*'s reference to the singing of angels. One of the aims of monasticism was to replicate on earth the worship rendered by the angels in heaven. What the story expresses is a belief that worship in heaven and worship on earth touch one another most closely during the taking of Holy Communion.

4. *The People.* The clergy moved outside to where the people were waiting. Communicants stood to receive the bread and wine, with kneeling a later innovation.[31] The men were bareheaded: the women veiled their faces. Warren highlights a regulation in the *Penitential of Cuminius* specifying 'women shall receive Holy Communion under a dark veil', and citing Basil as an authority.[32] This is bolstered by a ruling of the Council of Auxerre (575/585) to the effect that a head-covering should be worn by women.[33] If that were the norm throughout the Irish Church, then it would be so on Iona.

5. *Communion in Both Kinds.* Columba gave both bread and wine to laity and priesthood alike, as was standard practice in the early Church.[34] The withdrawal of the cup from the laity was a later feature of Latin Christianity. Warren cites a formula of administration at the close of the *Antiphonary* which he believes implies reception of the chalice.[35] Warren also compares the wording of the *Antiphonary* with the eleventh-century Irish *Drummond Missal* which assumes communion in both kinds.

---

30 Warren, *The Liturgy and Ritual of the Celtic Church*, 110f.

31 Dom Gregory Dix, *The Shape of the Liturgy*, 13: 'The practice of kneeling by anybody for communion is confined to the Latin West, and began to come in there only in the early Middle-Ages.'

32 Warren, *The Liturgy and Ritual of the Celtic Church*, 136; cf. *Penitential of Theodore*, VII:3: 'Women may receive the host under a black veil, as Basil decided', cited by McNeill and Gamer, *Medieval Handbooks of Penance*, 205. McNeill and Gamer (248) also refer to the *Confessional of Egbert*, Canon 37.

33 Council of Auxerre, Canon 42.

34 cf. Justin Martyr, *First Apology*, 67.

35 Warren, *The Antiphonary of Bangor: Part II*, 74, referring to Item 112; cf. Warren, *The Liturgy and Ritual of the Celtic Church*, 135.

THE EULOGIUM

The eucharistic bread was selected during the service, and its quantity would be chosen with a view to there being no leftovers. We do not know if unused eucharistic bread was retained as a Reserved Sacrament, but we can be certain that no consecrated bread would be disposed of carelessly. We also know that Columba respected the portion of the bread offered and blessed during the service but not selected for the Eucharist itself. This was the *eulogium*, and it was special in its own right.[36] It had been baked from flour ground with the special stone. It had been presented to the priests. It had been blessed (though not consecrated).[37] This 'blessed bread' could be eaten at the communal meal following the Eucharist, or it could be put aside for people in need. Adomnán gives examples of both scenarios.

Adomnán writes of an occasion at Cainnech's monastery at Aghaboe in Ireland, when the *eulogium* was divided on the refectory table and distributed as part of the communal meal of the day (II:13). This took place after None (3 p.m.) which raises an intriguing question. On a Sunday (which was the regular day for celebrating the Eucharist) the practice was for the main meal to be taken at 12 noon, and the main meal was only taken at 3 p.m. on working days. Does this mean that the Aghaboe incident took place on a weekday? If so, had there been a special Eucharist that day? Or had the *eulogium* been kept from the Sunday to be shared later in the week? Whatever the case, sharing the *eulogium* at the communal meal was a feature of Irish monasteries (II:4).[38]

Adomnán also records incidents in which 'blessed bread' was conveyed to needy people and seen as instrumental in easing their plight. Adomnán writes of boxes containing a 'blessing', with the 'blessing' being the 'blessed bread' itself. When Columba sent the monk Lugaid to help the holy virgin Mogain, who had broken her hip, he handed Lugaid a small pinewood box, saying, 'When you arrive to visit Mogain, the blessing contained in this box should be dipped in a jar of water, and then the water of blessing should be poured over her hip' (II:5). This was not the consecrated bread of the Eucharist, but the *eulogium*. Because it had been blessed in union with the bread

---

36 Anderson and Anderson, *Adomnán's Life of Columba*, 112, note 140.

37 Salt, as well as bread, could be blessed. Adomnán, *Life*, II:17.

38 cf. Bede, *Life of Cuthbert*, 31.

which was chosen to become the eucharistic bread, it was believed to be pervaded by a special holiness. The same idea is expressed in Adomnán's story of Columba sending the monk Silnan on a mercy journey (II:4). Columba said to him, 'Prepare to make a voyage tomorrow (if life continue and God will) after receiving from me bread that has been blessed with invocation of the name of God. When it is dipped in water, men and beasts sprinkled with that water will speedily recover health.' The next day Silnan received the bread from Columba's hands, but before he sailed off, Columba gave additional encouragement:

> Be confident my son, you will have favourable and prosperous winds, by day and night, until you arrive at the district that is called Ard Ceannachte, so that you may quickly cure the sick in that place, with the healing bread.[39]

Warren suggests that the *eulogium* concept came from the Middle East where, 'the custom was to bless a loaf at the conclusion of the Liturgy, which was then cut up into small pieces with a knife specially consecrated for that purpose, and distributed to the congregation, who came forward and received it at the priest's hands.'[40] Irish practice may well have evolved from this. When monks ministered to local Christian communities in villages out in the field, it would make sense to distribute the *eulogium* immediately after the service.

DAY AND TIME

Columba's regular practice was to celebrate the Eucharist on Sunday, the Lord's Day. When Adomnán describes Columba's last week, he writes that mass was celebrated 'as usual' on Sunday, indicating that Sunday Eucharist was the norm.[41] Warren sees no evidence for a daily Eucharist in the Celtic Church, concluding that it was only celebrated on Sundays, Saints' Days, feast days, and other special occasions as decided by the abbot.[42] One such time was when Columba became

---

39 Adomnán, *Life*, II:4 [Tr. Anderson and Anderson]; cf. Sharpe, *Adomnán of Iona: Life of St. Columba*, 324, note 239.

40 Warren, *The Liturgy and Ritual of the Celtic Church*, 139.

41 Adomnán, *Life*, III:23. Cassian, *Institutes*, III:11, states that on Sunday morning only one Office was celebrated before dinner and this involved the Eucharist. It was a long service, and Terce and Sext may have been included within it.

42 Warren, *The Liturgy and Ritual of the Celtic Church*, 140. The early Christian document *The Didache* states: 'On Sunday come together, break bread and return thanks after you

aware of the death of Colman of Leinster. He stopped his monks as they prepared to start their daily work and instructed them instead to prepare for the holy rite, which was to be followed by a special meal 'as on the Lord's Day' (III:12). The monks quickly put in place the normal preparations for the Eucharist. They went to church clothed in white 'as for a major feast'. After the Eucharist, they held the special communal meal. Because the day had become a eucharistic day, it was Sunday practice rather than normal weekday routine which was followed.[43]

In the primitive Church the Eucharist was originally celebrated in the evening but was moved to a morning observance in the following centuries.[44] The likelihood is that the regular weekly Lord's Day Eucharist on Iona was celebrated at an early hour. This would follow the general practice of Christendom, and it also meant that the night-fast need not be broken before communicating. An early hour was the rule in Irish-originated monasteries on the Continent, with threats of heavy penalties if not complied with.[45]

The time of day when special Eucharists took place is less certain. In his *Life of Columba*, Adomnán alludes to three special Eucharists, but with varying precision as to the hour they occurred. In his first example Adomnán is clear, writing that on the joint feast day for Columba and Baithéne (9 June), the commemorative mass was held at Sext which is mid-day (II:45). In a second example, the hour of the unexpected Eucharist to honour Bishop Colman is less certain (III:12). The monks were putting on their shoes before starting work when Columba informed them of the change of plan. But how early was that? Time was still needed for preparation, and although it could have taken

---

have confessed your sins, that your sacrifice may be clean.' Similarly, Justin Martyr only refers to the Lord's Supper on Sundays. Monasticism, in its search for spiritual intensity, increased the number of times a person communicated per week. Basil of Caesarea favoured four times plus saints' days (*Letters*, 93). Cassian, *Institutes*, III:2, wrote that desert monks communicated on both Saturdays and Sundays. Saturday Communion, in addition to Wednesday, Friday and Sunday, is also mentioned by Basil, *Letters*, 93. There is little trace of a Saturday Communion in the West. Extraordinarily, Herren and Brown, *Christ in Celtic Christianity*, 126f., 212, consider that the Eucharist was of minimal importance in the theology of the Common Celtic Church, largely basing this on early Irish texts not urging frequent communion. They miss the wood for the trees!

43 Sharpe, *Adomnán of Iona: Life of St. Columba*, 366, note 378; cf. Adomnán, *Life*, II:13.

44 Bradshaw, *Daily Prayer in the Early Church*, 41.

45 Warren, *The Liturgy and Ritual of the Celtic Church*, 142, referring to Strabo, *Life of St. Gall*, XXVI.

place at Terce (9 a.m.) it may have been as late as Sext (12 noon). In the third example of a special Eucharist, this time held to commemorate Brendan, Adomnán refers to rushed preparations, noting that it was early morning when Columba ordered Diarmait to get things ready (III:11).[46] But what does Adomnán mean by early morning? There are two possibilities. Brendan's Feast Day is 16 May when first light is ridiculously early, and that Eucharist could have taken place very early indeed. But there is also a tradition of commemorating Brendan on 29 November when first light on Iona is around 8 a.m., in which case the Eucharist could be celebrated no earlier than Terce and might have been held over until Sext.[47]

Warren is keen to argue that all eucharistic celebrations, including special or Festal Day celebrations, were held at an early hour.[48] However, Adomnán is clear that Sext was the hour for the Eucharist on Columba and Baithéne's joint Feast Day. The commemorative Eucharists held in honour of Colman and Brendan may also have taken place at Sext. It may have been that Sunday regular Eucharists were at Terce, and all other special Eucharists were at Sext, but we cannot be definitive.

Was there also a night-time Eucharist? Adomnán has two narratives which could be interpreted as affirming this.

1. *Mogain's fall:* The first story concerns Mogain, who stumbled and broke her thigh-bone when returning from the Oratory after a night service (II:5). Adomnán writes that the mishap took place 'in this past night', indicating that Mogain was returning home from a nocturnal service. The Latin text does not specify which of the night services this was but does state that her return home was 'post misam'. But how do we translate *post misam*? Scholars differ on this. Sharpe translates it simply as, 'after the night office'. With similar caution, the Andersons render it as, 'after the Office'. However, Reeves boldly states, 'after Mass'. Was the service a Mass? Or is Adomnán using *misa* in a broad sense to describe any service?[49]

---

46 Adomnán, *Life*, III:12, may have a similar implication.

47 Anderson and Anderson, *Adomnán's Life of Columba*, 198, note 221, referring to the *Martyrology of Oengus.*

48 Warren, *The Liturgy and Ritual of the Celtic Church*, 142.

49 Bradshaw, *Daily Prayer in the Early Church*, 132, defines *missa* as 'a unit of worship, comprising three readings, each followed by a prayer, and three psalms (two antiphonal and one responsorial).' Bradshaw sees these as 'base units', the number of which increased or decreased according to the length of night. The term had an elastic usage.

2. *Cruithnechan's vision*: The debate on 'post misam' carries over into a second instance, this time involving Columba's foster-father Cruithnechan, who saw his whole house 'bathed in a fiery ball of light' as he returned from church one night (III:2). The Latin text again has 'post misam', which Sharpe and the Andersons again translate as 'after the Office', and which Reeves again prefers to render as 'after Mass'.

Which translation is valid? On the one hand, it is argued that, in both incidents, *post misam* is not meant to refer to a nocturnal Mass. On the other hand, it is argued that, throughout his *Life of Columba*, Adomnán means the mass whenever he uses 'misa'. (Adomnán's text consistently spells 'misa' with a single 's'.) So how does Adomnán normally use the term? Does he use *misa* to refer to any service? Or does he have a restricted usage? The Andersons are adamant that in Adomnán's text *post misam* does not refer to the Eucharist.[50] Ryan brings some support to this, arguing, '*Missa* in [early] Irish documents denotes generally the whole liturgical service, from Matins and Lauds onwards, of which the Mass was, at least on Sundays and the greater feast days, a conspicuous part.'[51] However, the actual instances of Adomnán's use of *misa*, which the Andersons cite to prove their case, are inconclusive (especially since the Andersons make a prior assumption that the Mogain and Cruithnechan examples support their case!). But examination of instances of *misa* in Adomnán's book (outside the disputed cases) shows that *misa*, or its cognates, unswervingly refers to the Eucharist (I:40; II:45; III:11, 17, 23). Adomnán's actual usage of *misa*, putting aside the Mogain and Cruithnechan narratives, seems consistent. He uses it to mean the mass or Eucharist.[52]

---

50 Anderson and Anderson, *Adomnán's Life of Columba*, liii, 102, note 133. The Andersons cite '*misa*' in Adomnán's *Life*, II:5; II:2; III, 17; and III:23 in support of their conclusion. But in III:17 *misa* means mass or Eucharist; and in III:23 *misa* is used to describe the Lord's Day mass or Eucharist, though not a night-time event.

51 Ryan, 'The Mass in the Early Irish Church', *IQR* (1961), 372: 'The technical term for the mass in the languages of Western Europe came to be *missa*. Strange to relate, the word was not adopted into the Celtic languages, Irish and Welsh, in that sense. *Missa* in Irish documents denotes generally the whole liturgical service, from Matins and Lauds onwards, of which the Mass was, at least on Sundays and the greater feast days, a conspicuous part. The Irish word for mass is *oifrend, aifreann* (Welsh, *offeren*).'

52 cf. Ambrose, *On Psalm 118*: 'We must be prepared for the midnight hour. We must fortify ourselves by eating the body and blood of our Lord Jesus, which brings remission of sins, reconciliation with God, and eternal protection.' In this passage 'midnight hour' might be a general reference to Christ's Second Coming rather than to midnight as a time of day or a Canonical Hour, though context suggests the Canonical Hour.

Perhaps there were pre-dawn Eucharists. The *Rule of Columbanus* refers to the sin of those who communicate 'in their night garments'. Does that imply a night-time Eucharist, to which some arrived inappropriately dressed?[53] Not necessarily. The reference may be to monks coming to an early-morning, but post-dawn, Eucharist, inappropriately attired.

THE CELEBRANTS

A monk could celebrate the Eucharist only if he were also a priest. Adomnán gives us the story of a Munster bishop who visited Iona anonymously, presented himself as a priest (I:44), and was invited (as a priest) to take part in the Eucharist along with others. Columba then discerned he was actually a bishop, and exclaimed, 'Christ's blessings on you, my brother. Break this bread alone, according to the rite of a bishop.' But why did Columba stress 'alone' when he realised that the man was a bishop? This has generated speculation concerning eucharistic practices on Iona, with Warren concluding that Iona had a practice of needing at least two priests to consecrate the Eucharist, whereas a single bishop could do so.[54] Against this, in the story of the unworthy priest at Trevet (I:40), Adomnán's text appears to imply that the priest was a single celebrant. Sharpe thinks that Warren is wrong and, alongside the Trevet incident, cites the occasion when Columba was visited on Hinba by his fellow-abbots, Comgall, Cainnech, Brendan, and Cormac (III:17). On that occasion, despite Columba only being a priest and not a bishop, he was chosen to be the sole celebrant. This makes Sharpe interpret the Munster bishop story differently from Warren. Sharpe reads the words, 'Break this bread alone, according to the rite of a Bishop', as simply indicating that a bishop could act unassisted if he so chose.

It may have been that if a bishop were the celebrant, then priests could only be concelebrants if invited by him. That may have been what Columba was anxious to respect. An early Church Council of Arles (314) ruled that opportunity of celebrating mass should always be given to a visiting bishop. And the Second Council of Seville (619) prohibited priests from celebrating the sacrament in the presence of a bishop,

53 Columbanus, *Rule of Columbanus*, XII.

54 Warren, *The Liturgy and Ritual of the Celtic Church*, 128.

even though elsewhere in the West bishops and priests celebrated the Eucharist together.[55] Though the Seville Council was held twenty-two years after Columba's death, it took place before Adomnán wrote his *Life of Columba*, and Adomnán may have written its prohibition into his narrative. Sharpe's conclusion is that Columba was sensitive to issues of honour and precedence, and anxious to give way to a guest of higher status. In Sharpe's opinion, Iona did not have a peculiar custom. Rather, any invitation to concelebrate had to come from the bishop. Status was important in church life, as elsewhere.

Priests were permitted to celebrate the Eucharist twice on the same day, but no more than twice.[56] It is unlikely there were multiple celebrations at the monastery itself. What the regulation was addressing was the situation of monks out in the field, going from community to community. Even there they were not to over-repeat the holy mystery.

THE MEANING OF THE EUCHARIST

In the early Irish Church, it was believed that receiving the Eucharist affected a person's eternal salvation. This was why penitents, who were excluded from the Eucharist during their years of penance, were allowed last-minute access to the sacrament if they were at risk of death.[57] The saving power of the Eucharist is alluded to in the *Amra* (IV) when it states of Columba:

He was a terror to the devil,
To whom Mass was a noose (trap).[58]

In these lines the mass is described as a 'noose' or as a 'trap' to Satan. It caught him. It bound him. It fettered him. It took away his power

55 Sharpe, *Adomnán of Iona: Life of Columba*, 306, note 192.

56 Warren, *The Liturgy and Ritual of the Celtic Church*, 143, referring to Cuminii, *De Mensura Poenitentiarum*, XIV.

57 Cassian, *Conferences*, XXIII:21, stresses the importance of the Eucharist for sinners: 'We ought not to suspend ourselves from the Lord's Communion because we confess ourselves sinners, but should more and more eagerly hasten to it for the healing of our soul, and purifying of our spirit, and seek a remedy for our wounds with humility of mind and faith, as considering ourselves unworthy to receive so great grace.' This contrasts with some ascetics who taught that the Eucharist was a reward to be merited; cf. Herren and Brown, *Christ in Celtic Christianity*, 128f., 239, and 258: 'In the ascetic Irish monastic tradition, baptism initiates the spiritual life in Christ, while the Eucharist is the reward for achieving a high level of sanctity.'

58 P. L. Henry translates: 'The devil, full of fear of him, was fettered by the Mass.'

over the soul. And, in binding Satan, the mass enabled a communicant to escape from Satan's clutches and to be set free from the spiritual bondage which he had imposed.[59] When Satan was bound by the Mass, then his prisoners were liberated for a spiritual Exodus. They could now progress on their journey towards the promised land of eternal salvation. Throughout Irish spirituality, the Exodus motif of liberation, and its initiation of the pilgrimage journey, was a strong and a recurring theme. This meant that the Eucharist was more than a simple remembrance of the first Easter. In some way, though never explained exactly how, taking the Eucharist lessened the grip of Satan. It set sinners free. It put them in a better state of grace. And it prepared them for facing death.[60]

The *Bangor Antiphonary* uses high-sacramental language when referring to the bread and wine of the Eucharist, and Columba would employ similar terminology. This does not mean that Columba believed in transubstantiation, though there are some scholars who read this back into early-medieval Celtic eucharistic theology. MacLauchlan is of that opinion,[61] but MacLauchlan confuses high-sacramental language with the theology of a later era. Although Adomnán uses terms such as 'sacred mystery' and 'sacred offering', it is doubtful if there was belief on Columba's Iona that the bread and wine truly changed into the body and blood of Christ. A full doctrine of transubstantiation requires Aristotelian concepts of substance and accident, and we have no evidence that these were in Columba's mind or in the minds of his contemporaries. Herren and Brown refer to an 'inverted formula' in which it is not the bread and wine which are changed into Christ's body and blood, but Christ's body and blood which are changed into bread and wine, and they suggest that this idea can be found in Irish texts.[62] However, it is unclear whether the texts which we are examining can sustain this interpretation.

Columba embraced the high-sacramental theology of the Irish Church. That spirituality is reflected in the eucharistic hymns and

59 Elsewhere Satan's hold over a person is described in terms of them being held by HIS noose; cf. Beccán *Fo Reir*, XXIV: 'Royal kin of triumphant kings/ lord full of grace, thus may he guard us/ I'll take off the devil's noose/ his bard's prayer perhaps may save us.'

60 cf. *Voyages of St. Brendan*, VII: 'The monk received Communion, his soul left his body and was borne heavenwards by angels of light, as the brethren stood looking on. Brendan buried him where he had died.'

61 MacLauchlan, *The Early Scottish Church*, 185, citing Adomnán, *Life*, I:44.

62 Herren and Brown, *Christ in Celtic Christianity*, 126.

prayers of the *Bangor Antiphonary.* Item 109, the first in a series of seven Communion Anthems, states:

We have received the Lord's body,
And we have drunk his blood.
Of no evil shall we be afraid,
Because the Lord is with us.[63]

Similarly, Item 8, the *Sancti Venite*, sung at Bangor and on Iona as priests (and people?) communicated, starts:

Come forward, you who are holy.
Receive the body of Christ,
and drink the sacred blood,
by which you will be (were) redeemed.[64]

The *Sancti Venite* is similar to other communion chants found in early Irish liturgical texts.[65] It affirms that all powers shall bow before Christ. It links the Eucharist to the sacrifice of Christ on the cross. It sees the sacrifices of the old law as foreshadowing the ultimate sacred mystery. And it asserts that if the Eucharist is approached with right faith and with purity of intention, then God will bestow salvation and eternal life through giving heavenly bread and living water. In other words, given true faith and purity, any communicant who takes the visible bread and wine triggers a parallel reception of heavenly bread and the water of life.[66] This is not transubstantiation as such. Instead, the Eucharist is understood as an event of faith, in which taking the bread and wine activates a corresponding spiritual action in the soul of the believer.

The *Sancti Venite* presents the Eucharist as a potent force in God's mighty work of salvation. Satan and the powers of darkness are conquered through the sacrifice of Christ. Fear is taken away. As is the case throughout early-medieval Irish spirituality, the dominant emphasis is on the power of Satan being overcome. Men and women are

---

63 *Bangor Antiphonary*, Item 109, [tr. Morrison].

64 *Bangor Antiphonary*, Item 8:1, 2, [tr. Michael Sheane, *Ulster in the age of St. Comgall of Bangor* (Devon: Stockwell, 2004), 43]; cf. Curran, *The Antiphonary of Bangor and the Early Irish Monastic Liturgy*, 47; and Walpole, *Early Latin Hymns: with Introduction and Notes*, 345.

65 Curran, *The Antiphonary of Bangor and the Early Irish Monastic Liturgy*, 47f.

66 Woolfenden, *Daily Liturgical Prayer: Origins and Theology*, 294, cites Hilarion who wrote: 'Orthodox theology regards the sacraments as sacred actions through which an encounter takes place between us and God.'

victims of Satan's oppression. They need liberation. Participation in the Eucharist enables this to happen. The *Sancti Venite* makes this explicit:

This sacrament of Body and blood,
Frees all from the jaws of Hell.

Other eucharistic references in the *Bangor Antiphonary* express a similar belief. Redemption is through the body and blood of Christ [cf. Item 10:4, 6], which is received by means of the bread and wine. Right faith is required in order to truly receive. In all of this, the eucharistic event is profoundly connected with the defeat of Satan, and with the liberation of men and women. They are released from fear, from demonic captivity, and from Satan's authority. Christ is the ransomer from the bondage of death:

Offered was he, for greatest and for least,
Himself the victim, and himself the priest.[67]

As Iona's abbot, it was Columba's responsibility to safeguard the Eucharist, as it was his responsibility to ensure that his monks arrived safely in the heavenly kingdom. Pilgrimage through life was full of peril, even for those freed from Satan's clutches through Christ's liberating power, which was mediated by Baptism and the Eucharist. But was their destination truly assured? Might they be recaptured? Columba was a trustworthy captain of their Ship of Faith, but that ship sailed on tempestuous spiritual oceans. Might they yet flounder? Did their faith have a vulnerable stress-point? Was there provisionality in relation to their final salvation? This becomes a central issue in the following chapters on Columba's theology.

67 *Bangor Antiphonary*, Item 8:5, 7. (Stratman)

PART FOUR
THEOLOGIAN

CHAPTER 17

The Evangelical and Apostolic Teaching

> All we Irish, inhabitants of the world's edge, are disciples of Saints Peter and Paul and of all the disciples who wrote the sacred canon by the Holy Ghost, and we accept nothing outside *the evangelical and apostolic teaching*; none has been a heretic, none a Judaizer, none a schismatic; but the Catholic Faith, as it was delivered by you first, who are the successors of the holy apostles, is maintained unbroken.[1]

The title for this chapter comes from a sentence in a letter written by Columbanus, which was sent to Pope Boniface IV around the year 612. Though it was mischievous of Columbanus to boast that the Irish Church had never suffered error, he was keen to give that impression. His words represent how Irish Church leaders, including Columba, saw themselves. All agreed that orthodoxy of belief was essential for salvation.[2] What was believed really mattered. Of paramount importance was the identity of the true God as Father, Son, and Holy Spirit. The deities of pre-Christian paganism were different from the God of Abraham, Isaac, and Jacob. An Arian god was different from the triune God. And homage, worship, and adoration given to other divine beings was not equivalent to devotion offered to the Trinity. Columba and his contemporaries affirmed orthodox Nicene doctrine concerning God and Christ. And they understood salvation primarily in terms of conflict between Christ and Satan liberating sinners from satanic captivity, rather than as a satisfaction rendered to God.

---

1 Columbanus, *Letter V to Pope Boniface IV;* cf. Herren and Brown, *Christ in Celtic Christianity*, 47ff., 106. Columbanus' argument is that the Irish tradition was bound to the teaching of Peter and Paul as expressed in Scripture. But Pope Boniface is only the worthy successor of the apostles if he maintains their teaching. [My italics]

2 Herren and Brown, *Christ in Celtic Christianity*, 50.

This notion of spiritual warfare against Satan is key to unlocking the spirituality of the Irish Church. It informed Columba's interpretation of the cross. It directed his thoughts on the atonement. It pervaded his theology of the Eucharist. It lay behind his methodology of evangelism. It moulded his piety and his daily living of the Christian life. However, it also fostered ambivalence concerning assurance of eternal life. This was because the paradigm of spiritual warfare not only embraced Christ's victory over His enemies at Calvary but included ongoing struggle in relation to Satan's campaign against the people of God. All believers were mindful of these realities. Each day, the soldier of Christ was conscious of taking to the field of spiritual battle. For Columba and his monks, spiritual warfare was not something on the periphery of Christian faith. It was at the heart of things.

Traditional works on Celtic theology focus on a range of questions. Where did the beliefs and practices of the Irish Church come from? Which elements carried over from pre-Christian thinking? How did faith develop as the centuries passed? All of these are important questions, and it is possible to study Columba solely from within these parameters. However, our aim is to set Columba within the context of a wider Christendom. He studied and worshipped as any other young monk would study and worship anywhere in Europe. Irish monastic libraries had the same books as other monasteries had. Irish liturgies echoed those in use across the Church. There were local variations, but Ireland (as much as Gaul, or Rome, or Egypt) was part of one faith.[3] And because Columba's spirituality was formed by the teaching he received and by the liturgy he participated in, then he absorbed the orthodoxy of that Universal Church. He imbibed the beliefs and worship of an international faith. Indigenous Irish culture impacted on him: that is undeniable. However, he was pre-eminently the product of a supra-national Christian orthodoxy. The Irish Church had no desire to be different. Champions of the Celtic Churches defended their orthodoxy fiercely, Columbanus most of all.

A liturgy can become a protective-fortress for right belief. The daily chanting of doctrinally orthodox hymns, and the daily recitation

3 Markus, *Conceiving a Nation*, 137.

of approved creedal statements, act as potent safeguards, ensuring adherence to established Christian teaching. Monasteries were places where the faith could be accurately preserved, with Basil viewing this as one of the great pluses of monasticism.[4] Although the Roman Church criticised the Irish tradition on issues such as the date of Easter and the type of tonsure, it never accused it of heresy in its doctrine of God, Christology, or soteriology. When Bede describes Aidan of Lindisfarne's Columban theology, he goes out of his way to affirm it as orthodox in every respect, apart from the Easter question. Bede could never 'approve or commend Aidan's failure to observe Easter at the proper time', but he knew that Aidan 'believed, worshipped, and taught exactly what we do, namely: the redemption of the human race through the Passion, Resurrection, and Ascension into heaven of the Man Jesus Christ, the Mediator between God and man'.[5]

In homologating Aidan's theology in such sweeping terms, Bede affirms that the core beliefs of the Columban tradition are those of his Church. But is Bede over-polite? Does he approve too easily? Does he write in warm terms out of a sentimental respect for the memory of Aidan and Cuthbert? Does generosity of spirit blunt his critical evaluation? But Bede was not alone. Wilfrid had little of Bede's magnanimity of spirit, and was consistently hostile to the Columban tradition. Wilfrid could be rude, abrasive, and confrontational, with his attitude reflected in Eddius' *Life of Wilfrid* in which he is quoted as saying: 'Was I not the first to root out from the Church the **foul weeds** planted by the Scots?'[6] Yet, despite this hostility, Wilfrid is nowhere cited as arguing that the Columban Church was at fault in its core theology.[7]

It is the Irish Church's adherence to traditional orthodoxy which lies behind Bradley's assertion that any attempt to make Columba's faith coterminous with modern liberalism will fail. Columba was no liberal in the modern sense. The emphasis in Columba's poem, *Altus Prosator*, is on God's sovereignty, human sin, the Fall of humanity, the power of divine judgement, the apocalyptic nature of Christ's second coming, and the reality of hell.[8] Bradley is spot on.

---

4 Morison, *St. Basil and his Rule: A Study in Early Monasticism*, 30.

5 Bede, *History*, III:17.

6 Eddius, *Life of Wilfrid*, 47.

7 Eddius, *Life of Wilfrid*, 10.

8 Bradley, *Argyll: The Making of a Spiritual Landscape*, 58f.

GOD THE TRINITY

Beccán's praise-poem for Columba, *Tiugraind Beccain*, describes Columba leaving Ireland under God's protective providence: 'In the Trinity's care he sought a ship.'[9] Columba's God was the triune God of Father, Son, and Holy Spirit; and adoration of the Trinity is a consistent feature of early Irish texts. Early Irish Church theology was decisively anti-Arian. It affirmed the deity of all three persons of the Godhead, and it was belief in this tenet which was considered to make a person's religion a distinctly Christian faith. When a person acknowledged the triune God, then they honoured the true God of heaven and earth, rather than a false idol.[10] Columba expresses reverence for the Trinity in the opening stanza of his *Altus Prosator*:

The High Creator, the Unbegotten Ancient of Days,
Was without origin of beginning, limitless,
He is and He will be for endless ages of ages,
With whom is the only-begotten Christ,
and the Holy Spirit,
Co-eternal in the everlasting glory of divinity.
We do not confess three gods, but say one God,
Saving our faith in three most glorious Persons.[11]

This is classic Christian orthodoxy, perfectly dovetailing with the Nicene and Athanasian Creeds. Three key statements stand out: 'Co-eternal', 'We do not confess three gods but say one God', and, 'Our faith in three most glorious Persons'. Although these are not taken word-for-word from either the Nicene or Athanasian Creeds, they accurately reproduce their theology, whilst retaining a freedom of

9 Beccán, *Tiugraind Beccain*, 9.

10 Markus (*Conceiving a Nation*, 126) lists four fundamental elements of Christian doctrine which a person becoming a Christian would be expected to assent to. (1) the unity of God as creator of all things. (2) Jesus Christ as God's revelation in history, and his death and resurrection as a source of hope for eternal life. (3) The calling to moral goodness under the guidance of God's Holy Spirit. (4) the church as God's people and the community where this faith was expressed and taught. What he omits in this list of key beliefs for baptismal candidates is: (i) an awareness of the triune God; and (ii) an awareness of having been rescued from hell and judgment. Both of these ranked high.

11 *Altus Prosator*, Stanza A. The last two lines replicate sentiments found in Basil, *Letters*, 8: 'Against those who cast it in our teeth that we are tritheists, let it be answered that we confess one God not in number but in nature.'

phraseology. Nicene orthodoxy was hard-wired into the faith of the Irish Church. It was integral to Columba's personal piety.[12]

All early-medieval Irish Church documents exhibit a similar orthodoxy, with the *Bangor Antiphonary* avowedly trinitarian from beginning to end. A strong Nicene doctrine of the Trinity is particularly evident in Item 12, a hymn which may have been derived from the fourth-century philosopher-theologian Victorinus.[13] A clear trinitarian doctrine of three persons and one Substance is also found in Item 13. Other hymns and prayers throughout the *Bangor Antiphonary* consistently affirm the deity of Christ and the trinitarian nature of God.

However, it is Item 35 of the *Bangor Antiphonary* which stands out in any discussion of its doctrinal teaching. Item 35 is a statement of faith used at Bangor, which is unique in some of its phrases and expressions. D. S. Nerney, in three articles on Item 35 published in the *Irish Theological Quarterly* in the early 1950s, terms it the Bangor Symbol because it only appears in the *Bangor Antiphonary*, though probably not originating there. The Bangor Symbol summarises Christian doctrine as it was understood in an early-medieval Irish monastery, and the theology of this unique creedal statement, which Bangor monks affirmed week by week, if not day by day, merits closer examination.

In essence, the Bangor Symbol is a beefed-up version of the Apostles' Creed and anti-Arian in its core theology.[14] Though the Irish Church never suffered directly from Arianism, it viewed Arianism as the ultimate heresy. Consequently, it regarded anti-Arian statements as benchmark statements of orthodoxy, and as yardsticks in defining Christian identity. This is why the Bangor Symbol describes not only God the Father as

---

12 J. E. L. Oulton, *The Credal Statements of St. Patrick: As Contained in the Fourth Chapter of his* 'Confessions', (London: OUP, 1940), 32, argues that dissemination of the Nicene Creed was so gradual that it was not used in any Western Latin liturgy until 589 in Spain. That date may be queried, but Ireland's adoption of its terminology points to strong links with the Greek Church.

13 Curran, *The Antiphonary of Bangor and the Early Irish Monastic Liturgy*, 66f., suggests the Marius Victorinus link. Warren thought Item 12 was of Irish origin. Oulton, *The Credal Statements of St. Patrick*, 1, notes similarities between 'Patrick's Creed' and a passage of the *Commentary on the Apocalypse* by Victorinus, and concludes (16) that the author of 'Patrick's Creed' knew Victorinus from a recension by Jerome. Item 12's 'Light from Light' is highly reminiscent of Nicaea. 'Patrick's Creed' is also discussed by O'Loughlin, *Celtic Theology*, 41f.

14 Adamson, *Bangor: Light of the World*, 53, incorrectly states that the Symbol is an adaptation of the Nicene Creed. Nerney, 'The Bangor Symbol: Part I', *ITQ* (1952), 367, affirms it as a recension of the Apostles' Creed with Nicene elements.

'almighty', but gives God the Son and God the Holy Spirit the same attribute of 'almightiness'. Nerney suggests that this radical attribution of 'almightiness' to all three persons of the Trinity (individually as well as collectively) is a deliberate ploy to counter Arian teaching. Arians were prepared to speak of Jesus as 'a god' but not as 'The God'.[15] But in making a threefold attribution of 'almightiness', the Bangor Symbol allowed no ambiguity on this major issue. Son and Holy Spirit are Almighty God, as much as the Father is. Warren identifies this insistence on the deity of each of the persons in the Trinity as a distinctive mark of the Bangor Symbol.[16]

Nerney argues that the Bangor Symbol's intense anti-Arian stance indicates an origin in south-east Gaul around 537.[17] He suggests it was adopted in Ireland because it expressed the Irish Church's own understanding of Christian faith. And he argues that it was used widely across the whole early-medieval Irish Church.[18] If so, it would be known to Columba, and would be part of the Iona liturgy. One clue that the Bangor Symbol may have been used in the Columban tradition is that the much later *Book of Deer* reflects Bangor wording in not having 'dead' in its rendering of the Apostles' Creed's phrase 'crucified, dead, and buried'.[19] However, Nerney's argument that the Bangor Symbol was shared across the Irish Church does not depend on possible residual traces in the *Book of Deer.*

The following table sets out the Symbol with a translation. Highlighted in bold is wording which replicates the Apostles' Creed.

The Bangor Symbol	
Credo*[20] *in Deum Patrem omnipotentem, invisibilem, omnium creaturarum visibilium et invisibilium conditorem.	I believe in God the Father almighty, invisible, creator of all things visible and invisible.

15 cf. Oulton, *The Credal Statements of St. Patrick,* 31.

16 Warren, *The Antiphonary of Bangor, Part II,* 63.

17 Nerney, 'The Bangor Symbol: Part I, III' in *ITQ* (1952, 1953), 372, 393, 398. Nerney comments on its strongly anti-Arian agenda seeing this as pointing to a non-insular origin, since the insular Church was not itself plagued by Arianism.

18 Nerney, 'The Bangor Symbol: Part I' in *ITQ* (1952), 375.

19 Nerney, 'The Bangor Symbol: Part II' in *ITQ* (1953), 277. Yet the *Book of Deer* only uses 'almighty' for God the Father.

20 The Bangor Symbol uses 'credo' five times. Nerney, 'The Bangor Symbol: Part I', *ITQ* (1952), 376, suggests this may have divided the Creed into successive interrogations at Baptism, and into strophes for antiphonal chant in the liturgy.

The Bangor Symbol	
Credo et in Jesum Christum, Filium ejus unicum, Dominum nostrum, Deum omnipotentem, ***conceptum de Spiritu Sancto, natum de Maria Virgine, passum sub Pontio Pilato, qui crucifixus et sepultus descendit ad infernos, tertia die resurrexit a mortuis, ascendit in coelis, seditque ad dextram Dei Patris omnipotentis, exinde venturus judicare vivos ac mortuos.***	And I believe in Jesus Christ, his only Son, our Lord, God almighty, conceived by the Holy Spirit, born of the Virgin Mary, suffered under Pontius Pilate, who was crucified and buried,[21] descended to Hell, on the third day rose from death, ascended to heaven, seated at the right-hand of God the Father Almighty, from where he will come to judge the living and the dead.
Credo et in Spiritum Sanctum, Deum omnipotentem, unam habentem substantiam cum Patre et Filio. ***Sanctam esse***[22] ***ecclesiam catholicam, abremissam peccatorum, sanctorum communionem, carnis resurrectionem.***	And I believe in the Holy Spirit, God almighty, possessing the one substance with the Father and the Son, [through whom there exists] the holy catholic Church, the forgiveness of sins, communion of the saints, and the resurrection of the flesh.
Credo vitam post mortem, et ***vitam aeternam*** in Gloria Christi. Haec omnia credo in Deum. Amen.	I believe life after death, and eternal life in the glory of Christ. All this I believe in God. Amen

It was commonplace for local traditions to re-write confessional statements in their own words, without feeling they were departing

21 Warren, *The Antiphonary of Bangor: Part II*, 63, reproduces two versions of the Apostles' Creed, neither of which has 'dead'. One is from an eighth-century manuscript; the other is a Gallican Creed contained in a letter from Cyprian, Bishop of Toulon, to Maximus, Bishop of Geneva, c. 524-533. The Gallican closely approximates Bangor. Both are based on the Apostles' Creed, but with local variations of phrase and style.

22 The use of 'esse' is puzzling. Warren, *The Antiphonary of Bangor: Part II*, 48, suggests that it is sometimes redundant; cf. Nerney, 'The Bangor Symbol, II' in *ITQ* (1953), 279. Nerney suggests that it could be construed in two ways: either (a) 'I believe that the Catholic Church is holy' or (b) 'I believe that there is a holy Catholic Church, remission of sins, etc.' He prefers the second, with 'esse' used prospectively to profess faith in the remaining articles.

from official truth.[23] Hence the Bangor Symbol replicates the Apostles' Creed, but with supplementary phrases which nail it to Nicene orthodoxy. The base text is the Apostles' Creed. Words and phrases are added so as to remove any doubt on major issues. This was standard practice as shown by Cassian in his *Institutes*.[24] An Arian might put his or her own spin on the Apostles' Creed and repeat it quite happily: but an Arian could never accept Bangor's enhanced version.

The Bangor Symbol has some statements not found in the Apostles' Creed or in the Nicene Creed. For example, as well as ascribing Almightiness to the Son and Holy Spirit as well as to the Father, it also states that the Holy Spirit 'possesses the one substance with the Father and the Son'. (Item 10 of the *Bangor Antiphonary* also speaks in terms of the Holy Spirit being of 'one substance' with the Godhead.) Other Creeds only use the phrase 'of one substance with the Father' in relation to the Son. Even when the 381 version of the Nicene Creed clarified that the deity of the Holy Spirit was equal to that of the Father and the Son, it never expressed the deity of the Holy Spirit in such terms. The Bangor Symbol is making an unequivocal declaration on a major issue. This is a significant variation, though consistent with Nicene orthodoxy.

1. *God the Father.* The Bangor Symbol mainly reproduces the Latin of the Apostle's Creed. 'I believe in God the Father almighty' replicates the opening phrase of the Apostles' Creed, rather than that of the Nicene Creed ('I believe in one God'). Conversely, the Bangor Symbol replaces the Apostles' Creed's 'Creator of Heaven and Earth', with '[God the] invisible, creator of all things visible and invisible', which is from the Nicene formula.

2. *God the Son.* The Bangor Symbol stays close to the Apostles' Creed, with the significant addition of 'God almighty', making the deity of the Son crystal clear. Nerney reckons that this triple predication of 'omnipotence' to Father, Son, and Spirit, was characteristic of Gallic recensions. Ambrose and Augustine had used the same triple 'almighty' (*omnipotens*) to stress that God the Son was God *omnipotens*,

---

23 Nerney, 'The Bangor Symbol: Part I' in *ITQ* (1952), 375, notes that between the fifth and eighth centuries there was a family of Celtic variants of the Apostles' Creed.

24 Cassian, *The Seven Books of John Cassian*, Book VI:4-7, discusses various Creeds based on the Apostles' Creed but strengthened by Nicene theology. The modern common text of the Apostles' Creed is from the seventh or eighth centuries.

contrasting Arian teaching that God the Son was only God *perfunctorie*, not *omnipotens*.[25]

3. *God the Holy Spirit.* The Bangor Symbol builds on the Apostles' Creed, but with intriguing alterations. As noted, the Holy Spirit is, 'God almighty, possessing the one substance with the Father and the Son'. This dramatically transforms basic Apostles' Creed theology into Nicene orthodoxy. And, in using the phrase 'one substance' in connection with the Spirit's relationship to the Father, it offers a supercharged version of Nicene theology. Significantly, however, the Bangor Symbol does not speak of the Spirit 'proceeding' from the Father as in Nicene theology. Was the Nicene text not consulted directly? Or did Bangor regard the 'one substance' wording as an improvement? In connection with this, and in relation to Iona's overall theology of the Holy Spirit, Clancy and Markus express concern that Columba's *Altus Prosator* does not mention the Holy Spirit apart from a brief appearance in the opening stanzas.[26] Nevertheless, what it does say of the Holy Spirit is fully orthodox, and the *Altus Prosator* is not the only statement of Christian faith which fails to develop a fuller theology of the Holy Spirit. The doctrinal concern of the early-medieval Irish Church was Arianism with respect to God the Son. Adomnán, in his *Life of Columba*, certainly recognises the place of the Holy Spirit in the Trinity (II:32, 23), and he refers to the Holy Spirit working in Columba's life (III:2, 18). In his Second Preface, he describes the link between the Holy Spirit and Columba's name, a name which marks him as a man of the Spirit.[27]

4. *The Church.* The section on the Church in the Bangor Symbol has no '*credo*' as in the Apostles' Creed. This reflects the Nicene Creed whose Latin text also has no '*credo*' in relation to the Church (though 'I believe' is inserted into English translations at that juncture). Nerney makes the point that Bangor has simply '*credo*', rather than '*credo in*', for its last two sections.[28] Hence, it reserves '*credo in*' for faith in the persons of the Trinity: this is an important peculiarity which Nerney links to later recensions, and which earlier creeds did not always observe.

25 Nerney, 'The Bangor Symbol: Part I', *ITQ* (1952), 372f., 376f., 381ff.

26 Clancy and Markus, *Iona: The Earliest Poetry of a Celtic Monastery*, 67f.

27 Bruce, *Prophecy, Miracles and Heavenly Light?*, 161; cf. Appendix 1.

28 Nerney, 'The Bangor Symbol: Part II' in *ITQ* (1953), 280.

5. *The Affirmation.* The Bangor Symbol has the sequence: (i) forgiveness of sins; (ii) communion of saints; (iii) resurrection of the body. This differs from the traditional sequence in the Apostles' Creed which is: (i) communion of saints; (ii) forgiveness of sins; (iii) resurrection of the body.[29] Warren views the term '*abremissam*' (forgiveness) within that series, as highly unusual, with a fifth-century Gallican text the only other known occurrence. This supports the theory that the Bangor Symbol originated in Gaul.[30] Concerning the resurrection, the Celtic Church anticipated a bodily, physical resurrection, and monks were buried with their fellow-monks in expectation of this. Columba prophesies of Libran (II:39: cf. III:23) 'You will die in one of my monasteries; and your part in the kingdom will be with my elect monks, and with them you will wake from the sleep of death into the resurrection of life.'[31] Monks envisaged living the heavenly life with their community.

6. *The Christian Hope.* The closing words are brief, and appear to be original to Bangor: 'I believe in life after death, and eternal life in the glory of Christ.[32] All these things I believe in God. Amen.' This may reflect a confession of faith made by catechumens at baptism, with the form of words fixed through many years of usage. If so, this may be why Bangor prefers it over wording such as 'one baptism for the remission of sins'.

The Bangor Symbol is a form of the Apostles' Creed but strengthened by a selection of formidable, theologically orthodox, phrases. Just as Bangor quarried from a range of liturgies for its liturgy, so it quarried from a range of the Church's Creeds for its Creed. Creative editing was widespread throughout Christendom. It was only later that official versions became the norm. There was strict orthodoxy of doctrine: but there was

29 Nerney, 'The Bangor Symbol: Part II' in *ITQ* (1953), 282: 'The insertion of the article on the remission of sins between the article on the Holy Catholic Church and that on the Communion of Saints is not found in any Western recension of our acquaintance though Zahn states that it appears in an Armenian creed.' Nerney argues that early recensions simply had: *Credo Sanctam Ecclesiam, remissionem peccatorum*, but when the 'communion of saints' was added it was normal to place it immediately after the article on the Church as its sequel and complement. This makes the order in the Bangor Symbol doubly unusual, perhaps echoing a very early form; cf. Warren, *The Antiphonary of Bangor: Part II*, 62.

30 Warren, *The Antiphonary of Bangor, Part II*, 62.

31 MacDonald, 'Adomnán's Monastery of Iona' in Bourke (ed.), *Studies in the Cult of Saint Columba*, 33.

32 Nerney, 'The Bangor Symbol; Part II' in *ITQ* (1953), 392, suggests this reference is to the General Judgment when Christ comes again with majesty to judge the living and the dead.

also a freedom of expression. Columba's Iona may have produced its own doctrinal formula, but there is a high likelihood that the Bangor Symbol was used across the Irish Sea. This may have been Columba's Creed.

GOD THE SON

Consistent with the Irish Church avoiding any taint of Arianism, Columba's *Altus Prosator* strongly censures any incorrect beliefs concerning Jesus. In his opening lines Columba commits to a high-Christology involving the full deity of the Son of God.[33] Deeper into his poem Columba condemns all who doubt the relationship of the Son to the Father:

> The raging anger of fire will devour the adversaries,
> Who will not believe that Christ came from God the Father.

Adomnán has a similar high-Christology when he writes that Columba followed the stainless faultless Lamb, 'to whom with the Father be all honour and power and praise and glory and everlasting kingdom in the unity of the Holy Spirit, for ever and ever'.[34] The wording echoes Revelation 5:13, which may have been used as a doxology on Iona.[35] For Columba and Adomnán, Jesus was to receive the same honour, power, praise, and glory as God the Father. He was to be worshipped as God. This replicated Patrick, who refers to 'Christ my God' in his *Letter to Coroticus*.[36]

The collects of the *Bangor Antiphonary* echo this high-Christology. In these collects it is God the Son who is routinely addressed in prayer. As noted previously, out of the eight collects which may be used after singing the 'Song of Moses: six of these are addressed to Christ; one is addressed to God the Father; and the other is indeterminate.[37] Moreover, Warren suggests that all seven of the collects for use after the *Benedicite* are addressed to Christ.[38] As previously noted, even when

---

33 *Altus Prosator*, Stanza A.

34 Adomnán, *Life*, III:23.

35 The *Bangor Antiphonary*, Item 13, depicts Patrick singing Psalms, Hymns, and the 'Apocalypse'. The latter is a reference to singing the various doxologies and angelic songs referred to in the Book of Revelation.

36 Patrick, *Letter to Coroticus*, 5. Dales, *Light to the Isles*, 34.

37 *Bangor Antiphonary*, Items 62, 68, 71, 76, 81, 88, 91, 94; cf. Warren, *The Antiphonary of Bangor: Part II*, xxi.

38 *Bangor Antiphonary*, Items 63, 69, 72, 77, 82, 89, 92.

a collect starts with 'God' (*Deus*), it may be addressed to Christ as much as to the Father. with Warren citing several examples of collects referring to 'God' (*Deus*) but clearly addressed to Christ.[39]

Liturgical material changes slowly. Prayer styles embedded in a liturgy remain constant for generations. Prayer in the *Bangor Antiphonary* would differ little from prayer practised at Bangor by Comgall in the sixth century. Comgall's prayers would differ little from Columba's prayers on Iona at the same time.

GOD THE CREATOR

Columba's *Altus Prosator* affirms God as the High Creator. Almost incidentally, it also reveals that Columba was not a flat-earther, with Columba using the Latin *globus* (globe) to refer to the earth as a ball-like sphere:

By the divine powers of the great God,
is hung the globe [*globus*] of the earth.
And the circle of the great deep around it,
is held up by the strong hand of almighty God,
with columns like bars supporting it.[40]

Clancy and Markus suggest that here Columba draws on the Vulgate rendering of Job 26:7, 11, with its representation of the earth resting in the hand of God. That may be. But Columba is also following in the footsteps of Church Fathers such as Justin Martyr, Novatian, Augustine, Eusebius, Jerome and Leo the Great, who describe the earth as a globe.[41]

1. *The Purpose of Creation.* In the *Altus Prosator* Columba reflects on why God created the world. He concludes that created entities came

---

39 *Bangor Antiphonary*, Items 71, 72, 73. Warren, *The Antiphonary of Bangor: Part II*, xxi. Though Item 3 of the *Bangor Antiphonary* was probably composed after Columba's death, its theology is that of the early-medieval Irish Church. In stanza 20, it gives a superb description of the true humanity which Christ had in the Incarnation: 'Tiny of stature he is contained by a manger; but in his fist the world can be enclosed' [Tr. Herren and Brown, *Christ in Celtic Christianity*, 287].

40 *Altus Prosator*, Stanza M.

41 Justin Martyr, *On the Sole Government of God*, 3; Novatian, *On the Trinity*, 8; Augustine, *Tractate IX on John's Gospel*, II:14 (though in his *Commentary on Psalm 150:2* Augustine may be implying that the phrase 'globe of the earth is a figure of speech); Eusebius, *Oration in Praise of the Emperor Constantine*; Jerome, *Letter 60: To Heliodorus*, who refers to 'inhabitants of the globe from India to Britain'; and Pope Leo the Great (d. 461), *Letters: Book V: Epistle 18 to Bishop John*, who wrote, 'Nations rise against nations, the globe of the earth is shaken.' Over against this, Lactantius, *Institutes*, III:24, was less enthusiastic. Theophilus of Antioch, *Book 32*, was also sceptical about the earth being a sphere.

into existence in order that the Trinity might not be 'unproductive in all works of bounty'. Does Columba imply that God can only be God in His perfection of goodness if He creates nature and heavenly beings? That may not have been Columba's intention, but is a possible reading:

He created good angels and archangels, the orders
Of Principalities and Thrones, of Powers and of Virtues,
So that the goodness and majesty of the Trinity
Might not be unproductive in all works of bounty,
But might have heavenly beings in which He might greatly
Show forth his favours by a word of power.[42]

If Columba is stating that God's act of creation is a necessary consequence of God's bountiful nature, rather than being a truly free act of His will, that would be alien to Christian tradition. Christian orthodoxy affirms God as complete and sufficient in Himself in every aspect, and that His act of creation was a sovereignly free decision of the divine will. Does poetic exuberance take Columba beyond this? Or is Columba using the example of a 'busy' God to teach his monks that true godliness should go hand in hand with productivity?

2. *The Harmony of Creation.* Much clearer is Columba's thought that every part of the natural world is in harmony: or at least it *used* to be in harmony before the Fall.[43] Stanza P of the *Altus Prosator* describes the Tree of Life in the midst of Paradise whose leaves, 'bearing healing for the nations' do not wither or drop. This hints at a future restoration of what God first made as perfect. The poem goes on to describe how God's original flawless creation was spoiled by the sin of fallen angels and the sin of humanity, and how man lost his glory. Despite the Fall, God, through grace, maintains the created order in existence and allows it a continuing life-giving and life-sustaining potential. But the Fall means that the thunder of God's Law, glimpsed at Sinai, will lead inexorably to trembling at God's judgement seat.[44]

42 *Altus Prosator*, Stanza B.

43 *Altus Prosator*, Stanzas E and F.

44 *Altus Prosator*, Stanzas E, F, L, N, Q, R, S, Z. Basil, *The Shorter Rule*, Qu 2:45f., views the Law positively and part of God's cure for fallen humanity: 'When man was deceived by the craft of the serpent and fell into sin and through sin fell headlong into death, God by no means despised him, but gave him the Law for a help, set angels over him, checked the impulses of vice by the severity of threats, stirred desires for the good by the most lavish promises, and declared beforehand the end of either course in many images.'

In the *Altus Prosator* there is a clear awareness of the brokenness of Creation. At the same time there are texts within the Columban family which recall the ideals of a pre-lapsarian Eden, and of a primeval harmony between humanity and nature. An example of this is Adomnán's tale of the white horse which carried milk-pails to the Iona monastery (III:23).[45] One day, as Columba neared his death, the white horse nestled into him, and began to mourn 'like a person', pouring out its tears in the saint's bosom, and 'weeping aloud with foaming lips'. Adomnán makes Columba say that, although humanity alone has rationality, from time to time God may give animals an ability to empathise with humans, despite animals having no rational soul.[46]

Other near-contemporary texts reflect similar beliefs. Bede writes of Cuthbert spending hours of intense prayer, standing waist-deep in the sea, after which two great sea otters came and frolicked around his feet.[47] Though various interpretations of this story have been proposed,[48] it undoubtedly points to a (temporary) restoration of an Eden-like, human/animal relationship, made possible because of Cuthbert's saintliness. In similar fashion, other early-medieval Irish documents focus on a special bond between saints and the birds of the air, possibly because birds were associated with the upper atmosphere and hence with heaven.[49] Sacred woods are also prominent in early Christian writings from Ireland and Iona; but whether that was due to Christian theology, or to the lingering influence of pre-Christian religious thinking, is debated.

3. *The Dysfunctionality of Creation.* Despite allusions to a harmony of creation before the Fall, and despite hints of a restoration of that harmony in the future, the same literature speaks of dysfunctionality and brokenness in the here and now. There is an antagonism between nature and humanity. Both of these opposing themes (harmony and brokenness) crop up in early texts, and they also represent two

45 Finlay, *Columba*, 25, detects echoes of a 'Celtic warrior-aristocrat and his horse' motif; cf. Bruce, *Prophecy, Miracles, Angels and Heavenly Light?*, 108, who discusses possible eschatological references as foretastes of a restored creation.

46 Bruce, *Prophecy, Miracles, Angels and Heavenly Light?* 128, suggests that Sharpe's translation of II:4, 'At once men and beasts regained their health and praised God in St. Columba with exceeding gratitude' is consistent with Adomnán having an eschatological view of nature restored and healed in which even 'brute' beasts articulate praise to their Maker.

47 Bede, *Life of Cuthbert*, 10.

48 Benedicta Ward, 'The Spirituality of St. Cuthbert' in Bonner (ed.), *St. Cuthbert: His Cult and his Community*, 71f.

49 Finlay, *Columba*, 23.

contrasting modern ways of interpreting early Celtic spirituality. Modern Celticism tends to stress that the early monks lived in concord with nature, and contrasts that harmony with modern industrialised society which exploits and abuses nature. But scholars such as Clancy, Markus, Meek, Raikes, Bitel, and Bradley are anxious to demythologise any false romanticism attached to the period.[50] Clancy and Markus stress that real-life hermits were not living in comfort with the natural world, but were struggling to survive in a harsh northern climate. They would never have had a rose-tinted view of nature, and the period should not be interpreted through New-Ages eyes:

> A real hermit, living in a damp stone or wooden cell, fasting in hot and cold weather to subdue the flesh, terrified of thunder and lightning, … is not the author of these [later romanticised Celtic] nature poems.[51]

Meek similarly rejects a romanticised version of the Celtic past: 'I applied the axe of reason to the root of the sentimental tree of wishful thinking which purported to represent the lineage of Columba and the other saints.'[52] Meek stresses that Columba did not preach kindness to all; nor was he unaffected by wild and dangerous nature; nor did he see harmony between paganism and Christian faith; and any interpretation of early Celtic theology which assumes otherwise is far from the mark. For these scholars, the early literature conveys images of monks living in uncomfortable, bare, ascetic conditions. The monks were battling storms, fearing drowning, dreading sea monsters, resisting wild beasts, and suffering cold and wet for most of the year. Such monks would not recognise the dreamy unity between humans and nature which is so beloved of modern Celtic spirituality. And anyone who has lived through

50 Clancy and Markus, *Iona: The Earliest Poetry of a Celtic Monastery*, 90. Meek, 'St. Columba and Celtic Christianity' in Randall (ed.), *In Search of Colmcille*, 40. Raikes, *Light from Dark Ages? An Evangelical Critique of Celtic Spirituality* (2012), 19 notes, 'The Celts recognised also that the creation was fallen, transient, corrupt, and needing redemption.' Betel, *Isle of the Saints: Monastic Settlement and Christian Community in Early Ireland*, 31f., who writes., 'Small boys in monastic communities slipped and drowned … monsters lived in rivers, lakes and seas … the denizens of the wilderness were animals and demons … who inhabited the wild for one purpose only: to prey upon those foolish enough to leave the safety of home.' Ian Bradley, *Argyll: The Making of a Spiritual Landscape*, 58f.

51 Clancy and Markus, *Iona: The Earliest Poetry of a Celtic Monastery*, 90; cf. *Noli Pater*, 1, 2.

52 Meek, 'St. Columba and 'Celtic Christianity', 37.

a cold, wild, wet, and storm-lashed Hebridean summer, to say nothing of a hurricane-blasted Hebridean winter, would agree! The ancient literature sets Columba and his colleagues in conflict with nature as often as they are at peace with it. In Adomnán's *Life of Columba*, storms bring danger and have to be calmed; monsters from the deep are dreaded not welcomed; the wild must be tamed not cossetted. The world has not just been *affected* by the Fall; it has been *infected* by it. It needs to be redeemed. Nature is not what it was created to be. It is not always a friendly environment, but a hostile one. In line with this, Columba's *Altus Prosator* sees the natural world as doomed to destruction and in need of redemption. And the struggles and tensions which exist within nature are symptomatic of that deeper spiritual battle against the demonic, whose leader is Prince of this world. Nature is fallen, not perfect. Nature is an enemy needing to be subdued, as much as an ally giving assistance.

Columba starts his *Altus Prosator* by celebrating the goodness of God's original creation, but soon paints a darker picture of nature corrupted and broken. This is echoed in the short prayer *Noli Pater Indulgere*, the first six lines of which may have been written by Columba, and in which the elements are portrayed as a threat to humanity:

> Father do not allow thunder and lightning
> Lest we be shattered by the terror and the fire of it.[53]

Despite all this, there is another side, recognised by Raikes despite her disquiet with some over-romanticised appraisals of the early Celtic period. She suggests that, because Celtic spirituality was less influenced by Neoplatonist thinking than was the continental Roman Church, it had a different view of the relationship between the divine and the natural world. Celtic spirituality may not have suffered from Neoplatonism's inbuilt dualism between the spiritual and the material. This may have made Celtic spirituality more comfortable with the concept of God's immanence to His creation. It was more at ease with connections between God and nature, despite retaining an awareness of nature's brokenness.[54] At the same time, Raikes dismisses any superficial

53 *Noli Pater*, 1, 2; cf. Clancy and Markus, *Iona: The Earliest Poetry of a Celtic Monastery*, 86.

54 Raikes, *Light from Dark Ages?* 14. Yet O'Loughlin, *Celtic Theology*, 34, adds the reminder that though the 'Celtic saints' had a strong presence of God's immanence, that was not always comfortable: 'Their sense of God was very often that of a mighty power hovering over every situation. The closeness is the overpowering closeness of the stern, all-seeing master.'

correspondence between the spirituality of the ancient Irish Church and modern Celtic spirituality. The early medieval Irish Church did not have a spirituality brimming over with pure waters of peace, harmony, and environmentalism. Concord with nature was not uppermost in monks' minds as they battled to survive in challenging conditions.

Romanticism has viewed the early Christian centuries as a Golden Age, before capitalism and industrialisation spoiled everything. This has fed a desire to interpret Columba as an open and inclusive figure, living out a pure faith before divisive doctrines, damaging schisms, ecclesiastical-power abuses, and exploitative developments, ruined a spiritual Eden of nature, society, and Church. Stories of animals in peaceful coexistence with monks; legends of horses and sea otters sensing the needs and moods of holy men of God; and accounts of a fondness for trees, woods, and wild places; have all been marshalled as evidence of a time when faith had a green-edge, when nature was not exploited, and when creation itself responded.[55] This is also the preferred narrative for theologians who want to move theology away from notions of atonement through the cross, to an emphasis on peace, ecology, and the environment. There is an undoubted attractiveness in this approach. And there are elements within it which do resonate with early-medieval Irish Christianity.[56] But much of it is unrealistic idealisation. For sixth-century monks, nature was feared as much as loved.

GOD THE JUDGE

The hymn *Cantemus in Omni Die* was penned after Columba's death, but comes from the heart of Columban Christianity. It describes the world as having perished; humanity as languishing; and there being a need to be saved 'from flame of the dread fire'.[57] These ideas were widespread in the literature of the era. Such sentiments prompt Clancy and Markus to dismiss interpretations of Celtic theology which represent Columba and his contemporaries as unconcerned with sin

---

55 cf. Adomnán, *Life*, III:23 and Bede, *Life of Cuthbert*, 10. Herren and Brown, *Christ in Celtic Christianity*, 229, discuss the significance of animal representations in the highly illustrated Chi-Rho page of the *Book of Kells*.

56 Jackson, *A Celtic Miscellany*, 278, highlights early works from Celtic spirituality which celebrate harmony between saints and nature. He includes the tenth-century, 'The Wish of Manchan of Liath' (280), and the ninth/tenth-century 'St. Mael Anfaidh and the Bird's Lament for St. Mo Lua' (296). These are later than Columba's era, but from the Irish tradition.

57 *Cantemus in Omni Die*, 12.

or with judgement. Clancy and Markus insist that Celtic Christianity highlighted the fallenness of the created order. It emphasised sin. It stressed the need to escape hell. On these issues it was the same as other Christian traditions. Aware of attempts to make Columba and his era reflect a modern worldview which downplays these elements, Clancy and Markus note, in connection with *Cantemus in Omni Die*:

> When the wishful thinking of modern writers asks rhetorically of Celtic Christianity, 'Where was original sin and the alleged corruption of nature? Where the need for a redeemer?' the Iona monks themselves answer, 'Here!'[58]

1. *The Fall.* In the *Altus Prosator* Columba describes a created order in which things are not what they were intended to be. In teaching that Satan fell from heavenly glory, not once but twice, Columba is following Cassian on the double-fall of Satan.[59] Satan's first fall was because of pride. Satan's second fall was rooted in envy of humanity. He was envious because humanity was now called to share in God's glory to replace him. He had forfeited that destiny because of vanity.[60] This second fall took Satan deeper into his rebellion of ungodliness.[61] It generated his visceral hatred of humanity, placing men and women in a perilous situation. It means they are surrounded by demonic ill-will which seeks to entrap and bind sinners.[62]

2. *Hell.* The destination of those who fall from heaven and into Satan's hands is hell. Columba is stark:

> It seems doubtful to no one that there is a hell
> down below,
> Where there are held to be darkness, worms and
> dreadful animals:

---

58 Clancy and Markus, *Iona: The Earliest Poetry of a Celtic Monastery*, 191f. Though elsewhere (89f) they give later examples of a romantic view of a harmony between the Celtic mind and love of nature, they add: 'If we are to allow the early Irish monks to speak to us in their own voices, rather than simply projecting our needs onto them, we must go back to the texts and attend more closely to such evidence as we have. … A real hermit, living in a damp stone or wooden cell, fasting in hot and cold weather to subdue the flesh, terrified of thunder and lightning, as the author of the *Noli Pater* evidently was, is not the author of these "nature poems". Negative views of nature abound in Celtic poetry and prayers.'

59 Cassian, *Institutes*, XII:4.

60 Clancy and Markus, *Iona: The Earliest Poetry of a Celtic Monastery*, 57f.

61 *Altus Prosator*, C, G, H.

62 Clancy and Markus, *Iona: The Earliest Poetry of a Celtic Monastery*, 58.

Where there is sulphurous fire burning with
voracious flames:
Where there is the screaming of men, weeping
and gnashing of teeth.[63]

For Columba there are two possible outcomes. One is heaven. The other is hell. There is no universal salvation. There is no future repentance once a person stands before God's judgement seat.[64] This was reality for Columba. He and his monks lived every day with the possibility that hell might be their destiny, and the *Amra* (VII) suggests that fear of eternal damnation lay behind Columba's exile and asceticism. He gave up princely privileges. He renounced possessions. He repudiated chariots. He embraced exile. All in order to avoid the risk of rejection when he stood before the Son of the King at the Last Judgement. The *Amra* (VII) also reminds its readers why Columba was buried in Britain, rather than in Ireland. It was 'for fear of hell'. Columba needed to keep the terms of his exile even in death. If he failed to do so (even as a voluntary exile) then he jeopardised his soul and risked everlasting loss.

3. *Judgement.* The awful possibility of hell as the final destination of the soul is referred to several times by Adomnán. Columba, by the Holy Spirit, is able to see, 'the souls of the just carried to the heights of heaven by angels, but those of the wicked taken to hell by devils' (I:1). Robbers have been 'snatched down to the depths of hell, a wretched end, but one well-deserved' (II:22). He notes with approval that a man who killed a girl 'shall descend to hell' (II:25). The reality of hell was woven into the spirituality of the Irish Church, and the liturgy reflected these deep-seated beliefs. As priests took the Eucharist, they sang of their relief that they had escaped from the 'jaws of hell'.[65]

GOD THE SAVIOUR

In the few texts available to us, Columba rarely mentions the cross. There is one reference in the *Altus Prosator*; but the *Noli Pater Indulgere* and the disputed *Adiutor Laborantium* have no mention of the cross at all. And in his one brief allusion in the *Altus Prosator*, Columba makes no apparent link to the atonement,

63 *Altus Prosator*, Stanza N.
64 *Altus Prosator*, Stanza S.
65 *Bangor Antiphonary*, Item 8.

When Christ, the most-high Lord, comes down from the heavens,
the brightest sign and standard of the cross will shine forth.[66]

In this extract Columba refers to Christ's Second Coming. He features the cross because it symbolises how Christ, who was once so despised in being nailed to it, will at that point be acknowledged and honoured as the King of Glory. The cross will become His standard of glory, and no longer His symbol of shame.

What is absent in the *Altus Prosator* is an explicit connection between the cross and the atonement. Columba moves from meditating on the fallenness of humanity, to describing the judgement seat of God and the coming of Christ in triumph.[67] He has no intervening reflection on how redemption was achieved at Calvary. He offers no clear model of the atonement, whether penal substitution theory, ransom theory, or moral influence theory. Nevertheless, the lack of a specific atonement model and a dearth of references to the cross in the *Altus Prosator* does not mean that, for Columba and his monks, the death and resurrection of Christ were unrelated to salvation.

This is because the link between the death of Christ and God's mighty act of salvation was emphasised on Iona every time the Eucharist was celebrated. The *Amra* (IV), written within a year of Columba's death, articulates this connection between the Eucharist and salvation when it states that Columba was a terror to the devil to whom the mass was a 'noose'. In other words, the act celebrated at the centre of the Eucharist was what trapped the devil, despoiled him, and 'killed his power'.[68] The language of captivity and deliverance saturated the

66 *Altus Prosator*, Stanza X. The limited content of Columba's *Altus Prosator* contrasts with the broader content of the Anglo-Saxon Caedmon's poems who, according to Bede, *History*, IV:24, 'sang of the creation of the world, the origin of the human race, and the whole story of Genesis; sang of Israel's exodus from Egypt, the entry into the Promised Land, and many other events of scriptural history; and sang of the Lord's Incarnation, Passion, Resurrection, and Ascension into heaven, the coming of the Holy Spirit, and the teaching of the Apostles. He also made poems on the terrors of the Last Judgement, the horrible pains of Hell, and the joys of the Kingdom of Heaven.'

67 *Altus Prosator*, Stanzas P, Q, R, T, X.

68 Cassian interprets the atonement in terms of despoiling Satan and also in terms of paying a debt; cf. Cassian, *Institutes*, III:3: 'At the Sixth Hour the spotless sacrifice, our Lord and Saviour, was offered up to the Father, and, ascending the cross for the salvation of the whole world, made atonement for the sins of mankind, and, despoiling principalities and powers, led them away openly; and all of us who were liable to death and bound by the debt of the handwriting that could not be paid, He freed, by taking it away out of the midst and

mind-set of Columba and his monks. Within this context we begin to see that the single reference to the cross in the *Altus Prosator* does have a soteriological dimension. It is a reference to Christ's triumph over Satan. It is that triumph which brings salvation. Christ conquers Satan on the cross; and His subsequent triumph brings captive sinners home.

The complementary concepts of entrapment, despoliation, and setting-free are also high profile in the *Bangor Antiphonary*, which is more evidence that the theology of salvation centred on victory, release, and triumphal home-coming. Importantly, the *Bangor Antiphonary* has explicit references to the redeeming power of the blood of Christ. Item 8 speaks of, 'drinking the holy blood by which you were redeemed'.[69] The same hymn declares that it is through the sacrament of the body and blood that Satan has been despoiled, enabling the saints to escape from the 'jaws of hell'. Item 27 states: 'O Lord our God, you have redeemed us with your holy blood.' Similarly, Item 41 is a collect which states that the Lord has mercy on His church by 'redeeming it through his blood'.[70] The words of the liturgy ensured that monks never forgot that the cross, the blood of Christ, and the atonement were inextricably connected, though how that shed blood made atonement was not explained. Nevertheless, the effects of the shed blood were fully described, with Item 109 declaring: 'We have received the body of the Lord, and have had his blood to drink. We will fear no evil for the Lord is with us.' The overall consequences of God's actions in Christ on the cross, mediated through the Eucharist, are the triumph of Christ and the breaking of the rule of Satan. With the breaking of his rule, men and women are redeemed.

Columba believed that Christ's resurrection victory made redemption and liberty possible for those who had been held captive. In line with this, the *Amra* (IV), immediately following its statement that the mass

---

affixing it to His cross for a trophy, [i.e. fixing the bill of debt to the cross (Colossians 2:14)].' Herren and Brown, *Christ in Celtic Christianity*, 230, cite Augustine's description of the cross in which Christ's death was the bait by which the devil was caught.

69 *Bangor Antiphonary*, Item 8:1. See also: Items 27, 34, 41.

70 *Bangor Antiphonary*, Item 41. Herren and Brown, *Christ in Celtic Christianity*, 280, suggest: 'the Christology of the [later] *Celi De* reveals a clear shift from the Christ who saves by teaching and example, to the Christ who saves by shedding his blood.' They imply there was little emphasis on the 'atoning blood of Christ' in the earlier period. Against this view is the fact that the prayers of the early Irish Church, and the centrality of the Eucharist (with its constant emphasis on the redeeming power of Christ's blood), point in quite another direction.

is a 'noose' to Satan, declares that Christ 'suffered briefly until he triumphed: he was a terror to the devil'. This makes the triumph of Christ centre-stage. Christ allows Himself to be subjected to death. He is exposed to all of Satan's hostility. But He is strong enough to triumph and overcome. That victory creates the opportunity to set free all held captive by the Evil One. The imagery feeding into this theological mind-set is profoundly influenced by terrestrial warfare, in which a victorious General would sweep into his enemy's capital after a decisive battle and release all imprisoned there. In like manner, Christ descended into hell itself to free its captives after the battle on the cross. Christ is the Harrower of Hell, a theme discussed further in the next two chapters.[71] But what is already clear is that the dominant motif is that of the triumph of the strong man over the forces opposed to him.

Did Columba think at all in terms of Christ satisfying God's righteousness? This is not emphasised in his writings. Nor is it high-profile in the theology of the early-medieval Irish Church. The theme which is explicit, and which delivers the logic and vocabulary of early-medieval Irish theology, is the triumph of Christ over all that Satan could throw at Him. Because of Christ's triumph, Satan lost his authority to keep men and women captive. The evangelistic mission of the Church was empowered by that triumph. And the missionary task of the Church lay in bringing that victory of Christ to dark and pagan places.

The paradigm of the triumph of Christ and the breaking of Satan's rule saturates the thinking of Columba's Church. Maximising the fruit of that victory involves monks, as soldiers of Christ, engaging daily in spiritual warfare on earth. Their warfare is parallel to, and part of, a warfare waged by the angels in the heavenly places, and it is waged in the knowledge that the triumph of the resurrection means that there is only one ultimate victor, Christ Himself. Here and now, there is an urgency to gather as many souls as possible into Christ's victorious triumphal procession. Their task, with God's help, is to seek out and destroy the authority and rule of Satan wherever that holds sway. But

71 Herren and Brown, *Christ in Celtic Christianity*, 138, suggest that the harrowing of Hell is an un-Pelagian concept since it implies that the just who lived before Christ were unable to save themselves. Yet it is consistent with semi-Pelagianism.

it is anticipation of that final triumphal procession which explains why the one reference to the cross which we have from Columba's own pen comes in the context of Christ's anticipated return in glory:

> When Christ, the most-high Lord, comes down from the heavens,
> The brightest sign and standard of the cross will shine forth.[72]

The cross is mentioned in the context of the triumph of the returning Christ, because the cross was where the triumph of Christ over Satan was actualised. Christ's triumphant return is possible because of the cross. Furthermore, because victory climaxes in resurrection, the *Altus Prosator* goes on to affirm the resurrection of both body and soul:

> At the blast of the First Archangel's wonderful trumpet,
> the strongest vaults and tombs shall break open,
> The chill of the men of the present world melting away,
> The bones gathering to their joints from every place,
> Their ethereal souls meeting them,
> Returning once more to their own dwelling-places.[73]

This triumph meant that the early Irish Church viewed the day of a believer's death as their 'natal day' and the day of their true birth (II:45). After Columba's own death, when the young monk Fintan mac Tulchain met two of Columba's monks and asked after their abbot, he was told, 'Truly, our patron is in the best of health since only a few days ago he departed to Christ' (I:2). If the *Bangor Antiphonary* reflects early-medieval Irish spirituality as we think it does, then its Item 3 suggests that resurrection puts the Church 'among the Trinity'. The destiny of the believer is nothing less than participation in God.

Christ's death and resurrection released souls from Satan's captivity. This was foreshadowed by Israel's release from bondage in Egypt at the Exodus. But the Exodus narrative also reminded Christians that long years of desert pilgrimage followed Israel's release from bondage. Only after many years was the promised land reached. And in the spirituality of the Irish Church, that time of earthly pilgrimage, between liberation and glory, was not without risk.

---

72 *Altus Prosator*, Stanza X.

73 *Altus Prosator*, Stanza T.

CHAPTER 18

The Tendency of the Times

Was the early-medieval Irish Church tainted by Pelagianism? The British Church was certainly affected, with envoys sent from the Continent on at least two occasions to shepherd it back into the mainstream. Pelagianism took off in Britain around 429, and Bede claims that although the British Church instinctively recognised it as suspect, its leaders struggled to refute its arguments.[1] Help was sought from Gaul, and Germanus of Auxerre, along with Lupus of Troyes, were sent to Britain. According to Bede, they were entirely successful. The 'abominable heresy' was put down. Its authors were refuted. And the people were re-established in the 'pure faith' of Christ.[2] Bede's account is good propaganda. It represents his Roman Church coming to the rescue of the British Church. Nevertheless, Pelagianism resurfaced, prompting Germanus to return.[3]

Ireland may not have been immune. In 431, when the Church in Gaul was helping the British Church to combat Pelagianism, Rome sent Palladius to 'the Irish who believed in Christ to be their first bishop'.[4] However, Palladius may have been dispatched to combat heresy as much as to engage in evangelism, with Pelagianism in his sights.[5] Patrick was then commissioned to aid Palladius, but Palladius died before he arrived. Indications that Pelagianism had indeed taken root in Ireland may be implicit in Bede's observation that in the seventh century Rome was concerned that Pelagianism was reviving in Ireland. The heresy 'reviving' may indicate that it had previously affected the

1 Bede, *History*, I:17.
2 Bede, *History*, I:18.
3 Bede, *History*, I:21
4 Bede, *History*, I:13.
5 Dales, *Light to the Isles*, 30: Dales sees Palladius as having two objectives: combating Pelagianism; asserting Roman authority. McNeill, *The Celtic Penitentials*, 72, notes that a well-known early Irish Christians was Celestius, an able propagandist of Pelagianism, and renowned throughout Europe before Patrick.

island. Its recurrence certainly worried Pope Honorius in 634 and Pope John IV in 640, with each writing to the Irish Church about the matter.[6]

Pelagianism was a complex phenomenon. At its core it denied original inherited sin and taught that salvation could be achieved by human effort alone. Augustine of Hippo opposed Pelagianism tooth and nail, stressing that salvation is totally dependent on divine grace, with no merit attached to human effort or the human will. Critically, Augustine insisted that any good achieved by a man or woman is itself entirely the gift of God: 'God does not crown your merits as your merits, but as *His* own gifts.'[7] The logic of Augustine's position made him develop a robust doctrine of predestination, with human decision, human will, human merit, and human goodness, having no decisive role in a man or a woman's salvation. Cassian's semi-Pelagianism, with its combination of divine grace and human effort, emerged as a middle-way between the polarities of Pelagius and Augustine. Cassian believed that grace was indeed vital, but linked the necessity for divine grace with an equal necessity for human response and human virtue.[8] And it is because Cassian's thinking affected continental Christianity, as much as it affected Christianity in Ireland, that he is a central figure in this chapter.

Warren is aware of accusations of Pelagianism existing in the early Irish Church and is anxious to give it a clean bill of health.[9] But were Honorius and John IV seriously misinformed? Or had they a right to be worried? Though it is still a matter of debate as to whether pure Pelagianism permeated Ireland, the influence of semi-Pelagianism is much clearer. In semi-Pelagianism, divine grace and human merit cooperate in a person's salvation. And under this description there is little doubt that the early-medieval Irish Church had clear semi-Pelagian features. The growing

---

6 Bede, *History*, II:19; cf. Herren and Brown, *Christ in Celtic Theology*, 82ff., and 278ff.

7 cf. Augustine, *On Grace and Free Will*, XV: 'It is His own gifts that God crowns, not your merits, if, at least, your merits are of your own self, not of Him. If, indeed, they are such, they are evil; and God does not crown them. But if they are good, they are God's gifts, because, as the Apostle James says, "Every good gift and every perfect gift is from above, and cometh down from the Father of lights." ... God does not crown your merits as *your* merits, but as His own gifts.'

8 Cassian, *Institutes*, XII, 4:2, 3; cf. Cassian, *Conferences*, XIII, 'On Grace and Free Will', especially the 'mysterious manner' in which *both* grace and human effort play their part. This prompted Augustinians to label Cassian as semi-Pelagian. Semi-Pelagianism permeates Benedict's *Rule*: cf. VII: 'The ladder erected [to heaven], is our life on earth.'

9 Warren, *The Liturgy and Ritual of the Celtic Church*, 26.

importance of penance as a prerequisite to maintaining a heavenly hope, is itself enough to prove the case. Early-medieval penance was inherently semi-Pelagian, insisting as it did on penitential actions helping to purge the soul as a precondition to final salvation.

Michael Herren and Shirley Ann Brown, in their 2002 landmark study, *Christ in Celtic Christianity*, make a strong case for semi-Pelagianism being endemic in the early Irish Church, and argue that semi-Pelagianism was in fact embedded throughout the entire Common Celtic Church.[10] From a different viewpoint, Helen Conrad-O'Briain published an article (also in 2002) entitled, 'Grace and Election in Adomnán's *Vita Columbae*' in which she interprets Adomnán and his tradition as Augustinian through and through.[11] Conrad-O'Briain was hampered in that she was unable to draw on Herren and Brown's research, and her arguments are critiqued by Tomas O'Sullivan (who broadly endorses Herren and Brown) in a chapter entitled, 'The anti-Pelagian motif of the "naturally good" pagan in Adomnán's *Vita Columbae*', as his contribution to Jonathan Wooding's book, *Adomnán of Iona; Theologian, Lawmaker, Peacemaker*.[12] We return to these works later in this chapter.

MUTUAL NON-CONFORMITY

There is a major question. If the Irish Church was semi-Pelagian, and if the Roman Church was Augustinian, why was the Irish Church's

10 Bonner, 'Review of Herren and Brown, *Christ in Celtic Christianity*' in *Peritia*, vol. 16 (2002), 510-13, challenges Herren and Brown's central thesis of a common Celtic Church inspired by Pelagianism. Gilbert Markus, 'Pelagianism and the Common Celtic Church: A Review of Herren and Brown *Christ in Celtic Christianity*', *Innes Review*, vol. 56 (2005), 165-213, similarly argues that each example which Herren and Brown cite could be reinterpreted as Augustinian. However, O'Sullivan, 'The anti-Pelagian motif of the 'naturally good' Pagan', 257, argues that the weight of evidence and Adomnán's phraseology are suggestive of a non-Augustinian theology. What was decisive in the whole matter was the feeling that if human effort did not contribute toward salvation, then there was little value in the ascetic self-discipline to which monks had dedicated their lives (265). Marion Raikes, *Light from Dark Ages? An Evangelical Critique of Celtic Spirituality*, 24f., rejects the thesis that all Celtic theology was tainted by Pelagianism; but does not cite Herren and Brown on *semi*-Pelagianism despite her work being published in 2012, ten years after theirs.

11 Conrad-O'Briain, 'Grace and Election in Adomnán's Vita S. Columbae' in *Hermathena*, 172 (2002), 25-38.

12 O'Sullivan: 'The anti-Pelagian motif of the "naturally good" pagan in Adomnán's *Vita Columbae*' *in* Wooding (ed.), *Adomnán of Iona*, 253-73. O'Sullivan (256) inaccurately states that Herren and Brown identify Pelagianism as the operative theological paradigm in these narratives. What they identified was semi-Pelagianism.

tendency towards Pelagianism not used as an argument against it at Whitby in 664?[13] If the two traditions diverged in this important area, why did the Roman Church not take the Irish Church to task? Why is there no indication of this in the Whitby debates? Why was that fault not exposed and exploited?

We have two near-contemporary accounts of the Whitby debate. One is in Bede's *History*. The other is in Eddius Stephanus' *Life of Wilfrid*. Bede could be a generous writer, and it is conceivable that Bede was reluctant to impugn the memory of Columban churchmen such as Aidan and Cuthbert who were held in awe as holy men of God. Did that inhibit what he wrote about Whitby? Did Bede have no appetite to record anything which would diminish Iona's reputation, since Northumbria owed much of its Christian faith to Iona? However, even if Bede was tempted to give a sanitised account of Whitby (and that is conjecture), Eddius Stephanus, the biographer of Bishop Wilfrid, was not. Eddius had no inhibitions when writing about the Irish/Columban tradition. It is he who records Wilfrid as boasting, 'Was I not the first to root out from the Church the foul weeds planted by the Scots?'[14] 'Foul weeds' is strong and insulting language. Eddius has no hesitation in piling abuse on the Irish Church. Yet, despite Eddius' readiness to smear, he includes no criticism of Iona's theology in his account of Whitby. Thus, neither the polite Bede, nor the hostile Eddius, indicate that Iona was suspect in relation to Pelagianism, which was a touchstone heresy of the day. The reverse was true. Bede delivers a celebrated imprimatur on Columban theology, stating that Aidan:

> Believed, worshipped, and taught exactly what we do, namely the redemption of the human race through the Passion, Resurrection, and Ascension into heaven of the Man Jesus Christ, the Mediator between God and man.[15]

Bede homologates the Irish Church's doctrine of salvation through Christ, with no hint that Pelagianism or semi-Pelagianism affected this

13 Yorke, *The Conversion of Britain: 600–800*, 116, concludes that the charge of Pelagianism was not raised against the Irish Church because it was not Pelagian. At the same time, she allows Cassian's semi-Pelagianism as a characteristic of the Irish Church, but does not follow through on this, despite semi-Pelagianism (officially) also being deemed a heresy by Rome.

14 Eddius, *Life of Wilfrid*, 47.

15 Bede, *History*, III:17.

core doctrine. Bede was well aware of the menace of Pelagianism. He wrote about pre-Roman churches in Britain and Ireland being affected by Pelagianism. He knew that Augustine of Canterbury had been sent to Britain by Pope Gregory in 597, with the specific aim of introducing a 'correct and pure' Catholic faith which was properly linked to Rome. He was to replace a 'corrupted' version which had rooted itself in Britain. Despite all this, in Bede's accounts of Whitby, there is no sign that the Irish tradition was branded as Pelagian.

Were Bede and Eddius inhibited in what they wrote because their work had to be acceptable to the Northumbrian royal house? Both knew that the Northumbrian royal family came to Christian faith through Iona.[16] Both knew that when the royal family returned to Northumbria, they brought that spiritual legacy with them. And both knew that Oswald sought help from Iona in evangelising his kingdom. Did this back-history dampen their criticism of Iona's theology? Was it impolitic to imply that the royal household had adopted a contaminated faith? But if Bede's writings might conceivably have been influenced by this, not so Eddius' works. The readiness of Eddius to term Irish/Columban traditions as 'foul weeds' shows that he saw no need for a diplomatic silence on its perceived demerits.

Why then was the Irish Church not accused of Pelagianism or semi-Pelagianism at Whitby? Our argument is that the matter was never raised, because the Roman Church, officially Augustinian, was *de facto* semi-Pelagian in its day-to-day piety, and so shared the same theological position with Iona. This made Rome blind to the presence of semi-Pelagianism in its neighbour. The whole Church, Roman and Celtic, continental and insular, had a common, semi-Pelagian, spirituality. Although the official theology of the continental Roman Church was Augustinian, its practical piety was more nuanced. At Rome as well as on Iona, it was assumed that although baptism cleansed a person from past sins, it was the subsequent quality of a pilgrim's life, in conjunction with his or her fulfilment of penance, which determined his or her eternal destiny. Such a theology necessarily involves a combination of divine grace and human effort. And it was that theology, with its interdependence of grace and effort, which was the *de facto* day-to-day mind-set of all European Christendom. Any semi-Pelagianism in the

16 Bede, *History*, III:1.

Irish tradition would go unrecognised by Bede and Wilfrid, because it was no different from their own spirituality. Both Iona and Rome rejected full-blown obvious Pelagianism. Both rejected its denial of original sin. Both rejected the notion that unaided human effort could bring salvation. But both accepted a combination of grace and effort. That constituted semi-Pelagianism.

NATURAL GOODNESS

These issues come into sharp focus when we consider the conversion narratives in Adomnán's *Life of Columba* which involve the phrase 'natural goodness'.[17] The first account concerns the conversion of a family in Glen Urquhart, near Loch Ness (III:14). Adomnán writes that Columba was with his monks in Pictland when he said to them:

> 'Let us make haste to meet the holy angels who have come from the heights of heaven to bear away the soul of a heathen man, who has spent his whole life in *natural goodness* and is now very old. But they must wait till we reach the place, so that we may bring timely baptism to him before he dies.' Though St Columba was an old man, he hurried on as fast as he could ahead of his companions, till he reached the fields of Glen Urquhart. There he found an old man called Emchath, who heard and believed the word of God preached to him by the saint, and was baptized. Thereupon, [Emchath] departed happily and safely to the Lord in the company of the angels that had come to meet him.

The second account is Adomnán's story of the conversion of a family on the Isle of Skye. Columba struck the ground by the seashore with his staff and said:

> 'Today, in this place and on this patch of ground, an old man – a pagan but one who *has spent his whole life in natural goodness* – will receive baptism, and will die and be buried.' Only an hour later – look! – a little boat came in to land on the shore, bringing in its prow a man worn out with age.

17 Sharpe offers the English phrase 'natural goodness' in his translation on three further occasions (II:18; III:6; III:19). But in each of these the Latin is *bonae indolis*, which Anderson and Anderson translate more precisely as 'of good ability'.

> He was the chief commander of the war-band in the region of *Ce*. Two young men carried him from the boat, and set him down in front of the blessed man. As soon as he had received the word of God from St Columba, through an interpreter, he believed and was baptized by him. When the rite of baptism was finished, as the saint had predicted, the old man died on the same spot and they buried him there and raised a mound of stones over the place. It is still visible there today by the seashore. The stream in which he had received baptism is even today called by the local people 'the water of Artbranan'.[18]

Both narratives give insights into Adomnán's understanding of how Columba and his monks evangelised. The word was proclaimed. Faith was born. Baptism took place. But in the Irish tradition, baptisms normally took place only after a period of instruction and preparation, so why was baptism granted immediately in these cases? Was it because the converts were at the point of death? Was it to seal them into the Church before Columba moved on, given their geographic isolation? Or was immediate baptism appropriate because, as Adomnán expresses it, the candidates had spent their whole lives in 'natural goodness'? Had that prepared them morally for the rite? What does Adomnán mean by natural goodness? There have been several interpretations.

1. *Montalembert:* The Roman Catholic scholar Charles Forbes Montalembert was the Duke of Argyll's *bête-noir* when the Duke wrote his book on Iona. Several of the Duke's broadsides were aimed specifically at him, not least because Montalembert argued a strong case for Columba's faith dovetailing with Roman Catholic beliefs. In Montalembert's analysis of Adomnán's *Life of Columba*, he notes the expression 'natural goodness' in the conversion narratives. Montalembert paraphrases it as 'natural law' because he interprets the two men's pre-conversion lifestyle as the outcome of them having recognised, and having lived in accordance with, the 'light and virtues of the law of nature'.[19] This enables Montalembert to see 'natural goodness' as resonating with the Roman Catholic notion of natural law which teaches that all moral law given by divine revelation is consistent with the laws of nature and

18 Adomnán, *Life*, I:33 (my italics).

19 Montalembert, *The Monks of the West from St. Benedict to St. Bernard: vol. II*, 49f.

the human reason. In Roman Catholicism, natural law is based on the conviction that if human reason were able to probe deeply enough, it would find that the very structures of the natural world demand the specific moralities which come through divine revelation and the teaching of the Church.[20] Every divinely revealed moral precept is an expression of principles embedded deep within nature. Interpreted through this lens, the conversion narratives concern men who have discerned, through natural law, the requirements of God's righteousness and have lived accordingly. This idea was common among some of the Church Fathers, with Basil teaching that the written Law cultivates and nurtures powers which are implanted in the soul by the Creator.[21] For Montalembert, it was because the two men recognised this implanted Law and obeyed it in their lives, that they were on the threshold of acceptability to God, needing only faith and baptism to complete the journey.

2. *Herren and Brown:* Herren and Brown go further. They view the references to 'natural goodness' as examples of clear semi-Pelagianism.[22] For them, Adomnán's narrative implies that the two men had lived lives full of natural goodness without help of divine revelation. All they now required was to hear and respond to the Gospel in order to complete their salvation. These men showed what the natural man is capable of morally, and were proofs that men and women are able to live good lives before God. The good life is possible, and this is what Adomnán means when he describes their state as one of 'natural goodness'. For Herren and Brown, the narratives underscore the semi-Pelagian theology of the Irish Church. Good lives prepare men and women for salvation. But they still need faith and baptism. If Adomnán had taught that the men's morality on its own had been sufficient for salvation, then that would have been undiluted Pelagianism. But, because Adomnán makes it clear that the grace of God, through faith and baptism, is also

20 This definition was given by Cardinal A. G. Cicognani to Karl Barth on behalf of Pope Paul VI in a letter dated 11 November 1968: 'As for Christians, revelation does not suppress natural law, which is equally divine, it simply elucidates it, completes it, makes its observance possible through the Holy Spirit, and above all orders it to the supernatural calling of the children of God which remains their sole salvation. This fact, that natural law finds itself thus ordered to salvation, explains why its prescriptions can be the subject of the church's magisterium.' (J. Fangmeier and H. Stoevesandt (eds), *Karl Barth: Letters 1961-1968* (English translation: Edinburgh, T&T Clark, 1981), 357f).

21 Basil, *The Shorter Rule*, Qu. 2:59.

22 Herren and Brown, *Christ in Celtic Christianity*, 95f.

required, then he is describing semi-Pelagianism. Tomas O'Sullivan accepts Herren and Brown's analysis. He agrees that the conversion narratives are indicative of semi-Pelagianism. For Herren, Brown, and O'Sullivan, Adomnán is not expressing an Augustinian position. Neither is he promoting pure Pelagianism. Adomnán is replicating Cassian's middle-way theology, in which human response and human goodness are both involved in salvation.

This middle-way theology was thriving on the Continent as well as in the Irish Church. By the close of the sixth century, during the papacy of Gregory the Great, there was discomfort with Augustine's full-blown doctrines, resulting in Cassian's middle-way becoming the *de facto* theology even in Rome, albeit with no fanfare. Officially Rome never moved away from Augustine. But Cassian's semi-Pelagianism underpinned the day-to-day beliefs of most Christians. Cassian's theology made moral effort worthwhile. And by the time of Whitby in 664, middle-way theology was unquestioned. Popular faith and piety across Christendom absorbed Cassian's ideas rather than Augustine's logic, and the growing discipline of penance contributed to this. Penitential exercises involved human response, human will, human effort, and human application. Across Christendom it was accepted that only through such exercises could sins be shriven. To all intents and purposes, this made penance part of a semi-Pelagian Gospel. All of this was believed, without protest, on Iona, on Lindisfarne, and at Rome.

3. *Conrad-O'Briain:* Helen Conrad-O'Briain resists this interpretation.[23] She accepts that in this area the theologies of Iona and Rome were the same, but she attempts to prove that they were the same

23 Conrad-O'Briain, 'Grace and Election in Adomnán's Vita S. Columbae' in *Hermathena*, 172 (2002), 25-38. She focuses on Adomnán, *Life of Columba*, I:33 and III:14, arguing that they were read by minds who assumed 'an essentially Augustinian field of reference'. She maintains that in I:33 Columba displays prescience participating in God's foreknowledge, and in III:14 Columba acts as an instrument of God's providence in fellowship with the angels. She writes that when Adomnán wrote his *Life of Columba*, he was anxious to present a Columba who was orthodox in his understanding of the relationship between good works and grace. However, she assumes throughout her article that the Roman Church followed an orthodox Augustinianism, an assumption which we question. A weakness of Conrad-O'Briain's thesis is that she does not consider the option of semi-Pelagianism, which needed faith and grace to complement moral virtue. She insists that the original readership 'would not read Artbranan's and Emcath's salvation as the result of their ethical lives, but their ethical lives as a result of their salvation, a paradox which resolves itself when viewed through the eyes of God.'

because both were Augustinian. She believes that Adomnán's 'natural goodness' passages can be harmonised with Augustinian theology and claims that if we assume Adomnán's original readers had an Augustinian mind-set, then all the features of these conversion stories (including the notion of 'natural goodness') fit that assumption. She points out that Augustine viewed all human goodness and all natural goodness as a gift of God's sovereign will, with nothing to do with human merit. Therefore, if we read Adomnán's narrative with that in mind, the theologies of Iona, Rome, and Augustine are one and the same. But does Adomnán view human goodness in an Augustinian way? Take, for example, Adomnán's story of the upright and pious blacksmith Columb Coilrigin as illustrative of the centrality of good works and human merit in Adomnán's understanding of salvation:

> [Columb Coilrigin] has been fortunate in *procuring with the labour of his own hands the eternal rewards that he desired to buy*. See now, his soul is being carried by holy angels to the joys of the heavenly country. For whatever he was able to gain by practising his craft he laid out in alms to the needy. (III:10) [my italics]

Columb Coilrigin's actions were commendable and well worthy of a Christian. That is undeniable. But it is Adomnán's assumption that Columb Coilrigin's salvation was due, at least in part, to his meritorious good works through the labour of his own hands, which raises questions. Nowhere in this story does Adomnán indicate that he is working with Augustine's description of a 'good work' in which no merit is applied to the human agent.

There are stress points in Conrad-O'Briain's analysis. Because of publication dates she could not interact with Herren and Brown's study of the theology of the Celtic Church. Nor does she explore the links between Irish theology and Cassian. Nor does she consider the possibility of Cassian's system being a more natural context in which to interpret the notion of natural goodness. Nor does she consider the option of semi-Pelagianism, as distinct from full-blown Pelagianism. Nor does she reflect on what was the *de facto* theology of Rome in contrast to its *official* theology. Nor, in her study of Adomnán's *Life of Columba*, does she analyse how Adomnán uses the concept of predestination. Though she is not alone in this.

PREDESTINATION AND CONDITIONALITY

Adomnán's use of 'predestine' and its cognates takes us into new territory. Our argument is that when Adomnán refers to predestination in his *Life of Columba*, he does so in a non-Augustinian manner, confirming that the underlying theology of the Irish Church was of a semi-Pelagian variety. There are five passages to be considered.

1. *Columba and King Diarmait's son:* Adomnán describes Columba speaking to the son of King Diarmait, with Columba saying, 'You should take care my son, for though God has predestined [*praedistinatam*] for you the prerogative of the kingship of all Ireland, you may lose it by the sin of a family murder.' (I:14)

2. *Columba and Feradach:* Columba heard news of a murder committed by a man called Feradach. Adomnán puts the following words into Columba's mouth, 'It is not only in my sight but in God's that Feradach has betrayed our trust. His name will be *removed* from the Book of Life.' (II:23)

3. *Baithéne and Fintan mac Tulchain:* Baithéne, Columba's eventual successor, is reported by Adomnán as declaring, '[Fintan mac Tulchain] is still a youth, spending his time in the pursuit of good and the study of the Scriptures. He will beg you to receive him as one of your monks. But God knows this is not what is predestined [*praedistinatum*] for him, that he should be an abbot's monk. No, he has been chosen by God to be an abbot of monks himself and one who leads souls to the kingdom of heaven.' (I:2)[24]

4. *Columba's mother and the Angel:* Adomnán uses the terminology of predestination in his account of an angel speaking to Columba's mother before Columba's birth. The angel announces, 'He [Columba] has been predestined [*praedistinatus*] by God to be a leader of innumerable souls to the heavenly country.' (III:1)

5. *Brendan and Columba:* Adomnán places similar words into Brendan's mouth, with Brendan saying about Columba, 'I do not

24 Charles-Edwards, 'The Structure and Purpose of Adomnán's *Vita Columbae*' in Wooding (ed.), *Adomnán of Iona*, 205-18, discusses this. His view is that there was nothing Pelagian about Adomnán's portrait of Columba, in spite of the natural goodness of Artbranan and Emchath, and he concludes that Adomnán managed a balance between predestination and personal goodness. Like others, Charles-Edwards does not consider the option of semi-Pelagianism.

dare to spurn this man whom God, as I have had visible proof, has predestined [*praeordinatum*] to lead the nations to life.' (III:3)

The latter three extracts could each be interpreted in an Augustinian sense, since, in each case, what was predestined came to pass. Fintan mac Tulchain *did* become an abbot of monks (I:2 and II:31). Columba *did* become a 'leader of innumerable souls to the heavenly country'. And Columba *did* become a significant international figure for the Gospel. However, the first two citations do not conform to Augustinian notions of predestination and election. The first two extracts assume that, although God may have sovereign purposes for individuals, God's sovereign purposes are not fixed immutably. Diarmait's son could lose what had been predestined for him. Feradach's name could be erased from the Book of Life. In these instances, predestination did not make an issue unchangeable. These demonstrate that, for Adomnán, predestination indicates God's desire for the future, rather than God's sealing of the future. Predestination signifies divine intention, not divine determinism.[25] God might predestine something, but it may not occur. It is this which lies behind Columba's revealing comment that Feradach's name could be removed from the Book of Life. It also lies behind another incident in which God predestined something which might not actually come to pass, namely Diarmait's son gaining the kingship of all Ireland. God's predestined plan for the King's son might yet fall.[26]

In writing as he does, and in employing the vocabulary of predestination as he does, Adomnán voices notions which no true Augustinianism would allow. No one who was Augustinian in the manner in which Conrad-O'Briain claims Adomnán was, would write such theology. Nor would the critical phrases be penned by accident. If Adomnán were fully Augustinian, he would never allow such sentences to flow from his pen. His theological sensitivities would prevent him from making such statements. He would know the implications of what he wrote.

Few as they are, these instances reveal a non-Augustinian theological understanding. They promote a notion of predestination which is loose

---

25 cf. Herren and Brown, *Christ in Celtic Theology*, 100.

26 Adomnán uses the same term as the Vulgate version of Ephesians 1, normally translated as 'predestined'.

and conditional. They allow the possibility that a man or woman's eternal destiny might still be in doubt even after coming into the grace of God through faith.[27] For Adomnán in particular, and for Columban theology in general, predestination indicates God's preferred destiny for a person, but that destiny could go astray. A predestined kingship could be lost. A predestined calling could be missed. More seriously, a soul's eternal destiny could be forfeited. A name written in the Book of Life could be expunged. This is a spirituality rooted in Cassian's middle-way theology. The Irish and Columban traditions followed Cassian, not only in their form of monasticism, and in the shape of their liturgy, but in critical aspects of their theology.[28]

The early-medieval Irish Church, including Columba and Adomnán, had a theology with significant semi-Pelagian elements. And yet, it would be misleading to imply that early-medieval Irish Church leaders were debating concepts of human free will and human merit. The sixth-century Irish Church was comfortable with semi-Pelagianism, but not because it was wrestling with the same questions as had occupied Pelagius and Augustine. The spirituality of the Irish Church was not driven by that particular philosophical stand-off, but by the existential reality of spiritual warfare against Satan and his demonic hordes. What it found was that the semi-Pelagian solution fitted that context as comfortably as it fitted the quite different context of the original debates in southern Europe. The formative influence on Columba's thinking was not a search to solve a series of philosophical questions. Nor was it the Augustinian doctrine of election. Nor was it the abstract Pelagian notion of human free will. Instead, it was the question of spiritual warfare. And a theological system which combined human striving and divine provision in that area of spirituality was welcomed.

27 *Bangor Antiphonary*, Item 12, focuses on Christ's predestination 'for us' rather than our predestination 'for Christ'.

28 Dales, *Light to the Isles*, 31, notes that Faustus' work, *Concerning Grace*, which vigorously opposed Augustine's predestinarian theology, was brought to Britain in the late fifth century, after being approved at the Council of Arles in 472-3. Faustus was a protégé of Cassian, and insisted on the important role of the human will in cooperating with the work of divine grace in a person. Faustus was also abbot of the monastery at Lerins for twenty-six years up to 459 when he became Bishop of Riez. Lerins was influential on the Irish tradition.

It is true that from time to time Columba and his monks may have reflected on the nature of the will and on the notion of accrual of merit through moral endeavour, but these were not what drove the underlying logic of Iona's thinking. Iona's liturgy, doctrine, and evangelism, were driven by thoughts of cosmic spiritual warfare. And this thinking was not limited to the Irish Church. It was the prevailing mind-set of Christendom. Salvation was understood in terms of God's actions in Christ to set men and women free. It was metaphors associated with battle, conquest, triumph, despoilation of the enemy, and liberation of the captives, which dominated the spiritual imagination and the theological vocabulary. Salvation occurred when men and women were freed from the clutches of Satan into whose hands they had fallen by their sin. The cross and the blood of Christ, were instruments in that spiritual struggle against demonic power.[29] The death of Christ was not cited principally to explain how the price of sin might be paid, or how God's honour might be satisfied. These ideas were not totally absent; but the main thinking was elsewhere. The keynote theme of 'the triumph of Christ over Satan, and the setting free of God's people' occupied prime position. That was the day-to-day unifying principle.

This is illustrated by an example in Bede's account of the seventh-century Canterbury mission. Pope Boniface sent a letter to King Edwin of Deira (a kingdom north of the Humber) urging Edwin to convert, because Christian Faith 'will free you from Satan's bondage; and through the liberative power of the holy and undivided Trinity you will inherit eternal life.'[30] Pope Boniface also wrote to Edwin's Christian queen, Ethelberga, again emphasising liberation as the hallmark of salvation, and stressing that Christ saves men and women by redeeming them from 'the Devil's enslaving tyranny by the shedding of his own precious blood'.[31] Boniface's sentiments exactly parallel those of the Irish Church of the same era. Salvation is understood in terms of liberation from Satanic bondage.

But this powerful theology of victory, triumph, and setting free, came with a price. Because the images which were used to explain spiritual

---

29 Herren and Brown, *Christ in Celtic Christianity*, 281, regard the motif of the cosmic struggle against the devil as gripping the imagination of Irish writers from the seventh century onwards. Adomnán was a seventh-century monk.

30 Bede, *History*, II:10.

31 Bede, *History*, II:11.

warfare were borrowed from human warfare, then they also allowed the possibility that liberated souls could yet be lost. It was a reality of human warfare that there were fatalities, even on the victor's side. In all wars there were some who never made it through, despite initially seeming to triumph. When the imagination transferred imagery from human warfare to spiritual warfare, it retained and included the possibility that, in the struggle and conflict against spiritual powers, some may be lost even though the war itself was won. Whereas models of the atonement which major on Christ paying the price of sin once-for-all, or which focus on God's immutable decree of election, make an individual's salvation irrevocable and permanent, a model which saw the atonement in terms of struggle and conflict brought provisionality.

Ireland and Iona had a semi-Pelagian spirituality. However, whereas Augustine and Pelagius debated divine sovereignty, human free will, and human merit, the issue in Ireland and on Iona was spiritual warfare. Holiness or merit in themselves did not bring salvation. What holiness and merit did do was to enable men and women to engage more successfully in spiritual warfare: but it was the warfare as such which was decisive. Good works were preparatory factors for battle. Good works honed the spiritual warrior to peak condition. But the spiritual battle was the action arena. However, all warfare brings with it chance and uncertainty, even for those on the victor's side. And it was the importation of such contingencies (so obvious in human conflicts) which profoundly affected any guarantee of an assured heavenly hope for an individual. It was this which allowed the possibility that names could be removed from the Book of Life.

CHAPTER 19

The Triumph of the King

Columba's spirituality was shaped and coloured by his core belief in the triumph of Christ over Satan which resulted in God's people being set free. This dovetailed easily with semi-Pelagianism, because what fed semi-Pelagianism in Ireland was not the original controversy concerning human free will and human merit, but an all-enveloping consciousness of spiritual warfare. This cradled Columba's understanding of the Christian Gospel. And in Ireland and on Iona the triumph of Christ was imagined in highly realistic terms.

The early-medieval Irish Church rarely debated the question of how Christ's death on the cross brought atonement.[1] The literature of the period has only occasional references to concepts such as the price of sin being paid on the cross. In place of this, there is a consistent emphasis on the triumph of Christ who, through the cross, cancelled the demonic captivity to which men and women were subject. In death, Christ entered the depths of hell. He then emerged from hell in triumph, with freed captives in His wake. Christ overcame the strong man's stranglehold over humanity.[2] Christ harrowed hell. He despoiled Satan. He liberated those held captive by the Prince of Darkness.[3] The *Amra* (IV) references this, with Satan, the erstwhile captor, himself becoming bound:

[Columba] suffered briefly until he triumphed,
He was a terror to the devil, to whom Mass was a noose.

---

1 Herren and Brown, *Christ in Celtic Christianity*, 65, point out that Pelagianism, in emphasising Christ as law-giver, teacher, and model, left little room for a divine Redeemer. Yet, the Irish Church's semi-Pelagianism was often overridden by orthodox creedal statements and by orthodox liturgical practices. The liturgy protected the doctrine.

2 Jesus has 'the strong man' as a metaphor for Satan. (Matthew 12:29; Mark 3:27; Luke 11:21). Bruce, *Prophecy, Miracles, Angels and Heavenly Light?*, 83, notes that Adomnán uses it similarly (II:8); cf. O'Loughlin, *Celtic Theology*, 99.

3 Herren and Brown, *Christ in Celtic Christianity*, 159f. Holding slaves was part of life in early-medieval societies. In this context, being set free from bondage to another was strongly relevant; cf. Yorke, *The Conversion of Britain: 600–800*, 73f.

Beccán's honour-poem to Columba, *Fo Reir Choluimb*, has similar thinking:

> Royal kin of triumphant kings,
> Lord full of grace, thus may [Columba] guard us.
> I'll take off the devil's noose.[4]

Both extracts employ the concept of a noose or trap. In the *Amra*, the mass is described as a noose to Satan. In the *Fo Reir Choluimb*, the Christian is someone who has taken off the devil's noose and has been set free. Taken together, these describe how Christ reversed the effects of the Fall of humanity and turned Satanic captivity on its head.[5] The cross, the death of Christ, the resurrection, the ascension, are all placed within the context of spiritual struggle against a demonic power which has imprisoned humanity. The entire Christian Gospel, and the whole life of Christian pilgrimage, is read as a dramatic narrative in which Christ engages with Satan in a life and death wrestle over souls. Sin gave Satan a hold over men and women. Humanity has to be set free from his grip. Salvation occurs when sinners are released from Satan's noose, and when Satan is caught in Christ's noose. Christ triumphs and overcomes the Enemy. But Christian believers continue in spiritual warfare until the end of their earthly pilgrimage. Engagement with Satan, grappling with the enemy, and (hopefully) triumphing in victory, are all part of life for every Christian.

ENGAGING THE ENEMY

Columba, and the early-medieval Irish Church, were drawing on concepts which had strong roots in the Church Fathers when they thought in terms of Christ engaging with Satan at the cross. The Church Fathers interpreted Ephesians 2:2 to mean that the air was Satan's natural environment. And they believed that when Christ was

4 Beccán, *Fo Reir Choluimb*, XXIV. The notion of being 'chained' and of Christ loosing such chaining through the cross is also present in Item 3 (*Precamur Patrem*) of the *Bangor Antiphonary*: '[Christ], with the old adversary subdued, loosed the pole from the knotty chain of death … Fixed on a cross He shakes the pole wondrously, and He veils the illumination of the sun for three hours … The man [Adam], gnawed fiercely by knots for thousands of years, He extricates from the savage beast of hell … He placed the Church in the Trinity.' [Tr, Howlett, 172f.]

5 Cassian, *Institutes*, XII:8, portrays God using the principle of opposites as a mechanism to conquer Satan: 'God, the Creator and Healer of all, knowing that pride is the cause and fountainhead of evils, has been careful to heal opposites with opposites that those things which were ruined by pride might be restored by humility.' Here, Cassian applies the principle of 'healing opposites with opposites' to salvation; cf. Basil, *The Shorter Rule*, Qu. 2:48-54.

lifted up into the air on the cross, He entered Satan's territory, engaging him full-on. Athanasius' statement is worthy of repetition:

> By what other kind of death could this [salvation] have come to pass, other than by one which took place in the air, I mean the cross? For only He that is perfected on the cross dies in the air. Whence it was quite fitting that the Lord suffered this death. For thus being lifted up He cleared the air of the malignity both of the devil and of demons of all kinds, as He says: 'I beheld Satan as lightning fall from heaven'; and made a new opening of the way up into heaven as He says once more: 'Lift up your gates, O ye princes, and be ye lift up, ye everlasting doors.'[6]

Athanasius returns to the theme in his *Festal Letter* for the year 350:

> Our Lord Jesus Christ, who took upon Himself to die for all, stretched forth His hands, not somewhere on the earth beneath, but in the air itself, in order that the salvation effected by the cross might be shown to be for all men everywhere: destroying the devil who was working in the air: and that He might consecrate our road up to heaven, and make it free.[7]

Christ engaged with Satan directly 'in the air'. The battle climaxed when Christ embraced death and descended into the abyss of hell where Satan held men and women in miserable captivity. In entering hell, Christ went to the ultimate Far Country. As Son of God from heaven, He went not just to the earth but to the desolation of hell itself. Columba refers to this deliverance in his *Altus Prosator*:

> Under the earth, as we read, we know there are inhabitants,
> Whose knee bends often in prayer to the Lord,
> But for whom it was impossible to open the written book
> Sealed with seven seals according to the warnings of Christ,
> Which he himself had unsealed after he had risen as victor,
> Fulfilling the prophets' foreseeing of his Coming.[8]

---

6 Athanasius, *On the Incarnation*, XXV.

7 Athanasius, *Letters* 22; cf. Athanasius, *Life of Anthony*, 21: 'Great is their number in the air around us.'

8 *Altus Prosator*, Stanza O.

Columba's poem reflects Revelation 5:3 where those who are held 'under the earth' are souls who belong to Christ but are imprisoned and unable of themselves to open the scroll sealed with seven seals. Instead, Christ comes to the place of their captivity, and sets them free. Herren and Brown view this despoiling and harrowing of hell as a dominant motif in Celtic theology. Christ's battle was won when, because of His mighty strength and greater virtue, He overcame Satan, plundered hell, and in resurrection power rose to eternal life, accompanied by those whom Satan had held captive. Christ became the victorious warrior *par excellence.* He led His people in the ultimate Exodus.

This vivid drama of redemption filled the mind of an Irish monk as he meditated on the power of Christ's death and resurrection. He did not think of Christ's death primarily in terms of paying the price of sin, or in terms of satisfying God's honour. His instinct was to think of the cross in terms of Christ's battle against the old enemy. Other notions are detectable in the literature, but centre-stage is occupied by thoughts of warfare, engagement, conflict, battle, and victory. All the decisive metaphors involve conflict and warfare scenarios. The texts are rich in word-pictures which feature: battle, wounds, struggle, victory, setting free, temporary set-back, possible recapture, and eventual triumph. The monkish mind operated as a picture gallery of images, rather than as a debating chamber of ideas.

An example of this is Item 3 (*Precamur Patrem*) of the *Bangor Antiphonary*, which was composed soon after Columba's era.[9] *Precamur Patrem* is an extended hymn on the life of Christ in which the central theme is light, both the light of creation and the light of salvation. In creation this eternal light (rooted in the Trinity) dispels the primordial darkness of the world, and in salvation the same light vanquishes Satan, the author of death. Christ Himself, as eternal light, is the agent of both creation and redemption. He lives on earth. He descends into hell. He harrows hell. He sets free the saints. *Precamur Patrem* vividly illustrates the type of spirituality which nurtured Comgall, Columba, Columbanus, and other Irish saints. Its main theme is Christ's rescue mission, described in terms of liberation and deliverance. This was the paradigm for understanding redemption, and *Precamur Patrem* is not an isolated example. Elsewhere, in Item 13 of the *Bangor Antiphonary*,

9 Curran, *The Antiphonary of Bangor and the Early Irish Monastic Liturgy*, 50.

Patrick is portrayed as Christ's representative on earth, who was appointed to redeem innumerable numbers of men and women from the captivity of Satan.[10] The concept of release from bondage was regarded as thoroughly biblical, with Paul describing evangelism as releasing men and women from the power of Satan and freeing them for God (Acts 26:18).

Warfare metaphors shaped every aspect of faith in early-medieval Irish Christianity, moulding its understanding of salvation, lifestyle, daily piety, and evangelism.[11] We discuss evangelism in later chapters, but we can note at this point that the missionary monk saw himself as a co-warrior with Christ and, through prayer and proclamation, he participated in Christ's ongoing campaign of cancelling the rule of Satan over subject peoples. When Christ broke Satan's rule in a new locality, then the fundamental change which took place was that the men and women who lived there now belonged to Christ's kingdom and not to Satan's. It was not argument, disputation, or discussion which moved a person from hell to heaven. It was Christ winning a spiritual battle against Satan over their souls: a battle thought of in almost physical terms.

FREEING THE CAPTIVES

Christ's mission of warfare and rescue was an emphasis of the Roman Church as much as of the Irish Church, with the letters of Pope Boniface to Edwin of Deira and his Queen Ethelberga striking examples of the genre.[12] In the Church Fathers, Christ's victory over Satan was seen as the central act of redemption. Cassian describes the cross as the place where Satan's power was broken, and, in a passage in which he reflects on the importance of each of the Canonical Hours, he writes:

---

10 *Bangor Antiphonary*, Item 13:21. In referring to the 'bondage of man' and to 'enslavement to the devil', Item 13 includes both human and spiritual slavery. Patrick and Israel were in human bondage before experiencing a human exodus. But humanity is also enslaved to Satan, requiring a spiritual exodus. Item 13 combines the historical and spiritual Exoduses.

11 e.g., *Bangor Antiphonary*, Item 60.

12 Bede, *History*, II:10. Ryan, 'The Mass in the Early Irish Church' in *IQR*, vol. 50, no. 200, (1961) 372, points out that in the Stowe Missal (c. 800), there are a number of prayers between the Epistle and Gospel, including one found also in the Bobbio Missal: 'Almighty, everlasting God, who hast redeemed thy people by the blood of thine only begotten Son, bring to nought the works of the devil, burst the chains of sin, so that they who have obtained eternal life through the confession of thy name may incur no debt to the author of death.'

> At the sixth hour the spotless sacrifice, our Lord and Saviour, was offered up to the Father. Ascending the cross for the salvation of the whole world, he made atonement for the sins of mankind; and, despoiling principalities and powers, he led them away openly. And all of us who were liable to death and bound by the debt of the handwriting that could not be paid, he freed, by taking it away out of the midst and affixing it to his cross for a trophy.[13]

In this extract Cassian also alludes to Christ dealing with a debt which could not be paid by sinners. Hence, the debt motif is not absent. But the debt motif is subsumed within the more fundamental idea of Christ despoiling principalities and powers. It is in the background, not the foreground. The real driver which underpins Cassian's theology is engagement with Satan. Christ ransacked Satan's kingdom. And, just as a victorious military general took possession of the assets of his defeated foe, so Christ seized and liberated those under Satan's thrall. The logic of the faith is worked out within this powerful idea of victory over the Evil One, and this has practical day-to-day consequences. In a believer's daily battle with Satan, Christ's own victory over the Evil One is both an inspiration and an empowerment.

What this means is that although Columba's *Altus Prosator* refers to the cross on only one occasion, the death and resurrection of Christ are central in his understanding of salvation. They are interpreted within the warfare and rescue scenario. The *Altus Prosator* has no mention of paying a debt. Nor does it refer to satisfying the honour of God. Nor are there references to Christ exchanging His righteousness for our sin. Instead, it moves directly from the fallenness of humanity to the judgement seat of God and the coming of Christ in triumph.[14] This quick movement of thought is consistent with a theological paradigm majoring on warfare and rescue.

DYING THE DEATH

Freeing the captives was a costly action for Christ. Each time Columba and his community celebrated the Eucharist they re-emphasised Christ's death and His shed blood. At Bangor the community prayed

13 Cassian, *Institutes*, III:3, alluding to Colossians 2:14, 15.

14 *Altus Prosator*, Stanzas P, Q, R, T, X.

for a Church which had been redeemed in 'your holy blood', and they sang of 'drinking the holy blood'.[15] Iona would make comparable statements. The liturgy meant that thoughts of the blood shed on Calvary were ever-present in Columba's faith. They were reinforced at every Eucharist. It was the death of Christ, as the crucial eucharistic event, which trapped the devil and killed his power. This is what the *Amra* (IV) means when it states that the mass is a noose to Satan.

But why did Christ's death on the cross bring that outcome? Did the monks think in terms of Satan being tricked into harming a sinless man, and thereby being 'trapped' through having acted unjustly? Or was Satan trapped because Christ, in His death, paid a debt which Satan had thought unpayable. Or was death the only portal through which Christ could enter hell? Whatever the reasoning, it was because Satan had been disempowered and dispossessed that the *Amra* (IV) could describe the outcome of the first Easter events in terms of the triumph of Christ: 'He suffered briefly until he triumphed: He was a terror to the devil.' What the Amra celebrates is a decisive spiritual battle and a glorious triumph. Christ fought hand-to-hand with Satan on the cross. He went to hell itself. He robbed Satan of his captives. In triumph He returned. He will return again. This is why it makes perfect sense that the single reference to the cross in the *Altus Prosator* comes in the context of Christ's anticipated return in triumph and glory.[16] The *Altus Prosator* is recognising the consequences of God's actions in Christ

Consistent with this, the crucial article of belief for the *Altus Prosator*, separating a believer from an unbeliever, the saved from the lost, is the confession that, 'Christ came from God the Father'.[17] This occurs in the concluding stanza of the poem, and, as such, it summarises the theological emphasis of its author. The statement that 'Christ came from God the Father' is not just a recognition of Christ's divine origin and divine authority. It is more than that. To make such a confession involves a man or a woman actively rejecting the spurious authority of any other spiritual force. Making that confession shifts men and women from being submissive to Satan's false and usurping dominion, to accepting the true authority of Christ. In stating 'Christ came from

15 *Bangor Antiphonary*, Items 41, 8.
16 *Altus Prosator*, Stanza X.
17 *Altus Prosator*, Stanza Z.

God the Father', Satan is disowned. His rule is declared deceitful. His authority is deemed invalid. His enslavement is exchanged for liberation. Men and women transfer from a false master to the true Lord.

Clancy and Markus are concerned that Columba's *Altus Prosator* lacks expressions of mercy and tenderness, and never mentions God's patience with sinners.[18] But in sixth-century spirituality God's mercy was not expressed through sentimental words. It was communicated through describing how God in Christ took to the battlefield on behalf of His people. In Christ, God campaigned deep into Satan's heartland of sin and death. It is God's readiness to do what needed to be done to overcome the enemy which shows His love and the quality of His mercy. In the *milieu* of the time, the power and victory of Christ on behalf of those in bondage was synonymous with the love and mercy of God. Curran recognises this way of thinking. Curran notes that Item 11 of the *Bangor Antiphonary* has no explicit reference to any 'love' the martyrs have for Christ, salvation, or holiness. Instead, the emphasis is on the martyrs being fortified by Christ and by the Holy Spirit, so that they may crush the devil, overcome death, and march victoriously out of this world.[19] The triumph of Christ on behalf of humanity says all that needs to be said about God's love for His people.

DICING WITH DESTINY

The triumph of Christ over Satan governed not only Iona's theology of salvation, but its understanding of the Christian life. Take, for example, Adomnán's lengthy story about Columba going to a lonely place on Iona for prayer, and later reporting that he had seen, 'a very black host of demons fighting against him' (III:8). Columba prevailed because angels assisted him, making the malevolent spirits flee from Iona. Finlay interprets the host of demons in psychological terms, with the story representing an inner conflict in Columba's soul, perhaps reflecting Columba's mood on a day of wild weather and dark forbidding clouds.[20] But Adomnán would see himself as recording history rather than spiritual metaphor. For Adomnán, Columba was confronted by real hordes of darkness and not just by his inner emotions. What

18 Clancy and Markus, *Iona: The Earliest Poetry of a Celtic Monastery*, 68.

19 Curran *The Antiphonary of Bangor and the Early Irish Monastic Liturgy*, 80, dates Item 11 to the sixth century.

20 Finlay, *Columba*, 126.

the story illustrates is a fundamental truth: the life of a man of God involves repeated battles against demonic spiritual beings.

This world-view dominated the age. Satan was despoiled by Christ, but he counter-attacks. Thus, believers face demonic onslaughts throughout their earthly pilgrimage as Satan strives to reclaim sinners. This desperate struggle for repossession peaks at the moment of death. At death the soul leaves the body; but it has to transition to heaven through the air, a region which Satan sees as his own. Because no pilgrim's life has been perfect, then, at death, sins and imperfections might yet make a soul vulnerable to Satan's grasping hands. On coming to faith in Christ the soul was released from Satan's bondage. But Satan can repossess. He can drag pilgrims back to hell before they reach glory.

At the moment of death there is a cosmic spiritual struggle involving Christ, Satan, angels, and demons. All might yet be lost for some who have been liberated. That was an anxious possibility for any monk and is a typically semi-Pelagian feature. Nothing was sealed. Nothing was certain. Doubt remained concerning the assured salvation of believers. And Adomnán's *Life of Columba* has several instances of believers at risk.

1. *The Good Briton.* There was a contest over the soul of one of Columba's monks of British origin (III:6). Just after the monk died, Columba commented: 'I have just now seen holy angels fighting in the air against the powers of the Adversary: I give thanks to Christ, who watches over the contest, for the angels are victorious and they have carried to the joys of the heavenly kingdom the soul of this pilgrim who is the first of us to die here in this island.' There was no doubt that the deceased monk had been a Christian. Nor was there doubt that he had lived a virtuous Christian life. And in his case, Columba did see him safely transported to the heavenly kingdom. Nevertheless, despite the monk's obvious piety and goodness, that destiny was not assured until angelic forces overcame Satanic adversaries who sought to reclaim him at death.

2. *The Grasping Leader.* Columba was in his hut with his friend Colgu mac Cellaig, when suddenly Columba said, 'At this moment devils are dragging off to hell a grasping leader from among the chief men of your district' (I:35). Later, Colgu discovered that a man of his own district, Gallan mac Fachtnai, had died at that hour.

3. *The Drowned Monk.* Columba had a vision of monks drowned in Ireland and said to his monks, 'We must bring the help of our prayers

to some of St. Comgall's monks who are drowned in Belfast Lough at this time. See, even now, they are battling in the air against the powers of the Adversary who are seeking to snatch away the soul of a visitor who was drowned along with them' (III:13). In this instance Comgall's drowned monks were in no spiritual danger, but their visitor was. Comgall's drowned monks became part of a spiritual army battling in the air to secure the soul of their visitor who risked being claimed by Satan. Their salvation was safe, but not his. His soul was in jeopardy as it attempted to transition from earth to heaven through the air where Satan, the Prince of the powers of the air, could pounce.

4. *Neman mac Gruthriche.* One of Columba's most solemn warnings was given to Neman mac Gruthriche, 'Your enemies will find you lying in bed with a whore, and there you will be cut down. Devils will seize your soul and take you to the place of torments' (I:39). Neman's danger was not death as such. The real danger was Satanic forces claiming him at the point of death. Waylaid at the final stage of pilgrimage, he would be deprived of the kingdom of God.

Within this understanding of the Gospel, true reality is not what is visible to mortal eyes. True reality is Christ and His angels battling Satan and his demons. The battle concerns human souls. And the crisis is most intense at the moment of death because death is when final possession of a soul is sealed. A soul is vulnerable at that moment. It has to cross a region inhabited by Satan and his devils. And all that occurred previously during a person's life, was preparation for that struggle for possession when death came. God and Satan, angels and the demonic, heaven and hell, fight for every soul. This is one reason why monks never saw themselves as escapists from life. They were frontline soldiers in the army of Christ, who were tasked with aiding the release of men and women from Satanic captivity, and with interceding for souls at the vulnerable hour of death.

REACHING GOD'S HEAVEN

Could it be known if a particular soul reached heavenly glory? The only certain proof was if angels were observed escorting that soul through the dangerous regions. Bishop Colman's soul 'was carried away among the choirs of angels and ascended beyond the starry sky to paradise' (III:12). Emchath of Glen Urquhart 'departed happily and safely to the Lord in the company of angels' (III:14). A soldier of Christ named

Diarmait, was brought to paradise by the angels of God (III:7). The soul of the humble but pious blacksmith, Columb Coilrigin, was seen carried by heavenly angels to the delights of the heavenly kingdom (III:9). Columba saw heaven opened and Brendan's soul being met by choirs of angels (III:11). On another occasion, Columba became aware that, although the soul of a virtuous woman had gone straight to paradise, the soul of her husband (despite him being a 'devout layman') was being fought over fiercely and was in danger of being lost. In that instance the woman herself, together with holy angels, fought against the powers of the Enemy 'and because the man himself was always righteous, his soul is rescued from the devils' assaults and is brought to the place of eternal refreshment' (III:10).

As for Columba himself, there was no doubt. The *Amra* (III) declares that he was transported to glory in the company, not just of angels, but of archangels,

He reached the apostles, with hosts, with archangels,
He reached the land where night is not seen
He reached the land where we expect Moses.
He reached the plain where they know the custom of music,
Where sages do not die.
The King has cast off His priest's troubles.[21]

Death was a time of crisis. All resources were needed to ensure a safe crossing between earth and heaven. Release by Christ from Satanic captivity was a start, but also required were a virtuous life and heavenly assistance during the final transition. The battle was only over when it was fully over. Charles-Edwards points out that nine chapters of Book III of Adomnán's *Life of Columba* concern Columba seeing angels conducting souls to heaven after death.[22] He also identifies Adomnán's concern with the moment of death and its consequences as a major theme of Book I, especially in the fateful story of the whoring Neman mac Gruthriche, whose soul would be seized by devils (I:39). For him

21 Adomnán refers to Columba's transition in (III:23). The monk, Ernene moccu Fir Roide, claimed: 'On the night of Columba's blessed and blissful passing from the world to the heavens, I and the men with me were hard at work fishing in the fishful River Finn, when all at once we saw the whole sky light up.'

22 Charles-Edwards, 'The Structure and Purpose of Adomnán's *Vita Columbae*.' in Wooding (ed.), *Adomnán of Iona*, 212.

there would be no angels battling with demons on his behalf. There were no helpers to assist him. His wickedness left him exposed and defenceless at his death. Neman's eternal fate was settled according to whom he belonged in his last hour.

CHAPTER 20

The Threat of Recapture

Thoughts of battle between the forces of Christ and Satan shaped Columba's entire spirituality. This warfare and rescue model of salvation drew on familiar analogies from real life, but all metaphors can overreach themselves. In human warfare there are individuals, belonging to the winning side, who fall in the conflict and never share in the final triumph. Moreover, in human warfare single foot-soldiers from a victorious army can be picked off, even by a retreating and defeated enemy. Within the faith-understanding of an Irish monk it was easy to transfer these scenarios to the spiritual realm. As such, the model allowed for uncertainty concerning the final destiny of individual soldiers of Christ. Not all would make it.

The pilgrim journey was full of risk, especially at death. Would Christ or Satan take final possession of a soul as it attempted to transition from earth to heaven? The outcome would be influenced by how the soul had been prepared for death. Good deeds and a holy life were not sufficient in themselves. These were only part of spiritual conditioning preparatory to the final struggle between the forces of heaven and the legions of hell. Good deeds and a holy life affected how much of a grip Christ or Satan could obtain on a soul; but it was the battle itself which determined the outcome. And in the final struggle any moral or spiritual deficiencies might yet be made up by urgent prayer offered by those on earth, or by great numbers of heavenly beings engaging in the conflict. But it would be easier for the angels to triumph if the believer had lived a godly life during the years of earthly pilgrimage. And triumph they must. But then again, nothing was certain. Nothing was totally assured. Souls had to be striven for. There was real risk of being reclaimed by Satan. A name could vanish from the Book of Life.

UNCERTAINTY AND INSECURITY

Adomnán did not believe that whatever was predestined was immutably fixed. The sixteenth-century Reformers, influenced by Augustinianism,[1] taught that, because of God's eternal election, and because the price of sin was paid in full upon the cross for the elect, then the status of a saved soul could never alter. Reformed Calvinism rooted atonement in the immutable decree of God and in the full payment of the price of sin by Christ. A person was predestined or not. The price was paid or not. God's wrath was satisfied or not. And because sin cannot be punished twice, then any soul was secure if redeemed through God's decree and Christ's once-for-all, sufficient sacrifice. Assurance does not lie in personal righteousness. Nor does it lie in holiness acquired through life. Assurance lies in God's decree and in Christ's work. Nothing can undo such a redemption. But this emphasis is lacking in Columba's spirituality as portrayed by Adomnán.

One reason it is lacking is because early-medieval spirituality envisioned the salvation event within a warfare and rescue narrative. Columba understood redemption through images, and not through philosophical concepts. In human warfare, even a winning side suffers losses: so also in spiritual warfare. The final outcome will be an overwhelming victory for Christ, but some individuals might stumble on the life-pilgrimage to heavenly glory. They will be recaptured and lose their place in Christ's great triumph. Adomnán's high-profile stories of struggles over souls at the moment of death testify to this belief that a defeated foe could still disrupt the triumph of the victor.

But what kind of theology can allow for an eternal destiny being forfeited? How can liberation be negated by recapture? How can Satan re-enslave any of Christ's people? Semi-Pelagianism permits such thinking, because any system based on a combination of grace and human effort always allows a degree of doubt concerning the final outcome. Whenever elements of personal merit and goodness

1 Augustine does not subscribe *simpliciter* to the concept of 'once saved always saved'. Confusingly, he employs the term 'salvation' in two senses. Sometimes it means 'permanent salvation' for all eternity. Sometimes it means 'temporary salvation' whilst on earth. The difference between the two is that the 'elect' have a salvation that endures; whereas, though the 'non-elect' have a salvation that is *real* (in that they belong to the Church and have, temporarily at least, been freed from Satan's bondage) yet that is only *temporary* in relation to eternity. God gives the elect the extra gift of perseverance; cf. Augustine, *On the Gift of Perseverance*, XXI.

contribute to salvation, it is always possible that an individual's merit and goodness may prove to be inadequate and insufficient. However, although the early-medieval Irish Church adopted semi-Pelagianism features, the classic semi-Pelagian debates on free will and accrual of merit were not drivers within the Irish context. Instead, early-medieval Irish spirituality was energised by the paradigm of warfare and rescue. Total vigilance was needed from each warrior if they, as individuals, were to survive the campaign. What was possible in human warfare was, *mutatis mutandis*, possible in spiritual warfare. A soldier of Christ, whose defence was down, might yet be picked off by an enraged and wounded foe. The mind-set was not 'once saved, always saved'. The paradigm allowing this outcome was spiritual warfare.

The monkish imagination was fuelled by such images, with the daily liturgy driving these images ever deeper into the spiritual subconscious through repetition. The presence of warfare language within the liturgy is unsurprising, since participation in worship was itself regarded as a key aggressive action in the battle against Satan and his forces. Monks prayed because they were soldiers in a conflict.

EXODUS AND ESCAPE

Christ's descent into hell to despoil Satan and deliver God's people from spiritual captivity, reflected Moses going into Egypt to confront Pharaoh and release God's people from political bondage. 'Egypt' had a threefold significance in early Christian theology. It could refer to the historical Egypt and the events of the biblical Exodus. It could be a metaphor for an ungodly world.[2] Or it could be a synonym for Satan, with some early liturgies referring to Satan as the 'Egyptian', echoing the Apocryphal Book of Tobit which represents the devil (Asmodeus) fleeing to the extreme parts of Egypt where an angel bound him.[3] All of this fed a theology in which Moses leading Israel from Egyptian bondage was the governing archetype for Christ leading His people from Satanic captivity. Significantly, the archetype included not only the event of initial liberation from captivity (leaving Egypt and crossing the Red Sea) but Israel's many years of desert pilgrimage. The freed Israelites, pursued by hostile forces, prefigured

2 cf. Jerome, *Letters* XLVI.

3 Warren, *The Antiphonary of Bangor, Part II*, 92.

Christian believers who, although liberated from spiritual bondage, were pursued by Satan as they pilgrimaged towards glory. The trials and tragedies of Israel's subsequent forty-year desert pilgrimage after that dramatic release, were sober reminders of what might yet befall a Christian pilgrim.

The events of the historical Exodus and its aftermath anticipated the spiritual Exodus gained through Christ. The Exodus motif was high-profile at Bangor and on Iona, not least because the liturgy centred on the Psalter, and the Psalms return again and again to the Exodus theme. The Exodus narrative became the principal Old Testament event for interpreting Christian doctrine. Thus, the opening Item of the *Bangor Antiphonary* is the Song of Moses with its joyful celebration over deliverance from Pharaoh and his hosts.[4] This triumph song is given prime position, setting the tone for all that follows. Bangor regarded the Song of Moses as not only commemorating Israel's deliverance from Egypt, but the Church's deliverance from Satan.[5] This emphasis recurs in many other hymns and collects of the *Bangor Antiphonary*, which adopt the language and imagery of the Egyptian deliverance.[6] One example is Item 68:

> O God, who every day lifts up the yoke of Egyptian slavery from your people, and, by washing in a spiritual stream, leads them by conquering evil into a promised land; grant us victory over hostile attacks of enemies, that defeating our darkness we may be led to our inheritance in the sanctuary prepared by your hands, O Saviour of the world.[7]

In this prayer the Exodus experience is linked to monks living the Christian life in the present. It calls for protection during the coming day. It speaks of struggles faced during a believer's earthly pilgrimage on the way to the ultimate sanctuary of heaven. It has sharp awareness of ongoing conflict with evil. Importantly, throughout the collect there is consciousness of a still-present enemy, and awareness of a need to defeat darkness. There is need for ongoing protection against this ever-hostile enemy.

---

4 *Bangor Antiphonary*, Item 1.

5 cf. *Bangor Antiphonary*, Item 91, *Miriam's Song* (Exodus 15:21).

6 e.g., *Bangor Antiphonary*, Items 3, 5, 9, 10, 62, 68, 71, 76, 81, 94, 95, 99, 127.

7 *Bangor Antiphonary*, Item 68. (tr. Woolfenden, 274).

The *Bangor Antiphonary* has frequent prayer to the Saviour, asking Him to protect His people, just as God defended His chosen people from Pharaoh and from the pursuing hosts. Item 91 asks God to defend His people from the *vetus inimicus*, the old enemy.[8] Item 81 has similar sentiments:

> Christ, God, who for the salvation of your people was helper and protector; (Israel), whom you led from Egypt through the dried sea; save us in this way from the yoke of sin. Who reigns for the ages.[9]

Throughout the liturgy there is no suggestion that once God's people have been set free they are safe for ever. The enemy pursues as Pharaoh pursued. Hostile attacks continue. But what kind of damage can a pursuing host inflict? Can it only wound a liberated captive? Or can it deal a fatal blow?

PURSUIT AND PILGRIMAGE

In theory, the paradigm of the Exodus and Israel's subsequent desert pilgrimage could be a metaphor for the spiritual life without implying that some who were once rescued might be lost. But that was not how the Church Fathers applied the Exodus motif. They allowed the possibility that saved souls might yet perish. They read the Scriptures with that in mind, and that was also how the early-medieval Irish Church interpreted the narrative. It knew that when Pharaoh thundered in pursuit of newly-liberated Israel, his aim was not simply to harry Israel as they journeyed, but to recapture and re-enslave.[10] It is true that none of God's people were recaptured by Pharaoh, but the attempt was made and the possibility had been real. More seriously, despite escaping through the Red Sea, very few of that generation actually reach the promised land. And, given that the whole of Israel's Exodus experience (Liberation, Red Sea, and Desert Pilgrimage) was used to shed light on

8 *Bangor Antiphonary*, Item 91; cf. Warren, *The Antiphonary of Bangor: Part II*, xxi, 45.

9 *Bangor Antiphonary*, Item 81.

10 Warren, *The Antiphonary of Bangor: Part II*, xxi, points out that collects used in the Daybreak Office, 'ask our Lord as the "*Salvator mundi*" [Items 62, 68, 71, 91] to protect his people from the *vetus inimicus* [Item 91] and from all danger, as once he defended his chosen people in the Red Sea from Pharaoh and his pursuing hosts.' These collects do not assume that the baptised are safe, otherwise baptised monks would not pray in such terms.

the Christian's experience, it was accepted that perishing on the way could and would take place. Satan could stop a soul from reaching the promised land. He might attack even as late as at death itself. This is what Adomnán and Columba believed.[11]

In the biblical narrative, the Red Sea, once crossed, became a barrier between Israel and Egypt.[12] This encouraged the Church Fathers to interpret the Red Sea crossing as a metaphor for baptism. Baptism dealt with a believer's past. It was a firewall between believers and their original sin plus their pre-baptismal actual sins, just as the Red Sea was a firewall between Israel and Pharaoh's host. The Irish Church linked the Red Sea crossing and baptism in similar terms.[13] However, within that model, baptism only related to cleansing from past sin. That left post-baptismal sin as a problem. Even though a spiritual Red Sea was crossed in baptism, that gave no protection from the guilt of future sins. And, just as there was a testing post-Red Sea, desert pilgrimage for Israel, so there was a testing, post-baptism pilgrimage for the Church.[14]

Israel's post-Red Sea years proved troubling. Many who had been protected by the Red Sea from the vengeance of Egypt, were lost to God in the wilderness wanderings. As far as the Church Fathers were concerned, this meant that Israel's hazardous post-Red Sea desert pilgrimage highlighted a core spiritual truth: some whom God had once delivered might yet be doomed. This interpretation lay behind the Patristic reading of several New Testament passages, including

---

11 cf. O'Loughlin, 'The tombs of the saints; their significance for Adomnán', in Carey, Herbert, Ó Riain (eds), *Saints and Scholars: Studies in Irish Hagiography*, 1-14.

12 cf. O'Loughlin, *Celtic Theology*, 100, 103ff., who discusses the importance of the historical Exodus and escape through the Red Sea as in Muirchu's *Life of Patrick.*

13 Herren and Brown, *Christ in Celtic Christianity*, 258: 'In the ascetic Irish monastic tradition, baptism initiates the spiritual life in Christ, while the Eucharist is the reward for achieving a high level of sanctity.'

14 For Basil of Caesarea, *On the Holy Spirit*, 31, the Red Sea brings the departure of Pharaoh and is a type of baptismal washing which occasions the end of the tyranny of the devil. Despite this, for Basil, the future pilgrimage after baptismal washing (as with Israel's future pilgrimage after the Red Sea), involves jeopardy. Ultimately, full salvation comes from imitation of Christ: 'For perfection of life the imitation of Christ is necessary, not only in the example of gentleness, lowliness and long-suffering set us in His life, but also in His actual death.' (*On the Holy Spirit*, 35). Basil stresses that a person has to be born of water (baptism) and of the Spirit (evidenced in the new life being led). It is through a life led by the Holy Spirit that a person achieves restoration to paradise. What Israel did after the Red Sea deliverance affected their final destination. Similarly, what believers do after the cleansing waters of baptism has huge importance.

1 Corinthians 10:4,5 where Paul writes that, although Israel 'drank from the spiritual rock that accompanied them', God still struck down those who displeased Him. It also included the Church Fathers' interpretation of Jude's statement: 'I want to remind you that the Lord delivered his people out of Egypt, but later destroyed those who did not believe.' These were read as solemn warnings of what could yet befall a liberated Christian believer on his or her journey.[15] Loss and recapture were possible outcomes, even after a mighty act of divine deliverance. Commenting on Jude, Chrysostom writes:

> We must not only be delivered out of Egypt, but we must also enter into the promise. Since the Jews too, as Paul says, both went through the Red Sea and ate manna and drank spiritual drink, but nevertheless they all perished.[16]

Similarly, Clement of Alexandria warned believers against sinning, because even those whom God had once saved might yet be destroyed.[17] Other Church Fathers taught the same. It was accepted, without question, that disobedience could result in some freed souls never reaching their final destination. Though saved from 'Egypt' they might not persevere to the fullness of that salvation. Early-medieval Irish theology took these assumptions on-board. Recapture was still possible. It was not 'once free always free', or 'once saved always saved'. A believer could lose his or her destiny. This is what lies behind Adomnán's portrayal of Columba's theology. Just as some in Israel were lost to God despite a glorious deliverance from captivity, so also, heaven-losing possibilities lay in wait for all Christian pilgrims.

AIDING THE JOURNEY

The Red Sea was an archetype for baptism. Alternatively, the Red Sea could signify the waters of death, and in this reading it was even easier to envisage the possibility of recapture until the final crossing had been

---

15 cf. 2 Peter (esp. 1:10); 1 Corinthians 10:5-11 (esp. v. 5); Hebrews 3:18–4:2 (esp. 3:19; 4:1, 2); and Jude 9 with the struggle over the body of Moses.

16 John Chrysostom, *Homilies on Matthew*, 39. Elsewhere, Chrysostom refers to the possibility of a believer losing his or her salvation because godly living has not been added to initial faith; cf. Chrysostom, *Homily* 64. Augustine, *On Psalm 78*, implies that not all were truly saved in the first place.

17 Clement of Alexandria, *The Instructor*, III:8.

accomplished. Under both interpretations, the moment of death was approached with real fear. Iona monks saw themselves as having been released from captivity to Satan by the triumph of Christ but were aware of still being harried by demonic forces. They knew there would be a struggle between angels and demons when they died. Only when they touched the solid ground of the heavenly kingdom would they be safe from being reclaimed. This meant that pilgrims who were approaching death wanted the crossing to be as rapid as possible. They wanted to die where it was safest to cross; where the waters of death were shallow; where the ford was narrow; where the transition through the air was better guarded; and where it was better patrolled by heavenly beings.

Adomnán never writes in terms of souls being weighed on scales to determine their fate.[18] For him, as for Columba, what is decisive is warfare in the heavenly places. The holiness of a life only indirectly affects the outcome of the struggle, with the decisive reality the battle itself. This struggle over a soul at death is similar to how the New Testament describes the archangel Michael contending with Satan over the body of Moses (Jude 9). Moving from this world to the heavenly kingdom is a crisis-event. It is hemmed around by anxiety and uncertainty. Nevertheless, there are ways of making a good outcome more likely.

1. *The Holy Companion.* A pilgrim could seek the aid of a holy man of God.[19] A successful transition at death is more probable if there is help from a great saint. This belief may have grown from early Irish law which gave high-status persons authority to conduct those of lesser rank to the borders of a territory and grant them safe passage to the next.[20] In a folk-understanding of Christian faith, this may have been applied to the journey from earth to heaven, with the journey less risky if a figure of spiritual high-status accompanied the pilgrim. This is what Beccán seeks when, in his poem *Fo Reir Choluimb*, he asks Columba to guard him when he goes 'the road of fear', the 'way of death'.[21]

18 cf. De Paors, *Early Christian Ireland*, 148, who refer to later high-crosses which have Michael weighing the souls of the dead and Satan attempting to upset the balance.

19 cf. Charles-Edwards, 'The Structure and Purpose of Adomnán's *Vita Columbae*' in Wooding (ed.), *Adomnán of Iona*, 212, on the role of angels at the death of a person. He sees this as on overt theme of Book III, leading to the final chapter on Columba's own death.

20 Clancy and Markus, *Iona: The Earliest Poetry of a Celtic Monastery*, 153.

21 Beccán, *Fo Reir Choluimb*, 1. In exchange for praising Columba in his poem, Beccán hopes for his soul to go to heaven. Dallan Forgaill, near the close of the *Amra*, also envisions

2. *The Holy Place.* Transition is also easier if death occurs at a holy place. Men with blood on their hands sought to end their days on Iona because Iona was regarded as nearer heaven. The journey through the air was shorter. There was less possibility of being ambushed en route. And Iona was where Columba could best be appealed to as protector. The combination of these factors, a shorter journey on the one hand and a holy helper on the other, meant that Satan had less opportunity to reclaim his captive at the moment of death. Some kings and noblemen spent their final years on Iona because of this belief. After Columba's death, Iona became regarded as a 'thin place' and as a special gateway to heaven.[22]

3. *Penance.* Believers who fall into serious sin cannot be reconverted or rebaptised. For them, a different mechanism has to apply. That mechanism is penance. In order to maintain a place in Christ's kingdom when serious sin has been committed *after* having become a Christian, penance has to be completed. Baptism relates to past sins: but penance enables a believer who sins subsequent to baptism to be forgiven. It was the responsibility of the abbot to determine which penance was appropriate. Columba's reputation was such that his judgements were trusted unreservedly. If he said that such-and-such was the appropriate penance, his monks were confident that such penance would be accepted by heaven itself. The issue was sealed once heaven was reached: Item 14 of the *Bangor Antiphonary* has the repeated refrain 'guarded by angels, and will endure for ever', specifically applying these words to those 'whom God has taken to the heavenly dwellings' [Item 14:6].

Battles between the forces of Christ and the forces of Satan lie behind Adomnán's entire narrative. Angelic struggles with the demonic are at the heart of Columba's spirituality. These are not later intrusions into the original Columban narrative, as the Duke of Argyll thought when he found Adomnán's *Life of Columba* frustrating and disappointing.

Columba's help after death: 'He will urge me past torments.' cf. Charles-Edwards, 'The Structure and Purpose of Adomnán's *Vita Columbae*' in Wooding (ed.), *Adomnán of Iona*, 216f.

22 The Welsh island of Bardsley, 'Island of a Thousand Saints', is also described as a 'thin place'. In medieval piety it was believed that dying on Bardsley avoided purgatory, which was a development of the original idea of avoiding ambush. The term 'Iona is a thin place' was used by the novelist Evelyn Underhill and adopted by George MacLeod.

Instead, they express Iona's fundamental understanding of God, Christ, the world, and Satan. These were daily reality in the minds and imaginations of Columba's monks.

Moral endeavour did not earn salvation through accumulation of merit *per se*. What it did do was to determine how much a soul could resist Satan's clutches at death. This fed into an overarching paradigm in which the whole of life and faith was understood in terms of spiritual battle. In the 'natural goodness' conversion stories, the lives of particular pagans were so pure that Satan had no hold when the Gospel was introduced, giving an easy victory for Christ. Outside of this, assurance was uncertain. Predestination was seen as divine intention rather than as an immutable destiny. Ongoing spiritual battle lay behind everything. The spiritual life focussed on making a pilgrim less vulnerable, and less likely to be ambushed or recaptured. All pilgrims were safer if their lives were marked by piety and holiness. But in the final struggle at death, as the ultimate crossing was made, it was the angelic armies of the Redeemer who had to be at hand to aid the pilgrim.

PART FIVE
EVANGELIST

CHAPTER 21

The Call to Mission

The village of Alpbach lies in the mountains of western Austria, and a leaflet in its parish church informs visitors that Christianity was brought to the region by Irish and Scottish monks in the seventh and eighth centuries. As the historian Gougaud wrote in his work on early Irish missions to Europe: 'There are many towns and villages in lands watered by the Marne, the Meuse, the Rhine, and the Danube, in which the memory of Irish missions is still celebrated.'[1] For four centuries Irish monks penetrated deep into continental Europe. They evangelised. They built churches. They established communities. And their activities beyond the island of Ireland ranged much wider than the relatively local areas of Scotland and Northumbria.

The Irish Church had a missionary ethos. Each monastic family was autonomous. Each was able to make strategic decisions without requiring permission from a higher authority. This created a culture of initiative and enterprise.[2] Such potential became actual action on the ground because the Irish Church was also inhabited by a dynamic driving-force which energised its whole outlook. That driving-force was its theological motif: 'The triumph of Christ over Satan, and the setting free of God's People'. Christ was King. He was victor over Satan. He was liberator of men and women held in bondage. The faith of the Irish Church was saturated by this axiom. It meant that the whole of life was viewed as a missional-enterprise in which Satan's strongholds were to be stormed and brought into subjection to Christ. When this took place, and when Satan was toppled from his position of a false authority over men and women, then humanity was set free from thraldom and set on a pilgrimage towards heavenly glory. Ailred's twelfth-century *Life of Ninian* may have been penned half a millennium after Columba's

1 Gougaud, *Gaelic Pioneers of Christianity*, xiii.

2 cf. Markus, *Conceiving a Nation*, 134.

era, but perfectly expresses this link between spiritual warfare and evangelism:

> Grieved that the devil should have found a seat in a corner of this island in the hearts of the Picts, Ninian set himself as an able athlete to drive out his kingdom, taking for this end the shield of faith, the helmet of salvation, the breastplate of love, and the sword of the spirit which is the word of God. Fortified with such arms, and the companionship of holy fathers, as if surrounded with heavenly troops, he invaded the empire of the strong man armed, about to deliver many captive vessels from his dominion. … Renouncing Satan, and all his works and pomps, they are joined to the family of believers by faith, and word, and sacraments.[3]

There was also an eschatological dimension to evangelism. It was believed that Christ would not return in glory until the Gospel had been taken to the ends of the earth. This is one reason why Christianity was taken to Britain and Ireland. These islands were viewed as the geographical extremities of the world, and therefore had to be evangelised before Christ returned. Indeed, His return might be hastened if these 'edge-people' were converted.

The Irish Church was a mission-orientated Church. But what was the aim of evangelism? What were souls to be saved from? Was Columba truly an evangelist? How did monks relate to non-Christian religion? What were the tools used in evangelism? What was the response when evangelism took place? This group of chapters explores these issues.

RESCUING THE LOST

The primary aim of mission in Irish Christianity was to save souls from eternal loss in the terrors of hell.[4] Some modern interpreters underplay

---

3 Ailred, *Life of Ninian*, quoted by MacLauchlan, *The Early Scottish Church*, 70.

4 Herren and Brown, *Christ in Celtic Christianity*, x; cf. Yorke, *The Conversion of Britain: 600–800*, 100, who discusses A. D. Nock's distinction between 'natural' and 'prophetic' religions. Natural religion is characterised as the desire to control natural forces and processes and in which religious ritual focussed on aiding daily life through such forces. Prophetic religion (such as in Judaism, Christianity, and Islam) has an emphasis on achieving salvation for an individual's soul through faith and/or appropriate behaviour. Yorke points out that people would not necessarily be aware of a need for salvation until it had been impressed upon them. Nor would they have assumed that religion came with a specific moral code.

this crisis-driven motivation, preferring to view Celtic Christianity within the parameters of peace, justice, and respect for nature. There is no doubt that these issues were important for Columba and Adomnán (especially Adomnán) but only as part of their task. Gilbert Markus, in two very readable publications, *The Radical Tradition: Saints in the Struggle for Justice and Peace* (1992) and *Conceiving a Nation: Scotland to A.D. 900* (2017), chooses to focus on Adomnán's peace and justice work as representative of the missional activity of the early Irish Church in Scotland, and there is little doubt that Adomnán was outstanding in this area. If Adomnán lived in modern times he would be a Nobel Peace Laureate for his work on the *Law of the Innocents*. But the core concern for Columba, Adomnán, and others, was to rescue souls from an eternity in hell. That had prime importance. That was a greater task than liberating men and women from the political or social captivities of this life. Peace and justice work was not what Columba or Adomnán would themselves define as pure mission or as pure evangelism.

We have already cited Bradley's statement that Columba's emphasis was on the sovereignty of God, the reality of human sin, the depth of the fall of humanity, the power of divine judgement, the seriousness of Christ's second coming, and the reality of hell.[5] These issues reflect the heart of Irish and Columban evangelism. There was a relentless pursuit of perishing souls. Souls needed to be saved from a lost eternity and the horrors of hell. Souls needed to be liberated from their captivity to Satan. And, after release, souls needed to be helped to complete their journey to heaven. That was the existential crisis which mission addressed and which drove evangelism.[6]

EVANGELIST OR REFORMER

In popular legend, and in older academic studies, Columba has been portrayed as a frontline evangelist and termed the 'Apostle to the Picts'. However, that particular epithet is rarely applied to him now. There is an awareness that others evangelised the Picts more effectively than

5 Bradley, *Argyll: The Making of a Spiritual Landscape*, 58f.

6 McNeill, *The Celtic Penitentials*, 77: 'The Christian religion was [interpreted primarily as] a means of escape from sin and its spiritual penalties.' Bruce, *Prophecy, Miracles, Angels and Heavenly Light?*, 103f., demonstrates that for Adomnán the coming of God's kingdom was not the coming of a set of ethical ideals (which Harnack saw as the essence of Christianity) but the in-breaking of the rule of God as supernatural events.

Columba ever did. There is also a suspicion that Columba's story has been misread, and that Bede's version of history, which represents Columba preaching to the northern Picts and turning many to Christ, may distort historical reality.[7] The *Old Irish Life* encouraged the older interpretation of Columba, focussing on him as a pioneer missionary in Ireland before ever coming to Scotland, and giving him a legacy of having established over three hundred new churches in Ireland. But did these accounts feed a skewed understanding of what Columba actually busied himself with during his Iona years?

James E. Fraser queries whether Columba was at all a pioneer missionary evangelist during his Iona period.[8] Fraser bemoans the fact that the overwhelming majority of the written sources available to us come from Ireland and the Iona family of churches. Do these give a misleading impression? Do they encourage the notion that Argyll and Pictland were Christianised exclusively by Irish monks? Do they foster the belief that Iona was the springboard for this? Do they make us assume that Columba was at the centre of it all?

Fraser is determined to eliminate as much of the Iona 'myth' as possible. Along with others, who are similarly frustrated by the lack of non-Iona early sources, he suggests that later Iona scribes rewrote history so as to place their monastery, and Columba its great founder, at the centre of achievements which had been the accomplishments of others. Fraser insists that if we read the early sources aright – sources such as the *Amra Choluimb Chille* and even Adomnán's *Life of Columba* – we see that they do not in fact major on Columba as an evangelist. Fraser argues that we read that role into these texts because of a later perception that Columba was a great missionary. Fraser's view is that Columba's forceful personality occupied itself in restructuring missions and monastic settlements which already existed in Argyll and Pictland before he arrived on the scene, rather than in evangelism. In Fraser's opinion, it was later writers who created the myth that Columba was the first to take the Gospel to such places. For Fraser, Columba was an organiser and a reformer, and his contribution should be appreciated in these terms. James Bruce agrees with Fraser to a certain extent, pointing out that Adomnán's *Life of Columba* has

---

7 Bede, *History*, III:4.

8 Fraser, *From Caledonia to Pictland: Scotland to 795*, 103ff.

few accounts of preaching tours or of Columba founding churches in Pictland, sharply contrasting with what Columba did in Ireland before 563.[9] Nevertheless, Bruce does not follow Fraser entirely.

Linked to this discussion is the question of why Columba left Ireland in the first place. One explanation is that Columba exiled himself because of an altruistic desire to evangelise the lost. Another focusses on Columba gaining as many new converts as souls perished at the Battle of Cul Drebene. Both theories depict Columba leaving Ireland in order to evangelise. In the first, his incentive is purely selfless. In the second, it includes an element of cleansing his own soul from guilt. Yet, although the two scenarios have differing motivations, both involve a commitment to evangelism. But might both sanitise reality? Might it be that Columba left Ireland because Ireland had become too hot for him? Or, as Máire Herbert suggests, did Columba leave because it was impossible for him to live a truly monastic life in a land where his people had prominence and power?[10] Was the noble aim of evangelism written in later?

Fraser argues that, whatever the reason for Columba's exile, he continued on Iona what he had excelled at in Ireland, namely reform and reorganisation. Columba's natural gifts lay in leadership, administration, diplomacy, teaching, and the instruction of existing believers.[11] Columba was essentially an improver, who made his mark by reinvigorating and regularising existing communities which had been planted by others. This was Columba's core contribution. It was not pioneer evangelism.[12] Fraser suggests that this more easily dovetails with the portraits of Columba painted by Dallán Forgaill in his *Amra*, and by Adomnán in his *Life of Columba*. Fraser concurs with a widely held view that it was Bede's treatment of Columba in his *History* which

9 Bruce, *Prophecy, Miracles, Angels and Heavenly Light?*, admits that some of Adomnán's *Life of Columba* is closer in flavour to the accounts of the contemplatives Antony and Benedict than to missionaries Martin, Germanus, and Patrick, though Bruce is careful to qualify the impression that Columba did not engage in missionary work.

10 Herbert, *Iona. Kells and Derry*, 28.

11 cf. Sheane, *Ulster in the Age of Saint Comgall of Bangor*, 26: 'The main task that Columba set himself was the training of monks.' Also see MacDonald, 'Adomnán's Monastery of Iona' in Bourke (ed.), *Studies in the Cult of Saint Columba*, 27: 'It is also, surely, a noteworthy reflection of the kind of community over which Adomnán has Columba preside that he accords his exemplary abbot no explicitly pastoral role outwith the monastery, and only a very limited missionary one.'

12 Fraser, *From Caledonia to Pictland: Scotland to 795*, 103f.

created the myth of Columba the great missionary. In this view Bede's conclusions were influenced by the northern Picts of his era, who, more than a hundred years after the event, wanted to claim Columba as the man who had evangelised them directly, making them exaggerate Columba's personal contribution to their own Christianisation. Fraser argues that Columba's most meaningful contact with Picts was with the Picts of Tayside, and not with those further north as traditionally thought. In Tayside Columba encountered existing Christian Pictish communities which had been established long before he arrived.[13] He reformed these communities. He did not evangelise them from scratch. However, Fraser's conclusions about the true geographic focus of Columba's activities are based on a few words in the *Amra*.

Putting aside the issue of location for the moment, what about Fraser's assertion that Columba was less an evangelist and more a reformer? It is undisputed that earlier Irish monks, plus other Christian influences from the south, impacted Scotland long before Columba came to Iona. It is also undisputed that, during Columba's own lifetime, other monks and other missions, not under his authority, were evangelising the land, including monks from the island centre of Lismore. History ranges beyond Columba and Iona; and there is a need to interpret that history more evenly and more broadly. Despite this, does Fraser push his argument too far? Does he overreact to the dominance of the Iona narrative? Is he unfair to Columba as an evangelist? Crucially, does he define missional activity as Columba or Adomnán would define it? Does his understanding of what constitutes mission and evangelism affect his conclusions?

Does Adomnán present Columba as an evangelist? Adomnán may sometimes give us a lopsided picture of Columba, but his portrayal of Columba is the only detailed near-contemporary record available to us, apart from the *Amra Choluimb Chille* and a few literary fragments. In Adomnán's book, it is significant that he does depict Columba as an evangelist, and, in so depicting him, Adomnán reflects what the Iona tradition always understood to have been an important part of Columba's calling. Adomnán's allusions to Columba as an evangelist occur in several passages.

---

13 Fraser makes much of references to the Tay in the *Amra*, I and VIII. But, to argue that Adomnán was only tangentially interested in the north of Scotland is to miss the wood for the trees. In his *Life of Columba*, I:1, Adomnán mentions two great kings, one of whom is Bridei of Pictland. At the start of his book Adomnán highlights his interest in the north.

1. In Adomnán's account of the message given by an angel to Columba's mother Eithne before Columba's birth, the angel says that the child has been 'destined by God to lead innumerable souls to the heavenly kingdom' (III:1). Adomnán sees this as defining Columba's God-given destiny and calling. Columba had a divinely appointed task of leading souls to heaven.[14] Some of that task could be achieved on Iona itself, with Columba helping the monks of his community complete their personal pilgrimages safely. But other aspects could only be realised in the field, and in bringing new converts into the kingdom.

2. In the Second Preface of his *Life of Columba*, Adomnán writes that for thirty-five years Columba lived as a good soldier of Christ on Iona. Adomnán's use of the term 'soldier' is key. A soldier is part of an army. He engages the enemy. He is a frontline combatant in battle. This repeated description of Columba as a soldier indicates that Columba is more than a reformer. He takes the fight to the enemy. He pushes back the boundaries of Satan's rule. This presupposes missional activity of some type. Sometimes the theatre of combat will be on Iona; at other times it takes place on the islands of the Hebrides. Occasionally, it occurs in the vast hinterland of mainland Scotland.

3. Far from portraying Columba only as a leader and reformer, Adomnán has several narratives involving conversions through Columba's agency. Pagan individuals and pagan families were brought to faith in Christ (I:1, 33; II:32, III:14). These were all one-off incidents, and as such, do not fit in with any pre-conceived theory that true evangelism in the early-medieval period had to involve the conversion of kings followed by a mass conversion of their peoples. Nevertheless, it was evangelism. Significantly, Adomnán constructs these narratives to make them echo accounts in the Acts of the Apostles of the conversion of individuals and their families. For Adomnán, similarities in *modus operandi* between Columba and the apostles was further evidence of Columba as a true man of God, and proof that Columba was equivalent to an apostle. As such, the conversion of individuals and families, rather than of great kings and whole nations, do not diminish Columba as an evangelist. Instead, these incidents reveal him as a living embodiment of a New Testament apostle. For Adomnán, an evangelist is a man who does what Paul and others did in New Testament times. Under that

14 cf. Bruce, *Prophecy, Miracles, Angels and Heavenly Light?*, 211.

criterion, Columba was an evangelist even if he did not bring whole nations into faith.

Despite this evidence, Fraser insists that Columba was not a true evangelist. To support his case, he points to the *Amra*'s description of Columba as 'teacher' in its declaration that Columba was the 'teacher who would teach the tribes of the Tay'.[15] Fraser suggests that the *Amra* deliberately describes Columba as 'teacher' and not as 'evangelist'. However, in early Christian literature, 'teacher' meant 'evangelist' as much as it meant 'instructor'. When Jesus commanded His disciples to evangelise the world, He commissioned them to be 'teachers' (Matt. 28:19f). When Paul wrote to Timothy about his missionary calling as a herald of the Gospel to the Gentiles he wrote in terms of being a 'teacher' (1 Tim. 2:7). Moreover, the *Amra* also states that, in Tayside, Columba stopped the mouths of the 'fierce ones' and turned them to the 'will of the [heavenly] king'.[16] As with much in the *Amra*, the expression is enigmatic, but it more readily refers to pagan forces resisting Columba, than to Christian monastic communities obstructing Columba's reforms![17] Stopping the mouths of the 'fierce ones' indicates spiritual warfare against Satan's forces. It fits less well with Columba arguing with fellow believers who were dragging their heels on his reorganisation of their communities.

Fraser's thesis is intriguing, but not watertight. He epitomises an overreaction to Iona-centricity, and he falls into an ABC (Anyone-But-Columba) methodology. Rightly, he publicises the importance of non-Iona missions which have long been under-represented in the written historical record. But he does not prove that the earliest Iona sources know nothing of Columba as an evangelist.[18] The opposite is the case.

MISSIONARY METHODOLOGY

Fraser's argument is linked to a particular missiological model which assumes that missionary monks operated with a top-down policy, in which they sought first to convert the chiefs, who then brought

15 *Amra*, I.

16 Bruce, *Prophecy, Miracles, Angels and Heavenly Light?*, 109.

17 Yet, Markus (*Conceiving a Nation*, 122) interprets the *Amra* as indicating that Columba was teaching existing Christian communities in Tayside, turning them 'to the will of the King'.

18 Charles-Edwards, 'The Structure and Purpose of Adomnán's *Vita Columbae*' in Wooding (ed.), *Adomnán of Iona*, 212.

their tribes into line.[19] In this model Christianisation came through cultural conformity and coercion. Fraser takes pains to describe this process, assuming it to have been standard missionary procedure.[20] He accepts, almost without question, that Christian pioneer evangelism across the centuries had two stages. First, there was the individual conversion of a potentate. Second, there were communal conversions with mass baptisms. And because Adomnán's *Life of Columba* does not have examples of this two-stage phenomenon, then Adomnán is not presenting Columba as an evangelist.

It is true that a top-down methodology was employed in some places in some eras, especially when missionary work became entangled with imperialism. But it was by no means a universal practice. It was just as common for missionary work to begin with the conversion of low-status individuals and families. This was the case in New Testament times, and it remained so in later centuries, especially in situations where permission to evangelise a people was granted by a power-figure despite that power-figure himself not converting. This is what we have in Adomnán's *Life of Columba*. Adomnán depicts Columba in discussion with great men on a range of issues. But when Adomnán describes Columba making a missional-impact, it is not with major chiefs and leaders but with lower-status individuals and their families. Nevertheless, that was still evangelism, operating as part of a recognised mission strategy. It may not have been a top-down approach, but it was still frontline mission. Adomnán never claims that Columba converted any kings. What Adomnán does record in some detail are individuals and households coming to faith one-by-one, with the Skye and Glen Urquhart conversion narratives prime examples of the genre (I:33; III:14). These families consisted only of local prominenti, who were not on the same level as Bridei and his retinue. Moreover, in neither

19 Fraser, *From Caledonia to Pictland: Scotland to 795*, 85f. Yorke, *The Conversion of Britain: 600–800*, 98f., 256f., has a more detailed analysis of this approach leading to the Christianisation of societies, citing three stages: (i) control of external collective behaviour; (ii) control of external individual behaviours, and (iii) control of internal individual behaviour and consciousness. Yorke's fine book on the Christianisation of Britain from the seventh to the ninth centuries assumes this process, in which individual consciousness (individual piety) is largely the result of the Christianisation of society rather than the cause of it, though she does allow for a varied picture. Undoubtedly, this sometimes happened. Our argument is that, in Pictland, Columba operated at a stage prior to such a process.

20 Fraser, *From Caledonia to Pictland: Scotland to 795*, 89f.

the Skye nor the Glen Urquhart narratives does Adomnán give any suggestion that other conversions took place outside the immediate families. For Adomnán, the top-down model does not apply on any significant scale. Instead, he portrays Columba following a New Testament model involving the conversions of households, and not the mass conversion of tribes.[21]

Fraser assumes that the top-down coercion model was standard practice in frontline mission. In not seeing Columba successful within that model, Fraser concludes that Columba was not a regular evangelist. But Adomnán represents Columba's strategy in the field as mirroring New Testament practices, not later movements. And any evaluation of Columba as an evangelist has to be calibrated in accordance with that approach, rather than in relation to another methodology. Fraser misunderstands the nature of evangelism in the sixth century. James Bruce notes this modern academic concentration on aristocratic and political conversion, and he reckons that it seeks a mark of success which does not concur with the gospel as understood by Adomnán.[22] In Adomnán's narrative Columba brought men and women and households to faith on a one-by-one basis. Columba did engage with great overlords such as Bridei, but probably only in order to gain permission to operate within their domains. The overlord himself did not necessarily convert. Elsewhere, the reverse could also be true: in Ireland, conversion of the Ri did not always result in the conversion of the kingdom or tribe.[23]

It is understandable that Fraser, and others, assume the dominance of a top-down coercion methodology. There are well-publicised and deplorable instances of this in some early missions when rulers forced their subjects to convert and be baptised on pain of death. There were similar instances in some later Roman Catholic and Protestant missions, especially missions closely allied to secular imperial ambitions. Some communities were forced with threats to conform

21 Yorke, *The Conversion of Britain: 600–800*, 120, discusses alternative theories to a top-down process in the conversion of southern England following Augustine of Canterbury's 597 mission, but concludes that this is difficult to assess for lack of evidence. Evidence will always be less obvious for a from-below strategy which deals with relatively unimportant people. Nevertheless, Yorke indicates awareness that the top-down strategy was not the only methodology.

22 Bruce, *Prophecy, Miracles, Angels and Heavenly Light?*, 217.

23 Sheane, *Ulster in the Age of Saint Comgall of Bangor*, 28.

to the religion of the colonial power. But far more numerous, though far less publicised, are missions which strove to stay independent of political power. These include most nineteenth-century Protestant evangelical missions. They could not operate with a top-down model because their understanding of what it meant to be converted was inimical to any system of imposed conformity.[24] Evangelical piety looked for the heart being moved in each individual as evidence of true faith. This automatically precluded the validity of forced conversion. The likes of Robert Moffat of the London Missionary Society, who was based at Kuruman in southern Africa from 1820 until 1870, never operated with a top-down methodology. Moffat sought permission from a Chief: and, with permission granted, he strove to bring individuals and families to faith, even when the Chief had not, and would not, accept Christian faith personally.

Other missions, more closely aligned to State interests, understood conversion differently. Some saw mission in terms of a cultural Christianisation of communities, in which individual faith of the heart was of minor importance. They worked on the assumption that Christian beliefs would follow cultural Christianisation. But evangelical missions saw it in reverse. For them, individuals had to come to a personal faith of the heart before groups of converts could then become the building blocks of a Christian society. What we have in Adomnán's portrayal of Columba is closer to Moffat's approach than to a top-down model. As Kenney observes, the early pattern of evangelism in Pictland involved the establishment of small cells of Christians, independent of royal patronage.[25] There was an awareness that the mission of Christ and the apostles did not include the conversion of kings. In this respect Columba's evangelistic missions replicated Christ's.[26] Royal patronage, with its opportunities and problems, with its blessings and curses, came later.

24 cf. David Livingstone, *Missionary Travels and Researches in South Africa* (1857), 107ff.

25 Kenny, *The Sources for the Early History of Ireland*, 425.

26 Bruce, *Prophecy, Miracles, Angels and Heavenly Light?*, 215. Bruce points out that some commentators view Columba as an unsuccessful evangelist because there is no evidence of conversions on a national scale following the conversion of rulers. Bruce criticises such commentators for having a preconceived view of how evangelism took place: 'As Patrick observed earlier for his own mission, the time had not yet come for the conversion of kings.' (*Confessions*, 52)

CHAPTER 22

The Weapons of Warfare

Missionary monks carried little: satchel; prayer book; crosier; hand-bell; possibly items for a portable altar. Not much more.[1] These were the physical tools for ministry, to be used in conjunction with prayer, praise, preaching, signing the cross, and blessing.[2] Open-air ministry drew crowds. After watching and listening, the onlookers asked questions, wanting to know more about the faith which had come into their midst.

Not everyone was welcoming. When Columba and his monks recited Vesper prayers outside Bridei's Pictish stronghold, druidical priests arrived and tried to disrupt the worship (I:37). Adomnán claims they were attempting to ensure that their own people could not hear 'the sound of God's praise from the brethren's mouths'. In response, Columba chanted Psalm 45 (Vulgate 44), and Adomnán writes that Columba's voice was miraculously lifted up in the air like some terrible thunder, so that the king and his people were filled with unbearable fear. The words of Psalm 45 were apt for opposing devilish powers:

Gird your sword on your side, you mighty one;
clothe yourself with splendor and majesty.
In your majesty ride forth victoriously
in the cause of truth, humility and justice;

1 Martin Goldberg, 'Ideas and Ideologies' in Clarke et al. (eds), *Early Medieval Scotland*, 142ff. Some hand-bells were bronze, but most were brazed iron, i.e., coated with bronze. The hand-bells sounded a variety of signals to the community: call to prayer; moments during ceremonies; heralding announcements; clamour at time of danger; slow peal marking death, etc. They were part of the ritual of early Christianity; cf. Foster: *Picts, Gaels and Scots*, 88.

2 The *Bangor Antiphonary*, Item 13 (*Audite Omnes*) describes Patrick's ministry in terms of preaching the Gospel, administering baptism, strengthening those who have believed with the heavenly food of the Eucharist, preaching in deeds as well as in words. Patrick is depicted as the true and faithful shepherd feeding his flock with true doctrine, the substance of which is the blessed Trinity and the divinity of Christ. As such, Item 13 describes essentials of early Irish mission; cf. Curran, *The Antiphonary of Bangor and the Early Irish Monastic Liturgy*, 42.

let your right hand achieve awesome deeds.
Let your sharp arrows pierce the hearts of the king's enemies;
let the nations fall beneath your feet.[3]

The story can be read as Columba drowning out the opposition by the sheer power of his voice. But more is involved. Columba responded to what he saw as a demonically inspired disruption. And he acted on the principle that if God's name is exalted in praise and in prayer then God's enemies will be scattered. Columba's tactic was based on Psalm 68 (Vulgate 67): 'Let God arise, let his enemies be scattered, and let those who hate him flee before him.'[4] Glorifying God publicly was itself a weapon against Satan and his legions. Columba was not outshouting the Pictish priests. He was exalting God's name. He was affirming God's glory in the midst of His enemies. And this public exaltation and affirmation was itself a powerful weapon in spiritual warfare. Psalm-singing was especially effective, since it employed God's own words about Himself as recorded in Holy Scripture. When God's name was lifted up and proclaimed, His enemies were set at naught.

DISABLING THE ENEMY

Souls only had hope of heavenly glory if they were first set free from Satan's captivity. Consequently, the first step in mission was to disable Satan's bogus authority over places, tribes, and individuals. This was in line with the thinking of the monks of the eastern Mediterranean who sought out the demonic in its desert-heartland in order to overcome it and cancel its power. They put themselves in harm's way, and they engaged with the forces of evil, as co-warriors with Christ against principalities and powers. Columba and his contemporaries took the same principles into their mission field. The first necessary and unavoidable task was to engage with Satan and overcome him. All else flowed from that. It was only when Satan's rule was broken that men and women could see the light and begin respond to the Gospel. Consistent with this, the *Bangor Antiphonary* depicts Patrick as appointed to redeem innumerable numbers from the captivity of Satan.[5] Columba agreed with this. He saw it as a biblical principle of

3 Psalm 45:3-5 (NIV).
4 cf. Numbers 10:35.
5 *Bangor Antiphonary*, Items 13, 21.

evangelism, involving the release of men and women from 'the power of Satan to God' (Acts 26:18).

1. *Opposing Paganism.* Confrontation with, and victory over, hostile spiritual powers was integral to the early-medieval Church's approach to evangelism. Confrontation also defined its attitude towards non-Christian religion in general. All non-Christian religious practice was viewed negatively. It was interpreted as a manifestation of Satan's rule. Pagan religion was not seen as an early harbinger of a future, more-perfect knowledge of God, only requiring fine-tuning in order to dove-tail with Christian faith. Nor was pagan religion viewed as primitive evidences of the Spirit of God working anonymously and secretly within the souls of men and women. Nor was it seen as a stepping-stone towards a fuller and a better faith. O'Loughlin suggests that early Irish missionaries recognised a working of the Holy Spirit in people in their pre-Christian religion, and he claims that missionary monks built on that foundation, but there is little evidence of such an approach.[6] The opposite was the case. When Irish missionaries took Christianity to the unconverted, they demanded that new believers abandon heathen observances and heathen cults. Following Patrick's example, they insisted that converts totally renounce former fidelities.[7] In his *Confessions* Patrick claims that, when he was abducted by pirates, he twice refused to participate in pagan-associated actions: one involving 'sucking their breasts', and another involving eating honey which had been offered in a pagan sacrifice.[8] Even if Patrick is depicting his youthful self as having followed a purer faith than might have been the case in reality, it is clear that when he writes the *Confessions* he wants to show himself as having a policy of no compromise with pagan religion. New converts were to see pagan religion as the domain of evil demons. Pagan religion was not inspired by the Holy Spirit but

6 O'Loughlin, *Celtic Theology*, 97. O'Loughlin has a view of mission similar to that of J. V. Taylor, *The Primal Vision.* Taylor argues that the fault of many Christian missions to Africa was that they failed to recognise that God's Spirit had already been at work in African religions and that these religions should not be seen as the enemy of Christianity but as having lasting spiritual value in themselves. Markus, *Conceiving a Nation*, 129f., appears to support Taylor's view, arguing that the eighth-century prologue to the Gaelic law-text *Senchus Mor* regarded aspects of pre-Christian native law in Ireland as having been given to 'righteous men and poets' through the Holy Spirit.

7 Patrick, *Confessions*, 45, 60, etc.

8 Patrick, *Confessions*, 18, 19.

was the product of spirits who were enemies of the true God. It was to be replaced, not absorbed.[9] That was the official line.

Adomnán boasts that Columba drove druidical wizards away in confusion and defeat (II:11). Columba drowned out those who disrupted Vespers (I:37). He overcame the sorcerer, who appeared to draw milk from a bull (II:17). He twice confronted and defeated Broichan, King Bridei's principal druidical advisor. On the first occasion, aided 'by an angel', he brought Broichan near death (II:33). On the second occasion, this time aided 'by Christ the Lord', he reversed contrary winds which had been summoned up by Broichan, and sailed against them (II:34). Adomnán's narrative never presents Columba as working with the representatives of pagan religion. He always works against them. Adomnán never represents Columba as recognising value in pre-Christian practices.[10] Moreover, wherever missionary monks encountered non-Christian religion, the initial missional activity was not about persuading men and women intellectually. The first task was to engage demonic forces and destroy their authority.[11] Non-Christian religion was an enemy. It was not a first building-block of spirituality, only needing redirection. Non-Christian religion was formed and inhabited by the demonic. It was not indwelt by God's Holy Spirit. It was to be put to flight. And elements of pre-Christian religion which seeped into early Irish Christianity did so unofficially.[12]

---

9 Bede, *History*, I:30, notes that Pope Gregory advocated a replacement-strategy to be adopted by the Canterbury mission of 597. Pagan places and pagan feasts should become Christian places of worship and Christian festivals. In theory, pagan elements were being replaced. In practice, many pagan features were absorbed into the new faith and only thinly Christianised. Yorke, *The Conversion of Britain: 600–800*, 133, 248ff., notes that the conversion of Britain and Ireland was largely peaceful with no accounts of pagan sites being deliberately destroyed. Instead, they were adapted into the new faith in line with the policy advocated by Gregory. The official policy was total rejection of pagan beliefs.

10 This is the case even if later documents such as the *Senchus Mor* or the *Canones Hibernenses* appear to, as suggested by Markus, *Conceiving a Nation*, 130f. Yet, even in the *Senchus*, the 'good' is in relation to pre-Christian native laws for society, and not in relation to the validity of pre-Christian religion.

11 The sixteenth-century *Aberdeen Breviary* has a strong emphasis in its prayers for Columba's Feast Day (9th June) on Columba defeating the demonic, with Columba removing the 'filth of demons by his holy preaching' (MacQuarrie [ed.], *Aberdeen Breviary*, 135). The *Breviary* was compiled and printed several centuries after Columba's era, but preserves a way of interpreting Columba's ministry which resonates with that of earlier centuries.

12 Bradley, *Argyll: The Making of a Spiritual Landscape*, 119f., draws attention to a fourteenth-century carving from Oronsay depicting a man in armour, the tip of whose scabbard rests on the back of a small leering devil. Though later than Columba's era, it expresses a similar spirituality.

2. *Overpowering Demons.* Columba believed in the reality of the demonic, and never dismissed the powerful Pictish deities as non-existent.[13] Nor did he interpret the demonic metaphorically as the personification of malicious forces such as hunger, poverty, famine, war, or tyranny. Demons were real. Men and women had to be set free from concrete demonic beings, and not just from the grip of mistaken illusions. In accepting the reality and power of demons, Columba saw his task in terms of actualising the victory of Christ over the demonic wherever it was encountered in places or in people. As a soldier of Christ, actively battling against Satan's legions, it could be said of him as it was of Patrick, that he:

> Could never have said to an Irish wizard, as children of the Enlightenment now say 'Your magic is an imposture; your spells cannot really raise spirits or control the forces of nature; you cannot foretell what is to come.' Instead, he would have said, 'Yes, you can do such miracles by the aid of evil powers, but these powers are subject to a good power whose religion I preach, and are impotent except through his permission.'[14]

Satan's hold had to be broken. Only when his grip was shattered could the Gospel begin to bless a people. This need to break the devil's grip over a people, lies behind Adomnán's story of a sorcerer who, 'by the art of the devil' seemed able to draw milk from a bull (II:17). Adomnán tells us that it was Columba who had, in fact, made this devilish activity possible, because, in deceiving the sorcerer into thinking he had the power to draw milk from a bull, Columba was able to destroy his credibility when the 'milk' was found not to be milk at all, but blood 'deprived of its colour by the devil's cheating'. Significantly, Adomnán adds: 'It was not in order to confirm these sorceries that the saint had ordered this to be done, but in order to *defeat* them in the sight of the people.' Sorcery was to be defeated. And it had to be seen to be defeated. Columba did not just have a more powerful magic. If that were all it was, then Columba might be just a more powerful druid.

13 Finlay, *Columba*, 126.

14 J. B. Bury and Jon M. Sweeney (eds), *Ireland's Saint: The Essential Biography of St. Patrick*, 93.

What was happening was much deeper. The power of the demonic was being made subject to the power of Christ. Satan was not simply weaker than Christ; he was made subject to Christ. This was what set people free, enabling them to begin to recognise the triune God and to begin to respond to His claims. And it was belief in the specific identity of God as Father, Son, and Holy Spirit, which was crucial in assessing if a man or a woman were now a Christian.[15]

3. *Overcoming Satan.* No Gospel progress could be made until Satanic pseudo-authority was broken. Any attempt to evangelise without first establishing the triumph of Christ over powers which held a particular locality in bondage, was a fruitless exercise. Consequently, establishing the victory of Christ was the essential opening step in evangelism. This direct engagement with Satan's forces in a spiritual conflict is expressed in the eighth-century *Patrick's Breastplate*, which depicts a Christian entering the field of battle, clothed in the ultimate spiritual weaponry which is God's triune name itself: 'I bind to myself today, the strong Name of the Trinity'.[16] The name of the triune God was wielded as a weapon whenever the sign of the cross was made; whenever He was called upon in prayer; and whenever He was proclaimed. The story of Columba vanquishing a great boar on the Isle of Skye is in this vein. The boar was a cult animal in pagan Pictish religion;[17] and the narrative can be read as a metaphor of how the power of God, through Columba's ministry, overcame pagan religion:

> Entering a dense forest, Columba encountered a boar of amazing size which was being pursued by hunting-dogs. Seeing this, the saint stood still and watched it from a distance. Then he raised his holy hand and called on the name of God with earnest prayer, and said to the boar: 'Go no further, but die where you are now.' The saint's voice rang out in the forest, and the beast was unable to move any further but at once collapsed dead in front of him, killed by the power of his terrible word. (II:26)

---

15 cf. Yorke, *The Conversion of Britain: 600–800*, 135.

16 This version: Cecil Frances Alexander (d. 1895). Hughes, *Early Christian Ireland: Introduction to the Sources*, 241.

17 Yorke, *The Conversion of Britain: 600–800*, 106f., discusses the significance of the boar and other cultic animals in early-medieval non-Christian religions.

The forest was dense. The boar was of incredible size. The saint raised his hand. He prayed. The great beast perished: 'killed by the power of his terrible word'. The spiritual importance of this story goes beyond Columba neutralising a dangerous animal; and there may be an implicit reference to Psalm 80, since several of the Church Fathers saw the wild boar of Psalm 80 as a demonic power which was despoiling God's vineyard of Israel (the Church). Following the Fathers, Adomnán may have had that Scripture in mind.[18] Despite its fearsome appearance, and despite its association with demonic powers, the Skye wild boar was conquered through Columba raising his hand, through prayer, and through proclamation. Significantly, the boar was not an exotic creature from faraway lands, known of only by hearsay. It was a real-life, local, wild beast. As such, it represented real-life, local, spiritual powers. Victory over it symbolised victory over the fiercest of local indigenous spiritual authorities.

Martin Carver, writing about the Columban-inspired Pictish monastery at Portmahomack, notes that fierce beasts such as serpents (signifying death) and composite beasts (signifying terror), are frequently depicted in insular art as having been tamed by Christ.[19] They are put under his rule. One carved stone at Portmahomack has a lion and a boar occupying adjacent niches. Lion and boar were noble, powerful, and dreaded beasts, but they had become subject to Christ with all that that represented. The Enemy had been overcome.

Narratives of demonic powers being defeated through Columba's ministry, also confirmed that Columba was a workman used mightily by God. Columba was called to the heart of spiritual warfare. He was

---

18 Psalm 80:13 (NIV). Several Church Fathers link overcoming wild boars to overcoming dark spiritual forces. They may have been alluding to the myth of Hercules defeating the Erymanthian Boar, but more likely they were referencing 80:13 and its imagery of a wild boar despoiling God's vineyard (Israel/the Church). Augustine, commenting on Psalm 80, suggests that because a boar is the same as a savage swine, then the boar should be compared to the Gadarene swine which were inhabited by the demonic. Eusebius, *Church History*, X:4, comments on Psalm 80, pointing out that what appeared to be a wild boar, was in reality something else masquerading as a boar, which attacked God's people. The wild boar was the 'enemy of the vineyard of the Lord'; cf. Jerome, *Apology*, II:24; and Gregory of Nazianzus, *Orations*, XLIII:41, who writes of God's vine being ravaged by 'that wicked wild boar the devil', but though it ravaged God's vine (Israel), the true vine (Christ) triumphs.

19 Carver (ed.), *Portmahomack on Tarbat Ness: Changing Ideologies in North-East Scotland*, 157. This interpretation is more likely than the passivity of fierce animals being an eschatological reference to a time when the lion lies down with the lamb.

placed at the centre of Christ's mission. He was tasked with advancing the triumph of Christ upon the earth. Against all later detractors, this was further proof of the validity of his ministry as God's chosen vessel.

FREEING THE MIND

Satan's binding of men and women resulted in their minds becoming clouded, preventing them from being able to see the truth. Minds as well as souls were held captive, and only when Satan's false authority was removed was there even the beginning of an understanding of what the truth might be. This was why liberation from demonic captivity had to precede intellectual understanding. Only when liberated, was the mind free to be rational and free to believe.

This principle is illustrated in Adomnán's story about a well which Columba visited (II:11). Adomnán tells us that the foolish people worshipped it as a god because the devil, 'clouded their senses' (Sharpe's translation), 'deluded their understanding' (the Andersons' translation). Clouded senses and deluded understanding prevented them from recognising the truth and gave Satan control of their thinking. The well also brought illness in the form of leprosy. In Adomnán's narrative Columba viewed the well as a critical battleground where Satan's false rule had to be broken. Hence, Adomnán portrays Columba making his way 'fearlessly' to the well, to the glee of pagan priests who were convinced that Columba would succumb to its powers. But the outcome was rather different. Columba blessed the well. He washed in its water. And, by the power of God, the well was changed. The influence of Satan over the well was broken. Instead of being a place of harm it became a place of healing. After Satan's rule was broken, a well which caused illness now gave healing, and a power which had 'clouded their senses' was removed.[20]

PROCLAIMING THE WORD

In his *Life of Anthony* Athanasius mentions two types of weaponry which were to be used against Satan and to advance the Gospel. These were proclaiming Christ and making the sign of the cross.[21] In his earlier book, *On the Incarnation*, Athanasius already spells out the

---

20 cf. Bruce, *Prophecy, Miracles, Angels and Heavenly Light?*, 81f. Yorke, *The Conversion of Britain: 600–800*, 255, interprets the story as involving the Christianising of a previously pagan site.

21 Athanasius, *Life of Anthony*, 78.

importance of signing the cross and confessing the name of Christ when engaging in spiritual warfare:

> Anyone may put what we have said to the proof of experience in another way. In the very presence of the fraud of demons, and the imposture of the oracles, and the wonders of magic, let him use *the sign of the cross* which they all mock at, and but *speak the Name of Christ*, and he shall see how through Him demons are routed, oracles cease, and all magic and witchcraft is confounded [my italics].[22]

Proclamation and signing the cross were major weapons. If used aright they caused demons to flee and rendered malevolent spiritual powers powerless. These spiritual weapons were so important for ordinary believers living their day-to-day Christian lives that Cyril of Jerusalem (d. 386) expounds on them at length in his lectures to candidates for baptism.[23] The Irish Church inherited this spirituality, and the self-same spiritual weapons of proclamation and signing the cross are high-profile for Adomnán.

Proclamation includes preaching, but is more than preaching. Proclamation occurs whenever Christ's name or God's name is glorified and made public. When Columba raised his voice in psalm-singing outside Bridei's fort, that was a proclamation of the glory and majesty of the true God. And in heralding the true God, it was a potent weapon. Strategy for mission was based on declaring, exalting, making known, announcing, lifting up, celebrating, and triumphantly praising the triune God, in situations where Satan claimed to rule. Proclamation unleashed a spiritual power which made Satan's strongholds fall. That was how spiritual battle took place. It was not

22 Athanasius, *On the Incarnation*, XLVIII.

23 Cyril of Jerusalem: 'Let us not, therefore, be ashamed of the cross of Christ, but, even though another hides it, do you openly seal it on thy brow, that the devils beholding that royal sign may flee far away trembling. Make this sign when you eat and drink, sit or lie down, rise up, speak, walk; in a word, on every occasion, for He who was here crucified is above in the heavens' (*Catechetical Lectures*, IV:14); 'Many have been crucified throughout the world but none of these do the devils dread, but Christ having been crucified for us, when they see but the sign of the cross the devils shudder' (XIII:3); 'Let none be weary: take up arms against the adversaries in the cause of the cross itself: set up the faith of the cross as a trophy against the gainsayers. For when you are about to dispute with unbelievers concerning the cross of Christ, first make with your right hand the sign of the cross of Christ, and the gainsayer will be dumb. Be not ashamed to confess the cross' (XIII:22; cf. XIII:36).

through argument or reason as such, but by glorifying God and His Christ, declaring that the King has come, and proclaiming him as the Victor who is establishing His rule. This was what lay behind preaching and making the sign of the cross. In similar vein, prayer was not an exercise in quiet meditation, but a spiritual weapon against the legions of evil. Praise and prayer were inextricably linked since praise was the same as prayer, albeit in a sung or in a chanted form. In a frontline missionary situation, which involved facing down the demonic, such as outside Bridei's fort, prayer-praise was Columba's weapon of choice.

Adomnán has only a handful of references to Columba's preaching ministry. Columba preached frequently as abbot and monk, but because Adomnán is focussed on supernatural events in Columba's life such as prophecy, miracles, and angelic visitations, he has little reference to the content of Columba's sermons.[24] Adomnán does record prophecies which Columba uttered, because each fulfilled prophecy indicated divine approval of Columba's mission. But Adomnán skips over Columba's conventional preaching, and only uses the term 'preaching' twice, though it is implied in a number of other passages.

In the province of the Picts, the preaching (*predicante*) of Columba was heard by a man who believed the word of life and was baptised, along with his wife, children, and servants (II:32). Likewise, Emchath of Glen Urquhart came to faith after hearing and believing the word of God preached (*praedicatum*) by Columba. He was baptised along with his son Virolec, who also believed, and with his whole household (III:14). On another occasion, although Adomnán does not use the term 'preach' in his story of the old man on Skye who was converted, he does write that the old man 'received the word of God from the saint', believed, and was baptised (I:32). In this context 'received the word of God' is equivalent to hearing God's word preached.

---

24 In the context of the Northumbrian post-Whitby Church, Bede, *Letter to Egbert*, 5, sets out what he regards should be in a monk's preaching to scattered communities: 'Preach in each hamlet the word of God and offer the heavenly mysteries and above all perform the sacrament of baptism whenever the opportunity arises. In preaching to the people, this message more than any other should be proclaimed: that the Catholic faith, as contained in the Apostles' Creed and the Lord's Prayer which the reading of the Gospel teaches us, should be deeply memorized by all who are under your rule.' Though this may describe preaching to communities already deemed to be Christian, the message to the unconverted would be similar.

In each of these incidents Columba is in a frontline, evangelistic setting. Each time Adomnán refers to what was preached as either the 'word of God' or the 'word of life'. On other occasions, such as when Columb mac Áedo was cut to the heart concerning his love of money after hearing Columba's comments on wealth (I:50), Columba may not have been preaching as such, but discussing issues with those around him.

Adomnán gives sparse data from which to construct Columba's preaching, but what we do have is in line with the early Irish Church's understanding of proclamation as a heraldic activity.[25] Preaching heralds both the name of Christ and the name of the triune God. Preaching brings the true God into geographical and spiritual regions where Satan claims to rule. Just as Christ (the incarnate Word of God) through being lifted up on the cross, engaged Satan, and overcame him, so also Christ (the proclaimed Word of God), through being lifted up in preaching, engages Satan and overcomes him. If the Eucharist reiterates the cross and its victory, so also does preaching. Satan, already defeated at the cross, has to renounce control of places and peoples which he seeks to retain as subject to himself. And with Satan's dominion shattered, there can now be effective teaching, instruction, and understanding.

Whenever Christ was glorified in the midst of hostile powers, the demonic stranglehold over men and women was broken, and faith could follow. Emchath of Glen Urquhart lived all his life in natural goodness, so Satan had very little hold over him. Emchath's captivity was a weak captivity, enabling him to respond quickly and instinctively to the Gospel (III:14). The presupposition behind Adomnán's account of Emcath's conversion is that because Emchath's natural goodness kept his senses clear, then, when God's Word was proclaimed, he was able immediately to hear plainly, understand clearly, and respond freely.

SIGNING THE CROSS

Irish monks made the sign of the cross with the right hand (III:23), but followed a version of the Eastern style rather than the Roman style. This involved extending the first, second, and fourth fingers, whilst closing the third finger down over the extremity of the thumb which

25 O'Loughlin, *Celtic Theology*, 95ff., discusses Muirchu's account of Patrick's decisive encounter with pagan power, and identifies Patrick as Christ's herald and champion on a night of deliverance and baptism.

bent across into the palm.[26] The Roman method was to extended the thumb, the forefinger, and the middle finger, and to bend the third and fourth fingers into the hand. Images of the Roman style only occur on later Iona crosses, carved after Roman practices displaced Celtic ones.

Drawing the sign of the cross 'in the air' and holding up the right hand in blessing 'in the air', brought Christ into a realm which Satan regarded as his own territory. As such, making the sign of the cross was an act of spiritual aggression. It was not a sentimental way of expressing good wishes! In Adomnán's *Life of Columba* making the sign of the cross is almost always associated with spiritual warfare. When Adomnán describes Columba driving out a devil from a milk pail, he remarks that 'the devil could not withstand the power of that sign' (II:16). In the same vein, the sign of the cross was involved in every act of consecration in order to expel the demonic. It was used over tools before use (II:29); to restrain a river monster (II:27); to unlock castle gates (II:35); and to deprive a knife of its power to harm (II:29). Making the sign of the cross is also implied when Columba banished evil spirits (II:17); stopped a wild boar (II:26); endowed a pebble with healing properties (II:33); and enabled the godly woman Mogain to be healed (II:5).

At the miraculous opening of the massive doors of Bridei's fort, the action of Columba making the sign of the cross is central in Adomnán's account (II:35). When Columba arrived at Bridei's fort, the gates were slammed shut against him. But Columba made the sign, and, 'only then did he put his hand to the door to knock'. Adomnán constructs the story carefully to make it clear that before any human hand could intervene, the doors opened of themselves: more accurately, they opened because of divine power acting on Columba's behalf. Bridei and his council were stunned. Columba was looked on with a new respect. Bridei now welcomed Columba with words of peace; and 'from that day forward for as long as he lived, the ruler treated the holy and venerable man with great honour'. But the story is not just about Columba as a miracle-worker. Opening the gates was a spiritual victory over demonic powers, the same powers which were imprisoning the king and his people. In Adomnán's narrative, the power of signing the cross at the gates of Bridei's fort was a harbinger of spiritual conquests to come.

---

26 Warren, *The Liturgy and Ritual of the Celtic Church*, 100.

Signing the cross was a Christian exercise from early times, with the practice increasing during the fourth century, partly in imitation of Anthony of Egypt. In the fourth century, Lactantius (d. 320) wrote a lengthy exposition on the importance of the sign of the cross and its power to make devils flee, teaching that when the sign is made, then the demonic has to yield and retreat from ground it once held.[27] In this respect signing the cross was similar to preaching the word. It was a heraldic action. And, because it was nearly always accompanied with proclaiming the name of Christ and confessing the name of the triune God, then it announced God's presence, exalted Him in the midst of His enemies, and put these enemies to flight. Athanasius reinforces this conviction in his *Life of Anthony*, in which signing the cross is a vital and important weapon in Anthony's battle against Satan and demonic powers.[28]

Signing the cross made two powerful theological statements. First, it was invariably accompanied with confessing the Trinity and/or the deity of Christ, hence was a public witness to the identity of the true God. Second, it openly declared the victory of Christ on the cross over Satan. Both aspects of this theology are strikingly presented by Athanasius: 'Their so-called gods are routed by the sign of the cross, and the crucified Saviour is proclaimed in all the world as God and Son of God.'[29] Severus' widely read *Life of Martin* has a similar emphasis on the power of signing in spiritual warfare. Severus explains that Martin protected himself against all dangers, both human and demonic, by the **sign of the cross** and with the help of prayer.[30] All of this had been part of Cassian's spirituality, with Cassian writing that when demons attack, monks ought to:

> Beat them off with the sign of the cross and drive them far away; and when they rage furiously against them they should

27 Lactantius (d. 320), *Divine Institutes*, IV:27; cf. Herren and Brown, *Christ in Celtic Christianity*, 191.

28 Athanasius, *Life of Anthony*, 13, 23, 78, 80.

29 Athanasius, *On the Incarnation*, LII.

30 Severus, *Life of Martin*, IV:5, XII:3; cf. Cyril of Alexandria (d. 386), commenting on Isaiah XIX:19: 'He, in this place, calls the sign of the holy cross, with which it is the custom of believers to be fenced round, a *pillar*. For this we have ever used; overthrowing every assault of the devil, and repelling the attacks of evil spirits. For an impregnable wall is the cross unto us, and our glorying in it is truly salutary. God forbid that I should glory, save in the cross of Christ.'

> annihilate them by the constant recollection of the Lord's passion and by following the example of His mortified life.[31]

Drawing directly on Athanasius' work, Cassian cites Anthony's example: 'These most savage demons did not even venture to approach [Anthony] as he was now signing his breast and forehead with the sign of the cross.'[32] Cassian also refers to Abbot Abraham:

> Pestered with tears and prayers by a woman who brought her little child, already pining away and half dead from lack of milk. He gave her a cup of water to drink signed with the sign of the cross; and, when she had drunk it, at once most marvellously her breasts that had been till then utterly dry flowed with a copious abundance of milk.[33]

This extract is intriguing because Adomnán also includes stories about Columba using the sign of the cross in relation to milk, though not woman's milk (II:16 and II:17). What is common to both is that the milk has its life-giving goodness released through the sign of the cross.

Teaching from the major Church Fathers fed the spirituality of the early-medieval Irish Church. Hence, when Irish monks bound themselves to 'the strong name of the Trinity' as they battled against Satan, they did so by making the sign of the cross with their hands, and by confessing Christ and the triune God with their lips. In word and in action they heralded the presence of the true God and the triumph of Christ. They brought these realities into situations where Satan claimed to rule. Throughout Christendom, the sign of the cross was a sign of deliverance. Adomnán describes it as 'the saving sign of the cross' (II:16). It was not simply a reminder of an event in the past. Instead, in being a proclamation of the divine name and the triumph of Christ, it was an instrument of Christ's power to deliver His people from the Evil One. Columba made the sign of the cross in circumstances where Satan's power had to be broken. As with preaching, the power of the sign lay in the exaltation of Christ. The demonic must yield before Him when He is exalted.[34]

---

31 Cassian, *Institutes*, I:8.

32 Cassian, *Conferences*, VIII:18.

33 Cassian, *Conferences*, XV:4; cf. XV:10.

34 cf. *Voyages of St. Brendan*, XXIII.

An object or a person could also be blessed 'in the Name of the Lord', or 'in the Name of the Trinity'. Blessing in the name of the triune God had real power. It was far from being an expression of good luck, or pious well-wishing, or an impartation of magical powers. Blessing was a spoken way of invoking God's presence. Blessing claimed a situation or a person for God and, in so doing, put that situation or person under divine rule. Monks did not bless sick people as a maudlin expression of sympathy, but as an active means of aiding recovery. Illness was believed to have been caused by spiteful spiritual forces, but when the sick were blessed, then God's rule was claimed over them, expelling Satan's influence.[35]

Columba's final actions on Iona were to bless the island, including its animals, produce, and people (III:23). Jennifer O'Reilly interprets the whole of the long final chapter of Adomnán's book as six scenes in which Columba systematically blessed the whole island from periphery to centre, containing within his blessing, its inhabitants, stock, barn, grain, draught-horse, monastery, and company of monks. She notes in particular that, when Columba blessed the monastery, Adomnán gives him words suggestively reminiscent of Old Testament prophecies that the holy citadel of Jerusalem would one day be revered by all and draw peoples from far and near (cf. Isaiah 2:2-3). Then, in the church at midnight, at the close of that last day and just before he dies, Columba's final action was to move his hand visibly, 'as much as he was able', in order to be seen to bless the brothers. Only after the holy benedictions were complete did he breathe out his spirit.[36]

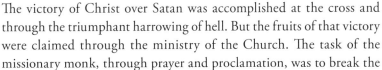

The victory of Christ over Satan was accomplished at the cross and through the triumphant harrowing of hell. But the fruits of that victory were claimed through the ministry of the Church. The task of the missionary monk, through prayer and proclamation, was to break the rule of Satan over individuals and communities. Once that rule was

35 cf. Adomnán, *Life*, II:7 and II:11. In the story of Columba curing a well of evil powers the sequence is: (1) Praying; (2) Blessing (claiming the well for Christ); (3) Acting in faith through touching the well and drinking the water, knowing that previously to do so was to be struck down.

36 O'Reilly, 'Reading the Scriptures in the Life of Columba' in Bourke (ed.), *Studies in the Cult of Columba*, 95f.

broken the Gospel could take root. But the necessary precursor to faith, and the *sine qua non* of evangelism, was that enslavement to Satan had to be dissolved before hearing, believing, responding, could even begin. The *pre-evangelium* was not an accommodation of the Gospel to the indigenous religious context: it was the breaking and expulsion of the authority of Satan in the lives of those to whom the Gospel was preached.

The power of preaching lay in it being a heraldic proclamation of Christ's victory and authority. The primary task of preaching was to announce the presence of the true King who was the conqueror of Satan at Calvary. Once Christ was lifted up through proclamation, the powers of the demonic were engaged, overcome, and scattered. The missionary monk brought the presence of the triumphant Christ, with His infinite conquering potential, into a situation.[37] Through prayer, preaching, demonstrations of power, signing the cross, and blessing, Christ's presence was introduced and Satan's power was broken. These were powerful weapons in warfare against demonic forces.[38] This entire evangelistic strategy was rooted in the motif of Christ the King, Victor over Satan. Columba's successful involvement in spiritual warfare proved he was God's true and chosen servant in this most important of all tasks.

---

37 O'Loughlin, *Celtic Theology*, 99, writes of the great Easter Vigil in terms of 'Light and life, Christ, have triumphed and the victory is proclaimed in the dark territory that was formerly controlled by the great enemy.'

38 McNeill, *The Celtic Penitentials*, 101, suggests that Columba, in his confrontations with Broichan, ritually cursed Broichan (cf. II:33). McNeill argues that Columba drew on pre-Christian druidical influences. But it can as easily be interpreted as Columba drawing on the Old Testament concept of 'cursing' as the antithesis of 'blessing'; or drawing on the New Testament example of Paul's declaration 'let him be anathema!'

CHAPTER 23

The Response of Faith

Political, social, cultural, economic, and psychological factors can all affect the response to a new idea or a new faith. But missionary monks believed that it was soul-awakening through God's Holy Spirit which advanced the Gospel. Identifying causes of events is an inexact science, and any historian's conclusions are always affected by his or her presuppositions. With this in mind, Fraser suggests that because many older scholars were themselves Christian believers, they too readily assumed that Christianisation occurred because of the essential truth of the Christian faith and because it had a higher religious development.[1] They presupposed that Christianity's ideas about God, humanity, death, and eternity were more advanced than anything which indigenous paganism had to offer. Consequently, Christianity overawed the populace and triumphed. But was this the case?

Fraser's argument is linked to his assumption that Christianisation was a two-step process, beginning with the conversion of a local king or power-figure, which was followed at his command by communal conversions and mass baptisms. Because Fraser takes this as the standard model for missionary advance, he questions the validity of conversions which such a process produced. He points out that modern missiologists judge these to be invalid conversions because few would dare opt out of the collective decision of their community or disobey their king. Fraser concludes that because a top-down enforcement model was at work, then Christianisation was not about men and women coming to faith through free response. Instead, Christianisation occurred because it offered outcomes which raised its status and appeal in the eyes of elites: and the people had to follow.[2] Critical factors persuading a king to adopt a new religion included whether it would bring military success, national

1 Fraser, *From Caledonia to Pictland: Scotland to 795*, 85.
2 Fraser, *From Caledonia to Pictland: Scotland to 795*, 89f.

well-being, dynastic stability, and glory and riches. If Christianity could meet these demands of elite culture, then 'conversions' would take place. True soul-change played a minor part.

History does have examples supporting Fraser's thesis. When Edwin of Deira (d. 633) adopted Christianity as the faith for his people, he consulted his Privy Council on the benefits which would accrue to the kingdom if Christianity became its faith. To some extent, his final decision was not driven by belief in the truth of the new religion, but by its political and economic advantages.[3] A decision was made by elites, and the people followed. Examples of more brutal impositions of Christianity by a 'converted' king can be cited, and it is undeniable that some rulers did command their people to line up for baptism as part of tribal obedience.

Nevertheless, in the Irish missions to Scotland of Columba's era, there are no recorded instances of a top-down enforcement process taking place. Fraser's model does not fit. Despite this, and despite many other exceptions, it has become almost automatic to assume that whole communities were Christianised because the powerful decided so, rather than through a genuine upsurge of faith. But verdicts need to be arrived at on a case-by-case basis.[4]

THE RESPONSE OF THE HEART

It is true that, in tight tribal societies, the lead given by the chief was critical because inclusion, acceptance, conformity, and obedience, were core to identity and belonging. It is also true that any notion of personal faith choice may have been an alien concept and should not be read back from later Western culture with its emphasis on the individual. Yet, although it would appear that forces of conformity were so strong that individual expression was unthinkable, history records a more nuanced reality. In major independent evangelical missions of the nineteenth

3 Bede, *History*, II:13. In Bede's account of King Ethelbert of Kent converting (*History*, I:26), Bede is anxious to convey the impression that Ethelbert did not compel his people to accept Christianity. Bede knew of compulsion being used elsewhere and did not approve of the practice. It may be that Bede 'protests too much'. He admits that Ethelbert 'showed greater affection for believers since they were his fellow-citizens in the kingdom of heaven'. In other words, Ethelbert rewarded those who followed his example. He may not have coerced directly, but he made life more difficult for those who remained pagan.

4 Sheane, *Ulster in the age of Saint Comgall of Bangor*, 28, points out that in Ireland conversion of the Ri did not automatically mean the conversion of the kingdom or tribe.

century, such as those of the London Missionary Society, the top-down enforcement model was virtually absent. Evangelical missionaries looked for a 'response of the heart', because that was the only type of conversion which they regarded as genuine. In the tradition of the Great Awakening and the Evangelical Revival, 'response of the heart' was the *sine qua non* of evangelical mission. Mass Christianisation of society without confirmation of individual responses, was not on the radar. What LMS missionaries did do was to seek permission from tribal chiefs to evangelise their people. When permission was granted (which it was not always) this could lead to ones and twos coming to faith. These individual conversions were permitted by the chief, even though he had not yet converted and in some cases never did.[5]

There are strong parallels between LMS scenarios and what we know of Columba's work. The top-down enforcement model is absent from Adomnán's *Life of Columba*, with Adomnán concentrating on Columba bringing individual families to faith, and with the great Pictish overlord, King Bridei, most likely never converting.[6] Just as, in nineteenth-century southern Africa, Mothibi of the Batlhaping, and Moselekatse of the Ndebele gave Robert Moffat permission to preach Christian faith to their people at a time when neither were themselves believers, so Bridei allowed monks to evangelise in Pictland. Mothibi, Moselekatse, and Bridei did not see their authority compromised if some under their rule adopted a new faith. Moselekatse gave permission even though he knew that Christianity was incompatible with his own status as a 'god' to his people. Moselekatse never became a Christian. Mothibi eventually converted. Bridei probably never did. Yet neither Moselekatse nor Bridei were weak kings. They were warrior despots.

There were some missions which were satisfied if a converted ruler imposed the new faith on his people. In such cases societal Christianisation was seen as more important than individuals being persuaded in mind and heart about the new faith. In these instances,

5 Bruce Ritchie, *The Missionary Theology of Robert Moffat* (Ph.D. Thesis, University of Malawi, 2006).

6 Hughes, *Early Christian Ireland: Introduction to the Sources*, 225. The De Paors, *Early Christian Ireland*, 73, emphasise that in Ireland the primary unit of society was not the individual citizen but the family, and public responsibility for individual acts rested not on the individual but on his family. We note, however, that when the Church imposed penance it was imposed on the individual who was deemed responsible for an act of murder or theft or sexual impropriety.

mass Christianisation was seen as a way of accelerating the absorption of indigenous peoples into the culture of the colonial power. But that was not the methodology of independent evangelical missions. The aim of the evangelical missionary was to gain a surrender of mind and heart to Christ. A top-down enforcement model of Christianisation contradicted and negated that aim. Thus a notion of imposed Christianisation by the will of a king or chief, is insufficient to explain all missionary advance, whether in the nineteenth century or the sixth century.

Another issue raised by historians is that all the early sources for Scotland were written by monks. Did they give sanitised versions of history? Was the truth bloodier and more disturbing? But Gordon Donaldson judges that there are few signs of conversion by coercion in early missions to Scotland, even though intimidation occurred elsewhere.[7] Similarly, the National Museums of Scotland text, *Early Medieval Scotland*, concludes there was 'no invasion and no external power forcing people to adopt new beliefs, in contrast to how the Carolingian emperors forced conversion on the Slavs and pagan Saxons through warfare.'[8] Admittedly, some of the early military successes of the Christian settlers of Dál Riata against the Picts would boost the spread of Christianity. And it is almost certain that if a king did convert, then he would use his position to 'encourage' his people to follow him. Nevertheless, the only known example of ruthless coercion within Scotland occurs late in the tenth century in Orkney, where Scandinavian practices prevailed. Olaf Tryggvason, on his way home to Norway in 995, enticed Earl Sigurd of Orkney on to his ship off South Ronaldsay and commanded him on pain of death to receive baptism and make his people follow suit.[9] This replicated shameful incidents elsewhere in Scandinavia and on mainland Europe, where brutal kings commanded their people to convert or die. But that was not the normal scenario in Scotland.[10]

---

7 Gordon Donaldson, *The Faith of the Scots* (London: Batsford, 1960), 16.

8 Goldberg, 'Ideas and Ideology' in Goldberg (ed.), *Early Medieval Scotland*, 196. For further discussion of this theme in relation to the 'peaceful' Christianisation of Ireland, see: Bruce, *Prophecy, Miracles, Angels and Heavenly Light*, 46ff.

9 *The Orkneyinga Saga*, 12.

10 Woolf, *From Pictland to Alba*, 14, 26, distinguishes between conversion to Christianity which required an act of faith, and 'Christianisation' which was the adoption of a Christian way of life by a community. He argues that in the sixth and seventh centuries kings negotiated the conversion to Christianity of their peoples *en masse*. This is a sweeping assumption.

Columba was involved with several powerful monarchs. Yet not one of them was converted through him. Conall of Dál Riata was Christian before Columba arrived. Bridei of the Picts probably remained a pagan. Áedán of Dál Riata was ambivalent, and most of his subjects were already Christian. Rhydderch of Strathclyde received Christian faith from the British Church, rather than from the Irish Church. Hence, Columba was never involved in a situation in which he or his monks converted a major chief and the rest of the tribe followed. Although it might be argued that happened in the nuclear family units which Columba preached to, such as Emchath's family in Glen Urquhart (III:14) and the Pictish layman's family (II:32), the conversion of a nuclear family unit is different in scale and type from mass conversions of a whole people following a major chief's change of religion. In his conversion narratives, Adomnán describes the New Testament model of household conversions, rather than a model of conversion through imposition by the State. Columba's experience was repeated in the ministries of other Irish missionaries in Scotland. Advance was not made in quantum leaps following the conversion of a power-figure. Advance occurred by small steps, with individuals and families coming to faith.

THE NEED OF THE SOUL

Did people convert because of Christianity's message of life after death? Finlay suggests that, if accounts of druidical religion by writers such as Caesar, Strabo, and Tacitus are accurate, then the Christian Gospel may not have offered any more than what people already believed.[11] The druids already preached about immortality and the paradise of *Tir nan Og* (The Happy Isles beyond the Setting Sun). Indeed, belief in life after death was so strong in pre-Christian druidical culture that debts could be repaid in the afterlife by the deceased. This meant that pre-Christian societies in Ireland and Scotland were untroubled by the problem of death, unlike avant-garde Roman society which had demythologised its religion. In Rome Lucretius taught what many believed about death, that 'the end is sound slumber and a long good

11 Finlay, *Columba*, 27ff. This is missed by Yorke, *The Conversion of Britain: 600–800*, 135, 216, who suggests that it may have been the Christian teachings on life after death which distinguished Christianity from non-Christian beliefs.

night'. But the Celts were different from elite Romans: and on the issue of life after death, Christian faith was not introducing something totally absent from their religion.[12]

Why then was Christian faith adopted? Was it its ethics? Or was it welcomed precisely because it dovetailed with existing beliefs about death? Or were other factors at work? Finlay puzzles over this because he previously assumed that resurrection preaching would be the main thrust of Irish evangelism. But the unique selling point of Christian faith may not have been the hope of immortality as such, but how that immortality could come about. Christianity taught that eternal life was now possible specifically because Christ had overcome Satan's power and Satan's obstruction of a heavenly hope. Christian faith answered the 'how?' question. It was the triumph of its God which made it different. For those who listened, the victory of Christ made sense. It explained how the demonic was dealt with, taking away the greatest obstacle to that hoped-for life after death.

THE CASE OF KING BRIDEI

Adomnán's *Life of Columba* refers to King Bridei five times. Is there enough information in these stories to indicate whether or not Bridei was converted through Columba?[13]

1. In the first story, Columba took a white stone from the river and blessed it so that it might work a cure (I:1). Adomnán notes that the stone 'when dropped in water floated like an apple in defiance of the natural order; this miracle of God happened in the sight of King Bridei and his household'. The druid Broichan was cured by drinking the water on which the stone had been placed. Smooth white quartzite charmstones have been found in pre-Christian Pictish contexts, and the incident may reflect an unstated accommodation to pre-Christian beliefs.[14]

---

12 Goldberg, 'Ideas and Ideology' in Goldberg (ed.), *Early Medieval Scotland*, 175: 'The new faith came as a comprehensive philosophical package through its central texts, but it was one that was still open to debate and modification through the centuries … In much of Scotland there was no Roman transition to introduce Mediterranean models of practice and worship that Christianity later used and adapted across the rest of Europe. Instead, we must expect a more direct interface between Christianity and the existing belief systems of people beyond the frontier … but [there is an] absence of data about these belief systems.'

13 cf. Yorke, *The Conversion of Britain: 600–800*, 130f.

14 Jill Harden, *The Picts*, 43; and Yorke, *The Conversion of Britain: 600–800*, 251f.

2. Adomnán refers to Bridei in the story about the power of Columba's singing outside Bridei's fort (I:37). Columba's voice was 'miraculously lifted up in the air like some terrible thunder' so that the king and his people were 'filled with unbearable fear'.

3. Bridei's third appearance is when Columba pleaded for the release of an Irish slave-girl, who had been captured during a Pictish raid on Dál Riata (II:33). Pleas had no effect on Bridei until Columba took drastic action. Using supernatural power, he brought Broichan to the point of death. This terrified Bridei, since Broichan was his foster-father as well as his chief druid. Bridei relented and set the girl free. The story shows Columba fulfilling one of the precepts of his teacher Finnian, who expected clerics to be involved in redeeming captives.[15]

4. Adomnán mentions Bridei in the story of Bridei's fortress gates opening when Columba made the sign of the cross and put his hand to the door to knock (II:35). The king and his council were totally taken aback, and they received Columba with a new respect which lasted the rest of Bridei's life.

5. The fifth occurrence was when Columba asked Bridei to give protection to the monk Cormac Us Liathain, who was seeking 'a place of retreat in the ocean' (II:42). Cormac is described elsewhere as a truly holy man, 'who no fewer than three times laboured on the ocean in search of a place of retreat yet found none' (I:6). There were so many monks looking for uninhabited islands that Cormac could not find one. Bridei was the overlord of Orkney, and Columba persuaded Bridei to ensure Cormac's safety if Cormac arrived there. Adomnán adds that it was because of Columba's appeal to Bridei on Cormac's behalf that Cormac was delivered from imminent death in the Orkneys. There may be more to this story than first appears, with subtle political machinations in the background. Nevertheless, Adomnán presents the story as Columba entreating Bridei for protection for Cormac.

Nowhere, in any of these stories, is there an account of Bridei's baptism. Nor is there any reference to a gift of land from Bridei to the Iona mission. Nor are there instances of the founding of churches and settlements by Bridei, such as frequently accompany high-status conversion narratives in Ireland.[16] Nor does Adomnán record Bridei taking part in

---

15 *Penitential of Finnian*, 30, 31.

16 Finlay, *Columba*, 131.

any Church activities. If Adomnán's narrative reflects the Iona tradition, then the Iona tradition was silent concerning the conversion of such a great king. Moreover, nothing in Adomnán's five stories about Bridei corresponds to the traditional image of missionary preaching.[17] Columba does not stand before Bridei explaining the message of the cross, resurrection, and judgement. Nor does Columba call Bridei to repentance. Adomnán does not portray Columba preaching to Bridei as he portrays Columba explaining Christian faith to Emchath of Glen Urquhart, the old man on Skye, or the Pictish layman. Why is this?

1. If Columba did appeal to Bridei to convert but without success, then it may be that Adomnán does not want to record failure. Chronicling failure would not aid Adomnán's primary goal of presenting Columba as a man empowered by the Holy Spirit. The post-Whitby environment cast doubt on Columba's credentials. That doubt could only be removed by accounts of Columba's successes. Hence, Columba's *preaching* to Bridei may not have been chronicled by Adomnán precisely because it failed; but the mighty *wonders* which Columba performed in Bridei's court were clear successes, therefore Adomnán documents these in detail.

2. Another possibility involves redefining 'proclamation'. If proclamation is any public affirmation of the triumph of Christ over the forces of Satan, including demonstrations of power, then Columba did proclaim Christ to the king. Columba, clothed with power from God, triumphed over the powers of evil in Bridei's presence. Significantly, other early accounts of Irish Church evangelism do not always preserve sermons, but do record the triumphs of Christ in setting the demonic to flight. In this interpretation, Columba *did* proclaim the triumph of Christ, and *did* declare the majesty of the true God to Bridei, but in mighty acts rather than in words.

3. A third option is that Bridei converted.[18] But the only ancient or semi-ancient text to state unequivocally that Bridei personally converted and was

17 Bruce, *Prophecy, Miracles, Angels and Heavenly Light?*, 102, points out that Adomnán has little of Columba's preaching and records only the fruitful words of his prophetic revelations and small sections of significant conversations. Bruce suggests that Adomnán focusses on the establishment of God's kingdom by 'virtue', which includes powerful, supernatural actions of which preaching is but one part.

18 The possibility that Bridei came from a Christian family, was baptised as an infant, and was already a Christian, is speculated by W. Douglas Simpson, *The Historical Saint. Columba*, 2nd edition, 1927). This theory is discounted by most modern scholars, though

baptised is the later *Pictish Chronicle*, which is of doubtful value and which we consider below. Some read Bede's *History* as pointing to Bridei's conversion, but that interpretation is doubtful.[19] Bede states that Columba arrived in Pictland in the ninth year of Bridei's reign, and that Columba converted that people to Christian faith by his preaching and example.[20] Bede does not state that Bridei himself converted. If Bede believed that Bridei became a Christian through Columba's ministry, it would be unusual for him not to make that clear, since, elsewhere in his *History*, Bede fulsomely chronicles the conversion and baptism of kings. Hence, just as Adomnán has no account of Bridei's personal conversion, neither has Bede. It is more likely Bede believed that Bridei permitted his people to adopt Christian faith without doing so himself. Such a scenario would not be unique in Bede's *History*, with Bede referring elsewhere to examples of mission-tolerance by unconverted monarchs.[21] Bede's knowledge of Columba in Pictland probably came from Christian Picts of his own era. They may have wanted to convey the impression that their countrymen responded more positively to Columba's mission than had been the case.

4. It is the *Pictish Chronicle* which asserts unambiguously that Bridei converted to Christian faith through Columba's ministry, stating that Bridei was baptised in the eighth year of his reign by Columba.[22]

Markus (*Conceiving a Nation*, 120) revives the idea. The *Old Irish Life* (Skene, *Celtic Scotland*, vol. II, 504), portrays Bridei as positively hostile to Columba's mission.

19 Hughes, *Early Christian Ireland: Introduction to the Sources*, 225, argues that Adomnán is to be preferred to Bede.

20 Bede, *History*, III:4.

21 Bede, *History*, I:25.

22 W. A. Cummins, *The Age of the Picts* (2009), 93ff., builds his entire Columba account on the *Pictish Chronicle*'s version of events, speculating from an unreliable source! Cummins argues that Bridei had been brought up in the household of Broichan, and not only was Bridei a pagan but he had been given a highly conservative education and was steeped in the traditions and practices of the old religion. Cummins speculates that Bridei may have been deliberately trained to be a bulwark against the creeping Christianity of the south. Cummins further argues that the southern Picts would have nothing to do with the pagan king of the north, choosing Gartnait as their king and happy to let the Pictish kingdom remain divided; however, Bridei would have none of it, wanting to be king of all the Pictish provinces. Cummins then argues that Bridei realised Pictland could only be united if it shared one faith, and, because southern Pictland showed no signs of reverting to paganism, he decided to change. Cummins proposes that after putting Dál Riata to flight, Bridei went to Ireland to find out more about Christianity and was baptised soon after. This was why he offered Iona to Columba, and why Columba left Ireland on his mission. Bridei then ruled as a Christian king, eventually ruling the whole of Pictland jointly with Galam Cennaleph. After Galam's death Bridei was undisputed king of all the provinces of the Picts. Cummins's evidence is thin.

Cummins, in his book, *The Ages of the Picts*, accepts this at face value, and builds his entire Columba section on it.[23] Cummins concedes that Adomnán does not mention Bridei's baptism, but suggests that the *Pictish Chronicle* supplies what Adomnán omits. Thus, Cummins treats the *Pictish Chronicle* as complementary to Adomnán's *Life of Columba* rather than as an alternative account. However, there are well-known problems surrounding the *Pictish Chronicle.* First, its earliest text (the A-Text) is no earlier than the tenth century. Second, it is a composite document sewn together from diverse sources. Third, it has known inaccuracies. Fourth, the later medieval kings, for whom it was written, wanted a Pictish heritage and also wanted Columba to be part of their narrative. Added to these points are profound questions arising from neither Bede nor Adomnán making any clear statement concerning Bridei's conversion or baptism. Bridei was the most powerful monarch in Scotland north of the Forth/Clyde line, described by Bede as 'most powerful king' (*rege potentissimo*).[24] If such a man had converted then the Iona tradition would have gloried in it. Adomnán records the conversion of three relatively obscure families. Why omit the conversion and baptism of a man such as Bridei?

Iona knew nothing of Bridei's supposed conversion or baptism. If it had, it would have celebrated this trophy of the Gospel. It would not suppress something as massive as Bridei becoming a Christian believer. It would glory in such a triumph. What we find in Adomnán's *Life of Columba* is Columba exerting influence over Bridei by the mighty works he is able to perform, but we do not find Bridei's conversion. Bridei gave an attentive ear because the gates of his fort were miraculously opened. Bridei freed the slave-girl because Columba brought Broichan to the point of death. Bridei agreed to protect the monk Cormac, possibly because the request flattered his ego by acknowledging that his power stretched to the Orkneys. The one undisputed outcome of Columba's meetings with Bridei is that, for all of Bridei's reign, and for years afterwards, Iona monks had unrestricted and unmolested freedom within Pictland.[25] There is no recorded persecution of Christian monks

---

23 Cummins, *The Age of the Picts*, 95.

24 Bede, *History*, III:4.

25 Adamson, *Bangor: Light of the World*, 84, building on the *Old Irish Life*, alludes to a sub-strata of tradition which holds that Columba and Moluaig of Lismore visited Bridei jointly, and that Bridei preferred Moluaig to Columba because Columba was too close to

in Pictland until the massacre of the monks of Eigg around 617, more than thirty years after Bridei's death, which was due to local tensions.

COMMUNITIES, FAMILIES, INDIVIDUALS

Despite Iona not employing a top-down enforcement model in its evangelism, communal responses to the Christian Gospel did occur, and the monks would not be surprised by this as it fitted into their overall worldview. Their understanding was that if the power of Satan over a people were broken, then that whole people was set free to know the true God. Therefore, the phenomenon of whole communities coming to faith could and would occur. Once a community or nation was liberated, a domino-effect should take place, resulting in faith becoming widespread. Defeat of Satan meant defeat of darkness. Defeat of darkness meant that people saw the light. In seeing the light, the natural response was to embrace the Gospel. Within this thinking, the *objective* work of frontline evangelism consisted in breaking the rule of Satan; and the *subjective* work of evangelism occurred when a liberated people freely responded to God's truth. Irish missionary monks expected spiritually liberated communities to embrace faith as a group, and there seemed to be biblical precedence for such thinking. In the Exodus narrative it was the whole nation of Israel which shared in the deliverance which God wrought on their behalf. In a monk's mind, this paradigm should apply to whole nations in their own age. That was the expected domino-effect consequence of the triumph of Christ. Coercion was unnecessary. No need for a power-figure to command his people to follow his lead. Response would flow naturally once Satan's dominion was broken.

Donaldson points out that when communities change their belief systems, there can be a temporary dislocation of values.[26] Social problems erupt when society adopts unfamiliar beliefs and rules, since old sanctions, rooted in traditional tribal beliefs, lose their authority. Did that occur in the evangelisation of Scotland? Probably not, and for two reasons. First, at no point did evangelisation initiate regime

---

the Gaelic-speaking leadership of Dál Riata and the Ui Néill. Adamson thinks this explains why Moluaig evangelised largely Pictish areas and why Columba stayed within the sphere of Dál Riata or Scottish [Irish] influence.

26 Donaldson, *The Faith of the Scots*, 4.

change: the governors of society remained constant. Second, because conversions started at a low level, family by family rather than by dramatic imposition from above, then there was no single moment when a whole society had to readjust. There is also evidence, especially in Ireland, of tribal laws carrying over from pre-Christian contexts into the Christian era. This encouraged continuity and stability.

At the same time conversions were not unopposed, and the story of the Pictish layman and his family is one example of a tussle between the new faith and the old religion (I:1 and II:32). When the Pictish layman heard Columba preaching, he believed and was baptised along with 'his entire household' including wife, children and servants. But after Columba moved on, druids attempted to undermine the family's new-found Christian faith. They introduced doubt when one of the sons in the family died. But Columba returned. He asked where the dead boy lay, and, after intense prayer and tears, he declared, 'In the name of the Lord Jesus Christ, wake up again and stand upon your feet.' According to Adomnán, the boy fully recovered, 'Mourning gave way to celebration, and the God of the Christians was glorified'. In this incident validation of new faith in 'the God of the Christians' came through a visible exercise of divine power.

THE THEATRE OF MISSION

How geographically widespread was Columba and Iona's missionary influence? If all legends are to be believed, then Columba evangelised not only the Inner Hebrides, the Loch Ness area, and Tayside, but also Harris and Lewis, other islands of the Outer Hebrides, St Kilda, the Moray Firth region, part of Aberdeenshire, and the district around Kingussie and Newtonmore![27] We know that two Anglo-Saxons were on Iona during Columba's era, Genereus the Baker (III:10) and Pilu (III:21); but whether they took Columba's influence back to their homelands, or whether they lived out their days on Iona is unknown.

---

27 Reeves, *Life of Saint Columba: Founder of Hy*, xlix-lxxi., gives an extensive list of foundations in Ireland and Scotland, traditionally thought to have been created by Columba himself though few were; cf. Colin Scott Mackenzie, 'St. Columba's Church' in Randall (ed.), *In Search of Colmcille*, 128. Mackenzie notes three early dedications in Lewis, one in Berneray of Harris, one in north Uist, one in Benbecula, one in south Uist, and one in remote St. Kilda. Mackenzie points out that the monk Catan has more claim to Lewis, and that Columba was first connected with Ui, near Stornoway, only in 1433 in a Papal letter.

The *Book of Deer* portrays Columba and the monk Drostan arriving in Aberdour on the extreme east coast of Scotland and founding a settlement at Deer at the request of the local ruler (Mormaer) of the district. The name Drostan may be Pictish, and the account may be a rare example of the name of a native Pictish Christian surviving. Achievements of Pictish Christians are usually underreported or ascribed to monks of Irish origin. John Stuart, in his 1869 study of the *Book of Deer* on behalf of the Spalding Club, is content to repeat the Columba and Drostan legend uncritically, though modern scholars hesitate to give it any historical validity.[28] The *Book of Deer*'s statement that the local Mormaer gave land to Columba at Deer 'in freedom for ever' may be a later monastic claim to land rights, attempting to legitimise that claim by grounding the claim in a supposed ancient gift granted to Columba, who was the most revered saint of the Scottish Church. There may be a basis for the claim, but probably not.

The *Aberdeen Breviary* was published in Edinburgh in 1510 as Scotland's first full-scale printed book, and is a major collection of legends concerning Scottish, Irish, English, Welsh, Pictish, and Scandinavian saints. It includes several stories of Columba roaming far and wide over the north of Scotland, and, although it refers to Drostan as Columba's nephew, it knows nothing of them evangelising the north-east as claimed by the *Book of Deer*.[29] On the other hand, the *Aberdeen Breviary* has Columba travelling to the Molindar burn, near modern-day Glasgow, to meet Kentigern, though not as a missionary.[30] It also portrays Columba meeting with the martyr-king Constantine.[31] In its ninth of June entry for the Feast of Columba, it expounds at length on the great man, with the opening antiphon placing Columba within a context of spiritual warfare:

> Father Columba, recognising the warfare of his struggle,
> Defeated multitudes of demons, relying on Christian strength.

The *Aberdeen Breviary* celebrates Columba's life: his birth in Ireland; his quasi-kingship role as 'head over the peoples of the isles'; his accomplishments as the 'father and founder of monasteries'; and his missionary successes as an evangelist who 'converted pagans by the

28 John Stuart, *The Book of Deer: Edited for the Spalding Club* (1869), iii ff.
29 MacQuarrie (ed.), *Aberdeen Breviary*, 5, 353f. (14th December).
30 MacQuarrie (ed.), *Aberdeen Breviary*, 35 (13th January).
31 MacQuarrie (ed.), *Aberdeen Breviary*, 81 (11th March).

power of his miracles'. As with Adomnán and the *Old Irish Life*, it mentions his visit to King Bridei and the fortress-gates incident.[32] Moreover, without mentioning specific locations, it gives Columba an important role in the overall evangelisation of Britain:

Leaving his beloved homeland of Ireland,
He came to Britain through the grace of Christ;
Through him the King received the peoples of Britain,
By a worthy beginning of life.

This panegyric is characteristic of how Columba's missionary role was seen in the centuries after his death, with the *Aberdeen Breviary* also recording legends in which monks, trained by Columba, arrive in various locations as evangelists, including Machar (Mochumma/Maurice) who made an impact both in Mull and Aberdeenshire.[33]

In addition to claims made by the *Book of Deer* and the *Aberdeen Breviary* there are innumerable local legends of Columba founding churches in various areas. As Columba's reputation grew after his death, many Christian settlements wanted him to be part of their foundation story, and wrote his name into their history, at times replacing the names of the local saints who did the actual work. A church might also be named after Columba because it was believed that some of his relics were stored there. This exercise of claiming Columba for a group's Christian history was similar to the practice of the northern Picts, who gave Bede the impression that their predecessors had responded enthusiastically to Columba's preaching, a claim which Adomnán never makes. In later years, as Roman influence grew, Columba's name was itself replaced in some places by the names of Paul or Peter.[34]

---

32 As well as drawing on Adomnán's *Life of Columba* and the *Old Irish Life*, the *Aberdeen Breviary* also uses Bede's *History*, especially in its material for Ninian's Feast Day (16th September), quoting Bede directly and repeating Bede's description of Columba's mission to the provinces of the northern Picts. MacQuarrie (ed.), *Aberdeen Breviary*, 342, suggests that a version of the *Old Irish Life* was brought to Iona sometime between 1164 and 1203 and used as a source of a Benedictine office for St Columba.

33 MacQuarrie (ed.), *Aberdeen Breviary*, 269ff., 275 (12th November). MacQuarrie (379) notes that though Aberdeen is not mentioned by name, the *Breviary* refers to Machar making his dwelling at a river mouth shaped like a bishop's staff which is a description of the site of St. Machar's Cathedral at the crook at the mouth of the Don.

34 Bede, *History*, V:21, writes that, under Nechtan's influence in the early eighth century, 'the reformed nation [Picts] was glad to be placed under the direction of Peter, the most blessed Prince of the Apostles, and secure under his protection.'

If we dismiss the myth that Columba was everywhere, what can we know? Adomnán is definite that Columba ministered around Loch Ness and in Skye. The *Amra Choluimb Chille* refers to him being active in Tayside. And Columba would definitely have been active in his homeland of Dál Riata.

More precise clues to the extent of early Iona missions may exist in archaeological evidences from Iona's retreat centres, and from places of exile used by anchorites. Two caves on the Ross of Mull have excited particular interest. Ewan Campbell, building on an RCAHMS 1980 Archaeological Report, suggests that early religious carvings in these caves make them viable contenders as 'deserts' for anchorites or penitents. His comments occur in an article on crosses with distinctive expanded terminals, and on the distribution of these crosses throughout the Inner Hebrides.[35] Campbell argues that the type of cross in question is linked to Iona, and their distribution indicates that the area of Iona influence may not have been as geographically extensive as once thought. Although Bede claims that Iona was the head of many monasteries throughout Dál Riata and Pictland, this may not have been the case. Campbell points out that only three monasteries are actually mentioned by Adomnán as daughter houses of Iona: Mag Luinge on Tiree; Cella Diuni on Loch Awe; and Hinba. Further evidence that Iona had a restricted area of activity also lies in the place-names mentioned by Adomnán since, apart from locations on the sea-route to Ireland and locations mentioned in connection with Columba's journeys to Pictland and Skye, Adomnán's place-names are restricted to Tiree, Mull, Morven, Ardnamurchan, and Lorne. Significantly, crosses with Campbell's distinctive expanded terminals all fall within this restricted area of northern Argyll, making him conclude that this was the true sphere of influence of Iona during Columba's years. If correct, Campbell's work confirms that, although Columba's Iona mission was highly active, it did not in any way extend over the whole of the north of Scotland. Nevertheless, it was substantial.

35 Ewan Campbell, 'A Cross-marked quern from Dunadd and other evidence for relations between Dunadd and Iona' in *PSAS*, 117 (1987), 105.

CHAPTER 24

The Baptismal Ministry

When Columba was travelling on the Ardnamurchan peninsula, a child was brought to him for baptism (II:10). The parents may have been Dál Riatans rather than Picts, and were presumably themselves baptised believers and part of a local Christian community.[1] Adomnán tells us that no water was available, so Columba knelt, prayed, blessed a nearby rock, and water 'bubbled out of it in great quantity', enabling the baptism to take place. The Ardnamurchan peninsula is not noted for lack of water, but there may have been an uncharacteristic dry spell, which can happen if the wind is from the east for an extended period. More likely, Adomnán wants to compare Columba with Moses who also brought water from a rock (Exod. 17:6).

At the baptism Columba prophesied that the child, after a squandered youth, would live into extreme old age and be a soldier of Christ all his days. The story is in Book II of Adomnán's *Life of Columba*, a section which focusses on miracles of power, often accompanied by prophetic insight (II:1). But it is the miraculous feature of water issuing from a rock, accompanied by Columba's prophetic insight, which is why Adomnán narrates the story; and the baptism as such is incidental to the miracle and the prophecy. Nevertheless, the story reveals aspects of Iona and Columba's approach to baptism.

BAPTISM AS A SEAL

Our aim is not to expound the full baptismal theology of the early-medieval Irish Church, but to discuss what we can deduce of Columba's baptismal practices. Adomnán has three major conversion stories: Emchath and the Glen Urquhart family (III:14); the old man and the Skye family (I:1, 33); the Pictish layman and his family (II:32). All exhibit a similarity of style and structure. All would be rooted in authentic incidents remembered

1 Markus, *Conceiving a Nation*, 119. In the *Old Irish Life* this incident is translocated to Derry.

in the Iona oral tradition. All may have been documented by Cumméne before being published by Adomnán. And all include the baptism of converts. In each case the Word of God was proclaimed, heard, and believed. In each case the new believers were baptised almost immediately, even though the norm in settled Christian communities was for baptisms only to occur on specified dates of the Christian Calendar, and after an extended period of catechetical instruction.

Catechumens who had been baptised as infants were not rebaptised. Catechumens who came as adult converts were baptised at Easter, Pentecost, or Epiphany. Exceptions to the prescribed dates for baptism were possible, especially if a new convert was near death. Immediate baptism was also advisable if new converts, living far from regular Christian ministry, were to be established into their Christian profession.[2] In remote areas a monk might not pass that way for years, and this was the case in many places, with Bede writing in his *Letter to Egbert* that, even in more populated southern lands, there were isolated communities which hardly saw a priest from one year to the next.[3] On a psychological level, it was important for new converts to be sealed into their new faith by baptism. This was vital if they were expected to continue as believers on their own.

In two of the conversion stories (I:33 and III:14), 'natural goodness' was a precursor to hearing and believing. It created a readiness of response and may also have contributed towards suitability for baptism. Though natural goodness by itself was not enough for salvation, and though a man such as Emchath still needed to hear the Word and believe, his natural goodness indicated that in the spiritual battle over the soul, Satan had less hold over him than over others. It may be because of this that Emchath was considered holy enough to be baptised.

INFANT BAPTISM

Adomnán describes baptism as a 'ministry' (I:33). And the Ardnamurchan incident features Columba in a ministry of baptising infants, complementing his baptism of adult converts elsewhere. The *Bangor Antiphonary* taught that infants were born as children of God 'from

2 Herren and Brown, *Christ in Celtic Christianity*, 134, argue that, in the Common Celtic Church, Baptism and the Eucharist were symbols of the merits of human nature, rather than as panaceas of grace applied to human nature, and that a person merited baptism only after a long period of preparation.

3 Bede, *Letter to Egbert*, 5, 7.

the font'.[4] In the early-medieval Irish Church, baptism was certainly understood to 'do something' in salvation. As such, for monks like Columba, baptism was more than a sign or symbol. In the *Bangor Antiphonary* one phrase which occurs in several collects and is placed alongside references to baptism (as well as references to the Eucharist), is 'the blood which redeems'. This comes within a context of connecting the waters of the Red Sea and the waters of Baptism.[5] In the theology of the early-medieval Irish Church, baptism was necessary in order to deal with original sin, and it established an impassable protection between the believer and his or her original sin, just as the Red Sea was a firewall between Israel (the Church) and Pharaoh.

This is why the immediate baptism of children had high priority, and is why the *Penitential of Finnian* laid down severe penalties for both priests and parents if children died unbaptised. If the priest was at fault, he had to do penance for a whole year with bread and water. If the parents were responsible for their child dying unbaptised, they were given the same penance and forbidden from sharing the marriage-bed for twelve months.[6] Because of this, and because of his enthusiasm to evangelise wherever possible, Columba readily agreed to the Ardnamurchan parents' request.

Herren and Brown discuss whether the earliest Celtic Churches also had a 'Blessing' ritual as a substitute for infant baptism.[7] If so, did it point to a stronger Pelagian element in the Celtic Churches than otherwise supposed? Pelagians did not believe in transmitted original sin, and hence baptism simply absolved an individual of actual sins which he or she had committed. Hence, for Pelagians, infant baptism was unnecessary since an infant had no original sin and few actual sins! Far better to wait until later in life. However, Herren and Brown reckon that Pelagius' possible alternative ritual for children may not have differed much from baptism, though it was termed a 'blessing' rather than a 'baptism'. Significantly, the *Penitential of Cummian* (XI:19) has severe penalties for a person blessing an infant instead of baptising it, indicating that the Irish Church of his era disapproved of the practice.

---

4 *Bangor Antiphonary*, Item 12. (tr. Howlett). Stratman's translation is: 'You were born by the Holy Spirit of the Virgin Mary, for the adoption of sons who were brought into being from the font of baptism to live for you.'

5 *Bangor Antiphonary*, Items 68, 76, 88, 94.

6 *Penitential of Finnian*, Canons 48 and 47.

7 Herren and Brown, *Christ in Celtic Christianity*, 73, 122.

The *Penitential of Finnian* also implies that deacons were permitted to baptise, though only a priest could consecrate the Eucharist. This permission may have been a functional necessity given the scarcity of priests, plus the anxious desire of parents to have their infants baptised as soon after birth as possible.[8] This elevated deacons above ordinary monks who, unless they also became ordained deacons and priests, were not allowed to baptise or to receive alms.[9] Controversially, Yorke suggests that pre-Christian Celtic societies practised infanticide as a legitimate way of restricting the population, and that the Christian practice of the immediate baptism of infants was a means to stop this, since baptised infants were deemed to have souls.[10]

CONVERSION BAPTISM

Apart from the Ardnamurchan infant, Columba's other baptisms involve adult converts from paganism, as described in the three conversion narratives. In addition to these, MacQuarrie ventures that the anointing of Áedán as King of Dal Raita (III:5) may have incorporated a baptismal ceremony, but this is speculative.[11]

None of the well-known conversion stories recorded by Adomnán are included in order to teach Columba's theology of baptism, but are recorded to prove Columba's God-given ministry. Each highlights miraculous powers and/or supernatural knowledge granted to Columba, and the baptisms are subsidiary to that aspect of the story. This aim, of demonstrating Columba's saintliness by describing the powers given to him from God, is at the core of one other baptismal occasion recounted by Adomnán. In his opening chapter, Adomnán tells of how King Oswald of Northumbria in the 630s was inspired by the deceased Columba to do battle against his enemies (I:1). Because Oswald's army saw Columba as the inspiration, guide and protector of their king, then the victorious soldiers believed and were baptised. This incident, which headlines Adomnán's whole book, is an important statement to any Northumbrian readers that Columba was a true man of God.

---

8 *Penitential of Finnian*, Canon 49.

9 *Penitential of Finnian*, Canon 50.

10 Yorke, *The Conversion of Britain: 600–800*, 222.

11 MacQuarrie, *The Saints of Scotland: Essays in Scottish Church History, 450-1093* (1997), 77f.

POSTSCRIPT

CHAPTER 25

Retrospect

In the autumn of 1773 Dr Samuel Johnson and his friend James Boswell travelled to the Western Islands of Scotland. Despite rain, wind, storm, and discomfort, the famously irascible Johnson relaxed and softened as the tour progressed, and the island experiences of the Hebrides appear to have contributed to his mellowing. He wrote of finding civility and elegance on Raasay where he was received by Malcolm MacLeod, whom he described as 'a gentleman'. He was awestruck at Kilmuir on Skye, when he met the Jacobite heroine Flora MacDonald. He treasured his extended stay with MacLeod at Dunvegan Castle, almost becoming the owner of a small island. Johnson enjoyed Dunvegan so much that he wrote of having 'tasted lotus' there, and of being in danger of forgetting to depart and move on. This was a remarkable confession from a man who saw London, and all it could provide, as necessary for life to have any meaning.

By the time Johnson's party reached Iona, he had adopted a romantic disposition towards peoples and places which hitherto he had regarded as wild and 'savage' – though, in the eighteenth century, 'savage' meant 'unspoilt' as much as meaning 'primitive' or 'hostile'. All of this, plus Iona's unique ability to enchant, moved Johnson to rhapsodise on the island's virtues, and he later wrote a sentence which has been repeated innumerable times in guide-books. 'That man is little to be envied, whose patriotism would not gain force upon the plains of Marathon, or whose piety would not grow warmer among the ruins of Iona.'[1]

This was no throwaway line. It was high praise. Johnson adored the classical age: and for an eighteenth-century intellectual such as Johnson, the Battle of Marathon in 490 B.C. was a defining moment, not only for antiquity but for the whole history of civilisation. For Johnson's generation, with its enthusiasm for the glories of antiquity,

1 Samuel Johnson, *A Journey to the Western Islands of Scotland* (Penguin edition, 1984), 141.

the victory of the Greeks over the Persians at Marathon represented the defeat of barbarism. It epitomised what was good in the human spirit. It symbolised the triumph of the noblest aspects of human achievement. Hence, when Johnson compared the impact of Iona on his spirit, with the impact of Marathon on the course of civilisation, he was not spinning idle words.

But which Iona had affected Johnson? Was he aware of Adomnán's *Life of Columba*? Did he know anything about the early-medieval monastic community of Columba's era? Or were Johnson's feelings for the spirituality of the island entirely a product of him viewing the ruins of the later medieval Benedictine Abbey, plus a general sense of mysticism? Whichever was the case, Johnson's inner mind saw civilisation and culture, despite his physical eye only seeing the remnants of a medieval monastery. The anti-Presbyterian Johnson noted with approval that, though the ruins were Catholic in origin, they had been left largely undisturbed. To his thinking they were protected by the very 'venerableness of the place', with one sad exception in the form of a marble altar which 'the superstition of the inhabitants had destroyed'.

What Johnson and Boswell viewed were the remains of a Benedictine Abbey, built in 1203 by Reginald, Lord of the Isles, almost certainly on the site of Columba's monastery.[2] These later Lords of the Isles respected early holy sites, increasing the likelihood that the Columban-era church lies under the present buildings. However, clear proof is lacking, and anything beneath the current structures is now inaccessible to excavation. Reginald's father, the great Somerled, had earlier built the chapel now known as the Chapel of St Oran, though his simple construction would be dwarfed by Reginald's building. Reginald wanted to transform the Church of the West Highlands. He wanted to bring it in line with developments throughout Europe. And his Benedictine Abbey soon replaced any vestiges of the old Columban monastery. In time, an Augustinian Nunnery was built close by, and near the Nunnery was erected the chapel of St Ronan which acted as the parish church.[3] The buildings were connected by criss-crossing

2 Ritchie and Fisher, *Iona Abbey and Nunnery*, 7. Clarke, *Early Medieval Scotland*, 90f.

3 Ritchie and Fisher, *Iona Abbey and Nunnery*, 25, are of the view that *Teampull Ronain* was built c. 1200, though 1992 excavations revealed traces of an earlier and smaller chapel, which perhaps dated back to the eighth century.

tracks, and, at some point in the late fifteenth century, Maclean's Cross was erected where the tracks met.

The Benedictine Abbey subsequently fell into disrepair, needing restoration even before the Scottish Protestant Reformation of 1560, after which the whole way of life associated with Abbey and Nunnery came to an end. The buildings were abandoned. They became increasingly ruinous. Then came the twentieth-century rebuilding, inspired by Lord George MacLeod of Fuinary, who hailed from the same family as Norman MacLeod whom we met in Chapter One. What the modern visitor sees is a restored medieval landscape. Yet, here and there, are faint traces of Columba's island base, including the ancient graveyard of the *Reilig Oran*, noted by Johnson as the hallowed resting place of many Scottish kings, though Johnson was aware of a lack of evidence for as many regal burials as are sometimes claimed. On leaving Iona, he reflected:

> We now left these illustrious ruins, by which Mr Boswell was much affected; nor would I willingly be thought to have looked upon them without some emotion. Perhaps, in the revolutions of the world, Iona may be sometime again the instructress of the western regions.[4]

If the physical remains of Columba's monastery are irretrievable, Columba's thinking and spirituality are not. Columba is fortunate in having had an able propagandist in Adomnán. Yet, even without his Boswell, Columba was such a massive figure that non-Adomnán sources, such as Dallán's *Amra* and Beccán's poems, would give him lasting fame. Columba came to Iona with a faith moulded by the piety, liturgy, and spirituality of the Irish Church. His theological education was that of any young monk in Christendom. His faith was rooted in Creeds and Liturgy which were part of the heritage of the whole Christian Church.

Patrick wrote in his *Confessions* that Ireland was at the furthest extent from Jerusalem where the Gospel had first been preached, and it was widely believed that when the Christian message reached Ireland it

4 Johnson, *A Journey to the Western Islands of Scotland*, 144.

had reached every place on earth.[5] Similarly, when Adomnán wrote *The Holy Places* he placed Jerusalem at the centre of the terrestrial world, with Ireland and the Hebrides on its remotest edge. This was a point of pride for Columbanus who revelled in this status for his native land, writing to Pope Boniface IV: 'For all we Irish, *inhabitants of the world's edge*, are disciples of Saints Peter and Paul and of all the disciples who wrote the sacred canon by the Holy Ghost, and we accept nothing outside the evangelical and apostolic teaching.'[6] Existing on the edge of the world invested the Irish Church with a certain kudos and prestige, though others saw it as equivalent to being 'out in the sticks'. At Whitby, the hostile Wilfrid sneered sarcastically at the remoteness of the Irish and Columban Churches, 'Do you think that those few men, in a corner of the remotest island, are to be preferred before the universal Church of Christ throughout the world?'[7] Ireland and the Hebrides were remote, and those who shared Wilfrid's hostile attitude to the Christianity which flourished there, regarded that remoteness as a cause of error and as an explanation of the Irish Church's inability to keep in step with Christendom.

That was not how Columba saw things. For Columba, neither Ireland nor Iona were cut off from Christendom. Columba lived at a time when travelling inland was fraught with difficulty, with rough ground, impenetrable forests of trees and scrub, unknown peoples, and unknown terrain, making land journeys hazardous. In contrast, the sea was a freeway not a barrier. People and ideas came by the sea to Ireland, Iona, Dál Riata, and Pictland. Like local Churches anywhere in Europe, Columba's Church absorbed indigenous influences, sometimes consciously, sometimes sub-consciously. It had its quirks, but, at core and at heart, it was steadfastly orthodox in its trinitarian faith and its anti-Arian doctrines. If it suffered from semi-Pelagian tendencies, so did all Churches from the Greek East to the Latin West.

What has emerged in our exploration of Columba is that he is to be understood within this global context of an international Christian faith. He was a believer whose spiritual life and worship was nurtured by the Church Fathers. In placing Columba within this setting, we

---

5 Patrick, *Confessions*, 38f.; cf. Thomas O'Loughlin, 'Living in the Ocean' in Bourke (ed.), *Studies in the Cult of St Columba*, 14.

6 Columbanus, *Letter V to Pope Boniface IV* [my italics].

7 Bede, *History*, III:25.

also see that, for him, the existential issues which confronted the spread of the Christian Gospel were not the intellectual ideas of the freedom of the will or the accrual of human merit (so dominant elsewhere), but the issues of spiritual warfare against demonic powers. That was the dynamic at the heart of Columba's thinking. It pervaded his work. It shaped his worship. It informed his theology. It drove his evangelism.

However geographically extensive or limited Columba's actual field of mission was, he worked within it as a soldier of Christ, taking the battle to the enemy and seeking to overthrowing its strongholds. The victory of Christ over Satan had to be actualised in each local setting. Men and women needed to be set free from Satan's dominion. Some modern readers interpret that in terms of setting men and women free from social, legal, political, and economic burdens which can be demonic in their own right: but that would be an importation of contemporary thinking into the story of a sixth-century saint. Columba wanted men and women set free from an actual spiritual bondage to Satan, though he and his successors (notably Adomnán) were also aware of the important broad humanitarian aspects of the Christian Gospel.

Every great figure has successes and failures. On the credit side, Columba and his Irish monks, alongside native Pictish Christians, took Christian faith deep into Scottish culture and religious belief. They pursued that goal with courage, determination, tenacity, and resolution. They ensured above all, that the God who was worshipped at the heart of that faith was the triune God of Father, Son, and Holy Spirit. On the debit side, Columba's faith was dogged by a penitential theology which contained within itself problems which were to be played out in the following centuries, and this expanding system of penance eventually eroded the New Testament understanding of radical divine grace at the heart of the Gospel.

In terms of his personality, spirituality, temper, and ambition, Columba was a man of clay, sharing this with every Christian past and present. But Columba was also a light. And that light shone brightly from Iona. Alongside other heroes of the faith, women as well as men, Columba cleared a Christian pathway for those who followed.

Bibliography

ADOMNÁN'S *LIFE OF COLUMBA*

Anderson, Alan Orr and Ogilvie, Marjorie (eds), *Adomnán's Life of Columba* (Thomas Nelson & Sons Ltd, 1961; revised edition, Oxford: Clarendon, 1991). (Latin/English)

Reeves, William, *Life of Saint Columba, Founder of Hy* (Edinburgh: Edmonston & Douglas, 1874). (English)

Sharpe, Richard, *Adomnán of Iona: Life of St. Columba* (London: Penguin, 1995). (English)

OTHER EARLY LIVES

Anon., *The Old Irish Life of Columba*, in William F. Skene, *Celtic Scotland.*

Anon., *The Old Irish Life of Columba*, in Máire Herbert, *Iona. Kells, and Derry.*

O'Donnell, Manus, *The Life of Colum Cille* (ed. Brian Lacey: Dublin: Four Courts Press, 1998 edition).

WORKS BY ADOMNÁN

Adomnán, *De Locis Sanctis*, in Meehan (ed.), *Scriptores Latini Hiberniae, Volume III.*

Adomnán, *The Law of the Innocents*, in O'Loughlin (ed.): *Adomnán at Birr, A.D. 697.*

Adomnán, *The Holy Places*, in O'Loughlin, *Adomnán and the Holy Places.*

EARLY TEXTS

Athanasius, *Contra Gentes and De Incarnatione* (Oxford: Clarendon, 1971).

Athanasius, *Letters and Selected Works*, vol. iv, NPNF Second Series (Massachusetts: Hendrickson, 1994).

Basil, *Ascetical Works*, tr. Monica Wagner (Washington: Catholic University of America Press, 1962).

Basil, *Letters and Selected Works*, vol. viii, NPNF Second Series (Massachusetts: Hendrickson, 1994).

Basil, *The Rule of St. Basil in Latin and English*, tr. Anna M. Silvas (Collegeville, Minnesota: Liturgical Press, 2013).

Cassian, John, *Sulpicius Severus, Vincent of Lerins, John Cassian*, vol. xi, NPNF Second Series (Massachusetts: Hendrickson, 1994).

Clancy, Thomas Owen and Markus, Glibert, *Iona: The Earliest Poetry of a Celtic Monastery* (Edinburgh: EUP, 1995).

Cyprian, *Hippolytus, Cyprian, Caius, Novatian*, vol. v, ANF (Grand Rapids: Eerdmans, 1981).

Dallán Forgaill, *Amra Choluimb Cille*, in Clancy and Markus, *Iona: The Earliest Poetry of a Celtic Monastery.*

Dallán Forgaill, *Amra Choluimb Cille*, in Henry (ed. & trans.), *Amra Choluimb Cille: Dallán's Elegy for Columba.*

Haddan, W. and Stubbs W., *Councils and Ecclesiastical Documents Relating to Great Britain and Ireland*, ii (Oxford: OUP, 1873), 119-21.

Henry, P. L. (ed. & trans.), *Amra Choluimb Cille: Dallán's Elegy for Columba* (Ultach Trust, 2006).

Jackson, Kenneth Hurlstone (ed.), *A Celtic Miscellany* (London: Penguin, 1971).

Mackinnon, Donald, *A Descriptive Catalogue of Gaelic Manuscripts in the Advocates' Library, Edinburgh, and elsewhere in Scotland,* (Edinburgh: Brown, 1912).

Martyr, Justin, *The Apostolic Fathers with Justin Martyr and Irenaeus*, vol. i, ANF (Massachusetts: Hendrickson, 1994).

Meehan, Bernard (ed.), *Scriptores Latini Hiberniae, Volume III* (Dublin: The Dublin Institute for Advanced Studies, 1958).

O'Hara, Alexander, *Saint Columbanus: Selected Writings* (Dublin: Veritas, 2015).

Patrick, 'Letter to the Christian Subjects of the Tyrant Coroticus', in *Confessions* (London: Aziloth, 2012).

Severus, Sulpicius, *Sulpicius Severus, Vincent of Lerins, John Cassian*, vol. xi, NPNF, Second Series (Massachusetts: Hendrickson, 1994).

Tacitus, *Agricola*, tr. Anthony R. Birley (Oxford, OUP, 1999).

Tertullian, *Tertullian*, vols. iii, iv, ANF (Massachusetts: Hendrickson, 1994).

Various, *Lactantius; Venantius; Asterius; Victorinus; Dionysius; Apostolic Teaching and Constitutions; 2 Clement; Early Liturgies*, vol. vii, ANF (Massachusetts: Hendrickson, 1994).

Warren, F. E. (ed.), *The Antiphonary of Bangor (Antiphonarium Benchorense): An Early Irish Manuscript in the Ambrosian Library at Milan, Part II* (London: Harrison, 1895).

COLUMBA AND IONA

Bardsley, Warren, *Against the Tide: The Story of Adomnán of Iona* (Glasgow: Wild Goose, 2006).

Bourke, Cormac (ed.), *Studies in the Cult of Saint Columba* (Dublin: Four Courts Press, 1997).

Bradley, Ian, *Columba: Pilgrim and Penitent* (Glasgow: Wild Goose, 1996).

Broun, David and Clancy, Thomas Owen, *Spes Scotorum, Hope of Scots: Saint Columba, Iona and Scotland* (Edinburgh: T&T Clark, 1999).

Campbell, John Lorne, *Canna, The Story of a Hebridean Island* (London: OUP, 1984).

Clarkson, Tim, *Columba* (Edinburgh: Donald, 2012).

Finlay, Ian, *Columba* (London: Victor Gollancz, 1979).

Hutchinson, Roger, *Father Allan: The Life and Legacy of a Hebridean Priest* (Edinburgh: Birlinn, 2010).

Johnston, Bob, *Dalriada: The land that Scotland forgot* (Gigha: Ardminish, 2004).

Kennedy, Donneil, *The Land below the Waves: The Island of Tiree, Past and Present* (Tiree: Tiree Publishing Company, 1994).

Lynch, M. (ed.), *The Oxford Companion to Scottish History* (Oxford & New York: OUP, 2002).

McNeill, F. Marian, *Iona, A History of the Island* (7th edition; Moffat: Lochar, 1991).

MacQuarrie, Alan, *The Saints of Scotland: Essays in Scottish Church History, 450–1093* (Edinburgh: Donald, 1997).

MacQuarrie, Alan (ed.), *Legends of Scottish Saints: Readings, Hymns and Prayers for the commemorations of Scottish saints in the Aberdeen Breviary* (Dublin: Four Courts Press, 2008).

Marsden, John, *Sea-Road of the Saints: Celtic Holy Men in the Hebrides* (Edinburgh: Floris, 1995).

Marshall, Rosalind K., *Columba's Iona: A New History* (Dingwall: Sandstone, 2013).

Meek, Donald E., *The Quest for Celtic Christianity* (Edinburgh: Handsel, 2000).

Menzies, Lucy, *Saint Columba of Iona: A Study of his Life, his Times and his Influence* (London: 1920).

O'Loughlin, Thomas (ed.), *Adomnán at Birr, AD 697: Essays in Commemoration of the Law of the Innocents* (Dublin: Four Courts Press, 2001).

Randall, John (ed.), *In Search of Colmcille: The Legacy of St. Columba in Ireland and Scotland* (Laxay: Isle of Lewis, Islands Book Trust, 2015).

Simpson, W. Douglas, *The Historical Saint Columba* (3rd edition; Edinburgh: Oliver & Boyd, 1963).

Wooding, Jonathan M., *Adomnán of Iona: Theologian, Lawmaker, Peacemaker* (Dublin: Four Courts Press, 2010).

Articles (Columba and Iona)

Bulloch, J. P. B., 'Iona's knowledge of the outer world', *SCHS*, vol. XII (1956), 1-20.

Bullough, D. A., 'Columba, Adomnán, and the Achievement of Iona', *SHR*, vol. 43, no. 136 (1964), 111-30.

Campbell, Ewan, 'A Cross-marked quern from Dunadd and other evidence for relations between Dunadd and Iona', *PSAS*, vol. 117 (1987), 105-17.

Campbell, Ewan, 'Were the Scots Irish?', *Antiquity*, vol. 75 (2001), 285-92.

Clancy, Thomas Owen, 'The real St. Ninian', *The Innes Review*, vol. 52 (2001), 1-28.

Clancy, Thomas Owen, 'Nechtan son of Derile' in Lynch (ed.) *The Oxford Companion to Scottish History*.

Clancy, Thomas Owen, 'Philosopher-King: Nechtan mac Der-Ilei', *SHR*, vol. 83, no. 2 (2004), 125–49.

Colker, Marvin L., 'Review of Anderson and Anderson (eds), *Life of Columba*', *Speculum*, vol. 38, no. 1 (Jan. 1963), 105-7.

Cowan, Ian B., 'The Post-Columban Church', *SCHS*, vol. XVIII (1974), 245-60.

Egan, Rory B., 'Stesichorus and Helen, Dallán and Columba', *The Classical World*, vol. 87, no. 1 (1993), 64-7.

Enright, Michael J., 'Review of Wooding (etc.) *Adomnán of Iona: Theologian, Lawmaker, Peacemaker*', *The Journal of the American Society of Irish Medieval Studies*, vol. 5 (2011), 224-6.

Evans, Nicholas, 'The Calculation of Columba's Arrival in Britain in Bede's *Ecclesiastical History* and the Pictish King-lists', *SHR*, vol. 87, no. 224, Part 2 (Oct. 2008), 183-205.

Fraser, James E., 'The Iona Chronicle, the Descendants of Áedán mac Gabráin, and the Principal Kindreds of Dál Riata', *Northern Studies*, vol. 38 (2004), 77-96.

Harden, Jill, 'Following in St. Brendan's Wake: Distant Early-Christian Islands between Ireland and the Faroes' (Groam House Lecture, 31st August 2017).

Lacey, Brian, 'The Battle of Cul Dreimne: A Reassessment', *JRSAI,* vol. 133 (2003), 78-85.

Lacey, Brian, 'The Amrae Coluimb Cille and the Ui Neill', *JRSAI,* vol. 134 (2004), 169-72.

Laing, Lloyd, Laing, Jennifer, Longley, David and MacDonald, A. D. S., 'The Early Christian and later medieval ecclesiastical site at St Blane's, Kingarth, Bute', *PSAS*, vol. 128 (1998), 551-65.

McCormick, Finbar, MacSween, A., Dore, J. N., O'Berg, A. and Wilthew, P., 'Early Christian Metalworking on Iona: Excavations under the 'infirmary' in 1990', *PSAS*, vol. 122 (1992), 207-14.

Meek, Donald E., 'Columba's Other Island? Columba and Early Christianity in Tiree' (Lecture given at the Tiree Feis, July 1997, transcript).

O'Neill, Pamela, 'When Onomastics met Archaeology: A Tale of Two Hinbas', *SHR*, vol. 87, no. 223 (April 2008), 26-41.

Picard, Jean-Michel, 'The Purpose of Adomnán's *Vita Columbae*', *Peritia*, vol. 1, (1982), 160-77.

Picard, Jean-Michel and Balbulus, Notker, 'Adomnán's Vita Columbae and the Cult of Colum Cille in Continental Europe', *PRIA, Section C: Archaeology, Celtic Studies, History, Linguistics, Literature*, vol. 98C, no. 1 (1998), 1-23.

Sheehan, Ronan, 'Sub Nomine Columbae: In the Name of Columba', *Field Day Review*, vol. 8 (2012), 180-205.

Smith, J. Huband, 'Iona', *UJA*, vol. 1 (1853), 79-91.

Veitch, Kenneth, 'The Columban Church in northern Britain, 664–717: A Reassessment', *PSAS*, vol. 127 (1997), 627-47.

Whitaker, Ian, 'Regal Succession among the Dál Riata ', *Ethnohistory*, vol. 23, no. 4 (Autumn, 1976), 343-63.

Woolf, Alex, 'Dun Nechtain, Fortriu, and the Geography of the Picts', *SHR*, vol. 85, 2, n. 220, (Oct. 2006), 182-201.

IRELAND

Alcock, Leslie, *Arthur's Britain: History and Archaeology, 367–634* (London: Penguin, 1971).

Anon., *The Voyages of St. Brendan* in Webb and Farmer, *The Age of Bede*, 211-45.

Bitel, Lisa, *Isle of the Saints: Monastic Settlement and Christian Community in early Ireland* (New York: Ithaca, 1990).

Bury, J. B. and Sweeney, Jon M. (eds), *Ireland's Saint: The Essential Biography of St. Patrick* (Massachusetts: Paraclete, 2008).

Byrne, Francis John, *Irish Kings and High-Kings* (London: Batsford, 1973).

Carey, John, Herbert, Máire and Ó Riain, Pádraig (eds), *Saints and Scholars: Studies in Irish Hagiography* (Dublin: Four Courts Press, 2001).

De Paor, Máire and Liam, *Early Christian Ireland* (3rd edition; London: Thames & Hudson, 1961).

Dougherty, Martin J., *Celts: The History and Legacy of One of the Oldest Cultures in Europe* (London: Amber, 2015).

Haywood, John and Cuncliffe, Barry, *The Historical Atlas of the Celtic World* (London: Thames & Hudson, 2009).

Hughes, Kathleen, *Early Christian Ireland: Introduction to the Sources* (London: The Sources of History, 1972).

Kenney, J. F., *The Sources for the Early History of Ireland: Ecclesiastical* (2nd edition: Dublin: Four Courts Press, 1968).

Laing, Lloyd, *The Archaeology of Late Celtic Britain and Ireland* (London: Methuen, 1975).

Marshall, David, *The Celtic Connection* (Grantham: Stanborough Press, 1994).

Meehan, Bernard, *The Book of Kells* (London: Thames & Hudson, 1994).

Petrie, George, *The Round Towers of Ireland* (2nd edition; Dublin: Hodges & Smith, 1845).

Severin, Timothy, *The Brendan Voyage* (London: Arrow, 1979).

Sheane, Michael, *Ulster in the age of Saint Comgall of Bangor* (Devon: Stockwell, 2004).

Stokes, George T., *Celtic Church: A History of Ireland from St. Patrick to the English Conquest in 1172* (6th edition, London: SPCK, 1907).

White, Newport J. D., *Saint Patrick: His Writings and Life* (London: SPCK, 1920).

Articles (Ireland)

Hunwicke, J. W., 'Kerry and Stowe Revisited', *PRIA: Section C: Archaeology, Celtic Studies, History, Linguistics, Literature*, vol. 102C, no. 1 (2002), 1-19.

O'Riain, Padraig, 'St. Finbarr: A Study in a Cult', *JCHAS*, vol. 82 (1977), 63-82.

SCOTLAND

Anderson, Alan Orr, *Early Sources of Scottish History: 500–1286*, vol. I (revised edition, Stamford: Paul Watkins, 1990).

Anon., *The Orkneyinga Saga*, tr. Hermann Palsson and Paul Edwards (London; Penguin, 1981).

Ascherson, Neal, *Stone Voices: The Search for Scotland* (London: Granta, 2002).

Babbage, Charles, *Passages from the Life of a Philosopher* (London: Longman, Roberts & Green, 1864).

Bainton, Ronald W. B., *The Prehistoric Rock Art of Argyll* (Poole: The Dolphin Press, 1977).

Bannerman, John W. M., *Kinship, Church and Culture: Collected Essays and Studies* (Edinburgh: Donald, 2016).

Barnett, Ratcliffe, *Makers of the Kirk* (London: Foulis, 1915).

Beveridge, Erskine, *Coll and Tiree, Their Historic Forts and Ecclesiastical Antiquities* (Edinburgh: 1903).

Bradley, Ian, *Argyll: The Making of a Spiritual Landscape* (Edinburgh: St. Andrew Press, 2015).

Burleigh, James, *A Church History of Scotland* (London: OUP, 1960).

Cameron, Nigel de S. (ed.), *Dictionary of Scottish Church History and Theology* (Edinburgh: T&T Clark, 1993).

Campbell, George Douglas, *The Reign of Law* (London: Strahan, 1867).

Campbell, George Douglas, *Iona* (Edinburgh: David Douglas, 1889).

Campbell, George Douglas, *Autobiography and Memoirs* (London: John Murray, 1906).

Clarke, David, Blackwell, Alice and Goldberg, Martin, *Early Medieval Scotland: Individuals, Communities and Ideas* (Edinburgh: National Museums of Scotland, 2012).

Clarkson, Tim, *The Men of the North* (Edinburgh: Birlinn, 2012).

Collins, G. N. M., *Donald MacLean D.D.* (Edinburgh: Lindsay, 1944).

Cowan, E. J. and McDonald, R. Andrew, *Alba: Celtic Scotland in the Medieval Era* (Edinburgh: Tuckwell/Donald, 2012).

Cummins, W. A., *The Age of the Picts* (Stroud: The History Press, 2009).

Donaldson, Gordon, *Scotland: Church and Nation through Sixteen Centuries* (London: 1960).

Feachem, Richard, *A Guide to Prehistoric Scotland* (London: Batsford, 1963).

Ferguson, Ronald, *George MacLeod: Founder of the Iona Community* (London: Collins, 1990).

Foster, Sally M., *Picts, Gaels and Scots* (London: Batsford, 1996).

Fraser, James E., *From Caledonia to Pictland: Scotland to 795*, NEHS, vol. 1 (Edinburgh: EUP, 2009).

Grosjean, Paul, *Scottish Gaelic Studies II* (University of Aberdeen, 1928).

Harden, Jill, *The Picts* (Edinburgh: Historic Scotland, 2010).

Hardinge, Leslie, *The Celtic Church in Britain* (London: SPCK, 1972).

Henderson, George and Isabel, *The Art of the Picts: Sculpture and Metalwork in Early Medieval Scotland* (London: Thames & Hudson, 2004).

Hunter, James, *Last of the Free* (Edinburgh, Mainstream, 1999).

Lane, Alan and Campbell, Ewan, *Dunadd: An Early Dalriadic Capital* (Oxford: Oxbow, 2000).

McCrorie, Ian, *Steamers of the Highlands and Island* (Greenock: Orr, Pollock & Co., 1987).

MacDonald, W. J., *Church of Scotland Gairloch and Dundonnell: A brief history of Gairloch Parish Church 1255–1992* (Gairloch: 1991).

Mackay, John, *The Church in the Highlands: or the Progress of Evangelical Religion in Gaelic Scotland, 563–1843* (London: Hodder & Stoughton, 1914).

Mackenzie, Donald A., *Scotland: The Ancient Kingdom* (London: 1930).

MacLauchlan, Thomas, *The Early Scottish Church: The Ecclesiastical History of Scotland from the First to the Twelfth Century* (Edinburgh: T&T Clark, 1865; reprint Forgotten Books, 2015).

MacLean, Colin and Veitch, Kenneth (eds), *Scottish Life and Society: A Compendium of Scottish Ethnology; vol. 12, Religion* (Edinburgh: Donald, 2006).

MacLeod, John, *Banner in the West* (Edinburgh: Birlinn, 2009).

MacNaught, John C., *The Celtic Church and the See of Peter* (Oxford: Blackwell, 1927).

MacPherson, John, *A History of the Church in Scotland* (Paisley: 1901).

MacQuarrie, Alan, *The Saints of Scotland: Essays in Scottish Church History AD 450-1093* (Edinburgh: Donald, 1997).

MacQuarrie, Alan, 'Early Christianity in Scotland: The Age of Saints' in MacLean and Veitch (eds), *Scottish Life and Society: Volume 12: Religion* (2006).

Magnusson, Magnus, *Scotland: The Story of a Nation* (London: Harper Collins, 2001).

Markus, Gilbert (ed.), *The Radical Tradition: Saints in the Struggle for Justice and Peace* (London: Darton, Longman & Todd, 1992).

Markus, Gilbert, *Conceiving a Nation: Scotland to AD 900* (Edinburgh: EUP, 2017).

Maxwell, Herbert, *The Early Chronicles relating to Scotland* (Glasgow: Maclehose, 1912).

Marshall, Rosalind K., *Scottish Queens: 1034–1714* (Edinburgh: Donald, 2007).

Metcalfe, W. M. (ed.), *Pinkerton's Lives of the Scottish Saints,* vol. 1 (Paisley: Gardner, 1889).

Oliver, Neil, *A History of Scotland* (London: Phoenix, 2010).

Pallister, Marian, *Argyll Curiosities* (Edinburgh: Birlinn, 2007).

Ritchie, Anna and Fisher, Ian, *Iona Abbey and Nunnery* (Edinburgh: Historic Scotland, 2004).

Ritchie, J. N. G., *Brochs of Scotland* (2nd edition; Oxford: Shire, 1998).

Ritchie, J. and A., *Scotland: Archaeology and Early History* (Edinburgh: EUP, 1991).

Schapera, Isaac (ed.), *Livingstone's Missionary Correspondence: 1841–1856* (London: Chatto and Windus, 1961).

Scott, Douglas, *The Stones of the Pictish Peninsulas of Easter Ross and the Black Isle* (Balintore: Historic Hilton Trust, 2004).

Simpson, W. Douglas, *The Ancient Stones of Scotland* (2nd edition, London: Hale, 1968).

Skene, William F., *Celtic Scotland: A History of Ancient Alban. Volume 2, Church and Culture* (first published 1877; American edition, New York: Books for Libraries, 1971).

Smyth, A. P., *Warlords and Holy Men* (Edinburgh: Hodder Arnold, 1984).

Tranter, Nigel, *The Story of Scotland* (Glasgow: Wilson, 2000).

Watson, W. J. *The History of the Celtic Place-Names of Scotland* (1926).

Woolf, Alex, *From Pictland to Alba, 789–1070: NEHS, vol. 2* (Edinburgh: EUP, 2007).

Articles (Scotland)

Alcock, Leslie and Elizabeth A., 'The Context of the Dupplin Cross: A reconsideration', *PSAS*, vol. 126 (1996), 455-7.

Macdonald, George, 'On Two Inscribed Stones of the Early Christian period from the Border District', *PSAS*, vol. 70 (1935/36), 33-9.

Mann, John C. and Breezet, David J., 'Ptolemy, Tacitus and the tribes of north Britain', *PSAS*, vol. 117 (1987), 85-91.

Meek, Donald, 'Surveying the Saints: Reflections on recent writings on Celtic Christianity', *SBET,* vol. 15 (1997).

NORTHUMBRIA

Adams, Max, *The King in the North: The Life and Times of Oswald of Northumbria* (London: Head of Zeus, 2013).

Bede, *Ecclesiastical History of the English People* tr. Leo Sherley-Price (revised edition, London: Penguin, 1990).

Bede, *Life of Cuthbert* in Webb and Farmer, *The Age of Bede*, 41-102.

Blair, Peter Hunter, *The World of Bede* (London: Secker & Warburg, 1970).

Colgrave, Bertram (ed.), *Two Lives of Saint Cuthbert* (Cambridge: CUP, 1940).

Eyre, Archbishop Charles, *The History of St. Cuthbert: or, An Account of His Life, Decease and Miracles* (London: Burns & Oates, 1887).

Hamilton Thomson, A., *Bede: His Life, Times and Writings* (Oxford: Clarendon, 1935).

Magnusson, Magnus, *Lindisfarne: The Cradle Island* (London: Oriel, 1984).

Morton, James, *The Monastic Annals of Teviotdale: The History and Antiquities of the Abbeys of Jedburgh, Kelso, Melrose, and Dryburgh* (Edinburgh: Lizars, 1832; Forgotten Books reprint, n.d.).

Stenton, Frank, *Anglo-Saxon England: The Oxford History of England, Volume 2* (3rd edition; Oxford: OUP, 1971).

Stephanus, Eddius, *Life of Wilfrid* in Webb and Farmer, *The Age of Bede*, 105-82.

Stranks, C. J., *The Life and Death of St. Cuthbert* (London: SPCK, 1964).

Webb, J. F. and Farmer, D. H., *The Age of Bede* (Penguin Classics edition; Harmondsworth: Penguin, 1965).

MONASTIC LIFE, WORK, AND SCHOLARSHIP

Anon., *The Monastery of Tallaght*, tr. E. J. Gwynn and W. J. Purton, *PRIA*, vol. XXIX, Section C, no. 5 (Dublin: Hodges, Figgis & Co., 1911).

Benedict, *The Rule of St. Benedict.* in Timothy Fry (ed.), *The Rule of St. Benedict in English* (Collegeville, Minnesota: The Liturgical Press, 1982).

Bonner G., Rollson, D. and Stancliffe, C. (eds), *St. Cuthbet, His Cult and Community to A.D. 1200* (Rochester: Boydell Press, 1987).

Carver, Martin, *Portmahomack: A Monastery in Pictland* (Tarbat: Highlands & Islands Enterprise, 2007).

Carver, Martin, *Portmahomack: Monastery of the Picts* (Edinburgh: EUP, 2008).

Carver, Martin, Garner-Lahire, Justin and Spall, Cecily, *Portmahomack on Tarbat Ness: Changing Ideologies in North-East Scotland, Sixth to Sixteenth Century AD* (Edinburgh: Society of Antiquaries of Scotland, 2016).

Chadwick, Owen, *John Cassian: A Study in Primitive Monasticism* (London & New York: CUP, 1950).

De Hamel, Christopher, *Meetings with Remarkable Manuscripts* (London: Penguin, 2017).

Gougaud, Louis, *Gaelic Pioneers of Christianity: The Work and Influence of Irish Monks and Saints in Continental Europe*, tr. Victor Collins (Dublin: Gill, 1923).

Haslehurst, R. S. T., *Penitential Discipline in the Early Church* (London: SPCK, 1921).

Herbert, Máire, *Iona, Kells, and Derry: The History and Hagiography of the Monastic Familia of Columba* (Oxford: Clarendon, 1988).

Herity, Michael and Breen, Aidan, *The Cathach of Colum Cille: An Introduction* (Dublin: Royal Irish Academy, 2002).

Howlett, David R., *The Celtic Latin Tradition of Biblical Style* (Dublin: Four Courts Press, 1995).

MacLean, Donald, *The Law of the Lord's Day in the Celtic Church* (Edinburgh: T&T Clark, 1926).

McNeill, John Thomas, *The Celtic Penitentials and their Influence on Continental Christianity* (Paris: Librairie Ancienne Honoré Champion, 1923).

McNeill, John Thomas and Gamer, Helena M., *Medieval Handbooks of Penance: A Translation of the Principal* Libri Poenitentiales *and selections from related documents* (New York: Columbia University Press, 1938).

Montalembert, Charles Forbes, *The Monks of the West from St. Benedict to St. Bernard: vol. v* (Edinburgh: Blackwood, 1877).

Montalembert, Charles Forbes, *The Monks of the West from St. Benedict to St. Bernard: vol. ii* (Boston: Donahoe, 1872).

Morison, Ernest Frederick, *St. Basil and his Rule: A Study in Early Monasticism* (London: OUP, 1912).

Watkins, Oscar D., *A History of Penance Vol. II: The Western Church from 450 to 1215* (London: Longmans, Green & Co., 1920).

Articles (Monastic Life, etc.)

Esposito, M., 'The Cathach of St. Columba', *JCLAS*, vol. 4, no. 1 (Dec. 1916), 80-3.

Hull, Vernam, 'Cain Domnaig', *Eriu*, vol. 20 (1966), 151-77.

Joynt, M., 'The Cathach of St. Columba', *ICQ*, vol. 10, no. 39 (July 1917), 186-204.

McNamara, Martin and Sheehy, Maurice, 'Psalter Text and Psalter Study in the Early Irish Church (A.D. 600–1200)', *PRIA, Section C: Archaeology, Celtic Studies, History, Linguistics, Literature*, vol. 73 (1973), 201-98.

Meyvaert, Paul, 'The Book of Kells and Iona', *The Art Bulletin*, vol. 71, no. 1 (1989), 6-19.

Moore, Philip S., 'Review of Owen Chadwick, *John Cassian: A Study in Primitive Monasticism*', *Speculum*, vol. 26, no. 3 (July 1951), 497-8.

O'Loughlin, Thomas, 'The Library of Iona in the Late Seventh Century: The Evidence from Adomnán's *De Locis Sanctis*', *Eriu*, vol. 45 (1994), 33-52.

O'Neill, Padraig P., 'Welsh *Anterth,* Old Irish *Anteirt*', *Eriu*, vol. 41 (1990), 1-11.

Robinson, F. N., 'Review of MacLean, *The Law of the Lord's Day in the Celtic Church*', *Speculum*, vol. 2, no. 4 (Oct. 1927), 491-2.

LITURGY, THEOLOGY, AND EVANGELISM

Adamson, Ian, *Bangor: Light of the World* (Newtonards: Colourpoint, 2015).

Billett, Jesse D., *The Divine Office in Anglo-Saxon England* (London: Henry Bradshaw Society, 2014).

Blaes, Arnold, *The Canonical Hours: Their Origin, Symbolism, and Purpose* (Conception: Conception Abbey Press, 1956).

Bradshaw, Paul F., *Daily Prayer in the Early Church: A Study of the Origin and Early Development of the Divine Office* (Eugene: Wipf & Stock, 1981).

Bruce, James, *Prophecy, Miracles and Heavenly Light? The Eschatology, Pneumatology, and Missiology of Adomnán's* 'Life of Columba' (Milton Keynes: Paternoster, 2004).

Comaroff, Jean and John, *Of Revelation and Revolution: Christianity, Colonialism, and Consciousness in South Africa, vol. 1* (Chicago: Chicago University Press, 1991).

Constantelos, Demetrios J., *Understanding the Greek Orthodox Church* (4th edition; Massachusetts: Hellenic Press, 2005).

Curran, Michael, *The Antiphonary of Bangor and the Early Irish Monastic Liturgy* (Dublin: Irish Academic Press, 1984).

Dales, Douglas, *Light to the Isles: Missionary Theology in Celtic and Anglo-Saxon Britain* (Cambridge: Lutterworth, 1997).

Dix, Dom Gregory, *The Shape of the Liturgy* (2nd edition, London: A&C Black, 1993).

Donaldson, Gordon, *The Faith of the Scots* (London: Batsford, 1990).

Finney, John, *Recovering the Past: Celtic and Roman Mission* (London: DLT, 1996).

Germanus, *Expositio Antiquae Liturgiae Gallicanae*, in Ratcliff (ed.), *Expositio Antiquae Liturgiae Gallicanae* vol. XCVIII.

Herren, Michael W. and Brown, Shirley Ann, *Christ in Celtic Christianity: Britain and Ireland from the Fifth to the Tenth Century* (Woodbridge: Boydell, 2002).

Holmes, Dom Augustine, *Pluscarden Abbey* (Derby: Heritage House Group, 2004).

Landau, Paul Stuart, *The Realm of the Word: Language, Gender and Christianity in a Southern African Kingdom* (Cape Town: David Philip, 1995).

Livingstone, David, *Missionary Travels and Researches in South Africa* (London: Murray, 1857).

Messenger, Ruth Ellis, *The Medieval Latin Hymn* (Washington DC: Capital, 1953).

Moran, P. F., *Essays on the Origin, Doctrines, and Discipline of the Early Irish Church* (Dublin: Duffy, 1864).

O'Loughlin, Thomas, *Celtic Theology* (London: Continuum, 2000).

Oulton, John Ernest Leonard, *The Credal Statements of St. Patrick: As contained in the Fourth Chapter of his Confession* (London: OUP, 1940).

Raikes, Marian, *Light from Dark Ages? An Evangelical Critique of Celtic Spirituality* (London: Latimer Trust, 2012).

Ratcliff, E. C. (ed), *Expositio Antiquae Liturgiae Gallicanae* vol. XCVIII (London: Henry Bradshaw Society, 1971).

Stratman, Paul C., *The Antiphonary of Bangor and the Divine Offices of Bangor* (Beaver Dam: Stratman, 2018).

Taft, Robert, *The Liturgy of the Hours in East and West* (Collegeville Minnesota: The Liturgical Press, 1986).

Thomas, A. Charles, *The Early Christian Archaeology of North Britain.* (London: OUP, 1971).

Walpole, Arthur Sumner, *Early Latin Hymns with Introduction and Notes* (Cambridge: CUP, 1922).

Warren, F. E., *The Liturgy and Ritual of the Celtic Church* (Oxford: Clarendon, 1881).

Warren, F. E. (ed.), *The Antiphonary of Bangor (Antiphonarium Benchorense): An Early Irish Manuscript in the Ambrosian Library at Milan, Part II* (London: Harrison, 1895).

Woolfenden, Gregory W., *Daily Liturgical Prayer: Origins and Theology* (Aldershot: Ashgate, 2004).

Yorke, Barbara, *The Conversion of Britain: 600–800* (Harlow: Pearson Longman, 2006).

Articles (Liturgy, etc.)

Barclift, Philip L., 'Predestination and Divine Foreknowledge in the Sermons of Pope Leo the Great', *Church History*, vol. 62, no. 1 (March 1993), 5-21.

Bonner, Gerald, 'Review of Herren and Brown, *Christ in Celtic Christianity*', *Peritia*, vol. 16 (2002), 510-13.

Campbell, Ewan and Maldonado, Adrián, 'New Discoveries from Iona', paper presented to the 8th International Insular Art Conference, University of Glasgow, 10th–14th July 2017.

Conrad-O'Briain, Helen, 'Grace and Election in Adomnán's *Vita S. Columbae*', *Hermathena*, 172 (2002), 25-38.

Markus, Gilbert, 'Pelagianism and the Common Celtic Church: A Review of Herren and Brown, *Christ in Celtic Christianity*', *Innes Review*, vol. 56 (2005), 165-213.

Nerney, D. S., 'The Bangor Symbol, I', *ITQ*, vol. XIX, no. 4 (Oct. 1952), 369-85.

Nerney, D. S., 'The Bangor Symbol, II', *ITQ*, vol. XX, no. 3 (July 1953), 273-86.

Nerney, D. S., 'The Bangor Symbol, III', *ITQ*, vol. XX, no. 4 (Oct. 1953), 389-401.

Reeves, W., 'The Antiphonary of Bangor', *UJA*, first Series, vol. 1 (1853), 168-79.

Ryan, John, 'The Mass in the Early Irish Church', *IQR*, vol. 50, no. 200 (Winter, 1961), 371-84.

Stancliffe, Clare, 'Venantius Fortunatus, Ireland, Jerome: the evidence of *Precamur Patrem*', *Peritia*, vol. 10 (1996), 91-7.

Names and Places Index

Subjects and Texts Index

B

C

D

E

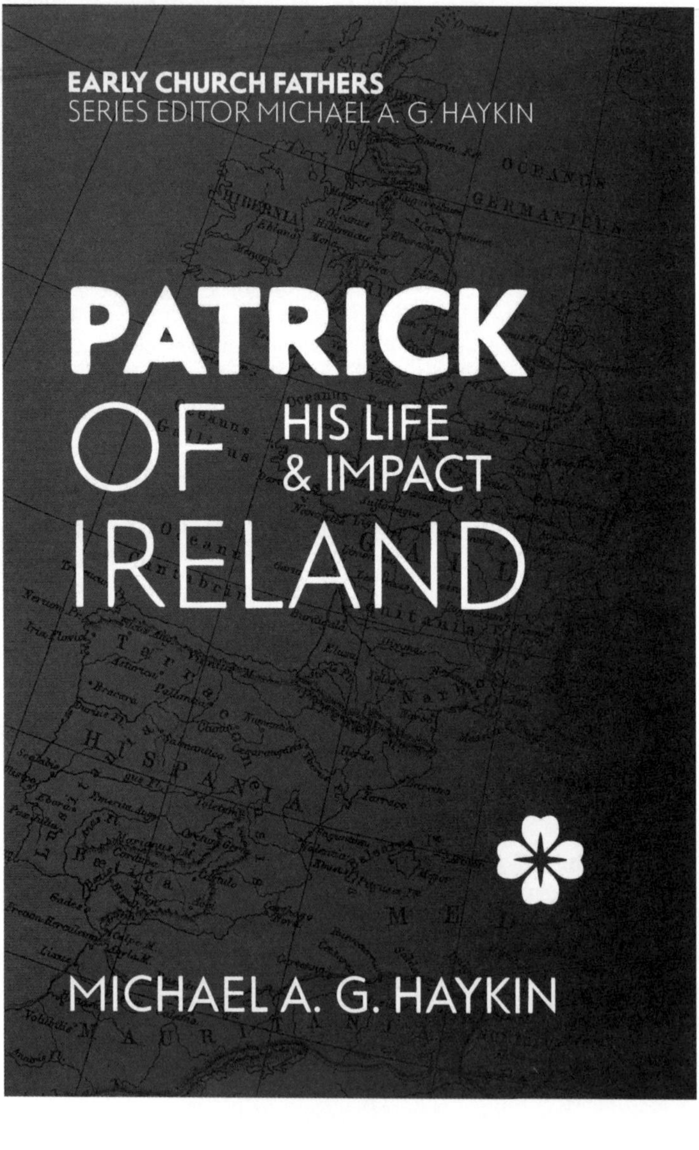
EARLY CHURCH FATHERS
SERIES EDITOR MICHAEL A. G. HAYKIN
PATRICK OF IRELAND
HIS LIFE & IMPACT
MICHAEL A. G. HAYKIN

Patrick of Ireland

His Life and Impact

Michael A. G. Haykin

Patrick ministered to kings and slaves alike in the culture that had enslaved him. Patrick's faith and his commitment to the Word of God through hard times is a true example of the way that God calls us to grow and to bless those around us through our suffering. Michael Haykin's masterful biography of Patrick's life and faith will show you how you can follow God's call in your life.

Early Church Fathers: this series relates the magnificent impact that those fathers of the early church made for our world today.

> *A fine balance between a biography of an extraordinary servant of Jesus Christ and an explanation of the beliefs that sustained Patrick.*

Michael Ovey
(1958-2017) Principal, Oak Hill Theological College, London

> *Judicious… knowledgeable…insightful… Readers will be impressed.*

D. H. Williams
Professor of Patristics and Historical Theology, Baylor University, Waco, Texas

> *To read this account is to fill us with thankfulness for the Lord's work in history and with hopefulness for… another era of lost–ness.*

Edward Donnelly
Principal, Reformed Theological College, Belfast, Northern Ireland

978-1-52710-100-5

Christian Focus Publications

Our mission statement –

STAYING FAITHFUL
In dependence upon God we seek to impact the world through literature faithful to His infallible Word, the Bible. Our aim is to ensure that the Lord Jesus Christ is presented as the only hope to obtain forgiveness of sin, live a useful life and look forward to heaven with Him.

Our books are published in four imprints:

CHRISTIAN FOCUS

Popular works including biographies, commentaries, basic doctrine and Christian living.

CHRISTIAN HERITAGE

Books representing some of the best material from the rich heritage of the church.

MENTOR

Books written at a level suitable for Bible College and seminary students, pastors, and other serious readers. The imprint includes commentaries, doctrinal studies, examination of current issues and church history.

CF4•K

Children's books for quality Bible teaching and for all age groups: Sunday school curriculum, puzzle and activity books; personal and family devotional titles, biographies and inspirational stories – because you are never too young to know Jesus!

Christian Focus Publications Ltd,
Geanies House, Fearn, Ross-shire,
IV20 1TW, Scotland, United Kingdom.
www.christianfocus.com